BEAZLEY

BEAZLEY

A biography by Peter FitzSimons

To Garelan

With thanks for your

friendship

[signature]

■ HarperCollins*Publishers*

HarperCollins_Publishers_

First published in Australia in 1998
by HarperCollins_Publishers_ Pty Limited
ACN 009 913 517
A member of HarperCollins_Publishers_ (Australia) Pty Limited Group
http://www.harpercollins.com.au

Copyright © Peter FitzSimons 1998

HarperCollins_Publishers_
25 Ryde Road, Pymble, Sydney, NSW 2073, Australia
31 View Road, Glenfield, Auckland 10, New Zealand
77–85 Fulham Palace Road, London W6 8JB, United Kingdom
Hazelton Lanes, 55 Avenue Road, Suite 2900, Toronto, Ontario M5R 3L2
and 1995 Markham Road, Scarborough, Ontario M1B 5M8, Canada
10 East 53rd Street, New York NY 10032, USA

National Library of Australia Cataloguing-in-Publication data:

FitzSimons, Peter.
    Beazley : a biography
    Bibliography.
    Includes index.
    ISBN 0 7322 5876 6.
    I. Beazley, Kim C. (Kim Christian), 1948- . 2. Australian
    Labor Party - Biography. 3. Politicians - Australia -
    Biography. I. Title.
324.29407092

Typeset in Sabon 10.5 on 14
Cover photograph: Robert Garvey
Printed in Australia by Griffin Press Pty Ltd on 79 gsm Bulky Paperback

5 4 3 2 1
02 01 00 99 98

For Lisa, Jake, Louis and Billi the kid

10 DOWNING STREET
LONDON SW1A 2AA

THE PRIME MINISTER

Kim was always a guy who stood out – in every way! Early on, even at
University, he was streets ahead in terms of political savvy and intellect. Later, as I
was still struggling to get on in the Labour Party, he made huge efforts to help me with
advice, friendship and encouragement. I remember in 1982 he arranged for me – then
not even in the UK Parliament – to meet Hayden, Hawke and Keating when I was in
Australia, shortly before their election victory. It was incredibly decent of him, and
showed what I have always found about him: no side, no love of status or position and
a good friend.

Then later again, when Kim was a rising star in Government, we met regularly
in the UK and Australia, discussing political issues and where the centre-left should
develop.

His outstanding characteristic in my view is his judgement. He has a lightning
quick appreciation of people and situations, and I have rarely found his judgement of
either to be at fault. Like any of us he has ambition, but I always found he had it under
control, if you know what I mean. He knows what he wants and will fight hard to get
it, but he is essentially a principled and straight man. As you can see, I am proud to
call him a friend.

Tony Blair

June 1998

CONTENTS

'Kim is essentially a man who has got the cloud-lands and the grassroots. When I say the "cloud-lands", I mean up there he is thinking, he is a thinker, but he also knows that if you are going to be able to translate your ideas into action, you have got to be "down there" at the grassroots, and I just found him from the word go, a charming, good man — and I formed the view very early that he could go where his father hadn't been able to go.'
Bob Hawke, November 1997.

'Kim sought to bring a genial, scholarly approach in an adversarial system, and where reforms have to be made it's certainly running against the culture.
I think he believes you can draw on the better instincts of people and draw the political power from them to make valuable and good political changes. I believe that too, but there'll come a time when those forces don't want to give you the power or don't want to give you the room to make the policy changes. And that's where people have to be very persuasive, very determined, very urgent, because without that sense of urgency for the changes and persuasive determination, you basically don't get there. As a minister Kim has been able to get those changes where he needs them through the years ...
Provided that the agenda he wants is one that he feels urgent about, passionate about, then he'll be able to draw the power down ...'
Paul Keating, May 1998.

'Kim has a wide range of personality styles. He can be mild and persuasive, or good humoured and entertaining. But when he's got to be, he can be as tough as blazes, and in fact on that day when I was digging my toes in, he went for me and I remember thinking "he reminds me of a tough rugby union forward, hitting the ruck without any apologies to his opponents".'
Bill Hayden, 1998.

CHAPTER ONE

IN THE BEGINNING — BORN A BEAZLEY

> 'Life is a game of whist. From unseen sources the cards are shuffled, and the hands are dealt.'
> *Eugene Hare.*

Labour. Fourteen hours of it. But finally it was done. At nine pounds four ounces, he was big from the beginning, and when his mother first laid eyes on him she gasped: 'Oh, what a beautiful baby! He looks like he's already three months old!' Father was ushered inside from the waiting room, and the young couple gazed down upon their firstborn, on this 14th day of December, 1948.

He was named on the spot: Kim Christian Beazley. 'Kim', because that was the first name of his father and also because the Rudyard Kipling story by the same name was a favourite of theirs, and they wanted their boy to be just like its kind and resourceful hero. 'Christian', because that was their religion and it was their firm intention from the beginning that it would be his. And 'Beazley' because this child was from that moment the twig nearest the ground on the Beazley family tree that had been growing strongly in those parts since the mid-1800s. To friends, the Beazleys would sometimes refer to young Kim as their 'honeymoon baby'. He was that. They had married on 7 February 1948, and their hoped-for baby had been conceived in the final days of their post-nuptial holiday in Sydney.

Theirs was a union which had its misty origins some 12 years previously within the halls of the Perth Modern School, at that time the Western Australian capital's finest academic establishment. Betty Judge, as she was then, had won a scholarship to the school, to the pure delight of her struggling and war-widowed mother, who had encouraged Betty to concentrate on her education above all else. Although she was three years behind the rather dashing Kim Edward Beazley at the school, she had certainly noticed him around the place, as had a lot of her schoolgirl friends. She thought he not only 'wrote beautifully' in the school magazine, but was also impressed when he had topped the state in both History and English.

Kim, for his part, had not noticed her particularly — not yet. At that stage he had an extremely narrow focus, making the absolute most of this educational opportunity, for he too had come to the school from extremely modest circumstances. He had grown up in the mean streets around Fremantle, the youngest of seven surviving children of a particularly hard-drinking father and an especially devoted mother. His father had once been a respectable land estate agent and secretary of the Northam Church of Christ, but as the grip of the grog tightened, he had drifted to being a worker in a wool store and Secretary of the Northam Racing Club. Under such difficult circumstances, his youngest son had felt that if he had a chance to lift himself, he was morally obliged to do so. As one whose nomadic school years had encompassed Beaconsfield State School, Fremantle Boys Central, and then Perth Modern, his education was everything to him, and he was determined not to be distracted by deep friendships at school.

Both of them ended up at the University of Western Australia, Kim in 1936 to study Political Economy and Betty in 1939 to study Arts. This time he noticed her, for she was what he was not: gregarious, vivacious and bubbly. *And* she was willowy, already an athletics champion of great repute, shortly to prove herself as the fastest 880-yard female runner in the country, when she won that event at the Australian Athletics Championships in early 1939. But it was her mind rather than her athletic ability that attracted him — she was a first-class scholar — and they came to be friends, if not romantically involved. For a brief period in 1940, when Betty was doing some 'prac' teaching at Midland Junction School and Kim was himself working there part-time, a spark of something stronger than friendship passed between them, but did not spring into life. Before anything *might* have developed, Betty had secured her Arts degree from UWA and moved to be the sports mistress back at Perth Modern, and thence to Melbourne University for two years to continue her sterling amateur athletics career and to study for a diploma of Physical Education.

Kim, meantime, had begun his formal academic career, tutoring at the University of Western Australia in Modern European History and Political Institutions, as well as teaching at Claremont Central School and working as an adult education lecturer on international affairs at various institutions around Perth. In conjunction with these jobs, he had also worked locally as a wireless operator for the Australian Military Forces on secondment from UWA during the war. While it would seem that he would have little time left, Kim Beazley at this time was working assiduously for the Australian Labor Party.* This had become his passion since witnessing first hand the harshness of the Depression, and thinking 'there must be a better way to do things'. He saw the Labor Party as a vehicle for this 'better way'.

By 1945 — at a time when Betty was back at Perth Modern as a Physical Education teacher — Kim Sr had risen so high in the estimation of the Western Australian Labor Party that, upon the untimely death at the age of 60 of the Honourable Member for Fremantle and Australian Prime Minister, John Curtin ('I am too tired to live,' he had said shortly before dying), it was Kim Edward Beazley who, at 28, was chosen to contest the August 18 by-election. He won by 14 000 votes against Liberal candidate Don Cleland, and so began his political career. The following year in the general election he expanded that margin to 20 000 votes, and in 1947 something at last *clicked* between Kim and Betty.

They had come across each other again at a meeting of the Council for Anglican Youth at St George's Cathedral in Perth; Kim had offered to see her home to East Fremantle on the bus, and the two had proceeded to walk half-a-dozen times around the block before she went inside. During their whirlwind courtship, one thing had impressed Betty Judge about Kim Beazley above all other things. While standing doing the washing-up with her at her mother's place,

---

* While in its early history it was sometimes spelt as the Australian Labour Party, to avoid confusion it will henceforth be referred to with the modern spelling.

he had, almost off-handedly, recited to her an entire scene from George Bernard Shaw's play *Saint Joan*.

'*Oh, do stop talking about God and praying,*' he had burst forth as part of an exceedingly long dialogue that he had word perfect, '*I can't bear people who are always praying. Isn't it bad enough to have to do it at the proper times?*'

Betty has never forgotten it. 'He just went straight through from beginning to end,' Betty recalls, 'and I thought, "Oh gee, this is good!".'

The young couple were engaged after only three weeks of formal courtship. In her last days of being single, the bride-to-be confirmed her place in the annals of Australian athletics by winning another 880-yard race, in her fastest time yet. She broke the Australian record, her misfortune in this regard was that even though she was confirmed as the fastest woman in the land over this distance, it simply wasn't an Olympic event.

Those athletic triumphs were behind her now, as she lay in the maternity ward of the King Edward Memorial Hospital. The event was now upon her that she had always hoped would come. Raising a family was to be her new focus. Within four days the young couple took their baby home to their rented premises in 2A Tyrell Street, Nedlands — the lower storey of a solid two-storey brick home of classic English design, within walking distance of their old UWA stamping ground. It was a modest residence, albeit on a very large block of land with a large umbrella tree out the front, just next to a shady pergola at the side, and a large hammock beneath a canopy of trees at the back. For the young couple it was just the kind of place to settle down to start raising their boy, and they did just that. Father and son had a very strong bond from the beginning. To Betty, her husband seemed an extremely devoted father, and her son a particularly happy child. 'Beautiful and so happy,' is the way she recalls him.

Her son was never much of a grizzler, and Mrs Beazley would often pause in her work about the kitchen to watch father and son. Young Kim would be in his highchair, and the older Kim sitting directly in front of him, with 'Kim Snr just talking to him, talking and saying words, words, words'.

This had quite an effect it seems, for both parents remember that it was when Kim Jnr was only 10 months old that he looked at the kitchen window and out of a clear-blue sky said his first words:

'wind blow curtain', prompting as Betty Beazley remembers 'great astonishment from all of us'. They were convinced he hadn't fluked it though, for shortly afterwards he looked through that same window and uttered his next words: 'Benny cut lawn'. The occasional gardener, Benny, was in fact cutting the grass with his whirring push-mower at that very moment.

While having a man to mow your lawn was one of the signs at the time of middle-class gentility, the Beazleys were still far from rolling in it. It would be some 24 years from young Kim's birth — and when his father was a full-blown Minister of the Crown — before his parents owned their own home outright, and the common feature of many of the foodstuffs that came into the house, was that they were 'on special'. The young couple's finances were further strained at every election, as they dipped into their own meagre bank account to make up the difference between the funds they had raised and the real cost of the campaign. The costs were justified, though, as the young parliamentarian continued to be returned in his seat, and he could again head off to Canberra to represent his Fremantle constituents. Occasionally, Kim Snr would take Betty and Kim Jnr with him.

'Typicality' has to start somewhere. Typical of Kim Jnr on his first aeroplane trip — as a one year old, to Canberra of course — was that he was calm and happy all the way. It was as well that his typicality was thus, for there were to be roughly a thousand such cross-continental trips in the next 50 years of his life. For his first entrance to the national capital, he was carried down the steps of the DC4 by a famous Liberal friend of his father's, and the man who would one day be Governor-General, Sir Paul Hasluck.

When Merrilyn Christine Beazley was born on 31 January 1951, Kim was just over two, and both parents were keen that their son not feel left out.

'I always made sure,' Betty recalls, 'that when I was feeding Merrilyn as a baby, I'd have Kim right beside me on the couch, reading him a book, so he was a part of it all. Most of my feeding was done like that, with Kim right with us all the time, so there was no chance that he would get jealous.'

As Merrilyn grew, his parents were pleased to note that her older brother seemed innately protective of her. If she was sucking her thumb or crying, he often enquired of his parents 'Does that mean she is hungry, does that mean she is tired?' When she began to toddle, she only had to take two steps towards the front gate, and the three-year-old Kim would come running to his parents to tell them that she was too close to the road.

Even if still at a level no higher than a footnote, the life of this young Beazley family was interwoven with the affairs of the nation. On the night of 13 June 1951, both parents and children were in Canberra for the Jubilee anniversary of the opening of Federal Parliament. At late-afternoon tea of that day, Ben Chifley, the former Prime Minister and then Opposition Leader, was at his usual table at the Hotel Kurrajong — the accommodation of choice for most Labor MPs when in the national capital — and was chatting at his table with Arthur and Mrs Calwell, as was also his wont. Presently Mrs Calwell enquired of Ben Chifley whether he would be attending the ball that evening at Parliament House.

'No,' the 66 year old said. 'I'm doing something that I like very much, I'm going to bed and reading. And will you be going yourself?'

'No,' Mrs Calwell replied, 'I too am doing something I like very much, I'm looking after the Beazley children.'[1]

That night, Mr and Mrs Beazley were indeed tripping the light fantastic, dancing to the big band, when they noticed someone coming in and whispering in Prime Minister Menzies' ear. The Prime Minister nodded gravely, and asked the band-leader to stop the music, as he had an announcement to make.

'Ladies and gentlemen,' they remember him saying, in his famous stentorian tones, 'it is with very great regret I have to tell you that the Leader of the Opposition has died. We have lost a very great Australian...'

People wept, the band packed up, and the room broke up into small, grieving knots, with the Member for Fremantle being particularly affected. Chifley was more revered by his colleagues than any other Labor leader, and although certain policy differences (relating to the ALP's attitude to communism in particular) had resulted in Kim Snr and his chief becoming less close than they had earlier been when he was sometimes described as 'the protégé of Prime Minister Chifley', the younger man had remained an enormous admirer.

Five years to the day after they were married, Kim and Betty Beazley had three children: Kim Christian, Merrilyn Christine, and David

Christopher Beazley, who was born on the 7th of February, 1953. 'I think they were trying to make a point on what our future religious beliefs ought to be,' their oldest child would drolly note of the commonality of their second names, years later. That point was that his parents were not only Christians, they were *serious* Christians, devoted to raising their children to believe in the Holy Trinity. 'Jesus Christ be Thou our guest and may this food and we be blessed,' was the grace said at the family table before both lunch and dinner; church on Sunday at the nearby Anglican Christ Church, Claremont, was the spiritual and temporal anchorstone of their week; both parents would regularly read the Bible, and bedtime was always preceded by long prayers.

This commitment to Christianity would grow deeper still. In the middle of 1953, Kim remembers being told that his father had 'gone away ... to see the Queen'. He had. As part of a Commonwealth Parliamentary Delegation from Australia, the Labor parliamentarian of eight years standing had been chosen to represent both Australia and the Australian Labor Party at the Coronation of Queen Elizabeth II, at Westminster Abbey on June 2. As it was this trip which would entirely change the life of Kim Snr, and that of his family, it is as well to dwell on the circumstances and content of this sojourn.

A couple of years before, in the confines of Canberra's Parliament House, the Member for Fremantle had met and talked with people from a visiting delegation of a group called Moral Rearmament. They were a spiritual/ideological/religious movement devoted, as they saw it, to changing the world for the better, and a couple of days before departing for England Kim Snr decided to look them up. A few telephone calls later and he had not only the address in Britain of 'the only people I knew there, but also a luncheon invitation and ...'

And this must be the place. A day or so after arriving in London, the Member for Fremantle turned up at the designated address — 45 Berkeley Square — but had there been some mistake after all? A prominent blue plaque on the wall clearly announced that this was the very home where CLIVE OF INDIA had resided. The Australian was very impressed that he was actually standing in front of the former residence of such a famous historical personage, and as that was clearly the address he had written down as the centre of Moral Rearmament in Britain, he knocked.

Welcome. Welcome. Welcome. Lovely to see you, and thank you for attending this luncheon. At the lunch he met a wide variety of people from many walks of life, including British parliamentarians, authors, high-ranking civil servants and one or two members of the British aristocracy. He was not only enormously impressed to be meeting such people, but in the course of talking to them, was able to learn a little more detail about this movement that he had first encountered two years previously.

Its beginnings were in May of 1938, when Frank Buchman, a young man from Pennsylvania and a devout Baptist by extraction, had first publicly proclaimed the need for 'moral and spiritual rearmament'. At the East Ham Town Hall, in London, he and 60 local mayors and councillors who had shared the platform with him, called for 'absolute moral standards of honesty, purity, unselfishness and love', as they asked their listeners to recognise that 'when people *listen*, God speaks'.[2] From that meeting began a burgeoning global network of like-minded people who were dedicated to building a system of human governance 'where every human need is met'.

In essence the movement stood as a direct counterpoint to the growing mood of the times that everything is relative, that in the final analysis there can be no absolute values of what is right and wrong. Moral Rearmament, or MRA or 'the Oxford Movement', as it was variously known, was about *change*, he was told, changing the structures of the world for the better, through individual actions. As Cardinal Franz Koenig of Vienna had put it, when talking of the work of Buchman: 'He stood out against the notion that we could build a better world without God ... His strength was to show that the teaching of Jesus Christ is not just a private affair but has the great force to change the whole structure of the social orders of economics, of political ideas, if we combine the changing of structures with a change of heart.' Integral to this, Kim Snr was further told, was taking time out, each day, to reflect on one's actions. Mahatma Gandhi had once made a remark that, 'the only tyrant I accept in this world is the "still small voice" within'. What MRA wanted was for everyone to listen to this voice, for it was, they were positive — the voice of God. It was merely up to the individual to stop long enough to *listen*.

'The outcome of the lunch,' as Kim Beazley Snr recalls, 'was that I was invited to go to the town of Caux in Switzerland after the Coronation, for a conference. Caux was the international centre of Moral Rearmament.' MRA held these conferences regularly but they were most definitely for individuals rather than titles. He would be going as Kim Beazley, citizen of the world, rather than the

Honourable Member for Fremantle. The aim was for people to meet as individuals, and talk as individuals, and reach agreement as individuals about what was right in the eyes of God, and *then* resume their formal titles, to make the world a better place.

When the Coronation was over, Kim Snr did indeed journey to Caux, and there at the MRA conference he met such notables as the Foreign Minister for Denmark and the German Minister for Refugees. As one who had made his living prior to becoming a parliamentarian by lecturing at the University of Western Australia in both world history and international politics, he was very impressed to meet such people in the flesh and he would often tell people afterwards: 'I learnt more about international affairs in seven weeks at Caux than I had ever learnt doing a degree in it at the University of Western Australia.'

He was captivated. All up, MRA was an extremely heady mix for him. Prior to departure he had been most interested in ideology, politics and religion, but as separate issues. As his daughter Merrilyn would later note, 'The thing about the Moral Rearmament was that it quite genuinely combined all three! It was absolutely intoxicating to him.'

While Kim was in Caux, Betty Beazley was back in Perth doing what she would in fact spend a large part of her married life doing — waiting for her husband to return home, and coping the best she could in the meantime. She remembers clearly that as he walked back into their home at 2A Tyrell Street — bearing the suitcases that had sustained him for the previous three months away — she turned to her widowed mother and said, 'How changed Kim is!'

At that point, she knew nothing in detail about Moral Rearmament apart from the fact that Kim had travelled to Switzerland, and talked to people about it, but as she recalls, 'I got very interesting letters back from Caux and very honest letters — some of the things I knew already and some I guessed at. But from the moment he walked back through the door, I had a wonderful feeling. His attitude was different. He'd always taken an interest in the children but it was even more so now. He was so different, and so clearly very happy, that I thought "Goodness, well whatever has caused this I'm all for it".'

Betty Beazley thus underwent her own informal 'conversion' to the cause and shortly thereafter things really did change around the household.

The central plank of the Moral Rearmament ethos was to constantly analyse your past actions and future intentions according to the four eternal verities — absolute love, absolute honesty, absolute purity, and absolute unselfishness — to see how you measured up. With that in mind, time was set aside each morning while Kim and Betty Beazley were still in bed to do just that.

'We'd look for anything that needed to be put right,' Betty explains, 'and what we felt about God, or what was the best for the coming day. And then we'd write it down afterwards in a book and then read it out to one another with the kids listening.'

In this way, as the precepts of MRA maintained, they would receive God's 'guidance'. Something that Betty Beazley personally wanted to change about herself, was the fact that she was 'a bit of a nagger'. 'Actually, I was a terrible nagger,' she says, 'I couldn't stop it immediately, but I'd admit it, and I'd say "sorry about that yesterday", and it helped to start breaking it down.'

Inevitably the three children would come to be drawn into this formally introspective start to the day. 'They would come in and see us and ask us what we were doing,' their mother recalls. 'And we said "Well we're thinking of yesterday and if we've seen anything that was wrong we're putting it right if we can and we're planning the new day". And they said "Oh, we can do that" and so they would tell us their new thoughts and write them down. It became part of their life even though they didn't realise it, and I think the fact that we always had those things in mind — honesty, purity, love and unselfishness — must have had a big input into their bringing up and thinking of people around them.'

A side-effect of trying to identify these thoughts 'that came to you from God in the clarity of the morning', as Kim Snr describes it, was that it reinforced the absolute authority of the parents over the children. As Merrilyn notes, 'If you maintain that your directions are coming from God, then what you do is you pass on your directions as coming from God to your children. So therefore it's not just a question of disobeying your parents, you're also disobeying God.'

This would prove to be a problem for Merrilyn in particular, for the 'moral improvement' of the morning would soon be consolidated in the evening by a review of the day just gone, and an examination of any sins that might have been committed during the day. In the memory of all, it was usually Merrilyn who provided the longest list, invariably having committed many acts of childish naughtiness including failing to have done the washing-up as she was supposed to, speaking back to her mother and simply running away at the first sign of trouble. (This was a particular problem when, of all three of the children, it was Merrilyn who had inherited her mother's speed.) 'My sins usually revolved around disobedience and impurity,' Merrilyn remembers of her time in both childhood and adolescence.

Not young Kim though. Neither he, nor his parents, nor Merrilyn remember his own daily sin-lists being long at all, so he had no need to add lying to the list. 'He just wasn't that sort of boy,' says his mother, 'he was a very easy child.' For Betty, this was just as well, because there were always long days for a child to fill, and it would have been nigh on impossible for Betty if Kim had been difficult too.

Outside of the Moral Rearmament ethos and the fact that their father was so often away in Canberra, the basic pattern of life for the young Beazley children at home in those summer days was typical of the times. The children would play in the morning, have lunch, and then go to bed for a sleep. Some days it was simply too hot to sleep — for in a Perth summer the sun does not so much shine, as *beat* — but on those occasions, Betty Beazley still insisted that they put their heads down for a rest. If it was still too hot to sleep, they would be provided with pencils and huge sheets of butcher's paper to while away the time with drawing. Merrilyn would draw all sorts of things, from flowers to houses to cats and camels. Kim would draw one thing over and over again.

'Ships,' says Mrs Beazley. 'He would draw ship after ship after ship.'

Why young Kim loved drawing them so much at such a young age, above all other things — in fact everything — she wasn't quite sure. Perhaps it was because of the stories he'd heard about his paternal great-grandfather, a sea captain, or perhaps because he would often see ships going to and fro off the coast at Fremantle and they lit his imagination; but like the man who liked two kinds of music — Country *and* Western — young Kim only liked drawing two kinds of ships. Big ones and bigger ones. During such times, the children would count down the days till their father returned from Canberra. And then the phone in the hall would ring.

'They were great moments, when Dad rang,' Kim recalls, 'and we would all crowd around wanting to have a chance to speak to him, and find out what he'd been up to. There was never any sense from him of trying to cut it short, either for reasons of expense or his own time.' At other times the children wouldn't wait, and would call him direct in Canberra. It was expensive, but some things simply were never skimped on.

'They always had the right to use the telephone,' Betty Beazley recalls, 'and when he was a bit older young Kim in particular would talk to his father long-distance nearly every day.' And then the day would come. The day their father would arrive home after completing a 36-hour journey from Canberra, taking him via Melbourne, Ceduna, Forest and Kalgoorlie, before making the last jump home.

The front door would click open, the doorway filled by the largish frame of Kim Snr, prompting the children to rush around and embrace him. One of the pleasures that young Kim took on just such occasions is passing surprising. That is ... he liked nothing better than to sniff his father's suits. Initially he would get a glorious sniff in the warm embrace after his father first came through the door, and then later when his father had undressed and changed and was perhaps in the kitchen chatting with his mother, Kim would often steal into his parents' room to really *bury* his head fully into the soft fabric, and breathe deep. It was the cigar and cigarette smoke that did it for him. His father was not a smoker, but in the days before 'No Smoking' signs, his clothes would retain the smell of the inner atmosphere of the aircraft cabin.

'It was terrific, it was exotic, it was a smell from other places, of places far away from Perth.'

It smelt, basically, like *elsewhere*, and it was common for young Perth children of that generation to have a strong desire to go there. For so many of their contemporaries, 'the East', as they called it, or 'the other side', represented a more sophisticated world; one they would see pictures of and hear about, but never actually visit.

On the other hand, Perth was the most isolated city on earth, and certainly the most provincial capital city in Australia. It was dependent for its survival almost entirely on the vast rolling hectares of agricultural pursuits and scattered mining endeavours stretching into the hundred horizons around. It was, at the time young Kim was growing up, essentially a country town, with just a quarter of a million people living there, in a state that could claim only double that. No-one locked their houses at night, nor their cars in the street. In terrible heatwaves people sometimes slept on the beach. Children were not warned about 'stranger danger' for the simple reason that they were taught to be open and friendly to everyone, to start from the presumption that even the people they didn't know wished them well. The population was overwhelmingly of English stock, with most families having lived in the city for several generations.

That held true for Kim Jnr, with roots from both sides of the family stretching back to just after the time that the Englishman, Captain James Stirling, had sailed well up the Swan River in 1829 and made the picturesque settlement at a site well away from any possibility of naval bombardment. The city was built on a sense of vulnerability from its very beginnings then, and Perth could still be harsh. For most of the rest of the next half-century, one disembarked from the ship from England, bearing either a gun or leg-irons. Betty's forebear, Lieutenant Charles Heal, had arrived on 20 January 1830 as a gun-toting officer of the Royal Navy, on the good ship *Minstrell*; while John Beazley, the son of a London carpenter, had first set foot on Perth soil in 1859 in chains, having been convicted of larceny[3] two years earlier in Middlesex — before being made a free man a year later and going on to a sterling career first as a builder, then as a Rechabite preacher who fulminated daily around the Perth settlement against the hideous evils of alcohol.

While the family shield thus, could justifiably have guns, leg-irons and a Bible to honour its past, the fact that it would also have to include a plane to honour Kim Snr's frequent departures and returns on the same, meant that things were often a little out of kilter for Betty Beazley.

'When my husband would return,' Betty Beazley says, 'I had to keep re-thinking what our relationship was, and at one stage I thought "now when Kim does come okay, hand the reins over to him," and in one way I found that was quite hard although it was the sensible thing to do. But I did it deliberately, so Kim took as much responsibility bringing them up as I did.'

In raising the children, Kim Snr notes that 'they certainly had discipline'. And they did. Much of it was the discipline that came from having such a strong-willed father and resolute mother who had clear expectations of just how their children should behave. Never did the failure of the children to meet those expectations though, result in anything remotely resembling a smack. In all her days under her parents' roof, Merrilyn remembers only one occasion when her father's emotions manifested themselves in the form of physical anger. After attempting to cook a meal for his children, he burnt three chops and, in a rare fit of pique, hurled them into the ceiling. His daughter fell about laughing, and he sheepishly eventually joined in. In total, Kim Beazley Snr's approach to his children was an odd combination of the generous and the forbidding — he was a giving, attentive and endlessly patient father, though he was equally not one to be crossed.

Kim Jnr barely crossed him at all, and his father would take a particular pride in his eldest son's progress. When Kim was still only four his father remembers being struck by his enormous 'clarity of expression, the way he would clearly pronounce each syllable and construct sentences so there could not possibly be any misunderstanding'. It was as if he were meticulously thinking everything out, before he would let it come out of his mouth. 'Dad, did you see the little girl that walked by a little while ago?' he would say. 'She was wearing a very nice, very bright, red dress.' Mostly though, at least when his father was home, the elder son would do far more listening than speaking.

Of the many things that Kim Beazley Snr was notable for in his relationship with his children, one was that he never spoke down to them, but had the happy knack of pitching his talks to them at a level that they could still reach if they stood on their toes. It was a way of doing things, of teaching, that he had honed to a fine edge as a successful university lecturer, and he applied this to his children. For young Kim, father's good, God-fearing and highbrow ways were nevertheless punctuated by frequent flights of fancy. Should Kim Snr happen to be home on one of Perth's rare cold nights, they would get the fire going. The two would often lie down on the carpet in front of the fire, with the lights turned off, the flames throwing crazy shadows across the room. Merrilyn and David were usually already asleep, so they would speak very quietly, almost whispering.

'And then,' Kim Jnr recalls fondly, 'Dad would imagine things in the flames, and you'd sit there and he'd tell you what he imagined he saw. He'd identify animals in the flames — "there's a lion, there's the shape of the wolf, there's a dragon," and then weave stories out of them. I would just sit there, enthralled.'

Some time shortly thereafter, for it was never long in coming, the son would regret it keenly when he would spy his father through the open bedroom door, packing his bags. He seemed always to be going to the airport, or just coming back from it, and these impressions were not simply the children's youthful fancy.

'I would be away in Parliament on average about 30 weeks of the year,' is how the older man remembers it. This did not include the frequent overseas trips he was obliged to make as a member of various parliamentary committees, which required foreign study trips. He was away so often and for so long that although his older son was later sometimes known as 'Kim Jnr' to distinguish him from his even more distinguished father, he never went by that sobriquet in the family home — nor was there any other version of it.

'The truth of the matter,' says the eldest son, 'is that Dad was so often not there that we didn't really need another name.'

CHAPTER TWO

'POLITICS IS THE FAMILY BUSINESS'

'More controversy has raged around the studious figure of Mr
Beazley than any other rank-and-file Labor member.'
Sydney Daily Mirror, *25 February 1962.*

'Basically my poor old man was the most isolated politician I
think in Labor Party history.'
Kim Jnr, on Kim Snr.

There was a green and leafy park. And a house right beside it. And
that was where the Beazley family lived now. It was Claremont
Park immediately adjacent to 1 Thomson Road, Claremont,
where the family had moved when Kim was five years old. The house
was a big bungalow-type dwelling, that the children often referred to as
their 'barn'. Constructed of solid brick, with a high corrugated-iron
roof, the house was on a large expanse of ground and really did have
barn-like aspects, with the notable exception that in its interior ran one
solid wall with no thoroughfare between, dividing the house in two. The
Beazley family lived on one side of this wall, while 'Nana' — Betty
Beazley's mother — lived on the other. Nana was an ample, grey-haired
woman of strong will and firm views — Kim Jnr used to always think
there was an uncanny resemblance between her and pictures he saw of

Queen Victoria — and she was the babysitter of choice as the children were growing up, and a constant warm presence in their lives.

Claremont was at exactly the halfway point between the centre of Perth and the working port of Fremantle, a suburb that was old and traditional, populated by a rising working class, that could, at this stage, still be counted on to deliver a slim majority to the ALP in Kim Snr's electorate. It was very, very green. Apart from the enormous park, with its bowling green on the far side, everywhere the streets were lined with trees and the mighty Swan River was only a kilometre to the south, where the famous Claremont Baths were situated. About 200 metres to the north of the Beazley household ran the Stirling Highway, and on the other side of that, a light railway that also joined Fremantle to Perth.

It was, all up, not only a lovely part of the world to grow up in, but also convenient. It was far enough away from the hurly-burly of the city that you could get peace and quiet, but close enough to both town and 'Freo' — as the folk that lived around called Fremantle — that you could jump on a bus and be at either place in half an hour. However the principal axis of Kim's own world back then, ran only about 60 metres. That axis had the family home at one end, the park in the middle, and Claremont Primary School at the other extreme.

'Our house was the focal point of everybody's social activities,' he remembers. Everybody would congregate on our front verandah and then go down to the park, so you had a pretty gregarious sort of existence.' The school meanwhile was a classic of the genre of that period, coming complete with large playgrounds, white wooden schoolrooms, fixed wooden desks with inkwells, a blackboard at the front and, taking pride of place on the wall, it would soon have the requisite portrait of the Queen of England in a shimmering gold dress and crown.

'Good mooooorning boys and girls.'

'Good mooooorning Mist-uh Sergeant . . .'

Perhaps the most marked thing about Kim's academic beginnings in early February of 1954, was that because he was born on December 14th, in the last gasp of 1948, and the cut-off point for admission to Western Australian schools was 1 January, it meant that throughout his schooling career he would always be close to the youngest of the class. He had only just begun to attend Claremont Primary though, when his life was changed, with the Queen of England once again in the far distance . . .

On 1 February 1954, the newly crowned Elizabeth II had landed in Sydney on her first trip to Australia, and the political establishment was quick to work itself into a highbrow lather to welcome her. A fortnight later, Mr and Mrs Beazley flew to Canberra for the weekend to attend a ball in her honour, leaving the children at home in the care of Nana and a supplementary babysitter. While they were away, young Kim noticed that his legs 'felt funny'. In his parents' absence, the babysitter called the doctor, and it was this medical man who addressed Betty Beazley on her return.

'Mrs Beazley,' he said, 'I'm sorry to have to tell you that your son has got polio. We've already put him in hospital.'

What made matters worse still for Betty Beazley was that at that moment she was feeling more than a little crook herself. On the plane she'd noticed that she hadn't even been able to swallow mashed potato, so badly did her throat hurt. Initially she had simply put it down to the fact that she had 'always been a terrible traveller on the plane, so I just took it that it was my usual travel sickness'. It wasn't. After examination, the doctor gave her his diagnosis: 'My dear, I'm afraid you've had raging polio all weekend.'

In Australia in 1954 there was a lot of it about. At that time the country was still two years away from the mass immunisation programme orchestrated by the Commonwealth Serum Laboratories, meaning that the virus — which was spread from person to person — was free to roam essentially where it pleased. Some time in the previous week or so it had likely made its way into the Beazley household and settled first in the intestinal tract of either Betty Beazley or her oldest son. Now both had to — in the classic medical approach of the time — 'wait and see' just how badly the potentially paralysing disease would affect them.

Young Kim seemed strangely accepting of his misfortune — his father noting that he 'never whinged' — but the youngster was nevertheless rather put out, to feel 'vaguely paralysed'. Claremont Primary was put on hold while he remained in the nearby hospital at Graylands to recover, with his mother visiting daily despite her own illness, as well as his father when he was in town. 'I remember,' Kim Jnr says, 'wandering around in this khaki gear that the hospital issued and chatting to blokes in iron lungs. I thought that khaki gear was terrific — the khaki pants had buckles on the side and the khaki shirt epaulettes — and I thought it was really cool.' At least the prognosis, when he eventually was discharged from the hospital six weeks later, was good. The doctors noted that his calves had lost a lot of muscle, but he would neither be obliged to walk with a limp for the rest of his days, nor be disabled in any significant way. If he followed the long course of rehabilitation they recommended, the sole remaining legacy that they predicted — correctly as it turned out — was that he would have particularly thin calves for the rest of his life. When both mother and son were well enough to get out of bed, Betty Beazley supervised for long hours the rehabilitation exercises that the doctors had deemed necessary for her son. Plus a few other exercises besides . . .

While Kim had been ill, none other than the great Australian Test cricketer, Sir Donald Bradman, had written to Kim Snr, commiserating with his family's misfortune, and recounting how his own son had got polio a few years previously, and recommending some exercises that had been particularly beneficial to him. If Sir Donald thought it was a good idea, Kim Snr thought it was a *great* idea, and the younger Kim soon found himself on the living-room floor for hour after hour trying to scrunch up a tea towel with his toes and draw it towards him, repeating the exercise endlessly, until he could no more. He hated doing it, but his parents insisted that he keep at it — his father over the telephone, his mother more often than not right beside him. Gradually, the strength did indeed return to his calves though such exercises continued for a long time thereafter. His strength was sufficient that he was able to return to school to try to catch up the best he could. Despite this enforced break from school, Kim was obviously a bright kid, though in his parents and teachers' eyes, he lacked the drive to push himself to achieve his best academically. 'I don't know why it was,' Kim Jnr says, 'but I just didn't feel the need to be competitive in my schoolwork. I didn't particularly mind what sort of results I got in tests or whatever, though I was quite happy to be at school.'

When the school day was over at around 3.30 pm, the children would always return to the park. One of his school friends and neighbourhood playmates then, Chris Smith, remembers 'We used to play sword fights with pickets and that sort of caper, I remember standing on this box and bashing Kim on the head with a picket and the box broke and I slipped down the fence and scratched myself. We were having a war. I was Sir Lancelot and he was Sir Galahad. They were the games we played — war games — running around with swords and things and beating each other over the head.'

In one incident that made a deep impression on young Kim at the time, he and some of his mates were playing just such games in the park when they heard a strange crackling sound. It was coming from above. They looked up in the sky to see, silhouetted against the clouds and burned into Kim's memory forever, the young fellow who lived right over the road, David Mills. He was being fried in the sky. The lad had climbed up onto the shed in the corner of the park that housed the generator for the electricity system of the park, and grabbed onto the covering of a wire that led from the top of the roof to nearby lights. The wire was covered by plastic, but that hadn't stopped him. He'd peeled back the plastic to expose the metal, gripped it hard, and his body suddenly became the shortest circuit for the electricity to get back to Mother Earth.

Even as the children watched in stunned amazement, his body was shuddering as the waves of electricity passed through it. Luckily, it was one of those rare times when Kim's father was in residence. Alerted by all the shouting, he came bounding from his front garden where he'd been watering the hydrangeas, assessed the situation in an instant, and grabbed the lad to pull him down. It was precisely the sort of thing that would have got him electrocuted himself, bar the happy circumstance that he was wearing rubber-soled shoes, and so he lived to bring the boy to the ground. For a long moment it looked as if his father's efforts were going to come to nought, that their neighbourhood playmate was actually lying before them *dead* — 'all you could see were his opaque eyeballs,' Kim Jnr recalls now — but Kim Snr did not accept that was the case definitively and even as some of the children started to wail, immediately placed his mouth over the boy's and began puffing, circulating air into the lungs, even as he rhythmically began pounding his heart.

And one and two and *press*, and three and four and *breathe*, and five and six and *press*, and seven and eight and *breathe* ...and ... at last David Mills was kick-started back into life.

He started to breathe in his own right. Relief.

After the ambulance had taken him, the two, father and son, walked back to the family home with the seven-year-old Kim still shaking his head in wonderment at what he had just seen.

If that day had been typical of most days, they would have returned to see the five-year-old Merrilyn pinballing her way round the furniture or from her mother's legs to the kitchen table and back again, while the toddler David would more often than not be sitting in his highchair, rather passively looking around him.

From this vantage point David would have seen a comfortable and correct family home in the understated fashion of the day. There were family photos on the mantelpiece, beside a set-piece wind-up clock, wooden floorboards covered with the odd rug, and mostly well-worn furniture that his parents had picked up from here and there, some of it inherited through the maternal side of the family — specifically from the family of Betty's father, Tom Judge, who had fought for Australia in World War I with the Tenth Light Horse, and died four years after returning, from wounds suffered during his service. Though Betty Beazley simply had no time to become too devoted to housekeeping, the place was always neat. The one distinction between this home and most of that era was that the bookshelves all around groaned from the weight of the many worthy tomes heaped upon them. For his own literary diet as a lad Kim Snr had had to walk two miles to the Fremantle Literary Institute, and was determined that his own children should have a supply of books that was far more readily accessible.

Even from a very young age, Kim would, as would each of his siblings, have assigned daily chores to do — in return for 'a couple of bob pocket money a week' — to keep the house properly functioning. Young Kim's particular job was to chop the wood for the fireplace in winter, and keep the water up to his father's hydrangeas in summer. When Kim Snr wasn't there, young Kim had to water them each evening, weed them, and reset the nets and gauze that protected them from the hot Western Australian sun that would have knocked them stone-dead otherwise.

This association with things natural did not stop at the hydrangeas. Claremont at that time, as now, was home to a large bird population, and it was typical of the approach taken by Betty Beazley that she not only nurtured a particular flock of magpies, but she also gave them names, and encouraged her children to regard them in the same manner. 'Matilda' was the old grandma of the flock, and a little bit crotchety. 'Derby' seemed to be the male leader, with confidence enough to simply come through the front door and walk down the passage like he owned the joint. The Beazley family saw themselves as their protectors, and it was something that the flock seemed to appreciate. While they could be terrible pests to other neighbourhood children, dive-bombing them from on high, they never did that to Kim, Merrilyn or David, who would daily feed them by hand. On one occasion when a newly born bird fell out of the nest, and was injured, the children quickly gathered it up before their own dog Paddy could get at it. They named it 'Francis', put it back in the tree, and then set the sprinkler running under the tree all night so that no passing cat would be tempted to dine. When it still seemed to be ailing, their mother organised for a veterinarian student at the nearby university to come and take care of it. Later on, Merrilyn would note that episode in particular, and the nurturing of the birds in general, as the beginnings of her own concern for the environment.

'John', one of the sons of Derby, was not as lucky as Francis. John was the baddest of the bad'uns — constantly swooping on people and pecking them — and one day Betty Beazley looked out the window to see a man with a gun standing there. 'So I walked out,' she recalls, 'and I said "What's happening?"'

'We've had a complaint about a magpie that's attacking people,' the man replied.

'Oh yes I know, that's John.'

The man paused, wondering . . .

'That's John,' she repeated, 'please don't kill the wrong one.'

With that she took the man to the tree where the flock usually settled in the heat of the day, saw John, and pointed.

'That's the one,' she said.

And the man shot John dead.

Kim was not at all upset, in Betty Beazley's memory, because 'he knew it was the sensible thing to do'.

Kim Jnr's greatest playmate in those earliest days was Merrilyn. Though there was a two-year age gap between them and though they had entirely different personalities — her volatile, him calm — they still hung close both in the park and around the house. For the two of them, most days in summer would begin with an early walk down to the Swan River and a long swim — followed by the trek back, breakfast, and then to the very best part of the day of all.

Battleships.

The game was to painstakingly build your own battleship out of Builder Blocks (a precursor to Lego) and then throw marbles from the other side of the room, and see who could destroy the other's first. Kim invariably won, for a simple reason . . . 'His battleships were always so well made,' Merrilyn remembers. 'He would spend hours and hours designing them and then building them, and they would always be made in such a way that even when you got a direct hit, they could survive. He put these defensive things on them, so no matter how many marbles you threw at them you couldn't win. My designs were intricate, his were blocky. I was determined I was going to beat him at it, but I never could.'

What Merrilyn didn't necessarily know at the time, was that her older brother was getting a lot of advice from their father — mostly over the phone — about how the World War I Dreadnoughts had been built. 'Dad would teach me,' Kim Jnr recalls. 'He would say to me the Dreadnoughts had a reinforced hull at the waterline, so you always had your base stronger than your superstructure and if you put four Builder Blocks adjacent, and then built a line of three on top of it, you actually had a very strong ship indeed and a hull that could survive just about any marble thrown its way.'

Invariably Merrilyn's boat was blown away first or sometimes she simply tired of the game, but her brother Kim always wanted to play on. David would sometimes watch from a couch, but never participate. He didn't get in their way, ever. When Kim Snr returned, he too would spend hours with his older son playing the same game, providing far stiffer competition, but still rarely winning. Young Kim built good ships. Maybe too good. By the by, Merrilyn noticed what her brother started marking on his primary school exercise books: *Kim Beazley, Ruler of the World.* 'It made me think my brother was probably headed for a big career,' Merrilyn recounts with a laugh, though her brother would always maintain that it had been written by a friend, as a joke.

Further cementing a military mind-set in young Kim was a bona-fide air-raid shelter in the Beazley backyard. It had been built in the early 1940s, only some 15 years previously, at a time when many in Perth lived in fear that someone in Tokyo would give the order to wipe out the Western Australian capital with bombers, sent from the Indonesian Archipelago which was entirely controlled by the Japanese. On one occasion when young Kim had asked his father about the shelter, his father had told him that all of Claremont Park had also been dug up with slit trenches during the war, to prepare against the day of invasion. Although that specific fear had faded, the general one — a pervading sense of isolated vulnerability — had not. A common theme among Western Australian politicians as Kim was growing up was the need for Perth and Western Australia to be better defended. The shelter was something of a feature in the neighbourhood, and with good reason. No-one else had one and it was pretty close to the first domain of which young Kim was ever the kingpin. A wooden trapdoor opened to reveal 13 steps leading down into a quite spacious room deep beneath the soil, replete with bunks and cupboards that had once been well stocked with provisions. 'We played all sorts of games down there,' Kim recalls now, 'and it was one of our favourite places to go. The best thing early on was when you were having sword fights and war games and so on, you could take people prisoner, and then lead them away to the air-raid shelter. Or if one of your friends had been taken prisoner, you could lead a raid to rescue them ...'

The 'arts' were also a feature in their young lives, if initially only by accident for the oldest Beazley child. When Kim was seven years old and Merrilyn five, it was decided that Merrilyn would learn the piano, and with that in mind Mrs Beazley booked prim Miss Hill from around the corner to give her daughter six months worth of after-school lessons. The problem was that Merrilyn was at that stage of her life where, as Betty Beazley recalls it, 'if you mentioned anything, she'd immediately be against it,' and the young girl ended up protesting so strongly that she didn't want to learn the piano, that her mother eventually gave up. Betty Beazley decided there was only one thing for it — Kim would have to take her place. 'So I said to Kim,' she remembers, ' "oh look, you'll be starting your music lessons this year" and so off he went, and it wasn't until quite a few weeks later that he said "Why am I learning music?" But you know he accepted the fact that it was part of life and he did them well.'

And so it went, young Kim pounding away at the piano day after day, as Merrilyn played carefree in the park, and David watched them both.

For Kim, it was, yet, something that fitted well with Winston Churchill's famed bit of advice to his son Randolph: 'Politics is like piano-playing — the earlier you start, the better.' At politics, the oldest two of the Beazley children not only started early, they stayed with it. Just about everything of significance that happened to them, seemed associated with politics in some way. One of the greatest joys Kim Jnr can remember of his early life, for example, was when the family went on a trip to Canberra when he was about eight years old, and he was able to actually embark upon a ship for the first time.

'It was called the *Dominion Monarch*, and I remember everybody sitting rugged up on deckchairs drinking Bovril, and everybody else being vehemently sick, but not me. It was terrific being on that ship, looking out at the horizon all around, and I adored going to Canberra. We always thought of it as interesting and exotic. Apart from Dad's job, there was snow in Canberra, and that just bowled us over.'

On arrival, the family would most often move into the famed Hotel Kurrajong in the suburb of Barton where many of the leading politicians of the day resided when Parliament was sitting. The hotel, with many elegant verandahs and radiating courtyards, had been designed by the same man who had designed Parliament House, which was fitting — for in some ways the life within the hotel also resembled Parliament, with all sorts of rules and regulations, conventions and traditions, which were not immediately apparent to a small boy. When, for instance, to get out of the rather closed atmosphere of the hotel room in the early morning young Kim would wander around, he frequently gravitated to the enormous lounge — effectively a kind of 'political club' smoking room. As he remembers it, 'always the lounge would be completely empty, but I'd go and sit on a chair and then this lady would appear from nowhere, and she'd say "You can't sit there, that's Senator Arnold's chair!"

'And then I'd go and sit in another chair and she'd say, "No you can't sit there, that's Mr Calwell's chair". They were hoping I would sit on the floor, because there were obviously places for longstanding members. That was what the Kurrajong Hotel was like.'

He sat on the floor. That was what he was like.

While they were there, Kim Snr would inevitably be taken up with the politics of the day, and the family would pass the time 'rambling around Canberra'. A trip to see their father in action in Parliament was always on the agenda, although in those early days, neither Kim nor Merrilyn nor David had much idea of what was actually going on. 'It was just Daddy talking to a whole bunch of other men,' Merrilyn recalls 'or sitting down and listening to what they had to say.' Kim remembers the special delight of being in the Speaker's Gallery — situated just behind the Opposition front benches, on the ground level, and 'feeling like we were almost out there on the floor of the house'.

If it was an enormous pleasure on such trips for the whole family to be reunited in Canberra, there was much pain when the time came for Betty and the three children to return home. The constant separation from her husband made things very difficult for her. Without him, a lot of responsibility devolved onto young Kim to, in effect, 'be the man of the house', as the concept of the time went, and perhaps because of it mother and son have always had a particularly close bond. He remains a great admirer of her role in their upbringing. 'It was really Mum's day-to-day view about life that dominated what we did,' he says. 'Mum was home all the time, and so you could always get to her with any of your concerns and she was always very gregarious, my mother, while my father was not. She loved people being around, loved talking to them, loved having friends in for lunch, getting on with the housekeeping.'

Things could be extremely difficult for her though, as she acknowledges. 'The family, at one stage ... did go through difficult years, because of me bringing up three children and Kim being away,' she says, 'but we managed.'

Looking back on it, Merrilyn is full of sympathy for what her mother had to get through.

'My mother was left alone for extremely long periods with three kids,' she notes. 'One of them Kim — highly intelligent, physically damaged by polio. The middle one myself — too much energy, too much intelligence, a lively little devil. The third one, very, very young — and she had to look after us. In those days no Prozac, no Valium, no Serapax, nothing to help her. So where does she turn? She turns to religion ...'

Specifically, she turned to Moral Rearmament. The family's devotion to the way of life that Kim Snr had brought back from Caux did not lessen when Kim Snr was away in Canberra and, if anything, the reverse applied. Betty Beazley's commitment to it soon matched her husband's, if not surpassed it.

Betty and the three children still started every day seeking 'guidance' from God, finished it with a review of how their day had gone, and lived the MRA life between times. The family would also come to see a lot of the small but growing number of Moral Rearmament adherents then in Perth. At meetings held roughly monthly at other people's houses and their own, the movement's followers would pray together, sing together, discuss how they could attract more followers, and generally reinforce each other's faith.

It was at such meetings that the children would be encouraged to learn songs from MRA, including one that would become the family favourite, written by a Burmese woman of the faith. With matching hand movements, it went:

When I point my finger at my neighbour,
There are three more pointing back at me.

They say, 'see here my lad,
Maybe you are just about three times as bad.'
When I point my finger at my neighbour,
It just ain't honest.
In my heart I feel that I first must deal
With the three that are pointing at me.

The women of the movement were, at Betty Beazley's invitation, frequent visitors to the house, and she remembers them as 'always being very helpful to me'. The children, and Merrilyn particularly, were less keen on their presence. 'I thought they were interfering sort of people,' she recalls, 'and I did not like having them around, even if I could see that Mum really needed them there to help. Her stability and sheer existence depended on this network of female friends, our "aunties", as we called them, who supported her for the months and months Dad was away.'

Kim, for his part, was more understanding. As far as he knew, that was simply the way every family operated. 'It was just the way it was,' he says now, 'and it wasn't a bad thing.'

For all that, Moral Rearmament still did not replace the role of more traditional Christian upbringing in the young family's life. Kim Snr had not been brought up in the Church of England himself — having been raised in a particularly evangelical strain of the Churches of Christ — but he was very keen that his children all knew the Scriptures. 'So we sent them to the Baptist Sunday School,' he says, 'although Betty and I went to the Church of England church. It's an eclectic thing, maybe a bit strange, but the Baptist Sunday School certainly taught them the Scriptures.'

Teaching their children these religious texts was important for the Beazley parents on two counts. 'Even if you regard it purely as literature, as a literary background, it's important,' Kim Snr says. 'But also what you gave them were the moral stories of Christ's teaching. Things like the Good Samaritan ...'

For Kim Jnr, later on, his first experience of speaking in public would be around the age of eight, behind the lectern on a Sunday morning, reading from the Bible. 'The reading today comes from'... he intoned, while consciously projecting his voice so the children at the back could hear, and quelling his initial desire to go back, sit down, and not say a word. He would occasionally do the same thereafter, both in Sunday School and more rarely, at church. So it was that the foundation stones of both his Christian beliefs and public speaking ability were laid at one and the same time.

And yet, there were still more religious influences around him. Nana, living on the other side of the house and frequently around their side, was deeply committed to her own variant of Christianity. The passion of her life was a slightly mystic religious movement called 'The Seekers', which believed in such things as faith-healing by the 'laying on of hands', and an almost literal interpretation of the words of the Bible. Her principal pleasure was to go in her 1927 Chevy to The Seekers' Centre in suburban Perth, to engage in a lot of singing and praying, and she would occasionally take young Kim along for the ride. Although it brought home to him the fact that there were all kinds of religion in this world, Kim claims little influence from being exposed to The Seekers at such a young age.

'I never really could figure out what they were,' he says, 'but I was just happy to spend some time with her, and if that is where she wanted to take me, that was fine.'

At other times the two would head off into the vast hinterland of Western Australia, to spend the night at an out-of-the-way place called the Narrogin Inn, about 30 km out of Perth. He remembers such trips with acute pleasure, because in his young life there was one thing he did on those trips, that gave him joy like no other thing. The Chevy had a running board on the side, and sometimes, if they were on a very isolated country road and Nana was in the right mood, she would let him stand on the running board as she tootled up hill and down dale. There, with the speedometer just nudging 30 miles an hour, her young grandson would cling to the open window frame and thrust his head forward into the rush of the oncoming wind. 'I liked that,' he says, 'it made me feel very, very alive.'

Somewhere in the course of Kim's studies at Claremont Primary, probably around fifth class, the children studied the concept of 'democracy'; how it was the fairest of all possible systems for the people to not only express their desires, but actually realise them. 'Politics', they learnt, was a system whereby the democratic will of the people could find expression in the actions of the government of the day. Far from feeling the buzz of finding himself on suddenly solid ground as the teacher steered the whole class on to his turf — he had, after all, been to Canberra several times and seen with his very own eyes Parliament in action — young Kim actually felt the reverse.

Though he never boasted about it or anything, all the other kids knew his Dad was in politics, and it placed a special kind of pressure upon him. 'I would always get quizzed by the other kids after class,' he remembers, 'and I always felt under pressure to get my essays right because I was supposed to know. My concern was that I should know enough and be right enough so that when I was asked a question on something I wouldn't be embarrassed by having the wrong answer.' Another thing about these lessons irritated him. While the teacher described democracy as being well-ordered, cool and logical, he certainly had the impression that what his father was involved in was not quite like that. 'Politically it actually felt like my family was always under siege, and that they were always going for Dad,' he recalls. 'I was always hearing talk of one political crisis or another that Dad was in.'

As a matter of fact, Kim Beazley Snr *was* pretty much always under siege. An article in Perth's *Sunday Telegraph* in 1956, by the famed political commentator, Alan Reid, sets the tone:

> *Canberra, Sat: Just over a decade ago, a young Lochinvar, bestriding the white horse of youth and ambition rode out of Australia's West to adventure in the realm of politics.*
>
> *The Lochinvar was Kim Beazley, then young, eager, vital and still flushed from winning for the Labor Party the Fremantle seat.*
>
> *Today, changed and sombre, more a melancholy Hamlet than a blithe Lochinvar, Beazley faces the prospect of being carried back on his shield to the West.*

Other stories sound a similar note. A dusty file in the offices of the *West Australian* newspaper bears witness to just how accurate Kim Jnr's memory of his father's plight was.

> *'Wolves Draw in on Beazley'*
> *'Beazley has Fight Ahead — Unionists'*
> *'Left-Wing Gauntlet at Beazley's Feet'*
> *'Dowding will Fight Beazley'*
> *'Kim Beazley: How Long will he Survive in Politics?'*
> *'DLP Makes Effort to Unseat Beazley'*

As such headlines indicate, 'situation normal' for the Honourable Member for Fremantle around that time was always to be holding on to his political career by the barest of all bare threads. Though in his first six years he had been mooted as a possible future Labor Party leader, his time in the party had been made more turbulent by the famous Labor Party schism that occurred through the first part of the 1950s — when two diametrically opposed views emerged as to what the ALP's approach to Communism should be. One section of the party, broadly Catholic and broadly known as 'the Groupers', were implacably opposed to Communism and agreed with Sir Robert Menzies that the Communist Party Dissolution Bill of 1951 should be passed. This would have not only made the Communist Party illegal, but also ensured that all Communists were ineligible to hold any office in any union, and could be summarily expelled from the Public Service. Another section of the party, while not wishing to embrace Communism, abhorred the breach of civil rights that making illegal *any* political party would entail. Kim Snr, while not a Catholic, was in the former group, while the ALP leadership was broadly in the latter.

The fact that a referendum called by Menzies, seeking authority to pass the Bill, failed to receive a majority from the Australian public did nothing to stop the issue festering within the Labor Party. Passions were further intensified when on 13 April 1954, Menzies was able to announce in the House of Representatives that a Russian spy by the name of Vladimir Petrov had 'defected and supplied ASIO with oral and documentary information concerning Soviet espionage in Australia'.[4] A Royal Commission into the 'Petrov Affair' was immediately announced, ensuring that the renewed bout of fear and loathing of the Communists throughout Australia would remain at fever pitch right through to the day of the Federal Election on May 6, and the Liberals were able to narrowly obtain a highly improbable victory that might otherwise have been denied them.

Within the ALP the resultant tension climaxed in a famous scene in October 1954 when the party leader 'Doc' Evatt withstood a challenge to his leadership — or lack thereof in quelling what many of his fellow Labor MPs including K.E Beazley genuinely saw as the Communist threat — and then stood on a table in the Caucus, shouting 'Take their names! Take their names!', referring to all those members of the Caucus who had voted against him. For many with their names so taken it was the beginning of a long period of exile within their own party — though some would quickly leave to join the DLP — but for Kim Snr such isolation was nothing new. He had already been accused of privately warning Menzies, in the Prime Minister's office, that Communist sympathisers were working in

Doctor Evatt's office, and also of warning him that the Communist Party had donated 13 000 pounds to the Labor Party to help them fight the referendum to shut them down.

For the record, Kim Snr acknowledges going to see Menzies, but maintains that it was not for the specific purpose of tearing down people in Evatt's office.* 'I spoke about not really that,' he says, 'I spoke about experiences in Europe when I went to Caux that stemmed from people in Australia. I didn't make a particular point that they were from Evatt's office. One of them — Alan Dalziel — was, but that sort of thing has unnecessarily been made a big deal of.'

Unnecessary or not, it *was* perceived to be a big deal. Perth's *Sunday Times* recounted the episode in 1956 and concluded a long article with the following chilling paragraphs:

> *Beazley is supposed to have impugned to Menzies the trustworthiness of certain members of Evatt's personal staff. From that hour, Beazley was marked for political destruction.*
> *Now the time for the kill is drawing close.[5]*

The final split came in 1956–57 when 'the Groupers' separated from the Labor Party to form the Democratic Labor Party. Although Kim Beazley Snr did not go with them, he was for a long time isolated within the loyalists who remained, suspected of being a Grouper in a very thin disguise. Somewhere in the mists of his mind, young Kim retains a snatch of conversation overheard between his parents, where the possibility of them leaving the ALP to join the DLP was raised, only to be immediately dismissed, with both parents saying, as he remembers, 'No matter what, we could never do anything other than vote Labor'.

'That in many ways cemented me in the Labor Party, that incident,' Kim Jnr recalls.

Kim Snr's 'different-ness' from all of his parliamentary colleagues was compounded in part by his conversion to MRA. In reference to Kim Beazley Snr's trip to Europe in 1953 which prompted his conversion, none other than Gough Whitlam maintains that 'the Coronation was his ruination', though this was only in reference to his

---

* This strong stand by Kim Snr against Communism fitted in well with the precepts of Moral Rearmament, which from its foundation had stood four-square against the evils of that ideology. MRA founder Frank Buchman was particularly fierce in his opposition to 'the anti-Christ of Communism', something that accorded well with Kim Snr's own views. As Kim Jnr recounts: 'Dad, though a man of the Left, was deeply hostile to Russian Communism, and really, it was the spiritual denial and the diminution of the value of an individual, which probably put him in that position.'

subsequent parliamentary career. There is no doubt that Kim Snr was clearly happier after his 'conversion' than before it.

Nevertheless, a central problem lay in the fact that the principal tenets of Moral Rearmament espoused values that were not necessarily conducive to effective political manoeuvring, that sometimes required getting down and dirty. The young parliamentarian cared very little anyway what flak he got, for he was quite clearly a man on a mission. 'Moral Rearmament aims at change,' he explained to his parliamentary colleagues, 'national change, international change, personal change.'

And he was just the man to bring about this change. He was, from the moment of arriving back in Australia from Switzerland, fully committed to doing his bit to reorganise the way the world worked, whatever the cost might be to him personally — and that too, was always a central part of the MRA ethos. Always but always, he would essay to steer by the four points of his personal compass: 'Is it absolutely honest, is it absolutely pure, is it absolutely unselfish, is it absolutely loving? Now if an action fails those four tests it probably doesn't come from me because I'm not like that. So this was the way you were trying to find what is God's mind, without dogma ...'

If Kim Snr felt he had received 'guidance' from what was on God's mind, then he did not hesitate to say it, regardless of whether party 'dogma' might say otherwise. This was a large source of the trouble for Kim Snr within his own party, because when party decisions conflicted with his own conscience he tended to speak out. Many in the Labor Party took an exceedingly dim view towards those who dared to publicly air their differences with the party. The unofficial rule of the era, expounded by the Scottish-born Labor MP Jack Dedman,[6] described as a 'stern Socialist disciplinarian', was 'One toot and ye're oot!'

Kim Snr was very nearly 'oot' on two occasions for going public with his disagreement with Caucus decisions. The man that the famed Country Party leader Artie Fadden had christened 'the Student Prince', at one point made a call in a Sydney newspaper article for the complete overhaul of the entire ALP policy platform. On another occasion he specifically voted at the famous Labor Party National Conference in Hobart in 1956 against the wishes and instruction of the Western Australian LP, who had made him their delegate to the conference. Though he escaped expulsion for the latter offence, he was for his trouble suspended from representing the WALP at the National Conference for the next three years.

If young Kim understood barely a word of such things, he did at least pick up the name of his father's principal persecutor through it all — 'Joe Chamberlain'. Chamberlain was the Secretary of the WALP for nigh on 30 years, and practically the prototype for a certain classic breed of Labor/trade union figure of the time. Born at the turn of the century in Britain, he had served briefly for King and country in World War I, before deciding to try his luck in a new country altogether. In Western Australia he had worked his way up through the Labor Party to the point where he became 'the party's most significant backroom power-broker nationally',[7] and a very dangerous opponent indeed for Kim Snr. The two constantly fell out over Kim Snr's outspokenness, as well as having entirely different ideas on many issues. Chamberlain for example was strenuously opposed to the government granting any financial assistance whatsoever to Church schools, while Kim Beazley Snr took the view, 'that they're all Commonwealth citizens and you've got to do something for all of them'.

It would be a long time before Kim Jnr knew what Mr Chamberlain looked like, but as he was growing up, the very name 'Chamberlain' came to be synonymous with 'trouble'. While he was still too young to attend the many party branch meetings that his father was always heading off to, there was ample room for him to get some practical experience of nitty-gritty politics at the coalface, or more precisely, at the waterfront.

From the age of five Kim had been appearing in photos with Merrilyn and David in his father's campaign pamphlets; from the age of eight he was, after school and on the weekends, putting these pamphlets in letterboxes in the Fremantle area. Sometimes he would pass 'Old Mr Collins', a blind man formerly high up in the Waterside Workers' Federation, who would walk up and down the streets of Fremantle ringing his bell, and yelling his mantra of choice: 'Tonight, *tonight* at 8 pm Kim Beazley will address the electors of Fremantle on the corner of Alma Street and Vine Street ...' *ding-a-ling-ling* ... 'Tonight, *tonight* at 8 pm, Kim Beazley will ...' Such were the political methods of the time, and Kim Snr would sometimes regale his oldest son with stories of how, when he was first starting out in politics, he would drive around Fremantle with a loudspeaker on the roof. On one occasion he had pulled up alongside the young local Liberal candidate, Billy Snedden, who was standing on the back of a truck and fulminating about the inherent evils of the Labor Party — to the point where Kim Snr had to crank his own loudspeaker up and make reply: 'Oh what nonsense, Billy!'

There were others also involved in his father's election drives, including SP bookies and union organisers, all drifting in and out of the family home. Young Kim watched, listened and learned. Every Friday that Kim Snr was in town, the politician would catch the bus — the family could not afford a car until 1962 — down to an area on the Fremantle docks between Shed A and Shed B on the south wharf, where something that was colloquially known as 'the pick-up' would take place. When young Kim was on school holidays, he would always go with him.

These were the days before the imports and exports to and from Australia were mechanically moved around in massive containers, and most of the loading and unloading was done by hand, requiring an enormous number of men to do it. It was hard physical labour, not particularly well paid, and it frequently fell to newly arrived immigrants to do it, as well as to a scattering of born and bred Australians who were simply making a quid the best way they could. The pick-up then was a system whereby all those wanting to work the following week would gather at the waterfront on the Friday morning, and the fellows who ran the gangs to load and unload the ships would cast an eye over them to select those they wanted to hire on a weekly basis, depending on how busy they would be.

It was as concentrated a collection of Fremantle's blue-collar workers — and likely Labor voters — as the dockland suburb would see, and into the seething throng of oft-unhappy hopefuls, Kim Beazley Snr would weekly wade, with his notebook in one hand and frequently young Kim in the other, to see what particular problems they might have, and how he might help.

A lot of the new immigrants, particularly, would be having problems with the Department of Immigration, as well as their landlord who was more often than not the State Housing Commission. As young Kim watched, his father would meticulously write down their name, contact details, and the particulars of their problems. When the workers had problems with communicating in English, the politician would virtually act as an amanuensis, which, as he explained to Kim, is 'one who writes other people's dictation'. Many others of the men waiting for work who needed the politician's help were not immigrants at all, but were none other than Kim Snr's former schoolmates. As a former Beaconsfield boy he had been brought up in the heart of what was then working-class Fremantle, and in terms of the poverty of his beginnings, he could match it with most of them.

All up, going to the pick-up might have been a tedious, laborious duty for Kim Snr, but for him it was well worth it — both for the satisfaction of genuinely being able to help his constituents, and also for the political returns it offered. Those who had been helped by this rather distinguished looking, and certainly erudite, solidly built man rarely forgot it, and inevitably left him a little something in the ballot box — their vote.

Still more hands-on political education came spasmodically down at the old Trades Hall in Fremantle, the place where all the local unions would meet. From time to time, Kim Snr would journey down there, again often in the company of his oldest son, to debate particular trade union issues. Though young Kim could not venture inside — no kids allowed — he would sit outside the windows straining to hear what was going on. There he would stay, undoubtedly quite inconsequential to passers-by, this robust eight year old in short pants, and certainly inconsequential to the Communist organisers who sometimes would have small muttered gatherings outside to work out just how they were going to embarrass and harass that well-known antagoniser of the Communists, Kim E. Beazley, on this day.

These gatherings were more often than not led by the organiser Paddy Troy, of the Maritime Workers' Union, who had long sworn to do Kim Snr down. Listening in on these conversations, Kim Jnr recalls 'being very nervous about life by the end of the day,' and would often ask his father about him on their way home on the bus. The answer would always be along the lines of 'Yes, well, Mr Troy can be a bit of a trouble,' but young Kim shouldn't worry about it, because his dad had his measure.

If in the process of accompanying his father, he would get some rough idea of what the Labor Party was all about, still it was not detailed.

'Dad would not talk about this history of the Labor movement,' Kim recalls, 'so much as the people who were involved, what they were like, what their strengths and weaknesses were, and he'd also talk about how these people — people like Curtin and Chifley — had been able to do things that actually helped others.'

It was only later, much later, that the politician's son would read up on the origins of the Labor Party, and about such things as the famed

Tree of Knowledge up in Barcaldine in the central-west of Queensland in the 1890s where the shearers would gather after a day's work and maltreatment at the hands of the bosses, and decide over time that the only way they were going to definitively improve their lot and their ilk was to get themselves organised politically.

By the 1950s, the political seeds from such things as the Tree of Knowledge had been blown to all corners of Australia, growing differently according to the soil in which they were nurtured. In Western Australia the ALP's organisational structure was quite different from the rest of Australia. In the other states, industrial labour and political Labor had developed as formally separate entities (though the unions routinely contributed delegates to the various party conferences), but in the Beazleys' home state, meetings of the individual Trades Halls first dealt with the union agenda, before dealing with the Labor Party agenda. It was this historical quirk which meant that when the time came for preselection, every member of a trade union affiliated to the ALP living in the electorate could vote for who they wanted the Labor Party candidate to be. Whereas the average Labor Party electorate in the rest of Australia might have as few as 250 preselectors deciding who would carry the torch of the workers into the coming elections, in this part of the country, that number grew to 6000.

It was thus far harder for Kim Beazley to be manoeuvred out by machinations from head office, which was an advantage, but it also meant that as a candidate, he had an extremely populous patch to work. And, given that he was fiercely opposed in nearly every preselection battle he fought, work the patch he did. Vigorously. Kim Snr was always off to a good head start because of his sterling work at the pick-up, but for all that he still left nothing to chance. In young Kim's memory, before every election, 'Dad always spent more money on preselections than he did in the actual campaign, producing pamphlets and things which we would distribute, so it was a very intensely political life only half-understood by me at the time.'

But such understanding would come, by pure dint of exposure if nothing else. Always as part of securing the preselection, his father would move to workplace after workplace — to such blue-collar fountains as the Fremantle Power House where the workers of the Amalgamated Engineering Union were gathered — to speak to them and try to ensure their vote. On such occasions, Beazley Snr — who upon his retirement from Parliament many years later was described in *The Age* as 'the finest orator of his day' — showed a particular ability to connect with his audience. He would address them in his shirtsleeves, always a good Labor look, while his wide-eyed son would usually stand in the corner listening.

'I could just see the workers listening to him, and I'd watch the way he did it,' is the way the son recollects it now. 'No matter who they were, or what job they did, he would always assume that they were capable of comprehending a complex argument. He was just very, very good at getting his point across.'

The Beazley kitchen table was also a site for many informal meetings of his father's supporters around preselection time, and young Kim would again listen in from the middle distance as they discussed the prognostics for each individual union; just how many votes the Shop Assistants' Union could be counted on to deliver; how much Joe Chamberlain would have managed to turn the Waterside Workers' Union against him this time, and so forth. At other times he would accompany his father as he went to the same kind of meetings in other people's kitchens. It was politics at the cutting edge, and if young Kim couldn't claim to understand all the machinations in their entirety, he knew enough to know that, 'I was fascinated, and that I liked it a lot'.

On one occasion he was privy to his father's end of a telephone conversation. A branch of the Seamen's Union had delivered a preselection vote of 100–1 against Kim Snr, and his father had rung the boss of that branch for an explanation. How could this *possibly* be, his father had asked with some exasperation.

'Well,' the reply had come down the line, 'they were all at sea, and so not wanting to disenfranchise them, I voted for them ...'

Against such cruel numbers, the Beazleys, Snr and Jnr, knew that they could always count on the good ol' right wing Shop Assistants' Union to do the right thing and vote up big for the incumbent. Down in Fremantle, a plump Irishman by the name of Jim Feaney, who was an organiser for the Shops and Warehouses Assistants' Union, would set up his ballot box at the Plympton Hotel. When the shops closed the shop assistants would come in to cast their ballots and lay their bets with the local SP bookie, and, as Kim Jnr recalls, 'at the end of the day, no matter how badly the ballots had gone with other unions, the Shops and Warehouses Assistants' votes were always what counted. After they'd finished voting, there'd be a couple of thousand votes for Dad, and a couple of hundred for somebody else and the whole thing would be over.'

Young Kim had by this time perceived that politics was 'the family business,' as he would tell the political journalist Alan Ramsey years later,[8] but he would be ten years old before he realised just how dangerous such politics could be when you were on the wrong end of it.

The beginnings of his true political education came just before the 1958 General Election. As Kim remembers it, his father returned home one day to tell his wife and children that Sir Robert Menzies was going to be speaking at Fremantle Town Hall. It is perhaps a measure of how sheltered Kim had been from the hurly-burly of partisan politics to that point, that he remembers being excited at the prospect. Just to think that the Prime Minister was coming to speak about his father was thrilling. 'But then when Dad told me that he was actually going to be coming to speak *against* him, I was just panic-stricken from then on — obviously Dad was going to lose if the Prime Minister had this to say about him. He was going to be out of a job.'

His father tried to calm him, and explained that that was just the way politics was, but it was to no avail. For the next few days, Kim and his siblings were extremely worried at the prospect of the nation's most powerful man coming specifically to their neck of the woods, in order to give it to their father *in* the neck. The Prime Minister did indeed come to address 1000 Liberal die-hards while the children waited at home for something terrible to happen, and their father did *indeed* get criticised by him — the way it was written up in the papers the following day — but the important thing was that he was still standing when it was over. Kim Snr held on to his seat in the subsequent election, even if Labor, as was all too common, lost.

'I guess it was a salient lesson,' Kim Jnr recalls, 'that part of politics was the business of speaking against other people, but it wasn't actually something that should be *too* distressing. It was also about then that I realised that there was a party called the Liberal Party, who were in direct opposition to the "Labor" that I knew. It was, I suppose, from about then that I really became partisan.'

With that in mind, Kim Jnr now questioned his father even more assiduously whenever he returned from Canberra about events in the nation's capital — what was happening, who was in, who was out, who was on the rise, *what was happening*. 'We used to give Dad the third degree,' Kim Jnr remembers. 'He'd be at the top of the table and my sister and I and to a lesser extent my younger brother David, would grill him. I think every now and then he found it hard, it was just like an intelligence debriefing. My sister and I absolutely scoured his memory for news.'

The reason Kim Jnr in particular questioned his father so closely was not simply his growing fascination with the world of politics. He had an ulterior motive. 'I was looking for the certainty that Dad would get re-elected,' he recalls. 'I think it was as simple as that. When we were kids, his re-election was security, and we never had much security so it was all that we were worried about. I sat in a state of abject terror at every election wondering whether my father would win or lose.'

Between elections, because of the constancy of the political attacks on his father, a very strong desire emerged within him.

'Because my father was always in trouble,' he recalls, 'and people were trying to take his preselection off him, and he was always being condemned by the State Executive, I always felt that if I went into politics part of the job I'd be doing would be defending my father because he had had such a hard time. I wanted to help protect him.'

At this point it was not clear if his political education was distracting him from his school work, or the reverse, but nearing the end of his time at Claremont Primary, Kim's parents decided that he should go to high school at their own alma mater, the Perth Modern School. This was still a selective establishment of great repute, designed to cater to advanced students, which they felt their boy was. Their son had always achieved good results particularly in English, his teachers seemed happy with him, and they personally thought him most intelligent. There were a couple of exams young Kim would have to sit to get in — a preliminary one to thin the mob, followed by a more refined one to get the very top-notchers — but they didn't think those exams would be too much of a problem for him.

Kim duly sat the first of those tests, but as Betty Beazley recalls, 'To our horror we found that he didn't even get past the preliminary test, he wasn't allowed to sit for the final one so we realised at that point, that although he'd been getting good reports, something was wrong.'

It was nothing too serious, of course, just that their oldest son was not nearly as academically advanced as they thought necessary to embark on his high school career. It didn't seem to worry Kim at all but it did worry his parents.

There was only one thing for it. For once, Kim Snr was to be home for the next ten weeks over that summer of 1960, between parliamentary sessions, and he decided he would take it upon himself to personally tutor his son in all the things he thought the boy needed to know and give him a kind of crash course in 'Necessary Education'. So it was agreed. The Kims would sit daily at the dining-room table and get stuck into it. It was one of the few times in his young life when his parents took him entirely in hand and genuinely *made* him do something.

'This was,' Kim Jr says, 'the only real instance of what you might call vigorous parental action. Dad just sat down with me day in, day out, going through maths, going through English, going through everything. He was anxious about the entire curriculum. And it was day after day after day after day. Mostly my recollections of my father when I was a boy are of him in repose — quiet, very quiet — but he was not like that on this occasion.'

Such pressure to perform, to get himself up to speed at the hands of his redoubtable father was not without its trauma for the 11 year old. Outside the closed door of the living room, Merrilyn and young David could hear their father berating their older brother: 'Damn you for your inattention! Concentrate! Again, try it again! Damn you for your inattention!' They were harsh words, but still their father was not such a man that he couldn't laugh along with them when later the three children would march around the house together chanting in a singsong fashion, 'Damn you for your inattention, damn you for your inattention'. Whatever the travails of the learning, there was no letting up. As Betty Beazley remembers, 'There were tears, but it was done'.

CHAPTER THREE

HOORAY FOR HOLLYWOOD

'Fide et labore'
School motto for Perth's Hollywood High. It translates as
'Loyalty and Work'.

'Remember that as a teenager, you are at the last stage of your
life when you will be happy to hear that the phone is for you.'
Fran Lebowitz, Tips for Teens, *1981.*

Having failed to gain entrance to Perth Modern School, Kim was
sent to Hollywood High School instead. An urban speck amid
hundreds of thousands of square kilometres of dirt, Perth has
raw acreage in abundance, and most schools are well supplied with it.
Hollywood High was typical, with large sporting ovals beside newly
built double-storey brick buildings. In those early 1960s, Hollywood
was considered to be academically well above average for government
schools. Many of the students attending were the children of University
of Western Australia's academics, the campus of which was only a short
distance away. In the words of one of the teachers there at the time,
Hollywood was 'a good solid, no-nonsense school with a young,
energetic staff, working hard to build the school into a community. It
was a new school, one that the government wanted to use as a showcase
to demonstrate how good government schools could be.'[9]

The procedure at this school was that incoming students were
graded purely according to their primary school reports. But joining

the school as headmaster at the same time as the incoming class of 1961 was a Mr John Paul, newly landed from Kalgoorlie, and he decided that all of the First Form would sit for a test of his own making, to grade the intake according to ability. Fresh from a summer spent doing his tables and learning his grammar with his father, Kim sailed through the tests, and went straight into the top 'Professional strand' or 'A' class of the school. There were 12 classes in all in that year's intake — it was an exceptionally large school — and Kim was in 1P1, as in 1st Form Professional 1. The second-best class of the Professional strand was 1P2, and so on.

Every morning then, Kim would leave Thomson Road on his bike — waving goodbye to Nana, his mother, and Merrilyn and David who were still at Claremont Primary — and ride for 20 minutes down the Stirling Highway before taking a left up Smythe Street, and then turning right just after passing the entrance to the vast Karrakatta Cemetery on the left, to get into the school grounds.

Kim settled in to his classes, in much the same manner as he had at Claremont Primary, with enjoyment but still not a lot of drive, his good results in the initial test notwithstanding. Often, as he was sitting in class, he would daydream. 'He was a mild sort of kid,' remembers Brian Jenkin, his geometry teacher in the first year, 'though his mind could wander from the task at hand. He was never a problem in terms of behaviour, or anything like that, just a bit of a dreamer.' This memory meshes well with that of his other teachers. 'He was never the slightest problem in that way at all,' recalls Keith Punch, Kim's teacher in Mathematics and French for much of his high school career. 'He was a terrific kid to have in a class, not the shining light, but never a problem.' Which is much as Kim remembers it. 'There were serious students in my school and I wasn't one of them,' he says flatly. 'I was very average at Hollywood and I wasn't, except in History, an outstanding student at all.'

There was no mystery about why he was so good at History. Simply, whenever his father was at home, 'every evening at dinner would be like a tutorial from Dad, where he would talk about all sorts of things and what fascinated him most was the study of history'.

Such conversations could get very involved. 'Now as you know, Kim,' he might say, once fully launched, 'Otto von Bismarck gave the Kaiser three warnings: he said, "We need ships, but *not* warships". In other words if you go for warships you will alienate the United

Kingdom. Secondly: maintain the reinsurance treaty with Russia or you'll get a war on two fronts. Bismarck had always maintained the reinsurance treaty with Tsarist Russia.' Occasionally in the middle of such dissertations, Kim might hear the sounds of his mates fooling around outside in Claremont Park, but would envy them nought, and pick up the thread even if distracted momentarily ... 'Thirdly: there was Bismarck's famous dictum, "The whole of the Balkan Peninsula is not worth the healthy bones of a single Pomeranian Grenadier". The Kaiser ignored all three and so you got a World War. Do you understand how stupid he was to ignore those things?'

All of it would have been pretty dry stuff for some, but not for young Kim. As he had done with his father's political career, he listened and learned. The high points of his life, as he would later remember it, were such dinner-time discussions with his father, and his knowledge base of international history expanded accordingly. Merrilyn too, would join in, and endlessly pepper her father with much the same kind of questions that Kim did.

And David? David would not join in such discussions. If he was in the room, he was more likely to just sit there passively, listening or not listening, it wasn't easy to tell. He was a good boy, and very easy to get on with — he was one of theirs and they took care of him — but he was just different from them, their mother had told them. They had done some tests which showed that his skills lay in different areas to theirs, and that was that. The tests had shown that he had always been like that, and always would be. The children had known for a long time that their brother was a bit different, perhaps instinctively, but also because his passions lay in such different areas. Actually, it was one passion in one area. He loved trains, from almost the first time he saw one, and he would spend hours, days, standing on the overpass of the Fremantle railway line, not too far from the family home, waving to the engine drivers and ticking the trains off on his timetable as they went past. It came to the point where the engine drivers all came to know him, and would take him for rides in the engine cab, to Fremantle and back, and sometimes in the city. He could not have been happier, nor could his parents. Yes, David was a special child, their mother told them, and it was for this reason that instead of sending him to Hollywood, they would send him to Christ Church School for Boys, where he could get some 'Special Education', for children who needed special care, including some with mild intellectual disabilities.

In terms of that childhood, and his older brother's role in it, David remembers: 'Kim ... Kim was a good brother to me, very good brother to me, all the time a good brother to me, we played indoor cricket all the time in the sleep-out, I was cheeky to him and wouldn't give him the bat, cheeky a lot, but he was a good brother to me.'

One night, on the 20th February, 1962, the Beazleys left all their lights on. So did the rest of Perth. The whole city was 'leaving a light on', for the American astronaut, John Glenn, who that night was circling the earth three times in less than five hours. That evening, the young adolescent boy lying alone on his back in Claremont Park, watching the tiny speck of light whizzing through the heavens above was Kim Beazley Jnr. One man, in a tin can, was hurtling through space 200 kilometres above his head. The world was changing. Shortly thereafter a lot of Kim's friends expressed ambitions to be astronauts themselves, and one day fly the skies just like John Glenn. But not Kim.

The way his mother remembers it, her older son's ambitions were torn between going into politics like his father, or going into the Royal Australian Navy to be an admiral. His interest in the sea had blossomed from the days when he merely wanted to draw ships, and it was an interest nurtured most obviously by his father. 'Dad loved ships too,' Kim Jnr says of Kim Snr. 'He was brought up at Fremantle on the coast, had a grandfather who was a ship's captain, and he loved the sea, loved the idea of ships, and talked endlessly about the great naval battles.' Maybe, too, ships were simply woven into the fabric of Perth's soul. From the city's foundation they had been the principal point of contact with the rest of civilisation, an affirmation of the world beyond. Perth had always loved ships, just as it was now starting to love aeroplanes, and whatever else, Kim was a Perth boy to the bone. Often when his father was invited in his capacity as the Member for Fremantle to have a look over visiting ships, especially warships, he would take Kim Jnr with him, something that enthralled the boy.

His ambition to go into the Navy at that time in his life was strong enough that he informed his parents of his intention, and he even went so far as to send away, entirely off his own bat, for admission forms to the Flinders Officers Training School over on 'the other side,' a place designed to form 'tomorrow's leaders today'. As a matter of fact, young Kim was always going to send the application forms in 'tomorrow', but somehow never did. He continued to make the rather intricate model ships that had become his passion after the Builder

Block ships, for hour after hour after hour, but decided that someone else could sail the real ones.

If not an admiral then, what of the obvious — a politician? His memory is that aside from a general desire to protect his father in general political forums, 'I never really thought of becoming a politician myself, back then,' though others remember it differently. One day in the early '60s, a young teenager by the name of Robert Drewe was on his way down to the Stirling Highway with a mate to see if they could thumb a ride to North Cottesloe Beach, and had stopped at the park for a bit of a play on the way. There was this kid there fooling around, Drewe remembers, obviously a local, who said his name was Beazley, *Kim* Beazley. Fair enough, and good luck to you. But after the three of them had been playing for a while, out of a clear blue sky the kid Beazley suddenly asked Drewe and his mate what their fathers did. 'We were a bit astonished at this sort of request,' Drewe remembers, 'because kids didn't give a stuff what their fathers did. I told him my father sold tyres and tennis racquets, my mate told him what his father did, and then the kid said *his* father was a politician and we were particularly unimpressed — and he said that not only that but he was going to be one too.' And good luck to you again. As it happened Drewe wanted to be a writer, a fiction writer, but didn't go telling complete strangers about it. It wasn't the sort of thing you did. The two walked on down to the Stirling Highway, and got a lift to the beach.

Back at Hollywood, Kim Jnr had settled in comfortably. A curiosity of the school in terms of its sporting culture was that it played the game of rugby. Kim was enthralled and took it up with great enthusiasm, initially playing in the second row for the school's U/14 side. He loved the game and was actually quite good at it. His sometime teammate of the time and good friend, Greg Buchanan, also then living in Claremont, remembers him as 'one who had great physical courage when he played'. Kim's long-time rugby coach, John Brown, had a similar impression: 'Kim always gave it his all, and obviously enjoyed it hugely, without ever being an absolute stand-out player. He was a big sort of bloke even then, and always good to have right in the middle of the forwards. He wasn't one to score lots and lots of tries, but you could count on him to give it his all.' In terms of his other extracurricular activities, one thing he most definitely did *not* get involved in was debating, even though he was asked and the school had a good debating team. 'Debating never interested me,' he says. 'Not at all. Whereas I always regarded what Dad did in politics as debating *to a point*, debating at school seemed to be just debating for the love of arguing, and I always found it a bit superficial.'

After school, he and his neighbourhood friends were, as one of them describes it, 'the last of the Ginger Meggs generation'.[10] Television had not yet really hit Perth, and sport in the park and on the street remained the principal leisure pursuit. Rambling wild and wilder was the go, often with that most crucial accoutrement of Ginger Meggs himself: the 'billycart', or 'hill-trolley', as it is known in Perth. The tiniest of slopes at one end of Thomson Road could be used for the purpose, as could the quite steep street that led down to the nearby Claremont Baths.

A large part of Kim's out-of-school time was spent thus, gambolling around with such friends as Chris Smith, Greg Buchanan and Colin Wilson. It was the last, particularly, whom Kim probably spent most time with. Wilson had been with him all through primary school, was in most of the same classes at Hollywood, and as Kim remembers it, 'He was like me in that he tended to like the historical, English subjects rather than the maths, science, physics subjects. He was a very sober sort of bloke, and a good friend to have because he would never get you into trouble. He never considered that he had to *test* anything of you. He never was a competitor, he was the sort of bloke who was just always there, a solid performer, solid sportsperson, just always doing moderately well, and we got on very, very well.'

Kim would often go to Col's place at 11 Devon Street, Swanbourne — about 20 minutes walk away — just as Col would make the same trek to Kim's. When, as would often happen, the two would go to Thomson Road after school, they would hurl their school-satchels onto Kim's bed and rush out the gate to meet all the other blokes in Claremont Park, there to play endless games, year-round, starting with cricket in the summer. Three stumps up one end, one up the other, and they were into it. Kim's great hero was the Australian Test fast bowler, Graham McKenzie — a local player for Claremont no less, whom they had even seen around from time to time in the flesh — and Kim, with his spindly polio-stricken legs pumping, would run into the crease trying to imitate McKenzie's long, loping action, dreaming the dream of many Australian boys of that era. 'I was like all my friends,' he recounts, 'in that I wanted to play for Australia.'

(He never got close, but one of the proudest moments in Kim's young life came after he took a hat-trick for the Claremont Cricket Club 4th XI, with Chris Smith having taken one of the catches in slips. At the end of season wind-up, none other than Graham McKenzie himself presented him with a hat-trick trophy with the words: 'I haven't got one of these.')

When Perth's version of winter came around, the lads switched to playing Australian Rules Football. Kim could kick pretty well despite his seagull legs, and if McKenzie was his cricket hero, a bloke called John Gerovich was his Aussie Rules inspiration. 'Gero' played full-forward for South Fremantle, the club Kim's father was the Vice Patron of, and father and son would frequently go to watch the team play on Saturday afternoons. These were the only times when Kim Jnr heard Kim Snr swear, as he would often grumble 'bloody useless!' or some such in frustration when South Fremantle made a mistake, but the younger man only had eyes for Gerovich. 'Talk about "up there Cazaly",' Kim remembers, 'because this guy really did have a leap, and he'd kick 100 goals a season. If Gero was scoring 9 or 10 goals in a game you'd know that South Fremantle was sweet — they'd do fine.' Upon his return to Claremont Park, Kim would try and 'mark' the ball just like Gerovich did, and kick it on the fly like he did, almost before his feet had regained purchase on the ground. Gero could damn near *fly*. So it went on, for the lads of Claremont, through all their adolescent years. Throughout these fun times, their mate Kim was notable for a couple of things.

'He could never play on Sundays with us,' his friend Chris Smith recalls. 'There was something with his mum and dad that Sunday was God's day, and that it wasn't for playing games. And whereas we would all play pretty much until we couldn't see the ball any more, Kim always had to go at five or six o'clock, when his mum wanted him home by, and he'd look at his watch and suddenly be off.' The other times they lost their mate was when they engaged in the ever-so-slightly more nefarious activities of the Ginger Meggs generation. Down by Claremont Baths on the Swan River, there was an enormous clump of extremely thick bamboo, and within that bamboo were tiny clearings. It was the one part of the area where kids could have little fear of being seen by adults, and they used it for the obvious — smoking, drinking and, if they got lucky, maybe the odd bit of groping with the opposite sex. 'I remember Kim coming with us once or twice when we had some cigarettes,' Smith says, 'and he would take a couple of puffs, but then he'd stop, and say "That's not for me". He'd go back home. I don't think Kim was allowed to roam as much as the rest of us. Even though he was a big lad, he was the least rowdy of the lot, I think because he was more strictly controlled than we all were. The park was alright for Kim because his mum only had to look out the window and there he was. But I think less so, down by the river.' It was pretty much the same thing with the 'pinnies', the pinball machines that were to be found in George's Milk Bar on Bay View Terrace, just on the other side of Claremont Park, down by the Stirling Highway. 'You never saw Kim there,' Greg Buchanan relates. 'I think his parents had forbidden him to go. Mind you, my parents had forbidden me too, *strictly* forbidden me, but I was always there. Some of the guys put him down as a bit of a wuss, but he still wouldn't be in it.'

A similar lack of aptitude for getting involved in common adolescent vices was on display at Hollywood High. When they were all in their mid-adolescent years, the school community was, as Kim recalls, 'totally scandalised when it turned out that a couple of girls were running a racket of ill fame over the road at Karrakatta Cemetery'. This particular racket involved, not to put too fine a point on it, 'Gladwrap and elastic bands'. At least that's the way he remembers it. 'At Hollywood,' he recalls, 'Karrakatta was where you went for smoking, drinking and carousing, shall we say, and the teachers were pretty hard if you were caught out of bounds.'

Kim Beazley Jnr never was. Not early in his school career, not later. Never. Not because he was clever, simply because he never had any interest in those sorts of things. While his father was a God-fearing man to beat them all, and it is almost a cliché for the 'son of a preacher man' to turn out to be the wildest fellow in town — as a man by the name of Robert Hawke would prove to be at one time in his life — Kim did not come even remotely close to following that pattern. 'There never seemed to be much point in rebelling,' he says. 'I had my own views about Dad's religion, but I was much more interested in sport than I was in cutting loose.'

He did in fact push the boundaries, just occasionally. Every now and then as a young teenager he would make a trip up to the farm of some family friends they had met through the MRA Movement, the Richardsons, who lived at Miling, about 130 kilometres northeast of Perth. It was a time in his life when the strength of adolescence was first starting to flow into his limbs and he enjoyed the hard physical labour of bagging the wheat and stacking it up in the shed, and doing such things as repairing windmills and fences, 'dagging' sheep and occasionally butchering them for meat. He would always finish the day dead-dog tired, but it was a satisfying fatigue. In the twilight of the evening he would play cricket on the homestead's lawns with the Richardson boys, Frank and Howard, and with them would sometimes turn out on the weekends for the Miling Cricket Club. On one occasion when Miling played the nearby town of Bindi Bindi, Kim found himself as one of the opening batsmen against, as he remembers, 'a barefoot Aboriginal bowler who was as fast as hot lead'. Time and again the lad from Bindi Bindi charged in; time and again Kim would swing at the ball, and miss before he realised ... The guy was *so* fast, and so wild, that the wicket-keeper himself was obliged to stand a long, long way back from his usual position. 'So I said to my partner, "Whatever happens, as soon as he releases the ball, just run on through, and I'll do the same for you".' The ruse worked. 'We had an opening partnership of 62 to which my contribution was 3 before I got out, and sundries were 35! They just couldn't work out how to stop us, short of standing closer to the stumps, and that was too dangerous because the guy was so fast. They got very annoyed.'

Miling won, and the day finished in not untypical fashion for young men of that age, and of that era. Someone brought out some grog — Sparkling Porphyry Pearl. Kim knew he shouldn't, knew that neither his hosts the Richardsons nor his parents would approve, knew he was probably letting himself down, etc, etc, but he had worked up a serious thirst on the day and when one of the lads passed him a bottle, and all the others were looking at him, it wasn't like he had a choice. His manhood was at stake. He put the bottle to his lips, threw his head back, and took a big gulp. He liked it. Several gulps along he liked it well enough to be impatient for his next turn, and was soon knocking it back with the thirst of a sailor on Marseilles shore leave. 'We really got stuck into it,' he recalls now, 'totally plastered, and when we got home, I was feeling very much the worse for wear.' In bed, later, he noticed that the room around him seemed to continue spinning whether he closed his eyes or not, and on a tide of torment he finally drifted off into something that would have to pass for sleep ...

He could smell smoke. He could hear shouts. He sensed flames, flickering. Was this hell? Someone gripped him, had him by both arms, and was shaking him violently. The Devil? 'Kim, come quick, the top paddock's on fire.' And it really was. Around midnight, a bolt of lightning had struck the earth, setting alight the long grass, and that fire was now threatening the Richardson homestead. In as terrible shape as he was — he felt positively *dreadful* — he was handed a wet sack and sent in to battle the flames. There was searing heat, billowing smoke, frenzied insects all around, little creatures that might well have been rats running around his feet, and someone playing bongo drums nineteen to the dozen right in the middle of his skull. So it went for another couple of hours until they finally got the fire out. 'And that,' he asserts sagely now, 'was my experience the first time I drank.' It would be nearly a decade before the demon drink again passed his lips.

And girls? He was dead keen, but ... 'But I was hopeless at that sort of stuff,' he remembers. 'I was into sport and into books and that sort of thing. But I wasn't into girls in a big way, not at that stage.'

Which is not to say he didn't have his fair share of adolescent crushes. Very few of the girls at school took his fancy, one way or another, but his neighbourhood was not without pretty girls. One girl who fired his imagination like no other, lived just up the same street on the other side of the road. Her name was Janet Ranford: 'She was a bit of alright,' he still vividly remembers. 'She was a doll ... an absolute *corker*!' Long of limb, clear of eye, shapely and with long brunette hair, she was pretty close to young Kim's fantasy girl, even if she was five years older and ensconced at university while he was still in the early years of high school. Much to his chagrin though, it seemed Janet was already rather keen on someone else, some bloke she had met at university, some South African bloke by the name of Robert Holmes à Court. Kim used to see them tearing off up the street on a scooter on their way to University dances or some such, her long hair billowing behind her as she went.

Sigh.

Often, when Greg Buchanan would go over to the Beazley house, he and Kim would gravitate to the latter's bedroom. 'It was actually like a bedroom-cum-study,' Buchanan recollects, 'set up on a kind of enclosed verandah, and it wasn't really a typical boy's room. He was fairly ordered and he really had an extensive personal library of books.' The two would often sit on the bed and talk. 'I wouldn't say that I was a close friend of Kim's and maybe apart from Col Wilson, he didn't have really close friends,' Buchanan says, 'but Kim had people that he liked to have discussions with, and I was one of them. What I found interesting with Kim was that we could sit down and talk about a lot of things other than just who was kicking the most goals in the local competition.' Things like ... politics; not Liberal/Labor politics, but more along the lines of moral stands that should be taken on particular political issues. Buchanan explains: 'It was more that he was politically *aware* than anything and he had strong, well-developed views on social issues — large and small scale — things like the Apartheid system, which he hated. These views were much more developed than you would expect, far more mature and multidimensional than me. When I look back on it now, my arguments were based on just pure gut-reactions, whereas he'd obviously been involved and exposed to discussions with his father and of course had read all those books that were surrounding us.'

Those books. One day they were chatting, when Buchanan spied upon his mate's groaning bookshelves a big thick book called *Candide*, written by some bloke called Voltaire. Buchanan picked it up, and, immediately impressed by its weight, asked 'What the hell is *this* all about!?!?'

'It's fantastic,' he remembers the 14-year-old Kim replying, 'this is the book that really had a big effect on the French Revolution and . . .'

'The French *what*?'

So it went.

This devotion that young Kim had to reading such authors had been nurtured from his earliest days. Betty Beazley, who had done her thesis at University of Western Australia on the works of T.S. Eliot, would spend long hours reading book after book to her children on the couch, until Kim Jnr was eventually able to read them too, and would often take on the role of storyteller to his younger siblings. Perhaps the main impetus behind young Kim reading, though, went back to his father's tutorials at the nightly meals. 'What I was fascinated with was why was he so knowledgeable,' Kim Jnr says, 'How did he get to be that way, what had he done to know so much?' Part of the answer at least, he concluded, was that his father was always reading, and he resolved to do the same. And when his father was actually home on-site, the literary life of the family would be thrown a notch higher still. Apart from his own example to his children of constantly reading books, one of his passions was poetry, and he loved to recite to them some of the favourites that he had learnt off by heart. His favourite poet of all was a local Western Australian, John K. Ewers, who had also been a close-enough friend of his and Betty's to attend their wedding. Often he and the children would sit out on the verandah, looking out to the park, as he would recite his favourite poems for them. The best Ewers poem was about their very state, he would tell them:

There used to be a red road running o'er the rise,
Dipping down to fern land and climbing to the skies,
There among the tall trees the sleepy shadows lay,
And the forest birds were singing there the live long day.
I used to like to walk there, as the days grew old,
Beneath the stately gum trees, a fire with sunset gold
And watch the pale stars, steal there beyond the eastern hill,
Then trim my lamp a nearer star, within my window sill.
I used to hear the storm winds among the ravaged trees,
I used to see the Spring spread her dainty tapestries,
I used to see the summer come, with anger in her eye,
I breathed the very breath of life, beneath my virgin sky.
There isn't any red road there beside my cottage now,
The trees have bowed before the blaze, the shrubs before
   the plough,
There isn't any red road — they've covered it with tar,
And the birds which come to steal the grain, are strangers
   from afar ...[11]

Though Ewers had penned the poem some three decades previously, the theme of it had never been more pertinent to Western Australia than right then, in those early 1960s. All over the state at that time there were indeed red roads disappearing beneath asphalt as development money flowed in. Up in the Hamersley Region, a man called Lang Hancock had been sheltering from a storm by flying a plane between the walls of a 70-metre gorge and noticed rich veins of ore in the rock face. Investigation proved that as a matter of fact 'rich' wasn't the word for it. There was actually around a billion tonnes of iron ore there — around three times what Australia's presumed iron ore reserves were at that time — and by 1960 Hancock had opened a mine. Bit by bit, and then in a rush, Western Australians realised that there was a fortune lying to the north. Around and about Kim at Hollywood High, it was not unheard of for some of his schoolchums to simply up and leave — either to go and seek work on their own account, or in the company of their parents who were heading up that way hoping to make their fortunes. While the Beazley family was never remotely tempted by such a thing, there was no doubt they would be affected by it, for the realm that the 'family business' operated in, politics, would itself be transformed by the discovery of such wealth, as new political equations would come into play.

Over in Dallas, at 12.30 pm local time, on 22 November 1963, President John F. Kennedy was being driven along Elm Street in an open limousine at just over 11 miles per hour. At least two shots rang out. President Kennedy was first struck by a bullet which entered the back of his neck and exited through the lower front portion of his neck, causing a wound which might not necessarily have been lethal. However, almost instantaneously thereafter he was struck a second time by a bullet which entered the right-rear portion of his head, causing a massive and fatal wound. He was rushed to Dallas's Parkland Hospital, and declared dead shortly thereafter.

The emotional tidal wave of grief, outrage and despair that resulted did not stop at America's shores. To the west it rolled clear across the mighty Pacific and engulfed an Australia that was in the full grip of a Federal election campaign, with the Liberal Prime Minister Sir Robert Menzies genuinely struggling to hold on against the claims of Labor's Arthur Calwell — who in the previous election had taken his party to within two seats of victory. Political historians would argue for decades just what precise effect the tragedy had on the mood of the Australian people at the time, but the prevalent theory is that in the rushing floodwaters of midnight, people held on for dear life to what they knew, and after 14 continuous years of Liberals in office what they knew in Australia was the Menzies Government.

Whatever the truth of that, there is no doubt that on the night of 30 November 1963, the three Beazley children had begun watching the Federal election coverage on that strange thing called 'television' at a neighbour's house with joy in their hearts. Both of their parents had told them that this was it, that the wait was over and after almost 15 years of being in opposition, Labor was at last going to win, and that their Dad would in all likelihood make it into the ministry. There was the added bonus, in Merrilyn's memory, that 'a win for Labor would "legitimise" us. We were very much "outsiders" in a basically Liberal world, Labor people living in the increasingly up-market suburb of Claremont, but we felt that was about to change.'

This notion of being 'legitimised' is one that Kim Jnr at least partially endorses. Already once or twice at high school he had been called a 'Commo' by classmates who took him to be exactly that as the son of Western Australia's best-known and often *only* Federal Labor parliamentarian. It would be very nice indeed if his father could at least be part of the government of the day. It didn't happen. Before the children's horrified eyes, it soon became apparent that what their parents had promised wasn't going to happen after all. Labor was going down the all-too-familiar tubes, and the Liberals were going to remain in power.

To this day, Betty Beazley has never seen anything like it. 'The way those children *reacted*!' she exclaims. 'They swore and I hadn't heard them swear before. And they cried.' When Kim the younger challenged his father about it, to ask him how such a terrible thing could possibly have happened, the answer was firm, if sad. 'That,' his father told him a little lugubriously, 'is politics.' It was an election result that profoundly affected young Kim as he approached his 15th birthday. It was after this devastating loss — with Kim Snr having his own margin of victory cut in half from the last election, to only 5000 votes — that the youngster began to focus ever more assiduously on politics. As he recalls it, this focus was less on the Liberal Party and what they were doing, and more on the ALP — and, specifically, on what ailed them that they seemed never to be elected. 'So I would talk over with Dad all the specifics,' he explains. 'What was it that had caused the split and the DLP to be formed, would the Labor Party ever be electable if it persisted in its attitude of hostility to aid for non-government schools, was the Labor Party's position on White Australia right? Then, because of the nature of the times, there was an enormous amount of emphasis on foreign policy: was it right that we didn't recognise China? Should we be involved in the defence of Malaysia? Should the Indonesians have West Irian? I became conscious that there was a government that was taking decisions, many of which seemed misguided, but which were equally dangerous to oppose because an electoral wasteland confronted you if you didn't do it smart.'

One who observed the maturing of Kim's political ideas was a notable Caucus colleague of his father's, Dr Jim Cairns. He would see the teenager from time to time, both in Perth at the family home, and in Canberra when he was visiting.

'Kim was always a very big boy,' Dr Cairns describes, 'and I think very quiet, studious really, in most of his teens and later on. He was pleasant, he was nice, he was easygoing and he *listened*, he wasn't a great talker, he seemed to be learning all the time. If it was appropriate, he had relevant and sound things to say, and in the views I heard him express he had more the characteristics of [traditional] Labor than his father, who often found his own inspiration within his religion.'

At the end of Kim's penultimate year at Hollywood High, the headmaster, after consultation with his teachers, announced the school captain and prefects for the following year. Kim was named as a prefect, while one of his other friends, David Stanton, was the School Captain. Neither one remembers it being a big deal at the time, nor even if it was a tight vote. 'I remember Kim congratulating me immediately after the headmaster told us,' Stanton says, 'and I was pleased, but I don't remember there being any sense of disappointment from him.' 'It didn't worry me one way or another,' says Kim, 'and I was happy to be a prefect.' Being a prefect actually entailed very little in terms of enforcing discipline on his fellow students, though one job that did fall to him was to ensure that when he was riding home on the bus, he saw no smoking by Hollywood High people. He observed this duty in his own fashion. '"*Saw*" was the operative word,' he says with a laugh. 'If I didn't *see* anybody, they couldn't get in trouble, so what the people who wanted to smoke would do, was to crouch down behind the seats and I'd be sitting up the front, and it was as though the back of the bus was empty, you could only see the smoke curling up. I wouldn't do anything. But once or twice some students would sort of defy that, by suddenly sitting up there with a cigarette — so I'd put them off the bus, out on the road. This was universally approved by the bus company, because they'd broken the *real* rule. The real rule was not "Don't Smoke," but "Don't be *seen* Smoking".'

Real leadership for him would come as the captain of the school rugby XV in his final year — his first position of formal leadership of anything. As captain, it was his honour to run onto the field at the head of the team, as the school's cheer squad on the sideline chanted the famous school war cry.

> *Hooley dooley!*
> *Hooley dooley!*
> *Fight, fight, fight!*
> *Hollywood, Hollywood!*
> *Red and white!*
> *Red's for our courage,*
> *White's cause we're good.*
> *Come on team!*
> *Come on school!*
> *Come on Hollywood!*[12]

On the field, in the thick of it, with the boys of Christ Church or John Curtin High School coming at them, Kim does not remember himself as a standout inspiration to his teammates. While he didn't mind the odd firebrand speech under the goalposts to rouse the troops from their torpor and get them once again to go hard at their opponents, there is no memory of such speeches having particularly rousing results. 'Nobody took any notice of me,' he recalls, 'and I learned very quickly that you can't actually captain a team from the second row.' David Stanton, who played in the pack beside him, considers that a harsh self-assessment. 'I thought he was an excellent captain of a relatively young team,' he suggests. 'He was a very hard-working player, and I think really led by example more than anything else. But on occasions when he did make speeches, the guys listened. They were never violent speeches though; he was always very conscious of fair-play, and the most common theme of his speeches was, "we've got to work harder".' That year, they really did need to work harder as a matter of fact, because they were thumped on something like eight out of 10 occasions. At least though, at *least*, they held those fancy-pants schmucks from Perth Modern to only a 6–3 win over them. The Hollywood High boys had been totally outgunned and outclassed, but had lifted themselves way above their abilities to lose by only three points. 'A great game, even if we lost,' Kim says now fondly.

That year's school magazine, *The Prokyon*, records his efforts in the 1965 season:

> Kim Beazley — Captain. Second row forward. Lent much power to scrums, good tackle. David Stanton and he combined to form a powerful second row.

His cricket report, for the record, was similar in tone:

> K. Beazley — An accurate medium fast bowler whose good performances were due to persistent and relentless effort.

As the second-half of 1965 rolled on, it was time to stop focusing on extraneous things like rugby, and start focusing on final exams. In his ongoing formal education, he had been helped immensely not just by his father and his constant tutorials, but also, oddly enough, by the family's continued involvement with Moral Rearmament. One of the benefits of the Moral Rearmament Movement was that it had a philosophy of 'open house', of extending hospitality to MRA visitors who might be in your own area, as well as encouraging visits by locals who might be interested in learning something more of the movement. What this meant in the Beazley household was that it delivered up to the family table, month after month, people from all over the world, of diverse backgrounds and talents, as well as many interesting local people. It meant, effectively, that the already rich realm of ideas in the Beazley household was further enriched by visitors of exotic backgrounds.

One visitor who would become a family friend was an Aboriginal woman by the name of Marge Tucker, sometimes known among her own people as Princess Lilardia. Ms Tucker was a woman of particularly regal bearing, and the family listened, fascinated, to her stories of growing up in Moonachulla in northern Victoria, and the almost unbelievable things that had happened to her. They learnt how she was taken by the Aboriginal Protection Board at the age of 13 and sent to the Cootamundra Domestic Training Home for Aboriginal Girls. 'She had the most beautiful eyes I had ever seen,' remembers Merrilyn. 'Her physical presence was extraordinary. As she told her stories, she radiated a calm that I have never felt from any other human being.'

'It was just like taking little puppies away to drown them and watching the mother get up to follow them,' Ms Tucker recounted to one with a tape-recorder once.[13] 'That's how it comes to me now. I don't know whether it's still going on.'

'What I remember about Marge is her amazing natural dignity,' Kim recalls, 'and her kind, grandmotherly voice, which was very calm despite the horror of what she was saying. The way in which she addressed the stories was as an exercise in teaching, she was trying to teach us something new, some of the poisonous features of race relations in this country ... '

When the inspector came to school to take us away, another Aboriginal woman said to one of the boys: 'Run like mad to get their mother.'

My mother came running, still with her apron on. She put her arms around us, and we held on to her tightly. She said: 'They're not neglected. See, they're well dressed.' The last we saw of her, she was walking up and down in front of the police station, crying and wringing her hands.

Marge and her sister had been taken under the powers conferred by the Aboriginal Protection Act 1909, which allowed for the removal from their families of Aboriginal children defined as 'neglected'. In a later time, it would become clear that Marge Tucker's experience was far from isolated and, indeed, that there were so many similar cases that these children became known as 'the Stolen Generation'.

On matters of Aboriginal welfare, Kim Snr could take a very deep bow, being the man primarily responsible for introducing the concept of Aboriginal land rights onto the Labor Party platform at the ALP National Conference in 1951, and being the first one to speak on the subject in Federal Parliament, in 1952. He did so, he says, out of a deep-seated belief that 'if Aborigines owned land they would negotiate from a position of strength, if they don't own land they will always negotiate from a position of weakness'.*

Also welcomed into the Beazley family home through their MRA connections, and through general hospitality, were many Colombo Plan students from the less-developed countries of Africa and Asia. In Australia to further their studies, they told their stories about their own parts of the world. Sometimes, too, young teenaged Naval trainees would come out from a nearby base. While most of the visitors were people of mid-range accomplishments and background, others were international visitors of some standing, who were particularly fascinating to young Kim. One who entered their home who would prove to be quite an influence on Kim Jnr was Rajmohan Gandhi from India, none other than the grandson of Mahatma Gandhi. Rajmohan was one of his country's leading journalists, who went on to be a highly esteemed professor — and one of the key proponents of MRA in India. Sixteen-year-old Kim listened in awed silence as his father and the visitor would discuss in the most intimate detail the political affairs of the subcontinent, its history, and its place in the geopolitical world. He also heard them discussing how MRA could help save India, and how it was crucial that it do just that. The key, they thought, was to make the youth and the leaders of the land, in particular, believe in living a pure life, and to show them the virtues, the Godliness and rewards that such a life would bring.

---

*In terms of the influence that Kim Beazley Snr had on initiating the process of Aboriginal reconciliation in Australia, the citation at the Conferral of an Honorary Doctorate of Laws by the Australian National University, in September 1976, is revealing: 'It has become popular, over the last few years, to recognise the contribution of the Aboriginal people to this nation, and to recognise the injustices that have been done to them; but over the last half century this was far from popular; and in that time few people have done as much, and none have done more, than Kim Beazley [Snr] has, to bring about that change in attitude. His constant concern has been twofold – to ensure better education for Aborigines and a better place for them in our society; and at the same time full study of their situation and a better knowledge and understanding of them amongst other Australians.'

Mrs Beazley remembers another visitor — the young Marquis of Montrose from England, soon to become the Duke of Graham. She remembers him because when he was coming, 'we decided which room he would have and then we put all our very best things into that room, because though our home was quite ordinary, we wanted him to have our best'. Kim savoured such visits, and now credits them with 'helping to stimulate me intellectually, and open me up to the world'. The same view of such MRA benefits could not be ascribed to Merrilyn. She remembers railing against the strictures of MRA, and everything that came with it, with a force that shakes her still.

'I felt I could never invite my friends home because of the weirdness of my parents,' she says flatly. 'It was bad enough that they were weird being Labor in a Conservative State — my friends could have coped with that — but being weird in this MRA way, well that was just too much. Normal kid behaviour, normal teenage behaviour was very much frowned upon. It was a cult, let's not muck around about this, we are talking real *cult* stuff here. None of this Kim ever experienced, so he could never understand why I was unhappy about it. Because his path was clear, he was going to go into politics. A lot of the "Aunties" thought he could become a politician then he would be the person who would introduce Moral Rearmament to Australia. But the fate of females in MRA was to go and literally cook, wash dishes or be secretaries and if they thought I was going to follow this bloody route they had another thing coming.'

As a matter of fact the Beazley parents really would have to rethink a lot of things when it came to Merrilyn, and her battles with them over the rules of the house and of life in general were a fairly constant soundtrack playing in the background during Kim's teenage years and into early adulthood. When he got a lot older, Kim too would have his fair share of qualms about some of the ways of MRA, but never chose to confront them head on with his parents. There, too, was a crucial difference between the two oldest of the Beazley children. 'When faced with an obstacle,' one MRA elder at a camp noted, 'Kim will slip through the window, whereas Merrilyn will try to bash down the door.'[14]

One day, when Kim was nearing the end of Hollywood High, his father took him aside, to have a word with him. 'Look son,' he said, 'your life is yours. I have views on what you ought to be doing and views on how you ought to conduct yourself, but you must make your choices and I will not seek to impose on you my own views.'

Yes, Dad. Thus, at the age of 17, with a sharp brain and the strong foundations of his education already laid — Kim would get three distinctions and three passes for his Leaving exams, the distinctions for History, English and Music. The possible directions in which these could lead young Kim extended right around the compass. The words of his father meant that when it came right down to it, he could actually do anything, *anything* he wanted.

He made up his mind ... He would go to India to work for a year for the Moral Rearmament Movement, with Rajmohan Gandhi and 50 or so others drawn from the South Pacific. So he set out for India, while his mates scattered elsewhere. Greg Buchanan went to the Navy before finding his way to the Air Force; Col Wilson went into accounting, Chris Smith had already set off into the world of small business the year before. None were surprised at Kim's choice of going off to India. 'Not at all,' recollects Greg Buchanan, 'we all knew that Kim was heavily into Moral Rearmament and that was just the sort of thing he *would* do. It wasn't our sort of thing, but we wished him well, wherever it took him. We didn't see him too much after that.'

CHAPTER FOUR

PASSAGE TO INDIA

'Like the mountain climber who can see the mountain more
clearly from the plain ...'
Kahlil Gibran, The Prophet.

There is in travel parlance, something commonly known as
'India Shock'. It is that slightly catatonic state new arrivals
from the Western world can descend into, when finding that
nothing surrounding them in this new world, really *nothing*, is
familiar. People talk of looking out the window and seeing a man
walking a bear; of realising that the building in front of them was
constructed before Alexander the Great had left his crib; of tasting
curry that would not bow to the sun; of seeing things in everyday life
that they never suspected existed on heaven or earth. Kim Jnr had a
good measure of this condition, straight after he arrived in May of
1966. After a very welcoming reception at Bombay airport, he went
out into the harshness of India proper. Mick Lennon, who was one of
the Moral Rearmament elders from New Zealand — under whose
guidance Kim would be placed for a fair measure of the time he was
there — happened to be sitting beside him in the bus on the way from
the airport. He describes it thus: 'It was dark, but you could still see it.
Right there by the airport were people living in the most *appalling*
conditions, living in these kind of shantytowns if they were lucky with
hessian sacks for cover, and using the street gutters as their sewage
system. Other people with no arms were banging on the windows,

asking for money, howling at us, and I remember Kim was so shocked, I don't think he came out of his room for a few days.'

When he did emerge from both his room and his shock, a bit stronger and ready to face it, there were other things that horrified the young man from Perth — who to that point had led a reasonably sheltered life with little exposure to the seamy side of things. He was walking through a street in central Bombay, when a man approached him carrying a baby. It was dead. The Australian sensed instinctively that it was dead, and *newly* dead at that, for there is a total floppiness of limb in the recently deceased which a merely sleeping child does not display. The man wanted money. Money to eat, money to bury the child, money to make sure his other children could get medical care. Kim wasn't sure. He gave him some coins and notes of indeterminate value, outraged and disgusted in equal measure at what he had seen. It was, though — as is also a common experience in India — a disgust that would lessen with time, as he would often come to see beggars carrying dead children. In terms of props with which to separate tourists from their money, nothing had greater force, and this was a country where the truly unbelievable was average. 'India was full of extremities of poverty and filth,' he recounts now, 'and it took me some time to get over it; how it was possible to have some people literally starving right beside people who had excessive amounts.'

There was a similarity there to the same influences that had shaped and hardened his father's political attitudes during the Great Depression in Perth in the 1930s, the difference perhaps was that the foundations of Kim's own political beliefs were already substantially laid, and seeing the misery of such poverty close-up merely confirmed the rightness of those beliefs. And so to work. Serious work. He had come here in the company of no fewer than 40 other Australians of his age — together with a sprinkling of New Zealanders, Fijians and Tongans — with the declared intent of helping to save India. With Rajmohan as leader, they had formed a group called 'Sing Out Australia', and were a troupe moving from town to town, putting on shows replete with singing, dancing, poetry recitals, storytelling and whatever else they could develop along the way to fill up the two-and-a-half hours it ran. It was entertainment with a purpose, designed to appeal to two distinctly different groups — India's youth and its political class.

If all went wonderfully well, then the youth in the towns would be so enthused they would form up their own groups, like 'Sing Out

Bombay', 'Sing Out Bangalore', who would in turn spawn other groups, and so it would go in a kind of domino effect for Good. 'We wanted to give them an aim beyond just their self-advancement,' Lennon remembers. 'We wanted to show as an example the selfless way our own young MRA people were living, living for others and not just for themselves. And we also wanted to show the politicians, the joys of the Moral Rearmament way of life, and make them understand the possibilities of the future if they and their constituents embraced it. We wanted the revue to be a part of helping to create a clean and united India, with all the people working for the one cause, to bring an end to corruption. So we had stories of character-building stuff, things like how Australians had all worked together to do the Snowy River scheme.'

They wanted, in short, to do to individual Indian politicians and Indian youth much the same as had been done to Kim Beazley Snr, 12 years previously — convert them to the cause.

It was a task that Kim Jnr took extremely seriously, as the letters that he wrote home to his parents show. These snapshots of the 17-year-old soul reveal him to be an extremely serious, pious and intellectually mature young man, albeit a little self-conscious as he makes his way for the first time on his own on the moral high road of life. His first letter, addressed to Mr & Mrs Kim Beazley M.P. read:

5 May 1966
Dear Mum, Dad, Merrilyn, David and Nana,
Just a short note to let you know I am here. We had a terrific flight out from Perth and arrived in Bombay to a tremendous reception by a crowd of youth from the conference. They really are a fine bunch of people. We were rushed through customs and were welcomed with three songs and a garland of flowers each.

The first thing that strikes you about India is its age. You can see it is a very old country with great traditions. It is extremely poor too. I have never seen anything like it. To see the way people live in wooden constructions with a hessian bag for a roof really tears at your heart.

We had a hair raising bus journey of about 5 miles to the conference and tonight we are going to see the new Indian musical, 'India Arise'. It will be a tremendous evening, and it is being put on in one of the nearby fishing villages. Rajmohan is fighting a terrific battle over here [and] it is a privilege to be with him.

I was sorry to hear that Dad did not make the delegation. It must be a real battle in the ALP, but I am sure the right ideas will win through. It is wonderful to hear the way you are taking this move on, Dad, and the telegram you sent to the cast really moved us.
Best of luck in the battles over there,
Yours,
Kim.

The troupe of 'Sing Out Australia' began their quest in Bombay, being initially accommodated in a school in the fishing village of Andheri on the outskirts of the city, where they began rehearsals. 'The village was fantastic,' Kim remembers. 'You were right there beside the sea, you would look out and see the bay just off the coast of Bombay and the endless twinkling lights of the ships strung out across the Arabian Gulf and it was just magic. In the evenings, we'd sometimes walk along the beach and you'd see the villagers repairing their nets.'

Kim Beazley was a real song-and-dance man bringing a mix of skills to the revue, from singing to playing the piano, guitar and harmonica — all skills he had continued to refine while at Hollywood High. Each of the troupe would have something to offer. Kim reports: 'It was probably the singing that I did mostly, and also what I enjoyed the most. They were songs about reconciliation, about improving your life, songs about having good attitudes to other people.' One of his fellow troupe members David Lancaster, remembers Kim as 'a particularly good singer,' while another Australian, Hugh Nelson, comments that 'Kim's language and presentation skills were recognised early, so it was often him that would kind of open the show, saying things like "welcome ladies and gentlemen, we have a *wonderful* show to present for you here tonight" . . .'

After the revue, they'd ask the audience to make donations so they could continue to carry on their important work, and then the troupe members would mingle freely with the audience, talk to them about their lives, and see if they too would like to be part of the Moral Rearmament life. Would they perhaps like to start up their own troupe? If they did, the stars of 'Sing Out Australia' would be most happy to help train them.

Then they would head to the next town, to be billeted with friendly families, and hopefully to continue to inspire the people they met with the possibilities of living their life the Moral Rearmament way.

While Kim was emotionally and intellectually enthused by the project, he suffered one problem. 'Delhi Belly' — severe dysentery.

13 May 1966
Dear Mum, Dad, Merrilyn, David & Nana.
    . . . It was a great letter you sent me Dad, and I appreciate very much your guidance for me. I have the doubtful distinction of becoming Sing Out's first bad casualty. I'm in bed at the moment with a rotten bad case of food poisoning, but I am recovering. I was vomiting solidly all yesterday and fortunately haven't the strength to vomit any more.
    We had full houses on Sunday and Monday, smaller ones Tuesday and Wednesday and they are beginning to pick up again now.
    The Indian youth with the force are really terrific and you can really see them going somewhere. What we need to do is raise 10 000 more like them in the next six months. We are really fighting a battle to save a nation over here . . .
Yours,
Kim.

As the troupe began to settle in, Kim's former repugnance of India's surface squalor all but disappeared. 'I came to see it was the most interesting, exotic place I'd ever seen, I thought it was fantastic,' Kim comments. He also became close friends with other cast members, especially Hugh Nelson. They had known each other since childhood, having both been a part of the MRA network in Perth. Hugh had come to the only birthday party Kim had ever had, when he was seven — the Beazleys were never big ones for parties — and although they had seen each other from time to time since, it was only now living cheek by jowel by towel that they came to know each other well. 'I remember,' Nelson says, 'admiring just how committed Kim was to the cause. It wasn't a holiday for him, he really, really wanted to do everything possible to help the country.'

Commitment aside, the tour was not easy for the oldest of the Beazley children. As they moved from the west to the southeast of the country, staying with all sorts of families including the poorest of the poor, they were obliged to eat whatever was served, howsoever it had been prepared, and one way or another Kim Jnr did not react well to it. His Delhi Belly simply would not quit, and he continued to lose weight. If it was a physically tough life which weakened his body, he was still conscious that the experience was strengthening both his mind and his spirit. By the end of May, he was clear about the effect that India was starting to have on him, and the way it was changing his thinking. This letter reveals a much more serious and reflective young man.

> 22 May 1966
> ... It is also great to get the news from home, Mum. I think of home a lot. I have been very sick lately and I seem to get it in bouts, but this will wear off soon. Some people become conditioned to India slower than others ...
>
> I appreciated your news about Mr Calwell, Dad. One of the things I want more than anything else is for that man to get peace in his heart. I find it hard to get bitter now. Many of my old bitternesses against Mr Calwell, Mr Whitlam, Mr Menzies, the DLP and a whole host of other things have faded away since being here in India. There is not enough time left for bitterness in this country, and only just enough time for cures. So we must concentrate on cures.
> Yours,
> Kim.

This bitterness at Arthur Calwell was the product of having witnessed some of the caustic wrangles that his father and the then ALP leader Mr Calwell had been involved in over the years. 'Dad himself was pretty phlegmatic about these problems,' he remembers. 'But we kids would absorb those who were opposed to him or had created a problem for him, we'd sort of internalise these as enemies and I suppose Arthur Calwell was one of those.'

In the meantime, at least Kim's role in the show was going well. Now that the tour was getting into stride, all the cast members were working out where their strengths lay. Kim's starring role was to be a swaggie. Not just any swaggie, *the* swaggie, the one made famous in Australia's most famous folk song *Waltzing Matilda*. This was the swaggie who camped by a billabong, under the shade of a Coolabah tree, stole a jumbuck, was pursued by troopers — 1, 2, 3 — and then committed suicide by drowning himself in the billabong. (It's a long story.) In the final piece of the show, the entire cast would belt the whole song out, and then in the climactic scene Kim jumped from the lower tier of the stand into a coloured piece of plastic meant to represent a billabong, and then disappeared from sight. Until ...

Then you could hear it. It was the haunting melody of a harmonica, played by Kim the Swaggie, as he slowly reappeared playing the last bars of the song to the accompaniment of the cast softly singing the last words ...

'And his ghost ... may be heard ... as you pass by the bill-a-bong ... You'll come a'waltzing ... Matilda ... with me ...'

Thank you, and good niiiiiiight!!!!

Quite unlike the swagman, the real Kim was scrupulously honest to the point of disbelief.

30 May 1966
Dad, I am now staying with a young businessman named Siraan Singh Kahlan who will soon be visiting Australia. He may come up to Canberra so if he does can I give him a letter of introduction to you. Also your $20 got through Dad, but please don't send any more money by post, because it is supposed to be declared before entering the country. It is quite difficult to exchange this money, since we do it legally,
All the best,
Yours,
Kim.

Kim became progressively more impressed with Rajmohan Gandhi as time went on. Though he doesn't cite him as a role model when he was growing up, 'because I didn't have role models,' Gandhi was someone who impressed him. 'He was interesting because there was an element of his grandfather in him. He had this profound conviction that anything could be changed by moral crusade, you could cure corruption and all the other things that were endeavouring to break down the Indian political system with a crusade of integrity ...' Rajmohan Gandhi in turn remembers young Kim.

'One of the reasons he stood out,' Professor Gandhi says, 'was because there was quite an independence about him. I can't remember the detail, but while he was part of a group that believed similar things, did similar things and sang songs together, he still stood out as clearly being his own man. A lot of them, because they were so far from home, would form up into tight little knots, but Kim wasn't like that at all, he seemed more intent on doing his own thing. And the other thing I remember was that he was always inclined to debate and discuss, and ask me questions more than the others, was always trying to find out as much as he could about Indian politics and how it all worked. He loved discussing politics.'

> *17 May 1966*
>
> *I have written a letter to Arthur Calwell so I would be grateful if you could check up to see if he received it.*
>
> *We leave for Kerala on the 21st but we still need a great deal of money for the trip. We will do a two week tour of some of the main areas, including a trip to the site we have in Kerala. We will no doubt meet many of the leading Communists, and Mick Lennon, Jill Vertigan and myself are working on what we can say to them.*
>
> *Do please give us news from home and the situation there. We get absolutely nothing in the Indian Press. I would very much like to know how the election campaign is going and how you are going in your seat, Dad.*
> *Yours,*
> *Kim.*

The answer was 'mixed'. Although Kim Snr had at least partly recovered from the troubles of 'The Split', and was universally respected within the party for his intellect, there remained one key problem — that he was always disinclined to push himself forward. One article, printed in the *Melbourne Herald* in the middle of '66 that the Beazleys sent their son, illustrates something of the way in which he was seen by the media.

> *Many of the Government's shrewdest tacticians think that at any election the Government would have more to fear from an ALP team led by Mr Beazley than anybody else the party has to offer.*
>
> *...but Caucus colleagues seem to have overlooked [him] as a possible candidate ... In a time when personal ambition seems to be the force determining the ultimate promotion, [Kim Beazley] has been content to stand on the sidelines and let the self-seekers occupy the ring. He has a graciousness that some senior ministers think hampers him. One of Parliament's best speakers and most effective debaters, he has never in his career tried to hurt personally in debate, and that is a rare fault, if it is one, in present-day Canberra.*

In the meantime, Kim Jnr's own political education was continuing.

28 June 1966
Dear Mum, Dad, Merrilyn and David,
    We have now finished our major shows in Kerala and I have been sent as an advance guard to Bangalore. It is a little disappointing because I have missed the 1 hour show we were giving to Rotary in Kattyan (50 miles southeast of Cochin). It is a very important show because at it will be the leader of the National Congress Party in Kerala. As you know the Congress is split into the National Congress and the Kerala Congress. Unless these parties find unity, the communists with 38 per cent of the vote will be elected. It is strange because the communists treated the people of Kerala very badly and it speaks pretty poorly for the Congress Party. Very few politicians from any political party really care for the people of Kerala. All they want to do is exploit them for their own political power. The people of Kerala know this and are very angry, but since every politician does it, they get frustrated.
    We are going to do a more intensive time in Bangalore, and we are going to move in a big way in this city. We have major shows on the 9th, 10th and 11th but we will be concentrated mainly on the schools and the state governments, both of which are open to MRA.
    I need to be constantly thinking for India and Australia these days, because occasionally one gets frustrated with inefficiencies in railways etc, but we get through it alright. Our treatment here has been marvellous and some of us (not me!) are getting fatter. I do pray for you all very much these days and I am always grateful to receive your letters. You must keep [Sing Out West] living to a big enough aim, Merrilyn, it sounds terrific at the moment but the right aims are essential. It is the difference between a great work and a revolution.
Yours sincerely,
Kim.

India was not a place where the rollicking good times jumped out and grabbed you. There were other things that appealed to him though, first and foremost the opportunity to be immersed in a culture entirely different from the one he had known. His political mind was maturing, just as emotionally he was becoming more reflective. Again, his letters indicated that he had a growing consciousness of the way he had changed.

16 July 1966

I am finding very much these days, that it is one thing to do the guided thing in various situations, but it is also essential to change people. I have made a lot of mistakes in this field. I find it very hard not to get argumentative and intellectual with people but to really give them my heart.

I also need to care enough for people to be absolutely straight with them on points where I needed to change and on points where they need to. It is very hard for an approval seeker like me.

Dad, it is great to get your news clippings ... If the ALP could develop a heart it would be terrific.

I do feel that there are men in the ALP who are meant to and will change ...

All the best for Sing Out West.

Cheers,

Kim.

22 July 1966

You can talk all the theory you like about MRA, but the only way we are going to change the Communist world is by showing them that MRA-run economies really work. Most of the communists realise that their economies [have] not worked well but are understandably contemptuous of capitalist economies. 'Enough food for everybody' is not meant to be a theory, it is meant to be a commitment. Nothing yet tried since time began has filled this need. By changing the selfishness in capitalists, the waste due to carelessness and the lack of energy due to impurity and national aimlessness MRA will answer this need.

It is beginning to do it in Britain and we need to start it in Australia. Mt Barker is one of the richest areas in Australia and must (not can) set a pattern for Australia. If Sing Out West goes there without this in mind it will do nothing at all; if it goes there with this in mind the impact will shake the Kremlin and Washington.

Yours,

Kim.

By the end of July, the impetus of the show was starting to fade fast. After 12 continuous weeks on the road, living out of suitcases, sleeping in strange beds and eating food that did not agree with them, all the members of the troupe were tired, if not physically exhausted. The money to finance the show from donations had trickled rather than gushed in; some like Kim were actually sick, others had already returned home. The MRA elders of the troupe felt the best thing would be to disband the show and send small groups back to cities already visited to consolidate the gains already made and to help the groups that were starting up.

As Hugh Nelson describes, 'we were all asked to pray about and to think about what we would like to do when the show broke up, so we could get "guidance".' Each member of the troupe, of course, sought their own guidance, in the time-honoured fashion of trying to 'listen' to God speaking to them in the clarity of the morning. Quite severely weakened and very tired of the travelling, Kim decided to return to Bombay to take an entirely different tack. He joined *HIMMAT*, the weekly MRA newspaper, as a subeditor. 'It is a great challenge ...' he wrote to his parents, 'and I feel totally inadequate to the task, but I pray for God's guidance. My guidance was to go to Bombay which I will do. Bombay is the toughest city we have been to and it will be tough.'

It was that and not least of it was suddenly finding himself in the entirely different field of journalism. 'It was basically because I spoke good English, that I could do the subediting,' Kim remembers, 'rather than any nascent skills I might have had. Occasionally, very occasionally, I might also write an article for them, but it was mostly working on the journalists' copy that took my time, and then seeing to the production afterwards.'

The editor of *HIMMAT* at that time, Russi Lala, remembers the 17 year old with great affection. 'It was like the pulse of the nation was beating in that office, and Kim was very much in its rhythm. What struck me most was his buoyancy, the sense of hopefulness he had to him — and how perceptive he was because anything you talked to him about, you felt that boy was taking in, even at that young age.'

That buoyancy would be severely tested shortly after he arrived when he took a crackly phone call from his father. Nana was dead. She had succumbed to a bout of cancer as sudden as it was vicious. He spent the rest of the day wandering around Bombay in a daze, in the company of another Australian MRA member working at the newspaper, Roger Uren. 'Roger just kept talking to me,' he recollects, 'making sure that I was alright, and it was very good of him. Nana had been such a fixture in my life, I just couldn't believe she wouldn't be there when I got home.'

Moving him along from the depths of his grief was the ongoing stimulation of being in Bombay, a city full of never-ending new sights and sounds. He had arrived in the ancient city at much the same time as the monsoon season, and delighted in seeing the rain 'coming down in bucketloads' outside the window as he worked, and soaking him as he walked back after work to the nearby apartment he shared with six other newspaper workers. That apartment was in Bombay's Carmichael Road area, near the famed Towers of Silence where members of the ancient Parsi religion left their deceased loved ones to be eaten by the vultures who were on a constant circling brief for new offerings.

Every Wednesday night he would be responsible for going down to the printers near the Gateway to India monument, to oversee the layout of the cover of the journal and to ensure that the photographic plates being used on the archaic printing presses were perfectly aligned. Mostly he would leave the printers at 3 or 4 o'clock in the morning and head home through one of the seediest areas of the city, down by the harbour foreshores. 'It was terrible, and I remember seeing vans coming around to pick up the dead bodies off the street as I walked. They would take them away to burn them. I remember once talking to a bloke from the vans about this, and I asked "Aren't some of these people alive, that you are taking away and burning?" and he said "Well yes, sometimes they are," and I said "What happens?" and he said "They wake up pretty quick!".' To get to the bus that would take him home, he was obliged to go through the red-light area of town, where the tragic prostitutes ranging in age from 7 to 70 would have for the most part finished the night's activities and be cooking meals on tiny stoves set up on the footpaths outside the brothels. They would see him, sometimes gaily wave and make the curious 'sssssssssssssss' sound of Indian people — a rough equivalent of the Western 'pssssssst' — to enquire in fun if he was interested in a little action. Red-faced, Kim would walk on. 'I would talk to anyone except the poor girls ...' he recalls. 'As a 17-year-old kid this kind of stuff just blew me away. India was the real world, a vibrant society, poor, tough, violent, but very very stimulating for me. I really admired the people, and the way they coped with their hardships.'

Of all the experiences the city offered him, the least pleasurable — although it certainly gave him an adrenalin rush — came on an afternoon while he was heading into the Bombay CBD, and came across a large demonstration of angry farmers. 'They certainly weren't violent in any way,' he remembers. 'I was part of the scenery, I was just wandering along, and so were they.' Then, seemingly out of nowhere, the police charged. 'They had *lathis*, big long sticks with iron nobs on the end of them ... and the farmers became angry enough that that didn't work, so the police unslung their .303s and started firing into the crowd.' Screams, shouts, shots. Kim ran into a side street, aware that if he fell he would probably be trampled.

In the end, for all the stimulation of his time in this exotic, sad and inspiring land, it was once again time to take a different tack.

28 October 1966
Dear Mum, Dad, Merrilyn and David,
I received an invitation three days ago to go to Britain for the opening of the Westminster Theatre on November 22, and to work in Europe and Britain [for MRA] for some months after that. We are moving very much with the workers (particularly dockers) in Britain and Europe.

It has been a hellish three days thinking this over. I can truthfully say I have enjoyed working on HIMMAT more than anything else I have ever done in my life. It has been a wonderful experience. More than anything else I would like to return home to you in the next months. Russi Lala would have liked having me continue on HIMMAT.

I have had the clearest conviction however that it is right for me to go. Personally I would rather not, but I have made the decision to give my life to God and [know] that at times this will cost me a great deal. However I have the knowledge that He cares for me and knows what is best for me in every situation. I will be leaving on November 9.

... I will miss you terribly greatly over the next months with your being involved in so many things and as Christmas and my birthday draws near. I feel in my heart, that what I have decided is right. God has been so good to me these last two years and I am sure He will continue.

Britain is in such a terrible mess, and I don't really know what I can do, but God will give me a plan.

I do hope you get well soon mother, I pray that it is not serious. I hope you win your elections, Dad, and I am sure Merrilyn will pass her exams with flying colours.
Your loving son,
Kim.

His time in India changed him in many ways. He left the subcontinent with an immense intellectual interest awoken within him, both in Asia and Australia's place within it. During his six months there, he had become acutely aware that Australia was actually part of a teeming world of which it had little understanding, and that while it might fondly imagine itself to be a self-contained bit of Britain in the South Seas, that approach could not long endure. 'Here was this country on which we had very little impact,' he explains, 'in a region in which basically we were a last-ditch defence colonial power. And you just couldn't help but get a sense at the time that we were reading the Asian region all wrong. I think the thing that really put the zap on me was the huge population of India, [around 500 million at the time]. Looking back to Australia, I saw that basically we sit there in a continent which then occupied about 12 or 13 million people — which in India fitted into a couple of cities — and so there was this gigantic slice of humanity on our doorstep which Australia found hard to relate to and comprehend the massive significance of.'

Compounding this sense that his own country was blinkered when it came to Asia, was the escalation of hostilities in Vietnam, which involved Australian troops. Others of his age group might have had only the vaguest concept of the political implications of the Vietnam War, but Kim Jnr, raised on such discussions at the family dinner table, understood and followed all the arguments from the beginning. And, surrounded as he was by people who saw the Vietnam conflict from an Asian perspective, his time in India helped change his own view, which had initially been supportive of any move which helped beat the Communists — something that had, after all, been a kind of *raison d'être* of MRA in the first place. 'You wouldn't have found a single Indian there who thought the Americans had the slightest chance of winning the Vietnam War,' he relates. 'And for Australia, our whole relationship to Modern Asia was defined in terms of the Vietnam War, which was just a totally wrong reading of the Asian political landscape. Our Government had come to the conclusion that essentially this was an externally inspired revolt in Vietnam and as an externally inspired revolt, the same external force would move on to deal with other countries. But that theory was never right, the revolt in Vietnam was a home-grown one, and we Australians were pointing ourselves at an infrastructure which was well dug in, that we had little understanding of. At the end of the day, unless we had been prepared to become a permanent part of the Vietnamese population there was absolutely no chance of success. It was a *totally* useless exercise.'

It was some change from monsoonal Bombay to chilly London, in only 18 hours on the plane. On-site, he found himself orbiting the Moral Rearmament world centred around the same Clive of India house that his father had visited well over a decade before. For the next three months, he was billeted at MRA houses around London and in southern rural England, while he worked and trained for the movement. If many of the things that happened to him in his tumultuous year in India would stay with him for years to come, his time in England and a subsequent quick trip to Caux in Switzerland for an MRA conference, would not. 'I did a bit of work on producing literature and programmes and things for MRA musical activities,' he comments, 'because I'd picked up a few journalistic skills. But I can't actually recollect that much.' A part of his vagueness, perhaps, was that at the time he was simply so very ill, and was expending a lot of his energies simply trying to regain his weight and strength. He had, after all, lost nearly 20 kilograms while on the subcontinent.

Two letters give an indication both of how his thinking had changed, and of the shifting relationship with his father. His distance from Australia and his extraordinary experiences in India gave him a more concrete vision for politics in general and for the ALP in particular. Now, his letters also reveal a change in his relationship with his father. Not only does he express his general political opinions, he also offers guidance to his father.

28 November, 1966
Dear Mum, Dad, Merrilyn and David,
    I have just received some letters from you and Dad's cable yesterday. I was very sad to read of our defeat in the elections and was amazed to see Dad's marvellous increase. It is a real tribute. The result must be shattering to a lot of people. I am convinced that we need now to build a totally new ALP out of what remains of the old. A Labor Party guided by God with a genuine concern for Asia and the world would be a great thing for Australia and Asia.
    ...Bitterness is one thing I am steadily having to overcome. I get so colossally anti-American, anti-conservative, anti-Communist at

*times. It got very serious at one stage and I had a colossal fight
with one member of the cast (educated at Eton and Oxford). I had
guidance to apologise to him. This bitterness has been with me all
my life and must have dragged you all down many times. If you
are living for the classless society, which I want to see, you must do
away with it. It is a severe disease with many of us socialists and
makes a mockery of the basis of true socialism, the 'brotherhood
of man and the fatherhood of God . . .'*
Yours,
Kim.

2 January 1967
Dear Dad
    *. . . my guidance is that whatever happens in the leadership
battle, the ALP must become God-guided.*
    *Your questioning of me for ideas of what you could say at the
conference has forced me to do some quick thinking. I thought
the other day that people in Australia must open their hands,
hearts and heads to their neighbours. I think particularly Japan,
India, Indonesia, Thailand, Burma and Malaysia. That point you
made in one speech about fertiliser factories in India was a good
one. Maybe you could bring in a new vision for the labour
movements of Asia. We need in Australia a turnabout in our
attitudes to Asia and labour. I thought you might put these
questions. What would a revolution in Australia's thinking
mean? What is God's plan for India and Pakistan, Japan and
China, Malaysia and Indonesia? How are we going to create a
situation where another Vietnam is not possible?*
    *. . . I am glad to hear you had a good time with Arthur Calwell.
He sent me two warm letters. I hope we can do something for
him during the conference.*
All the best for the conference,
Yours,
Kim.

As his long haul away from Perth neared an end, the 18 year old had a
firmer conception of what he wanted to do, at least for the next few
years. 'I decided I didn't want to do missionary work any more,' he
explains, 'and that I wanted to come back and go to university. There
was no pressure from my parents.' The Kim who returned to the

family home, in late January of 1967 — and promptly moved into Nana's former bedroom, now that she had passed on, and the house had become whole again — was not the same one that had left over eight months earlier. He was, by the reckoning of his parents and siblings a 'different man', with the accent being on the last word. After he had travelled the world, fending for himself and being exposed to so many different experiences, a lot of his blond boyishness had gone.

'It was nothing precise,' Betty Beazley comments, 'just a sense that our son was growing up, that he *had* grown up.' Her son agrees. 'It was just a seminal maturing experience,' he says, looking back. 'I was confronted with slices of humanity and human possibilities which I would just never confront in Australia; dealing with a country that had experienced the mother of all Asian independence movements, in the company of a bloke who was the grandson of the fellow who led it, in Rajmohan Gandhi. Through him I was introduced to all sorts of backgrounds and attitudes in that country, and it all just blew my mind away ...'

CHAPTER FIVE

THE STUDENT

'There are ... two educations. One should teach us how to make
a living and the other how to live.'
James Truslow Adams.

T he University of Western Australia was established in 1913 on
65 hectares of land next to the mighty Swan River, and boasts
one of the most stunning campuses in the southern hemisphere.
It is a seat of learning that enjoys a high reputation both in Australia
and overseas. Kim Jnr, freshly returned from India, England,
Switzerland and a one-week stop in Lebanon on the way home,
arrived there in the first days of February of 1967, and found his feet
immediately. 'It was one of the happiest times of my life being at that
University,' he says fondly. The pleasures of the place for this new
student were many. It was beautiful, with large ovals and enormous
trees attracting a great variety of bird life, and the buildings — though
sprinkled with the usual phalanx of clumsy 1950s architecture —
tended towards the large, gracious and magisterial, predominantly in
the Spanish-Moroccan style.

Academically, the University was blessed with some of the leaders in
their fields in Australia, and Kim's great joy in his studies was that he
could now concentrate solely on the subjects that interested him —
History and Politics. Kim Beazley Snr believed his older son was best
suited to study Law — though he only ever said that to him once —
but Kim Jnr was equally of the opinion that studying Arts would offer
him a broader field of enquiry. For one thing, this would give him the
chance to explore the history and international relations of India,
which had so fascinated him in the previous year. After some

discussion, Arts it was, and with his experience of the last year in mind he was also certain that he wanted to study Indian History as a part of it. He also joined the University U/21 rugby side as a second rower, as keen as ever on a game that pleased the aggressive twin within.

Politically, the place was *jumpin'*. Menzies had gone just over a year before, love was free, the Vietnam War was raging, and as Kim remembers, 'the whole ambiance of life at university was to be tremendously politically engaged'. The UWA Guild of Undergraduates was a magnet for many of the students' political passions at that time. While all other campuses around the country had a separate Student Union and Student Representative Council — meaning separate administrative and political wings of student affairs — at UWA they were combined in the form of the Guild. The weight of the Guild of Undergraduates was further increased by the fact that students simply weren't allowed to opt out from involvement. Voting for Guild elections and for Guild referendums was compulsory — just like in Australian elections — and students declining to vote were fined. Those still declining to pay their fines were denied their exam marks until they paid.

What it meant, as Kim recalls, was that the affairs of the Guild 'were intensely political. Everybody was into it and there were endless general meetings on all sorts of political subjects and from the moment I arrived I went to all of them.'

Even more intensely political was the University ALP Club. While at other campuses such political clubs were mostly 'pretend politics,' at UWA it was real — the ALP Club was an official branch of the party, boasting some 400 members. Such numbers were all the more pertinent when it was noted that in the wake of 'the troubles' of the 1950s, Joe Chamberlain had himself wiped out much of the membership of the party to the point where there were only 1500 members left in the entire *state*. Thus, with over a quarter of the Labor Party's members in the West drawn from the UWA campus, the branch had the potential to make a real impact on the Western Australian ALP and from there — if the numbers fell right — even the direction of the ALP nationally. This was the same branch that Kim Snr had joined in 1937, of which he had gone on to become the President.

During Orientation Week, Kim Jnr was wandering around outside Hackett Hall looking at the campus's club stalls set up to recruit students when he saw the ALP Club stall. He had been waiting for this moment for some time. He immediately made his way towards it.

'I was incredibly anxious to join the Labor Party, just as I was most anxious to get a trade union background, because my whole life had been sort of leading me that way to that point.' He handed over the two-dollar membership fee, was given a pen, filled out the form, and received his ALP membership card in return. 'That really was a big moment,' says Beazley, remembering the instant when he tucked the card away safely into his rather thin wallet — for in his memory it was always all but entirely devoid of money — where it would remain until the days of dog-eared disintegration well over a decade later. 'I really thought that this is a moment of great significance in my life. It was very important to me, just being part of it.'

But now having joined the Labor Party formally, the question facing him was, what could he do for the party? Others might be happy to be simply passive members, but he actually wanted to do something. Without exception he attended all of the meetings held in various lecture theatres around the campus, and was always sure to move or second a motion, or make a speech, or do *something*. 'I wanted to train myself,' he recalls. 'I wanted to hone skills. Maybe it was, oddly enough, something to do with the MRA commitment, but I believed that anybody who joined the Labor Party had to have a view on the issues of the day, put them forward, argue the case. I suppose it was a developed sense of citizenship.' This environment was tailor-made for him to prosper. For many of his fellow students active political engagement was a new experience, Kim had something close to a 17-year head start on the lot of them. In the words of Geoff Gallop, a friend who would come to be a member of both the Guild and Uni ALP Club with him: 'He was a natural at it. The rest of us were still learning the processes of politics, but everyone knew that he was someone who was born and bred in the standing orders of the Labor Party, and because he'd been in a house where his father had had to fight for every preselection, he well and truly knew all the tricks of the trade already. The debates he was in were often vigorous, full-on, but there was a "human" quality there too, that even though he was engaged in heavy political debate he would want to make sure that at the end of it people were still capable of conducting a dialogue.'

Beazley later made the comment that during his time at university, 'when you ceased talking about foreign policy for 90 per cent of the time, the remaining 10 per cent was devoted to the odd bit of fine-tuning of social welfare legislation'.[15]

And therein lay another source of his rising strength. When it came to talking on the subject of the day, on foreign policy — about Vietnam, the Cold War, America's role in Europe, etc — Kim was again right in his element. Not only had he spent many long hours with his father discussing the finest details of modern and historic foreign policy, but now he was studying it. Others might speak from gut reaction, and sometimes half-formed ideas, but from the beginning Kim Jnr was notable in that he actually knew quite a lot about the subject at hand.

It was a reflection of the esteem in which he was held that in June of his first year at the university, he was elected by his peers at the ALP Club to be the Treasurer. If that seemed like an extraordinarily rapid rise for one who had joined the club only five months earlier, the answer, in the view of one of Kim's fellow branch members at the time, Bob McMullan was that 'apart from being President, the other positions weren't really that prestigious, and it was the sort of thing that if you put your hand up keen to get work, then you would advance. Kim *always* had his hand up. The other reason Kim was remarkable was that he was the son of such a famous person, who we all looked up to, and he was really the only one who readily admitted to being what we would call now, "right wing". He was a very, very busy member.' Lectures? He went to them too and enjoyed them for the most part, but his passion for politics always curtailed the time he devoted to his studies at UWA. Only six months after arriving on the campus, he ran on the ALP ticket for a spot on the Guild Council and won, thus becoming involved in such nuts-and-bolts decisions as how to improve the university's catering facility, how much money should be granted to the various societies competing for the limited dollars available, what hours the library should remain open, and so forth.

It remained the University ALP Club proper though which devoured his greatest energies. Again, for a man eager to make his mark in the labour movement, he had arrived at a propitious time. Then, as now, the structure of the State Executive* of the Western Australian Labor Party was such that many spots were reserved for the delegates of all affiliated unions. But so low were the stocks of the ALP in Western Australia — in the state election just gone they had received their lowest vote in 40 years — that not all of the unions could actually be bothered sending someone along to the interminable

---

* Between State Conferences, the State Executive is the principal decision-making body in every State ALP organisation.

meetings. It meant there was an immediate opening for a young man with Kim Jnr's talents and ambitions, not to mention his last name.

A friend and political travelling companion of his father's, Joe Berinson, was a mature-age Law student, and had become very friendly with members of the University ALP. Jewish, 40ish, brilliantish, Berinson was a member of the State Executive, and was mounting the beginnings of what would be a long, albeit informal, campaign to break Joe Chamberlain's stranglehold on the Western Australian Labor Party. He had the support of several unions, including the Municipal Workers' Union, and at Berinson's request to their head, Percy Norris, Kim Jnr was made that union's proxy delegate to the State Executive at the tender age of 18.

'Kim was obviously very bright,' Berinson recalls of that time, 'and obviously going somewhere ... though I wouldn't have known where.'

In the first instance he was going to the fortnightly State Executive meetings held in the dingy downstairs hall of the old Trades Hall building, in Beaufort Street of central Perth — and loving it. 'I was just very chuffed about being a member of the Labor Party, I just thought that was the bees-knees and to be an officer in a branch, to be a proxy delegate to the State Executive I was just in heaven.' And now that he was on-site and free to speak on the party issues of the day, Kim steered his energies by two particular stars. 'From the moment I joined the party,' he says, 'I had been very annoyed by a willingness on people's part to accept the idea of permanent Opposition and I knew that wasn't for me. I wanted to do whatever I could that would actually help the party get elected.'*

The other thing on his agenda was even more clear. Protect his dad. 'I was very conscious,' he recollects, 'of all those people over the years who had wished my father harm and I was very quickly in the business of retaliation.' That meant his target was first and foremost the man

---

* In this he was very much in tune with the prevailing attitude of the newly installed ALP leader, Gough Whitlam, who at the Victorian State Conference of 1967, as quoted in *The Light on the Hill*, expounded his own views on this subject: 'Let us have none of this nonsense that defeat is in some way more moral than victory ... This conference, comprising a greater percentage of union delegates than any other democratic socialist party on earth, must reject any idea that constant defeat and permanent opposition do not matter, that the labour movement can be strong and effective industrially, while being weak and ineffective politically. On the narrowest industrial views, this is patently false. I did not seek and do not want the leadership of Australia's largest pressure group. I propose to follow the traditions of those of our leaders who have seen the role of the party as striving to achieve, and achieving, national government of Australia.'

who sat at the middle of the table, right in the front of the room when the State Executive met. Joe Chamberlain. He had it coming.

While Labor Party members could be generally thought of as 'Left' or 'Right', in WA it was more a case of whether you were 'for Joe', or 'against Joe'. Young Kim was in good company in this latter group, for there were many others rising to the fore of the fight at that very time, similarly disposed to take on Chamberlain on each and every issue — from whether or not to grant State aid to private schools, to electoral tactics, to whether or not to give Gough Whitlam total support.

When Kim looked around the meeting of the State Executive of 105 people, fully 20 of them were from the University branch, and all of them were aligned substantially the same way — his way. Against Chamberlain. Berinson had helped to manoeuvre many others from the university onto the State Executive, including a young, part-time economics student with fire in his belly by the name of Brian Burke, who was representing the Water Supply Union. Other young warriors of the ALP were also there — most drawn from the same University ALP Club — and though they were spread across the Labor spectrum of belief, from Left to Right, they all seemed to be driven by much the same thing, the way Beazley saw it. 'We were all just sick of losing, and even though everyone didn't agree entirely with Whitlam, some thinking him unacceptably Right Wing, all agreed with the idea of winning. And everyone had just got a bit sick of Joe, basically. The other thing was, we weren't frightened of Joe, none of us. Because unlike the union officials on the State Executive, our jobs didn't depend on him.'

The approach that Beazley and his cohorts took to Chamberlain has an echo in a story told in Graham Richardson's book, *Whatever It Takes*.[16] It concerns the time when the then NSW Premier Neville Wran told the State ALP machine boss, John Ducker, that he 'wouldn't wear' a particular proposal at a coming State Conference. Ducker had heard him out, and then let him have it: 'I'll tell you what you'll fucking wear! Not only will you wear it, you'll fucking *move* it!' Or else ... Which Neville Wran eventually did.

Joe Chamberlain was similarly brought to heel, though this time at the hands of the party's rising young Turks. Chamberlain, who stood against everything that Gough Whitlam stood for, at one point proposed that the State Executive refuse an invitation to Whitlam to attend a coming conference. Kim Beazley Jnr and his closest colleagues strongly opposed Chamberlain and moved that not only would the Conference invite the Opposition Leader to visit, but that Joe Chamberlain himself would go out to the airport to greet him. And Chamberlain did!

The episode made quite an impression on Beazley. 'What we loved was a sense of political power, because in a funny sort of way we were very powerless,' he says. 'Nothing is more powerless than an environment where you can be conscripted and sent away to war, and the government of the day is omnipotent. You feel a sense of powerlessness and to actually get a situation where we could influence the course of events for a national political figure like Whitlam, was terrific.' Through this and other manoeuvres, Gough Whitlam came to be aware of young Beazley, and he was impressed. 'I used to see young Kim at the University of Western Australia in the Hackett Hall,' he recollects. 'He chaired several meetings when I was there and I got to know him quite well. I thought he had great political talent in that he understood politics intuitively and had courage. The thing that impressed me most, was that right from the beginning he had the courage to stand up to Joe Chamberlain — not an easy thing to do at that time.'

For all the political passion in such State Executive meetings though, they rarely descended into abuse, either from 'Beazley and co', or from Chamberlain himself.

'Chamberlain had vehemence, but always politeness,' Kim remembers, 'he was never abusive. I remember one occasion, something that happened with a guy I'll call "Joe Smith". He was one of Chamberlain's acolytes and I was opposing every single recommendation Chamberlain was putting before the Executive. And every time that I made an amendment or a statement, this chap would say, "If I had ever been as cautious as that where would *I* be now?" "If I had been as temporising as that where would *I* be now?" "If I had been as right wing as that where would *I* be now?".

'He went on like that, about eight times. Anyway we were all filing out after the meeting was over and Chamberlain called to me: "Kim, wait a minute." And I came back and he looked at me with a mischievous eye and he said "Kim, where *is* Joe Smith now?"' It was a style of politics that, though rough and ready, could still be notable for its basic underlying humanity, and to be fair to Chamberlain, it wasn't that he represented the forces of darkness. It was simply that by this time — as many of his supporters now concede — he had stayed at the helm of the Labor Party machine in Western Australia for too long, that the times had passed him by. This was doubly confirmed for Beazley Jnr when he and Chamberlain had another civilised conversation, in which the party boss expressed his extreme scepticism about all this new-fangled polling of public opinion that was going on. Chamberlain's view, as Beazley recalls it was 'that once you were made aware of what the public thought about something, it might make you change one of your own deeply held convictions and that wouldn't do at all'. Beazley walked away, quietly shaking his head. For his part, he was always keen to know the public feeling on given issues, and started from the assumption that the best way of influencing that opinion was via the media.

Of all the youthful Labor stars at that time, there is no doubt that Beazley was the one who played best in the media. In those early days of his formal political involvement, the reporters from the *West Australian* newspaper were banned from such meetings — because Chamberlain considered the paper 'a tool of the Capitalists' — but the journalists of the ABC were welcome, and they took a particular shine to young Beazley. One of the young journalists assigned to cover the meetings — and a fellow who became a great friend — was the ABC's Tim Blue, from the *This Day Tonight* programme. As Blue explains 'this was the time when television was becoming more popular and the ABC was just getting going with its current affairs coverage. We put Beazley Jnr on quite often because he was very lucid, presentable, good-looking and talked in a manner that all journalists love: "talent" that talks. He was seen as the glamorous rising youth of the labour movement, the acceptable face ...' Blue's other impression of Kim in those days was that after the formal part of the meeting was over, 'he would always be on the phone lurking ... he was a great telephone conspirator, manoeuvring, gathering the numbers. I think the weekends were spent manoeuvring too. That was what he did.'

As he made these first forays into the machine side of Labor Party politics, others besides Gough Whitlam began to notice him and genuinely appraise him for the first time. This was the young fellow they had heard about, the one who was starting to be known automatically as 'Kim Jnr'. Peter Walsh, who would later go on to be considered one of Australia's finest finance ministers, remembers his first impressions of Kim Jnr after seeing him at the WALP State Conference in 1967.

'He was a rosy-cheeked, tall, slender young man,' Walsh recollects. 'He would have been regarded as a bit precocious, in his confidence and the bombastic way he spoke. I don't know whether it was consciously — or if he had tried to copy his father's style — but there was a lot of Kim Snr there. He had a sort of certitude as he spoke, but also his style of speaking was something that's largely gone out of politics. It was designed to swing people emotionally, and it did. I thought it was pretty clear even from 1967 if not earlier that young Kim saw a future for himself in politics.'

Kim maintains that at that time he saw no such thing. 'In fact,' he says, 'I assumed I would never get into Parliament.' The reason, he says, is because he had the daunting example of his father before him. 'I always assumed that he was a very able bloke who got a long way in life but not all that far. I didn't see myself as being a terribly able person by comparison and so I didn't think I'd ultimately get very far in political life.'

Despite this modest view of his political prospects, he was nevertheless well-satisfied with his first year at university, and *particularly* with his involvement in the University ALP Club, and from there the State Executive. There was just one catch as far as the latter was concerned. While Percy Norris had been happy for Kim Jnr to represent the union over the previous few months, as the Christmas holidays were approaching he now thought it proper that Kim should also have a union ticket, and the only way he could have a union ticket would be if he had a union job and the only union job available was … gravedigger at Karrakatta Cemetery, right opposite Hollywood High School. Hey, there were worse jobs. It might be hard physical work, it may not have been too glamorous, but it would provide him with a bit of money, and, most crucially, he would get his bona-fide 'ticket' as a member of the Municipal Workers' Union.

So there he was. On a particularly hot December day of 1967, he turned up at 7 am, was issued a shovel and assigned to a gang of men. In fact the duties of the gang were not simply to dig graves, but also to tend to the cemetery as a whole, cutting grass, trimming hedges, weeding, and so forth. But genuine gravedigging was a part of it, and no mistake. 'The soil,' as he remembers it, 'was easy enough to dig, but there was a bloody lot of it. There's an awful lot of soil in a grave, let me tell you.'

To pass the time in between hurling the earth skywards — black soil first and then the softer yellow sand beneath — the men would discuss the possibilities of hitting bones. Human bones. Bones from previous burials that may have somehow remained there while the tombstones had been moved on. The discussions were mostly fun, but had a genuine point to them. Under the Award, as Kim recalls, 'if you struck bones then you got three dollars a bone, Unpleasantness Allowance. So we used to have long debates about what a rib cage would be worth, and somebody took the view that you'd only count a rib cage as one bone, so we thought well, what you'd have to do is smash it, wouldn't you?'

Careful though. No-one was to work *too* hard. While that was not an official union rule, it was enforced all the same. One of the foremen there got very annoyed with the newchum Kim because of the approach he took to knocking over jobs. One was not meant to knock them over, one was meant to chip away at them, or there wouldn't be enough work to go round, see? If everyone went at their bloody jobs like a bloody big bull at a gate, then they would need only half the bloody workers, get it, and then where would that leave everyone? Up shit creek is where it would leave them, and don't you forget it. 'It wasn't easy,' as Beazley recollects. 'I insisted on doing jobs that he would have done in a day, in about an hour or two. Well, I didn't actually insist on it, I just did it, and then he'd tell me that I had entirely the wrong approach, and I had to smarten up on that.' Which he did, more or less. Whatever his instincts about wasteful work practices, his duty then seemed clear.

'[I went along with it]. It was these fellows' jobs, not mine — I was out of that place in a couple of months but they had to live with it forever — if they wanted to organise their particular work practices then that was between them and their employer. I wasn't there to do them damage.'

Besides, and no doubt about it, sometimes it was bloody good to have a break. On another occasion, when they were clearing new land for the expanding Catholic sector, there was a giant tree which had been chopped down, and it was the job of the gang to dig out the huge roots that had sustained its growth for the previous century. So they dug and dug. In fact, they dug for days, and still couldn't get to the bottom of it, when at last it dawned. No-one was watching. They were well out of the way of head office, and the question had to be asked: why not play cards instead? So they played cards instead. In fact, they played cards for a couple of days, before resuming. There were also, though, many days of long, hard physical labour, which resulted in the 19 year old staggering home when day was done, where he would 'be so damn tired I'd be in bed by six. It was the hardest physical labour I've ever done.'

One who remembers him from that long ago time, and one who himself was a big lump of a lad, is Ken Sackville. He had started work with him on the same day, and had got to know him as the summer progressed. 'Kim was always talking, as we worked,' he relates, 'and he was a lot of fun. He was a good bloke, sort of wise for his age, old for his years, and always had lots of stories. He always seemed to know about things, without being a know-all, whatever sort of subject came up. A friendly bloke, for sure, and I don't want to lay this on too thick but there was always an aura about him. It was obvious he wasn't going to be making a career out of burying bones.'

As the new hands, it would frequently be the job of Ken and Kim to stay behind when all the other workers had gone home, and fill in the newly dug graves. It was a weird sort of thing to do, being the people who actually laid the sod for all time on one of their fellow humans, and it could engender a funny sort of mood. Not talking now, because it didn't seem right, just putting the sod on the coffin which would throw back a hollow sound at first, and then just *thud, thud, thud,* as the dirt hit more dirt still. 'Sometimes,' Kim Jnr's co-worker recollects, 'if we were in the area, on the way back to the sheds Kim would veer off a bit to John Curtin's grave ... and I'd walk on.'

The grave, simple and essentially unremarkable from the others around, stands beneath a large white gum, has a white marble plinth set above it, with the following words engraved.

JOHN CURTIN
MHR PC
Prime Minister
Of the Commonwealth of Australia.
October 1941 — July 1945.
Beloved husband of
Elsie.
Loving father of
Elsie and John.
Born 8.1.1885.
Died 5.7.1945.
His country was his pride,
His brother man, his cause.

'In my house John Curtin was a constant topic of conversation,' Kim Jnr remembers, 'and though he'd died before I was even born, he was like a family friend. Dad would often tell us about his life, tell us about things he did and what a great man he was. How his own father was always anxious to vote for Curtin, and was always worried about what would happen to Curtin in elections.' The John Curtin portrayed by Kim Snr to his children was one of the finest men who ever lived, a very down-to-earth human being with no arrogance who carried it through by simple integrity and enormous persistence. It was this man that the graveyard worker remembered as he stood before the grave.

While there was a solid core of workers who had been at the cemetery for many and many a moon, there was also quite a large casual staff which would turn over regularly, and it wasn't long before Kim and Ken could play the 'veterans'.

'I can remember,' Kim Jnr says, 'that the blokes used to say to the youngsters who joined up, all these poor young fellas coming in, pretty naive, "you'll have to do the night shift mate". They'd say you don't have to do it for the first week, but next week you'll have to, and they'd be in abject terror for the whole seven days.' It was a time too, when the young man who would go on to spend a good part of his life trying to reach the heart and soul of the working man — among other social groups — actually got to know a lot of them on an intimate basis. One was there, a gnarled and weather-beaten old man by the name of Jimmy, 5 foot 2 inches tall in the old money, who'd been working in that same graveyard for the past 40 years and was already suspicious that the day was not too far away when his workmates would dig *his* grave. Jimmy took it upon himself to teach young Kim one or two things about life. Actually, one thing. One thing that worked his spirit, that he wanted to make damn sure all young fellas understood, young fellas that he liked in particular, because if he understood one thing about life it was this: 'Kim', he would tell him once a day without fail, over smoko or morning tea, 'you must never gamble with your wages. You've got to earn that extra bit of money see, before you put it on the horses, never put your wages on the horses. When you want to gamble only gamble with the extra money you've earned, by cutting lawns, or fixing fences or things, see? *That's* the money you gamble with, got it?'

It was after one such morning tea, that the younger man looked up to see the Beazley family car being driven into the cemetery. It had some writing, some letters on it. What the ..? The letters 'A' 'A' 'B' 'C' were written on separate cards, hanging off a piece of string attached across the top front of the windscreen. They were his final results, from his first year at UWA. As he had been working, Merrilyn had gone down to the campus to get the results, and had decided to communicate them to him in this novel manner. 'The look of joy on his face was just incredible,' she reminisces. 'He was absolutely delighted.' (The 'C' was for French, which he did not particularly care about, as it was simply a requirement of doing History Honours.) Part of that joy, perhaps, was that the time for leaving the cemetery to Jimmy and the boys was drawing near. The job had served its purpose in ensuring that he continued to hold the crucial ticket of the Municipal Workers' Union, and in enabling him to remain their representative on the State Executive of the Western Australian Labor Party.

In 1968, the demands on Kim Jnr's time would be even greater as his involvement in his studies, his political life via the State Executive, the University ALP Club and the Guild became progressively deeper. His ever greater political sophistication also meant that conversations with his father now took on a different complexion. Now there was fractionally less listening on the part of the younger man, and more genuine discussion between them. Kim Jnr also became aware that he had a slightly different approach to that of his father. 'Dad was interested in a few different things. Dad had more of a focus on the Aboriginal issues, foreign policy issues, specific issues in education. Me, I had my own views too – they actually didn't intersect necessarily all that much. I was a bit more interested in the philosophy of the Labor Party, not the specific issues of Foreign Affairs like he was. My dad's politics revolved very much around individual issues and not the total approach. I was a bit of a "power realist", while I suppose he was more of a "moralist".'

A 'power realist', Beazley Jnr took to be one who started solving problems from the presumption of 'this is the way it works, this is the way it is, this is the way to fix it'. Now that he was studying Politics at university, he also had names for some of his beliefs. He was, he realised, a 'Social Democrat'. Labels in politics have always been as cheap as they are malleable, but Beazley would never waiver from defining himself thus, and nor would his definition vary. 'Social Democracy,' he asserts, 'has several levels. The first is a commitment to the notion of equality of opportunity for all. The second is that the objectives of equality of opportunity will not be achieved without an interventionist government, and that while there is a role for the free market, there is also a role for the State to deal with the consequences of market failure. And the third element of it is a profound commitment to the notion of democracy. This notion is that society is not a set of combative elements but has a sense of community, a coherence which is best expressed by a system of democracy that the ordinary person has access to. Those are the key three elements, and I have always been proud to call myself a Social Democrat.'

His father spoke of himself in such terms, somewhere between 'never' and 'rarely,' and the only real framework that his own ideas hung off was the one provided by MRA — 'was an action absolutely honest, absolutely loving' and so on.

For all these slight differences in approach though, neither father nor son can remember ever strongly disagreeing on political matters. 'That never happened,' Kim Snr recollects, 'because Labor was not in power in all the time they were growing up, so there wasn't a Labor Government with which to disagree. And we were battling ...' Nor did they go through the other more traditional blues between fathers and sons of that era, like the length of Kim's hair, or what he smoked or drank — something passing surprising for the era. For the youth of the Western world it was of course a famously heady time, many going off to Saaan Fraaan-cisco with flowers in their hair, and many of the rest pushing the envelope of excess to its perimeters. This was not the experience of Kim Jnr.

Years after this, American President Bill Clinton would notoriously claim that while he had indeed smoked marijuana in his time — he was, after all, a university student around the time of the Summer of Love, and who hadn't? — he had not inhaled! Kim Beazley does not make the same claim. Rather he claims, and is backed up by the testimony of his friends, never to have put a marijuana cigarette to his lips in the first place. 'Like cigarettes, marijuana was not my thing,' he says flatly. 'I just never trusted it. A lot of my time was spent with the University Labor Party branch, which was highly social, but it was also highly political and it was an era in which we were a bit boringly political. The politics was more important to us than the sex, drugs and rock and roll.' Although alcohol was banned in the Beazley household, and this could be a problem for the odd uni get-togethers held in Thomson Road — when Kim's friends would have to retreat to the backyard to do their drinking — it was still not a problem for him, because he never touched the stuff. What did it all mean? 'It meant I was the designated driver.' There were two crucial differences separating him from those very few others pursuing similar abstention when it came to such minor vices. First he did not flaunt it, and was what one of his friends called 'a closet teetotaller'. If you weren't right beside him over a fair period of time, you would perhaps never notice that he never took a drink. Second, even if you did notice it, there seemed to be no sense of moral forbearance or disapprobatory air about him. In the words of another of his fellow students, 'I don't think it was ever really a matter of moral rectitude — I just don't think it was a matter where he felt denial. I think that simply, for Kim, there were more important things to do and really, he just had a tremendous enthusiasm for life.'

The least that can be said of his socially conservative views, while all around him lived wild, was that it did not damage his political aspirations when it came to securing the votes of his student peers. By mid-1968, he had not only been elected as Public Affairs Officer of the Student Guild, but also President of the University ALP Club, less than 18 months after arriving on-site. As Public Affairs Officer, he was quickly notable for organising a series of seminars and lectures on issues such as Vietnam, apartheid, world poverty. Within the constraints of his allocated budget, he still organised for such speakers as Dr Jim Cairns and noted academics from all over Australia to visit the campus, and his own profile rose accordingly. On one occasion, in his role as incoming President of the ALP Club, he visited the home of his predecessor in the post, Jeremy Dawkins, to get some papers. Jeremy was not home, but his younger brother John (or Joe as he was often called) was, and the two had a brief chat. It was an uneventful beginning to what would, at times, be a less than smooth relationship over the next 30 years. From that point on, Kim and Joe would see each other around the campus as well as in the ALP Club and Guild, both of which Dawkins became heavily involved in. 'He loved farming and animals,' Kim remembers of Dawkins at that time, 'so he was always wandering around in elastic-sided boots and moleskins, which was pretty unusual for a bloke in student politics. The other thing that you'd notice about him was that to avoid being conscripted — he was six years in the Citizens Military Force and he remained permanently a private, he wouldn't ever take promotions — so we'd see him wandering around in Army uniform, which again was pretty unusual.'

Dawkins was, in short, the way Kim saw it, an odd sort of cove, and he could never quite work him out. John Dawkins, for his part, remembers feeling much the same way about the young Beazley, though also with a rough affection. 'He used to laugh a lot,' he recalls, 'but in a slightly self-conscious way. I always thought he was old before his years. He was "the 21-year-old statesman". We knew that his father of course was in Moral Rearmament, but in a funny way his father was a very Left Wing sort of religious man, whereas Kim Jnr was conservative in *every* way, really "God Squad". Not just politically, but no drinking, no smoking etc — what we always used to say, was "if Kim is as conservative as this now, how conservative is he going to be when he's his *father's* age?" Everyone was to the left of Kim in those days. I suppose you couldn't help but like him though. He used to talk about how his enjoyment was spending weekends looking after his brother.' And that was true. Sometimes Kim and David would play cricket together in the backyard, sometimes they would just chat. Other times, Kim might stand with David for a while on the railway overpass at Claremont, and watch the trains as they went past.

Kim's role as the Public Affairs Officer of the Guild saw him get progressively more involved in the anti-Vietnam War movement, which included helping to organise protest marches. Most of these demonstrations involved a large body of youth — well-armed with placards, angst and anger — marching along St George's Terrace, before finishing on the grassy expanse of Perth's Esplanade, with such leaders as Kim on bullhorns leading the chant:

'*Whaddawewan?*
An end to the war!
Whendowewannit?
Now!
Whaddawewan?
OutofVietnam!
Whendowewannit?
NOW!'

'There was nobody burning draft cards at those rallies,' he notes, 'because their objective was to broaden support in the broader community, so you usually eschewed radical action.'

In the case of Kim, burning his draft card was never on the agenda anyway. He comments: 'I was very opposed to the war, but I was not a conscientious objector nor was I a draft resister or a pacifist — I never had a pacifist bone in my body and never had an objection to the notion that you sometimes must take up arms. So I accepted the view that the Government had the right to conscript in emergency to fight for the nation, that it was not simply a burden that should be borne by volunteers. Personally I was on student deferment, but at the end of student deferment if the Government had told me to go, I would have gone, under protest. So my objection to the conflict was political, it was not moral, in the sense of how it affected me personally. I thought it was the wrong war, wrong time, wrong place, wrong calculations. I participated in the demonstrations and spoke out — but there was no chucking of anything. We had very big demonstrations but they were not violent, they were never violent.'

They were noisy though, and they did attract an enormous amount of media coverage. Kim Jnr's participation in such demonstrations was not something ever likely to please his father. Only the previous year, in a magazine called *Outlook,* the journal of the Australian Institute of International Affairs, the senior parliamentarian had maintained that far from such protests being a genuine expression of public outrage, they were at least in part inspired by the Communists, whose policy it was to have a trained core of their own professional demonstrators at every significant political meeting in Australia concerning Vietnam. 'This is to counterfeit indignant public opinion,' he was quoted in the magazine as saying. 'One wonders whether the primary aim of this is to lead the Labor Party up the garden path and induce it to concentrate on the issues most acceptable to the Communist Party.'[17]

Furthermore, Kim Snr was opposed to the modern practice of demonstrating generally, believing that the proper forum for defeating the Government's policies was the Australian Parliament, and the proper way for 'the people' to register their protest was at the ballot box to throw the Government out. Nevertheless, on both the subjects of Vietnam and the demonstrations, the older man kept his own counsel. 'I'm sure the demonstrations I participated in were a source of some embarrassment to him,' Kim Jnr comments, 'but he never ever said that to me.' In Kim Snr's words: 'You certainly don't *impose*, that's very foolish. You may recommend.' In this case he recommended nothing, and Kim Jnr saw fit to devote his heart and soul to the anti-war movement. Although he often spoke at the protest rallies, the experience of being the sole voice addressing 3–4000 people was not one that fired his soul.

'No,' he remembers of the time, 'I think I preferred the sort of parliamentary debate of the State Executive of the Labor Party or of the Labor Party branch. I regarded the mass meeting stuff as functional, it just went with the territory.'

If he was thus more at home in the structured environment of Guild meetings and seminars, it was probably also where he shone most. At endless general meetings of the Guild, the debate would rage: should Australia have its soldiers in Indochina, and should the Liberal Government have conscription? 'No!' and 'NO!' were the answers put to the students by Kim Beazley Jnr, at some length. A callow young woman by the name of Geraldine Doogue — just emerged from the Santa Maria College for the Sisters of Mercy — remembers passing by the stately Winthrop Hall on campus as he was saying it on one occasion in very early 1969, and being drawn to such eloquently expressed passion. She wandered in to see this young man she had never seen before, speaking — without notes — with a beguiling combination of emotion and certitude, on the Vietnam War and its horrors. He was urging his fellow students to oppose it with every fibre of their being, calling upon them to use their collective weight to stop the slaughter of their fellow Australians who were of conscription age as well as the North and South Vietnamese who were going under in this useless war. 'He looked,' she recalls, 'like a career politician, or at least a politician in the making. He looked like he was born to politics, that is my first memory of Kim. I thought then he was magnificent because he could speak on his feet without notes and he was convincing and he had great passion. I thought he was thrilling actually. It looked like he was in training for the big league.'

Another who was impressed was Geraldine's close friend since childhood and fellow student, Mary Paltridge. She listened frequently to such speeches by Kim, and though she was one of two daughters of the late Liberal Cabinet Minister Sir Shane Paltridge, and a member of the University Liberal Club, and was aware of his Labor pedigree, she was not at all put off. 'I would say,' she recalls, 'I thought he was pretty attractive goods on the campus, and so did a lot of others. But he certainly wasn't known as a ladies' man, he didn't seem to have a lot of trivial relationships, and he wasn't interested in promiscuity, even if I think a lot of the female students were interested in him.'

They certainly were. Tim Blue, by now also a part-time student at the University, remembers being in the company of a gathering of female students one night, which included Gloria Brennan — who would go on to be one of the most famous Aboriginal activists of her generation — when she made a casual remark that has stayed with him still. As Blue remembers it, 'she said she and her girlfriends had begun a competition to see who could be the first to sleep with Kim'. It was no big deal explained Brennan and her friends. They thought him cute, very presentable, politically connected, and a highly desirable catch. Plus, as Blue recalls, 'they also thought it would be good for him to loosen up a bit, because he obviously didn't mess around'.

Kim has no memory of hearing of such a competition, and is sure none of Brennan's crowd was designated the winner. There is no doubt that the mysteries of females were occasionally frustrating to him. Merrilyn's role of adviser was broken by her own three-year spell to India where she worked in the slums of Delhi as part of a welfare programme — before beginning what would turn out to be her own high-powered academic career. Merrilyn was a fairly constant adviser to her brother on matters of the heart. 'Kim would often come into my room, and say *"women!"* which would be the start of long conversations about them.' His major frustration, as she recollects, was that he could never quite fathom their feelings, what they were on about, how they said one thing but seemed to mean another, and so on. To this point at university he had had a couple of so-so romances that had gone nowhere in particular — one of which broke his heart for a short while — but by his own reckoning, 'there was so much else happening, that it wasn't a problem'.

One of the other things that was happening through all his political involvements was of course his studies, and through it all Beazley had still made time for attending his lectures the best he could. His 'C' for French would prove to be the worst result in his entire time at university, while elsewhere it was close to solid 'A's. It was, not surprisingly, given his background and his interest, History where he shone — winning the Convocation Prize for History in his second year, before doing Honours in the same subject the following year. The subject of that Honours thesis, was *Bombay Students and the Non-Cooperation Movement from 1920 to 1921*. In the course of his research he was actually to receive some hands-on experience of being part of such a movement.

In March of 1969, one student had been killed on the Stirling Highway for want of a walkway over, or a tunnel beneath, the road. After a series of letters and petitions had got them nowhere, the Guild — with Kim as one of the key organisers — decided that it was time to take some more direct action. In a manner of civil disobedience that would have done Mahatma Gandhi proud, the demonstration was relentlessly peaceful. On the afternoon of Friday March 28, around 400 of the students simply sat down on the bitumen during the afternoon peak hour, and blocked the traffic on the highway. As the police moved in to drag them off, Kim Jnr among them, they followed their instructions to a 't'. They allowed themselves to be put on the side of the highway, but then moved to the back of the sit-in. The human roadblock diminished not a jot, the stalled motorists got progressively more angry, the cameras of the media whirred, and within days the local authorities had agreed to build the tunnel. If that decision had been small potatoes in the general scheme of things, it was still an enormous satisfaction to those who had been involved in making it happen.

'I remember it as something that showed what could be accomplished with combined direct action,' Kim enthuses, 'though I must also say I was a bit amazed and a little embarrassed at how quickly they had caved in to us.'

The downside? The tunnel didn't actually work. Some of the students thought it unsafe, and refused to use it. Others didn't think it too dangerous, but simply couldn't be bothered climbing up and down the stairs that using the tunnel entailed.
In Kim's words: 'They wanted to cross exactly where they wanted to cross and not in the tunnel, so in the end it was a pretty futile thing.'
And wasn't that sometimes just the way of politics? For every problem a solution. Within that solution more problems. To those problems more solutions, and so on, on and on. It certainly kept a bloke busy ...

CHAPTER SIX

THE SON ALSO RISES . . .

'I shall never be as old as I was between 20 and 30 ...'
V.S. Pritchett.

In September of 1969, Kim Beazley again ran for the post of Guild President. Although he had also done that the previous year as a kind of trial run — and had gained the post of Vice President — this time he was all-out committed to winning. The Guild Council under the outgoing president, Sue Boyd, had determined that her reign would be the last in which the Guild President simultaneously held the post and pursued his or her studies. But Kim was not deterred, even though he knew that he would have to defer his Honours course to take up the full-time paid position if he won. His campaign was based on two central, simple promises. That was to introduce an on-campus medical service for students and to 'do away with the overseas student surcharge of $60 dollars'.* With his supporters, again mainly members of the ALP Club, he spruiked these promises all over the campus. 'I loved *all* of it,' he declares. 'I loved the politicking, I loved going around to the lecture theatres, and all the places that people would gather on the campus, sometimes standing on an actual kind of soapbox, and trying to get them to vote for me. I just found the whole thing enormously stimulating. It was a taste of electoral politics and I

---

* The latter was a highly unpopular fee imposed on all those UWA students from foreign countries. Candidate Kim thought it unfair to burden such students, many from poor families, while also noting that they all voted in the elections.

thought it was terrific.' And it worked. He won easily. An article in the undergraduate newspaper, the *Pelican*,[18] entitled 'The Great Helmsman and his Scurvy Crew', tells the story. A large photo of Kim with a caption beneath reading, 'Long may the red sun shine out of our great Australian leader President Kim Beazley', preceded the beginning of the story proper:

> *Predictions that the Guild Presidential race would be neck and neck proved wrong with a landslide in Kim Beazley's favour. Beazley was also the first Guild Councillor to make the quota with nearly a third of the votes for him alone, leaving the remaining votes to be fought over by twenty-three remaining candidates.*

He remembers his win to become the 58th Guild President of the University of Western Australia, as 'a very pleasing moment'. He had to delay taking up the appointment, nevertheless, because in the meantime he had been selected for a study scholarship for thirteen student leaders from around South-East Asia called 'An Experiment in International Living'. It was sponsored by the US Information Service, and involved the students going to the USA for ten weeks in order for them to get intimately acquainted with the country. Shortly after leaving Perth in early October of 1969, the young West Australian found himself in real 'Leroy Brown' territory. He found that it was just like the song.

> *On the south side of Chicago,*
> *On the baddest side of town ...*

Next time he looked up, he was staying with a black family in one of the ghettos on the south side of Chicago, where the hostile teenaged children called him 'honky,' and the liquor salesman father called Jack told him to 'Get down!' every time they went out together in the car, for fear that the rest of the neighbourhood would realise that there was a pasty white boy among them. The teenagers were firm believers in Black Power, the power of the streets and direct action; while the parents believed in Lyndon Johnson and Hubert Humphrey and the power of Congress to change things for the better. As opposed to the rather theoretical discussions Kim Jnr had enjoyed with his father around the family dinner table, it was obvious that *these* political discussions were very much grounded in the grassroots and were about real life-and-death issues.

When Kim was allowed to lift his head to window level, when the car was safely out on the freeway and he could look around, he saw an America in the grip of anti-Vietnam turmoil the likes of which Perth had never remotely experienced — for all the passion of their own protests. As he recalls, the experience opened his eyes: 'The trip was a seminal time in my life, because I had no idea a nation could be so vibrant, diverse, so anarchic. Even though I'd been very hostile to American policy on Vietnam, I came away with an enormous respect for the diversity of American society and the depth of its democracy. I liked their sense of freedom — intellectual freedom and political freedom.' What closed his eyes again was tear gas. A week after leaving the family in Chicago he found himself on Pennsylvania Avenue in Washington marching in a moratorium demonstration towards the Washington Monument. It was the largest protest he had ever seen — tens of thousands of angry people — so many, and in such a mood, that the Maryland State Guard had hurled the tear-gas canisters at them when one part of the crowd had tried to storm the Justice Department. (It was, and it was not, a great day for political freedom.) Kim was not involved in any part of the attack on the Justice Department, and kept marching, as best he could, for the cause — the cause to do everything possible to stop the Vietnam War.

Shortly after leaving Washington, the young Australian went to Cornell University in New York State, and arrived at a time when the Black Power activists had stormed and taken over the Students' Union, and it was the visiting students, as 'honest brokers', who were the first allowed in to talk to them. It seemed strange to the young Australian to find himself suddenly immersed in such potentially violent situations — anger and guns all mixed in together — but it was certainly a fast education in the ways of America. When he looked at the calendar again, he couldn't believe how quickly the ten weeks had passed. It was like being caught in a kaleidoscope, with the rapid-paced change of colours and scenery constantly bombarding him with different experiences, and stimulating different interests.

One by-product of his time in the United States was that it started what would become a close to obsessive fascination with the American Civil War and all the intricacies of its many battles, to the point, in the words of one of his later Labor Party parliamentary colleagues, that 'Kim even knows the names of the fucking generals' *horses*!'[19]

In late December, 1969, he returned to Perth, wiser for the experience, and certainly more broadened. Assuming the position of

Guild President occasioned the first widespread press attention he had received in his life, other than the ancillary attention he had received as Kim Snr's son. In January of the following year, as he was about to take up his post as Guild President, there was a positive flurry of publicity. 'Kim Beazley Jnr: A Future Prime Minister?' asked Perth's *Sunday Times*.[20] The short answer from young Kim was 'not likely,' while the suggestion of the paper was 'maybe'. At the least, the paper was clearly impressed with his résumé at UWA, though it implied that some people were saying it had a quality of 'purposeful design' that was 'Kennedy-like'. Kim Jnr would have none of this notion of Machiavellian planning, at least not in those terms. 'It is freely said around the campus that my father is grooming me as a possible future Prime Minister,' he was quoted in the article as saying. 'There is a general suspicion that I sought student office to further these ends. Some people off the campus have also suggested it ... but I have no immediate plans to enter Parliament ...

'As for seeking student office to further [political] ends, my father was displeased with my election because it meant suspending my studies for a year ... In the long term, I might like to try it, but not now ...' Another profile on the same day in the *Independent Magazine* was penned by Geraldine Willesee, daughter of the same Senator Don Willesee for whom Kim Jnr had done some informal campaigning work over the previous three years. The young Beazley recorded his ambitions in this first gasp of the new decade as being to 'accumulate enough degrees to become a lecturer'. And real politics? 'Maybe I'll stand for selection in the future. I'm interested in State political matters a little more at the moment though.' He also noted the influence of MRA on his life. 'We are a very privileged sect,' he said. 'With MRA, I have learned to be more concerned about things not directly affecting myself. I suppose the fact that I am in MRA will reflect in the things I do and the way I do them.' Finally Ms Willesee let the 'quiet-voiced young man,' who was nevertheless 'outspoken on most things,' have his say on just what he hoped to achieve as Guild President that year. 'I would like to see still more concern from the students for things around them, things like the quality of life in Australia.'

Shortly after these interviews had been published, the *West Australian* for the first time referred to the older of the Beazley men in a slightly different way. 'Young Kim was the first one to notice,' Mrs Beazley recalls. 'I can remember him coming into breakfast with the paper, laughing, and saying "aah, Mum, I have *arrived*, they have to refer to Dad as 'Kim Beazley *Snr*".' The theme that the media harped on, that the Beazleys had raised their son to be Prime Minister, did not please Kim Snr. 'We didn't raise him to be Prime Minister at all,' he said sternly. 'I personally thought that wasn't for West Australians. I think if you look at both sides of the House then everything to do with the Prime Ministership tends to oscillate between New South Wales and Victoria because they are influential states.'

First things first. For Kim Jnr that was to get the Guild of Undergraduates of the University of Western Australia running just the way he wanted it. A hiccup in his early days in the post was that the woman who had been selected to be the Guild Secretary had during the Christmas holidays changed her mind and did not want to fill the post after all. Kim's strong recommendation to the rest of the Guild Council was that the woman who should fill the vacancy was one Mary Paltridge. She was dedicated to the Guild, he said, was competent, and, from what little he knew of her, thought she would have good administrative abilities. Mary Paltridge accepted his nomination, and recalls it as something 'that pleased me on all sorts of levels, one of which was that I thought that this meant that he actually looked at me seriously'. What escaped neither of their attention was that it was obvious that they would, by necessity, be spending a lot of time together over the next year. (Someone who also had a slightly more-than-passing interest in who filled the post of Secretary was Betty Beazley, who had herself held the position back in 1941.)

Kim's championing of Mary for Guild Secretary nevertheless aroused some interested comment from their fellow councillors and friends. After all, of all the people in all of Perth, it was unlikely that there were two people with more directly opposite mainstream political backgrounds than Kim Beazley and Mary Paltridge. As the daughter of Sir Shane Paltridge, her political pedigree on the Liberal side of the fence was every bit as pure as his was on Labor. Her feeling for the Liberal Party had still been strong enough in 1969 that she had been a delegate to the Liberal State Conference and at the end of the year had handed out leaflets on behalf of Robert French, the UWA law student who had stood against Kim Beazley Snr in the Federal Election. Still, you could never really bet on what Mary was going to do next. She was also well known to her amused student friends for frequently farewelling her rather more formal mother, Lady Paltridge, when she dropped her at the University, and immediately kicking her shoes off to walk around the campus all day barefoot. While regarded as highly intelligent, she had failed one of her subjects in her first year at university, before knuckling down somewhat to get serious about her studies for her Arts degree. Whatever, as she said to her close friend Geraldine Doogue early on, it wasn't as if she and Kim were going out or anything, she had merely accepted his nomination to fill the post of Secretary of the Guild. She does admit, though, to being impressed with the way he went about things, and how, right off the bat, he fulfilled his two key campaign promises by getting a medical service on campus and doing away with surcharges for overseas students, before getting to the harder stuff.

'He didn't always get his way and he didn't always get it easily,' she emphasises, 'but maybe because of that, Kim grew up politically very fast running the Guild, and actually making things happen in *reality* and not just in theory as a lot of his political stuff had been to that point. He was always very clear about things. He tended to look at an issue, turn it around, then look at it every which way before making a decision. He would talk to people, take advice, come to a view as to the best way, and then was very cogent at arguing and pushing it through.'

Still, she says, he was not like the clichéd version of the ambitious young man, announcing to all and sundry that he was one day going to be Prime Minister of the nation, blah, blah, blah. 'It was never like that,' she says. 'Kim has always had a very clear view of his responsibilities in life and one responsibility is — in whatever sphere he works, and wherever one finds oneself — to leave the world a better place than you found it.' Neither Kim nor Mary can remember a formal moment when they started 'going out' together. 'We started to spend a fair bit of time together around the Guild more than anything,' is the way Mary remembers it, 'and it just went from there.'

For the newly installed President, it was a busy and turbulent time. In other generations such a position might have meant dealing only with relatively mundane issues of students' daily life, providing a little bit of background hum to the mostly humdrum. Not at this time though. During Kim's time, the Guild was in the forefront of all noisemaking. Nationwide, one of the key bodies to express student outrage at things that displeased them — actually most things generally — was the National Union of Australian University Students, and it was this body which was constantly seeking direction from individual Guilds and Unions for their stance on the issues of the day. With that in mind, the Guild often held general meetings, to in turn seek direction from their students, at which Kim would speak.

At the first such meeting of the year, Kim spoke passionately against a motion supporting abortion, and saw it defeated. The *Pelican* reported:

> *The superficial phrasing of the motion was a blatant insult to the intelligence and Mr Beazley was quick to point this out. However he then delivered a twelve minute speech against the motion; as usual Mr Beazley Jnr was a full bottle on his facts, if not on the slant he chose to give them. It seems however a pity that he should see fit to discharge [such] a heavy broadside ...* [21]

The anti-Vietnam War movement was something that also continued to generate a lot of heat. The unwritten rule was that police would not come onto the campus, meaning that draft dodgers found it a refreshingly safe place to be. It meant that the Guild building acted as something of a magnet for students in trouble, and the Guild President something of a lightning rod for the trouble they brought with them. Many of the students getting grief from the police were either far removed from their parents geographically, or alienated from them emotionally, ensuring that the President of the Guild often found himself fulfilling a kind of parental role, trying to sort things out. It was something that the police actually encouraged, so that the assorted meanderers who passed through their cells would actually have something done for them. It was not only that 'the buck stopped' with Kim, as Harry S. Truman's famous expression went, but rather that the bucks *went* from him, as time after time he was obliged to stand bail out of his personal funds for his troubled fellow students. At one time he was standing bail for ten of them at once, placing severe financial strain on an already depleted purse. It was, again, an education for him, albeit of the seamier side of life. 'I remember one awful case,' he says, 'of a German student who inadvertently killed his girlfriend by trying to perform an abortion on her. You just had to cope, and I guess I "got real" in a big way pretty quickly.' Beazley was personally deeply committed against the whole concept of abortion, but did what he could to help the guy anyway, 'because in that kind of situation it's no time for wagging a finger or discussing the rights or wrongs of it, the guy just needed help, and my first duty was to help him'.

Then there were the problems with the *Pelican*, edited by David Roe. Roe took quite a liberal view of what was permissible to publish, which the Guild President could live with, so long as the Guild did not get into expensive legal trouble because of it.

'He was a rather serious-minded person who I actually liked,' Roe recalls of Beazley. 'We had various ... I wouldn't call them *disagreements,* because he respected that the student newspaper needed to have a degree of editorial independence and he never tried to assert any kind of authority over that. But I think at times we did things that he didn't approve of ...' That was true enough. 'The editor of the student mag,' Beazley recalls, 'was putting out the odd [rather risqué] edition, so we had people being arrested ...'

In some respects, the way the Guild Council worked was like a mini-cabinet, with individual councillors having responsibility for individual 'portfolios,' and advising both the President and his fellow cabinet members of their recommendations, and then arguing for them. In Kim's year the councillor responsible for education — the Education Officer — was none other than John Dawkins, and as Kim recalls it, the younger of the Dawkins' boys was nothing if not enthusiastic. 'He was always wanting to change things,' is the memory Kim Jnr has of him. 'He was always interested in structures and channels and what influences what, and how do you take a paradigm and make it a totally different one and he was obsessed with that when he was wanting to restructure the Guild and undergraduates and *everything.* He would get very passionate about it. I suppose it was through things like that that I really got to know him best, but we weren't ever close.'

Through it all, as Mary noted, Kim was able to develop his political skills — and especially learnt how to make it happen while keeping the maximum number of people onside. Early in his term, for example, he decided that the Guild would have to increase its annual subscription fees in order to meet its budget, and be able to fund some of the campaign promises that Kim, for one, had gained power on. There was a predictable outcry from a number of students who simply did not want their own tight budgets to be stretched any further. Too bad. Guild President Beazley was in no doubt that the proposal simply had to go through for his organisation to do what he wanted it to do, and therefore called a general meeting to discuss the proposal at the extremely out-of-the-way Ross Lecture Theatre in the physics building on the edge of the campus. As recounted by one of his fellow councillors, 'there were a very large number of representatives of sporting clubs induced to turn up because they were going to get a bigger slice of the action as a result of this increase, so the fee increase was carried with an overwhelming majority. It had all been set up very nicely indeed.'[22] Kim Jnr was, in his way, very much the quiet manoeuvrer, something that fitted in well with what he had learnt from his father. He remembers it happening much the same way. 'I *had* to manoeuvre to get the people in sports councils to come in and back that,' he asserts, 'to make sure they got enough money out of it so they would be prepared to go and vote for us. I thought it quite justifiable.'

Because of all his activities with the Guild, he had stood down as President of the University ALP, but remained busily engaged in the State Executive. On 15 July 1970, on a whim, he decided to stand for the position as Junior Vice President of the Western Australian Labor Party. 'I was sort of a representative of the non-Chamberlain forces,' he explains, 'but I was a youngster, I was about 20, and we didn't have any real hope of winning, so I thought I'd stand and see what happened.' It happened! 'I won by three votes — a State Executive of 106 delegates, in a secret ballot. To my amazement and everyone else's, I won, and they could never get rid of me from that point on. Oh, it was huge!'

Being an active and fast-rising member of the Labor Party now, of course, brought him into constant contact with his own father, not just as father and son, but as ALP colleagues, comrades on the great road of politics. Mostly this was an enormous pleasure, to actually be able to lend support to his father on a range of issues by giving him his *vote*, whereas previously he had been able to offer only emotional and intellectual support. Sometimes, however, it could be painful. At a State Conference of the Labor Party around that time there had been many 'modern' issues appearing on the agenda, including the legalisation of abortion, the allowing of gay couples to adopt children, the abolition of censorship, up to and including the possible legalisation of incest (admittedly the proposal of only one delegate).

Eventually, Kim Beazley Snr was moved to take arms against a sea of troubles and by opposing end them. This was *not* what he had joined the Labor Party for, and most definitely NOT the sort of thing the party should be devoting itself to. And he was, by God, just the man to tell them that. With that in mind, just before morning teatime, he rose to the podium, stared balefully out at the room, and let 'em have it ... 'When I joined the Labor Party,' he famously thundered in ringing tones, easily powerful enough to project all around the room and well into succeeding decades, 'it contained the cream of the working class. But as I look about me now all I see are the dregs of the middle class! And what I want to know is when you middle-class perverts are going to stop using the Labor Party as a spiritual spittoon!?!' The meeting went berserk. Shouts, cheers, boos, whistles derisory, whistles celebratory, cat-calls. Order! Order! ORDER! Amid all the mayhem, Kim Beazley Jnr, son-of-a-gun-of-the-son-of-the-same, sitting at a table just in front of the podium, was seen to sink his head into his hands and ... was ... *shocked*. 'You have to remember,' he explains, 'I was just a kid who had all the correct attitudes. Actually most of the things he was expressing I was supporting, in fact all of them, but I wasn't quite prepared for the vehemence.'

His further education in the ways of Federal politics continued at this time with frequent trips to Canberra. One afternoon in mid-1970, when Kim Snr had once again organised for his son to witness proceedings from the Speakers Gallery, the UWA Guild President was most interested to see in action one of the hard rising young warriors of the party, a bloke he had already heard a fair bit about, but had never actually seen in the flesh before. His name was Paul Keating, he was the Member for Blaxland in NSW, a very dapper and well-groomed sort of fellow, who on this particular afternoon was tearing into the opposition in the manner of a starving dingo on a newborn lamb. Several things fascinated Beazley as he watched. One was Keating's extravagant use of language to nail home points, the way he was constantly drawing word pictures to emphasise his points. Another was the way his body language served to provide added firepower for his words — the jabbing finger, the slight swaying motion of a boxer putting his whole torso into every punch.

It was a consummate performance from a bloke a little over four years older than Beazley himself — so much so that when he was done, Kim had observed Opposition Leader Gough Whitlam half-rising from his seat to say something to Keating, only to see the latter make a quick retort and storm off. Kim was to find out shortly afterwards what it had all been about when his father invited Keating for a cup of tea, a chat and a chance for his son to meet him. Though it was a full 20 minutes after the event, the man who would become known as the Bankstown Bonaparte was still outraged by the hide of Whitlam, the *hide* of him! 'He said to me,' recounted Keating incredulously to the Beazley men, "that was very good, Paul, you should go and get yourself a university degree".'

'And ...? You said to him ...?'

'I said, "What for? Then I'd be just like you".'

Kim Jnr liked him. A lot. The guy had style, had panache, had *balls*. It was to be the beginning of a long relationship between the two, with the major foundations being laid over the next few years, as Keating would look up the Beazleys, father and son — separately or together — nearly every time he was in Perth to have a succession of long lunches or late-night dinners. 'Kim had a lot of his father's goodness,' Keating says of his impressions of 'Beazley the Younger' in those early days, 'but he also probably had more of an earthy grip on how the Labor Party moves, how power was actually worked and distributed, how to get on in it. I liked Kim [Snr], and I knew Kim Jnr was steeped in the Labor Party from him and probably shared a lot of his views. I *knew* he shared a lot of those views, and some of mine too, so there was a natural getting along from the beginning.' Back at the Guild, life continued apace for Kim. His image in the University at this time was as a kind of political holy-roller, with the *Pelican*, at one point, describing him as being 'the No.1 ticket-holder of the God Squad'.[23] As Robert French reports, 'he was seen by a lot of his fellow students as very serious, very straight, and they saw him as not having ready access to a sense of humour. But he was greatly respected. We all knew he had a link with Moral Rearmament so they were pretty serious people. He definitely wasn't a nerd, but he was about serious business.'

Within the pure political forum, at the University Labor Club and the wider Labor world generally, a similar seriously conservative image prevailed. It was not always an image interpreted in the best light, and in the memory of Peter Walsh, a lot of the comment turned on Kim's religious commitments. 'Dawkins was only one of a number of people who had a similar attitude,' Walsh recalls. 'Bob McMullan was in the same group basically. It wasn't vituperative so much as derisory. Basically they'd just sling off at the "God Squad".'

Beazley took it all in his stride. One common assertion of his peers at that time seems to have been that in the ongoing struggle between students and the administration, the Guild President came down too close to the administration side of things. A satirical story in the *Pelican* on 7 October 1970,[24] certainly promoted that view ...

> *The Guild President sauntered into his office, threw himself into a padded leather chair and contemplated the past eight hours. It had been a long day. What with the official opening of the tunnel, the inevitable cocktails, a goodwill tour of the schools, afternoon tea, the usual interview on* This Day Tonight, *more*

cocktails, talks with the Vice Chancellor, and now after all that, he was expected to sign the day's batch of letters. There was one to the press apologising for the last issue of Pelican, *another to the students of South Africa expressing support for anti-Apartheid policy, one to something called NUAUS, and a dozen more of equal importance.*

But the Guild President sensed that something was wrong. He decided it was the smell. He would have lit a cigar to drown it out, but had forgotten to get his usual quota from the Vice Chancellor's office. He looked around.

Like any alert, up-and-coming executive, it took the Guild President only seconds to find the source. And he was shocked. There, in the corner of his very own office, were ... were ... he spluttered over the word, were ... STUDENTS!

Horrifying thoughts flashed through his mind. Anarchy; Moratorium; Sex; National Service Sit-Ins (no-one could say the Guild President did not understand students — he read the papers.)

Later ...

Just then the Guild President's secretary dashed into the room.

'Guild President,' she said, 'it's the Vice Chancellor. He says it's an emergency.'

The Guild President, thinking quickly, picked up the special red phone, marked 'For Emergency Use Only'.

'Yes, Vice-Chancellor.'

'Ah, Guild President, we have a small problem here. Some twit from Admin has forgotten to get the party pies for the Senate meeting tonight. Would you be a good fellow and pick some up for us? I just hate a Senate meeting without them, don't you?'

The Guild President's face lit up. At last. A real chance to represent the students.

'Pelican used to take the mickey out of me, I remember that,' Beazley says. 'I think I must have been a pain in the neck. I guess it was the era, with governments falling on student power all over the world, and I guess we just took ourselves tremendously seriously. We had a foreign policy, we had an education policy, we had a poverty policy.'

At the end of his one-year term as Guild President, Kim could legitimately point to a raft of achievements — no fees for overseas students, on-campus medical facilities, greater student representation on faculty and academic boards, finances in place for the new Guild building, more parking available for the students — and more and more people were trotting out the 'he's a future Prime Minister,' line.[25] Still he claims not to have had his head turned by it. To any friends saying such things, Beazley would always deny harbouring any ambitions of the sort — despite his pedigree and past — and would never concede that he was definitely heading off into politics. His friends however, were in no doubt. 'I always thought that in that puritan upbringing of his,' Geraldine Doogue says, 'it was drilled into Kim that he is here to serve, that a man of talents is here to serve others, not himself — and it was always clear that politics was always going to be the best way for him to do that.'

With his term as Guild President completed, Kim again took up his Honours studies, including the completion of his thesis on the Bombay Non-Cooperation Movement.

He slipped back into his full-time studies quite easily, though in early 1971 things were clearly quite different for him to the way it had been in late 1969 when he had last been studying. For one thing he was now going out, for sure and for certain, with Mary Paltridge. The two were a common sight walking around the campus together, and though it was not often hand-in-hand — for Kim, at that stage of his life, tended to eschew overt displays of physical affection in public — it was well known that they were together. 'I think a lot of people were interested,' Mary recollects, 'because of the whole Liberal/Labor thing, and our different backgrounds, but really by that stage I'd moved well away from Liberal beliefs anyway, and believed most of the things that Kim believed, though *not* because he believed them.' Kim had also gained at least one surprising close friend in Robert French. French was in fact more than just a cap 'L' Liberal — he was also the President of the University Liberal Club, on the State Executive of the Liberal Party, and Kim Jnr had gone through a good pair of leather shoes in his efforts to trounce him in his guise as his father's opponent in the '69 elections. Their friendship had flourished nevertheless through the course of Kim's year as Guild President and thereafter, and it was one of the first signs of the notably ecumenical approach that Beazley would take to politics. Andrew Peacock would later comment that he always had the impression that Paul Keating found it difficult to talk to Liberals — class enemies and all that — but Beazley never had the same innate distrust. And French, for his part, had also come to be an admirer of the Beazley way, for all the obvious things, and one other thing besides. 'I can't ever recall seeing him in a situation where he appeared to be under any undue pressure at any stage.'

This, despite having a university résumé that would kill a brown dog — and this is the other thing that stood out about Kim Jnr at university. He was a young man carrying on a full-time relationship, who was studying for an Honours degree at a major university, had been playing for the University Rugby Club, was an executive member of the Australian Union of Students, on the Foundation Board of Murdoch University, Treasurer of the Asian Studies Association, Member of the University Senate, President of the Student Guild, President of the University ALP Club and on the State Executive of the ALP. And yet he never seemed busy or hassled by it all.

It seemed to Betty Beazley that no matter what time of night she might happen to pass her son's bedroom door there would be a light coming from under it, as he ploughed on through his books. It was a high level busyness, and a consistent accomplishment therein, which was noted by many people. One of those was Josh Reynolds, who was Secretary of the Rhodes Scholar Selection Committee in Western Australia, and he encouraged the young student to put his name forward. After reflection, Beazley did just that, filling out all the forms, organising all the referees as to his good character and so on, but without any great expectations of success. 'I didn't think I'd get it,' he says now frankly. 'Basically I'd been very happy doing [my studies]; I knew that I'd probably have to go into the Army the moment I'd finished them and so I wasn't all that fussed about the Rhodes, that was just too far down the track.' As it turned out, he was right in the expectation that he wouldn't get it, the scholarship being awarded to his mate Geoff Gallop instead, but it was hardly a crushing disappointment. 'I was too busy to have much time for moping, it was just like ... OK, what's next?'

In the first instance, what was next was more study, more of seeing Mary and, more politics — always more politics. Only six months after becoming Junior Vice President of the Labor Party, he had gone up to the next rung on the Labor ladder by being elected as Senior Vice President. The 'Junior' and 'Senior' appellations had in fact nothing to do with age and concerned only rank, and he had now gone from being the fourth-ranked official in the State Labor Party to the third. Under most circumstances the position of Senior Vice President was still not powerful in its own right, but circumstances would suddenly make it very powerful indeed. A meeting of the Federal Executive* of the Labor Party was scheduled for April, and the West Australian Labor Party had the right to send two delegates. They had chosen Joe Chamberlain and WALP President, Col Jamieson. At the last moment though, Chamberlain fell ill, meaning that under party rules the next cab off the rank to replace him was the WALP's Senior Vice President — Kim Christian Beazley. The irony in Kim Jnr suddenly gaining a role on the Federal Executive representing Western Australia was that his father had lost his own spot on that body just the year before, when one of the many coup attempts that were always being launched against him was semi-successful. One can only wonder what the ailing Joe Chamberlain thought about the fact that his position at the powerful meeting was going to the son of the man he had nailed the year before. But rules was rules was rules.

So at the grand old age of 22, Kim Jnr found himself on a plane bound for Adelaide to attend a meeting of the Federal Executive of the ALP. This was a particularly contentious meeting of that body in which to be making his debut, and Kim was in a delicate position. At that time the ALP nationally was dealing with the delicate issue of the restructuring of the NSW branch, and the Left and Right of the party had two clearly different views about how this should be done. The power balance between them was very evenly weighted, or at least had been before Kim Jnr had got the nod. Had Joe Chamberlain been there, the Left would have just had the numbers to force the intervention in their own manner. Now, though, with Kim Jnr's presence, the Right looked likely to be able to prevent that happening. All seemed lost for the Left, unless they could pressure young Beazley into changing his vote, but there would be time enough for that.

The young student found himself ensconced in the Adelaide Hotel, rubbing shoulders with the titans of the party, people such as Mick Young, Gough Whitlam, Bob Hawke and Lionel Murphy. Some he already knew through his father and from other Labor Party meetings over the years, others he would come to know over the course of the week. The Adelaide Hotel was one of the finest hospitality institutions in Adelaide, and was all the more impressive to young Kim who had been used to conducting student politics in tacky back rooms. Apart from the motions, and proposals, and rebuttals, and ballots, there was

---

* The Federal Executive is the body responsible for making key party decisions between National Conferences.

also great camaraderie amongst the Labor brethren, despite their inevitable disputes.

On the second day of the gathering, when the meeting had yet to struggle fully with how to restructure the NSW branch, the famed Labor warrior Lionel Murphy was desperate to get his Senate preselection ratified as he feared that if the NSW branch was left to its own devices he would be dropped to the highly dangerous third position, where he would be unlikely to gain a seat in the next election. With that in mind he wanted the Federal Executive to intervene at least to the extent of selecting the next ticket for New South Wales, and after every other item was considered Murphy would move a motion that the Executive consider the Federal preselection. 'Every time he moved it, we deferred it,' Kim Jnr recollects, 'and he must have raised it half-a-dozen times during the course of the day.'

That night, the elite of the national Labor Party machine gathered in the hotel's restaurant for a formal dinner – all waiters, crystal glasses and lovely crisp white napkins with *creases* — when Jack Edgerton, the notorious delegate from Queensland, stood up and started to clink his glass, calling for attention. The ALP table, and to a lesser extent the room around, immediately fell silent. This was after all, a man famous for his dry and biting wit, who could nearly always be counted on to say something memorable, be it a bitter attack or an amusing aside. At a previous ALP conference in Queensland, for example, he had upbraided Bill Hayden for pursuing a ban on boxing while simultaneously calling for the decriminalisation of homosexuality, and expressed himself in inimitable terms: 'Gawd, I can't follow delegate Hayden,' he had rasped. 'He's opposed to a bloke getting a punch on the nose, but doesn't mind if he gets a punch in the bum! Those supporting the chairmen to the right, poofters to the left!'[26]

On this occasion though, he had something rather more serious in mind, something he wanted the party to put right without further delay, and accord honour where honour was due. 'I want your attention ladies and gentlemen,' he repeated. 'I want to ask you a question that's on the list for every right thinking Australian. I want to know this: when is Lionel Murphy going to stop thinking about the Party and the country and start thinking about himself!?!?' The table dissolved into uproar — most of it laughter — as other mystified restaurant patrons looked on. As he remembers it, none laughed harder than the young delegate from Perth, having the time of his life.

'I was knocked out by it,' Kim Jnr recalls, 'I was just amazed by the whole show.'

Not that there wasn't pressure on him for all that. Far from it. With the meeting building to the climactic moment when they were to decide in what manner they would intervene in the NSW branch, Beazley was granted an exceptionally fast education in the ways of the political world. On the morning of the crucial vote, around about 5 am as he remembers it, the quiet of the morning was shattered by the telephone on the bedside table. The young Western Australian delegate groped for the phone through the darkness, and picked it up. 'Hello . . . ?'

'It's Bob Hawke.'

'Er . . . yes?'

'I want to talk to you about the way you're going to vote today . . .'

'Yes?'

'Well we #%#$# well want you to vote our way!!! You have got to understand how essential it is to restructure the NSW branch in the right manner.'

Or some such. These proved merely to be his opening remarks. There followed, as Beazley remembers it, an 'exceptionally hostile' diatribe from the then Left-aligned Hawke, detailing all the reasons why the man from Perth should support his side of the argument, and finishing with Hawke being a little softer, saying 'Now you don't want to wreck your political career, young man, by going along with all this crap do you? Just come along with us and vote the right way today . . .'

Later that same day, the young delegate came under similar pressure from his fellow Western Australian, Col Jamieson, who put it right on the line for him. No muckin' about. Taking him aside, Jamieson came straight to the point. 'Voting the wrong way is going to wreck your political career, son, so you bloody well better back us.'

At the limit, Hawke might have been able to get away with speaking to Kim like that in the morning — Hawke was after all ACTU President, there had been no history of tribal animosity between them, and Kim had been half-asleep besides — but there was no way the new delegate was going to take this from a long-time antagonist of his father. Sure, Jamieson was no political wallflower — he had been described by a Liberal opponent once as being as 'hard as flintstone and as rough as goats knees'[27] — but the young man stuck it to him anyway. 'Listen Col,' Beazley remembers replying, 'I don't actually *have* a political career at the moment, I'm just a student, and

I'm way down the track from you. On the other hand YOU are actually in Parliament at this point of time, and you would want to be asking yourself the question whether I might not do *you* some damage.' Where did the Beazley boy get off talking to his nominal party superior in such insolent fashion? A part of it was the payback for Jamieson's political harassment of his father, but there was, also, a generational divide the dimensions of which the older man could only guess at. 'I just didn't give a damn,' is the way Beazley explains it now. 'None of us did. Basically the student politics then was tremendously intense and aggressive. It was the anti-Vietnam War era, the student control of universities era. We were a bunch of pains in the neck when it all boils down to it.'

There was still something else that worked him, an exchange of conversation he remembered back in WA between Joe Chamberlain and one of Kim's university ALP colleagues, which the younger Beazley thought summed up perfectly the way things were. The university ALP straddled Left and Right in that, although its core feeling was mainly Left, it was nevertheless pro-Whitlam, and devoted to seeing a Labor Government in power, and Whitlam was clearly the best chance for that. Thus the conversation ... 'I can remember Joe complaining to one of the members of the branch, saying, "no I can't believe this, you agree with me against Vietnam, while Whitlam is maybe compromising on these things. Why are you like that, why do you oppose me?"

'And the kid said to him, "Well look Joe, some of us are being conscripted, some of us are draft resisters and may go to gaol, some of us are going into court whether we are conscientious objectors or not, and some of us have got to go in the Army and get shot at. Either way, *any* of those ways, life is pretty bad for us, now whatever Whitlam may be doing, what he's not going to do is impose those choices on us. But if you succeed, those choices will keep being imposed on us because your policies will *never* get Labor elected, while Whitlam will very probably get elected. So we can't support you."

'So it was the getting of wisdom for Joe basically.'

As a fractured footnote, Hawke remembers being impressed, both with the way Kim Snr's 22-year-old son had got to the conference in the first place, and how he had handled himself once he got there.

'Here was this young bloke at university taking on the entrenched power of the Chamberlain machine — I knew Chamberlain hated his father — and I actually had this fellow feeling with him because Joe also hated my uncle Bert [the former WA Premier Bert Hawke*]. Bert and Kim Snr were both, you would say, moderate Left, ideological fanatics going right back. Kim Jnr had already established a reputation as being prepared to get down into the tough nitty-gritty of factional politics. We knew Kim was solid when it came for the need to push a case hard.'

Clearly a good part of the bond formed between the former Rhodes Scholar Hawke and Kim Beazley was their common high academic standing, and in this field Kim Jnr continued to excel. Though at the end of 1971, Kim did not get First Class Honours as he had hoped, and was instead awarded an Upper Second, he was considered a strong-enough student that he was offered a scholarship by UWA to do a full-time Master of Arts research degree in Politics, which he immediately snapped up.

His intellectual interests and political passions had matured since the time that he had begun his studies five years previously, in part because of his experience with fighting against the Vietnam War. Years later, in a newspaper interview, he would say of himself and his political colleagues of the time: 'We were created out of the Vietnam War. We were different from the '50s and '60s. We learned that a government whose policies were incorrect could conceivably kill you. Therefore securing power was a very important aspect of one's political life.'[28] There is no doubt either — now that he had been studying it for four years — just how strongly Kim Jnr had become confirmed in his views that the 'policies were incorrect'. They continued to infuriate him on an intellectual level. 'I just thought Vietnam at the time was a product of our excessive dependence on America,' he says. 'And an inadequate understanding of the region with which we were dealing. It wasn't the basis on which we in Australia could relate sensibly to contemporary Asia. So that's what really got me interested in a bit of independence for Australian foreign policy and defence policy towards America.' With all of that in mind, he decided to do his Masters on *Australian Labor Party Attitudes to the American Alliance*, which involved writing a 120 000 word thesis on that subject focusing on how Labor factions of the 1960s reacted to specific foreign policy issues like Vietnam, Malaysia and the joint facilities. (Not too mildly, would be a fair summation.)

---

* Premier Bert Hawke had, in fact, been instrumental in ensuring that during the 'troubles' of the 1950s, when Kim Snr had disobeyed the instruction on which way to vote at the Hobart Conference, he had only been suspended, and not expelled.

In the middle of 1972, and now well into his Masters, Josh Reynolds again approached Kim to put his name forward for a Rhodes scholarship, and found him initially reluctant. 'I thought that as I'd missed the first time, it was most unlikely I'd get it the second, but I liked old Josh, and it was not exactly time consuming.' Still there was some reason for vague hope that he might win, he realised, as he was filling in the forms again. The Rhodes scholarship was judged on three criteria — on academic life, sporting life and contributions to the community and university. In all three, his credentials were full to overflowing, and he actually did feel a slight surge of confidence as he posted the application forms this time.

'It's time. Time for moving, time for changing, it's time to begin, yes it's time.'

The ALP campaign slogan of 'It's Time' was catchy and it took Australia by storm in late 1972. In the Federal election campaign, Mr Edward Gough Whitlam essayed to work the crowds into lather enough to wash away 23 years of Liberal rule, by putting an end to Billy McMahon's Prime Ministership. In Perth, the young Kim Beazley had signed on as campaign director for ALP candidate Alan Scott in the electorate of Canning — his father's seat of Fremantle was rock-solid safe, whereas Canning was marginal — and he was conscious that there was a different feel in the air this time to any other election he had ever known. His favourite campaign badge, which he and Mary wore throughout — his girlfriend, whatever her Liberal antecedents, was now totally, emotionally and intellectually committed to Labor — had a caricature of Billy McMahon displaying him as a winged nut, with the caption beneath, 'Stop laughing at Billy!' The thing Kim had noticed was that people *were* laughing at Billy, while also being inspired by Whitlam. 'It was a very good personal experience,' Beazley recollects of those heady times. 'It was the first time I was actually director of a campaign, and we really got stuck in. Some of the older members of the party were still doubtful that it could happen after all those years out of office, but the young people were deeply convinced that the government would fall and I was very much infected with that spirit at the time.' The memory of the election will never leave him.

'I can remember the thrill as Mary and I were driving up to the tally room, from the town of Kwinana, and stopping off on the way and seeing all our university friends — some of whom were draft resisters, all of whom had been activists on things like Vietnam — and as we were driving back and stopping off at booths, we were getting more and more results in over the radio, and everyone was talking, and overjoyed because after all that time we'd actually *done it*. For me, it was absolute seventh heaven. I'd been waiting my whole life for that win.'

And indeed he just about had. The Coalition had been in power for 23 of his 24 years of life. His father had been waiting even longer. Having come into Parliament in 1945 as a very junior backbencher of the Government, Kim Snr had been waiting 27 years for the possibility of being a minister and now that hour was upon him. He hoped. So did his son. 'I'd come to believe that nothing good ever happened to Dad,' Kim Jnr says, 'that generally speaking he'd have a bit of a surge and then he'd lose. So I guess in the euphoria of Gough's election win, there was still that inner worry: "Would Dad get there? Would he make it to be a minister?".' He would.

Though it was still unofficial, Kim Snr soon got word that he was earmarked for the Education portfolio — but in an entirely different field there was still more wonderful news to come for the Beazley family. On the following Monday evening, only three days after the election, at a reception at Perth's Government House they were officially informed Kim Jnr had been awarded a Rhodes scholarship to attend Oxford University and Balliol College from October of 1973. Because the academic years between the hemispheres were out of kilter, it would mean finishing his thesis for his UWA Masters Degree in his first few months at Oxford, but that was fine.

Mary was especially delighted, and remembers feeling, 'really excited for him, even though I knew it would be taking him away. We'd all been waiting for the call, and when it came, I think we both sensed that this was just a great turning point in his life.' When the news of Kim's scholarship got out, there was a measure of surprise from many people who had known him as a good, but not brilliant, student and sportsman back in his Hollywood High days. Now he was regarded as the best in the state. Chris Smith recalls his mother commenting, 'Kim Beazley? Kim *Beazley*?! How on earth did *he* get to be a Rhodes scholar?!?!' Many of his high school teachers confess to feeling the same way. Kim himself has the explanation. 'There was only one subject that interested me at school and that was History, where I always got distinctions. And I was also learning politics at home with Dad. What was I doing when I got to university? I was doing History and Politics. It wasn't too surprising that I went well.'

The ten months between being awarded the Rhodes scholarship and departing the following year was, as always, full. There was not only the first draft of his thesis to write, not only his continuing relationship with Mary, but as had always been the case since he had become an adult, there were plenty of activities to do with the Labor Party. And what a joy it was, to still be in Australia while the Whitlam Government got into stride. One of Beazley's childhood acquaintances, Robert Drewe, would later write in *The Australian* about the Labor Government's first three months.[29]

Australians blinked as, within weeks, we recognised China, ended conscription, abolished race as a criterion of our immigration policy, banned racially selected sporting teams, supported equal pay for women, began reform of the health service, put contraceptives on the medical benefits list, established the Schools Commission, moved to stop the slaughter of kangaroos and crocodiles, abolished British honours and searched for a new national anthem.

He concluded: 'Labor restored some dignity to the conduct of our national affairs at a time when we had all come more or less to expect nothing but ill from political action.' Kim Beazley Jnr felt equally enthusiastic and remembers the time. 'I think basically I was very proud,' he says. 'Proud of my father and the changes he was beginning to make in education, proud of the changes that the Whitlam Government was instituting, proud of the Labor Party generally, that we were a party capable of generating so much good social change. It was a very exciting time for me.'

By mid-1973 Kim Jnr was himself highly regarded enough in the WALP to be entrusted with the role of Acting Secretary, filling in for Joe Chamberlain who was again suffering a long illness. For the most part this role was a procedural, supervisory one, reading reports, signing cheques, and presiding over meetings. There was really only one decision he took during his stint that amounted to anything. In May of that year, the popular Labor man and Deputy Premier of WA, Herb Graham, suddenly retired from politics, resulting in a by-election. The man who gained preselection for the seat was one of Kim's oldest friends, Brian Burke. Burke was a year older than Kim, but of a similar background, and to some extent they had lived parallel childhoods. Tom Burke, Brian's father, and Kim Beazley Snr had been Labor parliamentary colleagues together starting in the mid-'40s, and were so close that when Kim Snr and Betty had married, it was Tom Burke who had been Best Man. The two had fought the good fight side by side on many issues and been united in their anti-Communist, anti-Chamberlain efforts. There was, however, one crucial difference between them; for while Beazley Snr had *in extremis* survived, Tom Burke had not. As a result of the infamous Split of the 1950s Tom Burke had, at the instigation and insistence of Joe Chamberlain, been expelled from the party in disgrace — entirely unfairly in the 20/20 vision of historical hindsight. Tom Burke's demise had been greatly upsetting to Kim Snr, so much so that Betty Beazley recalls it as, 'the only time I ever saw my husband cry'.

With such a background it meant that Kim Jnr and Brian had not only effectively grown up together, seeing each other at family gatherings and political meetings etc, but they then had joined the University ALP branch at the same time, gone on to the State Executive together, and been close friends and political fellow-travellers since. Another binding force upon them was that both had younger brothers with disabilities. Brian Burke had a younger brother with Down's Syndrome, while Kim's younger brother David also remained in need of special attention. Aside from all that, the Burke and Beazley Jnrs simply liked each other a lot. 'He was sort of one of those friends you "inherit" automatically,' Beazley says, 'when your parents know each other, and the families are friends. They are almost like cousins. But then we became friends, real friends. In the Labor Party you can have a lot of mates, but he was a friend.'

As with their fathers, though, there was one crucial difference between them. While part of Kim's political motivation had been to protect his father, it was always said of Burke that what he was about was *avenging* his father — who had died shortly before this preselection — and as a result of that had always been more vehement in pushing himself forward than Kim had ever been. Now, in the company of his older brother Terry, Brian Burke came calling on Kim in his role as Acting Secretary. They wanted, they said, as much money as Kim could spare from the ALP's electoral campaign fund. Kim checked the WALP's electoral account. There was 6000 dollars there. He withdrew it. All of it. And deposited it in Brian Burke's campaign fund. 'I thought he was a very good candidate,' he remembers, 'contesting a very tight seat, and he needed every bit of support we could give him.' Joe Chamberlain was not of quite the same generous viewpoint. Within days, 'Joe got up off his deathbed … and was outraged that I should do this, absolutely *outraged*. "That is *all* the money for the next State election", he said.'

And that, as it turned out, was the end of young Beazley's role as Acting Secretary. Old Joe would sooner die with his boots on than let young Beazley stay at the wheel a single minute longer. Coughing and wheezing all the way, he re-took possession of his desk, his office and his dignity, and kicked Kim out. Others of the Labor brethren were equally appalled that that much money had gone on the one by-election, and come the night of the count, the young Labor man remembers being more than somewhat nervous that Burke should do the right thing by him by actually winning. 'I was praying for a win for Brian,' he recalls, 'otherwise I was dogmeat.' Early on, it looked bad, as to the surprise and horror of all assembled, Burke fell behind in the counting. 'Luckily though,' ex-Acting Secretary Beazley recalls, 'Brian ended up winning it by 28 votes, so I didn't hear any more complaints about having overspent from that point on.' As it turned out, Burke probably needed nearly every last one of those dollars to get over the line. But in the end what did Kim care anyway? He would soon be flying away, away to Oxford.

Kim Jnr's life at home had changed during his university years. His sheer busyness prevented him from being at home as often or as long as he would have liked, though he ensured that he was there as much as possible to help his mother when she needed it. Part of her need, as it had always been, was assistance in caring for David.

David had left school before doing the Leaving and had gained work as a telegraph boy at Claremont Post Office. At one point he was in trouble with his supervisor for not getting through enough work. Kim Snr was in Canberra, Merrilyn had returned from India only to go off to New Guinea, so Mrs Beazley had called in Kim Jnr to see if he could help. As they would often do when confronted with a problem, the three sat down for some quiet reflection, to see what 'guidance' God would offer. '*Kim's thought was to go up and talk it over with the man,*' Mrs Beazley wrote down in her book of recollections, '*and my thought was to realise that the man was a father of two children and you wanted him to be kindly, and David's thought was to be quicker in his delivery of telegrams, with the result that David came home the very next day beaming, all was well and after that he and his superior were good friends.*'

Whilst in his time since India young Kim's iron-bound commitment to Moral Rearmament had loosened, it was a long way from unravelling entirely. Still, his academic and political commitments meant that he only rarely had time to attend MRA meetings. Moreover, his university friends had illustrated that it really was possible to live otherwise than ramrod-straight and straight forward-march. Yet despite this growing awareness, there was no strain with his parents. After all, it was not as if he was embarking on a career of sex, drugs and rock 'n' roll — and nor was he considering doing something even more heinous, by voting Liberal. But the main thing was that parental nagging or interference just did not fit in with their beliefs. 'My parents were the most complex parents,' he explains. 'They had their deep religious commitments and they used to tell us what their commitments were and involve us in understanding this. But part of their commitment was the very, very strong view that we would always discover the right way ourselves, and my father and mother, particularly after I left school, took the view that they would not direct me in any way, that I was on my own.'

In his entire adult life, in fact, Kim Jnr can remember only one occasion when his father broke that general rule and did gently try to guide him in one direction, an occasion so stunning that Kim Jnr would remember his words for decades afterwards, syllable for syllable, and also the way his father had looked, as he said them at the time: It was late afternoon in the autumn of 1973, and they were alone in the family living room. His father was standing, he was sitting on the couch, and his father's head was framed against the golden twilight coming through the venetians in such a way that while his face was quite dark, there was a kind of halo effect around his head.

'Son,' he said, 'I've never said anything about these sorts of things and this is the only thing I'm ever going to say, but it's this: if Mary were to come to you and say that it was "all off", you would feel, I understand, hurt, rejection, pride, these sorts of things, but if your underlying feeling would be one of relief underneath all of those things, if you can honestly say it would be one of relief then get out of the relationship now. But if you can say that that's not the case then I have nothing more to say.'

It was clear in the younger man's mind then, as now, that his father was telling him in the gentlest of all possible ways, that in his opinion Mary was not the right partner for him. But the son was equally clear of his own opinion. Simply, 'I thought he was wrong'. So wrong in fact, that it was not long after this that Kim Beazley Jnr and Mary Paltridge became formally engaged — not that either can quite remember how that occurred. As Kim now represents it, 'we were going out for a long time and we just sort of — sort of had a discussion about when we should have the engagement party before I went away'. Mary remembers things happening in much the same way. 'There was never the romantic dinner thing,' she explains. 'We just came to the conclusion that we were going to get married. Instead of talking about "when *I* do this", it became "when *we* do this".'

The last of the great romantics he was not, at least in terms of being a down-on-bended knee, flowers and chocolate kind of guy. For his Best Man, he chose Hugh Nelson, now Dr Hugh Nelson. Before leaving Australia, Nelson had not only been Kim's closest friend, but also embodied those things that Kim Beazley himself held dearest. Nelson was a religious man, a regular churchgoer whom Kim had seen constantly since their days together in India with Moral Rearmament, and he had studied medicine at UWA. In the words of Geraldine Doogue, who had in turn been chosen as Mary's bridesmaid, and who had gone out with Nelson for a while: 'Hugh was a very good man who fitted in with that missionary side of Kim, the "do good" part, the MRA part. He was a very serious young man ... a very, very serious young man.'

While tradition usually dictates that the wedding will gravitate to the place of the bride, on this occasion it would go north, north to the groom. It was decided that they would get married at Oxford the following year, at the height of the English summer — when all would be appropriately flowery and beautiful. Meanwhile Mary would continue her studies for a Diploma of Education in Perth, before taking up some part-time work as a relief teacher. Getting married any sooner was out of the question anyway, as under the terms of the Rhodes scholarship, Kim had to spend at least one year in residence at Balliol College and the college did not have any married accommodation.

The qualms of the Beazley parents about the engagement were at least matched by the qualms of Mary's surviving parent, Lady Paltridge. Though this woman clearly had an enormous affection for her future son-in-law, she was concerned at how such a marriage would look, what with her daughter — progeny of the finest Liberal from out of the West — marrying the son of an equally famed Labor man. With perhaps that in mind, on the day before the announcement was due to appear in the engagements section of the *West Australian*, she rang Mary's close friend, Geraldine Doogue, who was then working as a cadet journalist on the paper.

Please tell me, Geraldine, she had said, that the paper is not going to give Kim and Mary's union any more publicity than just that simple announcement.

As a matter of fact they were, Lady Paltridge, had replied Ms Doogue, eyeing before her the proofs of the front-page splash the following day on that very subject.

Oh dear. Was there nothing anyone could do to stop that front-page publicity going ahead — after all, their engagement was fine, but it didn't have to have publicity with it, did it? No, it didn't *have* to have publicity, and yes, there was something somebody could do to stop it. But unfortunately that someone had to have the words 'Editor-in-Chief' in front of his or her name. 'Cadet' Doogue would not suffice. 'Lady Paltridge,' she finished, 'there is nothing I can do about it, it is already done.'

'Oh dear, really, her father wouldn't have wanted this . . .'

And maybe he wouldn't have, but the story ran anyway. There was, predictably, a great flurry of interest about the impending union, but at all turns Kim and Mary endeavoured to play down the fact of their opposing political backgrounds — at least insofar as it concerned their own relationship. 'We are marrying each other as people not as politicians,' Mary told Perth's *Weekend News* in late July of 1973, 'I think our views coincide in most areas to a considerable extent. Though we don't mirror each other's opinions, of course.'[30] Mary was there just two months later at Perth airport, with the rest of the Beazley family, to farewell Kim on his way to England.

CHAPTER SEVEN

OXFORD

'There ... within a stone's throw, stood the twin towers of All
Souls, fantastic, unreal as a house of cards, clear-cut in the
sunshine, the drenched oval in the quad beneath, brilliant as an
emerald in the bezel of a ring.'
Dorothy L. Sayers on Oxford University, from
Gaudy Night, *published in 1935.*

It had been a miserably typical, dark, cold, bleak October day in
London. If the wispy sun had at least delivered *something* in the way
of light and warmth during the nominally daylight hours, the same
could not be said of the foggy moon that night. Up in Oxford town, to
the northwest, through the near-deserted gloom of late evening, a taxi
cab came to a halt in front of Balliol College on Broad Street, near the
heart of Oxford University. Out stepped Kim Christian Beazley — just
woken from a sleep on the night train from London — and he looked
up at what was to be his new home. It looked, sure enough, *old*. It
looked gothic. It looked a bit more than a fraction intimidating. As
opposed to the sort of farewell he had received when leaving Perth four
days previously, here there was no brass band awaiting him, no
outstretched hands, not a murmur of anything, just a huge wooden
gate, such as would have kept ten peasant soldiers and a ramming log at
bay, and within that gate a kind of small door, which he opened up and
staggered through, a heavy green Trunklite suitcase in each hand.

Through the door, still in the dark, he could see just one light on in
the building proper, and he ventured towards it. 'Yes?' said the porter
lurking just inside the door, looking distinctly uninterested. 'Hi. Kim
Beazley, from Australia. I am enrolled here.'

'Yes sir, your room is at Staircase 20, Room 5, and if you call out for Percy down the hall near the stairs, he will help you out.'

Percy proved to be a little bird-like man who twitched his way through lots of little bird-like movements, and who looked old enough to once have carried bags for Queen Victoria. Barely a word passed between them as they climbed up the ancient staircases to his room. 'I thought to myself, "What sort of place is this?"' Kim recalls. 'It was *freezing*. I had no idea what was going on, nobody knew me from Adam.'

That feeling of isolation and total anonymity was exacerbated the following morning. After an extremely restless night, he had risen early to have breakfast in Balliol's magnificent dining room — with its massive wooden arches stretching to meet way above oak tables, and stained-glass windows throwing light on to portraits of British Prime Ministers past, Balliol men all — and sat down beside a rather effete-looking young man with a bow tie who was eating and reading the morning papers. 'Gidday, Kim Beazley from Australia,' he ventured, after he had settled. The Englishman kept eating his breakfast and reading, for all the world as if he had not heard a voice. Thinking that indeed must be the case, the new arrival tried again, this time with a proffered hand. 'Kim Beazley from AUSTRALIA,' he said. Nothing. Not a flicker of acknowledgement. Cornflakes to mouth. Cornflakes to mouth. Sip of coffee. 'I've come to do a Bachelor of Philosophy,' he tried one last time, with just a hint of exasperation, and ... achieved exactly the same result. Eventually he resigned himself to just sitting there and having his breakfast in what seemed an extremely uncomfortable silence to him, but which was obviously fine to the man beside him. It was an unhappy beginning, to what in effect would be an even unhappier first month. 'I was incredibly homesick,' he says, 'and it was a pretty ordinary introduction.' He had left Perth as that year's version of the best and brightest, the single Rhodes scholar representative from all of Western Australia, *la crème de la crème de la* bloody-well-best-there-was, and arrived in Oxford as just another nobody from nowhere.

Shortly though he was able to right himself, to take stock of what was around him, and get into the rhythm of the place. Balliol College itself would come to please him greatly. It was a place of no little distinction, with *Time* magazine once noting that the college 'sits at the head of Oxford's intellectual table — a proud hatchery of Prime Ministers, archbishops, cardinals and viceroys'.[31] Past Balliol collegians who particularly impressed young Kim included Gerard Manley Hopkins, Graham Greene, Robert Browning, the founder of Modern Economics — Adam Smith — and a trio of former British Prime Ministers in Harold Macmillan, Lord Asquith and Edward Heath. Another former student, a Rhodes scholar in fact, whose former presence there was commemorated on the walls with a plaque, was Friederich Adam von Trott zu Solz, who had been executed for his plot to assassinate Adolf Hitler in 1944. Beyond that, the place was near *dripping* with history, something that thrilled Kim clear to the core. Established in 1263 by John Balliol, one of King Henry III of England's most loyal Lords, the college was the oldest standing at Oxford, and looked exactly that, with the workmanship visible on rough-hewn stone in the oldest parts of the college having been done by men who had now been in their graves for seven centuries.

By the Master's lodging, a stone cross marked the fact that two Protestant martyrs, Bishop Hugh Latimer and Bishop Nicholas Ridley had been burnt at the stake in 1555 at that very spot under the reign of Mary I. As the fire had started to lick at Ridley's feet, Latimer had made the famous comment to him, 'Be of good comfort Master Ridley, and play the man. We shall this day light such a candle, by God's Grace, in England, as I trust shall never be put out.'[32]

If in his early months there, Kim was moved by a desire to find his feet, there were another couple of resolutions he had made which continued to guide him. For starters, he was not looking to relive his life at the University of Western Australia, where he later estimated that 80 per cent of his time had been devoted to politics.[33] 'At Oxford it was totally different,' he says. 'My resolution was I am *not* going to get involved in politics here at all, *not at all*. I said to myself I am going to look back at my weaknesses. My weakness was that I had never put the time I really wanted into my study. So, here, I am going to finish my MA and I am going to treat this as building my mind more than anything else. I really thought if I'm going to come to a place that stood at the peak of British intellectual endeavours, then it was an opportunity that I ought to exploit.'

He kept this central commitment to himself, without shutting down the rest of his usual activities entirely. 'So I joined the Oxford Union but I never participated in any of the debates. I helped the British Labour Party in election campaigns and took out membership of the University Labour Club but I don't think I attended any meetings.'

This success in changing his approach, lifted his spirits enormously. 'It was freedom,' he says. 'Freedom from everybody's expectations of you. Freedom from any form of self-direction in one sense and anyone else's direction in the other, and just letting your mind go. It was an intellectual treat.' For young Beazley, this treat was principally served up by Alastair Buchan,* the former Head of the Imperial Defence College, former Director of the British Services Staff College, founder of the Institute of International Strategic Studies — a man near enough to being the doyen, and by some measure the founder, of the modern study of international relations. Professor Buchan, a tall, angular man, with a pronounced stammer, was as Kim remembers him 'a diffident Englishman ... just superb, and a great intellect'. Within the realms of world diplomacy, Buchan was regarded as being fairly and squarely within the British small 'c' conservative tradition of international politics, a realist school tempered by the notion that there were nevertheless certain moral principles of international relations which governments ought to adhere to — *Realpolitik,* with just a large enough dash of morality to sweeten but not weaken.

It was appropriate then, by virtue of his association with Balliol College, that he was also to become Kim's 'moral tutor,' an Oxonian institution whereby the distinguished professor was obliged to oversee his student's personal and spiritual life to ensure that all was as it should be. In reality, it meant the odd conversation here and there about this and that and nothing much in particular. The two got on well from the beginning, and spent many long hours discussing things after the academic requirements were fulfilled. Also constantly thrown into Oxford's intellectual mix were such luminaries as the famous historian A.J.P. Taylor, and even though he was not lecturing in any area that the Australian was studying, Beazley insisted on going anyway. 'You had to go and see him,' he says. 'You would walk into a lecture theatre and he would start, virtually at the sentence he left off on the previous lecture. He gave his lecture, without a note, speaking in paragraphs of logical order, and then he walked out at the end of it. He was quite a speaker.'

He soon learnt that there was a clear difference between the way Oxford went about educating its students and the way the University of Western Australia had done it. At UWA the meat and potatoes of

---

* Alastair Buchan was also, for the anecdote, the son of John Buchan, who had written *The Thirty-Nine Steps,* one of Kim Snr's favourite books and authors.

education was lectures, with tutorials for dessert, whereas at Oxford this intellectual diet was reversed. The University was fiercely protective of its reputation for 'intellectual rigour' — the phrase of choice when Oxford chose to describe itself (which was often). It judged that the best way of inculcating that in their students was to have endless tutorials. Even then, they were not the type of tutorials that Kim had known at home, where there had been up to 15 students and one tutor. At Oxford the tutorials were one-on-one, with the student having to present to the tutor 2–3000 word papers weekly on subjects that were mapped out at the beginning of each semester. The system was extremely demanding, requiring that students be highly prepared with command of an enormous breadth of information and *detail*. After reading an essay to the professor for the first 45 minutes of the tutorial, the student would then have to defend the intellectual reasoning from the probing of the professor or tutor.

Such tutorials required, Kim recalls, 'intense concentration,' as he tried to provide learned insights on subjects such as the origins of the Cold War, the role that ideology played in the development of Soviet foreign policy, and the reasons why America maintained a continued strong military presence in South-East Asia. It was not a case, as it had occasionally been at UWA when he had had a busy week, of 'near enough is good enough'. Turning up without the required essay was not only not done, as far as Kim knew it had never *been* done. 'Also,' he recounts, 'because I was a graduate student, on top of that they also had a weekly seminar for all the Bachelor of Philosophy graduate students and generally speaking you presented what you might have been working on — your thesis as work in progress — or somebody would set a task, or volunteer a task'.

His letters back to Australia noted that 'the writing they want of me is 50 per cent more than they ask of me at UWA',[34] and showed that initially he found the going pretty tough. The subject matter of his Bachelor of Philosophy was extensive in scope. It included courses on the international relations of the Middle East and South-East Asia, a course on pure international relations theory, and two on the history of the last two centuries of international diplomacy. He had also tutoring positions at the nearby New College and University College. The tutorials ran the same requisite 90 minutes, but this time it was him doing the probing. 'I found it immensely demanding in terms of the reading I had to get through to be on top of the particular subjects that they were examining,' he remembers, 'but I managed'. Just.

Phillip Asquith, an Englishman in a room two doors away from Kim's, remembers him well: 'He was always coming over and borrowing my Elton John album, and he was a real ... what we call "swotter". It didn't matter what time you were crossing Balliol Quadrangle, you could look up to Kim's room, on the second floor on the left, and you'd see him through the window, sitting at his desk, hitting the books.' The need for Kim to 'hit the books', was particularly great in his first few months at Balliol as apart from all his Oxford work, he needed to finish the 120 000 word thesis he had begun in UWA on *Labor Party Attitudes to the American Alliance*. He was able to accomplish this, by snatching a few hours here and there between other commitments, and finished it just before Christmas, 1974.

While the pleasures of the mind were paramount in his time at Oxford, he also found time for more temporal pleasures. At Balliol he was soon to make firm friends with Ian Pollard and Peter Pierce, the NSW and Tasmanian winners of the Rhodes scholarship in the same year as him. Over the road at St John's College, Geoff Gallop was also still in residence in the second year of his own Rhodes scholarship. With lots of other young males besides in this exclusive bastion of learning, replete with at least its fair share of 'Hooray Henrys' as they would become known, there were the odd acts of youthful excess being committed. Kim participated, in his own way.

He was already a little distinct from other Balliol students, in that he was formally engaged to be married. He was sending, and receiving, two or three letters a week to Mary back in Perth, and as he worked he would often contemplate the big photo of her on his desk. 'All the blokes used to come in and look at her photo,' Kim remembers, 'since they themselves had never let women in their lives, and were interested that I had'. In Perth, Mary noticed a slight change in the tone of the letters she received from Kim. 'It wasn't anything you could put your finger on,' she says, 'probably just a sense that he was getting more and more into his life there, that he was getting progressively more heavily involved in so many things that gave him a lot of pleasure, and I suppose too, that through being in such an international environment he was becoming a bit more worldly'.

One of the things her fiancé was heavily involved in while at Balliol was sport. One of his Rhodes scholarship conditions was that he had to play rugby, so he turned out for the Balliol College Rugby XV, and also decided to go on with it and play for their First XI, as enthusiastically as ever. In rugby he remembers himself as 'tremendously keen', while in cricket, Peter Pierce remembers that 'he was Balliol's opening bowler in those days and was terminally erratic — he blamed some medical condition for the fact that he couldn't get a line at all, rather than blaming the English pitches, as he should have'.

It was mostly through those sporting institutions that he came to do a lot of his socialising. And here, as opposed to the way it had been at 1 Thomson Road, Claremont, there was no firm MRA rule preventing him from drinking on the premises. Far from it. 'I probably drank more at Oxford than I have ever done anywhere else,' he recounts. 'You would get into these drinking competitions in which you would drink half Guinness, half whisky. The most drunken occasion I was at, I remember this bloke was still left on the floor when I turned up there at 12 o'clock the next day and was out to it, still totally tanked to the eyeballs.' If he did his share of carousing, he still provided no competition to the legend of Bob Hawke, who had passed through those parts many years before, residing from 1952–55 at University College, and who had left a longstanding impression in the *Guinness Book of Records* — by drinking two-and-a-half pints (1.42 litres) of beer in 11 seconds. To celebrate, Hawke 'went down to the pub with the boys for a few drinks'.[35] Beazley never even contemplated trying to tickle the toes of his fellow Australian's feat, but he does acknowledge that 'we were all, as Rhodes scholars, very conscious of Bob Hawke's drinking record'.

His own nights of wretched excess in the embrace of alcohol came most particularly in the time leading up to Christmas. As part of the tradition one would stand with one's fellow students in front of the roaring ancient fireplace that had warmed over a hundred generations of Balliol boys, and sing Christmas carols with high gusto as you knocked the mulled wine back. Kim observed the tradition in full. In this company of his fellow people of the pass-the-wine-please, he sang with the best of them, knocked it back, and sang some more. Sometimes Kim would get his own guitar out, and lead the singalongs, being particularly notable for having mastered the extremely difficult chords for the Bob Dylan classic, *It's Alright, Ma, I'm only Bleeding*.

Outside these academic, sporting and carousing commitments, one of his great pleasures while in Britain was to go up to London to haunt the bookstores — both new and second-hand — to check the latest editions and also to track down books he had long heard about, but which had been unavailable in Perth. Often Phil Scanlan, a fellow Australian student at Oxford, would accompany him. The two had met early in the piece, introduced by another Australian, and had immediately hit it off. Their passion was to talk about American/Australian relations, world politics of the day, and sport. Kim Beazley impressed Scanlan from the beginning. While a good many of their fellow students gained knowledge for the purpose of 'passing of exams,' with Kim Jnr, it was actually wider than that. 'What stood out for me about Kim in those days,' he says, 'was this remarkable grasp of world security issues and how consuming his passion for it was. It was a matter of enormous personal interest to him, well beyond just what his academic masters might have required of him.'

It was also obvious to him, by the by, just how proud Kim Jnr was of his father back home in Australia. 'Kim had a great sense of delight that his father, after nearly three decades in Opposition, had become a Federal minister at long last,' Scanlan recalls. 'He had a great sense of vindication for his father, and for the Labor Party — and wanted to follow it as closely as he could from that distance.' On one particular occasion, probably early in 1974, Kim was walking through Piccadilly, with Scanlan, when the topic arose of Kim's plans for his future career. The man from Perth had paused for a moment, and then come out with it. 'My ultimate ambition in life,' he said, 'is to become Australia's Minister for Defence. I can think of no higher calling, no greater pleasure, than being involved in organising our nation's security ...' The way Scanlan remembers it, on hearing this he had demurred: 'But surely Kim, if you are going to go into politics you'd want to be Prime Minister?'

'No, Defence Minister would be what I'd want, if ever I could get there.'

Any hesitation about attaining such a goal had little to do with his capacity or incapacity to do the job. As he explained to Scanlan, it was never going to be easy for him given that he would be launching from the Western Australian branch of the Labor Party, which was as turbulent to be in as it was weak to launch from. To attain his goal, he knew, he would always have to fight a rearguard action, much the same as his father had done, against the forces from *within his own party* that would likely always be seeking to oust him. He also considered that far from getting an easy ride because his last name was 'Beazley,' it was more likely to be a bit of a handicap for him. 'But,' he continued to his friend, 'I'll probably give it a go. I am going to have to prove myself to get preselection and then my major aim is to just get in there and perform. If I do become Defence Minister it will be a quite singular achievement at some future time in my life.'

A London cab roared past. In Piccadilly, a London cab was always roaring past, and this was no exception.

Although Scanlan was a little surprised that Kim seemed unlike every other prospective politician he had ever come across — and at Oxford you couldn't spit out the window without hitting one — in not wanting to become Prime Minister, he remembers having little doubt that his friend had the abilities to fulfil his ambition. 'If somebody else had said they wanted to be Defence Minister, you might have thought it was their ego talking, but not with Kim,' he says. 'He was obviously enormously capable in the field of international relations and Australia's defence, and he was not one to bluster about all the great things he was going to do in the future. If he said he wanted to be Australia's Minister for Defence, then I thought there was a very real chance that that was exactly what he would go on to do. But it really wasn't ego with him. He was someone who really wanted to rise high in the Labor Party to try and ensure "there are no second-class citizens in our country". It was something of a lot of importance to him, almost evangelical. That's the other thing he used to say to me, that: "the highest station in life is to be your fellow citizens elected representative — he really believes that."'

The two walked on their way, with Scanlan musing that his friend seemed 'very, very sure of himself, in terms of knowing exactly what he wanted to achieve'.

Kim would also go on trips with Peter Pierce. They would venture up to Stratford-on-Avon where there was always one Shakespeare play or other to be seen or they would go out to dinner together in the town of Oxford proper; and on many Sunday afternoons they would go to the flicks in Walton Street. 'There would always be a double feature on,' Pierce describes, 'and sometimes it would be a skin flick. Kim would be disgusted at the things he was seeing, no doubt for the first time — even if not really in real life — and then we would always repair for a curry at Uddin's Manzil Tandoor Restaurant. This was his first experience of X-rated movies so he certainly needed the curry at the end of it.' It was, in short, a very full life that he led, and an immensely satisfying one for him. Perth seemed a long, long way away, and that was not necessarily a bad thing. Sometimes, despite their constant exchange of letters, Mary seemed very distant, and he would not actually miss her that much. Strange.

He would meet others, as he moved around this world which contained some of the best and brightest people in the Commonwealth. One night in Geoff Gallop's St John's College room, he met a young man named Tony Blair, a very long-haired, friendly sort of fellow, who impressed Beazley. 'He seemed quite intellectual,' he recalls. 'A nice sort of bloke who I warmed to immediately.' Blair was also a very Christian sort of bloke, something that would further cement the bond between the two, the more they got to know each other.

Although they remained essentially close acquaintances in their time at Oxford together rather than warm friends, that night was the beginning of a friendship that would progressively deepen with the passage of the years, as they would invariably make contact when visiting the other's country. 'It was just one of those things,' says Kim, 'where we got on very well at the beginning, and then because of the kind of parallel directions our lives took, the relationship had a lot of opportunity to grow'.

Whatever Kim's intentions about minimising his involvement in politics while at Oxford, for a young man still working out his own political ideas it was nevertheless an extremely interesting time to be in Britain. The winter of 1973–74 was one of England's harshest on record, the forerunner to the famous Winter of Discontent. The Tory Prime Minister, Ted Heath, had spent most of that winter in a fight with the coalminers over their conditions and had mishandled the situation so badly that the coalminers had simply downed tools and upped pickets — and they were in for the long haul. Britain shook, Britain shivered, and Britain went to short rations of coal, meaning that businesses, factories, schools, universities — everything — went on to a three-day week. At Balliol, as Kim remembers it, 'you certainly noticed that it was a pretty tired old time when nobody had the lights on in the shop windows and you would see this one globe strung from a wire lighting the whole shop, it must have been a shoplifters' heaven at the time ... The whole country was pretty miserable.'

On the night of 28 February 1974, the day of Britain's General Election, Kim finished working at the library in the early evening, and wandered back to Balliol College with every honest intent of making an early night of it. But in the end, he could not help himself. That night, he and Peter Pierce went down to the bar at the Oxford Union for a drink, and suddenly found themselves in a room which had obviously been set up for a Tory party to celebrate what they clearly presumed was going to be a very big win for their side of politics. Each table had an ice bucket with a bottle of champagne in it with a blue Tory rosette around its neck. They had set up red, white and blue bunting, and had pinned up the odd Tory poster on the walls, with the slogan: WHO RUNS THIS COUNTRY ANYWAY?

What the hell? The two Australians started playing pool and drinking, and in Kim's own words, 'were pretty wiped', by the time the Tory team came in from their hustings when the polling had closed. The two Rhodes scholars from Australia settled down with the rest of them in front of the television as the first poll results started to come in. And then they started to snigger. And then laughed — loudly — as it became obvious that far from getting a famous victory, the Conservatives were losing seat after seat.

'Pierce and I were hooning around and cheering wildly,' Beazley recalls, 'when every Tory seat went down and the British were too polite to complain, but there was a sort of cone of silence around us as every succeeding Tory started to hit the fence. It was a terrific night, because it was completely unexpected. We just stayed sitting there in the middle, sort of tearing away. Proud Australians absolutely.'

The former British Prime Minister Stanley Baldwin had once said that 'there are three groups that no British Prime Minister should provoke: the Vatican, the Treasury and the miners,' and now here was at least partial proof of that dictum. Within days, Ted Heath's Tories were ushered towards what would be five years of oblivion, and Harold Wilson had formed a minority Labour Government. In the political instincts still under construction inside Kim Beazley Jnr's head, the episode provided one durable stanchion for future use. 'It taught me,' he explains with some feeling, 'that the industrial relations issue is one you want to be very careful of, that it can cut any particular way. Hitherto I had always thought it would cut only one way. Badly for Labor. The lesson I think I learned from it, was that governments are expected to *govern*, and if they try to blame other people for their failure to deliver an outcome, and if there is a substantial constituency which believes that they are crying poor and that really they should have been able to do it, then they will be thrown out.'

Back in Australia the plans for the wedding continued apace. One afternoon, Geraldine and Mary Paltridge were in the Doogue household discussing some of the finer details of the forthcoming nuptials, scheduled for late June, when another of Geraldine's close friends from UWA, Susie Annus, dropped by and joined in the whole conversation. Geraldine was about to resign from her job at the *West Australian* to spend at least a year in London, and was planning to travel to Oxford with Mary at Easter. (Though she would be leaving behind her fellow journalist, Tim Blue, whom she had been dating since meeting him on the night of Whitlam's election in '72, she thought they would cope the same way Kim and Mary had — by writing a lot of letters.) Susie — who incidentally Kim Jnr regarded as 'one of the nicest-looking sheilas around University' — was tentatively planning to join up with Geraldine in Europe later in the year, but a spontaneous change of plans occurred. As Susie Annus remembers it, 'Gerry said well, why don't you come now to London with me and then we can travel after the wedding, and Mary was there as well and she said, "yes, come to the wedding!".' Mary arrived in Oxford just before Easter of 1974, with Geraldine Doogue and Susie Annus following on a few weeks later. It was wonderful to see Kim again, but none of them could help noticing one thing. He had changed. It was as if either he had suddenly blossomed into full maturity and the flower was of an unexpectedly colourful variety, or at the very least as if a great weight had been lifted from his shoulders. As Mary saw it: 'He was away from the constraining influences of his parents and the rest of the MRA stuff for the first time, and it changed him.'

'I just couldn't believe it,' remembers Geraldine Doogue, 'how it seemed as if he was an entirely different man. I found a different Kim, like I found the first carefree Kim I had met in my life. He was like a young man with a burden lifted off him, in my opinion the happiest I had ever seen him. He was much more expansive, much quicker to laugh, a bit more of a kid, he was just I suppose in effect, naughtier ... he was not just the serious young man. I think it was because he was not on show, he wasn't a "Beazley in training".'

Perhaps more to the point, he was not the same man who had committed himself to marrying Mary nine months previously. As such, the two had a lot of talking to do, not all of it easy. Soon after she arrived the couple packed up and went to the scenic New Forest in the central south of England, near Bournemouth, with Peter Pierce going along for the trip. On the way, Pierce recalls, the atmosphere between Kim and Mary seemed 'slightly strained' for a young couple planning to spend the rest of their lives together, and now so recently reunited. That night, over a couple of quiet beers with Kim, in a pub over the road from the hotel where they were all staying, he found out why. 'This is a mistake,' Kim said.

'What's a mistake?' Pierce replied.

'Me getting married to Mary.'

Oh. Pierce did not really like to get into it too much — it was extremely dangerous territory — but was willing to lend an ear if Kim really wanted to go on with it. He didn't. They drank their bock beer, and left it at that. Each went back to his room. Pierce noticed that the film on the television that night was *Camelot*.

It was a difficult beginning to what would be a difficult couple of months for Kim and Mary. At least the weather was good. After the punishment of the previous winter, England turned on a summer the likes of which the locals had forgotten was possible, and the Australians lost themselves in events such as the boat race between Oxford and Cambridge, and the horseracing at Ascot. Between times, Mary, Geraldine and Susie took a lot of day trips to various tourist destinations, while Kim fulfilled his ongoing academic commitments, and one other political commitment besides. He took one day's break from his studies on 23 May 1974, to travel down to London and hand out 'How to Vote Labor' cards on the steps of Australia House, after Gough Whitlam had called the second Federal Election in 18 months. Labor won again, losing only 0.3 per cent from their popular vote in 1972, and Kim, as he remembers, 'felt exhilarated that everything was going so well for us'.

Such distracting times aside, the underlying tension between Kim and Mary did not dissipate as the wedding got closer. Occasionally Geraldine Doogue's mother, Peggy — who had come with her husband on a long sojourn to Britain, which was to include attending the wedding — was called in for her wise counsel. As an experienced older woman who knew a thing or two about relationships, she did talk to Kim at some length. Her efforts notwithstanding, there remained some small possibility that the marriage would end before it had even formally begun.

Late one night, with the wedding just a little over a week away, Kim found himself once again ensconced in deep conversation with Peter Pierce, and again expressed to him his doubts about the forthcoming marriage. This time though, he let it all out. There was no way around it, he told Pierce, he simply was not *sure* that Mary was the right one for him. It wasn't that there was anyone else out there who attracted him more, for there was not, just a nagging feeling that he was doing the wrong thing. Pierce in turn, as a good friend, laid it right on the line for him. 'Kim,' he said firmly, in the memory of the prospective groom, 'it's *too late* now, sport. All the invitations have gone out, your parents are on their way, everyone has journeyed here from Australia. St Aloysius Church is booked, the reception is organised, you simply can't pull out.'

The time was right. With all this flip-flopping about, all the angst and worry, the roller-coaster ride of emotions, there was nothing for it but to call in the 'Moral Tutor'! Some two days later, Professor Buchan did indeed pause in his otherwise academic conversation with the young Australian and, obviously taking his role as spiritual guide seriously, brought up the subject. 'Now Kim,' he began in his stuttering way, 'I understand you are getting married next week?' Kim nodded that yes he was, and was not at all surprised that the great man knew. The esteemed academic had after all not only received an invitation, but had also RSVP'd that he would be attending. But Professor Buchan continued, choosing his words carefully. 'Now one has, as I recollect, a tendency to get cold feet before one gets married and certainly it happened with one of my children, who did definitely get a sense of cold feet. I just want you to know that if you at any time feel that you need assistance you can ring me ... '

'So, now, about your essay,' he continued.

The prospective groom never called him. And that was pretty much the end of it. The voice within, telling Kim that this was the wrong move was stilled — ultimately his sense of honour clearly forbade him to do anything other than go through with it. On the morning of 27 June 1974 he was there waiting at the altar of St Aloysius Church, Oxford. Around and about him as he stood there in his formal morning suit, were perhaps 100 of his and Mary's nearest and dearest, including Kim and Betty Beazley, Lady Paltridge, several friends from Balliol and UWA, among them of course Susie Annus and Geraldine Doogue — the last of whom was now leading Mary Elizabeth Paltridge down the aisle towards him. She looked stunning, serene, happy. He felt, in that moment, good.

In the absence of Sir Shane Paltridge, a family friend was giving Mary away, and that man gently guided her to the position beside him on the left, with Dr Hugh Nelson manning the post of Best Man on the right. Two 'I do's' and they were through. 'I now pronounce you, man and wife.' Of all the symbols that indicated just how much their union was the joining of two individuals from wildly opposite empires, there is perhaps none better than the disparate sources of the 150 telegrams they received on the occasion. Three stand out:

> *Congratulations And Best Wishes For Your Happiness* — Officers And Delegates, State Executive Australian Labor Party (WA)
> *We Both Send Our Warm Good Wishes* — Robert Menzies
> *Congratulations And Our Sincere Wishes For A Wonderful Future Stop Warmest Regards* — Sir Reginald And Lady Ansett

Different worlds indeed ...

There were sandwiches and drinks back in the Senior Fellows Common Room at Balliol — a kind of regal afternoon tea — and then that evening the nucleus of the wedding invitees retired back to the house that Mary had been staying at in Oxford with some Moral Rearmament friends of the Beazley family. Pierce was incredulous that there appeared to be not a single drop of alcohol in the whole joint, and he insisted that Geraldine search the kitchen for cooking sherry, but to no avail. Susie Annus's new shoes were killing her, and she ended up walking back down the main street of Oxford to her bed and breakfast, barefoot. Kim and Mary, meantime, had gone off to spend their first married night together in, as Kim remembers it, 'a ghastly pub near Heathrow Airport, a shocker, with pipes outside, not inside the walls in this tiny cramped little room. At least it didn't cost us anything — we were as poor as church mice — but the bloody pipes kept clanging away all night.'

When they returned from their fortnight-long honeymoon in Tunisia, the couple moved into a residence on Iffley Road, only 100 metres from the Oxford Rugby Oval — a happy circumstance for Kim, but not the reason they chose it. The flat was the second floor of a three-storey house, with rear access up a set of iron stairs to a small kitchen with a living room and bedroom coming off it. The kitchen had a small table in it — which Kim immediately seconded as his study table, and it was in this room that they spent the vast majority of their time while there together. Their landlady, a widow with silver tresses and a very proper middle-class attitude to everything, was a constant visitor, with equally constant queries as to whether they and her flat were quite ok, with neither one doing damage to the other. There would be a few problems with her, sometimes when Kim and Mary would make too much noise upon coming home late, but by and large it worked well.

One theory of marriage is that it is only upon living together in legal bond that a couple truly get to know each other, and certainly there was something of that in the way Mary got to know Kim. She had always known that he liked books and intellectual discussions of course, but it was only when living in Iffley Road together that she realised just how deeply it ran. 'I discovered he just had this huge intellectual life,' she says simply. 'He has an extraordinarily avaricious curiosity, he reads an extraordinary amount and absorbs it all. He has a prodigious memory, which is probably why I ended up losing mine because I figured I'd never need it. He has a very analytical mind and he delights in the life of the mind — a true intellectual except not in that sort of detached peculiar way that people often think about intellectuals.'

Kim continued his life of study, deeply immersing himself in the academic realm of the University, while Mary concentrated on setting up their home to her satisfaction as well as working in Oxford's most famous bookstore, Blackwell's. As well as Mary's income from that, they were also able to live on the money provided by Kim's Rhodes scholarship, which provided around 1500 pounds a year. With a fair portion of that money, the Beazleys — there was never any question that Mary would retain her name — entertained extensively, both the large informal network of Australians of their generation who were around and about Oxford and London at the time, and other academics and students that Kim would meet in the course of his studies.

Those who Mary was less keen about entertaining were people from Moral Rearmament. She simply could not abide it, and did not mind telling Kim so. Having lived for the six weeks before the marriage with a family steeped in MRA, she was more certain than ever that she did not want to live her own life like that, and made this known to her new husband. Mary explains it thus: 'We would often discuss the sort of people we met through it, and they weren't actually the people that we were naturally attracted to. I was allowed to express views and frustrations and criticisms that he found very difficult to express and I suspect that sometimes my reactions allowed him to distance himself from Moral Rearmament and tell himself it was really for me. I found the whole Moral Rearmament thing very cloying and proper generally, and in England I found it distressingly so.'

When the two of them were up in London they would often be invited to dine at the magnificent Moral Rearmament headquarters in the same 'Clive of India' house that had started Kim Snr on MRA all those years ago. As Mary describes it, each visit would push them further away from the movement. 'It was a knock-your-eyes-out kind of house,' Mary remembers, 'and when we went it was always full on, a silver-service type affair'. The conversation, invariably of the deadly earnest variety, tended to centre on how Moral Rearmament was faring in its quest to change the world, and their hosts would often regale them with such things as how they had recently visited the House of Commons to talk to such and such about the situation in Outer Mongolia, and so on. 'They were very good people,' Mary acknowledges, 'and very well-meaning, but we used to sit there and think well yes, of course this is all very fine, but what do you think this *does*, do you really think this has *some effect on the world situation*!?!?!' Other things too, would not gel with them. One night that they were dining there, they began to chat with the young woman who was waiting on them, when they realised that she was — like Kim had once been — a missionary, giving up a year or two of her life to serve tables on people like them. 'This woman was a linguist,' Mary emphasises, 'who spoke five languages and was preparing meals in the kitchen and waiting tables. I said to Kim afterwards, I think this just shouldn't be. This is ridiculous.' And his reply? '*Mumble, mumble,*' is the way she remembers it.

There was however, to be no radical re-conversion on the way *back* from Damascus, for the son of Kim Snr. 'Although Kim never talked about Moral Rearmament,' Mary says, 'he'd been brought up with it, he had given up a year of his life to work for it and he had a lot of time for the people. So he couldn't cut himself adrift easily.'

He was more or less understanding of her objections. While the basic tenets of MRA were certainly ingrained in the foundation stones of his conscience, on the surface it was no longer a part of his regular day-to-day existence.

Spasmodically throughout his adult years, Kim Beazley kept a diary, starting in 1975. Most of the entries from that year are happy and up-beat, but as shown by his entry on 27 June 1975, on his first wedding anniversary, he could have the odd down day too:

I should have been keeping this diary up. Some laziness inhibited me. Perhaps that is a reflection of these strange last two years, more particularly this last one. The first year of Mary's and my marriage has passed in a daze. I love her but it has been so confusing. I guess my absurd nervousness has made it difficult. I fear my work. I fear not matching an overwhelming ambition by achievement.

This overwhelming ambition, Kim thinks now, was 'probably a combination of academics and politics'.

He continued to work on the former, while the latter worked on him. Despite the resolution he had made at the beginning of his time at Oxford, politics was never far from his thoughts. And while he had followed British politics with one eye from up close, he had continued to follow Australian politics the best he could with both eyes from afar. One of his father's colleagues whom young Kim continued to be interested in hearing about, was Paul Keating. The Member for Blaxland had by then been in Parliament for nigh on seven years, and was edging closer to his first ministry posting. So, too, had Kim Snr continued to follow Keating's progress with some interest. 'Watch that man,' he said to the young journalist Paul Kelly in the Kings Hall of Parliament House, as Keating had walked by around this time, 'he is a political killer'.

If that observation stands as rather perceptive in terms of the subsequent career of Paul Keating, Kim Snr does not claim the same prescience when it comes to his own son. 'At that stage I didn't even think necessarily that Kim was interested in formally going into politics,' he recalls.

Actually though, Kim Jnr was now more than merely interested. After discussion with Mary — who, as he describes it, 'was into me running for Parliament whenever I wanted to' — he decided to stand for preselection for the Western Australian State seat of Melville. By necessity of course, his would have to be an 'absentee' candidacy, through the post and over the phone, but this was as good a chance as any to have a go. Melville fell substantially within the boundaries of the Federal seat of Fremantle, a patch he had worked for most of his life, and with that in mind he thought he had quite a reasonable chance of getting the nod. The answer though, was ... 'No'.

By that time he had slightly cooled to the idea of a life in State politics anyway, and was just as glad to continue his studies unimpeded. He was still only 26, after all, and there was clearly plenty of time to get involved in politics. He threw himself into his studies with renewed vigour, and for the most part continued to enjoy it. One of the most important things about it,' he says of these studies, 'is the confidence it gave you. The whole course really gave you confidence in handling global political issues; you had a pretty fair understanding of how the world *actually* worked. You gained confidence that the views you held were not views that had been formulated in isolation, but came after being exposed to as good a thinking as existed anywhere in the world. The point was you were talking to the blokes who wrote the books, people like Michael Howard and Alastair Buchan were consulted across both sides of the Atlantic. They were always arranging seminars, people were drifting through, like Henry Kissinger.'

One of the results of such study, Beazley says, 'was that I got a much clearer cut understanding of the priorities of the great powers of the world, the United States, China and Russia, the Middle East, and a much richer view of Australia's role in global politics'. That view would show that in reality, Australia, his country, 'didn't feature much'. 'Australia really was, and had been for a long time, off the map,' he explains, 'which gave me a sense of perspective about how vulnerable we were. In Australia we had always based our sense of security on assumptions which were patently false and had very much disappeared. It may have been valid during World War II, to think America or Britain would rush to our aid but it clearly wasn't any more. It became clear to me that our vulnerabilities lay not so much in threats to Australia but in our own attitudes. We needed to change in order to be able to handle the sort of world which we would ultimately face. So I tended to think of things then in defence terms, and how you would build-up the self-reliant military strategy for Australia. It was for that reason I wanted to do something that was close to Australia, so that was why I had chosen to do my thesis on the Indian Ocean — *Super Powers in the Indian Ocean* — I wanted to do something where I could bring Australia in.'

These twin strands of sustained interest in the Australian scene, and his growing confidence in international affairs, showed up in a letter he sent to his parents.

16 September 1975
Dear Mum and Dad,

Thank you for your letters. You have no idea how the possibility of your coming in January excites us. I guess much depends on whether the Opposition forces an election. Dad seems in the midst of many battles so we pray for his peace of mind. I am always glad to hear of activities in WA especially in Fremantle.

I am at last getting down to work again. I saw Prof. Buchan yesterday and he was most helpful. I need to do more work on Soviet policy before writing on the latter in the Indian Ocean. Buchan had just returned from a conference of Sea Power in Sweden and is giving me the papers. He was full of advice about jobs etc. He seems concerned politics is boring and was pressing me to put in for a UN Agency or the World Bank. He clearly doesn't know Australian politics!

...

I am at a little loss to know how to construct the next chapter. I rather feel Kissinger has made a mistake in his Egyptian/Israeli negotiations. He has cut off the principal moderate Arab states from the potentially more radical, eliminating much of the former's moderating influence. He has also exhausted much of Israel's ability to compromise, well before anything like a final settlement has been achieved. In addition the massive arms aid will lower the effectiveness of American pressure on Israel in the future. In [putting] American personnel between Israel and Egypt, he risks direct American involvement in a future war. Nevertheless he appears to have bought time. What an unbelievably dangerous world.

Mary and I bought an Austin 1100, 1972 ...

...I never did hear how Dad's speech in reply to Fraser went. Would love to know of colleagues' reactions. We thirst for information here tho' what we do get usually makes us curl up with misery. Mary sends her love as I do ...

Much love,

Kim.

As Kim Jnr read the situation from afar, things seemed to be extremely turbulent for the Whitlam government in general, but at least they were going well for his father as Education Minister. Kim Snr was in fact being widely acclaimed for having established the Isolated Children's Grant, the AusStudy system, and for making universities and technical colleges free.*

As the tone of Kim's letter home suggests, not all was going well for the Whitlam Government. One troubling issue was the famed Khemlani Loans Affair, a move by the Australian Government to borrow Middle East petro-dollars at low rates, organised through a Pakistani international commodities dealer by the name of Tirath

Khemlani. The deal never came off, but the knowledge of the attempt was enough to set the hounds a'baying, and the Whitlam Government was clearly making very heavy weather of it indeed.

Kim was troubled by a conversation he had had with his fellow Australian, Joe Santamaria — son of famed political activist B.A. Santamaria — who was then a student at nearby New College. The younger Santamaria had shown him a copy of a speech which the Australian Governor-General, Sir John Kerr, had recently made to the Commission of Jurists in India, in which, by Kim Beazley's interpretation, Kerr appeared to 'massively expand what seemed to be the area of action of the Governor-General'. This caused Beazley substantial unease, though just why at the time, he could not say. Was Kerr manoeuvring himself to do something extraordinary?

In the flat, the phone rang in the very early hours. Kim staggered out of bed and down the hall to pick it up. Mary stayed in bed, semi-listening through her disturbed veil of sleep to see if the call bore an emergency of some nature ... and was instantly awake. It was indeed an emergency, albeit a political one. It was Kim's father on the phone, and the tone of her husband's voice told the story. 'What? *What?* WHAT?' Gough Whitlam had been sacked by the Australian Governor-General, Sir John Kerr, in an effort to break the deadlock caused by the Coalition — led by Malcolm Fraser — blocking supply. Kim Beazley Snr himself was no longer the Education Minister. As Kim Jnr recalls it, 'I was appalled, absolutely appalled, but the discussion very quickly moved on to the coming battle. There was simply no question in my mind that home was where I had to be, to go and be Dad's campaign manager.'

On that day of high drama, all the Australians in England were calling each other, and one of Kim's calls was to Geraldine Doogue, who had stayed on in Britain and was by then living with Tim Blue in London and working as a freelance journalist. 'I must go home,' she

---

* For the record, Gough Whitlam would later claim what his government had accomplished with education in Australia as 'the most enduring single achievement of my government'.

In *The Light on the Hill*, Ross McMullin does not disagree: 'Besides the needs-based funding for schools, there was the abolition of fees for tertiary students, vastly increased expenditure on technical colleges, including the construction of residential accommodation for students, and special initiatives covering isolated children, Aborigines and the handicapped. In no other sphere did the government take such giant strides towards Whitlam's fundamental objective, equality of opportunity for all Australians.'[36]

remembers him saying. 'Anybody who wants to be anything in Labor politics has to go home to Australia.' And that, clearly, was him. Very shortly afterwards, and with Mary's blessing, the angry young Australian was in a plane headed for Perth. Before leaving though, he had to make a quick stop at Trafalgar Square where a gathering of angry Australians was meeting to voice their outrage at what had happened. 'It was a rally of Australian students and Labor Party people in London,' he relates, 'and I was invited to say a few words'.

The pigeons in Trafalgar Square fluttered as the loudspeakers boomed. 'Workers united will never be defeated!' he recalls as the theme running through his impassioned diatribe. 'This is a *coup d'etat*! This is Australian democracy under threat! This is a blatant seizure of power by the Australian establishment!' His outrage at Sir John Kerr's actions would not fade, even with the passage of years. 'I think it was a completely unjustifiable move by a chap who was more concerned about his own position than he was about the future of the nation,' he exclaims now, 'and I thought it was disgraceful. It rightfully was an albatross about the neck of the Fraser Government.'

If from the distance of London he was appalled with what was happening in Australia, he was even more disgusted when he landed in Perth. Instead of the widespread public outrage he had hoped for all over the country, there seemed only pockets of disgust, but nowhere near enough of them to keep the Government in power. 'I thought that Australian politics must have gone completely insane,' he says now of his paramount feelings. 'I was absolutely outraged. I was enormously fearful of the community's attitude: how could a community be like this? What is wrong with our civic morality that we'd cop this sort of nonsense? Why are we so weak intellectually that we can't cope with this drivel? Look, the Australian people would not defend their democracy. The Australian people would kowtow to a blatant act by a couple of establishment cranks, to knock over a decent Labor Government.'

For Labor Party apparatchiks assigned the task of bringing the Whitlam Government back into power, there were at least some small signs of hope. At rallies held in places such as St Johns Square, in Fremantle — at which Kim Beazley Snr spoke — a lot of people turned out, and some confidence grew among Labor Party people that perhaps the situation might be salvageable after all. Kim Beazley Jr had no such confidence. 'I was out there doorknocking, talking to people, and I thought we'd be completely smashed,' he says now.

'I was just on an angry high with the entire campaign, and full of fear, and with a more realistic appreciation of what was happening to my father than anyone else.' That is, with the possible exception of his father. Kim Beazley Snr had long held the theory, and he expressed it at the time, that the Australian public was disposed to 'accepting authoritarian outlooks, and when the Governor-General had dismissed us, I thought they would go along with that'.

Both men were right. The public as a whole did indeed go along with that, to the extent that come election day, five weeks after the sacking, they handed out a thrashing to the Whitlam Government the likes of which had been previously unimaginable. Of the 127 seats in the Federal Parliament House of Representatives, 91 of them were now held by Conservative forces. Labor was all but wiped out, beaten back to a bloody rump. Even Kim Beazley Snr was threatened, and just managed to hold on to Labor's jewel in the western crown which was the seat of Fremantle. In the wake of that bitter defeat, it was not quite that young Kim swore on the holy skull of Gough Whitlam's Prime Ministership that he would one day become Prime Minister himself — to teach those conservative bastards a lesson — but certainly the whole affair was a powerful tonic to his own politicisation.

22 December 1975
Ghastly flight back to Britain. Mary met me at the airport. We had lunch at [a pub] with Peter Pierce and his girlfriend. The time in Australia was disconcerting. It was as if I had never been to Oxford or got married. I was thrust straight into the old political arena, stayed in my old bedroom. It was deeply nerve-wracking. Got word early of likely heavy defeat, which made the whole effort seem pointless. In the end the ALP was devastated. By and large the party is the collection of [hacks] we were reduced to in 1966. Unlike that time we do not even have the benefit of a leader likely to rebuild. Whitlam's governing style and the loans question [confounded] his regenerative leadership powers.
Dad hung on by 2000 votes.

Back into the rhythm of the University town, one of his and Mary's principal pleasures was to go for trips up to London, where they would often stay in the single bedroom basement flat of the now engaged Tim Blue and Geraldine Doogue. Mary would go shopping or 'touristing' with Geraldine to various spots around London, while Kim did with Tim what he would later become famous for doing — drained his brain of everything he knew about life from his unique perspective. 'I think he thought that my life as a journalist with the ABC was quite glamorous,' Blue recounts, 'and he would continually ask me questions about what I was working on, the political situation in various parts of Europe. We'd also talk about a lot of other things of course, like sport, but typical of Kim he was also trying to learn as much as he could about as much as he could. He is essentially highly curious across a great breadth of areas.'

Blue in turn, would occasionally ask his mate for his own perspective on the political situation back home; why, for instance, did his father resign from Whitlam's Shadow Ministry in March?' The short answer was because Kim Snr had been horrified at the Iraqi Loans Affair, a scheme whereby the Labor Party endeavoured to borrow 500 000 dollars from the Ba'ath Socialist Party of Iraq to fund its 1975 election campaign. Like the Khemlani Loans Affair, the money never showed and it was splashed all over the newspapers. Kim Snr took a very dim view of it indeed, and after calling for Whitlam to resign, who refused, he then tendered his own resignation.

As 1976 rolled on and the deadline for Kim's thesis loomed, many such weekends would be spent with Geraldine, Mary and Tim taking shifts at a battered old typewriter, with Geraldine being the envy of the others because she could use all ten fingers, while Mary and Tim were more of the 'hunt-and-peck' variety. As journalists, Doogue and Blue did a little editing along the way, joking about how many times their friend used the phrases 'in the Indian Ocean area' and 'the Indian Ocean Strategic Zone'. On one occasion Kim was highly offended when Mary opined to him in private that his thesis was 'one of the most dreadful pieces of writing I've ever read', but he would get over it. Mary had, after all, been feeling a bit out of sorts, for the very good reason that she had fallen pregnant. 'It was a crazy thing to do because we had no money,' Mary recollects. 'He didn't have a job to come back to — but we just decided we would.'

On other trips to London, Kim went up on his own and stayed for as long as a week at a time with Geraldine's mother, Peggy — who had stayed on for a few months in London after the wedding on a working holiday. Mrs Doogue lived at St John's Wood and the reason he enjoyed staying there so much was not simply because her place overlooked the famous Lord's Cricket Ground and he could sometimes see the Test cricket being played only a couple of hundred metres away for free. More to the point, hers was a place where he could get through an enormous amount of work, while making frequent trips to the library of the International Institute of Strategic Studies down by the Thames.

Whatever time Mrs Doogue went to bed at night, Kim would be writing at her dining-room table, with a cup of black coffee beside him which he would lugubriously sip on from time to time, while often staring, thinking, out onto the darkened hulk of Lord's below. Whatever time she arose in the morning he would be there also — often giving her the impression that he had not been to bed at all. Sometimes, in fact, he had not. His was an energy sometimes powered by desperation. To get through the workload required, while also being a new husband, and having the attractions of Oxford all around, was not easy, and he sometimes fell behind. 'I would go out during the day to work myself,' Mrs Doogue describes, 'so he just had the place to himself, but he could get into a real state, and he genuinely thought if he didn't have a really good tutor who understood his situation he might have failed'. Despite his desperate schedule, Kim and Mrs Doogue still found some time to talk together. She had come to know him as one of her daughter Geraldine's university friends, and had always found him to be 'the one who took life very seriously'. But now she discovered another side to him. 'Until he came to visit like that,' she says, 'I didn't realise how warm and witty he could be. I used to very much enjoy the time we spent together. He became like a son to me.'

Back at Oxford, life had settled into a fairly steady pattern. Kim would rise early to study, head off to the library; Mary would go off to work at the bookstore, and in the evening they would meet up again, have a quick bite to eat together, and then Kim would work into the night. A major upset to this routine, and his equanimity, occurred just a couple of months before he was due to finish. He was at a seminar one day, when one of his other key guiding academics, Professor Sir Michael Howard, came in, cleared his throat and with precious little preamble told them he had something very unfortunate to announce. Professor Alastair Buchan had, that very morning, suffered a sudden heart attack. He was dead. Dead at the age of 57.

Kim sat rooted to his seat, scarcely able to believe it, and was beset by grief, most particularly for Professor Buchan's wife, Hope, who he considered one of humanity's pearls, and who he knew would be entirely shattered by the loss of her husband. The very last thing he wanted to do from that point on was to continue with the seminar, but as he remembers it, 'that was where I got introduced to the stiff upper lip of the British, and I remember Professor Howard saying "Well Alastair would think us a pretty poor lot if we didn't actually get on with it", and so that's what we did. It got me a bit off-side actually ...' For all Kim's upset at the time, after attending Buchan's funeral and saying his prayers, there really was nothing for it but to press on.

At last though, the great moment came. After almost three years solid research, preparation, and actual writing he was able to personally tap T ... h ... e ... E ... n ... d, at the conclusion of his manuscript. Hark the herald angels sing. Glory. Hallelujah. 'It was a blessed relief to get the damn thing out of the way and typed up,' he remembers of the time. 'It was getting to the last blinking page that really drove me insane, and finally I'd accomplished it.'

With the thesis now done and submitted, there remained an excruciating waiting period, during which time he successfully completed his final exams, but at last he got the call. Deep within the bowels of one of the ivory towers for which Oxford is justly famous, right in the heart of the campus proper, he was summoned into the venerable presence of eight dons of the University, who questioned him closely about what he had written, *why* he had written it, what he had discovered, and what evidence and arguments he could produce to prove this discovery. This was all part of the Oxford tradition, and it led to a climactic point. The dons were in their full regalia of academic dress for the occasion, with gowns and mortarboard, as was Kim himself — setting off rather impressively his white shirt and white bow tie. The dons began to question him particularly closely on his thesis, something he had not been expecting, and for a small while he was worried. As the Australian knew, if at the conclusion of that interview, the dons said to him 'Mr Beazley, would you deposit a copy of your thesis in the Bodleian Library?' it meant that he had passed. On the other hand, if he had not passed, they would simply thank him for coming, and that would be that. No names, no pack drill, but very much 'see you later'. It was simply 'the Oxford way' of doing things.

The interview had however proceeded well, and the dons had seemed to nod approvingly at his answers. Around and about him, Oxford University was going about its usual business, but inside that room, illuminated only by the kaleidoscopic light coming through the stained-glass windows, it all seemed a very self-contained world where this was the only thing happening. His life, in their hands. At last though, 'Mr Beazley,' Professor Sir Michael Howard's voice echoed in the cavernous room. 'Would you deposit a copy of your thesis in the Bodleian Library?' As a matter of fact he would, Sir, and after shaking all their hands profusely, he left, the very proud holder of a Bachelor of Philosophy, from no less than Oxford University.

'I was beside myself,' Beazley recollects. 'I was finally finished!'

If Beazley's memory of the preceding scene is still lucid, so too does Professor Sir Michael Howard remember him. He had observed the Australian's form over the previous three years; had been one of his tutors through part of his course, and his most significant tutor in the wake of Alastair Buchan's death. 'He was obviously going to be highly successful at whatever he was going to do,' the Professor recalls. 'He had a great deal of drive, energy and intelligence and — bearing in mind what a problem the field of politics is, I wouldn't ever guarantee that anybody was going to go far in that — but obviously he was going to be a success in whatever profession he cared to take up.' That said, however, the Professor admits to remembering 'very little about the actual thesis'. 'But he wasn't a scholar, let's put it that way. He did not [invent] new concepts. He gave an extremely able summary of the situation with very sensible judgements, but I wouldn't say he had a strikingly original mind. He was though, one of the abler members of the seminar which Buchan and I ran, and I would have numbered him among the top five out of the seminar of 20 or so.'

So where to now, for the Oxford scholar? He had felt intellectually rewarded by the process of getting his Bachelor of Philosophy, but what did one actually *do* with it?

'Kim Beazley? Professor Vatakiotis ... from London University,' the rather dapper middle-aged man introduced himself. Most British academics either wore a bow tie, or were a sartorial shambles, this bloke was of the former variety. The Australian had been expecting him. He searched for jobs 'all over the place,' and bearing in mind that he had lost a preselection for a State seat, he decided that maybe it was not time for him to go back home yet. His supervisors at Oxford had suggested to him that there might be a vacancy teaching politics at the School of Oriental Studies at London University for someone with his expertise in South-East Asian studies, and upon learning of his interest, Professor Vatakiotis had journeyed to Oxford to interview him. A long conversation had ensued about the requirements of the job, the subject matter of the course he would be teaching, and so forth, before the delicate subject of money was raised. 'We'd be happy to pay you 3000 pounds a year,' the Professor began.

'Three thousand pounds?' Beazley had replied. 'You can't live in London for that!'

'Nobody does,' the Professor had replied. 'What you do is, you set up outside London in a village, arrange all your teaching on one day and just come in one day a week.'

Beazley lost interest.

'That's no good,' he remembers replying. 'I want to be at London University for the intellectual experience, the intellectual interchange with the other academics, not sitting in some village somewhere.'

Had the Professor come back offering enough money for Kim, Mary and their expected new baby to live in London, they might have reconsidered, but that offer was not forthcoming, so that was that. It was time for the young couple to head home, home to Australia.

CHAPTER EIGHT

HOME

'Home is the place where, when you have to go there,
they have to take you in.'
Robert Frost

'A man travels the world over in search of what he needs
and returns home to find it.'
George Moore

The old town looked the same, as they stepped down from the
plane ...

They arrived back early in July 1976, and moved briefly
back into Kim's childhood home with the Beazley Seniors and David,
as Kim began looking around for work. Having arrived home 'on
spec' as he called it, neither of them had anything lined up in the way
of employment. With Mary already into the second trimester of her
pregnancy — highlighting their need for at least one serious income —
they spent an anxious few weeks going through both the 'Men and
Boys' and 'Women and Girls' employment sections in the *West
Australian*. For Kim, it all seemed kind of surreal to be back in his
childhood home, with the same furniture, same books, David down
the road on the railway bridge, his father away in Canberra, all of it
the same as it ever had been — but *he* was now twice the size, a full-
grown man, with a degree from Oxford, and with a *wife*, and ... he
needed to get a job. When he was a kid he could wake up from a
dream, in the familiar surroundings of his room, to find that it had
been just that — a dream — but this of course was reality. Not a bad
reality, just a difficult one to get through. The pressure was doubly on

him, because Mary was progressively keener for them to move out into their own apartment with every passing day.

At last though, after several nervous weeks, a breakthrough on the job front.

Professor Geoffrey Bolton, at the newly established Murdoch University — of which Kim Jnr had been on the Foundation Board five years previously — offered him a short-term stint till the end of the year as a tutor. 'Those sorts of positions halfway through the year are virtually non-existent,' Kim recalls, 'so I was very lucky and very grateful to him when he did that for me'. Getting this job was not dumb luck however. 'Of course I offered him a job,' says Professor Bolton. 'I knew of him from his days at UWA, where I had also been a professor, and he'd had a very high reputation. When he applied, I corresponded with both Oxford and Balliol and they gave me outstanding reports in return; said he was an excellent scholar, who'd achieved excellent results.' With the job, the young couple soon settled into some rented premises on Preston Point Road in Bicton, not too far from the University, and Kim began to tutor on much the same subjects as he had with the Oxford undergraduates, though there was a clear difference at Murdoch. The new University was in the vanguard of an 'alternative' approach to education, trying to break the traditional mould of the way other universities had imparted learning since the Middle Ages. Student intake was not determined purely by marks, but on the basis of essays written by the applicants as to why they wanted to go to Murdoch; and when they commenced, their performance was determined on a non-exam based assessment.

The environment at Murdoch could not have been more different from Oxford. If it all meant that Murdoch did not have quite the same culture of 'intellectual rigour' that Kim had enjoyed at Oxford — and did not necessarily fit with his own precepts of how higher education should be — he still found the job very satisfying, and was sorry when the academic year ended in December. He was the more sorry because it also meant he was out of a job. He was now once again unemployed, with Mary just over a month away from having their first baby — and next fortnight's rent soon due. They were not exactly penniless, and always would have had their families to fall back upon if it came to it, but it was at least bad enough that for a few weeks, Kim considered applying for unemployment benefits. 'I would have gone on the dole too,' he says flatly, 'I was going to have a family to support after all, but ...'

But Professor Bolton came through for him again, and had convinced the board of Murdoch to appoint this 'outstanding young man' Beazley to a further three-year stint as a tutor.

Before he took up his post though, when the academic year formally resumed, there was one other enormous event that overtook the young couple's life. Jessica Katherine Beazley was born on 8 January 1977. The birth was not easy. The experience was harrowing, fretful and exhausting. And that was just Kim. As Mary recalls, 'he found it hard, *very* hard to be with me when I was in a lot of pain'. For Mary the important thing was how good Kim was with Jessica when they all went home from the hospital a few days later. 'Some men,' she notes, 'are all angles and fear and discomfort when holding really tiny babies, but Kim was never like that. He was always comfortable and confident and never had any hassle with things like bathing and changing her, no matter how messy she got. He was always a very natural kind of father.' The godfather of Jessica was none other than Robert French, another indication of just how far the relationship between the two men had progressed since the days of the 1969 election, when Kim had spent an enormous amount of time handing out leaflets on behalf of his father, and against French.

Settling in to the brand new two-storey building of Murdoch University fully now, Kim found himself in a corridor with people who already were, or would become, lifelong friends. His old UWA and Oxford chum, now *Dr* Geoff Gallop was there, lecturing in Social and Political Theory, and Kim would soon become close to Professor Bolton himself, and to other academics, Stuart Macintyre and Robert Pascoe. The latter was an academic involved as a tutor in the same area as Kim — the School of Social Inquiry. In Pascoe's recollection, the new tutor made an immediate impression on the staff and students at Murdoch. 'Most academics have a fairly dry attitude to their subject,' he says, 'but what Kim would do whenever he got the chance would be to regale the students with stories about the Vietnam War or stories about the American Civil War and he was actually a kind of storyteller as much as an academic. The students used to love him because he was really good at bringing his subject to life.' The really clear difference between him and his fellow academics though, Pascoe says, 'was that it was obvious that he had wider horizons than us. Most of us were involved in the University activities, but Kim was sort of bigger than the University.' For his part, Beazley remembers those early days at Murdoch University with enormous affection. 'It was just sheer delight. I had a lot of responsibility put on me because Murdoch had a very liberal attitude towards its tutors and allowed them to organise and lecture in courses — which I did do. I had a number of articles published in journals. It was a very rewarding time.' His Oxford thesis was published under the title of *The Politics of Intrusion: The Superpowers in the Indian Ocean,* and the young couple also bought their first home, at Bull Creek, close to Murdoch.

So it was: new baby, new home, new job, new life, same passion — politics. 'However much I enjoyed being at Murdoch,' he says now, 'politics was still the thing that gripped me. And I think because I was engaged in "outside" politics, I didn't engage myself heavily in what might be termed academic politics. So I just did my research and my teaching and then left the campus to do other politics.' This 'other' politics, was of course the Western Australian Labor Party and soon after returning from Oxford he had again made his way onto the State Executive, and shortly thereafter had been appointed the State ALP Treasurer. It was from this position that he became a delegate to the National Conference, held in Perth in July of 1977, where he came to know, once again, the joy of being in the thick of the action.

The Labor Party at that time, federally, was still trying to come to terms with the thumping dismissal notice handed to them by the Australian electorate in the 1975 election, and was searching for a way back from the wilderness. As the conference began, Kim remembers feeling 'a great sense that it was good to be back into it, back involved with the party at that level'.

Among other people, the National Conference again brought him in contact with one Robert James Lee Hawke, who was still the leader of the Australian Council of Trade Unions movement — and very much beginning to rise in the polls of who the Australian people preferred as their Prime Minister. More importantly from the point of view of whatever ambitions Beazley might have had in the Labor Party, Hawke was also by now the President of the ALP. And a wild sort of one he was too. All reports of Bob Hawke from this time — including from Hawke himself, as well as his biographer Blanche d'Alpuget, who was to become his second wife — paint him in this latter part of the '70s as a particularly hard-drinking, womanising good ol' boy, a curious combination of the outlaw and sheriff, town drunk and mayor, blue-collar boyo and white-collar caliph of the Australian labour movement. He was, in short, pretty much as close to all things to all people as you could get — the source of his later tremendous political strength — and equally about as far from the *modus operandi* of living as it was possible to get from the sober-suited Kim Beazley. Yet the two hit it off handsomely anyway. Despite their obvious surface differences, they actually had many things in common.

Beazley was a born and bred Western Australian, and Hawke had spent a large part of his formative years there; both gained the first of their degrees at UWA and were Guild President before winning a Rhodes scholarship; both had grown up in strict religious families, with Hawke's mother considering that to even *knit* on a Sunday was a sin; both had enormous intellectual capacity; both loved cricket down to the last ball bowled; both were fascinated with security and defence issues, and of course, they were both born, raised, bred and steeped in the Australian Labor Party.

When Hawke was 16 and attending Perth Modern School, his uncle, Bert Hawke — who went on to be WA Premier — had briefly considered standing for the suddenly vacated seat of Fremantle on the death of John Curtin. His declining to do so had opened the way for Kim Snr to take the seat, and the man who would go on to be ACTU President had followed closely Kim Snr's career since then. Kim Jnr, for his part, had followed Hawke's progress over previous years and deeply admired his capacity to communicate ideas with complex intellectual underpinnings in the fashion of the common man.

Beazley is forthright about his impression of Hawke in those days of the mid-'70s.

'I was very impressed. I liked all of it: his populist image, his intellect, his knock-about element ... I thought this is a guy who really knows how to *do it*!' 'It' in this instance was to know how to advance the labour movement, and Hawke certainly did that. While his rise to the top was still seven years away, his was a star that was clearly in the ascendancy. Hawke was equally impressed with the younger man. In the first instance, he could not help but make comparisons between the Kims, Snr and Jnr.

'I just liked Kim from the first time I met him and I very consciously started comparing him with his father, and I was glad to see he had the strengths of his father, but also not the weaknesses. I had a great respect for Kim Beazley Snr, but I think he was one of the great tragedies of Australian politics, and if he hadn't got diverted from politics by the MRA he could have and *should* have got the leadership of the party. He was a better intellect and orator than Whitlam but he just got diverted.

'He was a man of extraordinary talent. I had an enormous admiration for his intellect and a great sense of sadness that he, as it were, "MRA-ed" himself out of it. So from the beginning I was well disposed to the Beazley name and of course when I first met Kim I could see that he had the attributes of his father, the intellect, but he was much more a political animal than his father.

'Kim knew that politics wasn't a Sunday school meeting organisation and it was tough and rough, and while he is not a tough and rough person, he knew that that was part of it and he became active in the factional side of things. He knew that if you were going to be in politics you had to be in power, as it were, within the party and that it is no good just saying "Look I believe in this", and then sitting under the Banyan tree and waiting for the world to come and understand the brilliance of your ideas. You have got to go out there and make it happen.

'Kim had that sense of *realpolitik* that his father basically was lacking. He is essentially a man who has got the cloud-lands and the grassroots. When I say the "cloud-lands", I mean up there he is thinking, he is a thinker, but he also knows that if you are going to be able to translate your ideas into action, you have got to be "down there" in touch with the grassroots and I just found him from the word go, a charming, good man — and I formed the view very early that he could go where his father hadn't been able to go'.*

To this point in Australian Labor Party politics there had been broad groupings, but little in the way of formal factions. There were those who were thought to be generally 'Left' and those generally 'Right' but those people weren't locked in on pain of political death if they deviated from the Left or Right position on any given issue. But in Western Australia during the early 1970s, this began to change, with the Left becoming better organised, principally through the efforts of people such as John Dawkins and Bob McMullan, holding regular meetings to determine their position and ensure that all Left members held the same rough line. The result of this increased level

---

* This view, about the effect that Moral Rearmament had had on Kim Beazley Snr's political career, was very much the prevailing one. The official history of the first 100 years of the Labor Party, *The Light on the Hill*, records the view thus: 'Beazley's temperament had prevented him from living up to his initial sparkling promise. Austere, opinionated, and highly moral, Beazley exuded profound intelligence, but had made himself unpopular in Caucus by displaying his intolerance of excess in drink, smoking, profanity, and bawdy anecdotes.'[37]

of organisation was predictable. The Left began to hold progressively greater sway on Labor Party decisions in Western Australia. Further, it meant that those to the Right of the State Party had no choice but to get themselves organised and form their own formal faction. A similar process was underway, effectively all around the country, as the strengthening of factional politics achieved unstoppable momentum. Everywhere within the Labor movement loose affiliations of like-thinking members were being forged into strong bonds of disciplined and concerted action, and a lot of it was happening right then and there at that 1977 ALP National Conference. It was one of Kim Snr's long-time associates, Senator John Wheeldon, who initiated Kim into becoming more deeply involved himself.

The Senator had been a minister in the Whitlam Government and to that point had always associated with the Left, but post-Chamberlain he had become disaffected with that side of Labor politics and wanted to shake things up a bit. Shortly after the Conference began, Senator Wheeldon approached Graham Richardson, the then State Secretary of the NSW branch, together with NSW Party President John Ducker. Wheeldon wanted Richardson and Ducker to come and meet with him, with Kim Beazley Jnr and another 'son-of' in Brian Burke, with a view to creating an informal faction of the Right in Western Australia.

Normally, with such a Right proposal coming from the comparative wastelands of the Far West, neither Ducker nor Richardson nor anyone else from their faction could have got there quickly enough. In Paul Keating's words, 'Western Australia was real bandit territory, so anybody from there who espoused reasonable views and was enlightened, was newsworthy to Labor in NSW. Kim of course wasn't in Parliament but he always had the political leanings we wanted to encourage.'

And this was where this meeting came in. It had always been Ducker's view, particularly, that their own faction could not proceed from the point of view of 'fortress NSW' and that the only way forward federally was to encourage like-minded factions to grow in the other states; but on this occasion he had a couple of queries. First, was Wheeldon *really* changing stripes from Left to Right, and second, why did young Burke want to lunch with him when he had just personally savaged Ducker on the Conference floor on a matter of Industrial Relations policy? The answer to the first, as Richardson recalls it, was that Wheeldon* was indeed jack of many of the Left's electorally knuckle-headed policies, and the answer to the second was that Ducker shouldn't worry about that savaging, because that was 'just young Burkie sucking up to the right people ... but he is ok'.

The meeting took place in the salubrious Mediterranean Restaurant in Subiaco. In the course of the lunch, Richardson remembers doing what he pretty much always did in such situations — appraising his partners for their potential political worth to the holy cause of the Right. He had heard of young Kim, of course — of all the 'son-ofs' getting around in Labor politics, he was one of the best known — but was interested to make his own assessment. 'My impression of Beazley when I first met him? I sat back and listened and thought "What's this fellow like?" You worked out in a minute and a half, the guy was brilliant.'

Ducker and Richardson left the lunch, both impressed and heartened. To get a serious Right faction up and running in Western Australia would be enormously helpful to the party generally, and their own faction specifically. From his side, Beazley too was impressed. 'I liked them personally, and also their ideas,' he says, 'but what it meant mostly for me was that instead of feeling like an unloved minority, I felt like a loved minority. To that point I had an intense sense of isolation. I'd begun, I suppose, to feel a bit, "well, perhaps the Beazleys always are in minority, perhaps we never *do* get on", but it was heartening to know that there were a lot of other people out there like Richardson and Ducker, who felt the same way that I did.' Beazley also felt it natural anyway that he should gravitate to the NSW Right, because the way he saw it, they 'had actually stood for the things which gave Whitlam control of the party, and those things were necessary for the Labor Party to be reformed and for it to advance into a modern era, with an appropriate ideology.

'I guess my political education was a product of all the threats to my father in the '50s and '60s and those threats always came from the Left — even though my father was really in many ways *of* the Left. So I identified the genuinely Left positions with electoral failure and the one force in the party that seemed to stand out against all that was the

---

* For the record, John Wheeldon says he was not actually formally abandoning the Left: 'I certainly wanted to get Kim up and running because I thought he was a good candidate,' he recalls, 'and for a long time we'd been of similar opinions on many things. I don't think I'd actually turned Right wing but by then I'd become very disenchanted with some of the things the Left wing were doing in WA.'

New South Wales Right, so I attached myself to them. It was as simple as that, and once you build up the contacts, they stay ... '

It might have been as 'simple as that' to Beazley, but others would take a slightly more cynical view of Beazley's sudden affinity with the politically close, but geographically distant, faction. 'Beazley has always known that the path to power required that he was with the biggest faction, which was the New South Wales Labor Right, that is the Keating faction,' says one of his close associates of the time, 'and so he has always paid more attention to observing New South Wales politics than he has to Western Australian politics. He always said to me privately, the power of the party depends on the power of the party in New South Wales, that's where it all derives from ... '

Beazley's friend, Brian Burke, for his part, was equally devoted to the basic precepts of the Right, but in Kim's mind, at that stage, did not want to curb his field of action or appeal by labelling himself one thing or another. 'Brian always thought I was terribly limited,' Beazley remembers, 'and that I was unwise to associate so intensively with the Right. He thought what you needed to do in the Western Australian branch was to build coalitions. Brian was always building extraordinary coalitions, Left–Right coalitions, basically, and they always worked because they were attached to him as a person.' That, at least for the time, was not the Beazley way, and he was happy to help to nurture a faction of the Right in the West, although formally, it meant nothing in the way of regular meetings. Informally, though, he says 'it meant that we pushed to get our sort of delegates elected to Federal conferences and kept in touch with each other meantime'.

Beazley's own ambitions at this time were clear. 'I wanted to go into Federal politics,' he says simply. 'And if I succeeded in that, then what I wanted to be was Defence Minister.' The word around the traps was that the Prime Minister, Malcolm Fraser, would go to the polls somewhere near the end of 1977, or early '78. By September 1977, Kim's old sparring partner, John Dawkins, had already announced that he would stand for preselection for the seat of Swan. To that point, Dawkins had in fact done far better than Beazley in the political stakes, having been elected for the suburban Perth seat of Tangney in the second of Gough Whitlam's election victories in 1974, only to be swept away in the massive anti-Labor landslide of the following year.

One day Beazley went to see Dawkins at the Trades Hall building in Fremantle. In a twisted conversation, the way Dawkins remembers it, Beazley seemed to be ascertaining just what level of attachment he,

Dawkins, had to Swan. 'He had this conversation with me which I didn't understand until later,' Dawkins recollects, 'because he was talking about how keen was I to run for Swan and what of the other options, blah, blah, blah, blah, blah. It was quite a funny conversation, the context of which I didn't understand because everyone thought that his father was going on again.'

A few weeks later though it suddenly clicked — for Dawkins at least — when the almost 60-year-old Kim Beazley Snr suddenly announced that he was standing down from Fremantle after a 32-year tenure in the post ... and Kim Jnr nominated for the position on the first day nominations were accepted, 17 October 1977. Kim Jnr's decision to run in his father's seat was met with a gasp of complete non-surprise by everyone who knew him. At every stage of his career to that point, he had always been judged 'boy most likely to go into politics', whatever protestations he might have made at the time. 'Of *course* he was going to run for preselection,' says Geraldine Doogue dismissively, 'none of us doubted it for a second'. John Dawkins himself took an exceedingly dim view of the news, but bided his time for the moment. The amount of help that Kim Snr could offer his son in the quest to take over the Fremantle franchise of 'the family business', however, was limited. As the former Minister for Education recalls, 'By then it was a State Executive selection, and I then had no further connection with the State Executive. I don't think I went around saying "my son ought to be the member for Fremantle". I think there would have been a lot of people in the Labor Party who would have been highly resistant to the idea that seats are hereditary.'

There certainly were. Of all the things that the Australian Labor Party stood for, nepotism was not one of them. While in a country like the USA merely having the last name of 'Kennedy' put you halfway home to being elected, for many it was a point of pride that in Australian Labor Party circles it was more or less the reverse that applied. In their culture, progeny taking the privileged positions of their parents is something they like to hate the Tories for, but it is most definitely *not* the thing that the Labor Party does. At least not often. Shortly thereafter, John Dawkins was approached by his and Kim's long-time Labor Party colleague from university days, Bob McMullan, who, at the age of 26, had now taken over from the 74-year-old Joe Chamberlain as Secretary of the Western Australian Labor Party. Both McMullan and Dawkins at that time were very much of the Left. 'So McMullan came to me,' Dawkins explains, 'and said, "Listen we have got to stop Beazley getting the seat — we are not having nepotism around here — you have to run for Fremantle".' It should not have needed a lot to persuade Dawkins. Fremantle, for any prospective Labor parliamentarian, was the one seat in Western Australia that was just about guaranteed to be held for Labor come hell or high water. But ... Dawkins remembers saying to McMullan 'I don't particularly want to run for Fremantle, I am quite happy with Swan, but they said "no, no, no you have got to run for Fremantle..." In the end I said, "I will run on two conditions. One that you guarantee me that you have got the numbers, because I've already got the numbers for Swan, I haven't done the numbers for this one. Two, you have got to agree with me on who is going to replace me in Swan".'

McMullan, after some negotiation with other Labor heavyweights, agreed. With that settled, Dawkins arranged to meet Beazley at a café in Fremantle, to tell him his intentions as a courtesy. After a couple of cappuccinos Dawkins got to the point. 'Kim,' he said, 'I just wanted to tell you that I am going to withdraw my nomination for Swan, and am going to run for Fremantle instead.' Kim Jnr, as Dawkins remembers it, was more than merely nonplussed with the news that he would be having such stiff competition to gain preselection for his father's seat of the last 32 years, but his emotions heightened still when Dawkins made his next remarks to him. John wanted Kim to know that he reckoned that he and his father had been in cahoots on the whole timing of Kim Snr's resignation, and that was why they'd had that convoluted conversation of several weeks before where, it seemed to him, Kim had been testing the waters as to what Dawkins might do if Fremantle suddenly became available. 'I said to him,' Dawkins remembers, "well of course, you knew all this was happening and you just wanted me shoved out into Swan before all this happened!"'

It was one of the few times Dawkins can remember, that he ever saw Kim Beazley angry. Instantly angry, genuinely angry, like he really meant it. And he really *did* mean it. For instantly Beazley rose from the table, nearly turning over his chair in the process, and was suddenly towering above the diminutive and still seated Dawkins. 'If you put that about,' he exploded, in words that Dawkins remembers to this day, 'I'll go through you like shit through a goose!' With which, he left the café. 'He was clearly, very, very upset,' Dawkins says. 'He was very angry that I would say that this whole thing had been orchestrated by him and his father. Notwithstanding that, I am quite sure from this earlier conversation that he did know ...' Absolutely true says Beazley. He did know. But so did everyone. 'Everyone knew my father was going to retire,' he says. 'It was all very open. It wasn't like some amazing thing he pulled at the last moment. It was known that the '75 election was his last, and I had always operated on that assumption, as I think everybody did. I *was* pretty annoyed about that, because my father wasn't like that. And if we were going to do a trick, the way you would do the trick would have him put his nomination in, then wait until about two minutes before nominations close and have him withdraw his nomination and put my nomination in. If you wanted to run fast tricks that is what you would do. We didn't do anything of the kind.'

The upshot of Dawkins standing for Fremantle though, was that for Beazley the Younger it had all suddenly become very difficult ... and even then there were complications to the complications. A third man, Bill McKenzie, had partial backing from the Right and had also decided to nominate for the plum seat, making the competition even tighter.

The Western Australian Labor Party that year had introduced a new system of preselection whereby a Selection Committee appointed by the State Executive would join six 'local' delegates in each electorate to make recommendations to the Executive as to who the candidate should be. Beazley was not without his own platform to launch on the preselectors of Fremantle — being then the Secretary of the Fremantle Electorate Council, thus nominally the number two office-holder in the electorate, behind the President — but he always knew it was going to be tough. While Joe Chamberlain's departure as Secretary meant that the Left's hold over the Western Australian Labor Party had weakened somewhat, there was still no doubt they were far and away the most powerful faction, and Dawkins was very much a part of them. Beazley was not. Not even close. 'I felt probably pretty excluded by them actually,' Beazley remembers, a little morosely. 'I mean, at least I was flattered to this extent that the Left did not think that they could beat me with anyone less than John Dawkins — you could tell he was a good candidate. I was sad about it ... '

At last the great day came. In the case of Fremantle, the preselection committee met, argued, and selected ... John Dawkins. And that would have been that, bar one thing. The State Executive had been so appalled by the result in Swan under this new system, whereby Joe Berinson, who had been the highly regarded member for Perth from 1969–1975, was beaten by Dawkins' preferred candidate, Pat Fox, that they decided to ignore all the Selection Committee's recommendations, and do the preselection again themselves. Fremantle was thus in the balance again for the next fortnight, and this time they chose ... Dawkins again. It was over. The decision, when it came, hit the Beazley family with tremendous force.

In London shortly afterwards, Geraldine Doogue was awoken in her flat by a phone call. It was Mary. 'She was shattered,' Doogue relates. 'I was stunned at how shattered she was. I have never come across Mary as upset, except for the death of her father. She felt betrayed. Mary decided she never again would be as hurt, and she felt that you could never trust anybody in politics. It was a seminal event for her. She was saying, "people come up to you in the supermarket and are terribly pleasant and say 'hello' and then they will vote against you behind your back!" and she never forgot it. She had learned one of the bitter lessons in politics about the numbers and how you can never seriously count on them ... '

Kim's own surface disappointment was perhaps less. Stephen Smith, who was then, self-described, 'just a baggy-trousered electorate council delegate', had been on the State Executive which conducted the concluding preselection and had in fact voted for Beazley, remembers talking to the defeated candidate immediately after the Dawkins' win was announced. 'Kim was disappointed,' Smith remembers, 'but my impression was that you wouldn't have regarded his disappointment as being crushing.' Mary agrees. 'Kim was much more sanguine about it than I was, and I think you could say much more strategic — his attitude was that it was a setback now, but there was bound to be an advance later. He kept explaining to me how things worked, how it was indicative of how we would always have to struggle in the WALP. I don't want to minimise his disappointment, because it did get to him, but he was just not nearly as emotional as me ... '

Beazley simply got on with it regardless. Come 8 am on 10 December 1977, he was there on the steps of the Fremantle Town Hall, as a humble poll worker, handing out 'How to Vote 1 John Dawkins' tickets, when he had wanted to be *the man* with his face on the posters. Dawkins got up, Labor got thumped, Beazley went home. (Dawkins' win notwithstanding, an indication of how bad things were for Labor in Western Australia at that time was that they only secured 32 per cent of the vote, state-wide. Things were crook in Tallarook, and not much better nationally. For Gough Whitlam it was the end. He retired and was replaced in the leadership of the ALP by Bill Hayden.)

At least, in the wake of his disappointment at not getting Fremantle, Kim Beazley was able to draw some satisfaction from how well things were going for him at Murdoch University. 'There is no question,' says Professor Bolton, the man who had hired him and who would shortly make him a Senior Tutor and then Lecturer, 'that he was very much on track to becoming an extremely young professor. Everybody had the highest regard for him, for both his scholarship and for his ability to communicate what he knew to his students. He would have measured up without a doubt.' Clem Macintyre, who studied under Beazley for three years, is one who agrees that he had the goods as an academic. 'He was very relaxed in his lecturing manner,' he recalls. 'It was like he knew what he wanted to say to us, had plenty of time to say it, so there was no rush. His lectures would be entertaining and informative, not rambles ... but they'd take you through the field and they'd be gentle in their pace. You could sit back, enjoy it, get something from it. There'd be an anecdote or something in there.' This relaxed style did not extend to the way in which he gave his marks. Macintyre, who went on to be a distinguished academic himself, also remembers Kim Beazley as the last academic ever to give him a 'B' for an essay. 'We were at a reception,' Macintyre says, 'and he came up and said "I've given you a 'B'"', and I looked at him and said "You bastard!" But at the same time, he was saying "the work's good, it's solid but it's not exceptional", and I certainly didn't bear any grudge. I think he was very fair but he was certainly honest and demanding.'

The experience of Macintyre at the hands of the Oxford man was, by all accounts, not an isolated one. His old friend Tim Blue was also to get a close-up view of his old mate's style as an academic. Keen to continue to expand his qualifications, he had taken some leave from the ABC and enrolled as a mature-age student at Murdoch, and had undertaken his close friend's course. And was, for the most part, impressed. 'He was a good lecturer,' Blue recalls, 'inclusive, provocative, testing and no slouch. He was clearly not there just to collect the dough — he was there to ensure that his students had undertaken required reading and there couldn't be any bludging. You could see, too, the whole tradition of "Oxford rigour" coming out. I remember him roasting someone for five minutes in a tutorial on the exact difference between a neutral country and a non-aligned country.' Under Beazley the academic, as Blue remembers it, the message to his students was that the approach of 'she'll be right, mate,' simply wouldn't do. It had to be 'Get it Right, mate'. There was one problem with the Beazley approach, as far as Blue was concerned. When he received his results at the end of his first year under Kim's tutelage, he too was interested to note that he'd received solid 'A's and just one 'B'. That 'B' was in International Relations, the very course taught by his good mate Kim Beazley, the one who he was almost family to, the very same bloke who had conceived his precious first daughter in his own London basement, that was the one. 'Mate,' he challenged him shortly afterwards, 'what have you done to me? I did great stuff and you only gave me a "B"!' 'I'm sorry Tim,' Blue recalls him replying, 'but for an "A", you've got to show outstanding original insight and yours didn't have that, so I gave you a "B".'

Whatever the demands of his academic life, Kim had continued to be heavily involved politically. Heartened by his meeting with Richardson and Ducker the previous year, he had been a reasonably frequent visitor to the East, the more so because one of the early fruits of that lunch had been that the NSW Right had supported him to get on the National Executive of the Foreign Affairs and Defence Committee in 1978 — the body within the Labor Party responsible for generating policy on such issues. It was during one of these visits, in early 1979, that Stephen Loosley, himself a rising warrior of the NSW Right, met Beazley for the first time. As was the way of things then, Loosley gently tested Beazley out a little to see just how strong his commitment to the Right side of politics was. One didn't simply come straight out and ask it of course, in the manner of 'are you for the Right or the Left?!?,' but there was always a very quick shorthand method to determine the exact shades of a Labor person's political complexion. At that time it was to ask about British politics, and the whys and wherefores of the incumbent Labour Government. With some spectacular fireworks along the way, it was convulsing internally over some of the notions of the hard Left — led by Tony Benn — and was clearly well on its way to massive electoral defeat because of it. Among other things, Benn was advocating the 'nationalisation of the commanding heights of the economy' and if in Australia you expressed even the slightest support of this, then you were clearly of the Left yourself while, if you took the view, as such people as Neville Wran did, that such notions were electoral suicide and the first duty of the Labor Party was to stay in office, then you were of the Right.

To Loosley's satisfaction, Beazley came back with all the right answers, and was suitably appalled by the state of British Labour politics. Kim Jnr was of the Right alright. But was he in the correct geographical position to help that nascent faction? In his bleaker moments, the Western Australian told Loosley, he thought that he just wasn't going to be able to crack it in WA, that the numbers were simply too strongly stacked against him no matter what their fledgling Right faction did, that he would be better to pack up and start again, perhaps from NSW.

It was with that in mind, that he enquired of Loosley whether there was any chance that he could secure the vacant position of Assistant Secretary to the ALP in NSW, which had become vacant upon Leo McLeay's departure for Canberra? Not actually, Kim, no. Loosley, for one, didn't think that was a very good idea at all, because he had his eyes on that very position himself ... and would shortly get it. Graham Richardson has a similar memory of Beazley testing the waters in the eastern states. 'There was a time when he did want a seat here,' he recalls, 'because he was concerned that the West Australians would basically never give him one, but that concern didn't last long ...' One of the reasons it did not last long is because bit by bit, it became apparent that the Right of the Western Australian Labor Party, having at last got themselves organised — and being helped by an economic environment in the state far more disposed to the Right viewpoint generally — actually started to gain in strength.

Nothing was guaranteed of course, in politics practically nothing ever is, but as the last half of 1979 rolled on and the first rays of the next election started to appear on the far horizon, Beazley began to think it more likely that he might prevail in preselection this time. But which seat? Fremantle was out. John Dawkins had won it easily, was performing well and had no intention of stepping down from it, and it would be sheer insanity to take him on in what was now his own fiefdom. The seat of Swan, on the other hand, was a lot more feasible. It was held with a margin of less than 1 per cent by John Martyr, a man who had had an amazingly chequered political past, at various times representing both the ALP and DLP before finding his way to the Liberals. It would only take the very smallest of swings to Labor to secure it for whoever could gain the ALP's preselection. The seat had, nevertheless, two downsides. It was notoriously volatile, seesawing between Labor and Liberal 11 times since World War II, suggesting that it would probably he hard to hold thereafter; but Kim felt he could deal with that if and when he got to it. Secondly though, it was known that Peter Cook, the very well-connected Secretary of the Trades and Labor Council, was also very interested in running for it. Again, Kim felt that he would deal with that when it came to it, and put his nomination in regardless ...

Not for the last time in his political career, the prospective candidate was helped enormously in what happened next by Bob Hawke, although this time the aid came only indirectly. After a long run-up that would have done Dennis Lillee proud, Hawke had at last signalled his intention to run for Parliament. He would stand for the seat of Wills, in the industrial heartland of Melbourne, and thus resigned as President of the ACTU. It left a vacancy in the position and Peter Cook was the man earmarked to fill it. With that in mind, Cook pulled out of running for preselection for Swan, and that was that. As it turned out though, Cook did not get the ACTU position after all. But by the time he realised that it was too late, with nominations for Swan having already closed.

This time Kim Beazley would have the support of one of the men who had opposed him last time, in Bob McMullan — still the State Secretary — on the simple grounds, as McMullan recollects, that 'Kim was clearly the best candidate, and the party needed people like him'. Still, Kim left nothing to chance. One of the things that he was notable for at Murdoch was his capacity to do several things at once, and this included being able to mark exams while working the phone on a desk submerged in a deep blanket of paper. As it happened, he did an awful lot of 'working the phone' at this time as he tried to tie up any wavering preselectors for the vote to determine his political future. His colleagues could always hear him as they passed his office — 'Sure, sure, Steve, but this is really *important*, and what we've got to do is ...' — and would often look in, to their amusement. 'He was on the phone all day long,' recalls his fellow academic, Rob Pascoe, 'just constantly, and you'd hear Kim talking to so-and-so about this and so-and-so about that, but always about politics.' The other thing Pascoe noticed, was that on those rare occasions that his colleague put the phone down, he would often place it in such a way that there would be an added twist in the telephone wire. 'In the end,' describes Pascoe, 'it got to the point where his face was about two inches from the telephone. The phone cord had become just this mass of wire, because he'd been on it for months, and of course he was terrified that the essays were going to take over his life because he had to win the seat. So what he would do: he would be on the phone talking to all the number-crunchers in the ALP with his left hand closer and closer to the phone, and with his right hand he'd be marking essays furiously and it'd be like that every day.'

So passed the days of his lives at Murdoch Uni, as the time for the preselection vote drew nearer ...

Often, very late at night, Kim would find himself driving around Subiaco, not too far from where they were living, thinking about the campaign ahead. In the back of the car was Hannah, Kim's and Mary's second daughter, born on 8 July 1979. It was often Kim who was assigned to take the squalling Hannah in the car so that Mary and the two-year-old Jessica could sleep. Gliding softly through the darkened streets, with Hannah's eyes and mouth now mercifully closed, he would use the time to think of the upcoming preselection vote. It looked as if his assiduous working of the patch over the last three years was now paying dividends. No longer was he nude factionally; he had the backing of what could loosely be called, for something like the first time, the Western Australian Right.

On the day, in late November of 1979, Beazley romped home to win the preselection by a handsome margin. The question remained. Could he have beaten Peter Cook for preselection had they gone up against each other, head to head? 'No I don't think so,' says Beazley now frankly. 'Because Peter would have got a unified vote from the Left, he was a very effective and prominent trade union leader, and he was from the area, which I wasn't. I think he would have been unbeatable.' Peter Cook is of the same view. 'I don't think there's any doubt about it,' he says. 'I would have beaten him.' Score one up to political providence for Kim Beazley Jnr, then. (That particular scoreboard would tick over fairly regularly over at least the next 18 years on Beazley's account, as he would prove to be generally extremely lucky in his timing.)

In the midst of fighting his own battle to get preselected for Swan, Kim Jnr had remained heavily involved in the activities of the WALP State Executive, and in such capacity was also on the preselection committee for the seat of Kalgoorlie, way to the east. The two serious candidates presenting themselves for the nod were Graeme Campbell and Brian Conway. Beazley was organising the numbers for Conway, while Stephen Smith was one of those organising for Campbell. On the night of the ballot, Beazley wandered up to a group that included Smith and predicted: 'Well, Conway has got that in the bag.'

'No,' Smith rejoined, 'it'll be Campbell who'll get there by one vote.'

When the counting was completed, Campbell had indeed won by one vote on a countback, leading Beazley to jocularly say to Smith afterwards that the results must have been 'cooked' for him to so accurately foretell the result. The postscript to the story is that years afterwards, Beazley admitted to Smith that the result would have been entirely different, if he, Beazley, had actually voted for the man he was nominally organising the numbers for. According to Smith, 'Kim confessed to me that whilst he was supporting Conway, he actually thought that Campbell had a better chance of winning the seat, and so in the end he thought that as Conway was going to win comfortably anyway, he voted for Campbell!' So began one of the stormiest parliamentary careers in recent times for Graeme Campbell, and a singularly successful entrepreneurial career in the world of resources for Brian Conway.

If the warm inner glow from having won preselection himself for Swan would not fade a jot, it was time to get busy in actually *winning* the seat for the Labor Party. Swan then was certainly not the 'jewel in the crown' that Fremantle was to the Labor Party, but it had potential. Its great long diamond shape had one pointy end in the metropolis of Perth and the other running out to the bush. On one side it had 'workers' residential suburbs, while the other side encompassed more up-market riverside suburbs with a large group of Perth's wealthier retirees. In sum, the flavour of the electorate was marginally more blue rinse than blue collar, and it was never going to require anything less than a good effort to win it.

The election campaign ran for five weeks, but well before that began, Kim Jnr pounded the pavements in the classic fashion, following the well-worn tracks of many generations of previous politicians in the electorate. That is, he went doorknocking. The aim was essentially to move from door-to-door down a street, making contact with the people inside and trying to winkle a vote out of as many as possible. If it became clear that you already had their vote, the game was to move on as quickly and politely as possible, so as to get to the next mark. Ditto if it was clear that it would be a cold day in hell before they would ever vote for you — no point in wasting time over it. Kim, as Mary remembers it, was hopeless with both kinds of voters, and all others in between them on the spectrum. 'He couldn't get through enough to make it worthwhile,' she says. 'Kim *liked* doorknocking. Kim loves people, he always likes meeting people and chatting to them. To me, every time I got to a letterbox I was steeling myself to go and knock on the door, whereas Kim would always be thinking "oh, I wonder who lives here?"' Either way Mary could get through as many as 20 houses in an hour, while Kim would be flat out doing four. At those places where he knocked and no-one was home, he would slip his electoral card under the door. On one side was printed a photo of himself, beneath which were listed what he saw as his major selling points to the electorate:

* *Married, two children.*
* *W.A's Rhodes Scholar in 1973.*
* *Lecturer, Writer and Commentator on Foreign Affairs and Defence Issues.*
* *Convenor, A.L.P. Industrial Development Committee.*
* *Lives in Swan.*
* *Former Member Senate, University of WA and Planning Board, Murdoch University.*
* *Actively involved in Community Life.*

On the back he would put, in a handwritten note:

Sorry we missed you. Please contact me if I can assist you,
Kim C. Beazley.

One of the family for whom there was never any question of doing such a thing as doorknocking was Lady Paltridge. She would babysit for them while they did it, certainly, and cook many, many meals, but she would *not* doorknock. Her Liberal traditions simply would not allow it. Not to worry. As mothers-in-laws went, she could have been a lot, lot worse. 'I'm pretty sure I got her vote,' Beazley says now.

And his own parents? For the most part, his father kept a low profile even after the campaign proper had begun, although he would occasionally speak about the virtues of his son at coffee mornings and branch meetings. His mother proved to be a trojan. She hosted no fewer than six lunches at home in the family living room — ten dollars a ticket was the entrance fee — with a guest speaker at each one, the last of which was Kim Jnr himself. Many of Kim's and Mary's friends also pitched in to help raise money for the campaign war chest. Notable in this were their friends the Pascoes. Susie Pascoe was Lebanese by origin and particularly gifted at catering meals for enormous numbers. She put on several dinners at the Pascoe's home in East Fremantle, at which Kim spoke, where they were able to raise a lot of money. 'I guess we were doing it,' she considers, 'to raise campaign funds, and also to get a sense of camaraderie going among his supporters, that we were all together in the plan to get him to Canberra. I remember one of the guests commenting that the gatherings were "the Labor aristocracy of Western Australia", and in a way I guess that's right. We were sort of children of the late '60s, early '70s, who had a quite jaded attitude to conventional politics, and the collective feeling was that it would be great to get a good person like Kim to Canberra.'

Mary asked another old friend, Susie Annus, to provide some quiches for a fundraiser, and as she comments, 'of course I was happy to help, because apart from them being very good friends of mine, I thought Kim would be good in Parliament'.

Kim's veteran campaign manager, Fred McKenzie, who had seen a candidate or two in his time, was singularly impressed with the young Beazley fella.

'He was very friendly and very well met and a very easy candidate for one to be promoting. Right away I noticed a few differences about him. The main one I guess, is that he not only knew his subject well, whatever he was talking about, but he listened to what the people had to say in return. A lot of the blokes I'd had over the years, would turn up on the hustings and tell everyone all the things that they were going to do for them, but Kim was actually interested to know what the people wanted him to do if he got elected and I think the people sensed that right away. There were one or two problems, in that he was never the flashiest dresser, but he made up for that with his friendliness, so it didn't really matter that much. I never had any real worries about him winning.'

The campaign had the odd quirky moment. With just a week to go, all four of the principal candidates were invited to make a campaign speech from the back of a truck in the Midland Markets. It was organised by one of the market proprietors, Michael Johnson, who was nostalgic for the way electioneering had been in his youth. One newspaper report of the time set the tone:

Mr Martyr got a few cheers when the candidates were saying what they thought of specific issues. He wouldn't have a bar of a 35 hour week he said.

Mr Kim Beazley Jun was fairly quiet and apologised for having a bout of Labor throat.

One old chap got carried away and shouted repeatedly at Mr Martyr. This, and his having squashed his $1.30 sponge cake, caused his wife to tell him to shut up and come home.[38]

For the most part it was a quiet, and fairly genteel kind of campaign, though at one point John Martyr was disrespectful enough to claim to the press that 'It's the Beazley name I'm fighting against. This fellow is just the boy.'[39] Thirty-five years previously, when Kim Snr was having *his* first tilt at winning a seat — and on his way to making the Beazley name really resonate for the first time — his opponent had taken a different slant. 'I'm glad to learn that Mr Beazley is to be my opponent,' the Liberal candidate, Don Cleland, was quoted in the press as saying. 'I can assure him of a good, vigorous fight, and a clean one.'[40]

And so to the young man's finest moment in his political career to date. The Midland Town Hall had recently been renovated, restoring it to the sparkling Federation building it once had been, and both the ground floor and the second tier were filled to bursting with Labor supporters in general, and Beazley supporters in particular. The walls themselves sang with the colourful bunting, the posters, all the paraphernalia of politics, not to mention the excitement of the 31-year-old candidate himself. As the crowd roared its approval, Kim Beazley Jnr made a rather theatrical entrance, down the side of the hall in the company of Mary, and NSW Premier Neville Wran, who had come all the way from Sydney to speak in his support. Two decades previously Kim had been mortified to find that Prime Minister Menzies was coming to speak against his father at the Fremantle Town Hall; but now his emotions were at the other end of the scale that one of Labor's triumvirate of leaders for the campaign (Bill Hayden, Bob Hawke and Neville Wran) had come to speak *for* him. Beazley, in short, soaked it up. Every last drop. 'I'd never had anything like that for me before,' he recalls. 'I'd done things for other people in campaigns, but I'd never had anything like that done for me. It was ... huge. I remember looking around and thinking, "gee, I actually *am* going to go all the way".'

Mary remembers it just like that. 'It was the most exciting thing even to be involved,' she recollects. 'It was a real gathering of the faithful about to embark on a new age, with lots and lots of positive energy.'

As Kim sat on stage, with Mary beside him, his mother and father and two daughters beaming up at him from the front row, Neville Wran warmed to the theme of how lucky the electors of Swan were to have such an outstanding candidate as this; one who had already proved himself in any number of political forums; who had already shown beyond all dispute just how committed he was to his electorate; one who — and he hastened to add that he did not say this lightly — one who was destined to take, in the not too distant future, a position of leadership within the Labor Party. And so said all of them. 'And I *didn't* say that lightly,' emphasises Neville Wran now. 'Clearly Kim stood out as distinct from just another political hack trying to win a seat. He was essentially a decent human being, with a high intellect, a clear sense of integrity and an overwhelming commitment to the philosophy of the "fair go". I thought of him then, and still do, as an individual who believes that a part of government's function in society is to help equalise the distribution of the goodies amongst the population. In other words, Kim's always the fellow who would help the lame dog over the stile.'

A minor kerfuffle during the campaign came with the news that a local Catholic priest had been saying from the pulpit, as Mary relates, 'that the Labor Party was pro-abortion, and therefore Kim Beazley was going to be pro-abortion and therefore Catholics should vote against Kim Beazley. Then we heard that at the Saturday night mass the pro-life, quasi-DLP people had been putting out flyers to the same effect.' The problem was not merely that it was untrue; Kim Beazley had personally spoken out against abortion on many occasions — and the ALP platform did not have rock-solid policy on it, one way or another. The real concern, of course, was the effect that such assertions might have on the candidate's vote. 'Basically,' Mary continues, 'we knew this was a fairly working class parish which was in our territory and in lots of ways we also knew that Kim appealed to the sort of churchgoing element of the electorate, so it was really quite concerning. So I said to Kim, "I will take this on" — sort of like this is my territory, because I am a "Mick". These were my people, and they were stuffing us up. So I rang Brian and met with him on the Sunday morning and he typed out a statement ...'

'Brian' was none other than Brian Burke, not only one of Kim's oldest friends but also a highly committed Catholic, and then a rising force in the Western Australian Labor Party at a State level. He also got on very well with Mary. The purport of the statement that Burke typed out was that not only did he personally assure the parishioners that Kim Beazley Jnr was anti-abortion, but as God was his witness, Kim had always voted that way within ALP forums. They ran off copies, and within the hour Mary was knocking on the door of the priest to tell him of the distress with which she had heard — inaccurately no doubt — the things people were saying he had been saying from the pulpit. She knew they must be mistaken, but just to make sure she wanted to inform him that Kim's supporters would be there in force at evening Mass to distribute these statements from Brian Burke. As Mary recalls: 'The priest, indicated that of course he had never made any political statement from the pulpit, and so he would not allow us to distribute pamphlets within the church. I agreed that that was entirely appropriate, but that we would therefore be distributing them on the footpath, because that was obviously part of public property and he could have no objection to that. It was a very polite conversation and then I asked him the time of the evening mass, and indicated that that was very helpful because I had not in fact been able to attend mass earlier in the day so it would be very useful for me to attend mass that evening . . . '

It all happened as planned. The priest minded his 'p's and 'q's and did *not* say that Kim Beazley Jnr was pro-abortion; the pamphlets were distributed; the issue died and the damage was contained.

On the morning of Saturday 18 October 1980, as the polling booths opened Mary was there with Kim in the car, driving around from booth to booth to make sure everything was as it should be, while Lady Paltridge took care of their kids at her home. At the South Perth Civic Centre they found Kim Beazley Snr handing out how-to-vote Labor cards like all the other campaign workers. That night, he was still there, as the candidate again moved around from booth to booth to thank all the workers for their help. The two, father and son, clasped hands, with Kim Snr asking 'How do you think you'll go?' 'Oh, I'm going to win,' replied the younger man. He did. Daylight was second, and then came the Liberal candidate, John Martyr, trailing Beazley by 7904 votes in an electorate of 67 225 people.

There would be one small epilogue to the time Kim Beazley Jnr spent at Murdoch University. The academic who inherited the Beazley office was a particularly prim and proper woman. So the legend at Murdoch goes, she took one look at the twisted wreck of a filthy telephone on the desk — all strangulated cord caught up like a knotted fishing line — refused to touch it, and from a safe distance in a colleague's office called Telecom, declaring that the phone was 'unworkable'. After the usual long waiting period, the linesman came, picked up the phone and said there was nothing wrong with the line, it was fine.

'Look at it,' she insisted, 'it's just a mess of filthy wire, it's obviously wrong.' Whereupon the bloke from Telecom, a laconic Australian worker, picked up the phone and held it up above his head and then let the mouthpiece drop down, to begin a long crazy spin, going on for at least ten minutes, as all of the many Beazley political calls of the three previous years unravelled. 'Look m'am, it's all fixed,' the bloke said when it was done, put the phone back on the desk, and walked out the door. The still staggered academic remained mute in the doorway, disbelieving that anyone could make that *many calls.*

So ended the last physical sign of Kim Beazley's time at Murdoch University.

CHAPTER NINE

CANBERRA BOUND

'Politics is the art of the possible.'
Otto von Bismarck

arliament House, you little bah-yooty. While it was one thing to have come here many a'time alone or in the company of his father — as a visitor — it was quite another to be here as of right, as an elected representative of the people. The sentiment that filled this parliamentary newcomer most, however, was pleasure, not slackjawed wonder. 'I think unlike most new members of Parliament, I was tremendously familiar with it so I wasn't sort of awed. There were some who had a background with no politics, who were suddenly in the chamber and overawed by it, but I wasn't. I'd come to Canberra virtually every year since I was born, I had spent an enormous amount of time sitting in that very place when I was over there, so I had a great familiarity with the way it all worked...'

It was perhaps because of this familiarity, that in these beginnings he did not suffer the usual fate of new parliamentarians outlined by Jim McClelland, in 1972. 'The first discovery that a politician makes after a brief stint as a legislator,' the famed Labor Senator had noted, 'is that he is even more ignorant about public affairs than he had been prepared to admit to himself or those who elected him. The second discovery he makes is that there is a vast conspiracy to keep him in that state.'[41] With Kim Jnr, any such conspiracy would have been wasted. The way he felt, nothing was going to stop him. 'I think it helped,' he recalls, 'that I had such an enormous political background, and I think there was every goodwill towards me, particularly from NSW colleagues, perhaps dating back to that 1977 stuff or even earlier. And they just wanted to help me on. Bob Hawke knew me a bit then but he wanted to help a bit too, so there was just a very friendly atmosphere.'

A measure of that 'friendliness' was when, five weeks after the election, he topped the Caucus vote to fill the nine positions available to Labor on the Joint Parliamentary Committee on Foreign Affairs and Defence. From there he made his way on to a subcommittee with Liberal Jim Carlton, to write a review of possible security threats to Australia. These committees had the task of assembling information and analysing it to provide recommendations to Parliament about how it should proceed on various issues, and Beazley found a particular joy in participating.

'Only a couple of months previously I'd been lecturing to students about Australia's security, while here it was real, it was happening. I was helping to make it happen, and I never lost that sense of privilege I had to have the responsibility that was given to me.'

While his father had been obliged to spend the many months of his own time in Canberra staying at the Hotel Kurrajong, Kim Jnr was more fortunate. During the time he had been at Murdoch, his sister Merrilyn had married and was now living in Canberra with her husband Rob Wasson — then a research scientist at the CSIRO and soon to be a professor at the Australian National University — while Merrilyn herself was on her way to becoming a Fellow in the Social Sciences, at the same university. The couple were living in the Canberra suburb of Downer, in a tiny two-bedroom house, but no matter. Seeing as he was going to be spending a great deal of time in the national capital, they invited him to live with them, and as he was just as glad to have some close approximation of home while away from Mary and his daughters, he accepted. Merrilyn insisted that he should stay for nothing, but her brother was equally insistent that he pay regular rent. He explained that if he did not he would be in breach of all sorts of regulations governing parliamentary travel and accomodation allowances and that was that. Merrilyn still protested loudly, but was quietly unsurprised.

'He has a very strong sense of honour,' she says, 'and always has done.'

One problem with the small house was that it had extremely thin walls, meaning that little that was happening in one room could be kept from people in the other. This was a particular problem when the young politician was working on his maiden speech.

On the night of 3 December 1980, Merrilyn and Robert Wasson were kept awake until the wee hours as he practised it. They could hear the Member for Swan trying different forms and emphases for the speech he would make on the morrow in the sanctified chamber:

'I am *most* honoured ...'

'I am most *honoured* ...'

'Keep going Kim,' they would yell lightheartedly in return, 'but give it more *oomph*!'

At last it was his turn for real.

Kim Beazley Jnr rose to his feet, and with a nervous cough by way of getting his bearings, launched into his maiden speech while the House of Representatives did him the traditional honour of remaining essentially silent. It was an address which covered many of the subjects that were dear to Beazley's heart, his intellectual and political passions of the previous fifteen years, but now he had the real forum in which to indulge these passions, where what he said had at least the potential to make a difference. He began rather formally: 'I thank Government members for their indulgence. Mr Deputy Speaker, I join with the many honourable members who have congratulated you on your appointment to high office. I ask you to pass on my congratulations to Mr Speaker.

'I thank the electors of Swan most sincerely for doing me the honour of electing me to this House. I am uncomfortably aware that quite a number of previous members of this House have had occasion to extend their gratitude to the people of the same electorate ...' A small titter from the House at this wry aside, and then he began, in his manner, to put a well-aimed boot into the Government of the day. 'The only changed direction evident in the Governor-General's Speech is that instead of belt tightening homilies, the Australian electorate is now to be the object of pseudo-erudite expositions of Liberal philosophy. I expect underneath the steady drum roll of Government hyperbole we shall hear a subterranean scratching as the nineteenth-century liberal philosopher John Stuart Mill spins in his grave as he hears the views he popularised bowdlerised by his contemporary Australian disciples.

'That humane thinker — as do all rational men — became a democratic socialist late in life and recognised that political freedom, vital as that is, means nothing if the daily experience of the citizen is tyranny in the work place, exclusion from real knowledge of how he or she is governed, and inequity in terms of economic power.' After more remarks on the Government's general ineptitude and moral bankruptcy on all things economic, he moved on to the subject ever and always closest to his heart. Defence.

'I would like now to pass to the final portion of the Governor-General's Speech where Government views on national security issues were placed before us. The time has come for a serious Western Australian interest in the direction of Government defence planning. The Australian Constitution, in section 119, states: *the Commonwealth shall protect every State against invasion.* For most of Australia's history this commitment has largely been without meaning in terms of Australia's defence doctrine, force structure and deployment. Our defence effort has been focused on the southeast, northeast and in forward activities with our allies. In keeping with national Labor's long tradition, stretching through two world wars, of sound and innovative defence planning, the last Labor Government firmly based Australia's defence doctrine on the concept of defence self-reliance. Initially, and still formally, this Government committed itself to that doctrine as its 1976 White Paper indicated, and the Labor Party strongly supported it when it did so. It can do nothing else for, as Dr Ross Babbage, in a recent thoughtful work on Australian defence pointed out:

> ... because the forward defence concept is no longer viable, Australia's defence policy in the future is likely to be primarily concerned with the development of an independent capacity to secure the nation's immediate environment — the continent itself and its offshore islands and resources.

Western Australians have a right to believe that, as the Government recast its defence doctrine, priority would be assigned to the defence of the resources-rich northwest in particular. It is the Pilbara which is likely to be the object of the attention of any enemy in our region that wishes to harm us short of outright invasion ...

'So to us in Western Australia, promises of improved staging facilities on the west coast, of patrol boat bases in the northwest to cover the Cockburn Sound-Darwin gap, improvement of facilities at Learmonth and a joint training area at Yampi, a project announced incidentally by the previous Labor Government — all of which were contained in the 1976 White Paper — were very important.

'So too were undertakings to improve the capacities of Australian forces to move rapidly across the continent. I would also advocate that real defence self-reliance requires the permanent basing of some aircraft with a strike capability in Western Australia and of a significant portion of Australia's submarine force.

'Yet we must also be aware that not much of this is off the drawing board. A lot of it can be readily shuffled to the bottom of the pile of priorities. As long as the Government's commitment to the defence self-reliance concept endures, there remains a reasonable expectation that the strategic needs of Western Australia will be met, even if, as happened with much of what was announced in the White Paper, the schedule is dropped back three to five years.' From skewering the Government for its handling of defence, the junior politician finished on a rather more personable note. 'I have a family background which encourages me to see this Parliament as a great Australian "institution",' he said. 'I was taught by my father, who was a member of this Parliament for 32 years, to love its forms and possibilities. I feel it a great privilege to be a member of what ought to be the focal point of Australian democracy.

'I am aware that the power and functions of this Parliament over the years have gradually, and not always consciously, been whittled away by the exercise of executive power. I believe that we are starting slowly to whittle back — we have done it much more rapidly in the Senate — that encroachment on the authority of Parliament via the committee system.

'It is a system worth protecting and taking very seriously. I am very grateful to my colleagues for having appointed me to two parliamentary committees. I understand that there are many honourable members on both sides of this House who are determined to reverse the process of executive whittling away of parliamentary authority. I hope that in the coming years they will treat me as a friend.'

The last, particularly, was indicative of the kind of politician that Beazley intended to be. He sat down to murmurs of approval from his own side of the house, and by one account, 'a look from their side like there's a new boy in town'.[42] In hindsight, this maiden speech served as a neat foreword to the book of Beazley's parliamentary career for at least the next two decades, touching not only on the major themes that he would be devoting his energies to, but also setting the tone. It illustrated that he would often move from a uniquely Western Australian perspective; that paramount in his concerns were matters of national security; that he revered the whole notion of a parliament as the principal forum of democratic action; that he felt confident enough to comment on matters of the economy as well, and that while he would not hesitate to attack the opposing side of the house, it would rarely be in a vicious fashion. He was, clearly, off to a good start. And loving it. 'I just had an overwhelming sense of the tradition of the place,' he recalls. 'Here I was, I had finally moved forward from the Speaker's Gallery as a boy, onto the floor. This was the heart of Australian public affairs and here I was in the middle of it.'

However much he thrilled to the parliamentary life, neither he nor Mary was in any doubt about how much strain it placed on their home life, particularly with two young children. It was perhaps made worse by two things. First, from his beginnings as an MP, he was never content to be a mere 'moo-cow' of a member — watching the world go by as he grazed — but was immediately involved with his constituency. Syd Hickman, who was then working in his Swan electorate office, and would go on to be with him in one capacity or another for 12 of the next 17 years, remembers his time working for him as a simple backbencher as 'the hardest work I've ever done'. 'He was forever *creating* work for both me and him; he was going round visiting groups, meeting people, making speeches, trying to get a community centre up in Victoria Park,' Hickman recalls. 'I was writing press releases for all the local papers, and following up the things that he started but couldn't finish because he was always heading back to Canberra.'

And therein lay the second problem for Kim and Mary. For whereas in Kim Snr's early time in politics the difficulties of cross-continental travel at least meant that when he was home he was *really* home, in the days of jet travel that was rarely the case. Even when Kim Jnr was home, there was usually another flight back to Canberra or somewhere else beckoning. 'We coped,' Mary recounts of that time, 'just.'

Just as well he adored it all so much. And although he would never concede it, it was even possible that he had gained some advantage by not winning Fremantle three years earlier after all. By winning the marginal seat of Swan instead, the hard way, as opposed to waltzing in to the seat of Fremantle, he had been seen to pay his dues. Had he beaten Dawkins in 1977, the taint of nepotism would likely have hung around him in those early establishing years, and perhaps too, he would not have been able to garner and polish the political skills necessary to win Swan. By winning the far more difficult seat, his very presence in the hallowed halls was a significant contribution to the Labor Party. As it was, he came into the Federal Parliament with wondrous timing, as a young man about to hit his stride, in a Labor Party that would shortly be hitting *its* stride. The Government of Malcolm Fraser had been in office for five years and was already looking tired. The Labor Party under Bill Hayden had substantially reduced the Coalition's massive margin of 48 after the 1977 election to only 23 now, and the party had every reason to feel confident that come the next election it would be them calling the shots.

Of course for Kim Jnr there remained many things to learn in the rough and tumble of Federal parliamentary politics about how to carry himself, how to express his ideas to best advantage, generally how to get along. A lot of the fundamental principles of successful politicking he had already learnt over the previous three decades' involvement in the Labor Party at all levels of activity, but all that now was comparative Bush League. If there was a notable lack in his maiden speech of any invective, that too was to be the mark of the man.* There had been a rich tradition, particularly on the Labor side of the House, to employ colourful abuse as a political weapon. This extended from even the relatively benign John Curtin who once referred to an opponent as a man 'with the body of an ox, and the mind of a troglodyte ...'[43] to Paul Keating who used terms like 'scumbag,' 'piss-ant,' and 'mangy maggot,' as easily as he did lethally.

Beazley though, would remain a political orator in the manner of his father, rarely taking aim at an opponent personally. Occasionally, when the situation warranted he *could* trade abuse with the best of them — always though in his own rather highbrow fashion. It was probably the famed Liberal hard man, also from Western Australia,

---

* Whatever Beazley's own reluctance to engage in invective, he could still very much admire the verbal assaults launched by others in Parliament. A passage from Michael Gordon's book, *Paul Keating, A Question of Leadership*, illustrates the point: '[Beazley] saw Keating and Mick Young as by far the most effective "Fraser baiters". Young, he recalled, was much funnier, but gentler as well. "Paul would always assume that Fraser was listening to him in his office and he would begin his speech with, 'You can come out from under the desk now, Malcolm, I'm speaking.' When he was in the Parliament, Malcolm had this habit of sitting back in his seat, hooding his eyes and going stone-faced. When he did that, Paul told him 'you look like an Easter Island statue with an arse full of razor blades'".'

Wilson 'Ironbar' Tuckey, who had the dubious honour of being the first to experience this first hand:

'To describe the Honourable Member for O'Connor as a Liberal, is to place an orang-utan in coronation robes,' Beazley said to Tuckey in Parliament soon after arriving in Canberra. 'Those of us on this side of the House who have watched his slightly simian visage, as he jabbers and twitters on the Liberal backbench are presented with a vivid image of what is meant by monkey business in the Western Australian Liberal Party.'[44]

Simian visage? Simian *visage*? It was a far cry from Paul Keating's rather more visceral verbal assaults, but still effective. Tuckey had it coming, Beazley reports, because 'he was such a flaming know-all, a real pain in the arse who hated me enormously, and he was into us. I got more patient as the years went by.'

But Wilson Tuckey would not. Regarding Beazley's attacks on him, he says: 'Kim would always like to present me as some sort of dunce, but I used to remind him that the school I went to, Perth Modern, where my academic achievement to that point was fairly sensational . . . was the same school that wouldn't have him!'

Predictably enough, it was not in the realms of verbal abuse that Kim Beazley made his mark in that first parliamentary term, but more on the floor of the Parliament, driving hard at the Government on his two special subjects — Defence and Foreign Affairs.

On those subjects, Beazley was extremely busy for a 'first-termer' — the press noting that 'he got to his feet in Parliament at every available opportunity' — making more than 40 speeches in those fields from December 1980, to March 1983. Such speeches were notable, says one colleague, 'for their wide ranging content and depth of knowledge'.[45] In one of his early efforts he passionately called on the Fraser Government to donate food to Poland with all possible haste as a way of helping to forestall a Soviet military annexation. 'It is quite clear that a return to economic stability in Poland will be very important in discouraging Soviet intervention and consolidating the political and economic gains of Poland's free trade-union movement,' he said.[46] In another speech he noted the surprising frequency with which American 'hunter-killer submarines' were visiting Australia, and wondered what it meant in terms of the Australia/US security relationship.

'They appear for a week a month at HMAS Stirling,' he noted. 'It is my view from an assessment of the public record that the regular visits represent the tail and softer end of a substantial Australian contribution to America's anti-submarine warfare effort in the Eastern Indian Ocean. It may be that both activities ought to be approved. But neither should occur without full and frank public discussion.'[47]

In yet another, he demanded to know why in the previous Federal Budget, of the appropriation of 179 million dollars for Defence Capital Expenditure, only three per cent was earmarked for WA?[48] And, speaking of that, why had the Government been so foolish as to buy Hornet jet fighters and deploy them from Darwin, when this was obviously totally useless for Western Australia? 'Western Australia continues to be the poor relation in defence expenditure,' he thundered. 'The relatively low range of the new fighter — an operational radius of about 740 kilometres — makes deployment from Darwin useless for WA's purposes. It is not enough to say that the F–18 has a special capacity to operate from bare base facilities. Sustained operations off the northwest coast require that the bases be supported by appropriate air defence arming and supply facilities. There was no indication of this in the announcement.'[49]

What could his Labor parliamentary colleagues say, most of them, but 'Hear! Hear!'.

As one of them, John Brown, notes, 'most of us wouldn't have known a Hornet if it bit us on the bum. But it was obvious from the way he spoke that Kim not only knew what a Hornet was, he automatically knew what range it had, what other attributes, whether or not it was suited for Australian conditions and so forth.' Everyone could see that this was really a bloke who knew what he was on about.

'Plus he was a worker, actually a workaholic who really *knew* something about foreign affairs. It is one of the subjects about which very few people know anything. A lot of people like [fellow Labor MP] Kerry Sibraa were always on those committees but Kerry only used it as a vehicle for getting on a plane. He made Marco Polo look like a stay-at-home. The difference with Kim was he actually knew about it, and cared.'

During Kim Snr's time in Parliament he had always been known as a deeply committed Christian and a devotee of Moral Rearmament. To his colleagues in that first term, Kim Jnr was known as neither of these things. He was no longer emotionally bound up with Moral Rearmament as he had been, as one diary entry shows.

Sunday 6 June 1982.
In the afternoon went to opening of MRA House in Bateman. It
really was an odd occasion. The thing I feel is that MRA has
really lost its inspiration [for me.]

I don't know why I feel as I do about MRA, but it seems to
lack the old magic — a really inspired touch. It is no longer at
the heart of the nation's affairs, as it so often seemed in the '60s.
What used to inspire me so much is now a shell devoted to the
*desires of a 1950s middle class.**

And moreover, his Christianity was very much a private commitment. While there were other Christians within the parliamentary halls, Beazley steered clear of having any formal relationship with them.

'I have always been cautious about involvement in things like the Parliamentary Christian Fellowship,' he said, 'or involvement with folk who argue that there is a linkage between Christian belief, moral commitment and a political position. That's because I recollect how hard my father had said it had been for his Catholic colleagues after the Split, as some sections of the Church denounced them and they would have to go around searching for individual churches where they could feel comfortable. I have been reluctant therefore to argue about things like Aboriginal issues or social issues or whatever with the view that if you are a Christian you would have these views. My view is that if you are a Christian you will have *all* sorts of views.'

It was for the same reason that while he went to the church service that marked the beginning of every parliamentary session — and would have a particularly rich 'prayer life' in private — he would always decline to join in the prayers at Parliament itself, and has kept to that since. 'I don't mind the fact that they do have the prayers to start off with,' he says, 'but I always have a pretty fair idea about what we are going to do to each other during the course of that day, and to have prayers as a sort of justification to those proceedings is something which I think is a bit rich.'

This approach to Christianity — private commitment, public neutrality — was consistent with his approach in Parliament. For far from being a 'God-botherer' as some of his Western Australian colleagues thought he would turn out to be, he was the reverse.

---

* Reading back on such comments some 16 years later, Beazley would note that he must have 'really had a bad day, that day, because I seem to have taken a harsher view then than I feel now. I retain many friends within MRA ...'

In March of 1982, he made a strong attack on 250 000 dollars of a Commonwealth Youth Project being granted to a group called Jesus People Incorporated. 'It leads one to ask just how this 250 000 dollars of taxpayer's money is being spent,' he railed, before comparing the grant unfavourably with a group within his own electorate — the Victoria Park Youth Accommodation Coalition — which had only managed to secure 300 dollars from the same body, though wanting it for much the same purposes.

In Caucus during that time, Beazley performed well, but not *too* well. The unwritten rule of parliamentary politics, then as now, is that correct form for newcomers is to ease themselves into the life of the party, before becoming it. As his old Western Australian Labor Party colleague Peter Walsh — by then in Parliament for seven years — recalls of Beazley during this time: 'He wasn't one of the most garrulous people in Caucus but he used to speak with some passion and conviction occasionally.'

Which was as it should be. Michael Duffy, who sat on the seat beside Beazley in Parliament in that first term, remembers him during that time in much the same way: 'He was like all of us, I guess, in that he really wanted to prove himself, to show that he had what it took to do well in Parliament. He was almost obsessive about not stuffing up, but when he started to accomplish that and get noticed, he was never cocky, never over confident. He was a bloke who went about his work assiduously, worked very hard and it had a big personal toll at the end of the day ...'

At the end of the day, it was exceedingly rare that the new parliamentarian would make it home for dinner with Merrilyn and Rob Wasson. More often than not, he would be working in his office in the basement of the Parliament — preparing a speech or doing work for one of his committees — or otherwise he might be dining with colleagues.

One he saw a lot of, right from the beginning, was Paul Keating, just as he had seen a lot of him over the previous ten years, with one looking the other up whenever they were in the other's town. The two had already become close enough that Kim and Mary had the year before made him the godfather of Hannah, but this was still the first time that they had been able to spend extended time together, and both took full advantage of it.

As Brown recalls, 'you'd often see Paul sitting there with Kim chatting just before Parliament opened, and then you'd see them sitting there long after it closed. They were very tight.' To some, seeing the two close together like that so often could be highly amusing. For, peas in a pod, they weren't . . .

'Keating,' Paul Kelly wrote in *The Hawke Ascendancy*, 'brought to Caucus and machine politics the disciplined infallibility of his Catholicism. Dressed with the smart severity of a Jesuit, he slid along the parliamentary lobbies carrying ambition as an altar boy cradles his missal, reflexes sharpened to strike heretics.'

Beazley appeared the opposite in almost every way. Not only did he not have that aura of ruthless ambition about him, but to some observers it appeared as if he had got dressed each morning by putting 'Superglue' on his back and rolled across the clothes he had left on the floor the previous night; as if he had shaved with one end of a broken bottle. Still, most of his colleagues found such a look endearing. While the modern image of a politician in the electronic age was a blow-wave atop a freshly pressed European suit, Beazley provided a nice counterbalance. He looked to be a politician like they used to make them . . .

So, as a matter of fact, did Mick Young. Beazley had first come across Young way back at the meeting of the Federal Executive that he had attended in Adelaide in April 1971, when Mick had the role of ALP Secretary. They had seen each other around the traps since, but now their relationship really blossomed.

Young, the Member for Port Adelaide, had a singular place in the Federal Parliamentary Labor Party. It was a group that always had a disposition to honour its political forebears, and consequently a certain amount of parliamentary bar bragging rights could be extended to those whose background most resembled that of the party's sweaty blue-collar founders. Peter Walsh had been a red-dirt farmer, Bill Hayden a policeman, Gordon Scholes a train driver and heavyweight boxer. Even the relentlessly urban sophisticate, Paul Keating, could not only boast that his father had been a boilermaker and union official, but had himself in his youth briefly loaded wheat trucks for a living.

In these stakes, Mick Young beat the lot of them hands down. Whatever that distilled essence of something is that makes Australian males particularly *Australian* males, then Mick Young had it by the tankful. Young had left home as a teenager with the words of his mother ringing in his ears: 'Bank Commonwealth, join the Union and go to mass.' From there he had risen to be a shearer good enough to go close to the magic 200 sheep-a-day mark, a Union official conducting meetings in Broken Hill boxing rings, thence into the ranks of ALP officialdom, and from there to Federal Parliament. The descriptive term most often attached to him was that quintessentially Australian term 'knockabout', yet he was knockabout with a difference; for not only was he substantially self-educated, with a voracious appetite for reading books, he also came replete with a strong sense of justice and the crucial capacity to *make it happen* politically, built on the earthy skills and organising abilities that he'd gained from his previous experiences. He was, in short, close to the embodiment of Labor's historical roots — and the party loved him for it.

Beazley gravitated to Young naturally, and stuck to him ever after. Though he was never quite sure what it was that drew him to this man a decade his senior, it was sure that the South Australian was almost the archetype of that brand of politician that Beazley had come to admire most over the years — that is, those born into the Irish-Catholic culture. 'I think it is because they are very "people politicians",' Beazley suggests. 'And what happens to people around them is always important to them and so they are automatically gregarious. They think in raw dimensions; they have a critical intelligence which probably is fermented in years of struggle against the British Empire or against the imposition of somebody else's culture. I always liked them.' And Mick in particular.

And Young's attraction to Kim Jnr? As his wife, Mary Young, remembers it, 'Mick just liked him a lot from the beginning, and I suppose a lot of that was their common interests. When Kim would visit our home and stay with us — which was often — the two of them would just sit around having cups of tea and talking about things like sport and politics and history and books for hours and hours. Mick loved books too, and always thought that Kim knew so much about them. They just *clicked*'. In the words of one of their fellow MPs, 'they were closer than brothers'.

Not that all of it was high times and rollicking laughter. The two became a familiar sight, standing on the shore of Lake Burley Griffin, just down from Parliament House, talking over the events of the day. At such times, Kim Jnr inevitably became familiar with the Young approach to politics, and he is certain that he was influenced by it.

'Mick always had his first point of reference to the grassroots. He was very strong on that: "you've got to take them along with you, got to absolutely make them feel comfortable with you". But he also appreciated the fact that you had to push them in a particular direction, you had to *lead*. Simply reflecting their views was not something you should be doing. His belief was they put you in that sort of position because you had some notion about what ought to be done and sometimes it may fly in the face of what they want to do, and if it does then you've got to try to bring them along, but you can't just simply override.'

Because Young was very close to the warm beating heart of the Federal Parliamentary Labor Party, it also placed Kim Jnr closer to the centre of things than he otherwise might have been. Young was, apart from everything else, a binder *sans pareil*. Of all the disparate tribes that made up the party, Young was at least a de facto member of most of them, and it meant that the young man from Perth would get to know a lot of his fellow Labor Parliamentarians very quickly. This was in strict contrast to his father. In 1963, it had been written of Kim Snr that, 'there are men who have been around Parliament House for 20 years, and have never had a conversation with him,' but that was never to be the case with his son.[50]

'Wherever Mick was, there was a public meeting,' Beazley recalls. 'Huge numbers of people marched in and out of his life. He just loved people, and was enormously gregarious. And it was just an enormous pleasure — so many people, interesting people, around all the time.' A popular point of congregation was in that part of the Members Dining Room closest to the Parliamentary Bar, where Young would hold court while eating with his mates what he called 'bushwacker sandwiches' — corned beef, beetroot, onion, tomato and lettuce. 'You'd get fat on bushwacker sandwiches,' Beazley explains, 'basically because you'd eat them at about 11.30 or 12 o'clock at night.'

And in the end, the symmetry was neat, the chemistry worked. Mick Young was also very close to Bob Hawke — the two regularly made bets on the races together, as well as having shared a Canberra apartment in the early 1970s — and it meant that although Beazley and Hawke had an independent friendship, they now saw a lot more of each other than they otherwise might have. Now the Member for Wills, Hawke was already a man on a mission, and it was not a secret one. His desire was to be the Prime Minister. He had stated this since as far back as 1972 as ACTU President, noting 'if I went to the parliamentary sphere, I would want to go to the highest post possible'[51] — and now he was keen to take the first steps towards that by knocking off Bill Hayden as Opposition Leader.

Almost from the beginning, Beazley lent a willing ear to Hawke's plans. 'Basically I had endless conversations with him about what it was he was up to,' Beazley says, 'and it certainly wasn't something I hid. That old Parliament was a hothouse — we all lived in each other's pockets and you really knew people by their associations, seeing with whom they were associating, and I guess everyone knew I was particularly associating with Mick and Bob. Mick was a numbers man for Bob. So I'd attend all these meetings.' Beazley was always amused at such meetings to note how relentlessly optimistic Bob Hawke was when it came time to go through the list of Caucus one more time to determine who was likely to vote for and against him.

'If someone was friendly to Bob in the corridor, or at least didn't snub him,' he comments, 'like, really *snub* him, then he would always say, "you can put him down for me, I'm sure I've got him". It was just unbelievable! I've never seen blokes with confidence in themselves like I saw it with Hawke and Keating. Both had the absolute conviction that they would have to be everybody's logical choice as leader. I've never had such a profound conviction myself and it was amazing to see.' In these meetings with Hawke and Young, Beazley considered himself no more than 'a foot soldier' in Hawke's stalking and eventual assault on the leadership, but he was at least involved. 'He was not there in a [key sense,]' Hawke asserts, 'as he didn't have a position of leadership then, but he was certainly on board right from the word go.' Nevertheless, the Western Australian delivered to Hawke something more than merely his own vote and work for the cause. 'You have also to remember,' Beazley says, 'that Bob ... might never have been backed by the NSW Right, and those were the people with whom I was closest.'

Beazley felt no qualms about doing his bit to help overthrow the elected ALP leader, Bill Hayden. 'Not at all,' he says now. 'Whatever you might say about the fact that Bill had done a good job as Opposition Leader — he had — the fact is Bob was going to actually *win* the next election. It was as simple as that. Bob was what he said he was: "the man most likely to lead the Labor Party to victory." It wasn't a very difficult conclusion.'

In truth too, Beazley was more than usually interested in the electoral appeal of Hawke as opposed to Hayden, in that like all politicians, his bedrock need from election to election was to hold his own seat, and he was always acutely aware how volatile Swan had been in previous decades. There would thus be even more urgent and cogent reasons for Beazley to become active in support of Hawke when, in June 1982, with the next election now predicted to be only a little over a year away, Hayden made a blunder which Beazley felt not only threatened Labor's chances of winning the next election, but more pertinently directly threatened his chances of holding on to Swan. In the course of a newspaper interview, Hayden unilaterally announced that if Labor won the next election then American ships with nuclear capacity would not be welcome in Australian ports.

'I thought it was a ridiculous move,' Beazley says, 'and in Western Australia where they came all the time and were very favourably received, I knew we were actually going to get into serious domestic political trouble. It is part of the Perth ethos in a way, with these regular port visits in Western Australia. As well, there would be serious trouble with the American alliance, because such visits are the bare minimum functioning of that alliance — of all the things that you do, this is the least hard. It is an obvious concomitant of joint exercises, certainly joint naval exercises, that you can end up in each other's ports. And it wasn't necessary. Mere visits by nuclear warships don't make you a target. Secondly, the weapons themselves are safe enough, they don't pose any real danger. Reactors not quite so, but still very good — proper studies have been made as to what anchorages they should have so there isn't a problem associated with them.'

Beazley told Hayden all of the above in strong terms. The irony though, of him being so aggrieved about the actions of the Opposition Leader in this regard — whatever the rightness of his assessment of the political fallout — is that 20 years earlier it had been Kim Snr who Dr Jim Cairns had held responsible for introducing the first vestiges of a 'nuclear-free zone' on the ALP platform. As reported in the *West Australian* on 10 September 1966:

> *Jim Cairns says it was Kim Beazley who originated the nuclear-free policy of the South Pacific. Dr Cairns said Mr Beazley had been a member of the Parliamentary Labor Party's foreign affairs committee which drafted the policy early in 1962.*
>
> *'The ... draft, as accepted by the committee, was substantially his,' Dr Cairns said.*

Hayden eventually drew back from his previous blanket refusal, but it was too late. As Hayden describes the episode in his memoirs: 'The consequences of my behaviour were similar in effect to someone pulling the pin on a hand grenade but neglecting to throw the device away before it explodes.'⁵² That said, Hayden was still not *terminally* wounded, and there remained some work to do to bring him down.

As the time for the clash between Hawke and Hayden drew nearer, Beazley was given the specific task of 'working on' a Western Australian colleague, Gordon McIntosh, and the Victorian, Dr Andrew Theophanous, to try to secure their vote for Hawke. Dr Theophanous had the office next to Beazley at the time, and 'kind of remembers' Kim having a word with him about the virtues of Bob Hawke as a possible ALP leader, but as he says, 'it certainly wasn't anything heavy handed enough for me to really remember in detail'. But did he vote for Hawke? 'Yes, though I must say I think it was entirely because of conclusions I reached myself,' he says, 'rather than anything Kim said to me.'

Paul Keating was not a part of such 'Make Bob King' meetings, at least not at the first tilt, as he was still nurturing his own ambitions in that field, but he was certainly aware of what Kim, Mick, and Bob were up to. 'Keating saw himself as Hayden's successor, at that point in time,' Beazley suggests, 'so he wasn't there with us. He also felt, I think, that Hayden had given him trust and fairly good positions and that put him into a situation where he owed him a bit.' So Keating was not wholeheartedly beside them in the political trenches, when Hawke made his first leadership assault on Hayden on 16 July 1982, when Hawke went down by a mere five votes, 42–37. But, crucially, Keating had fully shouldered arms by the second attempt. And this time, it did not even have to go to the ballot. In one of the more noble acts of political self-sacrifice in recent decades in Australia, Hayden resigned in favour of Hawke on the 3rd of February, 1983.

When the denouement came, Kim Beazley was in Britain on a study tour with his old compadre, John Dawkins. After Dawkins replied to an urgent message from Australia, it was he who told Beazley the extraordinary news. All in the one day, Hayden had gone, Hawke was the man, and Malcolm Fraser had called an election, for 5 March. Beazley, as Dawkins recalls, sat down the better to absorb this most extraordinary conjunction of circumstances in Australian political history — appearing a little staggered, and a lot worried.

'Geez, I'll have to get back home to try and save the seat,' Dawkins remembers him saying, clearly perturbed.

'For Christ's sake, sit down, calm down, and relax,' Dawkins replied. 'In one month's time we'll be in Government, and we'll both be ministers.'

Beazley did no such thing, but was on the next plane home, and scrambling hard to leave no mailbox unfed, no door unknocked, to hold his seat. So it had been with his father over 32 years, so it was with him now. Beazley cared nought that the polls were promising, that his personal popularity in the electorate was high. If there was an election on, then he simply *must* be in trouble.

The new Leader of the Opposition, Bob Hawke, was predictably frantic in the time that remained to election day, but he was still able to make time to journey to Perth in support of his good friend Kim. The day began with a visit to the Midland Junction Railway Workshops about 20 kilometres from the Perth CBD — a railway workshop centre and great Labor support centre — and the crowds were not only huge, but they had that indefinable '*bzzzzzz*' about them that politicians with a keen ear always listen for, as it is considered to be the sound of coming victory. From there Hawke went to speak at a supporters' luncheon for Beazley in the Swan electorate, and there again, the two politicians seemed near swamped with enthusiasm. As Hawke sat down to thunderous applause, he knew, as he says, 'that the tide was with us. So I turned to Kim and said "I think we're looking alright here mate".'

'Oh, I'm not sure, Bob,' a clearly worried Beazley replied, and would have continued but for Mary breaking in with a slightly exasperated '*Stop* being so silly, Kim'.

'He is,' says Hawke, 'a professional pessimist.'

Mary's own theory on the source of Kim Jnr's pessimism has been well thought out over the years. It was because of the experience of his father. 'Kim Snr had all the gifts that would lead him to a great political life, and the circumstances both externally and of his own making were such that it never really came to fruition. He spent an awful lot of time fighting internal battles that really, in many ways he should never have had to fight. Therefore I think Kim's view was always that — even if he was perceived to have the potential and the ability — it doesn't ever necessarily mean in politics that you're going to win through. I think Kim has always been very clear about that, that just having the ability and the leadership qualities and the values that people aspire to doesn't necessarily mean that you are going to get up.' But he did, and handsomely as it turned out, by 16 000 votes. And so did Labor, by a majority of 25 seats.

The people had decided. Robert James Lee Hawke would become the 23rd Prime Minister of Australia ...

CHAPTER TEN

'YES, MINISTER'

'Kim is a work-doggie, he doesn't shun the hard stuff.'
Michelle Schofield, Beazley media adviser 1983–1990.

Amid all the euphoria of the Labor victory, there were still a few parliamentarians who were nervous. To the victors the spoils, and the most immediate spoil of victory was power — power in the general form of government itself, and the specific form of ministries. There were 27 of these laurels to be handed out, of which 21 were quasi-promised to those who had been in the shadow ministry and one which was *guaranteed* to Bill Hayden, that is Foreign Minister, as part of his deal when he stood down from the leadership.

That left five spots open for the young and the restless. There is always a lot of Party horse-trading at such times, and in the frenzy of the deal making, Beazley heard the rumble. 'I was being "got up",' he comments. Translation: in all the machinations of factional deals going on, Beazley's case was being pushed by party heavyweights, none other than Bob Hawke and Mick Young, and as Beazley heard it, 'Bob was pushing me overwhelmingly'. Beazley attributes this support from the newly elected Prime Minister to one clear thing: 'I was a supporter and he was good to his supporters.' Yet while it was gratifying, thrilling even, to have Hawke's support, he maintains that he didn't necessarily need it. 'Bob was supporting me, Clyde Holding and Barry Cohen. I think Barry and Clyde actually needed the leg up, but I don't think I did — I think I would have won the Caucus anyway.' Perhaps, but the push of Hawke behind him certainly counted for a lot, for when Caucus held a ballot to see which of their members should be in the Ministry, Beazley, in Parliament for all of three years, came in more than handsomely in eighth position. On the morning then, of 10 March 1983, he received a phone call. Could he come around to the Prime Minister's office?

When Beazley arrived, there waiting for him were Hawke, Gareth Evans, John Button, and Lionel Bowen — the Government leaders whose job it was to preside over such announcements. With precious little preamble, the Prime Minister got to the point. 'Kim, congratulations, we want you to be the Minister for Aviation and Minister Assisting the Minister for Defence, who will be Gordon Scholes.'

'Good,' Beazley recalls replying, 'thank you, I'll go along with that.' Handshakes. Off-hand pats on the back. Beazley was ushered to the corridor outside, still trying to absorb the news. It was, for this still only 34-year-old man, a special moment. Minister. *Minister*. Minister! 'More than maiden speeches,' Beazley says, 'more than winning seats, those are all fine, but being a minister, that really was something special from the moment I got it.'

He called Mary, who was thrilled not only that he had made the ministry, but also that her husband was filling the same portfolio that her father had occupied at one time. The new Minister for Aviation flew home to Perth that afternoon, and that night lay awake and listened to the planes from nearby Perth Airport coming in to land. It was a strange feeling to know that he was now directly responsible for not only their safety and well-being, but also for their organisation. Further, here he was still with a mortgage hanging over his head that he was, frankly, struggling to pay off, and yet he was in control of the destiny of billions of dollars worth of aircraft. In the silent watch of that night, after he had finally dropped off to sleep, a wayward Jumbo came in low over their Victoria Park home, waking both him and Mary. Mary rolled over and went back to sleep. Her husband didn't. He turned on the bedside lamp and looked at his watch. It was 4 am. 'I thought, well this is going to be *my* problem from now on.'

The first days of the Hawke Government were euphoric, just as the first days of any new government always were, and while Beazley felt it as much as most, he was keen not to lose his head.

'I wanted to go slowly, and find out just how everything worked, before making any significant moves,' he says now. The only exception to this approach, seems to have been one particularly injudicious comment made just a few days after being sworn in, when, after noting that 'the resolution of Sydney's airport needs is a high priority in my portfolio,' he breezily suggested that work 'could begin'[53] on a one thousand million dollar second international airport for Sydney as early as the following year.* 'Too many governments have been dodging the issue for too long,' he told the press shortly after taking over, 'and dodging it is now no longer possible. There needs to be fairly intense consultation, and we really only have a maximum of five years left to do it.'[54] He also announced in his first press conference, at the Rockdale Town Hall near Sydney Airport, that in keeping with the Labor Party platform developed by the previous Shadow Minister, Peter Morris, plans for a third runway for Sydney had been shut down. All up, he felt enormously lucky as he took up his new post. Here he was, in Canberra for less than three years, and he was a Minister of the Crown. It was impossible not to compare his situation with that of his father, who had been in Canberra for 27 years before he became a minister.

So the common political wisdom goes, there are only two kinds of minister in the Westminster system of government: those who run their departments, and those who are run by their departments. Kim Beazley Jnr, who had essentially imbibed politics with his mother's milk and his father's every utterance, was aware of this from the beginning, and was determined to be of the former kind. Not that that in itself was a defence against the mandarins' manoeuvrings. Even that very essence of a substantial politician, Paul Keating, was said to be feeling his way in the role of Treasurer for the first 12 months of his tenure. Like all of his colleagues, Kim Jnr learnt as he went. The change in status, from being a backbencher to being a minister was immediate — and it was not just that physically he moved from the anonymous and safe back of the chamber down to the very public front row. It also meant that he had the right to five personal staff to help him meet his ministerial demands, and a suite in the ministerial wing, right next to the House of Representatives. It was a welcome change from the dingy, deep, dark and nasty office he had been occupying for the previous two years, on the opposite side of the building from where the House of Representatives lay. Now when the

---

* Sydney's second airport had been a contentious issue in the New South Wales capital since 1949, when it was first considered that the facility at Mascot would soon be too small to cope with the air traffic that wanted to use it. By the time that Beazley arrived in the aviation post, a total of 13 Federal Governments had unsuccessfully tried to resolve the issue by finding a satisfactory site on which to build it.

bells rang, he did not have to immediately belt along at a fast clip from the basement to be sure to make it in time, but could take a leisurely stroll, as befitted a minister.

His staff were good, notwithstanding that one of them mentioned to the press shortly after Beazley took the post that the new minister owned only one suit. Other ministers might be mildly offended at such a thing being put about, and slightly embarrassed at the content. But for the Aviation Minister, it was simply a trivial truth. After first decorating his suite with the required number of model aeroplanes and brightly coloured crayon drawings from his two daughters, he got to work. 'I guess I wanted to deal with the problems that were before me,' he remembers, 'because I didn't actually have a particular vision for the industry — it was not something that I'd thought about a great deal. But you wanted the airlines healthy, and that required capital injections for the government airlines to begin with. You wanted an analysis of their financial structures, so they could operate effectively, you wanted Sydney airport sorted out, you wanted communities across Australia to be able to live with airports . . .'

The first and most obvious matter that needed his attention was the two government-owned airlines, Qantas and TAA. He had taken over the Aviation portfolio at a time when the industry was in the worst recession of its 50-year history, and both airlines were suffering badly. Qantas was expected to run up a record loss for the 1982–83 financial year, and it was also predicted that TAA would lose around $30 million. A fact that was impressed upon him early by the then CEO of Qantas, Keith Hamilton, was how much more expensive aviation had become in recent times. According to Hamilton, the effect of the explosion in prices of aviation fuel since the OPEC crisis of 1973, meant that it now cost Qantas as much to fly a plane three-quarters of the way across Australia as it had previously to fly all the way from Sydney to London.

They were hurting. At a bare minimum, they needed money enough to upgrade their planes. They wanted, between them, some 150 million dollars. The response of the Federal Parliamentary Labor Party generally to this request was not good. In the words of Peter Walsh, who was one of the Cabinet's most influential members on economic matters, as well as a member of the Expenditure Review Committee who would shortly become Finance Minister: 'At that time,' he says, 'there was a subsidy going into aviation for about $200 million which in present value dollars of course is almost $500 million, which to me raised the question, from a Labor ideological perspective if you like, why should a Labor Government support an industry which is used principally by upper-income groups, why should we be pouring money into it?' Beazley's approach was the reverse: 'I thought they were an important Australian industry that was hurting, and they needed our help,' he recalls. 'I took the view that you had to jolly the industry along, it was in a lot of trouble, so I tried to relieve the financial burdens on them, like the fuel taxes and the rest of it.' The issue was to be decided at a meeting of the Expenditure Review Committee* — during which Bob Hawke smoked cigars because his first grandchild had just been born — after a Cabinet meeting in Adelaide. Going into it, Beazley was nervous. 'I was worried,' he remembers, 'because the airlines had really taken a pounding, and I thought if I can't actually succeed with this I'm pretty well going to be a failure as a minister, because I'm going to have these two major airlines just limping along and they will take a long time to recover. I was a young minister, I really didn't know fully what I was doing. I could understand basically the economics of the situation but was doubtful whether I could convey it to the High Priests — in the form of Keating and Walsh.'

Walsh didn't get the nickname 'Sid Vicious' from Paul Keating for nothing. As acerbic as he was probing, Walsh questioned the new Minister for Aviation particularly closely about why such a vast sum was necessary. Beazley's line was that it was a simple choice. Pay up, or watch the airlines go under. Walsh's contrary assertion was that the Government business enterprises were simply going to have to start paying their own way.[55] To continue to reach into the public purse would only reward sloppy management and heighten the chances that more calls would be made on taxpayers' dollars. Walsh's preference therefore 'was to allow them to increase borrowings on which they would be legally required to pay interest, maximising the pressure to improve their performance'. Beazley countered that the airlines already had a terrible debt to equity ratio and any course of action that would worsen that ratio would be seriously detrimental. Walsh replied that if the airlines could not give a decent return on the equity that the Government and taxpayers had in them, then the best solution would be to flog them off. 'Hawke terminated the debate,' Walsh later

---

* The Expenditure Review Committee is the nucleus of Cabinet's economic expertise, with responsibility for overseeing/slashing all Government expenditure.

recounted in his memoirs, 'by saying, "That is an option which is available to our political opponents, but is not available to us".'

Beazley got the money, and as he recalls, 'straight out of the meeting I rang the airlines. I was pretty proud of myself, really chuffed. It meant that I got a bit of "cred" with the industry which, given the fact that I was 34 years old, I really needed.' What it meant at the time was that in early May Beazley was able to announce that Cabinet had approved a capital injection of 90 million dollars for TAA and a 60 million dollar grant to Qantas. If it was a seminal moment for Beazley politically, it was also, Walsh argues, a crucial time for the Labor Government. 'Though not apparent at the time, this was the start of the privatisation debate within the Labor Government,' he wrote.[56] Hawke's assertion that only their opponents could privatise public enterprises would not last long, and it would not be too much longer before one of his main strike-forces would be Kim Beazley Jnr.

Now that the most urgent need of finding a financial lifeline for the airlines had been secured, it was time for Beazley to look at the rest of the portfolio. One who assisted him in the process of sorting out what was what and who was who, was Treasurer Paul Keating, and the two continued to spend a lot of time together discussing things. 'Aviation policy in those days was the Two Airlines Policy,' Keating notes, 'which was Government dispensed policy that essentially underwrote costs to the two airline companies. One of those companies was Ansett, managed by Sir Peter Abeles, who was a great friend of Hawke's, so running the airline policy was a bit tricky. Kim realised that I knew all the bits and pieces — I knew the airline policy history, I knew the personalities, I knew the personnel, I knew where the threads were, so we'd talk together in a comprehending way.'

The Two Airlines Policy was a commitment by the Australian Government that only TAA and Ansett would be able to ply the major airline routes of Australia.* At the time, the deal had been a rather cosy one because it guaranteed that Sir Reginald Ansett — in all

---

* Whatever Kim's problems with the Two Airlines Policy, it was not something that was easy to discuss with Mary, because the man who had actually introduced the policy, back in the 1950s, was none other than Shane Paltridge.

'The ghost of Mary's father was actually around me all the time when I was in the portfolio,' Beazley recalls, 'because a lot of the people in the department had been there from that time and he was a longstanding, well-respected Civil Aviation Minister, so a lot of the older guys in the department had known him and would talk about him.'

likelihood the Liberal supporter who made the party's coffers burp the most often — faced a bare minimum of competition. But the political and economic verities had changed. While much of the rest of the Hawke Government was embarking on the beginnings of a frenzy of economic rationalism, Beazley was, by nature and learning, a little more cautious. As he would note to an interviewer shortly after taking over the post: 'In the '60s, when I joined the ALP, there was a long Labor tradition of state-owned industries — state shipping, state timber, the Midland Railway Workshop, power stations and the rest. The attitude was that the government ran the economy and delivered services to the people, including employment.'[57] So while others of his colleagues might seemingly be prepared to throw all of that over in a flash, Beazley's background bade caution. 'I think at the time when we looked at it,' he recalls now, 'it seemed to us that if we gave away the Two Airlines Policy you'd get one airline real quick, but all the same, you just couldn't keep on with it.' In any case the agreement still had until 1986 to run. In the meantime Beazley at least announced plans to review the policy: 'What I intend to have between 1984 and 1986 is an orderly review of the whole agreement,' he told the *National Times*, 'an 18 month period in which everybody gets a chance to have a say about what they think ought to be done with the aviation industry.'[58] It was, admittedly, pretty dry stuff. Yet while running aviation might not be the most fascinating area of government to be involved in, Beazley was not complaining. 'To be a minister is about the most satisfying life I can imagine,' he told Kerry Coyle of the *West Australian*, soon after settling in. And he meant it.

Now he comments: 'Looking back on it, it was an ideal portfolio for me to start with, because it was small and manageable, with a lot of technical activity in it, which I liked. It had a fairly coherent set of policies around it that you had to deal with. It was a very good intellectual discipline as a portfolio. Plus the excitement of new technology. One of the things for example we were active in was lobbying for an Australian navigation system, or airport approach system, called Interscan which . . .'

It was pretty dry stuff.

But through it all, Beazley established what was to become his signature style as a minister. He ran a relaxed office in all things bar work output, where it was expected that his staff would always be on top of it. 'I never saw him take anybody apart or be heavy with anybody,' his then Senior Private Secretary Damien Wallace recalls,

'he'd work his way through issues without getting people offside.'
Beazley was also exceptional, Wallace says, for being far more
accessible to members of the Opposition than was the norm. 'That
was the thing that most amazed me. There were bloody Opposition
backbenchers who'd come in and get just about as good treatment as
the Labor blokes! Like at a personal level. And there would be joking
conversations with them, Kim would be saying, "well look I don't
know what you're sitting with them for, you'd be far better in our
party, you're such a good member".

'There was this extraordinary skill he had, like with people who came
to a meeting wanting $50 000 to get some new facility or something for
their airport. He'd kinda be able to take them through it all so at the
end of it, they haven't got the $50 000, but they've got another couple
of ways to address their problem. And they felt — it was just so often, it
seemed to be some kind of magic — so many people thought, well
they'd actually learnt something from him.' After hitting his stride in the
new position, Beazley had the sense that he was both on top of the
Aviation portfolio, and performing well for the Government. Only a few
months after he took the post, the influential political journalist Alan
Ramsey wrote in the *National Times* that, 'there are those in the Labor
Party, admittedly mostly in Western Australia, who are convinced
Beazley will one day lead the party. He is said to be that good.'[59]

That sense that he was going well was heightened, oddly enough
amid great sadness, on the morning of 14 July 1983, when he received
a request to go and see the Prime Minister in his office. Bob Hawke
told him two pieces of staggering news. The first was that his four-
month-old government had suffered its first Ministerial casualty — he
was standing down Mick Young from his position as Special Minister
of State, because of a single indiscreet remark to a close friend in a
Canberra car park over the Combe/Ivanov Affair.* And the second
was that he wanted Kim to formally take over from Young as Special
Minister, while an inquiry was conducted into, among other things,

---

* The Combe/Ivanov Affair emerged when the chief of the Australian Security
Intelligence Organisation (ASIO) briefed Prime Minister Hawke that the former
Secretary of the Federal ALP, David Combe, had formed what the ASIO chief viewed
to be an improper relationship with a Russian diplomat, Valeriy Ivanov. The National
Intelligence Sub-Committee of Cabinet, of which Mick Young was a member, met to
discuss the information, and that night in the car park of the 19th Hole Restaurant in
Canberra, Young told his great friend Eric Walsh that the Government was about 'to
kick out a Russian'. With that, Cabinet security had been breached, and when Hawke
found out about it, he had taken action against Young.

Young's actions. On the spot, Hawke personally escorted Beazley out to Yarralumla, where the Governor-General, Sir Ninian Stephen, swore him in.

Beazley remembers being 'completely shocked' at the speed with which it was all happening, and as soon as he had taken his leave of Hawke back at Parliament House, he tried to track down Mick Young. He was not in his office, nor in the Parliamentary Bar, nor in the Member's Dining Room. No-one had seen him. Beazley realised that he must have decided to fly home to Adelaide and would, in all probability, be at Canberra Airport, which is where he in fact found him, at the gate, and ready to board. 'He was devastated,' Beazley recalls. 'I said, "you know mate, I'll just hold office and hold the fort until you get back", and that was that.' The upshot was the same. Only four months after being a humble backbencher he now had Aviation plus responsibility for such sensitive areas of government action as Federal Police and the conducting of elections. The appointment effectively doubled his workload. Far from putting a cleaver between Young and Beazley, his six-month stint replacing Young only served to bind them closer together. After his time in the sin-bin, Young was officially rebuked by the Hope Royal Commission for an action deemed 'unauthorised and improper' and he was allowed to resume his post.

The then Secretary of the Department of the Special Minister of State, John Menadue, remembers that 'some members of the backbench were anxious for Hawke to fill the vacancy so they could get a ministerial guernsey, but Kim was absolutely adamant that he would resist that pressure and he would not give any support to those urging that Mick should be stood down permanently and someone else appointed permanently as the minister. Mick was extraordinarily grateful for the loyalty that Kim showed to him, and appreciated Kim's loyalty'. Loyalty. It is a word bandied around a lot in politics, and always made to sound like a fairly simple, one-dimensional concept. You were either loyal or you weren't. The real problem though, was all the *competing* loyalties.

Sometimes being the Special Minister of State could place Beazley in a ticklish position. In early September 1983 while on a trip to New Zealand to try to convince the New Zealand Labour Party of the unsoundness of pursuing their policy of banning visits of nuclear ships to the country's ports, he was advised by his Department head, John Menadue, that there appeared to be some serious irregularities in the expenses claimed by the Labor Senator from Queensland, Mal Colston. It appeared that he had claimed some 6500 dollars to which he was not necessarily entitled, and because one of the responsibilities of the Special Minister of State was to oversee his parliamentary colleagues' entitlements, including the reimbursement of travel expenses, the problem in the first instance was Beazley's.

As Beazley recalls, '[the feeling of the department was that] perhaps what ought to be done was that there ought to be some police investigation associated with it. And I said that that should proceed.' Menadue wrote a contemporaneous note to that effect, which would emerge years later, first published in Victoria's *Sunday Age*: '*Spoke to minister during 3/4 September in NZ. He agreed the course of action — proposed investigation by AFP — was the appropriate course. It was decided in the meantime he would speak with PM and ministers and also ask Colston for further explanations.*'[60]

The official advice to Beazley, when he returned, was along similar lines.

> *We believe we have no option but to ask the Australian Federal Police (AFP) to initiate an inquiry into the payments by the Commonwealth amounting to $6444. In reaching this view we have had regard to the pattern of Senator Colston's previous claims against the Commonwealth viz irregularities.*[61]

The problem was indeed not a new one, as Senator Colston had already been obliged to pay back some 4000 dollars the previous year, when the Fraser Government had still been in power.

Gareth Evans, however, the then Attorney-General — himself a former Oxford University man — thought that was premature, although his own Department had already examined the position and recommended that Colston be pursued. After Beazley consulted with Evans, the bearded law-man wrote to Beazley formally confirming what he had already told him. 'This is to confirm my oral advice to you as to the most appropriate course of action to be followed in respect of the possible irregularities which have appeared in Senator Colston's chartered transport claims over the last two years. My view is that before entering on a police investigation, which might have quite profoundly disturbing implications for Senator Colston's apparently delicately balanced family situation, quite apart from causing grave damage, whether unfairly or not, to his reputation in the event that the fact of the investigation became public knowledge, Senator Colston should be asked to provide a full and detailed explanation of the circumstances of his claims and be given time to pursue any documentation required. In all the circumstances, and given in particular that any such possible irregularities are routinely handled in private commercial organisations and other institutional settings, I believe it would be premature to set in train a police investigation. In the event however, that Senator Colston's explanations were unsatisfactory, I agree there would be no alternative but to involve the police . . .'[62]

The person whose duty it was to talk to Colston, was none other than Beazley himself, and he did it on the afternoon of the same day that he received Evans advice. Not easy. Beazley did not like the Senator from Queensland — and never had — even from his first moments of encountering him in Parliament. Beazley comments now, 'I thought he was a guy always looking for the main chance, and my argument to him was that there was a substantial conflict of interest. What he was doing was hiring services from a company which had his wife as a director: charter services, cars and aircraft. Now, provided he actually received the services, he was allowed to do that — and we had no evidence that he hadn't received the services — but what I was arguing was that it was a conflict of interest, he shouldn't have done it and we wanted the money back. Colston at first would not do it — he complained and said he was justified in the claims that he'd made. I was saying that what we're doing is looking at this practice of yours of hiring services from this company, it's not transparent and it is a possible conflict of interest. And you shouldn't persist in this practice. He argued the toss and said it was all appropriate and above board — and I said, 'irrespective, *pay it back*'. Eventually he did — I then had a long argument with him because he kept trying to do it, kept trying to hire services off this company. So I had a rather bitter exchange of letters with him, trying to get him to stop and he didn't.'

Mick Young was back in the post from January 1984 onwards, and from then on Colston was his problem — and an ongoing one he would prove to be.

Gareth Evans' Department came to concur with the Attorney-General's views, and so the upshot was that the police were never called in to investigate something that would clearly have been politically explosive if it had ever seen the light of day. It would certainly have damaged the Hawke Government, especially in the wake of the Combe/Ivanov imbroglio which had already given it an air of scandal. From the point of view of Beazley though, that was where it was all left, essentially unseen for the next 14 years.

It re-emerged in the winter of 1997, during the Travel Rorts Affair, when Senator Colston — who had by that time left the Labor Party — was accused of over-claiming on his travel expenses. When Labor attacked, the Liberals dug out the fact that the same problem had existed in 1983, and that at that time Gareth Evans and Kim Beazley had done nothing, despite receiving two separate pieces of advice from their own departments that police investigation was warranted. Both Beazley and Evans were accused of gross hypocrisy for attacking the Liberals for appearing to protect Colston when they had been no better — and they were also accused of trying to cover up the fact that they had so acted.

Alan Ramsey, in a series of articles in the *Herald*, was particularly withering: 'It was the bureaucrats who wanted the police called in,' he wrote in the middle of April, 1997. 'It was the politicians who kept them out. Beazley and Evans, with the Government's apparent support, were responsible. Their departments acquiesced only after the two ministers resolved the "problem" behind closed doors.' Beazley's reaction to such accusations is short and sharp: 'Allegations like that, are exaggerated horse-shit.'

The political experience offered up to Beazley by filling the role of Special Minister of State was intense. For the first time he was able to take his seat at the Cabinet table by *right* — and not merely ushered in as a lesser-mortal minister with cap in hand, seeking approval for money from his more powerful Cabinet colleagues. One thing he proposed to his fellow Cabinet members, was that they pass enormous changes to the Electoral Act — concerning such things as campaign funding, requirements for equal electoral districts — as well as pass another Act which would have seen Parliament expanded considerably. Getting Cabinet approval for the first was relatively easy, but for the second, was very difficult. Beazley was determined nevertheless to push hard, convinced as he was 'that seeing as the last time the Parliament had had an increase was in the late 1940s, and it was definitely time to try and break the Gordian knot'.

At the Cabinet meeting, Bob Hawke, in his manner, sought the views of everyone around the table and when the 'yay's and 'nay's were added up, the only Cabinet minister under 'yay' was Kim Beazley himself. Not to worry. Hawke decided to invite the two key factional powerbrokers, Senators Robert Ray and Graham Richardson, into the room for their views, and when they spoke strongly in favour, Hawke concluded with 'So I take it we're all in favour then?' Everybody agreed that was so. It was another conspicuous victory for Beazley, and a sure sign besides, of the growing strength of the factional system.

Part of Beazley's job from that point was to help guide the legislation through both Houses of Parliament, and in this endeavour Beazley singularly impressed Senator Robert Ray, for one. At a key point in the Senate debate on the legislation, as Ray remembers it, he noted that Beazley was sitting in the Visitors Gallery, watching proceedings, and the Victorian Senator was not at all surprised.

'He was often there,' says Ray, 'because he made it his job to follow it, to understand what was happening. He was the only one to try and follow the procedures and to understand the Senate, how it operated, and this was quite unique [for someone from the Reps]. We used to get people who'd bring in Cabinet submissions with no knowledge of how they would be treated in the Senate; but with Kim, he always had a fair idea of what the Senate would do on things — maybe adjourn it to a committee for six months, may reject this, may disallow that, he *knew* — but most of the others never did try to master the complexity of it. Kim knew more about the Senate than any other Cabinet minister from the Lower House.'

During this time, Beazley also presided over the establishment of the National Crimes Authority, a kind of permanent Royal Commission, which would have the responsibility of coordinating state-based efforts against white-collar crime, particularly, into a national effort. Beazley had inherited proposals for the bare bones of this institution from Mick Young, and recalls his own job as 'putting the flesh on them'. Perhaps most instructive in terms of his future parliamentary career though, was the heat that was applied on him in Parliament as a result of work done by the noted crime-fighter and investigative journalist Bob Bottom, in what would later become generically known as the 'Age Tapes' Affair (as some of the transcripts would come to be published in *The Age*.) On October 4, 1983, using information garnered from Bob Bottom, the Federal Opposition Leader Andrew Peacock asked a question of Beazley in his role as Special Minister of State, as to whether it was true 'that the Australian Federal Police had detected, by use of telephone taps, the payment of monies to people in authority, including a [NSW] Minister, to ensure the early release of prisoners.'[63] As detailed in Bob Bottom's book,

Without Fear or Favour, Beazley took five hours before replying, using the time to consult with the Prime Minister, and then read from a prepared statement acknowledging the Federal Police telephone taps, and stated that 'offences under NSW law may have been committed in relation to the early release of prisoners'.[64] So began a long saga, involving transcripts of tapes that purported to implicate in corrupt acts most notably two high-profile Labor identities: the NSW Minister for Corrective Services, Rex Jackson, and later the former Labor Cabinet Minister and then High Court Judge, Lionel Murphy.

For the rest of his time as Special Minister of State, Beazley would constantly find himself the man obliged to defend the Hawke Government against Opposition attacks, while the Attorney-General, Gareth Evans, did the same in the Senate. There was a clear difference in the way they went about it. Beazley quickly worked out that the best way was to 'just hunker down behind the privacy provisions associated with the taping process. The Opposition was trying to get information about what was in the tapes. And I was up there just saying "listen, the relevant Act says that whatever happens to be in those tapes, it's not something that I can either read or bring into the Parliament".* Gareth used to have the other view, he was in the Senate hanging by the same issues and he would always be most discursive, speaking very liberally about it all, so I rang him up once and I said "Listen Gareth, my view on this is that you get down in the trenches and you pull the cover over the top of you" and Gareth said, "No, I prefer to be in the open field!".'

Therein too, lay the key difference between these two Labor parliamentarians of the same generation; but that difference would be played out in the fullness of time. Beazley suggests now: 'I think

---

* Bolstering Beazley's commitment to his parliamentary defence, were his genuine doubts about the accuracy of the transcripts. As Beazley remembers it, on one occasion when Bottom had made a very negative reference to a female NSW judge, he had, as Minister, insisted that the Federal Police go through all the tapes over three or four days 'to find if they actually had a tape in which there was something like this appearing. 'At the end of it, the Federal Police said, "yes we do have a reference to the particular judge concerned in the tape, but it's not what Bottom has said. What it is, is two crims talking about what a *hard* judge she is, and how they don't want to go up in front of her". So you couldn't rely on these darn tapes.

'I was also pretty confident that Lionel Murphy wouldn't do anything wrong himself; Murphy was not a corrupt man in any shape or form.' Murphy in fact died before that could be properly determined by the courts, while for his part Rex Jackson was, in 1987, sentenced to seven and a half years jail for having conspired to organise the early release of prisoners.

the *Age* Tapes Affair did me the world of good at one level, because it taught me to toughen up in Question Time. It really imposed an extra layer of toughness on the skin that stood me in good stead through time — that you needed not be panicked. It was a very useful baptism of fire, because I learnt that you don't necessarily have to … you never give *inaccurate* information … but you don't have to go down the road of chasing everybody's delivery. You can just lift your bat and let it go.'

Damien Wallace, who observed it all closely, quite separately uses the same cricket analogy: 'Kim played it as I guess a really good opening batsman would — absolutely solid, straight bat, straight bat, not touching anything outside the off-stump. Gareth on the other hand was always sparring outside the off-stump, banging them back over the fence every now and then, but causing heart attacks to everybody else with his loose language.'

Watching Beazley perform like this, day after day, John Brown, the then Minister for Sport, remembers noting how extraordinarily far the Member for Swan had come in a short time, in terms of his parliamentary performances. Only a few months previously Brown and his ministerial colleague Chris Hurford had sat in Parliament making bets as to how many times the Minister for Aviation would put his hand in and out of his side pocket while standing at the Despatch Box during Question Time — it was usually somewhere between 20 and 30. Brown comments, 'I had never seen anybody more nervous, but then this amazing confidence came, and Kim became a most assertive speaker. I think his great capacity has been his ability to still *connect* with his opponents. Mick Young did it with humour, Kim did it with dignity and with force of opinion rather than florid abuse. He always maintained that dignity that his father had. Kim was never someone who got involved in screaming or yelling matches but he was certainly very strong in his opinions and strong in his condemnation of the Opposition but never in a nasty way. I thought he really came of age as a parliamentarian while filling in for Mick that time.'

Despite the fact that he was enormously honoured to be selected as Mick Young's temporary replacement, it meant of course that the greater workload was a problem for a family man working on the other side of the continent from where his family was putting their heads on the pillow. In this fight between the competing interests of politics and family for which Beazley has often lashed himself — the truth of it was the family was too often on the losing end. He was an extremely devoted father, but the reality of it was that the pattern of life that he had experienced as a young child was now being visited upon his children, and all too frequently he was a good father at the other end of a long-distance telephone wire. Each night, he would try to call home some time around 7.30 pm — which was 10.30 pm Canberra time — and after chitchat as to how their day had gone, he would say, as his daughters remember it, 'Ok, let's say prayers together'.

Hannah: 'God Bless Mum and Dad, Claudia, Nanna and Pop, Bing, [*Aunt Merrilyn*], Rob, Anton, David and Grandma and God Bless Jessica most of all.' Jessica, right beside her sister, would be saying the same prayer in unison, breaking off only to finish with 'and God bless Hannah most of all'. Both girls would finish their nightly conversations with their father by saying: 'Love you Daddy, and sweet dreams.'

As Jessica recalls it 'we would always say that, because we were always paranoid that he would die in a plane crash coming back, and if that happened we wanted our last words to be really loving ones'.

This fear of a plane crash was not because it was their father *running* the planes — just perhaps a heightened sense around the household that plane crashes of any description were particularly bad news.

On his usual Friday night homecomings, both girls quietly talked to each other to try to stay awake until they could hear the front door click open. Then, when their father came in to check on them, as he usually did about 30 seconds later, they both pretended to be asleep, before springing out of bed and jumping all over him. It was something of a family ritual, hugely enjoyed by all. When he was home, he could sometimes be a bit distracted — as if he was physically present, but his mind was back in Canberra — though he was mostly a lot of fun. The favourite game that their father played with them at night-time was pretending to be 'Wanda the Wicked Witch' — by holding a broomstick, pulling an old jumper up in a hood over his head, using a torch for lighting effects, and putting on a high-pitched voice. As the two 'beautiful princesses' ran around their bedroom, the evil witch chased after them, screeching how she was going to turn all the people they loved into toads and toadstools. Finally Wanda would catch one of the princesses and would be about to turn *her* into a toadstool, but was always foiled in her dastardly plans by the other princess. 'We would just play that forever and ever,' Hannah recalls. 'We loved Wanda.' What Hannah remembers clearly was first learning to ride her bike, with the Minister for Aviation running along behind her, keeping her upright as she pedalled furiously. 'And then suddenly, he wasn't there any more, and I yelled out, "are you there Dad?" And this voice from a long way back yelled out "NO!" . . . just before I ran into these huge rosebushes.' For all the fun of such games and pastimes, their father could still be strict in the old-fashioned manner. When both girls were young and experimenting with saying rude words — like 'shit' and 'damn' — there was always the same result if they were said within earshot of their father. He washed their mouth out with soap. 'Actually,' Jessica remembers now, 'at first, he would wash our mouth out with soap. After that we would do it, while he supervised.'

When he was home and working, both daughters remember their father making a particular effort to take them with him when at all possible. As his father had done with him, he often took them to his electorate office and to various meetings, party gatherings, fundraising events and so forth. Both girls learnt to be patient because of it. 'When Dad said he'd be with us in two minutes, that he just had to make one more call,' Jessica Beazley remembers, 'you knew that there was no chance he'd be with us in two minutes. It might be ten minutes, it might be twenty minutes. We learnt to be patient, and we learnt how to entertain ourselves.' It was the way it was. Their father had commitments, important commitments, that he simply had to fulfil if he was to do his job properly. It went with the territory of being a minister, and there was nothing he could do about it if he wanted to do his job properly.

If Kim Jnr was, in large part, leading the life of his father, and the children in turn were leading something of the life he had known, so too was there similarity in the lives of the wives. Just as Betty Beazley had struggled with the long absences of her husband, so now did Mary. Whereas Betty had remained at home full time, though, Mary's energies were further dissipated because she was doing full-time remedial teaching at a nearby Catholic college, and was determined that her own professional life would not be swallowed, merely because her husband had a political career. 'I do as much as I can in the electorate,' she was quoted in a newspaper as saying, 'as long as it doesn't impinge on my work. I have other involvements during the week as well as my job that take up a lot of time.' In the *National Times*, she was even more blunt, 'I think within the constraints of responsibility which a marriage and children put on you as an individual, both should be free to do the work which is important to them. I'm not trying to say it's hunky-dory. There are times when I want to pull my hair out and I say "God, what am I doing?".'[65]

As such comments suggest, it was not easy for her. 'At the time prior to getting married,' she says now, 'I guess I was silly enough to think that because I had some experience, growing up in my own political family, that I knew what it was about, and Kim certainly knew what it was about and therefore we were in a better position than most people to cope with it. Which looking back was entirely wrong because I think that sort of anaesthetised us to some extent to the difficulties. But for me at that time, it was a terrible, terrible life.'

An entry in Kim's diary from the preceding Mother's Day gave his own spin on it.

Mother's Day.
My present to Mary was leaving on the midday plane to Canberra...
I dearly love Mary but I think it may be we are incompatible. I am always tired...

He was tired for good reason, even apart from the constant plane travel. When he *was* at home, each morning would invariably begin with the thump of ministerial papers arriving on the front verandah for him to go through, which would often take him until late at night. The sole advantage he had in doing such unending paperwork was advice proffered by his father, that he should pay particular attention to briefs that seemed too thick for the thin matters being covered, 'because they would be the briefs where the bureaucrats are trying to snow you with detail'. All up, this wasn't much of an advantage when it came to 'clocking off' and spending entirely unfettered time with Mary and the kids — for this rarely happened. The difficulties that the couple went through because of this workload and his long absences, were at least partially apparent to their friends. Susie Annus, in a discussion with her friend Geraldine Doogue around that time, tossed around thoughts as to who Kim might marry next, and concluded that, 'he will probably end up marrying some bureaucrat from Canberra'.

Kim Jnr himself, perhaps, had no time to think such things. For him it was always time to get back to work. He continued to be involved in things not strictly within his own bailiwick. On matters environmental, Beazley established himself early on as 'a pragmatist', very much in the Western Australian fashion, once defining a pragmatist as one who 'knows how to present a principled position in a way that does not rub the electorate's nose in it'.[66] The most contentious environmental issue in the early days of the Hawke Government was whether to allow the mining of Roxby Downs, in South Australia. Others within Caucus might have had to talk with their colleagues and toss and turn at night to decide what to do. Beazley did not. 'I voted to mine it,' he says. 'Absolutely. I thought that politically you could not sustain an effective Labor Party activity in South Australia if you didn't give them that economic break. I thought that Roxby Downs was of such vast significance to South Australia it would be irresponsible to stand aside from it.' Beazley's attitude was, in short, not untypical of the one that, as Peter Bowers once wrote in the *Sydney Morning Herald*, 'grips so many Labor MPs from Western Australia. Pussycat socialist instincts notwithstanding, these Labor men are essentially political products of a State whose macho entrepreneurial character is fired by the Golden Mile and mountains of less precious metals.'[67]

On social issues, Beazley also continued to mark himself as a conservative. At the party's National Conference in 1984, for example, he spoke out as strongly as he ever had on the subject of abortion.* 'I felt very strongly against abortion,' he comments, 'and fought very strongly for a conscience vote on that issue.'

The preservation of such a conscience vote, with Beazley on the winning side of the vote — among other things freed the party from being guided by what the factional bosses had decided between them should be the result, something that increasingly gripped the Labor Party at this time, as the factional system had taken a progressively more institutionalised hold.

The formalising of the factional system had received a big kick along around February of 1984, a little under a year into the Hawke Government's first term, when people such as Peter Walsh, Neal Blewett, John Dawkins and Bill Hayden had formed up their Centre Left faction. This faction was described by Bill Hayden as 'a lonely hearts club squeezed between two super powers,'[68] and had collected many of the parliamentarians who did not feel comfortable being a part of either the Left or the Right. The three

---

* Beazley would soften his stance against abortion over the years. 'Personally I'm still against abortion, but I don't think it's a matter for the Criminal Code. You've got to accept the fact that basically the community values are such that — at least in certain circumstances and maybe in all circumstances — abortion ought to be permitted. In those circumstances it's far more sensible for people who still have concerns with it, to see it located in the Health Act, rather than the Criminal Code as a matter of regulation.'

main factions by this stage each had national convenors, regular meetings and strict internal discipline. This Labor system of 'tribes within the tribe,' though it sometimes resulted in internecine warfare, did have some virtues.

To quote Bowers again, 'Factions are the Labor Party's peculiarly effective way of power-sharing. No single faction can monopolise power, so the factions have to deal with each other to apportion power. The factions give the Labor Party its volatile cantankerous character because their interrelationship can stabilise or destabilise the entire party. The factions are the inner binding that puts fraternal flesh and blood on the Labor collective. Loyalty to faction, more often than not, seems more important to Labor politicians than loyalty to the party at large. It probably has as much to do with mateship as politics. Being alone in politics is like being alone in a dark lane at midnight with strangers filling their socks with sand.'[69]

While Kim Beazley has never had an *image* of being a true blue factional warrior for his own tribe of the Right, he has, nevertheless, always been intimately involved. As Graham Richardson tells it, 'Kim wasn't beyond — in the Caucus — doing a deal with the Centre to do over someone in the Left. He was an active faction member, he wasn't just like, say, John Kerin, who joined the faction because he had nowhere else to go, and Michael Tate, those sort of people. Kim was committed, he was there, and in.' That said, Beazley was not much of a one for the active hand-to-hand combat in factional warfare. 'He wouldn't twist an arm,' Richardson recalls, 'but he was very persuasive and most of that sort of politics is about being persuasive. Hardly ever do you get a bloke in a room and say 'you fucking do this or I will bury you', I reckon I only did that myself about half-a-dozen times. Most of the people that I won over to causes, or policies, or to people, I won by persuasion and Kim was always very good at that.'

He was good, perhaps, in part, because he had a specific attitude about factional warfare. 'I thought differently to a few people in the Labor Party,' Beazley says, 'I always thought that there should be no enemies in the Labor Party. I thought that people in the Labor Party ought to be able to get on with each other no matter how different their ideological perspectives. So I operated on the theory that even though I'd been factionally engaged, my enemies were elsewhere.' For all that, there was absolutely no doubt where his greatest ally resided, and that was behind the big desk in the Prime Minister's office.

As opposed to the situation with the vast majority of the Caucus, and indeed most of the ministry, Beazley would have frequent occasion to discuss his views on such matters with the Prime Minister, and hear Hawke's views in return. The fact that Beazley held the dual posts of Aviation Minister and Special Minister of State meant that they often had cause to see each other, and an already close relationship became even stronger. When the midnight oil was burning in Hawke's office — which was mostly — it was common for Beazley to be in there till very late himself, talking things over. Beazley recollects, 'Hawke worked absolutely diabolical hours. I have never seen anyone work like him. Most of my meetings with Bob, over the years would be 12 o'clock, one o'clock in the morning. It was really the only time of the day when he could settle down and chew the fat politically, the rest of the time he was on the job. I have never seen anyone like it — he was the classic, great Walter Bagehot type of Prime Minister. Bagehot was the British Constitutional writer of the nineteenth century who said 'Great Prime Ministers are men of commonplace opinions and uncommon administrative abilities' — that's Hawke, absolutely to a tee. He had the average Aussie opinions on most things, but diabolically good administrative capabilities.'

If Beazley found great joy in spending such long hours in Hawke's company, so too did the Prime Minister. 'We used to enjoy many hours together, talking,' Hawke recalls. 'Kim Beazley has consumed more of Hawke's cigars than any other person on the planet. As time went on people used to say that it was like a father and son relationship, and in a sense I did look upon him as a son. I really loved Kim, I still do, and respect him enormously ...'

It was not that they couldn't have disagreements. Towards the end of 1983 they had a clear difference of opinion on the subject of superannuation payments to pilots. As reported in the *National Times*, 'Beazley strongly counselled caution and felt that the pilots, isolated from public opinion, would quickly come to heel. Hawke was gung-ho for taking them head-on in what would have been a clear — and very safe — demonstration of reassurance to the electorate that Hawke was going to be "fair but tough on the unions".'[70] Beazley's view prevailed, and eventually the pilots did indeed back down. A possible reason is that the pilots actually liked him. A long article in the *Financial Review* entitled, 'Kim Beazley Soars In A Tough Ministry', noted that the 'relations between the Federal Government's youngest minister Kim Beazley and Australian pilots are an example of the Hawke School of Consensus at its best,' and also quoted an unnamed representative of the Australian International Pilots Association as saying that Kim Jnr was 'perhaps the finest Minister for Aviation this country has ever had'.[71] Such an estimation was all the more impressive when compared with the pilots' estimations of Beazley's immediate Labor predecessor in the post, Charles Jones, who not only was known by them as the 'Minister *Against* Civil Aviation', but was also said by them to be 'crazy'.[72] Jones had returned the favour in kind, describing the pilots as being 'arrogant, selfish, contemptible people who have resorted to industrial thuggery'.

Such confrontational language in public, or private, has rarely been Beazley's way. In Parliament, however, he gave Ian Sinclair quite a heated time whenever the National Party member and Shadow Minister for Defence started ripping into Gordon Scholes for the way he had run the Ministry for Defence. In private, on the other hand, Sinclair and Beazley got on very well. 'He is a charming bloke,' Beazley says of the Tamworth man. 'A lot of the most intelligent of the National Party people you find are very like Labor politicians — they tend not to have the narrow free enterprise philosophy of the Liberal Party; they tend to be a bit more flexible in their view about protecting people's economic position and they also deal with the poorest part of Australia, which, no question about it, is the bush.' Things could still get quite heated between them, most particularly when Sinclair was going for Scholes' throat. One such occasion was in Parliament on the afternoon of Friday, 30 March 1984. Sinclair, a very effective boots'n'knuckles'n'all debater, was in full cry against Scholes, asserting in a censure motion that in the 12 months since the Victorian had taken over the portfolio, there had been an abject failure to address the deterioration in Australia's defences, resulting in serious problems such as morale, training and equipment. '[Scholes] is a nice fellow,' the National Party Member for New England acknowledged, while still adjusting his aim, 'but an *abysmal* Minister for Defence'. Sinclair proceeded to describe in detail the exact contours of the mess over which he claimed Scholes presided, to which the Defence Minister made reply, without appearing to undo much of the damage. He was followed by Kim Beazley — firing back that *all* of the problems in Defence could be traced directly to the general ineptitude of the previous Government and Ian Sinclair's own stewardship — and this was particularly well received by those on the Government benches.

'During the censure debate yesterday,' Amanda Buckley reported in the *Sydney Morning Herald*, 'Gordon Scholes gave perhaps the shakiest performance by a Hawke minister — in or out of the House. Unfortunately for Mr Scholes his speech was closely followed by a strong display from Mr Kim Beazley, who, in defending Mr Scholes, managed to provide a firm answer to those wondering about a replacement defence minister.' Later in the article she opined, 'The Government would be wise to restrict the use of Mr Scholes in debate. He has never managed to learn the elementary art of buttering up his opponents, even after 16 years in Federal Parliament. The Prime Minister, sitting behind Mr Scholes, barely managed to keep an even expression and looked immensely relieved when it was over. When Mr Beazley's turn came, a look of delight passed over the glum faces on the Government front bench and people started to file back into the House to see some action. By the time he had identified the Opposition, in Calwellian terms, as a "jibbering array of pathological exhibits", they knew they were back in government again.'

If Beazley sometimes felt frustrated at the way Scholes was handling things, he was careful not to push the minister too far. On one occasion when Scholes was keen that the Navy buy the SeaHawk helicopter, and Beazley was equally certain that a far more intelligent buy was the Lynx — which was cheaper, and in his opinion did almost as much — it was the younger man who backed off. Beazley and Hawke discussed it and decided that 'Scholes would be a terminally wounded minister', if he got rolled in Caucus on the purchase. 'So,' as Beazley tells it, 'I changed my view on it and helped him through with SeaHawk, and it ultimately got up.' (In fairness to Scholes, Beazley, 15 years later, would acknowledge: 'I think now on reflection that Gordon was right and I was wrong. The SeaHawk was a very good helicopter, and the right choice.')

For the rest he busied himself in his role as Minister Assisting the Minister for Defence, by regularly reading all the reports that came in from Defence sections around Australia, visiting a lot of Defence establishments when he could and keeping as up to date in the field as it was possible to be while also fulfilling his other commitments. At least one of Australia's defence forces knew he was there, and was most happy to have him in the post. Up at the Royal Australian Air Force's F1–11 base in Amberley just outside Brisbane, Flight Lieutenant Greg Buchanan took pride in the ascension of his childhood friend to the post of Minister Assisting the Minister for Defence. 'I used to say in the

Air Crew Room, "*I* know the man at the top," and it was always "shut up Buchanan, no you don't". None of them *ever* believed me.' Buchanan's solution was at hand when his flying partner, Flight Lieutenant John Parker, was asked to go to Canberra to demonstrate the F1–11 to the Assisting Minister. Before he left, Buchanan asked Parker to give the politician a 'big "hello" from his old friend Greg Buchanan'. Flight Lieutenant Parker obliged, somewhere in the skies above Canberra, and asked if the Minister did in fact know him. His passenger not only confirmed that he knew him, but asked him to give Greg a big 'cheerio' in return! Back at base, Buchanan started walking tall. 'I dined out for months afterwards on that,' he remembers with a laugh.

It was a fairly typical contact between Kim Beazley and his old friends from Claremont days. Only rarely did he see them, but sometimes through third parties he would vaguely get some kind of news about what they were up to. It was not an intended distance, so much as just the way it turned out after he had lost touch while in India, then at university, then in politics — and the distance was not just from his side. Twice in the mid-1980s, another childhood friend, Chris Smith, saw Kim on the other side of a Perth street, and would not walk the 20 metres it would have taken to catch up with him. 'I didn't think he'd want to talk to me, now,' Smith recalls, 'now he was a hot-shot.' Then there was Col Wilson. Somewhere in early 1983, for no reason Kim could think of, the vision of Wilson kept popping into his head, 'and I kept thinking I should get in touch with him, find out how he was going, what he was up to'.

One thing led to another, which led to another trip to another meeting and another ministerial manoeuvre, and he just didn't get round to it. 'Then finally I got news of him,' Beazley remembers. 'Someone told me that he was dead, that he had suicided six months before, around the time that I was thinking of him.' No-one ever established why Colin Wilson had taken his car out into the bush, connected a hose to the exhaust pipe and killed himself, but it left Beazley with a slightly haunted feeling for a long time afterwards, 'like maybe he needed me, and I just wasn't there for him. I felt I'd let him down badly'.

Other friends, particularly from university days, remained reasonably close, and he saw them when he could. Robert French was one, and he remembers noting how well his old friend seemed to be coping with the pressures. 'He was much the same as he had been at university, in that he never seemed, externally, overwhelmed by the pressures,' he explains. 'I think that is because he had the capacity to stand back and take a bit of an overview and also to accept the possibility of, this may all come to an end, I may lose the next election etc.' Tim Blue, for his part, also noticed a slight change, 'Kim was always an intellect of great generosity and all-encompassing to all sorts of points of view. You'd never imagine he was a schemer but once in the early '80s he said to me: 'I'm a politician and I think I am a very good one,' and I remember being taken aback at that because I didn't somehow believe that my intellectually curious and generous friend could be so expedient as to be a numbers-cruncher. With that once simple and noble desire to just do good, he'd now added a cynical but absolutely paramount key skill, of *how to count the numbers and do the deals* so as to get done what you wanted done. I didn't think he'd be like that.'

Brian Burke, who had become the Premier of Western Australia just a fortnight before the Hawke Government was formed, was another from the old days with whom Beazley remained intimate. Burke was doing well, extremely well it seemed, and was very popular. He was pursuing quite a radical idea whereby his Government would work in such close partnership with business, that in some ways they'd almost be *running* the Government like a business — meaning all West Australians would effectively be able to reap the benefits of the profits — and the early signs were that it was working well. As Blue recalls it, 'Beazley was always amusedly outraged by some of Burke's antics like in soliciting funds to pursue a corporatist government style of ideology,' but there was never a barrier between them on that count. That was just the way Burke did things.

Mostly, though, his closest relationships remained with his fellow Members of Parliament. He continued to see a lot of Michael Duffy, was near to inseparable from Mick Young, saw Hawke within the constraints on the Prime Minister's time, and was tight with Paul Keating and his wife Annita. Graham Richardson remembers one sign in particular of Beazley's closeness to the Keatings, 'In those times Beazley would receive a lot of invitations addressed to Mr and Mrs Beazley and because he grew tired of attending functions by himself — with Mary always 4000 kilometres away in Perth — Annita Keating would often accompany him when Paul was busy. Now no-one raised an eyebrow over that, which says a lot about the Keatings' relationship with the Beazleys at the time and about Paul's relationship with Kim. I can think of any number of people about whom it would not even be contemplated.'

In mid-October of 1984, when Beazley happened to be in Hawke's office, the Prime Minister confirmed that he was going to call another election for December 1, well under two years since the last one. 'It was sort of the prevailing theory at the time,' Beazley explains, 'that you should follow up one election win soon afterwards, so as to consolidate that first victory.' Going into every election, all established politicians look back on what they have achieved in the previous term. It is partly science, as it can give some guide to how they will fare at the ballot box, and partly nature — the polls providing a natural punctuation point for reflective pause.

As the December 1984 election approached, Beazley could take some satisfaction. He had acquitted himself well, being lauded for the way he filled in for Mick Young, he had given Gordon Scholes as much support as he could as Minister Assisting the Minister for Defence; and he felt that he had at least kept his end up as Minister for Aviation. He had not only secured the crucial capital that Qantas and TAA needed to keep going, but also had since that time freed them from some of the financial legislative shackles which had constrained them by, in effect, 'corporatising' them.

He could also point to the fact that with the aid of his Department he had transformed the infrastructure of Australian aviation from something that was regarded as simply a part of the public service — with millions of dollars spent every year to maintain it — to something closer to a self-sustaining part of the national economy. Despite Walsh's fears about letting Beazley have his financial way with the airlines, the new minister had helped to lessen the drain on the public purse that aviation had traditionally been. At the time Beazley had taken over the portfolio, the taxpayer subsidised 30 per cent of the cost of running aviation's infrastructure, though within the space of 18 months this figure had been reduced to almost nothing. One of his ways of doing this had been by introducing a 'Cost Recovery Policy Review', a study entirely independent of the Public Service, which had determined who should pay what costs associated with providing and maintaining the runways, control towers, firetrucks and so on. With minor adjustments, the guidelines had been not only accepted well but implemented by the industry. Beazley ensured that the airports started to control their own revenue stream — instead of the Government collecting it and doling it back out — and to manage their own affairs. It was a move which would soon see the establishment of the Federal Airports Corporation — which owned and managed the airports — eventually enabling the Government to sell them off.

He had received many plaudits for such moves. One *Sydney Morning Herald* editorial that pleased him so much that he filed it away in his diary for safekeeping, for everafter, was headed 'Praiseworthy Initiative', and noted that Mr Beazley's efforts were 'a matter of congratulation'. 'The new rules allow Qantas the sort of flexibility modern management needs, especially in a field as complex and competitive as international aviation,' the editorial ran. 'Its performance in the past financial year returns it to the heady days of the late 1960s and the early part of the 1970s, when it returned a handsome profit to its shareholders. It can take new heart from the confidence now being shown in it by the government.' The editorial finished by noting that Mr Beazley had done so well on these things, it gave rise to hope that he might also, at last, be able to sort out the problem of giving Sydney a second airport. Unfortunately the most notable black mark, of Beazley's time in Aviation was the failure to find a definitive solution to that very problem, as he had promised he would do in his first days on the job. That particular airport, some 15 years later, remains as unbuilt as ever — with not even the first sod turned on a decided site. 'I thought then that we could get it done very quickly,' he says now. 'And I actually think I got a solution to it, in Badgery's Creek then, but you know we didn't do it fast enough ... There wasn't enough time to get through what we wanted to do before the election came on.'

And sure enough, the election did come on ...

CHAPTER ELEVEN

ON TARGET

'I was conscious of a profound source of relief. I felt as if I was
walking with destiny, and that all my past life had been but a
preparation for this hour and this trial.'
*Winston Churchill, upon assuming the British Prime Ministership
during World War II.*

A t last it happened. The phone call came. The question was
asked again. Would he come around to the Prime Minister's
office? Would he what. This just might be *the* call he'd been
waiting for since, a few days previously, the seat of Swan had been
held by 'K. Beazley' for the third time in succession. The Hawke
Government had also won, albeit with a substantially reduced
majority. As a matter of fact this might be the phone call he'd been
waiting for since the late 1960s, when a particular ambition had first
been formed ...

'Kim,' Bob Hawke started out, knowing full well the effect it would
have on his close friend and quasi-protégé, 'we've decided we want
you to be the Minister for Defence.' Praise the Lord, and pass the
ammunition. 'I was absolutely *elated* at the news,' Beazley recalls,
'and staggered that only eight years after leaving the life at Oxford, I
would now actually be involved in doing what I had previously been
studying about.' If such comments indicate some surprise on Beazley's
part, Hawke for one is quite clear that he should not have been too
startled. In fact, making Beazley the Defence Minister at this time had
always been part of Hawke's plan from the moment he had formed his
Government the previous year. Hawke explains, 'I don't intend any
disrespect to Gordon Scholes, and he knows this, but when I acquired

the leadership in 1983, I didn't want to unnecessarily rock the boat . . .
and it just seemed to me intelligent to keep as far as possible, people in
their same positions where they had been doing good work as Shadow
Ministers. Now Gordon Scholes didn't begin to have the intellectual
capacity or the academic ways or experience of Kim and we all
acknowledged that, so what I had in mind was that I would make
Scholes Minister for Defence with the full intention that it would be a
one-term go for Gordon. I thought it was in everyone's best interests
including Kim's, that he started getting the experience immediately as
Minister Assisting and he was in an interesting and relevant portfolio
and so it worked out in 1984 . . . '

The other reason Beazley should not have been too surprised is
that over the previous 18 months, he had informally and gently
lobbied Hawke for the position. 'But Bob had always said to me,'
Beazley remembers, "look we could have made you Defence first time
round but it wouldn't have been right; Gordon had done the job in
Opposition".' Scholes, for his part, had been clearly demoted from
the powerful position of Defence, to the Minister for Territories, and
was not even in the Cabinet, but that was just the way it was. There
was to be no commiseratory phone call from his former understudy
in the portfolio. 'I didn't call him,' Beazley admits, 'It wouldn't have
been appropriate.'

Beazley was sworn in by the Governor-General on the 13th
December 1984 — a day shy of his 36th birthday, the youngest
Defence Minister in Australia's history — and intended to hit the
ground running, as there were so many things that he was keen to get
under way. Instead, something else entirely hit him before he could
really get started. There always comes a moment when a new Minister
takes over his portfolio when, after the handshakes and the hoopla,
the door to his office is shut, and 'The Briefing' begins. If the incoming
Minister is a strong one, then, for the mandarins, it is often the
moment when the former Shadow becomes the sun around which
their work life will henceforth revolve. If strength is lacking, it is the
moment when they first fit the Minister with a nose ring with which
they can lead him around the political bullpit.

This first briefing had gone quite well for Beazley, he thought, with
the distinguished Department head, Sir William Cole, providing a broad
overview of the Defence Department and its current position on a
variety of matters. But subsequent, more specific, briefings from sections
of the Defence Department went less well, and this particular evening

was one of them. Both of the men before him — Alan Thompson and Ross Thomas — seemed rather nervous, as if they had something delicate to impart, which they would really rather not.

'Minister we think there is something you should know ...'

'Yes ...?' said Beazley inquiringly, looking up from his desk. It was the Americans, they said. And this new MX intercontinental missile they had been developing. And how in the time of Malcolm Fraser a secret agreement had been reached whereby the Americans would be able to monitor the splashdown of test missiles in the waters off Australia, using Australian facilities such as airfields to fly out some of their planes.

Beazley was gob-smacked. There had been scattered media reports just before the election about this kind of testing, which were just as quickly denied, and caught up as he was in his own campaigning, Beazley had left it at that. Now, he couldn't. 'How could you people have *signed up* for this?' he remembers asking with no little exasperation. 'You *must* know that the Americans don't need to do this test — by just changing the azimuth they can get all the information they need on the accuracy of these rockets — testing them in their own territories. This is obviously just an American all-flags effort and it's one we could have ducked. How could you be *snowed* by them?' Beazley was further disbelieving that something like this could be happening, while he had not heard a word about it, even though he had been the Minister Assisting the Minister for Defence for the previous 18 months.

Yes, well, they said. The project was a particular commitment of the previous Secretary of Defence, in the time of Malcolm Fraser, and though it had not actually gone to the full Cabinet Security Committee, the decision to persist had been approved by Gordon Scholes, Bob Hawke and Foreign Minister Hayden in November of 1983, as they had not wanted to offend the Americans by reversing something that Fraser had agreed to. 'And I said,' Beazley recalls, 'that "it still shouldn't be too hard to refuse it, I think we should do so".' No, replied the Defence men. It was too late. The Americans were already far advanced in their plans and had already laid highly sophisticated sensors on the ocean floor to monitor the accuracy of the missiles.

'When are they going to fire the bloody thing?'

'We don't know, but sometime in the next two years.'

'You mean to say we've got to put up with this crap for *two years*?'

Beazley had had enough. He headed off to see Bob Hawke. The whole thing, he reflected on the way, had all the ingredients of a Defence Minister's worst nightmare. First and foremost it was a political problem within his own party, and from there to the wider electorate. When the Left of his party got hold of this bit of news, he knew they would go stark raving berserk, as would a good portion of the media and the public. Bob was in. Others in Cabinet might sometimes have to wait hours to see Hawke, but Beazley never. Within minutes the two were alone in the prime ministerial office. After the preliminaries, the new Defence Minister got to the point. 'I said to Bob,' Beazley recalls, 'are you aware of the *logic* of all this? This is a "King Hell" weapon this one, and this is not a good one for us to be involved with.' Hawke seemed little concerned. He noted that in the initial plan, the MX missiles would be flying over the Australian mainland and land in the sea to the south of Tasmania, but that he had insisted they land further out to sea, well into international waters and the Americans had in fact agreed to this. Beazley felt a surge of relief. 'That might mean,' Beazley surmised, 'that Australia doesn't have to facilitate the tests in any way at all.' Hawke agreed that might very well be the case, and Beazley returned to his office a little uplifted.

But it wouldn't be solved that easily. The Department informed him that to monitor the tests, the Americans already had a P3 Orion aircraft tooled up to calibrate the information that came in from the electronics in the warheads as they flew by, and the only place that aircraft could operate from really was Australia. As Beazley saw it, there was nothing further he could do. They would simply have to batten down the hatches and wait for the whole thing to first blow up, and maybe then blow over.

In the meantime, there was plenty to get on with. In the first instance he settled into his comparatively luxurious new suite, next to the Treasurer's office on the ground floor of Parliament House. He decorated it in much the same fashion as his last office, with letters and drawings from Jessica and Hannah pasted up on some double cupboard doors, plus this time a bewildering and growing array of military models, aeroplanes, ships, tanks, submarines, a large model of the newfangled space shuttle — the whole catastrophe. To one side of his desk sat a grey phone with a red button on it. It was the 'secure communications' over which the most difficult and urgent defence problems could be discussed, up to and including if Australia ever came under sudden attack.

Beazley set to, if not with the enthusiasm of a kid in a toy shop, then at least with the impatient joy of a skilled chess player who has for too long been forced to watch a fairly ordinary game being played, and now, at last, has the chance to guide one side of the board's fortunes himself. And certainly there was much to do, to organise over 100 000 soldiers, sailors, airmen, plus some 50 000 civilians under his control. The Defence Department controlled the largest organisation in Australia, both in terms of employees and annual budget — around 5.5 billion dollars at the time — yet for all that it was not considered well structured or efficiently run.

A little under a decade previously, Jim Killen — not long before he became Australia's Defence Minister in the Fraser Government — had told BBC listeners that Australia's defence forces combined 'would be unable to protect Botany Bay against an enemy on a hot Sunday afternoon ...'[73] Beazley considered that this was a ridiculous overstatement, but there was no doubt that Australia *was* vulnerable. Other Defence Ministers might have taken it for granted that there were no credible threats to Australia's security, Beazley most certainly did not. 'If you're a Defence Minister and historian,' he says, 'you know that there is a distinct possibility that your country can't survive. Generally speaking, the record of civilisations is that they collapse. At the end of the day the centre doesn't hold, so you become enormously conscious of the issues of survival. I guess part of the psychological buzz of being Defence Minister is that you find yourself satisfied only when you have some notion that you are actually able to affect the direction the country is going in some way.'

To those who would claim that this sense that the nation's very existence might be in peril was a tad on the melodramatic side, Beazley also had a clear answer: 'I suppose a farmer of Galilee in 15 AD probably thought the same, but if he was unlucky enough in his dotage to be in Jerusalem in about 63 AD you would have found a different answer. And if you were a late nineteenth-century Briton your sense of personal security would lie in the idea that Britain's empire would continue forever and that the sun would never set on it. But within that person's lifetime, to see what happened to that Empire would have been unthinkable. So you have got to look at these things within our own framework — it is not a given thing, and I never took Australia's survival as a given thing.' Herein lay the very heart of the approach that Beazley would take to all his portfolios over the years, the guiding principle underpinning most of his key decisions. And like Kim Snr's trip to Caux in 1953, because it is so close to the very centre of the man's following actions, through all portfolios, it is as well to dwell on it. Kim Jnr explains, 'All the time, from the day I went into politics or earlier than that, I've always thought that you've got to look at the logic of history, and that it is not kind to nations like Australia, occupying large areas with small populations, culturally different from the regions around them. I've always thought survival for Australia is going to be a close-run thing. I think we're quite capable of it, but we have to always properly situate ourselves internationally so as to do it. We cannot be totally self-absorbed, we do not have that luxury. But as a historian, I knew there is nothing inevitable in anything and there are *choices*. Even if some circumstances, economic or otherwise, drive you in particular directions, you will never be short of choices. The thing for me was to try and help the Government make the right choices for Australia.'

This notion of 'for Australia,' was one he would warm to, most particularly during his early days in the Defence ministry, telling friends that he felt that he was 'employed by Australia'. It wasn't quite 'playing for Australia,' as he had once casually dreamed of doing in his youth back in Claremont, but it was not half bad. As his friend and political travelling companion over the years Dr Geoff Gallop notes, 'Kim's paradigm — the model in his head that he works from — is international affairs, and Australia's place within that. An absolutely clear theme that comes through is that he is a great Australian nationalist in the sense that whatever portfolio he has he strives towards protecting the *national* interest, making the country stronger within that international climate'.

One of his long-term former staffers, Patrick Walters, agrees with this analysis: 'essentially what comes through for Kim when he studies the history of Australia, particularly from the end of World War I through to the 1960s is our strategic vulnerability. What he's always trying to solve in his own mind is "how do we address these weaknesses ourselves, how do we turn what we have in Australia to our advantage *strategically* because obviously we do have tremendous physical and intellectual assets".' Beazley saw it much the same way, 'There isn't anything that I have ever done in my life that I have thought more about than those issues,' he says now, 'and at the time I thought that I needed to pursue those things religiously because they were things that would mean that we would survive as a nation.'

Despite the gravity with which Beazley viewed his role as Defence Minister, there was no doubt how much he loved being in Canberra. 'For Kim, it was wonderful,' is the way his sister Merrilyn Wasson, with whom he was still living while in Canberra, describes it. 'It was everything he had ever dreamed of, every happiness. It was like living with sunshine, just joy — the joy of seeing a human being so completely fulfilled. Defence brought together a whole range of things for him. He loved toys, he loved history, loves that notion of strategy and he is Australian through and through. So when you put all of that into one bag it was a totally intoxicating mix for him.' Which again, is the way Beazley himself saw it. 'If I was going to isolate the best days in politics for me,' he says, 'I'd start with when I was first elected and the wonderful feeling of going to bed that night in the knowledge that I had won the seat of Swan, and the next great moment was waking up, knowing that I was Defence Minister, responsible for the security of the country.'

There was no secret whatsoever about which direction the new Defence Minister wanted to steer Australia's defence. Following the broad outlines that he had already enunciated in his maiden speech in 1980, and had then pushed in Parliament through more than 80 speeches on the subject since, he wanted to entirely reorganise Australia's defensive structure. His plan was for Australia to push towards a policy of self-reliance first and foremost, and to move away from the concept of 'forward defence' — the ability to project the nation's forces a great distance from our shores, to the aid of powerful allies who would hopefully do the same for Australia should the occasion arise. (As it had most famously done in prolonged military actions at Gallipoli, El Alamein and Vietnam.)

This notion of putting the defence of the Australian continent itself in the first rank of defensive priorities, had been strongly burning within Beazley since his days at Oxford. It was then he had realised just how vulnerable Australia was to international forces beyond its control. This recognition followed in the wake of Nixon's Guam doctrine of 1969 — whereby US allies were warned they would likely have to defend themselves *themselves* — and Prime Minister Harold Wilson's similar assertion in 1967 that Britain was going to substantially withdraw its own military forces 'east of Suez'.

'When you realised that,' he says, 'you realised there was actually no-one to be "forward" with any more! I think this was appreciated at an intellectual level in Australia from the mid-1970s onwards, but it was yet to hit at a real visceral level, to actually have an effect on the way things were organised.' Beazley was equally clear, in broad outline, how he wanted this change in strategic thinking to manifest itself, and in some ways that too could be traced back to his days in the backyard air-raid shelter at home in Claremont, pretending enemy planes were coming in to attack. 'I'm Western Australian born and bred so I have all the WA prejudices about defence,' he was quoted as saying in the *West Australian* shortly after taking over the portfolio.

The 'WA prejudices', were essentially that for those living in that part of Australia, it often seemed ludicrous, if not criminally negligent, for Australia to have the vast majority of its defence forces based in the southeastern corner of the country. This, when just a glance at a map, any map, showed that a serious attack on the Australian mainland was never going to come from those directions, short of the Tasmanians turning Bolshie or angry invading New Zealanders swapping rugby boots for rifles. Physically, then, Beazley wanted Army, Navy and Air Force facilities moved from the southeast to the northwest, and he also wanted a change in Australia's relations with countries around it. 'We are a country capable of pursuing a generally independent foreign policy,' he told Perth's *Daily News*. 'Australian nationalism has the capacity to express itself in both cultural and political terms and ought to be given that opportunity.'[74]

In terms of Australia's defence alliances, to Beazley's eyes, it was time for Australia to hasten a process already begun, but stalled somewhat, and move the country into a historic third phase. In the first phase Australia had looked to Britain for protection pure and simple, and in turn had provided soldiers to help in what had been essentially Britain's wars. In the second phase, in the famed words of then Prime Minister John Curtin, halfway through World War II, 'without any inhibitions of any kind, I make it quite clear that Australia looks to America, free of any pangs as to our traditional links and kinship with the United Kingdom'.[75] Not only had Curtin never accepted that Australia's security was guaranteed in World War II by Britain's garrison and navy base in Singapore, when Australia seemed endangered in 1942, he insisted — despite persistent resistance and intimidating pressure from Winston Churchill — that Australia's soldiers had to be brought straight home. And in the third phase, what Beazley wanted was to continue Australia's alliance with America so clearly enunciated by John Curtin, but in his own words, 'to have self-reliance within that alliance'.

Australia's history in regard to its alliance with America had not been particularly edifying since WWII. It had been summed up by the then head of the External Affairs Department in the early 1950s, Sir Alan Watt, when he wrote in 1967, 'Many nations must depend on others for their ultimate security but in most cases they try to maximise their own independence within a relationship of dependency. Australia has seemed intent on doing the very opposite: of maximising its dependence, first on Britain and lately on the US.'

'Absolutely true,' says Beazley. 'And absolutely wrong-headed. Australia had developed such a sense of dependency that it could not feel confident about its own capacity to defend itself in a way that gave independence to its foreign policy. And I thought, while you should struggle hard to maintain your alliances, and to be prepared, from time to time, to make sacrifices in your opinions to those alliances, at the end of the day the people that you can most rely upon happen to be yourselves.

'And if you do not have that sense of self-reliance then you don't have that integrity as a nation and maybe you don't have survivability as well. And therefore I've always regarded the Defence portfolio as central to Australian national survival for all seasons. Seasons with allies, seasons without allies. We needed to develop the resilience and toughness that comes with self-reliance both in terms of defence and also economically, otherwise you couldn't bet on the future of the nation.'

As always though, it was one thing for Beazley to have a clear idea of which way he wanted to guide the Department of Defence, and quite another to get it there. The Defence portfolio, it was said, was one which 'historically chewed up Ministerial reputations as tank tracks churn through mud'.[76] Few ministries[77] ever responded like a sleek racehorse to the guidance of a new jockey. Often they were bastard donkeys which simply refused to move one way or another. Upon Kim Beazley's arrival, Defence had more resembled a camel, which moved a little but only rarely in the direction desired, and even then, never with anything approaching grace. 'The first thing that struck me when I looked at the Defence Department,' he recalls, 'was how extraordinarily inefficient the decision-making process was. Basically it was structured to ensure that the military did not come to the conclusion that civilians were running them. Everything was done so that every decision was intensely bound up in committees made up of military people and their civilian counterparts.' In Beazley's eyes, it was these committees and their invariably 'lowest common denominator' recommendations that slowed everything up interminably. It seemed to him that to bring the camel to heel, he needed more information on what was going on inside the committees. 'Then,' Beazley says, 'it struck me like a silver bullet.' That was the realisation that the committee system was actually the best possible arrangement a minister could have, because all the minister need do was to call for the committee minutes to see what was the *real* argument in the Department. 'So I could say, "well it seems like a pretty good argument against this particular proposition which has appeared on this piece of paper — as though the proposition is unarguable — but I happen to know that ..."' He happened to know that there was an equally good argument against the proposal, and as a matter of fact he, as the minister in charge, thought the alternative argument was the correct one.

If this insight, in the long term, helped him greatly in mastering his portfolio, in the short term it was still not enough to get the camel to move in the direction he wanted. What he wanted was to develop a coherent model for Australia's defence, to which the entire Defence organisation could make reference in order to guide them in their choices on the myriad matters that came before them. The way Beazley saw it, an example of the Defence Department's lack of a coherent structure could be seen in the way they went about buying new equipment. 'It was still an old-fashioned service wish list,' he explains, 'dominated by the so-called "replacement syndrome" where because you had something that had worn out, you would simply pick something of the same nature 20 years on. What I wanted by getting this model together was to get self-reliance embedded into the philosophy of the defence forces.' The solutions to the problems of the beast, he decided, could not emerge from the beast itself. 'When I got there,' he recalls, 'the civilian/military monitoring of each other had reached the point of atrophy, everything was stalemated and ...'

And he would have to get back to it, for suddenly the situation that he had been dreading actually happened — the 'MX Missile Crisis,' as it soon became known, broke upon the Hawke Government. The blow-up was a big one. Brian Toohey, reporting from Washington, broke the story in the *National Times*, on Sunday, 1 February 1985. 'Sydney Role In U.S. Missile Tests' ran the headline, with details of the testing and who had agreed to what, and when. Among many other things, Toohey noted that while the MX came with the absurd official name of the MX Peacemaker, the real thing could deliver 20 times the explosive force that had destroyed Hiroshima, with extraordinary accuracy. Following the Toohey story came an article by Geoff Kitney looking at the political fallout and, to many, the headline seemed likely to prove prescient from the first: 'Why Bob Hawke Will Have To Say No'. The reason, Kitney posited, was simple:

> *A decision in favour of the US request would almost certainly shatter the credibility of the Federal Government's disarmament policies, already under challenge from within the ALP. Senior members of the Federal Government recognise that any Australian connection with the MX missile tests would provoke a furore within the party with the potential to seriously damage it.*

By the following day it was clear that every major newsroom in the country had decided that the MX Missile Crisis was a big story. It was on almost every front page in the country, and led all the electronic media bulletins. The whole issue, after all, was to be fought in a political environment where, in the elections just gone, the Nuclear Disarmament Party — whose sole platform was contained in their name — had come within 6000 votes of securing a Senate seat for the NSW frontman, Midnight Oil singer, Peter Garrett. And now the Hawke Government was lining up four-square behind American nuclear missiles? Roll the presses!

With the story now out, there was enormous pressure from within the Labor Party — most particularly from the Left and Centre Left — to dump the MX tests immediately, and rescind the agreement with the Americans. Beazley would not hear of it, and said as much at a press conference held the following day in Canberra. Against a hostile gallery of journalists, he held the line that it was the right thing for the Government to continue. 'I took the view,' he remembers of that time, 'that now the matter had became public, we'd collapse confidence in the American alliance if we didn't proceed with it. Once it was public then it had to be defended and I was defending.' Which was as well, because there were plenty of others who were attacking. On the first page of the academic thesis he had completed just over a decade previously, *Australian Labor Party Attitudes to the American Alliance*, he had written some rather portentous words:

Throughout the 1960s Australia's foreign and defence policies were a major source of dispute between Australia's predominant political parties. Central to the dispute were differing perceptions of Australia's relations with the United States of America. Of particular concern were the costs and benefits to the Australia/American alliance. Within the ALP the resolution of Party policy on matters related to the American alliance was a major source of factional and ideological strife ....

The last sentence had particular resonances for this occasion.

The ALP Left wing held a Sydney news conference addressed by the leading anti-nuclear activist of her day, Dr Helen Caldicott, where she called the agreement to cooperate with the MX testing 'a suicide pact'. Both the Left and Centre Left factions, particularly, became progressively more restless on the subject, even to the point of releasing independent statements where they publicly warned Hawke against continuing to support the MX testing. Victorian Premier John Cain said senior Federal Ministers had no moral authority to make the MX decision without consulting the rest of the Labor Party, while noting that his own Government would do everything possible to discourage Australian participation in the testing. The NSW ALP, while reaffirming support for the defence relationship with the US, announced a mass meeting of rank-and-file members in NSW to discuss the MX missile issue and other disarmament matters.[78] There was a very real possibility that a special National Conference of the Labor Party would be called to roll the Hawke Government's support for the MX testing.

In a way, it was just like a return to the old days of the Labor Party. Although a lot of heat had gone out of such issues since the terrible days of the 1950s and '60s, Foreign Affairs and Defence matters still constituted two of the key friction points enduring in the Labor Party factions. At this time, with Ronald Reagan in the White House having overseen the largest increase in military spending in American history in order to stop the '*evil empire,*' the Cold War had reached its zenith, and the USA and Russia were staring each other down in regions all over the world from Africa to Central America to Afghanistan. The Soviets had a real fear that the Americans would launch a *first strike* against them. While it would be unwise to assume that Mssrs Gorbachev and Reagan ever paused a single moment to consider how their actions would be viewed by the factions of the Australian Labor

Party, the reverse could never be said. Within the Labor Party, a lot of time indeed was spent analysing the actions of those gentlemen, and more importantly, working out what the Australian Government should do to help or hinder them. It was a serious business, vigorously pursued. In the immortal words of NSW ALP organiser John Della Bosca, 'in the realms of the ALP, the Cold War was fought by proxy by the factions'. Either way, as Beazley noted, 'the party was most uptight about it. Helping with the MX testing was not what they saw as a thing that should be done.'

In the midst of the vicious squabble, the question was put many times. Was it *still* too late to tell the Americans that the Australian Government had changed its mind and did not want the tests to proceed after all? After consultation with the Americans, Beazley determined that the short answer was 'yes, too late'. The Americans had gone to enormous effort to get to this point, making it unlikely that they could be easily persuaded to pull out of the agreement because of the embarrassment it was causing the Australian Government. Nor did they want to establish a precedent whereby foreign governments could simply walk away from military agreements. At that time in Europe the Americans were conducting particularly delicate negotiations with some NATO allies on the deployment of cruise missiles and Washington was not at all keen to give those allies even a whiff that it was *possible* to renege.

Beazley thus remained in the camp that the Australian Government would simply have to tough it out, and honour its commitment to the Americans. 'I thought,' he recollects, 'well it's only these P3 planes coming through Australia — that's all we actually have to do. It was exceptionally unwise that we got ourselves into that position, but I basically remained of the view that Bob should continue to support the tests.' Some indication though of just how isolated the Prime Minister was on the whole subject, was that close to the only public person beyond his immediate circle to support him was the Queensland Premier Sir Joh Bjelke-Petersen, who said if Hawke backed down then Queensland would fill the breach. 'We believe that it is our right and responsibility to offer our facilities to the Americans,' Sir Joh said.[79]

Bjelke-Petersen support aside, the other forces coming to bear on the Prime Minister were considerable. The key NSW Right powerbroker Graham Richardson himself was working on Hawke — who by this time was on a whirlwind world tour which would culminate with his arrival in Washington — to change his mind about continuing to support the Americans testing their missiles. As Richardson remembers the conversation, at one point when Hawke was in Brussels and he was in Japan, the Prime Minister said to him over the phone, 'Well mate, I could take Caucus on'.

'Yes,' Richardson says he replied, 'I reckon that's very courageous.'

'What do you mean?'

'Well, you are risking your Prime Ministership on it, and if that's what you want to do, well go for your life.'

'What do you mean, *what do you mean!?!*'

'Well if you get done, and if you stand up as the leader in support of the MX missile testing, and the Caucus roll you, you are fucked, that's it — it's all over Red Rover.'

'Oh you think so?'

'I think so.'

'...'

'Bob you have to go in and say to the Americans, "I am sorry boys I can't do it".'

Jessica and Hannah Beazley — now seven and five — were bouncing around in a two-room suite of Sydney's Regent Hotel. They were on one of their six-monthly trips to the east when they would stay for a couple of weeks — nearly always in Canberra — to be amused partly by their father's secretaries and partly by the Defence Minister himself. Usually on such trips their father would take them by the Prime Minister's office to see 'Mr Hawke', but this time they didn't because the PM was away 'on an important trip', they were told. On their own important trips to the national capital their father would move out of his digs at 'Auntie Bing's and Uncle Rob's' and stay at the Rex Hotel so that they would have room to spread out — and that is where they had been for the previous two nights, before going with their father on a quick overnight trip to Sydney because 'Daddy has to talk to some people'. Generally the girls loved such times with their father, and this particular night was even more fun than usual. After their father had returned late, relieved the hotel babysitter, and had at last got them to bed and nominally asleep, the phone rang and they could hear him talking quite tensely, 'Yes Bob,' 'Good Bob,' 'No Bob, I think it would be better if ...'

'I remember,' Hannah Beazley says, 'thinking Dad must be important because even though we hadn't really been listening we kept hearing something about "missiles" ... and that meant for me, war, and if Dad was talking about a war then he must be very important indeed.' So important was he, that every time the phone rang, their father would become so distracted that they could get away with sneaking back into his room and with suppressed giggles turning the television on, down low. Their father ignored it, mostly, unless they strayed onto the adult channel, when he would wave his arms violently, while continuing to speak to the Prime Minister, or one of his staff, or a Defence bureaucrat, or whoever else it was, until the girls got back to the cartoons or the movies. At last the phone call would finish, they would turn off the tube to bounce around on the bed with the man they called their 'big pillow' before he would at last get them down again ... and then the phone would ring, and they would do it all again. Finally, somewhere there in the night, there was a last phone call. Again it was the Prime Minister, again their father was speaking, but this time the tone had changed markedly. 'That's good, Bob,' 'That's terrific news, Bob,' 'I think that's far the best thing ...' Hawke had pulled it off. Against all expectations, the US Secretary of State, George Shultz, had agreed to do the MX testing in a fashion that would not involve Australia. And that was it. Lights out in the hotel suite, and no more phone calls in the time of the owls.

Later, Beazley was most laudatory of Hawke's role in the affair. 'He pulled off what, in the circumstances, can only be described as a miracle,' Beazley was quoted as saying. 'Without doing any substantial damage in relationship with the United States he got George Shultz against all the advice [he] was receiving to let us off the hook.'[80] The MX missile testing issue had been hosed down. The plaudits for Beazley's own role in the MX crisis were, oddly enough, warm. Though he personally had felt that the whole affair had been a debacle, and that his own role had been peripheral, the perception of the press was different.

'On balance it is skilful footwork for a young man after little more than two months in the job, manoeuvring through the ALP's Byzantine factions,' reported *The Bulletin*. 'But he needs to be good. The collapse of ANZUS is the biggest foreign and defence policy issue to face Australia since Vietnam.'[81]

ANZUS, the formal security relationship binding Australia, New Zealand and the US — not necessarily in that order — had indeed been under severe strain. Articles IV of the formal treaty commit each of the partners to meet armed attack on any of them, in accordance with the constitutional processes of each. The reason there was talk of the ANZUS treaty 'collapsing' was not just because of the fallout from the MX Missile Crisis, but more pertinently because on 14 July of 1984 when the David Lange Labour Government had come to power in New Zealand they had immediately begun the process of fulfilling one of their campaign promises. They moved towards making a unilateral declaration that US naval ships would no longer be welcome in New Zealand ports unless they were declared to be nuclear-free.* The US had taken an exceedingly dim view of this move by one of its military allies, and in order to 'punish' them had decided to deny them access to US intelligence on their region, which had previously been passed on to them daily as a matter of course by virtue of an ANZUS arrangement, whereby key intelligence was shared among the partners.

The Hawke Government too had been most disapproving of their ally's actions — notwithstanding that there was an enormous amount of sympathy and even admiration for it from the Labor Left — and one of Beazley's most urgent jobs in the aftermath of the MX crisis was to make a quick trip to New Zealand to try to get the defence relationship between Australia and New Zealand back on an even keel. 'What I was doing,' Beazley explains, 'was actively looking for ways to ensure that the cooperation between Australia and New Zealand was sufficiently deep to keep New Zealand in the defence race, so to speak. I was very worried that New Zealand would just drift off, that it would develop a fundamentally hostile position to the West or to Australia or whatever in the South Pacific. That would have been a disaster, because the New Zealanders have always been, ever since the Anzacs fought together at Gallipoli, an important part of our total defence posture. So what I was trying to do was to look at ways of collaboration and cooperation between us.'

Mission accomplished. While there Beazley unveiled his plan to pass onto the New Zealanders much of the results of Australia's own intelligence gathering — while still withholding anything of solely American origin — and also worked out with them ways to upgrade the defence relationship between the two countries, including an

---

* One who was not impressed with the Lange approach — oddly enough, given his prior stance on the issue — was the Foreign Minister, Bill Hayden. At one point, in Beazley's memory, he would note that David Lange reminded him of 'the cross-eyed javelin thrower at the Olympics, who, while he was not necessarily effective, certainly kept the crowd on its toes!'

increase in joint military exercises, and an expanded programme of joint weapon acquisitions. It was all done, in Beazley's words, to 'make sure that Australia can work with NZ to bolster joint political, economic and military activity in the South Pacific, to ensure that it does not become an area of instability or conflict'.

Back home in the Defence Department, Beazley had been continuing to try to find a way to break through the civilian/military 'Mexican standoff' that seemed to have become entrenched. 'So I decided to break the log jam,' he says, 'by finding someone who would be trusted by all sides, who was already cleared to the eyeballs for security reasons, to get in there and devise a document that would resolve the conflict by being able to exercise a single-minded judgement and not be bound down by the enormous process.'

Enter Paul Dibb, a former Defence Department analyst, and then academic at the Australian National University. Beazley had first got to know the ascetic academic, an Englishman by birth, during the days when they had been academics in much the same field of international relations, and they would come across each other at conferences, and realise that they were like-minded.

At the end of February, Beazley formally commissioned Dibb to objectively assess the structure of Australia's defence forces and report his recommendations of the way they *should* be structured, and where and how they should be placed both geographically and strategically, to best assure the security of Australia within a limited budget. This commissioning of Dibb was met with general approval by the media. *The Bulletin* noted at the time of his appointment that 'the advantage of using an independent consultant such as Dibb is that Beazley can walk away from the recommendations if they are seen to be politically unacceptable'.[82] That was always going to be unlikely, however, given that before he formally commissioned Dibb, the Defence Minister had an extremely good idea of the kind of report that Dibb would come up with, and judged that it would be *more* than politically acceptable. 'I found him ideologically and philosophically compatible,' Beazley recounts of his many meetings with Dibb before his official appointment. 'I also like his willingness to be *robust*, in judgements about wish lists.' Beazley wanted some hard decisions locked in, Dibb was judged to be the man for the job, and he set to work with a clear idea of what was required of him.

Around such events, Beazley remained busy on many other issues. In the aftermath of the MX crisis there had been an enormous resentment towards Australia's formal alliance with the Americans, and renewed attention focused on the most tangible signs of that alliance, which were the 'joint facilities'. Dotted in the wilderness at three points around Australia, these joint facilities were military monitoring establishments of nominally joint Australian/American complexion. The opposing view, put most stridently by the Left of the Labor Party and a good portion of the voting public, was that they were no such thing at all, but were rather wholly American ticks on the dogsbody of Australian sovereignty and they had no business whatsoever being there. Such views had been presented most stridently, and most obviously, at events such as the Palm Sunday demonstrations, which attracted some 600 000 people across the country in 1984, and which called for total nuclear disarmament and the removal of the joint facilities.

Beazley had never remotely agreed with this position, and was convinced that the joint facilities served a crucial role in ensuring the security of Australia. Not only that, he was determined not to follow the lead of previous Defence Ministers who drew as little attention as possible to the bases, for fear of making the natives restless. 'I thought we should talk about them all the time,' he explains. 'In terms of our security relationship with the United States they were a particularly tangible contribution that we were making, and so we should draw attention to them, and highlight that contribution.' Just what was that contribution? At first glance, it was not easy to see. 'Nothing was written down!' he says incredulously. 'Everything to do with Pine Gap and the rest was in the heads of the senior officers, but there was little documented. I had the impression that the previous governments preferred not to know ... '

Clearly what was needed was a solid body of information which not only he, but his successors and other officials, could consult when they needed to know more about these joint facilities.

'So I just said well ok what I would like to do is to get regular reports on what is happening with the joint facilities and the tasking arrangements associated with them. I didn't do that because I really needed them, all I needed was an officer to come over and say "this is happening", but what I wanted them to do was build up a record and at least if they had to write to me to brief us, there would be a regular record being created with the day-to-day affairs of the facilities.

When I stood up at the party conferences and said that "we have full knowledge, control and consent of these facilities", I needed to know in my own heart that I was actually in a position where I was telling the truth.' In the short term, there was only one way to find out. He was soon in one of the RAAF jets at his command touring the joint facilities. As the Australian Minister for Defence he essentially had access to all parts of the facilities, bar the women's toilets, and availed himself of this access to the full. So began one of Beazley's key contributions during his command of the Defence portfolio — the effective neutralising of the joint facilities as a political issue and the basic acceptance, though by no means universal, by the Australian public of their utility.

After ascertaining *exactly* what they did do, he started to inform the Australian public of just that. He ceased to talk about 'the joint facilities' generically as one amorphous mass and began to talk of them individually — Pine Gap near Alice Springs, Nurrungar in South Australia and the North West Cape in Western Australia — detailing as much as he could of what it was that they did without breaching classified security. 'I wanted to demystify them,' Beazley says, 'I wanted to openly point out their relevance to Australia's own defence; their relevance to what gave the global political system stability; their relevance to the capacity ultimately to disarm weapons of mass destruction'. As he put it broadly in a speech to the Australian Institute of International Affairs in July 1985, 'These joint facilities provide the United States with early warning facilities and with independent means of verifying Soviet compliance with arms control and disarmament arrangements. In so doing, they advance Australia's interests by contributing to the preservation of peace and the global power relationships upon which our freedom and way of life ultimately depend. At the same time, these facilities make a major contribution to America's security, without requiring of America commitments comparable with those it makes to its NATO allies, a commitment to risk nuclear devastation in their defence.'

When it came down to specifics, Pine Gap, he noted in this and other speeches, was an intelligence facility connected to the US satellite system. It had a crucial role to play in 'monitoring Soviet military development and in verifying whether the USSR was obeying arms control agreements'. If that meant it was connected to 'spy satellites,' then so be it — at least it was helping to prevent the Soviet Union and the USA turning each other into two super-sized car parks.

He also emphasised to the public that the US shared the information it obtained about Australia's local region which Australia could never have gathered alone. Nurrungar was essentially part of the US nuclear attack early-warning system, and therefore also played its part in keeping world peace, while North West Cape sent and received signals using Very Low Frequency, providing crucial communications for American *and* Australian submarines, as well as ships from the two navies operating in the Indian and Western Pacific Oceans.

Bit by bit in succeeding years, Beazley was able to change the basis of the arrangements with the Americans — despite some resistance from them — ensuring that there were progressively more Australians working there. The aim was to move to a situation, in Beazley's words, 'where Australia was not just hosting Pine Gap because it was good for the Americans, but because it was good for us ...' In the case of North West Cape this process continued to the point where by 1990 a process had been started that would see that base become fully Australian with nary an American in sight. Though this fitted the American's desire to cut their military spending budget, it also suited the Labor Government to be able to demonstrate Australia's sovereignty on these formerly contentious sites.

Beazley was working hard to make all this happen to his satisfaction, both when he was away on trips to the bases, and when he was back in Canberra. Either way it was hard yakka. As one of his staff, Karen Bissaker, remembers it, 'Kim would usually be in by about 7 am, we'd get there by about 8 am, and then, when Parliament was in session, we'd usually go through until 1 or 2 in the morning, before starting again the next day'. There were many things his staff were learning about him as they went. One was the speed with which he could 'get across a brief'. It was a crucial skill, for what came with the territory of being a Cabinet Minister was that you ended up standing in the middle of a swirling paper blizzard. It was not only the reports that came from one's own Department, from all its various sections, not only the submissions his Department prepared for Cabinet consideration, but as a Cabinet Minister himself he was automatically entitled to briefings from all other Cabinet Ministers on their proposals. In the face of such storms some Ministers took shelter, others would scan the papers as best they could, while still others like Paul Keating would most frequently get verbal summations of them from their staff.

But Beazley read them. All of them, and other things besides, including such international publications as *Foreign Policy*, *Foreign Affairs*, *Survival*, and the international defence journal, *Jane's Weekly*. 'It was extraordinary,' his then Private Secretary John O'Callaghan recalls, 'not how quickly he would read all the reports and magazines, but how he could retain an enormous amount of information, read it and basically quote it back to you verbatim. It wasn't speed reading in the sense of moving his finger down the page, but he would whip across them so fast you couldn't believe he was retaining it all, but he was. He could get across a brief in about a quarter of the time it took most Ministers, and keep the information.' The other thing the staff noticed though, was that for all his resolute purpose and eagerness to get on with it, 'Kim,' as they always called him — for he never wanted to be addressed as 'Sir' or 'Minister' — never seemed frantic in his day-to-day activities. Nor did he evince a sense of chafing at the bit to get everything happening yesterday.

This latter quality, Beazley himself says, could be traced perhaps to his training as a history academic. When you knew the history of the world since ancient times, it always helped to put in perspective the particular problems that one might be having in one particular week or month. 'My professional training such as it was,' Beazley suggests, 'actually helped me in relation to politics. I had a more relaxed appreciation of the swings and roundabouts of politics as a result. You tend to get less obsessed about what's happening on a day-to-day basis, and take a slightly longer view.' This 'longer view', the sense that he seemed to be in it for the long haul, showed up in many of his public comments. 'I have in mind Billy McMahon's record,' he would say during his first term as Defence Minister. 'Twenty-five years would do as a Minister. I enjoy parliamentary life and I think governments need professional Ministers. I see myself bouncing around in senior portfolios. I would like to do five or six years in each. That's when you make the most impact.'[83]

By assuming this perspective of the longer view Beazley demonstrated that he was an evolutionist rather than a revolutionist, always wanting to *create* the conditions where the environment he desired could grow naturally, rather than simply calling in the bulldozers and building that environment from the razed ground up. An important way of creating those conditions was by straight talking to his Defence personnel about the need for change, and he did it in his own way. 'When I moved around,' he explains, 'I would make a point of ensuring that as many as possible of the line officers in the department saw me. I wasn't just talking to Secretaries of a Department or [the] Chief of Defence, I was talking to junior officials, or senior officials, but as far down the line as I could go. When I went around the bases, I would always try and get myself into the Mess Hall, to talk to the soldiers across the board, to give them an understanding of what I was on about and to get an understanding of how they felt about life, where they were headed, those sorts of things.' Hugh White, who observed Beazley first as a journalist and then as his staff member, says of these sessions, that 'his great ability was to actually make them believe that it was possible for Australia to be self-reliant and that we could do it while still being part of a wider alliance. He had a way of being able to communicate it in a manner that they could understand, and also projected such confidence, that it started to rub off wherever he went. He was able to start to change the culture from within.'

One of the topics he discussed earnestly with such people, was the types of military equipment Australia needed to best assure its security. What was clear to him when he took over the portfolio was not only that a lot of the equipment was useless for Australian conditions — while it might still have its uses in some far-flung foreign war — but also that a lot of it was simply in bad repair. There had not in fact been major capital equipment purchases for Australia's forces since the days of the Vietnam War. Already, he had a couple of things right at the top of his shopping list that he wanted to organise as soon as possible. First and foremost among these were frigates and submarines. Beazley loved them both, but submarines most of all ... 'Basically,' he proposes, 'submarines are the poor man's small population weapon to cause maximum angst to a bigger enemy. They are not easy to detect, they are very survivalist, and they are capable of delivering a fair amount of [damage] on the fleets and land bases of an enemy.'

This knowledge of military needs stood in stark contrast to the notions of the previous Coalition Government which, ludicrously in Beazley's opinion, had wanted Australia to purchase an aircraft carrier from Great Britain — and was only saved from doing so because the aircraft carrier in question had been retained by the British for use during the Falklands War. In Beazley's own words: 'If your primary goal is to defend Australian territory, why would you need an aircraft carrier, when all of Australia is just one big aircraft carrier?' The other thing Beazley was keen on were frigates, the 'Anzac' type of frigate, to

Kim Beazley Senior and Junior.

Kim and his sister Merrilyn.

1 Thomson Road, Claremont.

He never quite made the Australian first XI as he had dreamed, but he loved cricket all the same.
Here, he is bowling at Cottesloe Beach.

Left: Kim, Merrilyn, David (seated) and friend on winter holidays in Canberra.
Right: A proud father sending Merrilyn, Kim and David off to school.

Kim's class school photo from Claremont Infants School, 1954.
Kim is fifth from the left, back row.

Kim's first trip to Parliament in the arms of his mother on the steps of Parliament House circa 1949.

The Hotel Kurrajong in the 1940s when it was a focal point for politicians and their families in Canberra.

Kim was elected Student Guild President at the University of Western Australia, 1970. He is pictured here with the Guild Council. Mary Paltridge is two from his left.

A proud mother and brother at Kim's graduation from the University of Western Australia.

Left: Both Kim and Merrilyn travelled to India in their late teenage years.
Right: Kim Beazley Jr and Mary Paltridge married in Oxford in 1974.

Kim and Mary were joined by their good friend, Geraldine Doogue,
who came to England for their wedding.

Kim was Minister for Aviation from 1983 to 1984.

He always wanted to be in the navy, but this would do.

KIM BEAZLEY
A.L.P. CANDIDATE FOR SWAN

- Married, two children.
- W.A.'s Rhodes Scholar in 1973.
- Lecturer, Writer and Commentator on Foreign Affairs and Defence Issues.
- Convenor, A.L.P. Industrial Development Committee.
- Lives in Swan.
- Former Member Senate, University of W.A. and Planning Board, Murdoch University
- Actively involved in Community Life.

YOU CAN CONTACT ME AT 19 CALE ST., COMO. PHONE: 450 4696.

Authorised by Fred McKenzie, M.L.C., 30 Great Eastern Highway, Rivervale.
Printed by Action Press, 28 Rudloc Road, Morley.

Above: Kim hand delivered his election card when he was the candidate for Swan and if someone wasn't home he would hand write: 'Sorry we missed you. Please contact us if I can assist you.' (Right)

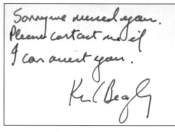

Kim Beazley has represented Fremantle since 1945. He is married with three children. Educated at Fremantle Boys' School (now John Curtin High School), Perth Modern School and the University of Western Australia, he is a graduate with first class honours of the Australian National University.

Kim Beazley is the Labor Party's spokesman on education. He has been on the governing council of the Australian National University for 22 years. He was formerly Vice-President of the W.A. Teachers' Union and a Counsellor of the Australian Teachers' Federation.

His service in Parliament has included Vice-Chairmanship of the Joint Parliamentary Committee on Foreign Affairs. In Parliament he has specialised in Education, Foreign Affairs, Papua New Guinea, Community Welfare and Aboriginal Affairs.

Concern with national issues has been matched with concern for the individual problems of electors. Kim Beazley has handled many thousands of cases for Fremantle electors on a variety of subjects – repatriation, immigration, housing, health, education and military service.

On Saturday December 2nd
VOTE

[1] BEAZLEY, Kim E.
for FREMANTLE

Remember voting is compulsory. Should you desire assistance to the polls or should you desire POSTAL VOTES (applications should be in by the 30th November, 1972), please ring the following numbers:
31 6175, 39 2685, 30 4060, 68 2816

Authorised by: G.J. Kerrigan, 14 Bolas Court, Myaree.   Printed by: Speed Eade Print, Maddington.

The election flyer Kim Beazley Sr used for his campaign for Fremantle in 1972.

Kim sharing a joke with the Dalai Lama during his visit to Australia in 1996.

Kim and British Prime Minister, Tony Blair, outside Chequers, July 1997.

On Sydney Harbour with US Secretary of Defence, Dick Cheney, and US Secretary of State, James Baker, and Foreign Secretary, Gareth Evans during the AUSMIN talks (late 1990).

With his best friend, Mick Young, during the Royal Australian Navy's 75th Anniversary celebrations on Sydney Harbour, 1986.0

Mr and Mrs Beazley.

Bob and Hazel Hawke with Kim and Susie.

Kim, his Dad and Paul Keating, taken on the day Kim became Deputy Prime Minister, June 1995.

Gareth Evans and Kim Beazley meeting with US President Bill Clinton immediately after Beazley gave his welcoming speech in Kings Hall, Parliament House.

Kim Beazley and Susie Annus were married 27 January 1990. The photos were taken on the UWA campus, their old stamping ground.

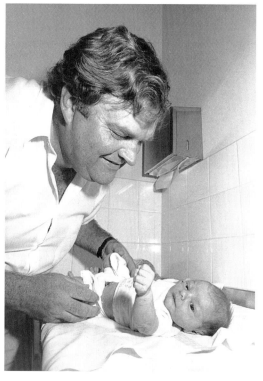

The hospital with Rachel on her first day of life, 18 January 1992.

Susie and Kim
at their Perth home.

Kim and Rachel
by the Swan River in Perth.

Left: 'As time went on people used to say that it was like a father and son relationship, and in a sense I did look upon him like a son. I really loved Kim, I still do, and respect him enormously.' – *Bob Hawke*

Below: Hazel Hawke flew to Perth to help Kim with his campaigning for the 1996 election.

Kim with his daughters, Hannah (left), Jessica (right), and Rachel.

be precise — bigger than a breadbasket, bigger than a patrol boat, but smaller than a destroyer. They were essentially a small style of warship. 'We wanted frigates,' he says, 'because they gave you mobility and firepower without the enormous expense of warships, and they were crucial for defending the sea approaches to Australia. When we didn't have an aircraft carrier, we could actually expand the size of the surface fleet, integrate its activities with the anti-submarine warfare capability of the Orion aircraft and the submarines themselves and get a useful surface fleet out of the frigates.' There was some salving of hurt too, with the Navy feeling pretty poorly at the time. 'I was terribly conscious of the wounds in the Navy of having lost its aircraft carrier. This was a bad thing for a nation whose defence is primarily maritime, to have a navy somewhat lost in its sense of how it fits into the nation's strategy, so I thought that the frigates would provide the sort of role that went missing.'

Stemming from this desire for such high-level military hardware though, were a couple of problems. The first was their sheer unadulterated expense. As a matter of fact, just about everything that Beazley wanted to do in the area of defence was expensive, from moving whole bases across the continent to buying equipment. At least though, he was not without his advantages when discussing his need for money with the most powerful financial decision-making body within Cabinet, the Expenditure Review Committee. The principal tactical advantage he had was the very complexity of the subject, and the fact that he was the only one sitting at the Cabinet table who had mastered those complexities.

The then Finance Minister, Peter Walsh, acknowledges how hard he and his Cabinet colleagues found it, when it came to trying to prune Beazley back. 'Defence took up about 10 per cent of the Commonwealth budget — that was one area that the Expenditure Review Committee never did seriously get into. Firstly, it's a bloody technical area so therefore unless you're up with that it's hard to argue with, and Beazley was right up to the state-of-the-art level on everything technically. Also so much of the Defence money is committed, locked in for years ahead. The short-term savings were always likely to be small, so defence was treated in a global context, cut 1 per cent off the estimates, and half a per cent next year, but there was no rigorous scrutiny of defence expenditure.' All of that said, there were still financial limits, and they were close to rock-solid ones. While the ERC might not have the capacity to take him to task on a particular item, they could and did set an annual limit on expenditure and, as Beazley knew, it was unlikely ever to move up significantly.

That left only one option for buying the equipment Beazley demanded, and that was to save money elsewhere within his portfolio. The most obvious place to start was in the netherworld of Defence Industries. Scattered around the country, these 15 defence factories — providing much of the production, storage and maintenance of the matériel needed for Australia's defence — were essentially leftovers from a bygone age where there was little accountability; successive governments, as a matter of course, had written big cheques with scant regard for what was provided. In the words of Syd Hickman, who was the first on Beazley's staff to really wrestle with the problem, 'these were absolutely disgraceful, they were the worst industrial sites in Australia bar none. Massive waste, hopeless. Brian Howe had run them, and being a Leftie, backed by the Metal Workers, was completely at the mercy of the workforce. So he'd come up with all sorts of crazy ideas about consultative committees and all the trendy Left bullshit. It was just appalling, it was unbelievable.' Hickman was far from alone in this assessment. In his own memoirs, Peter Walsh wrote: 'Howe had Defence Support, a portfolio subsidiary to Defence … Howe was a typical Victorian, sharing the Victorian Labor Government's woolly minded commitment to building a worker's utopia on a foundation of power sharing with unions.'[84]

Beazley resolved, one way or another, to clean 'em out. 'It was absolutely clear that we had to do it',' he insists, 'from pretty much the first moment we looked at it.' Whipping them into shape and reducing waste offered four neat paybacks to Beazley. First, it would give Defence a direct saving of money which it could then use to buy some of the equipment and weapons the country so desperately needed. Second, if they got it right, even the extremely high-tech submarines and frigates could be built in Australia, giving jobs to Australian workers and boosting the national economy. Third, if they *really* got it right, it might be possible to privatise some of those industries and raise capital for the Government. Fourth, and this was perhaps paramount in Beazley's thinking, there was a distinct military advantage in having the maximum amount of Defence's matériel needs produced in one's own country. In any protracted military engagement in the future, it was always going to be a colossal problem if ammunition or spares were coming from a country you were fighting against, or from that country's allies.

As 1985 progressed, and on into 1986, the Minister for Defence and his closest staff began to look at ways to cut down waste within these industries. One obvious way was to get the workers to actually *work*. Preliminary estimates showed that they were indeed among the most lax workplaces in the country. Just as he had done with the joint facilities and other Australian Defence establishments, Beazley now began to go from one defence industry site to another, to assess the severity of each situation, and to blow in the first stirrings of a wind of change that he would eventually turn into a tornado.

He appointed two men to the task of centralising management, eliminating duplication of effort, corporatising structure and introducing accountability measures. The results were near immediate. 'These facilities were hugely overmanned, with management that had major problems, but they were ultimately problems that could be solved,' Beazley reports. 'I remember the paintwork shops in Williamstown Naval Dockyard [in Melbourne], after we'd restructured the dockyard, had an 800 per cent productivity improvement!' Williamstown had indeed been a headache for the Defence Department. At the time that Beazley became Minister, the dockyard had two guided missile frigates under construction, but both were severely behind schedule and over budget, and there were serious concerns about just how long it would take to get them launched and operational. (At one point, according to Defence Department analysis, the frigates were moving further *away* from completion with every passing month.) Hugh White happened to be there one day when the Defence Minister addressed the workers of Williamstown about the need for them to adapt to the changing conditions.

'It was amazing,' White declares. 'Kim's great skill and ability is to induce in others an understanding of the inevitability of change, how they've either got to get with it or be bowled over, and on this day he did exactly that. What he basically said was that the workers could either change and build the frigates in the way he wanted them built, or he would get them built in Western Australia, and they better believe that was where he really wanted to build them, so it was up to them to decide how they wanted to handle it. He said it all without giving offense to them, with that kind of mirthless laugh he has, but there was no doubt they got the message. The thing was he'd worked it all out in his head what had to be done, and was sure of his ground. He has enormous self-confidence in his own judgement, and is very self-contained — ultimately he didn't care if these blokes liked him or not, that change was going to happen one way or another, and they sensed that. They fell in line pretty quick, and that was really the beginning of Williamstown entirely changing around.'

Another peculiarity of this venture to convince the workers at Williamstown and elsewhere that things were going to have to change, was that one of his key allies was none other than the head of the Amalgamated Metalworkers Union, John Halfpenny, perhaps Australia's most famous Communist of recent times.* Never mind that Kim Jnr had been brought up in a household where Communism was akin to Satanism, where a large part of his father's career had been sacrificed on the altar of anti-Communism at all costs, and never mind that as a 17 year old he had himself regarded the Communists as the political scourge of the earth — Halfpenny was extremely useful to him, and he was happy to have his help. 'He was a valuable adviser,' Beazley says of Halfpenny's contribution. 'He had an intricate knowledge of the unions that were active in the dockyards and a pretty good understanding of the cost structure of would-be employers and what would actually make a frigate go in Victoria and what wouldn't. If Melbourne was to be able to construct the Anzacs you just absolutely had to reform Williamstown, and Halfpenny understood that — he saw it as a way of keeping heavy engineering capability in Victoria. I don't think we could have done it without him.'

Halfpenny agrees with all of the above. 'I could see that Beazley was right in what he said, that unless Williamstown was reformed it would disappear. Personally, I think that Beazley was the first Minister for Defence that actually understood defence, and actually had a good command of the whole of the defence industry, and who very, very strongly believed that Australia should have a defence capability which relied heavily on a strong manufacturing capability. And even though one of my main missions in life is to be a peace activist, I also felt that we needed a good defence capability to defend your economic interests as well as territory. I had a view at the time, and still do, that the threat wasn't from the Cold War, but from Indonesia, and given that we should have a defence industry, it should serve two purposes: it should defend the nation's interests, but just as importantly it should foster and develop a strong manufacturing capability.'

---

* Halfpenny had in fact left the Communist Party of Australia, some four years before the time he was negotiating with Beazley.

The process would take time, just as it had with the joint facilities, but what Beazley was setting in train was a process which saw the Williamstown Dockyard become progressively more efficient and 'corporatised' to the point where within three years it was privatised, sold to a consortium of three corporate entities — and in the process he was creating a facility genuinely capable of producing the frigates and other matériel necessary for Australia's defence.

During these reforms, employment at the facility had been reduced from 2200 to 750 workers, 23 unions had been reduced to three and productivity had increased at least fourfold. 'We didn't make much money out of the sale,' Beazley notes. 'What we made money out of was getting our warships on time and getting off the books a hugely expensive operation, a drain.' That same 'closing of the drains' went on elsewhere, to the point where within five years of taking over the portfolio, Beazley could point to a record where subsidies paid by the Hawke Government to the defence factories had been cut by around $250 million a year,* with the total workforce cut from 15 000 to 8500. The former Office of Defence Production, also — which had administered it all from within the Defence Department — became a government-owned company, called Australian Defence Industries.

While Beazley was proud of such figures, there was also a fair measure of sadness thrown in. 'A lot of good people lost their jobs through this,' he recounts. 'And it was the only thing I felt sad about in the whole portfolio.' Against such sadness though would be the satisfaction of helping to create the conditions which would ultimately see six submarines built by Australian workers in Port Adelaide. When he had first mooted the possibility of building the submarines in Australia he had been howled down by his own Department, who had insisted that it would be close to impossible to build such highly sophisticated vessels on Australian shores, let alone launch them successfully beneath Australian waters. A submarine had never been built in Australia before, they pointed out, and it strained credibility to think that the country could now build six of the biggest conventional submarines outside the Soviet Union. Nevertheless Beazley, with the notable support of the Treasurer, Paul Keating, would not be put off, and insisted that they be built in Adelaide.

---

* There would remain, however, serious waste despite such measures. In 1997, The McIntosh Report of the Defence Efficiency Review, chaired by Malcolm McIntosh, estimated that a further 700 million dollars a year could be saved by improved efficiency.

He began a process whereby the design for the submarines would be put out to international tender, but they would be built by Australian workers, using foreign design and expertise. This would culminate in the tender being awarded to a Swedish firm, Kockums, which formed, with partners, an Australian company called the Australian Submarine Corporation.

Things were moving.

CHAPTER TWELVE

'BOMBER' BEAZLEY

'The [Defence] portfolio is so much at the heart of Australian
nationhood, that anything else is going to look pretty much
like a distraction alongside it.'
Kim Beazley, to the West Australian, *10 June 1986.*

As Beazley settled into the Defence portfolio he was clearly
getting things done. He was, in Hugh White's words, 'ticking
off things one by one on his agenda'. This streamlined
efficiency boosted his prestige in the party, and it also increased his
own confidence in asserting himself further. 'When Kim spoke on
Defence matters,' Stephen Loosley recounts, 'everybody listened to
what he had to say, and then people played around the edges of that.'
This point was brought home to Loosley in early 1986, when he was
Chairman of the ALP's National External Relations Committee, the
party body responsible for proposing the party's formal policies on
Defence, Foreign Affairs, Human Rights and Trade — (hopefully for
ratification in the party's coming National Conference). At the time
of this particular meeting, in one of the conference rooms at Old
Parliament House, the great issue of the day was President Ronald
Reagan's 'Star Wars' initiative, and as the Committee came to that
section of the platform, there was a buzz around the table as the Left
made their opposition clear. 'Well, the Defence Minister's with us,'
Loosley said, nodding to his colleague. 'Kim would you like to say
something at this stage?' Beazley leaned back in his chair with his

hands behind his head. He was clearly in an expansive mood, with, as Loosley reckoned it, the Left fully expecting him to blunt their criticism of his American friends and the wretched Star Wars proposal. 'Thanks Mr Chairman,' Beazley said, before pausing for a moment, perhaps for dramatic effect. 'The Strategic Defence Initiative will not outlive the Reagan Administration,' he said flatly. He then went on to explain, how he had recently been in Washington, talked with many of the Pentagon's strategic planners, many of whom he knew well, and had noted that when they all talked of America's defence thinking and forecasted military strategy and security policy for ten years down the track there was never mention made of Star Wars, nary even a whisper. Further, it was clear to him that there wasn't the budget there to sustain it. You only had to look at what the *research* on the project was costing them, he said, to know that even if such a thing were possible it would be too expensive to mount. He had concluded that in the Pentagon, Star Wars was treated as very much a second-order issue. It was fine for Reagan to score his political Brownie points by telling the American people that it was possible to mount an umbrella defence against incoming missiles — and have the added benefit of scaring the Russians in the process — but they in the Labor Party should base their policies on what was happening in the real world, and in the real world Star Wars was extremely unlikely ever to happen.

'Of course he was dead right,' Loosley says now, 'the only people who took Star Wars seriously were the Soviets. No-one in the American Defence establishment regarded it as being among their top priorities, essentially because of the technological impossibility of it, and Beazley just swept the debate away with him, because he so obviously knew what he was talking about. After that, Star Wars would be raised from time to time but no-one seriously treated it as a matter of serious contention inside the party.'

The Dibb Report — A Review of Australia's Defence Capabilities was tabled by Beazley in Federal Parliament in March 1986, and was regarded by him as the most crucial part of the process of changing the culture of Australia's defence community. Dibb's basic concept was the 'strategy of denial', the notion that Australia's comparative isolation from the rest of the world was, far from being its greatest point of vulnerability, in fact its greatest point of strength, and Australia's defensive approach had to reflect that.

Australia is one of the most secure countries in the world, ... ran the opening line of the report, before noting: ... but it would not be prudent to assume that we will always be able to conduct our affairs without challenge. [Australia's] sphere of primary strategic interest encompasses South East Asia and the South Pacific generally, and having a strong stable region free from external pressures is a fundamental security interest. While in defence terms, Indonesia is our most important neighbour, it is still important to recognise that, because of its proximity, the archipelago to our north is the area from or through which a military threat to Australia could most easily be posed.

To meet that threat, and beat the beggars back, Dibb posited a *'layered defence'*, whereby the sea around Australia could be regarded as an enormous moat, and *our most important defence planning concern is to ensure that an enemy would have substantial difficulty in crossing the sea and air gap.* And over there, for arguments sake, is a potential enemy, stirring.

First, we require extremely high quality and comprehensive intelligence about military developments in our region, as well as surveillance capabilities to detect and track hostile intruders in the sea and air gap ... The possibility of a surprise attack will be denied the enemy. Ensuring the 'transparency' of the approaches to Australia enhances the effectiveness of our weapons systems.

Second, Australia's air and naval forces must have the capacity to destroy enemy forces, at credible levels of threat, in the sea and air gap. This is a priority requirement. It means focusing on the north, which is our most vulnerable approach.

Third, closer to our shores, defensive capabilities are required to prevent enemy military operations in our focal areas, or shipping lanes or on our territory. These might include surface ships, mine countermeasures capabilities, air defence assets, and mobile land forces capable of being deployed rapidly and pre-emptively.

Fourth, if a landing on Australian soil should occur we would need ground forces capable of denying the enemy our vital population centres and military infrastucture ... Denial of enemy operations on our territory will require a demonstrable capability for highly mobile and dispersed ground force operations.

There was more, much more, a lot of it very detailed in how best to accomplish these goals, the kind of equipment it would be best to purchase, right down to the kind of radar, the need for medium artillery of 155 mm calibre ... six new submarines ... eight light patrol frigates, and how best all of the required purchases and changes could be financed. The review also had a long section on 'warning times', and the methodology to be used to assess the time necessary for a nominally friendly foreign power to change political complexion and pose various levels of threat to Australia's security.

The Review was a watershed in Australia's Defence policy, and the Defence Minister now busied himself in selling it to the Defence establishment, his parliamentary colleagues, the Australian public and the international defence community. His biggest problem in this regard would be with the Americans, and their interpretation of where Australia's pursuit of self-reliance might place them in the international sphere. As the then US Defense Secretary, Caspar Weinberger, remembers it: 'We had some worry that Australia might be pursuing a path of more isolationism. We had already had some unhappy results with New Zealand in that regard. The Dibb Report seemed to indicate more of a go-it-alone stance.' Shortly afterwards Beazley flew to Washington to meet with the Defense Secretary though, and Weinberger remembers the upshot: 'But I don't recall that Kim had any strong endorsement of that isolationist feeling, and he remained a strong supporter of continuing to work with us, and being a strong supporter of what we wanted to do.'

For those who knew the way Beazley operated, it was not at all surprising that he was able to quickly placate Weinberger's fears. For an obvious skill that he possessed at this point in his career, was the one noted by his old lecturing partner in politics back at Murdoch, Rob Pascoe, who had followed his friend's career with a professional eye since, and who now sometimes lectured *about him*. 'He's got an uncanny knack,' says Pascoe, 'of being able to understand the way in which people think, societies think, groups of people think, that's the first thing. I'd say he's got an amazing common touch and so his policy sense is always very strong. He can work out how a particular decision will affect different groups of people, and then work out how to make them accept that it actually is the best for them.' While not necessarily claiming the skill for himself, Beazley does note the importance of consultation generally. 'I think that is very important within every portfolio,' he says. 'Every portfolio has interest groups attached to it. People who are the beneficiaries or the potential dis-beneficiaries of decisions, people who have very sincere commitments to a series of views about policy matters, they have to be, whether they are Labor supporters or not, they have to be accounted for in the conclusions that you reach.'

An example of how Beazley was able to sell the Dibb Report to his own Labor colleagues, and its affirmation of the need for the Australian/American defensive alliance, was his constant assertion to his political kith and kin, that if it was not for that alliance being healthy, then the working class of Australia would be infinitely worse off. Beazley's premise was that the only way Australia could indulge in essential social security and social programmes, including education, was by having the US taxpayer subsidising the Australian taxpayer. If Australia had to be solely responsible for its own defence, then a much larger percentage of the Gross Domestic Product would have to go to defence, and Australia would have a lot less money for social welfare programmes. It was a position that Beazley genuinely believed, and also one that it was hard for the Left of the Labor Party to argue with. With Dibb's work now completed, Beazley's focus switched to working with the Defence Department to use his policy recommendations as the basis for a White Paper due the following year, which would be the official Government policy on defence.

If much of his thinking on the great affairs of the nation was up there in the 'cloud-lands', as Bob Hawke called it, still there was little worry about him losing touch with the grassroots of the way his fellow Australians were living their daily lives. By this time Merrilyn Wasson and her husband Rob had moved to the more up-market Canberra suburb of Lyons, and her older brother had continued to use their new house as his base when he was in town. For young Anton Wasson, then three years old, the presence of his powerful uncle was to provide him with his first memories, as whenever the official car came to pick him up Anton would stand there and wave as the big white car, sometimes with the flag of the Minister for Defence flying, glided in and out of the street, also frequently lined with the neighbours come to see 'The Man' go by. There was a very clear delineation in the Wasson household between Kim's work life and his 'home' life — although there was little of the latter, as he would usually arrive back around 11 pm at the earliest and be gone by 7 o'clock the following morning at the latest. On those exceedingly rare occasions when he was home with the family for dinner he might speak in general terms about what was on his agenda at that time, he was scrupulous never to discuss anything sensitive, and the Wassons, for their part, were just as glad not to be caught up.

There was, however, one time when Merrilyn Wasson was contacted by the Leader of the Government and pressed into service for the good of the nation. It was around April of 1986, and, after a parliamentary function that she had been invited to, she was asked by the Prime Minister to return to his office, as there was something he wished to discuss with her. After a little chitchat, he came to the point. Her mission, if she decided to accept it, was to get her brother to lose weight. It had been noticed that the Minister for Defence was starting to resemble a tank, if not a battleship, and the Prime Minister was concerned about his Minister's health and well-being. As Merrilyn remembers the conversation, the PM said that her brother was a brilliant man, was doing great work for the party, the Government and the country, was even then looking like a candidate to eventually succeed him in the top job, but he simply *had* to lose weight. The answer, Hawke told her, was the Pritikin Diet. Hawke himself was a devotee, had never felt younger or better, and if Merrilyn could just make sure that the fridge was always well-stocked with special low-fat Pritikin meals, he was sure that they could get Kim's shadow to less resemble an eclipse of the sun.

The second of the Beazley siblings tried, God help her she tried. She made all the Pritikin meals as requested, and they were disappearing as desired. 'The problem was though,' she explains, 'he was hitting the old Tim Tams. In fact I used to buy several packets of Tim Tams every week to keep up with it. He was really dreadful about this. Here I was making these Pritikin meals for Hawke but also buying Tim Tams because I knew what was needed. Kim eats when he's stressed about something and unfortunately that happened to be quite a stressful time for him.' Meanwhile, Bob Hawke and Mick Young were also on the attack. Whenever the Prime Minister chipped the Defence Minister about the need to exercise, as he recalls, 'Kim would reply "I'm swimming, I'm swimming". And I would say "well you are not swimming *e-bloody-nough!* and you are eating too much". God can he murder food, that man.' Mick Young, for his part, was able to persuade his mate — who was now almost double the weight that he had been when he left India two decades previously — that he simply had to get some exercise if he was going to be fair dinkum about shedding some bulk. For a short time, Young was even able to persuade him to take up running.

None of it seemed to make a substantial difference. Even when the Minister for Defence did indeed lose a lot of weight, it invariably came back just as quickly. In the end Hawke decided to leave him alone on the subject, on the grounds that 'Part of Kim's attractiveness to the people is that he is a sort of big, amiable, avuncular figure. They don't want a blow-wave, clothes horse fashion model. What comes through is a totally genuine fellow.' It was often like that. There would be a flurry of good intentions, diets etc, but inevitably things would work their way back to normal and Kim would live in the manner he wanted. Even Mick would drop off his case and leave him in peace.

Meanwhile, the closeness between the Minister for Defence and Mick Young kept growing, something that his staff took as a matter of faith. All calls from Young to 'the General,' as he delighted in calling him, were put through without question or hesitation. 'Mick was his sounding-board, Mick was his adviser, Mick had no hesitation in ringing him up and saying "Beazley, you should bloody well be doing this not that", and Kim would listen,' says Karen Bissaker. 'Or if Kim wanted some advice he would ring him and say "What do you think about this?" Mick was always there. He used to ring me every day — "tell Beazley to do this", or "get Beazley to call me". And if you wanted to find Kim of a night-time you would only have to go into Mick's office, or very late he might be in with Bob.'

For all Kim Beazley's growing success in the Defence portfolio, it was Bob Hawke and Paul Keating who remained the two big wheels on which the Government rolled. When they were aligned and in sync, things hummed, things *happened* — and the landscape through which they were travelling substantially changed to their combined will. The dollar was floated, the foreign banks allowed in, the financial system deregulated, powerful government institutions and longstanding traditions bowed as they passed. Beazley enjoyed the ride as much as anyone; the Australian public had responded by giving Bob Hawke record approval ratings — 75 per cent at his best — and Paul Keating had been voted the 'Finance Minister of the Year'[85] by a prestigious European financial magazine, prompting Hawke to describe him as the 'world's greatest Treasurer'.

When the two big wheels were out of alignment, though, and pulling in opposite directions, it could get very ugly. The first notable example had been the 1985 Tax Summit, when Keating had pushed his famous Option 'C' — a goods and services tax — only to find that Hawke had withdrawn his support at the crucial moment. 'That was the first one I put back in the memory, the first one I really didn't forgive him for,'[86] Keating would say later. While some in the Cabinet were close to Hawke, and others to Keating, none in the entire Caucus was as intimate with both men as Kim Beazley. The Defence Minister and Keating had been friends for 15 years, while the Prime Minister was his closest confidant in Canberra after Mick, as well as being as close as you would get to a political patron.

When Hawke and Keating were circling each other, then, it was Beazley, with the ear of both, who would often find himself in the role of pacifier trying to calm them down — although sometimes it was simply impossible to stop their anger flaring. One notable occasion came in the winter of 1986, at a time when Hawke was on a trip to Japan and China, and Keating had become highly concerned about the Current Account Deficit for the month of April just gone, which had shown that Australia had gone another 1.48 billion dollars in the hole. In an effort to communicate the seriousness of the situation to his fellow Australians, the Treasurer had gone on John Laws' radio programme, and in the course of the interview had pressed — advertently or inadvertently, no-one was ever sure — a button which sent Australia's political and economic cycle into spin-dryer mode. Nearing the end of the interview, Keating warned, simply, that unless Australia mended it's free-spending ways, and improved its manufacturing base, it risked becoming 'a banana republic'. Cue sirens. Within hours the value of the Australian dollar had fallen three cents against the greenback on the strength of the Treasurer's signal, or rather signal flare; the Australian stockmarket had lost serious wattage; and Hawke in Tokyo had been provided with a full transcript of what he saw as Keating's needlessly inflammatory remarks.

In the face of the ensuing crisis in public confidence in the national economy, Keating announced that a meeting of government, employer and union groups would be held shortly to examine ways to improve the Current Account Deficit — soon built up to be a full 'summit' by the media — and Hawke, who was now in Beijing, was almost made to feel as if Keating had seized the mantle of power from him. The whole episode culminated in an extraordinary meeting of senior ministers in Canberra, called by Hawke, where the Prime Minister spoke to them from Beijing via a telephone 'squawk-box' situated in the middle of the table. Hawke told his ministers, as recounted by Paul Kelly, that 'the planned economic meeting was not a summit, not a decision making meeting, and would not be held for a fortnight'.[87] Furthermore, all queries about the meeting should be directed to the Deputy Prime Minister, Lionel Bowen, until he, Hawke, got back in a few days time. In the course of Hawke's diatribe, Paul Keating sat at the far end of the table, with a pen and the morning papers, and started to tick off, one by one, points made by the Prime Minister that were exactly the same as had appeared in stories that morning which quoted an unnamed 'government source' and had damned Keating's actions in the strongest terms. To Keating, it was clear who the real culprit was, and eventually he could stand it no more, and made ready to speak. His colleagues knew from long experience that it was unlikely to be pretty, and conscious of Hawke's situation in Beijing, one of them warned him *sotto voce* to 'be careful, because the Chinese will be listening'.

'FUCK the Chinese!' Keating had roared in reply, before yelling down the line to Beijing. 'Just what's the *point* of this bullshit, Bob?'

'Who's that?' Hawke's voice had come from the squawk-box, for all the world as if he really wanted to know.

'Who the fuck do you *think* it is?' replied Keating. 'We've got problems here, and we're trying to solve them. Just what the hell do you think you're playing?'[88]

Essentially, Hawke was playing for keeps, reasserting control of the Government that bore his name. On this occasion, it worked, and although there would still be many more times when Hawke and Keating would combine to great effect, their personal relationship would never be the same, something that made things doubly difficult for Beazley. 'I never thought they had gone past the point of no return though and that was my mistake,' Beazley says. 'I always thought at the end of the day that that sort of fight could be ameliorated. The Labor Party had had those sort of titanic struggles before and generally speaking they were contained, so I was always hopeful that this one could be too.' In the short term, though, the problem for Beazley was that the air of fiscal crisis created by the 'banana republic' line meant that it was harder than ever to get the money he wanted for Defence. Keating tightened the purse strings across the board, meaning, as Beazley recollects, that 'it became harder'. 'We used to plan our budgets on having a real growth of three per cent, which we achieved once or twice, but after the whole "banana republic" thing, we found it almost impossible to get more than one or two per cent growth. What it meant, in short, was that some of the equipment purchases foreshadowed in the Dibb Report would have to be scaled back somewhat in the Defence White Paper then under construction, and the pressure on Beazley to continue rationalising the defence industries was all the greater.

Back in Perth, Mary Beazley would follow such goings-on with half an eye, knowing that she could have a fair stab at predicting what kind of mood Kim would be in on the weekend, when he was home, by what the front pages of the newspaper were saying. 'I was always interested in what was happening politically,' she says, 'and we would discuss it, but when it was intense like that it would really drain him. I guess what I most remember from that time though, is just night after night after night, being by myself with the kids; of coming home from work, playing with them, bathing them, making meals and feeding them and putting them to bed before eating myself, and then just the long evenings sitting around by myself. I read a lot which was fine, but it was just sitting around night after night by myself, always by myself. And then turning around and facing the whole rest of the night by myself and waiting for it to be 11 o'clock or half-past 11 so I would be tired enough to go to sleep.' The whole thing was not easy, and nor did it seem to be getting easier with the passage of the years. If anything, it was the reverse ...

While the Dibb Report was not official Government policy — and would not be until the White Paper endorsed an as yet indeterminate number of Dibb's conclusions — Beazley continued the process of moving Australia's defence structure from the south and east of the continent to the north and west. One of the things he announced in March of 1987, for example, was that the Second Cavalry Regiment based in Holsworthy just outside of Sydney would move to newly built premises at Darwin. 'I was very keen that we implement as many of the necessary changes as quickly as possible,' Beazley remembers, 'ensuring that the dispersal of our forces reflected the territory that we actually wanted to defend, so I had a lot of enthusiasm about upgrading facilities at Darwin ...' It was not an enthusiasm universally shared. One who was particularly trenchant in his criticism about the physical repositioning of Australia's forces was 'Diamond Jim' McClelland. 'Nobody, of course, fears an invasion by the

Japanese any more,' he wrote in the *Sydney Morning Herald,* 'since they have practically no armed forces (which may be one of the reasons why their economy is doing better than anyone else's ...) [And] it is hard to see the point of an invasion of this country by the Chinese or the Filipinos or the Indonesians, let alone the Sri Lankans or the Kampucheans. Old-fashioned imperialism, the grabbing of somebody else's land in order to exploit its resources and its people, is *passé* in the nuclear age ...'[89]

Beazley's essential defence of his own Defence policy was twofold. First, that the forces were *not* being situated at Australia's 'back door' at all, but were at last being put right next to the front door where they belonged, and further that prudent defence planning looked, almost by definition, to *future* threats every bit as much as it did to current threats. 'I was always conscious of the fact,' he articulates, 'that from the moment of planning the development of our submarine fleet to the time when they would be obsolete; was a greater period of time than separated my era as Defence Minister back to the conclusion of World War II. The point is that threats can emerge far more quickly than weapons ... and so anybody who takes the view that because at this stage of the game we face no threat — therefore we shouldn't acquire military expertise of a particular type or watch military developments — I think has an unrealistic view of Australian defence planning.'

Leisure for pleasure? Beazley had very little, and even then there were often signs that matters of Defence were not far from his thoughts. One notable occasion came during Australia's defence of the America's Cup sailing trophy which it had won so famously from the Americans in 1983, after they had held the trophy for the previous 132 years. On this particular morning, in early February of 1987, *Kookaburra III* was doing its best to hold off the claims of *Stars and Stripes* in the waters off Fremantle, and Bob Hawke, always a keen follower of the sport, was on a cruising yacht with other dignitaries and politicians, which included the Minister for Defence. As Hawke remembers it, there came a particularly exciting point of the race, when some 20 people had their eyes and binoculars straining to starboard to see which of the two sailing boats was edging in front ... while just one person, equally excited, had his binoculars pointed in exactly the opposite direction.

Kim Beazley. 'I looked around,' Hawke describes, 'and there was Kim focusing on these smudges on the far horizon, our naval ships, and he was saying "there's the *Derwent*, and there's the *Sydney*, and the *Adelaide*," and so on. He knew them all, just by their shapes on the horizon!'

When Beazley tabled the White Paper, titled *The Defence of Australia* in Parliament in March 1987, there appeared to be several changes of emphasis. The first and most obvious was a simple semantic change, that the 'Strategy of Denial' had now become 'Defence in Depth'. Beyond that though, defence commentators claimed that while the Dibb paper promoted a kind of 'Fortress Australia,' the White Paper was closer to the old notion of Forward Defence, that Australia was gearing up to head out into a hostile world again. Chapter One, page one, sounded like Dibb:

> *1.1 This Government's policy of defence self-reliance gives priority to the ability to defend ourselves with our own resources. Australia must have the military capability to prevent an enemy from attacking us successfully in our sea and air approaches, gaining a foothold on our territory, or extracting political concessions from us through the use of military force. These are uniquely Australian interests, and Australia must have the independent military capability to defend them.*

But after that, Australia's defence could sound like it had its passport in hand, ready to travel:

> *1.17. Options will always be available to Australian governments for assistance to Allies …*
>
> *1.36. Australia is a major power in the South-West Pacific. We have the capability now to deploy significant forces there …*
>
> *1.46 … Proposals for Australian defence involvement beyond our region of primary strategic concern will be considered on their merits.*

Despite such items, Beazley rejects the notion that he had changed emphasis. 'There wasn't all that much difference,' Beazley asserts. 'It was claimed to be different and in a sense it suited us to claim it was different, because the Americans actually did have a problem with the Dibb Report. The problem was based on a lack of understanding, a misunderstanding, but Dibb's report wasn't about strategic guidance, it was simply about the defence of Australia. The White Paper of course had to be about everything, had to take into account the alliance issues, the regional responsibilities and all the rest of it.' Something else that Beazley was particularly keen on came on page 35 of the White Paper.

4.9 — The Government has given high priority to the design and development of this network, based on the Australian designed Jindalee experimental radar.

The Jindalee radar, if it worked, would provide 'over-the-horizon' surveillance of Australia's northern approaches, at a distance of up to 1800 nautical miles off the coast.* The White Paper also announced a continuation of the programme to physically shift a lot of Australia's defensive infrastructure to where it would most likely be needed.

5.5 — An airfield will be built on Cape York Peninsula to complete a band of airfields across northern Australia.
— Naval facilities will be progressively developed in the north-west to enhance patrol operations in that region.
*— There will be further development of the naval base at HMAS Stirling** [in Western Australia] to allow more surface vessels and submarines to be based there.*

Perhaps most significantly, the document spelt out the details of what the Minister called in his preface, 'the largest defence capital investment in Australia's peacetime history'. This would include a spending programme for capital equipment of 25 billion dollars over the following 15 years, of which 7 billion dollars was earmarked for the continuing ship-building programme of the eight new light frigates and six new submarines.

Beazley was more than happy with the content of the White Paper, and was very up-beat about its likely effect on Australia's defensive capacities, when all of the changes and acquisitions had been accomplished and purchased. 'Then I think we will be able to say

---

* The Jindalee radar project was something that would prove to be extremely troubled. According to a report tabled by the Joint Committee of Public Accounts in March of 1998, the Jindalee was meant to be operational by 1997 at a cost of 1.1 billion dollars, but at the time of tabling was adjudged to be 600 million dollars over budget with an expectation that the earliest it could be operational was 2002.
** Apart from making good sense to Beazley strategically, it also did not do him any harm politically, on a local level. A later West Australian State Planning Commission estimated that the move would create 1000 jobs in the short term for construction of the expanded facility, 900 new jobs thereafter, and at least 50 million dollars injected into the economy of Western Australia.

seriously,' he was quoted in the *West Australian*, 'that in all of the foreseeable contingencies, we would have achieved a situation of defence self-reliance. There would be no holes.'[90] As the changes envisioned in the White Paper continued to unfold, Beazley showed impressive skill in manoeuvring the necessary reforms through his own Department. In order to get it through without encountering too much heavy resistance from his senior bureaucrats, he used the fact that he was privy to their annual leave schedules to institute major changes, that he thought they might be resistant to, while they were on leave. (One can't help making a comparison between this sly manoeuvre and Beazley's clever use of the student Clubs and Societies' members, and a little publicised meeting, to push through the fee-hike when he was Guild President.) 'I certainly did that sort of thing,' he acknowledges, 'but I wouldn't want anyone to think it was routine. Only the odd occasions.' Bit by bit, news of this got around his parliamentary colleagues. Perhaps Beazley had more guile than he had been given credit for after all. In the words of one of his long-time colleagues, 'there is no question that Beazley is a brilliant bureaucratic player'.[91]

From afar, Kim Beazley Snr watched the way his son was handling the Defence portfolio with warm approval. Occasionally, very occasionally, he and his wife would venture to the east to see him. Shortly after the White Paper had been released, Kim Snr did attend a Labor Party function in the NSW Parliament, where privately he spoke with enormous pride, affection and respect for 'the Defence Minister', as he called him. In the words of one person present, 'it was clear in his mind, that Kim Jnr was the standard-bearer for the future, no question at all'. Not that the father was unaware of the odd shortcoming of the son, for all that. Only a few days previous to this luncheon, a passing out parade had been held at Duntroon and Kim Snr had regaled the assembled company thus, with the line he said was then doing the rounds of Canberra, 'that while the Minister was standing to attention at the passing out parade ... unfortunately his suit was at ease!'.

Shortly after the White Paper was released, there came a reminder that the administration of Defence was not simply an academic exercise. A threat — or at least regional trouble — emerged from an unexpected direction. In Fiji's Parliament House, in the late morning of 14th May 1987, the Opposition MP Taniela Veitata had said in a speech to his parliamentary colleagues that 'Peace and harmony is the governing principle on which the Fijians have been running their lives since the advent of Christianity. This is in contrast to what Mao Zedong believes — that political power comes out of the barrel of a gun.'[92] It was clearly not a particularly prescient utterance, for only shortly afterward Lieutenant-Colonel Sitiveni Rabuka walked to the Speaker's dais and announced, 'This is a military takeover. Lie down and remain calm.' Only a mid-ranked officer of the Fijian Army, Rabuka had gathered enough disaffected sections of that army to mount a successful coup, based on the premise that the Indian–Fijians had taken over the country and it was now time to take it back, 'to ensure the birthright of the [native] Fijians'. He summarily revoked the country's 1970 Constitution, and declared himself to be the new leader.

Back in Canberra, Beazley was immediately on the case. 'We had the commander of the Fiji defence force sitting in my office so it was pretty dramatic,' he explains. 'We tried to work out what it was that Rabuka was going to do.' The most cogent factor to be taken into account from the point of view of Australia's security interests was that there were an estimated 4000 Australians in Fiji at the time. 'There were all sorts of decisions that had to be taken,' Beazley recounts. 'What level of danger were Australian citizens being placed in, could we afford to just simply trust them to the tender mercies of the new people in Fiji, or should we actually start positioning people in case they were going to lose control of the situation — deliberately or otherwise? Should we be facilitating counter-moves by other elements of the Fijian military then based in the Middle East? Were they going to be loyal to the commander in my office as opposed to Rabuka? Should we intervene militarily?' The fact that this last option was even considered, was an indication of how seriously the Minister for Defence regarded the situation in Fiji.

Journalist David Humphries, who talked extensively with Beazley at the time, both on and off the record, had the strong impression that what really got to the Defence Minister was the outrage of what Rabuka had done *vis-a-vis* democracy. 'Beazley made it very clear to me,' Humphries relates, 'that why he was so determined to proceed with the assault strategy was that the actions of Rabuka in Fiji, were in themselves an assault on the principles of democratic representation that he held so dear.' Beazley does not resile from this assessment. 'What had happened in Fiji was completely unacceptable and I was rather saddened by the fact that there seemed to be precious little we could do about it,' he says now. 'We had a situation where virtually a Labour Government in Fiji had been overthrown … on our patch, and about which it was not easy to do something.'

The problem in the first instance was that in order to 'do something' the Australian Government would need to have an invitation from the overturned Prime Minister, and that invitation was not forthcoming in the early days of the crisis. Actually no-one seemed to know precisely where the deposed Prime Minister Dr Timoci Bavadra was, or even whether he was still alive. In the meantime, Beazley's concern was that Australia's forces should position themselves in such a manner that they could react swiftly to any eventuality. With that in mind, he sought and was granted permission by Hawke and the Cabinet to send Royal Australian Navy ships into the immediate vicinity, while 120 soldiers from the Operation Deployment Force based in Townsville were flown by RAAF Hercules to Norfolk Island where they were picked up by *HMAS Tobruk* and waited off-shore, ready to assist with any evacuation of Australian expatriates. 'Operation Morris Dance' — a name Beazley is glad to acknowledge he did not make up — was quickly underway. 'Even so,' Beazley acknowledges, 'that was pretty unsatisfactory and I guess I just felt a sense of guilt about the fact that this fellow had been overthrown and there was precious little we could do about it. So that was the psychological environment if you like at the time ...'

Then occurred what appeared to be a breakthrough. The Defence Department got word that Bavadra was holed up in the New Zealand High Commission premises in Suva. It could not be confirmed because lines of communication into the building had been shut down, but intelligence reported that the building was now surrounded by Fijian troops, so the assumption was that the story was correct. As Beazley recollects, 'We thought he had escaped and we were looking at some way of getting him out ...' Bob Hawke happened to be in Adelaide at the time. He returned to Canberra to find that in his absence, his Defence Minister Kim Beazley and the Acting Foreign Minister, Gareth Evans, had cooked up a plan to save the day, and help restore stability to the troubled nation. The plan was simple, Beazley and Evans told him. They would send a helicopter from one of the RAN ships stationed off the Fijian coast, to fly in low over the houses of Suva, pluck Prime Minister Bavadra from the roof of the New Zealand High Commission building, fly him to a safe haven in Western Fiji, Bob would be your uncle, and as a matter of fact what did Bob himself think? Hawke, as he recollects, was staggered. 'I just couldn't believe it,' he says, 'just could not *believe* it! I said "You can't do that, you have got to be joking".' In the first instance, neither

Beazley nor Evans would be deterred. 'So I said,' Hawke relates, 'what we'll do is, we'll ask General Gration, and see what he thinks. I won't say a word, won't give any indication what I think about it, and we'll just see how he reacts, OK?' General Peter Gration, Chief of the Defence Force, was indeed summoned to the Prime Minister's office, and when he arrived the situation was explained to him ...

As Hawke tells the story, as soon as the General's eyes started rolling back in his head, he knew he had won the argument, and that was that. By the following morning Beazley had entirely dropped off the case. One who provides a perspective on such Beazley actions as the helicopters-to-Fiji episode is Hugh White, who worked with Beazley for over five years. When he heard about the helicopter plan, he was not in the least surprised, while being equally certain that the Minister for Defence never would have gone through with it. 'Kim would never *actually* have done it,' he says, 'but coming up with an idea like that is simply the way he works. His intuitive way is to throw out on the table wacky ideas as a way of narrowing options; he puts them out there, and even goes ahead with the idea to a certain extent, but it's all just part of getting his bearings in a situation. He gets rid of the flaky ideas early so as to get the solid stuff and nearly always shows great judgement. Far from being gung-ho and irresponsible though, as he is sometimes portrayed, he is actually very disciplined and controlled, certainly one of the most disciplined and controlled persons I have ever worked with.'

While not commenting specifically on the 'helicopters-to-Fiji' scenario, Beazley does acknowledge the central truth of White's assessment. 'I think it's important in every political gambit and in every crisis,' he says, 'to work out what all the options are and *then* determine which you should pursue. The good thing about that is, you may get into one of the options that you determine and suddenly find you've chosen the wrong path. It's good to have thought about a few alternatives and have argued them through; have your mind set to proper change.' The whole episode of the Fiji coup and Beazley's response to it, heightened the perception that the Defence Minister was far too gung-ho for his own and Australia's good — and often the accusers would be from his own party. By this time some of the backbenchers had long been calling him 'Bomber' Beazley and 'Kimbo'. John Dawkins, in particular, started calling him 'Dr Strangelove' after the famous film character who was the star of the movie which climaxed with a pilot with a cowboy hat riding a nuclear bomb down through the Russian skies onto the wicked Commies below. Bill Hayden delighted in calling him the 'Minister for World War III'. And even Bob Hawke, who might have been expected to leap to his protégé's defence — as he was wont to do — could not resist making a joke at his minister's expense when the subject came up. 'It's a paradox of course. Kim's a man of peace,' he told the ABC programme *Four Corners* when journalist Deborah Snow did an overview on Beazley's influence on Defence. 'He gives the impression, at times, that he wouldn't mind a little war as long as there weren't too many casualties. Just to see it all work, in actual fact. I'm joking about that, a bit.'[93]

On the same programme John Dawkins also weighed in with a not entirely untypical jibe at Beazley's expense. The relationship between the two had always been a bit strained, and while the tension was always more subterranean than apparent, the least that can be said is that on this occasion Dawkins did not seek to downplay any suggestion that Beazley might be trigger-happy. 'I wouldn't for a moment suggest that he would want to *start* a war,' Dawkins had said with a smile, 'but certainly he would not be unhappy if at some stage in his life he found himself as a member of a War Cabinet. We are certainly very conscious of his total fascination for the technology of the war machine ...' Oddly enough, none of these opinions or name-calling worried Beazley unduly. As a matter of fact, the *realpolitik* part of him even saw an advantage in it. 'No, no, why bother worrying about it?' he recollects as his main response to such jibes. 'Sometimes, it didn't do me any good in domestic politics — and probably got me more demonstrations than I would have attracted otherwise but ...'

But there were payoffs. 'Firstly it was useful that in terms of building a relationship with the military, that at least they have a Minister who takes them seriously. That was helpful. Secondly it doesn't do you any harm in the region just to keep people a little nervous, if they have a view of you that you are actually capable of being a bit wilful it doesn't do you any harm at all.' For all that, he rejects entirely any notion that he was, in *reality*, too jingoistic. Somewhat defensively, he responds, 'I did put the Army on alert four times,* that is true, but it wasn't because I was looking for trouble. It was just trouble had occurred and there had to be some sort of

---

* Specifically, the Operational Deployment Force, based in Townsville, had on four occasions been placed on alert after regional troubles, twice in Fiji, once in Vanuatu and once in Bougainville.

response, at least potentially, in case things went badly. And I didn't do it off my own bat I might add — I did discuss these things with the Prime Minister and others, and it was always a collective decision.'

Despite such criticism, most within the Defence community and parliamentary sphere conceded that Beazley had generally worked wonders with the transformation he had wrought in Defence in the very short time he had been at the helm. The long-time Secretary of the Department of Defence, Sir William Cole, was later quoted giving his own impression of the man he answered to for over five years: 'He is probably the most intelligent Minister that I have been associated with. He also came into the job with very good background knowledge, unlike most Ministers who have to learn the job.'[94]

The extent to which Beazley's astute handling of defence matters mattered electorally to the Hawke Government is unquantifiable of course, but there is no doubt that one particular episode was of significant benefit to them. At the height of the 1987 election campaign, just under three weeks before the July 11 polling day, Australia and America held high-level AUSMIN Talks, that is Australian United States Ministerial Talks — a direct descendant, once removed, of ANZUS — to discuss the security relationship between the two countries. Staging such sensitive talks during an election campaign was a clear breach of protocol, and had been noted as such by the Defence Department officials, but Beazley and Hawke had decided to press ahead regardless. If the Americans were willing, then so were they. Bob Hawke recalls that he had asked the Americans: 'If we have the talks can you do the right thing by us?' and had been heartened enough by their answer that they went ahead.

The talks were held at HMAS Watson, on the Sydney Harbour foreshores, and were attended on the American side most notably by the American Secretary of Defense Caspar Weinberger, and Secretary of State George Shultz. The talks went extremely well, and Hawke's admiration for Beazley was confirmed and deepened by the views of both George Shultz and Caspar Weinberger. 'Both of them said to me independently,' Hawke recounts, 'that neither of them had dealt with a more impressive Defence Minister. And I watched him when he was sitting down with senior officers, the brass ... they were in awe, they had never had a Minister who knew so much.' George Shultz confirms that his feelings towards Beazley then were much as described, commenting, 'I thought he was first class. He was well informed without being pushy about it. He seemed to be a very savvy guy who kind of understood the *nuances* of things, wasn't just on the edge of the obvious as so many people are. There's some other people who have a capacity for thinking more independently and they see the subtleties of issues and so their views are much more interesting and worth listening to. You go around the world and you see people in country after country and deal with them and after a while you have a sense of who among the people you're dealing with is a heavyweight, and you are then really interested to know what they think. Kim Beazley was outstanding in that regard. He's one of the "heavy cream" of people that I ran into around the world ... a first-class man.'

Caspar Weinberger felt much the same. 'I was always very impressed with him, and I think I mentioned to him that "I'm sure you will be a future Prime Minister". He was one of the finest defence ministers I ever worked with. And though I wouldn't want to criticise any other defence ministers, the difference with Kim was that while he was very aware of all the problems in the Pacific and the needs of Australia, he also had a good global view. He knew a great deal of what was happening abroad and how important it was ... he was not parochial at all. He knew Australia's needs, and they were first of course, but he knew a great deal about the rest of the world and that was very important.' (Beazley's relationship with Weinberger had thus come a long way from the occasion of their first encounter. On that occasion, during ANZUS talks in Washington, the Australian Minister for Defence had used one or two Australian colloquialisms during his opening remarks, only to see the American Defense czar at the opposite side of the negotiating table, interrupt him, turn to the American official beside him and utter just one word: '*Translation?*')

At the end of the AUSMIN Talks came the electoral pay-off. As the cameras rolled, and the tape recorders whirred, Defense Secretary Weinberger said: 'Defence self-reliance ... based on broad concepts of strategic responsibility and regional commitment, constitutes a strong foundation for the defence of Australia and for Australia's execution of alliance responsibilities ... I think the military relationship [between our two countries] is very strong, as strong indeed as it has ever been and we want to keep it that way.'

Headlines around the country the following day were to the order of the *Sydney Morning Herald*'s: U.S. Praise for Aust Defence Strategy.[95] It was all a clear indication, and was interpreted as such, of how much things had changed in terms of the security relationship between the two countries, most especially at a time when a Labor Government was in power in Australia. The situation was very different during the time of the Whitlam Government. 'Blinkered CIA chiefs had concluded that a wild revolutionary government had come to power in Australia,'[96] wrote Ross McMullin in *The Light on the Hill*; they were so alarmed that they 'even considered severing ASIO's links' with the CIA.

In this highly charged atmosphere, vivid rumours circulated that the CIA had been set loose to bug the Cabinet room.

Now, however, only 15 years later, two heavyweight Security and Defense appointees of the United States Republican Party* were essentially endorsing the defence operations of a Labor Government. And such endorsements had far more value to the Hawke Government than just a positive cosmetic image. It may even have been crucial. Of the 30 marginal seats in Australia leading up to Federal Election day in mid-July, a full 10 of them were 'defence seats,' where the bulk of Australia's defence personnel were congregated.

Just how much Beazley's and Hawke's astute manoeuvring of the American endorsement helped to secure those seats is debatable, but for the first time the ALP's own polling showed that the Party had succeeded in attracting over 50 per cent of the defence vote Australia-wide. This was some achievement; for just as the military establishment was made up of Tories, so too were the rank and file substantially made up of people from the bush, who often have a natural disposition to voting for the National Party. In the words of one defence man, 'in this particular election they basically said "okay, we think Beazley is not a bad bloke, we will vote for his side"'.

For the record, members of the Armed forces didn't always like the Hawke Government. On one occasion, not long after the Weinberger/Shultz visit had concluded, the Prime Minister and his Defence Minister were inspecting an Army corps on parade up in Townsville. All of the soldiers had their entire kit laid out on the ground before them and Hawke, being the chatty sort of bloke he was, wanted to engage some of the soldiers in conversation.

---

* One who was not surprised to see such a close relationship develop between Beazley and the two Republican titans was his long-time parliamentary colleague, Michael Duffy. 'My theory,' Duffy says, 'is that on things like defence and the American alliance Kim is very much to the Right, and that always motivated him. So much so I think if he was American he'd vote Republican rather than Democrat.'

In the middle of it all was one weedy sort of bloke, looking straight ahead in the military manner, but still not managing to supress a scowl. 'Gidday,' said Hawke, not at all perturbed. 'This stuff looks pretty good, does it go alright does it?'

'No,' replied the soldier with some feeling. 'It's shit. All of it's shit, and all of it always has been shit, whatever new stuff they give us, it's always SHIT!'

Later, Hawke, still clearly disquieted by what he had heard, and wondering if such discontent in the Armed Forces might be part of some deep-seated problem, asked the Defence Minister about it. Beazley put his mind at ease. 'They're infantrymen, Bob,' he told him, 'what some people call "grunts," and that's just the way they are. The thing is, just about every advance in weaponry and warfare techniques over the last 2000 years has been singularly devoted to more effectively wiping them out, and they're not happy about it. They never will be. Don't let it worry you.'

CHAPTER THIRTEEN

SKIRMISHES . . .

'You become much more patriotic in government. You get taken
out of the scrabble of politics and you have to think about
the nation. The sense of nationalism intensifies. We have all
changed a bit that way . . .'
Kim Beazley, February 1988.[97]

'I used always to talk to Kim a lot when the election campaigns
were on,' Paul Keating remembers. 'Because he would always see
everything through the eyes of his own seat and sometimes get
really down about it. I'd ring him some days and he'd ring me, and
some days he'd be going well, and other days he'd be really down. In
that '87 campaign, he'd say "I'm gone", "I'm gone", "I'm in trouble".
And I'd say, "we're going to win, because we *are* the government of
Australia, we look like the government of Australia . . . and who have
we got to beat? Only John Howard".'

The Treasurer was right. On 11 July 1987, Australia once again
went to the polls, and by 10.00 pm that night, Eastern Standard Time
— at which time John Howard, who had been the Opposition Leader
for the previous two years, had conceded defeat — it was manifestly
clear that the Hawke Government had won its third straight election
with an all but unbelievable *expanded* majority, from 16 seats in the
previous election to 24 seats this time. In the west, Kim Beazley held
Swan for the fourth time in succession.

In the wake of the election win, there was never the slightest
question of Beazley moving from Defence — he and Hawke never
even broached the possibility — and he was free to get on with the
restructuring programme he had begun. With the White Paper now

tabled, Beazley felt that 'we at last had in place a strategy of self-reliance,' and now turned his particular attention to Australia's defensive alliances in its own regional backyard. The White Paper had identified Australia's 'primary strategic environment' as being all of South-East Asia and the Southwest Pacific, the two designated areas from which the threats to Australia's security might emerge. In this area Beazley envisioned a different approach to the one that had for a long time been in operation. In former times, there was no doubt whatsoever about the role that the countries of South-East Asia played in the Australian defence scheme. They were variously known as 'The Threat,' the 'Yellow Peril,' 'The Teeming Hordes on Our Doorstep,' and so on. While those simplistic notions had largely broken down since the days of Sir Robert Menzies, Beazley's desire was to hasten this process, so that Australia's northern neighbours would be cast in an entirely different role – such as 'partners,' for example, 'allies,' and 'Australia's future'.

One part of this process was retrieving an old treaty from the Defence Department basement that had been close to long forgotten, dusting it off, and putting it in working order again. It was called the Five Power Defence Arrangement – between Britain, Australia, New Zealand, Malaysia and Singapore – and to that stage, if it was referred to at all, it was called the Five-Horsepower Defence Arrangement.[98] The FPDA had come into existence in 1971 in the wake of a failed attempt by Indonesia to move against Malaysia in the mid-1960s. While the agreement had provided a loose structure to coordinate various military exercises in those countries in the previous 15 years, Beazley wanted to revitalise it, and had signalled as much in the White Paper. 'I wanted to make sure,' he says, 'that we could use our defence forces effectively, diplomatically, in the region around us. That was the South Pacific and South-East Asia, so I wanted to breathe life back into the FPDA, and I wanted to make the Australian presence felt in the South Pacific.' For the record, this approach was entirely consistent with the approach long advocated by his father, who as far back as 1969, had told an MRA conference that 'Australia needed to stop worrying about being invaded by Asian countries and attend to its responsibility as a neighbour to these countries'.[99] It was also consistent with what Kim Jnr had written in a letter to his parents from India, in June of 1966, that: 'A Labor Party guided by God with a genuine concern for Asia and the world would be a great thing for Australia and Asia.'

But was it really the Defence Minister's role to institute that change in approach towards Asia? There were those who thought that organising such alliances was more properly the role of Bill Hayden, the Foreign Minister, but Beazley did not agree: 'Bill Hayden was not too interested in the South-East Asian area, the South Pacific,' Beazley says. 'Bill's focus was more — actually on the global issue, the arms control issues, the big picture issues.' David Jenkins of the *Sydney Morning Herald*, put it less kindly: 'While Foreign Minister [Hayden] was travelling to some of the better-padded hostelries of New York and Paris and addressing himself to global issues,' he wrote, 'the Defence Minister was back in Canberra setting the policy agenda in Southeast Asia and the South Pacific'.[100] Hayden had, in fact, labelled the FPDA as: 'no longer relevant' and a 'hangover from the colonial period'.[101]

The relationship between Beazley and Hayden was always quite a difficult one, in part because of the positions they filled. 'The art of diplomacy,' someone once said, 'is the art of being able to say "good doggie, good doggie", while you reach behind you for a big rock'. A cheap one-liner perhaps, but therein lay a tale; for if Hayden was in no doubt that the clearly defined role of Beazley was to provide only the rock, while he did most of the talking and forging of relationships, that was not *exactly* the way Beazley saw it. 'We needed to separate the diplomacy from defence,' he says, 'and not have our defence policy dominated by our diplomacy of the region. What you had to do was to use the forces that you developed for the defence of Australia to advance your diplomatic interests in the region.' Bill Hayden believed rather that 'essentially defence structure must follow diplomacy,' and this difference of approach was the source of conflict between the two.

Together with the revitalisation of the Five Power Defence Arrangement, Beazley was also instrumental in setting up a Joint Declaration of Principles with Papua New Guinea — essentially a security arrangement whereby if either country found itself under external armed attack, it would be obliged to consult the other. What was in it for PNG was clear. As a near neighbour who had seen Indonesia in recent times swallow both West New Guinea and East Timor to make them Indonesian provinces — as well as regular incursions across New Guinea's border by Indonesian troops in pursuit of guerillas — there was a clear motivation on their part to get a formal alliance with a powerful neighbour, to strengthen their defence. But its usefulness for Australia? Certainly Australia would always have taken a very dim view of any move by Indonesia on PNG, but if it actually came to it, one strong view had it that there would be very little that could be done that did not look like the Vietnam War. Foreign Minister Bill Hayden, for one, thought it was most unwise, and said so at some length both in Caucus and before the Cabinet. There was no benefit for Australia he said, just an increased likelihood that Australia would be sucked into a quagmire not of its making. 'I was never a keen Treaty signer,' Hayden says of his time as Foreign Minister, 'I think they tend to *imply* commitments, even if they are not explicitly there, you can raise expectations which you might then find difficult to meet.'

Beazley took precisely the opposite view that, just as the Dibb Report and the White Paper had highlighted the importance of the stability of the regions immediately to Australia's north, it was paramount that Australia do all it could to bolster that stability by confirming its commitment to a key ally. Just as the FPDA confirmed Australia's commitment to the defence of Malaysia and Singapore, the JDP would bring PNG 'into line' with them. He put this view to Hayden in Cabinet with a force that the then Foreign Minister will never forget. 'Kim has a wide range of personality styles,' Hayden says. 'He can be mild and persuasive, or good humoured and entertaining. But when he's got to be, he can be as tough as blazes, and in fact on that day when I was digging my toes in, he *went for me* and I remember thinking "he reminds me of a tough rugby union forward, hitting the ruck without any apologies to his opponents".' In short, Beazley smothered Hayden's objections with his all-out attack, and won the day. 'You wouldn't talk of the PNG agreement in terms of a hard and fast alliance,' Beazley says, 'but it was a formalised assumption of Defence responsibility. Hayden tended to be a bit less interested in the Pacific, whereas we tended to take a great deal of interest. We regarded it as an area of critical importance for Australia's defence.'

With such clear personal victories on the political stage, Beazley's prestige in Parliament continued to rise, and not only on the Labor side of the House. On one occasion around this time, when John Howard and Kim Beazley passed each other in opposing directions in the parliamentary corridors, there was the usual nod of friendly acknowledgement and semi-lifted hand of greeting. Howard happened to be with one of his heavyweight Liberal colleagues, and made a comment that this colleague would pass on to others. 'If ever there was a national crisis,' John Howard reportedly said in Beazley's wake, turning after him, 'and we had to form the one national government for the sake of the nation, then that guy is the one Labor man I'd be happy to serve under.'[102] The noted journalist Paul Kelly, who occasionally dined with John Howard, has a solid recollection of Howard speaking on much the same subject around this time, but with a different spin. 'If I had to form a government of national unity,' Kelly remembers him saying, 'the two Labor men I'd have in my cabinet would be John Button and Kim Beazley.' Further confirming John Howard's one-time high opinion of Kim Beazley, is a conversation he had five years later with radio broadcaster, Mike Carlton, at a lunch in London. When Carlton had asked Mr Howard which members of the Opposition he most respected, the reply had come without hesitation: 'Kim Beazley.'

Brian Burke, Beazley's old friend who had been the Premier of Western Australia for over four years, was another who was impressed with the way his ALP colleague had developed as a Federal politician. And there, around the middle of 1987, he was on the phone. Burke was always on the phone at that time, always urging Kim to do the same thing – come home, come home to take Burke's spot to be the Premier of Western Australia. 'He was going to go and do his Irish Ambassador stint and then come back as a Federal politician,' Beazley recollects, 'and his view was that I should return home to fill his position. He was constantly urging me to do it.' Beazley says that he was 'not particularly interested,' although Syd Hickman remembers having one particularly long conversation on the subject in Beazley's office, where, as adviser, he strongly advised his Minister that it would be extremely unwise to pursue such an option. 'He very seriously thought about it,' says Hickman, 'but it was a silly idea, and I told him "don't be crazy". I said, "Look, the Defence budget is vastly bigger than the entire budget of Western Australia — here you're dealing with big stuff, important stuff, talking to the Americans, working out alliances; there you're talking about potholes and primary schools and hospitals". And he sort of said "yes that's true". He probably never would have but he definitely did think about it.' Either way, the upshot was the same. Beazley did not take up Burke's suggestion, at least in part because he was already fulfilled professionally. 'I thought it was an exceptionally good thing to be Defence Minister of the Commonwealth,' he explains, 'which had been my only ambition. Ultimately I had no desire to swap that for being the Premier of Western Australia. And while I would never be dismissive of State politics, once you know what it is to be in National politics, I don't think you'd ever want to leave it for that.'

On Monday 8 February 1988, the Australian Labor Party was rocked by extraordinary news. Mick Young had decided to take his bat and ball and go home. Just like that, he up and quit politics. Precipitating his departure had been the Harris-Daishowa Affair, in which 10 000 dollars had been donated to the ALP by a logging company and was undeclared, all happening in an area of party operations that was Young's responsibility. The previous week, Young had been cleared of any wrongdoing in the affair — just as he ultimately had been the first time in the Combe/Ivanov Affair, and then in the famous Paddington Bear episode a year after that (where he had failed to declare the bear, so avoiding duty tax, when coming through Australian customs); but this time Young decided that he had had enough of it. No amount of pleading by Bob Hawke would change his mind. After spending half the night and part of the following morning in the effort, the Prime Minister finally accepted this, and called Kim Beazley late in the morning to tell him two things: first, that Mick had resigned, and second, that he wanted Kim to take over one of Mick's key roles for the Government, that of Leader of the House in the lower chamber — the position that decides on the legislative priorities on the house floor, how the debate will be run, who will speak, what tactics to pursue, and so forth.

Beazley was aghast at both bits of news, and proved powerless to alter either event. Mick, when he tracked him down, would simply not be dissuaded. He reluctantly put the phone down and then, thinking of some more arguments, called him back again, but his best friend's answer was the same — no. And nor would Hawke move from the view that Beazley should do as he had done in 1983, and take over Mick's role in Government. In Beazley's mind, being Leader of the House, at the very least, required intimate knowledge of the vast array of standing orders — the many precise rules under which debates in Parliament are conducted — and though he had a rough idea of a few of them, he felt he had no idea whatsoever of the arcane detail of them. There were, after all, over 400 of the brutes. 'You'll get the hang of it quick enough, Kim,' Hawke told him, 'you're made for the job'. Hawke himself had no hesitation about his appointment, though he now acknowledges that some others did: 'I think there was no-one who doubted Kim's present capacity and his [future potential],' he recalls, 'though one reservation that some people expressed was whether he had in a sense, enough "dog" in him. But [on balance] I think most people had seen him in action in factional manoeuvrings and ... knew how tough he could be. Personally, I never had any doubt that he could be tough enough if required.' Keating, weighed in on the subject too, publicly predicting just days after Beazley assumed the post: 'He'll develop a bit more hardness. None of us like it, but we develop it out of necessity.'[103]

Hawke had other reasons for putting Beazley in the job. 'He's always been a very good parliamentary performer and he loves it,' he says. 'He is good on his feet ... he actually loves parliamentary debate, parliamentary tactics and so he was ideal. And of course by that stage he was so well on top of his portfolio ... as Minister for Defence. Plus he had a sense of humour and one of the important features — and this is very important as Leader of the House — not only did he have the respect of his own people, but he was respected by the Opposition. Mick Young had that, Mick was incredible, he was so funny he could ridicule the Opposition and they were laughing with him, so it was very important to have someone in that position who could have the respect of the House as a whole, and that was Kim. Both blokes could deliver the barb without the venom ...'

Beazley was acutely aware of the Young legacy, and agreed entirely that Young had been a magnificent Leader of the House. He frankly could not see how he could measure up to him; but the other reason he didn't really want the job was simple workload. 'I was Defence Minister,' he says, 'and didn't want anything else.' Too bad, Bob had decided and that was that. As it happened, Hawke was right and Beazley would get the hang of it quickly enough. The next day the Clerk of the House of Representatives, Alan Browning, helped put his mind at ease by breezily asserting that, 'there are only about ten standing orders that you really need to know, like when the Opposition moves a motion of censure, and when ...'

And so on. On and on. At least that's what it was for Beazley night after night, thereafter, in an effort to master the massive brief before him. Over time, Beazley brought his own style to the role of Leader of the House, based largely on the perception he had garnered of the role — as always, started by what his father had told him — and then overlaid with his own experience. 'I have always loved the House of Representatives,' he says, 'I have always thought that you have to give the Opposition a bit of a go, that you can't be *too* hard. As it happens I think I was a fairly hard Leader of the House but I always thought that for Parliament to function as the founding fathers intended it to, there has got to be a bit of liberality in the way in which standing orders are operated, so I tried to be as fair-minded as I could on that.'

By Beazley's reckoning there were two other key strands to his role. The first was that the Leader of the House, 'carries the burden of the argument for the Government', and it meant that he would suddenly have to become far more intimate with all the policies that the Government was pushing. Perhaps more importantly still was Beazley's firm conviction that as Leader of the House, 'every Minister who got in trouble was entitled to a defence from the person in that position. So I would take on board all the censure motions, all the argy-bargy in the House and accept responsibility for it. Sometimes I would suggest to the Minister under attack that they not participate in the debate and I would do it all myself, and sometimes I would say I would go second.' Clearly, the role was one in which Beazley was well placed to rise in the esteem of his parliamentary colleagues.

It was a time when the Hawke Government was under attack from the Opposition on the parliamentary floor because of the disastrous run of messy imbroglios. As well as the Harris-Daishowa Affair, the Sports and Tourism Minister John Brown was also on the rack having been accused of misleading Parliament over the awarding of an audiovisual contract at the Brisbane Expo; Senator Michael Tate was being accused of misleading the Senate; and the Health Minister, Dr Neal Blewett, was fully immersed in the 'Medigate' Affair — where he was accused of releasing information to a Labor colleague which was in possible breach of legislation guaranteeing the confidentiality of doctors incomes.[104] Beazley resolutely defended each Minister in turn, expanding his level of governmental expertise and experience, and garnering warm feelings from his colleagues in the process.

Being the Leader of the House brought Beazley still closer to Hawke. Beazley says, 'it went with the territory'. It meant that late-night cigars in Hawke's office were an even more frequent occurrence, and it was during these sessions that Beazley became even more aware of how irrevocably the relationship between the Prime Minister and Treasurer Keating had broken down. There had of course been signs of this, with the two having had another particularly notable blow-up the previous year; but to this point, Beazley had not realised how deeply the feelings on both sides ran. 'It just became clearer that Paul was getting frustrated,' Beazley recounts, 'and that Bob was getting more and more morbid, and beginning to obsess about their conversations.' Beazley was aware that John Dawkins was getting around telling people that Hawke's time had come, but he had not realised just how active Keating was in destabilising Hawke. Frequently, when with Hawke, the conversation would turn to what Keating had said to the press gallery that day in his 'background briefings'. 'What Paul didn't quite realise,' Beazley explains, 'is that Bob had a big press office and an encyclopaedic knowledge of anything that Paul was likely to say in the press gallery. Paul had a very funny personality trait where he would divide what he regarded as "an analytical briefing," from an actual "full-blooded lobbying assault". So he'd go up into the press gallery and talk about all of his achievements and how Bob's nowhere near that, and refer to him as "old Jellyback," and he would assume that what he was doing was not undermining Bob at all, but simply advancing his own interests as a potential leader. This used to drive Bob *nuts*. Bob would hear about this sort of stuff and go nuts to me.'

Oddly enough, Keating also would 'go nuts' to Beazley after the Prime Minister inevitably upbraided the Treasurer for his disloyalty. On many occasions Keating waylaid Beazley and complained bitterly to him about the hideous injustices of what Hawke had said to him *this* time. 'He'd come to me,' Beazley remembers, 'and he'd say to me, "Kim, is there *nobody* loyal in this sort of thing? You know I've had to put up with an awful lot, I've done things for Bob. And I'm up in that gallery, and I am briefing them on what the Government is up to and now Bob thinks I'm being disloyal!"' Perish the thought. 'The thing is,' Beazley says, 'Paul would actually believe it. He'd believe that he wasn't undermining Bob. If you weren't actually so nervous about what was happening — it was exceptionally funny.' And if he had been in the mood, which Beazley rarely was, Keating would make it funnier still by invariably accompanying his diatribes against Hawke with imitations, mixed with an 'analysis of Bob's personal demeanour, and habits, and the shape of his face and his mannerisms and all the rest of it'. Despite this difficult situation, what always staggered Beazley was that, despite all their mutual antipathy, 'the Government still ran quite well, and Paul would still have a professional relationship with Bob. After all this he'd go in, sit down and they'd talk about the economy! I think that was for two reasons: firstly, Bob was a very professional Prime Minister and Paul was intellectually proud, and therefore he felt that it would be demeaning not to be able to conduct a portfolio rationally while nevertheless engaged in a contest with the Prime Minister.'

Beazley was never remotely persuaded by any of the arguments Keating used against Hawke. 'Keating was of a different political culture from anything that I had been used to,' Beazley comments. 'He was a real hard-scrabble politician, a real knock-down-drag-out politician. There was nothing more important to him than grabbing that top job and using it well. He is just about as hard-nosed as anyone I have come across and he would have his list of woes against Bob, but most of his woes were simply that Bob had a fair run as Prime Minister and Bob ought to go. It all boiled down to that in the end. He fashioned arguments after a while about "momentum being lost", and all the rest of it, but that was still what it boiled down to in the end — he wanted a go at the top job.'

Beazley, however, didn't – at least not at that time. When Beazley had taken Young's role as Leader of the House, Hawke had publicly praised him as 'a man of outstanding capacities', and said that he was a potential candidate for the PM's job. Beazley, typically, demurred. On ABC Radio on 16 February, 1988, he said, 'I think you have to have a particular burning desire to have [such ambitions] and that doesn't reside within me'. Regardless, the media speculated that there was a subterranean contest between Keating and him to be the heir apparent, and in the ensuing months, nay *years*, Beazley found himself obliged to quell that speculation. 'I have made it adequately clear that I'm not Keating's competitor,'[105] he flatly told David Humphries of *The Age* in March of that year. 'You have to make a judgement about the quality of someone's mind, their policy making capacity, their ability to develop the flexible approach necessary in a leader. And Keating's got all that. I think his claims are great and when the time comes — it's not going to be for a while yet anyway — I think that it's all very much in the interests of the Party to see that [the succession] is not an unstable process.'

In another interview, with Nikki Savva, for the *West Australian*, he sounded a familiar theme: 'There is no way, shape or form I will contest the deputy leadership or the leadership of the party,' he said. 'It's not what interests me and there are big contenders. There's a big contender for the leadership when it becomes available and that will probably not be for some considerable time — and that's Keating and I will support him.'[106]

Such machinations, together with being Leader of the House and Defence Minister, and still the Member for Swan, kept him very busy. But, perhaps, that was just the way Kim Beazley was, whatever his situation — busy. To his colleagues and friends, there seemed *always* to be an air of 'public duty' about him, and always had been since the days of spreading the word in India, a sense that his own desires and needs had to be sacrificed for the greater public good. It was something that fitted very well within the Moral Rearmament culture that he had grown up in, and while it was most admirable in the strictly personal sense, the truth of it was that it also placed a great strain on his family in general, and on Mary in particular.

During Easter of 1988, only two months after he had taken over the role of Leader of the House, Mary had had enough. She told him that the marriage was over, that he was to move out. It was *over*.

Beazley was devastated. Looking back on it, it is obvious to him now that the split had been a long time coming — maybe from the moment he said 'I do', and even before. But when he had made his vows at the wedding in Oxford he had never questioned that his marriage to Mary was for life, had never considered that when he was in Perth his head would not be under the same roof as that of his daughters. Mary would have none of it. Of course there had been happy days in their marriage, many of them. As recently as the previous Australia Day, at the climax of the Bicentennial celebrations, the two had a wondrous day together out on Sydney Harbour with the Hawkes, with Prince Charles and Princess Diana, and other dignitaries — but that was the *point*. Such happy days invariably involved the distraction of other people being around, other things happening. When it was just the two of them, left to their own devices, they were simply not happy. At best, their relationship had become as Princess Diana had seemed to Mary on that day: 'a bit remote and very uncomfortable.' At worst, it was ... far worse. 'So what I said,' she remembers, 'was that from my point of view there was no way our marriage could be brought back to life, and that he would have to make his arrangements to leave over the next few weeks.'

Unknown to Kim, Mary also made one phone call to Mick Young, telling him what had happened. 'He's going to need you, Mick,' she said, 'please stick close to him.' Young was supportive of his bereft mate, as was the Prime Minister. In many late-night conversations with Hawke at the Lodge, Beazley shared some of his pain, and told

Bob that he was even contemplating resignation ... 'He did talk to me a lot about it,' Hawke recollects, 'and I just told him that I supported him. He had this wrenching feeling that his continued absence was a problem — and he felt particularly badly in regard to the girls, whom he adores. I just said "well, sure that's a factor but you have a vocation in politics and there are prices that are paid. You shouldn't be ruthless, but you have an enormous contribution to make and you could be Prime Minister one day".' Their conversation finished up with the younger man sticking to his guns regardless, and telling Hawke that he was 'still going to talk to Mary and if Mary said that my resignation would hold the thing together then I was off. For my sake, for the kids' sake, for a way out of the sheer acrimony and all the rest of it, I thought that was the only way to go.'

With all that in mind, the Minister for Defence continued to fight a furious rearguard action to keep his marriage and family together. In long conversations with Mary he confirmed that he was prepared to resign, that he was certain that things could get better, that they could make it, that he would organise himself to spend more time in Perth, that for the sake of the children they both should do everything in their power to give it another go. But nothing worked. Seeking counsel elsewhere — most particularly about the mysterious whys and wherefores of women, of how their minds worked on such matters — he received some very salient advice from Carolyn Tannock, the wife of an old friend, Professor Peter Tannock. 'She said to me,' he recounts, "when women actually finally decide to do these things, their mind is already made up, and you can't change their minds on it, no matter what you do. They are not like men in these matters — men will often send out quite overt signals, while women send out covert signals and if you haven't picked them up by this point in time and she has got to that point of saying it really is over you are not going to talk her round".'

Bit by bit, slowly, slowly, he came to accept that the marriage really was finished. When acceptance finally did hit, he recalls, 'it was so sad. It was the most depressing moment of my life. I loved her'. As is the way of such things, both consulted a lawyer — the same one as a matter of fact, in the early stages — though there was actually very little in dispute, and absolutely no acrimony. Both agreed on two central things. The marriage would be dissolved and Mary would keep custody of both girls; and she would keep practically all the capital assets, including the house (and its mortgage), because that was, after all, where the two children would continue to live. He would walk away with a 25 000 dollar lump-sum payment to try to get started again, and Mary waived all rights to his future superannuation payout, which given the length of his parliamentary service would ultimately be a considerable amount. They also agreed to actually stay living together in the same house for another month or so, as both Kim's parents and Lady Molly Paltridge were looking forward to attending the opening of the new Parliament House in early May, and they felt that it would put a serious crimp in their celebrations if they knew their respective children were getting divorced.

That opening of the new Parliament came and went — with a good time had by all — and finally it was time. Jessica, 11, and Hannah, 10, were told, the terrible day came, and their father moved out on a Saturday morning. 'It nearly ripped us apart,' recalls Hannah, who was just 10 years old at the time, 'but I guess in the end we could see it was probably the best thing.'

For Kim there was nothing for it but once again to move back home with his parents for a few weeks, to have a place to sleep while he found himself some new digs. After apartment-hunting he found a bachelor's pad which was – not by pure coincidence — a mere hundred metres from the WACA, Western Australia's principal cricket oval and a place that Beazley loved to go to watch a game when possible.

There is some evidence that his personal unhappiness briefly affected his performance in his portfolio. Sleep was a problem and he was constantly troubled by odd dreams. This as well as 'the round eternal of the taxbook and the journal,' the constant travel between Canberra and Perth, the demands of being Minister for Defence and Leader of the House, was enough to wear any man down.

On one occasion when he had just returned to Perth from roughly his 25th cross-continental trip of the year — and it was still only the middle of the year — he was in his flat sleeping the sleep of the dead and the dead-exhausted when he thought he heard the phone ringing. He groped through the darkness and picked it up. 'Minister,' a very crisp official voice came back, 'this is the Watch Office. Minister, we have a situation ...' The 'Watch Office' is another name for the Australian Defence Force Command Centre, in the bowels of the Department of Defence building in Canberra — a rough equivalent of the 'War Room' so frequently displayed in Hollywood movies. A 'situation' was military-speak for 'potential problem of the first order'.

'We have a situation,' he remembers the voice continuing, 'what has happened is that there is a foreign fishing boat in our territorial waters which has failed to heed an order by our own naval vessel to stop.' Beazley, still not quite emerged from his deep sleep, nevertheless managed to gather himself long enough to ask 'Well what have you done so far, Commander?'

'We gave the order for him to stop and we have fired a shot across his bow and he has not responded to that either,' he remembers the voice at the end of the line saying. 'Minister, we want permission to fire into the ship — we will try and fire into a part of the ship where we don't see any personnel, to try and avoid taking a life.'

'Ok, shoot,' Beazley recalls saying, before rolling over and going back to sleep.

The following morning he went into his Perth office and regaled his staff with the story of this extraordinary dream he had had the night before, how he'd had some weird ones since he and Mary had split up, but this one was a fair dinkum *doozy!* Everyone laughed, and got on with the business of the day. Two days later, Beazley was still in his Perth office when the phone rang. This time the voice was less crisp than agitated. *Officially* agitated. It belonged to Admiral Michael Hudson, Chief of the Naval Staff and he came straight to the point.

'Minister you had an extraordinary call the other night.'

'What?' replied Beazley, still entirely unclear about what the man could be referring to.

'Yes, you were called by the Watch Office the other night about a foreign fishing boat . . .'

'WHAT!?!' Beazley interrupted.

'Yes, the call should never have come to you it should have gone through me, before it got anywhere near . . .'

'What *happened*?'

'Well fortunately,' Beazley remembers the man replying, 'the person handling the signals had the presence of mind to transmit the order in clear English so it wasn't coded, and the fishing boat must have been listening because instantly the order was transmitted to the patrol boat he stopped.'

Beazley breathed again. 'It was a lesson to me,' he says now, 'not to make decisions in the middle of the night when I'm not awake.'

Even with his new-found responsibilities as Leader of the House, and his continuing role as Defence Minister, Beazley still managed to keep his international connections going, making frequent trips overseas. On one such occasion, in the middle of 1988, he journeyed to England, and while there, went to meet with his old mate from Oxford days, Tony Blair — by then a rising force in the still moribund British Labour Party. Beazley had often looked Blair up over the previous few years, just as Blair would seek him out when in Australia, as they found they had an enormous amount in common in terms of their political ideas. In the company of his former press secretary, Michelle Schofield, who was then living in London, Beazley was invited to dine with the Blairs in their home in suburban London. Late into the night the four discussed the whys and wherefores of politics, both domestically and internationally, and Blair seemed particularly interested in how Labor in Australia was faring with all the economic changes they had instituted. Michelle Schofield remembers the Blairs as nice-enough people, but she had no particular presentiment that their host would go far. As she recalls, immediately after they had taken their leave from the Blair's home though, 'Kim turned to me and said, "he's going to be Prime Minister one day".'

Back in Canberra, Beazley slowly began to feel more comfortable living the life of a single man again. It was not easy at first — he hadn't dated anyone other than Mary for the previous two decades, and had never been noted as a 'player' in Canberra during the marriage — but he gave it a go anyway. 'It was a very important time for him,' says one friend about this period in Beazley's life, 'because it meant that he could actually do things that he didn't do as a young man growing up in a very restricted family. It actually gave him a moment of liberation so it was both exhilarating and at the same time terrifying for him — he had women everywhere — and he made it very clear around Parliament House that he and Mary had broken up because he didn't want people to get the wrong idea.' His romantic life for this brief stretch of time was not so much fast free-wheeling, as coasting along on an entirely unfamiliar road, but this too began to pall, and he went into something of a mild melancholy as a result. Nothing serious, just a general feeling that things were not as they should be, and the way to make them right was not obvious to him.

On the 10th October, 1988, Mrs Peggy Doogue barely recognised him. There before her, at her granddaughter Eliza's fifth birthday party at the McDonalds Restaurant in the Sydney suburb of Cremorne, was Kim alright, a man she had come to regard almost as a surrogate son over the years; but this was most definitely not the man she knew. 'I looked at him, and I thought, "Oh my God, what's happened to him?"' she recalls. The man she knew always had the light of vitality in his eyes, a spring in his step whatever weight he might be at the time, a laugh never too far from his lips. But this bloke was drooping, with the life seemingly drained clear out of him, a spiritual shell. 'Kim, whatever is the matter?' she asked gently as the pack of five year olds careened around them. It was Mary he said. As Mrs Doogue knew, they had separated, and he was struggling. Whatever troubles they might have weathered during their marriage, it had never occurred to him for a single instant that they would not remain married for life, and now that it had dissolved, it was hitting him pretty hard. On top of that, he was hurting financially. The trouble at the moment was that he was finding it a colossal inconvenience not even having a car when he was in Perth. As a matter of fact, he was saving up to buy himself one, and hoped that in a couple of months he would have enough money to get it. And, well, just between the two of them, he was lonely.

Mrs Doogue listened, staggered in spite of herself, that the man before her was responsible for a portfolio with a budget of well over 10 billion dollars a year, and yet he was saving up to get four wheels beneath him! On that subject there was little she could do, but on the fact of his loneliness, maybe she actually could help. 'Why don't you give Susie Annus a call?' she asked, 'Why don't you take her out to dinner, or something like that?'

'Susie?' she remembers him responding, 'Is she single these days? I thought she was still with what's-his-name.'

'No, she broke up with him, a while back ...'

Only three or four days later, Susie Annus, now a television producer for Channel Nine in Perth, returned from the studio to see a single message sitting on her desk: 'Kim Beazley phoned and will phone later.' Hello? Why would Kim Beazley be phoning her? They were friends certainly, more or less, and had been for the last 18 years. But it certainly wasn't like him to call her up out of the blue like that.

The following day she was at her desk when the phone rang, and a sixth sense told her it was going to be him. It was. Hi. How are you? Wondering how you were getting on. Was chatting to Peggy Doogue the other day about you, and thought I'd give you a call, and ... was wondering if she would like to have a bite to eat sometime. She would. He said he would book somewhere and call her back later. He did. He had booked a table for two at his favourite, The Mediterranean restaurant in Subiaco. 'And I thought hang on —

The Mediterranean — that's a very swish restaurant, that's a bit sort of *romantic*, just for two old friends.' Too late. The table was booked, and she had said yes. It went well and they talked into the night. 'My former summation of Kim was that he was terribly serious,' Susie Annus recalls. 'I never thought of him as having the humour and the warmth and the fun that he did in fact have. It wasn't a night where he spent it crying on my shoulder. He had a lot more humour and warmth to him than I thought he would have and we basically just kept chatting. And then he took me home and gave me a peck on the cheek and said 'Can I call again?' and got back into his parents' car which he'd borrowed for the night.' Perhaps only a fortnight later she got a call. It was Kim's close friend, Rob Pascoe, calling from Melbourne. 'Listen, I believe you're going to dinner with Kim at Rob and Val French's next Saturday night?'

'Yes ...' replied Susie, wondering how on earth such a thing was worthy of comment from someone she barely knew, who was clear on the other side of the continent. 'Well, I just wanted you to know, it's actually going to be a surprise 40th birthday for Kim,' Pascoe replied, 'and there'll be about 100 people there, so you should be prepared ...'

She felt unwell. An event that she thought would be an intimate soiree she'd be attending with Kim on the quiet, was in fact going to be a rather grand public occasion, where she would suddenly be on display on the arm of someone still married to someone who was a friend. 'But there was nothing, I could do,' she explains. 'It made me uncomfortable, but I just had to go through with it ...'

There were two things that struck both Justice Robert French — he had become a judge in 1986 — and Robert Pascoe, who had organised the party. First, how well Kim and Susie seemed to go together, and secondly how many people that they had invited to the function hadn't actually seen the guest of honour for years and years because he had been taken away from the world he grew up in, the world of Claremont, Hollywood High and UWA. It was almost, mused Justice French, as if the people at the party were of a world from which Kim had long ago departed and to which he was just now starting to return. 'With Kim, there is an internal Labor Party world, the intricacies of which we were certainly not privy to; there was a governmental world that he inhabited, dealing with bureaucrats and officials; and an international world that he inhabited in terms of his relationships with Defence Ministers from other countries. There are whole worlds in which he moves which are quite distinct from the world in which we move. We talk about it, but you can never give other people a clear window into what it is like. After he started going out with Susie, I thought he moved back into our world a bit more.'

That other political world was always there, though, always calling him. In December of 1988, Beazley had to journey to New Zealand to hose down a growing controversy concerning Australia's request for New Zealand to buy four Anzac frigates that were under production in Australia, at a price the New Zealand public thought too high. The ill-will towards Beazley personally was compounded by the fact that New Zealand's Government, led by David Lange, continued to be aggressively anti-American in its approach — still refusing access to all nuclear-powered vessels — and Beazley was seen as the representative of a government that was toadying up to the Americans.

The tone of the times was set when the Defence Minister landed at Wellington airport to see a huge banner, black painted on white, saying — 'Frig off Beazley'. As he was driven into Wellington proper, he couldn't help but notice posters on seemingly every telegraph pole and spare patch of wall, with a rather unflattering likeness of himself dressed as a Mafia don, puffing a cigar and wafting the smoke into a skeleton. *'Beazley's Offer You Can't Refuse,'* it said in big letters beneath the drawing, before getting to the punchline: *'Of Course We Can. Tell Mr Beazley Yourself. Say No To The Frigates.'* The personal danger for the Australian Defence Minister was considered so high by the New Zealand Government that the extra security of 30 armed men was provided for him during his stay, to forestall any nasty 'incidents'.

The day after arriving, Beazley went by Royal New Zealand Army helicopter to the Waiouru Army Base outside Wellington, and from there to a nearby open field where he observed the New Zealand Army going through some military exercises, before returning back to the base — to where a shamefaced colonel was awaiting him. Alan Ramsey, of the *Sydney Morning Herald*, would later tell his readers what happened then.[107]

'Do you want the good news first or the bad news?' Beazley swears the New Zealander asked him. The good news, said the high-ranking officer with an encouraging smile, was that they were now convinced nobody was trying to kill him. 'The bad news is we've blown up your briefcase.' In his absence, security had given Beazley's luggage a very thorough going-over. The only item that worried them was the briefcase. It held a number of briefing papers, nothing too important, but although the briefcase was shut tight, Beazley had left the key in the lock. Security X-rayed the briefcase and 'thought' they saw a wire running from the lock around the perimeter inside. This, they felt, 'suggested' perhaps an explosive device wired to detonate when the key was turned to unlock it. That's what they told Beazley, anyhow. So they blew it up. 'I thought it was the funniest thing I'd heard in years,' Beazley remembers of the moment. The New Zealanders did, eventually, buy the frigates. All things considered, it was a pretty good trip back from New Zealand to Australia, the more so because in contrast to the hostility that had surrounded him there, he knew he would soon be seeing Susie again, who was on his mind a lot these days.

Their relationship had progressed a long way, despite not inconsiderable resistance from her. Only a little over two months after they began going out together, now in January 1989, the two went for a quiet meal at a Greek restaurant, and were enjoying themselves immensely, when out of a clear blue sky, the Minister for Defence said, 'I think Greece would be a perfect place for a honeymoon, don't you?'

No Susie Annus *didn't*. At least not that quickly she didn't, sport. Her instinctive reaction was 'this man has to be saved from himself. He has to be made to understand that though such high morality is admirable, it isn't necessary that if you take someone out more than three times you should think that there's an obligation to marry them'. She admired his old-fashioned sense of chivalry but had a more worldly-wise approach herself, which recognised that 'anyone just separated is a loose cannon, and will be going through a lot of vulnerable periods'. For all that, she could not help admiring the gentle way in which he guided her into having a relationship in the first place. 'As Kim says, I galloped down to the bottom of the paddock and he had to gradually haul me back which is what really intrigued me about Kim, and the reason I think I really became interested in him was because his people skills are incredible. He knew exactly what was going on in my mind, which was "this is too difficult," "this is not something I want to get involved in," "I know Mary, I know you," "this is too hard". But he still hauled me back, gently, gently.' He was, to her eyes at least, a quite different sort of bloke from the rather austere student prince she'd come to know just under two decades previously. 'I think he was just much more comfortable with people, much more attuned to people than he was when I first knew him,' she says.

Back at the office in Canberra, his staff noticed a sudden up-tempo in the drumbeat of the Defence Minister. The relationship clearly had an enormous impact on him, both personally and professionally. Personally, and obvious to all, there was a newly bright mood around him all the time. Kim's personal assistant, Karen Bissaker, noticed it about two months after she had first made reservations for Kim's and Susie's first dinner date. 'He turned to me and said, "you know I have never been happier, she is the most wonderful person," and he said "I think I am falling in love with her".' The Prime Minister also noticed a difference in his favourite minister. 'When he went with Susie,' Bob Hawke says, 'it was palpable, the change in him. He became a new man.'

If things were falling into place for him in his 'civilian life,' so too were they professionally, with seeds that he had planted in his first years in Defence, now starting to present a handsome harvest. What Bob Hawke would call in his memoirs, 'the most massive peace time reorganisation of the defence forces in Australian history,'[108] was well underway. A lot of the defensive structure of Australia — in terms of airbases, military bases and naval facilities — was continuing the long haul of moving them from the southeast to the northwest of Australia. The submarines were being built in Adelaide.* Construction of the Anzac frigates would commence in the newly privatised Williamstown Dockyard later that year, meaning that because of Beazley initiatives the biggest naval shipbuilding programme the country had ever seen was under way.**

It is true that the Defence Minister was putting resources into the Navy. In the previous four years Naval deployments to the South Pacific had doubled, pleasing him greatly, as it had always been his belief that it was important that 'the Australian flag be shown in those areas as much as possible'.

---

* And Beazley was nothing if not proud of those submarines. In a speech in 1987 he had boasted that 'The six new Kockums type 471 submarines to be built in Australia to replace the Oberons will be the largest, longest ranging and most lethal conventional submarines in the Western world when they enter service in the 1990s.'

** If all of that sounds expensive, it was. And though Beazley had managed to pay for a lot of it by the savings made in defence industries, that did not entirely meet the added expense. In her report on *Four Corners*, Deborah Snow asserted: 'As the Minister continues to fuel his hungry capital investment programme, the real pinch is coming elsewhere in the Defence Forces. Manpower and day-to-day operations are hurting. To take just one example, the massive new Tindal Air Base cost over 200 million dollars. It is meant to house our frontline fighter squadron, yet it has got only two-thirds of the pilots it needs for minimum efficient operation and pilots are now leaving the RAAF at twice the rate they were five years ago.'

Planning was well under way for a major military exercise called Kangaroo '89 which would be held in the north of Australia later in the year. The joint facilities were now becoming less of an issue — though still flaring occasionally — and he had just the previous year negotiated an extension of ten years on the American's lease on the bases, with barely a word of protest emerging from anywhere. That included from his own party, which had quietly agreed with Beazley's assertion that the party platform should be changed to allow that extension. A further measure of the dominance that Beazley had in the ALP on such matters, was that the National Conference of the ALP had also allowed him to change the platform so that if Australia was ever at war, an ALP Government would be free to introduce conscription.

And where was the Opposition in all this? Exactly. Through it all, the Opposition had, in the words of one of their unnamed members quoted in the press, 'barely laid a glove on him,' although that was perhaps in part because they had been entirely preoccupied with their own travails, with Opposition leader John Howard finally being felled from the post by a coup at the hands of Andrew Peacock on Tuesday, 9 May 1989. The vote had been a thumping 44–27 against Howard.

Something else that had pleased Beazley, and made his worklife easier was the fact that Gareth Evans had taken over the role of Foreign Minister when Bill Hayden had left to take up the post of Governor-General in August of 1988. Even though professionally things had sometimes been strained between Beazley and Hayden, personally they had had quite cordial relations, and on the occasion of Hayden's final Cabinet meeting both Peter Walsh and Beazley had been notable for being the only two in the room who had spontaneously stood and applauded as Hayden had left the room.

Despite respecting Hayden, Beazley knew that it was always going to be easier working with Gareth Evans. They were like-minded on most issues, and enjoyed constantly bouncing ideas off each other to get input, with Evans later crediting Beazley with providing, 'a lot of valuable contributions,' to Australia's Regional Security White Paper. 'There had been a degree of tension between Hayden and Beazley,' Evans says, 'which evaporated completely once Kim and I started working together. We both made it a primary objective to find common ground and for the first time in Australian history, you had Defence and Foreign Affairs actively working with each other to produce an integrated view of the world.' Beazley agrees. 'Under Hayden,' he says, 'I was always a bit worried that Foreign Affairs had let issues in the South Pacific and South-East Asia drift, and had focused instead mainly on the great global issues, the arms control issues, the UN-type issues. For them that immediate region had lost a degree of focus and really it was Defence who was fascinated with Five Power Defence arrangements and putting life back into that, and it was Defence interested in the Pacific Patrol Boat programme and in keeping a western posture in the South Pacific. So in many ways Defence made the running. But when Gareth took over we just dropped it all. Foreign Affairs seized the agenda back again, because Gareth was fascinated with those areas and I think we had probably been acting a little bit outside our brief and we didn't need to act outside our brief any more because it was 100 per cent again in Foreign Affairs' focus.'

In all his time in Defence, Beazley had never hidden the fascination he had with things militaristic. During the *Four Corners* interview in May, 1989, as an example, he had been forthright: 'I just recollect I had this burning desire at about the age of 13,' he told ABC journalist, Deborah Snow, 'I really must join the Navy. Every time I get on board a warship now it resumes. I look at the fellows who are commanding warships now and they are all my age or perhaps slightly younger, but about my age, certainly my age at the time I was first appointed as Defence Minister and I keep thinking whenever I see these Commanders, well that's about the rank I would have and this is what I would now be doing if I had actually gone through with it.'

Snow: 'You get a fleeting desire to change places?'

Beazley: 'Not a fleeting desire, a frequent one.'

While all who knew Beazley accepted that he loved Defence, some of his parliamentary colleagues, especially opponents and members of the media, went further. Since the days when he had first been called 'Bomber' and 'Kimbo,' they were continual assertions that he had taken Australia's defensive capabilities over the line into *offensive* abilities. One journalist who particularly goaded him on this subject was Brian Toohey, who had five years before broken the story of the MX missile testing. In a heavy column attack in late May of 1989, which was syndicated around the country, Toohey asserted that although the Defence Minister had formally committed Australia's forces to embracing Paul Dibb's defensive posture of self-reliance, 'Beazley has [now] abandoned all of these policy restraints almost unnoticed ... and [Dibb's] carefully argued report has largely been tossed overboard.

'At the recent opening of the F18 fighter base at Tindal in the Northern Territory, Hawke read out a line written by Beazley in which he boasted that Australia could "deploy more forces, more quickly, to South-East Asia in support of our friends and allies than we have ever been able to do before ... " The revival of forward defence doctrines, especially when devoid of the intellectual rigour we have come to expect from Beazley, entails such serious distortions to his earlier plans to defend Australia, especially in terms of the cost of building extra range into new submarines, frigates and fighters, that we will end being branded as trigger happy neo-colonialists poking our noses into someone else's guerilla war.' There was more, a lot more, but the theme was the same. Beazley had taken things too far.

But if Toohey's journalistic attack stung when it was brought to Beazley's attention by one of his staff, what goaded him more was public criticism from within his own political camp — most particularly from the Left — that his collective initiatives amounted to no less than a 'new militarism'. In a speech in Adelaide, in late 1989, to a Labor business forum, Beazley made reply to such attacks. 'The idea that Australia might be seen as aggressive or militaristic is certainly novel,' he said. 'It is certainly ironic that some elements of the Left now seek to assail our efforts to achieve genuine self-reliance — a defence posture that embodies long-held Labor principles. While I think these views reflect an inadequate grasp of the imperatives of defence self-reliance, I welcome the assumption that we can now have confidence in our ability to defend ourselves.

'Without that rationalisation and overhaul of our dockyards, we could not have contemplated a nine billion dollar programme embracing six submarines and eight frigates.' However much he didn't mind being called 'Bomber,' or 'Kimbo,' there were few things more inclined to get Beazley riled than the notion that Australian Defence under his guidance had itself become 'Rambo-esque'. He explains, 'That suggestion appeared in a number of books at the time by a number of academics and they basically didn't like the fact that we actually took defence seriously; that we had acquired a large amount of equipment or were in the process of doing it; that we still had a relationship with the United States and that our self-reliance was based not on a non-defence strategy but a *real* defence strategy. They felt that the atmosphere that we were encouraging, in which we assigned significance to the military in Australia, was of itself militaristic; the fact that we had been prepared to contemplate intervention in places like Fiji; the fact that we would have our people in peacekeeping forces and things like that; they thought that all meant we were encouraging a militaristic view of society.

'It was complete and utter crap. I said in reply basically we are a peace loving people, we have a minimum defence for this country, no more than that but a confident one and that is all that we were aspiring to — we are not aspiring to direct and dominate other people, but we were aspiring to protect Australian interests if they were in any way under threat.'

Early one morning in late November of 1989, Susie Annus was heading into the Channel Nine network building in Perth, and left a message with the receptionist that if Kim Beazley were to call, she was to please put the call through to Studio 'C'.

'Kim Beazley...?' the receptionist had whispered back conspiratorially. 'Isn't it *terrible* about him?'

'Isn't what terrible?' Susie had replied quizzically.

'You know ... Haven't you heard? He's left his wife, to run off with a much younger woman.'

'No. That's not true,' returned Susie, bemused. 'I can assure you that's not true.'

'Well I can assure you it is true, a *very* young woman, I have it from an *excellent* source and ...'

'Well I'm a pretty good source myself and I can promise you that it's not correct.'

'Oh? And how well do you know him?'

Susie Annus leaned forward, so as not to miss her, and put a conspiratorial lilt in her own voice ...

'*I'm marrying him in eight weeks time*,' she whispered. '*But don't tell anyone.*'

In Perth, on 28 January 1990, just a few months after the marriage between Kim and Mary had been legally dissolved, Kim Beazley and Susie Annus were married. It had been a low-key proposal — 'I think it was just a matter,' Susie recalls, 'of "well we are going to get married, when does it fit in with your schedule and when does it fit in with mine?"' — and it was a low-key wedding, essentially just for family and very close friends. There had been a minor fear that the ceremony would be disrupted by disaffected airline pilots protesting at the role that the RAAF had played in transporting people around

Australia during their recent severe industrial trouble, but either because wiser counsel prevailed or because it was absolutely pouring on the day, the pilots didn't show.

They were married in the Anglican Christ Church, Claremont. This was the same church that Kim Snr and Betty had been married in over four decades before, and where Kim had been baptised. Susie's preference was to marry in her own Catholic church, but that was out of the question because of the doctrine that Catholics could not marry divorcees. Geraldine Doogue once again had pride of place — last time bridesmaid, this time matron of honour — with Jessica and Hannah as bridesmaids. Kim was in the same spot, as were his parents in much the same position as they had been in the church in Oxford in 1974, as was Lady Paltridge, while Susie Annus had moved from the fourth row up to the altar. Of the principal players the only person missing from the previous wedding, was Mary. (And she had sent a generous present, with all her best wishes for their union. She'd heard that Kim and Susie were going out one day, while driving along with Jessica, and her oldest daughter had mentioned, out of the blue ... 'actually, Mum, you know who Dad's going out with now ..?') The other notable change of personnel was that the jocular and knockabout Mick Young had replaced the serious and intellectual Hugh Nelson as Best Man — perhaps a sign of how the groom himself had changed in the ensuing two decades. In his speech, the groom did not neglect to thank Mrs Peggy Doogue for bringing them together.

Susie went househunting for their new base, knowing that her husband had only one requirement. It had to have a big verandah, so he could sit outside with his cigars and his books for long hours. She found just the place, in a leafy part of South Perth, just a kilometre or so from the Swan River. It was a largish, unpretentious bungalow; with a particularly deep verandah at the front, and a pool at the back for Kim to take his preferred form of exercise. By putting in all of the proceeds of the sale of her house and the bachelor apartment he had bought only 18 months before, and then borrowing heavily, they were just able to secure it. Kim then took both of his older daughters shopping so that they could have their own complete wardrobe of clothes when staying with him and Susie — basically whenever their father was in town — meaning that they could move more easily between their mother's and father's houses, without the constant hassle of packing and unpacking.

Susie's introduction to the real hurly-burly of politics was quick in coming. Only a fortnight after returning from their three-day honeymoon at the Esplanade Hotel in East Fremantle — where they had spent a fair amount of time in front of the television watching the Australian Commonwealth Games team rule victorious in Auckland — Bob Hawke called an election for 23 March 1990. Susie had now signed on for her husband's usual white-knuckle ride in campaigning, but it was just possible that the happiness they had found together had changed Kim from his previous ever-pessimistic outlook. Four days before polling day, Stephen Smith — by now the Secretary of the WALP — was in his office, personally signing off on the last of the direct mail to go out to the razor-edge seats of Cowan and Stirling, when his old friend Kim dropped by. 'He asked me how I thought we would go,' Smith remembers, and I said, 'I think we'll win six seats reasonably comfortably, but Cowan and Stirling will go right down to the wire.' And he said, "No, we'll hold eight, no problems."

'It was amazing! Here was Kim, the great pessimist, the great worrier, famous for it, and he was confidently saying we'd win eight seats. He walked out of the office, and I spent the rest of the day going through the entire campaign to make sure that I had missed nothing because if *Beazley* was saying that we are going to win eight, then I knew something must be wrong.'

Going into that 1990 election, Beazley's own stakes as a Cabinet Minister were at an all-time high and, as he had done with Aviation, he could look back with some satisfaction at what he had accomplished during his time in the Defence portfolio. In terms of his future leadership aspirations, what perhaps was most important was his own party's estimation of how he had performed. There was not universal praise. 'I think he was the most dangerous person that the defence of Australia ever had,' his parliamentary colleague Leo McLeay would say, looking back on it eight years later. 'It was all big toys — all of a sudden he got all the toys he would have liked in his life and he was having a dream run with the Prime Minister, the Prime Minister was willing to indulge him in that. He was also probably more slavishly pro-American than most other Defence Ministers we've ever had.' Aside from such jibes that 'Bomber' Beazley had appeared to enjoy it all a little too much, and had been too keen on the big-ticket defence items, in terms of his strategic repositioning of Australian defence, the estimation seemed to have been all but universally high. 'His strategic view was probably the best, was a better thought out one than most other Defence Ministers we've had,' McLeay concedes.

Others were markedly less qualified in their praise. In the words of one of the NSW Right's key powerbrokers, Stephen Loosley, who had been the Chairman of the ALP's National External Relations Committee, 'his achievement in Defence was phenomenal, in that he completely modernised Labor and Australia's defence policy in the 1980s. In his time, he took Labor policy from the ragged residue of opposition to American policy in Vietnam, to a position where even a left of centre Australian Government could cooperate quite openly and very effectively with a Republican administration well to the right of centre in Washington DC; one that could fit quite easily into a Social Democratic perspective on the Cold War; one that was made relevant to the Australian public and to the Labor Party itself nationally; that fitted into an industry policy, that fitted into an international relations perspective.

'And he did it all by arguing on a very high intellectual level ... It was a landmark performance by him, and acknowledged as such by all of us.' Paul Keating himself says that 'Kim's great contribution was to take Australia/USA problems off the map.' From that USA perspective, former Secretary of State, George Shultz, puts it more widely still. 'Internationally, he caused people to have a lot of respect for Australia and Australia's defence posture and its capability to think things through. He put Australia on a path to self-reliance.'

CHAPTER FOURTEEN

THE BATTLE ROYAL

'I can stand brute force, but brute reason is quite unreasonable.
There is something unfair about its use. It is hitting
below the intellect.'
Oscar Wilde, The Picture of Dorian Gray, *1891.*

Euphoria. The Hawke Labor Government had achieved its fourth straight election victory. Just as Beazley predicted, Western Australia had delivered eight of fourteen possible seats to the House, including Beazley's own.

Beazley got the summons. Kim, the Prime Minister told him on this morning of late March 1990, we've decided to move you on from Defence and make you the Minister for Transport and Communications. As Hawke jocularly explained it to Beazley, in words that would resonate in his ears for years, 'you have been working for yourself for the past five years, now you have got to work for Australia!' In the face of the obviously crestfallen Beazley, Hawke recalls following up a little more gently. 'Look, Kim,' he said, 'you are the best Minister for Defence this country has ever had, or likely to see, but the time has come when you have got to get a broader experience. This is not a demotion, this is in recognition for how good you are and you have just got to go forward on your experience ...' There were many who saw Hawke's moving of Beazley from Defence to Transport and Telecommunications as a part of Hawke's plan to 'groom' Beazley as a future Labor leader.* Bob Hawke agrees with them. 'I was thinking then about the future, his capacity for leadership,' Hawke says. 'Of course I wanted him to have rounded skills, and experience.' Others in Caucus, however, thought that the Prime Minister was simply putting Beazley in the key position of 'Minister for Bob's Mates'. He would after all, have the portfolio most directly responsible for such people as Kerry Packer, Rupert Murdoch and Sir Peter Abeles. It is a charge that still riles Beazley. 'That was an accusation made,' he acknowledges, 'but it was rubbish. Bob put me there I think for several reasons, firstly he did want to broaden me out and have me up there as an alternative leader. Secondly, I think he gave it to me because he thought I would be relatively hard-nosed, but also politically sensitive in dealing with the people who were influences [on] the media. So while I would not necessarily do what they wanted — I would not be in their pockets — I would also not be silly enough to grandstand in relation to them. I think he would have been aware of that, but I think those two reasons were subsidiary. I think the *main* reason he put me in there was that he had to present a justification for his further continuance as Prime Minister. He had been by now in power for seven years — he had just won an election against the breaks, and he was conscious of the fact that press opinion and a fair amount of public opinion was saying, "this Government has reached its use-by date".

'So what he decided he would do was take on the full micro-economic reform — the privatisations, the competition in relation to telecommunications, the works, and make it the centrepiece of his next three years. After we won the 1987 election, to a certain extent I think we had run out of ideas, and then after that Bob got onto micro-economic reform and I was the point man for the search.'

Which was fine for Hawke. Beazley remained less enamoured of the move and, by his own admission, he would spend a lot of the next few years 'pining for my old portfolio'. 'The hardest thing I had to do in

---

* One who was particularly glad to see Beazley move on from Defence to a more 'economic' portfolio was the Governor-General, Bill Hayden. On the day that Hayden left Parliament, in August 1988, he remembers having a long conversation with Bob Hawke on the subject of Beazley. 'I said to Hawke,' Hayden recollects, 'I know Kim doesn't want to shift out of Defence, he loves it, but you have to think of the future of the party and what will happen when you decide to retire, and you need to have a few people around capable of taking over apart from Paul Keating. I told him he ought to think of putting Kim in as Finance Minister, because Kim was undoubtedly going to be a party leader at some time, and he'd need that strength behind him.'

politics was to leave Defence.' In fact, the way he saw it, in the previous six years his focus had barely shifted from his own portfolio. 'I didn't care about anything else,' he says. 'From 1984 to 1990 the Defence portfolio absorbed me heart and soul, and I had become obsessed with it. I had a lot of other things going on, like marriages collapsing and other marriages starting up in that period, but I had become very narrow which is I think one of the reasons why Bob wanted me to move out.' While that may be doing himself a disservice, for his Cabinet colleagues had long noted that he was usually well-briefed on matters even far outside his own portfolio, it was true that he had not necessarily been a 'player' on all the major political issues of the day. Or at least not the winning player.

In the wake of the election just gone, Graham Richardson had been credited with saving the day by steering Labor towards a strong commitment to the environment, but he remembers that Beazley, 'thought politically I was mad'. (However, he would eventually back Richardson on the issue in Cabinet.) Nor, in the preceding seven years of Government had Beazley been particularly involved in the debate about floating the dollar, about how to deregulate the financial system, whether or not to allow in foreign banks, and so on. While he had certainly spoken on economic issues in Cabinet and at Federal Conferences — simply because all delegates of substance do — he had not been notable for saying anything *crucial* to sway a particular debate one way or the other.

The only notable exception to this was in 1985, where he was one of just five Cabinet Ministers to support Paul Keating's famous and doomed Option 'C' — essentially a goods and services tax proposal. In so doing he was, for one, going against Bob Hawke, who was quite opposed to Keating's proposal, but Beazley remembers well the reason for his support. 'I think the point about Option "C", at that point of time,' he explains, 'is that curiously in some ways it was the soft option. If you went down that road you didn't have to do all the budget cutting that we subsequently did — and you did not need to take on fights which actually looked a bit harder, such as putting in place capital gains taxes. In hindsight it was a totally aggressive tax which hurt the poorer people most, but at the time it was ... "here's the poor bastard trying to fight our tax policy and the Treasurer, now and then, needs a bit of support". I think that was about it.'

With Transport and Communications Beazley would become a player, a serious player, in matters of economic import for the first time. Hawke was impatient for him to get stuck into it immediately, and with that in mind wrote him a formal letter, on the 8th of April, a fortnight after the election, detailing exactly what he required of him.

> Dear Kim,
>
> In the important growth area of telecommunications, we must significantly increase competitive influences so that benefits to the economy of the new technologies which characterise this sector, are maximised ...
>
> Further signals to the industry on our attitude to telecommunications growth will be provided by the decisions on mobile phones; competition between the public carriers; and the future viability of AUSSAT. If competition and the growth of the industry are to be fully advanced we will need also actively to address even wider issues. In this context we will also need to consider how we fund essential community service obligations ...
> Yours,
> Bob.[109]

Telecommunications, then, was to be his principal focus. Around that though, Beazley's new portfolio made him powerful across an extraordinary range of territory, from having responsibility for the ABC, to working out the future of Qantas and Australian Airlines, to administering and changing if necessary such things as the cross-media laws. For Beazley, this range was at once both intellectually stimulating and aggravating.

'It was not at all like Defence,' he says. 'There you could work a lot of decisions off one coherent philosophical base, and fit everything into that. In Transport and Communications though, while there was a similar amount of detail that you had to get across, you couldn't find the same coherence to all the decisions you had to make.'

There was one key decision that would be most troublesome to him, a decision which flowed from Hawke's letter and subsequent discussions with both the Prime Minister and his advisers. The brief was to take Australia's telecommunications structure as it stood — at the time, then publicly owned and consisting of Telecom, the Overseas Telecommunications Corporation and AUSSAT — and fashion them into a form whereby some of it would be at least partly privately owned, and all of it would be fully competitive and up-to-speed for a nation operating in the international marketplace. Telecom was responsible for Australia's domestic telephone services, while OTC was responsible for international telephony, and AUSSAT was a government-owned satellite system, which provided 'domestic business communications links and broadcasting television to remote areas'.[110] The first two generated good revenue for the Government, while the last was crippled by debt and was an enormous drain on Government finances. Hawke spelt out the need for structural change in his memoirs. '[It] was important,' he wrote, 'not only to give industrial and domestic users access to the most efficient services and equipment but also to position Australia to take advantage of a huge export potential. The nations of the Asia-Pacific region contain half the world's population but only 17 per cent of its five hundred million telephone lines. By 1990 the rapid economic growth and rising living standards of these countries were reflected in a burgeoning demand for new and better telecommunications services.' In short, the 'clever country' had to be in a position to take advantage of the changed conditions.

Determining how to do that was never going to be easy, and it would be complicated further by one P.J. Keating, who had been elected unopposed to the post of Deputy Prime Minister after the election, in the wake of Lionel Bowen's retirement from politics. Never mind that many thought the whole issue was in an area well outside of the Treasurer's bailiwick, the man himself did not see it like that and was into the telecommunications' issue like fury from the beginning. 'I had Ministerial responsibility for the Industries Assistance Commission,' Keating remembers of his reasons, 'so involvement came to me under the aegis of "structural change". And after the May Statement of 1988, where we put in place the big first round of tariff cuts and a lot of other micro-economic reform, structural change was hot, hot, on the agenda of the economy, in the decisions of the Cabinet. We were not going to be easily thwarted, so it became an urgent topic.'

Paul Kelly has noted in *The End of Certainty* that this was a time in Keating's career when he 'moved to stake his claim to the leadership on policy grounds: he threw himself at the micro-reform agenda and ridiculed Hawke's technique of "reform by consensus". The battle was telecommunications reform ...'[111] To independent observers the three principals in this battle — Hawke, Beazley and Keating — had distinctly different ways of arriving at their key decisions. Hawke tended to find his inspiration securely within the popular mainstream of thought. One of the Prime Minister's favourite passages, quoted in

Stephen Mills' book, *The Hawke Years*, and coming from the English essayist, F.S. Oliver, gives some indication of that: 'An artist, starving in his garret because he has ventured to outrage the popular taste, may yet paint masterpieces; but political masterpieces can only be made by a politician working in energetic partnership with a prevalent opinion.'[112] Keating, on the other hand, cared less for putting prevailing popular opinion into his own mental equations. Keating's close adviser, Don Russell, once described for Michael Gordon the process whereby the Treasurer devised his policies. 'He thinks things through in a very systematic way with a big frame of reference — a model in his head of how things impact — and he refers problems back to that. When he works out the course of action which is most sensible, that's when he takes his punt. Rather than having a bit of everything and thereby having nothing, once he works out what the best option is he then puts the risk on that. Because his judgement is pretty good, and he does understand how the system works, that's how he gets the results.'[113]

The way Beazley came up with his ideas was a mixture of the two, though perhaps closer to the Hawke method. John O'Callaghan, Beazley's own long-time adviser, was one who observed the process. 'Because Kim is a person of such intellect,' he says, 'he generally has a pretty good idea in his own mind as to what he wants to accomplish strategically and philosophically — and those two words definitely go together — where he thinks through what he wants to do and what outcome he thinks he wants. He then develops a kind of template from there, a rough sketch, and draws everyone else in, getting their opinion, adjusting it accordingly if they have good things to add to it, and giving a lot of people ownership of the outcome.' Patrick Walters adds: 'It's his strategic cast of mind that keeps coming through with Kim. He does not just play the short-term political card. Kim is always thinking on that kind of plane rather than the majority of us who [mostly] think hard politics. When it comes to these big structural decisions I think what differentiates Kim from his colleagues is his ability to think about the long-term consequences rather than just the short-term political gain.'

Using these different methods, with Hawke in the role of key adjudicator, Beazley and Keating on this occasion emerged with two quite different models for telecommunications reform — though both included the central feature of placing Telecom in a competitive environment where it would actually have to work for a living. In broad terms the two models were:

Beazley: Telecom and OTC to amalgamate into one publicly owned 'Megacom,' with AUSSAT to be sold as the foundation stone for another telecommunications carrier, as part of the licence cost of gaining entry to the market. This other carrier would be likely foreign owned, though with an obligation to sell down over time. A duopoly would be created in the first instance, with a review after a period of time to determine whether other competitors should be allowed.

Keating: Telecom to be maintained in public ownership, with OTC to be sold to the highest bidder. No duopoly, all competitors welcome from the beginning.*

An earlier version of Keating's model did not include the open competition stanchion, but that did not last long. And Beazley had an argument against having open competition from the beginning: 'You wouldn't get any decent open competition unless you had first established the two major players, which meant that people who wanted to put services over the lines could play the two carriers off against the other. So you're only going to have genuine open competition when Telecom's monopoly had been substantially diminished. The key was to firmly diminish that monopoly by establishing a solid competitor and *then* reviewing the possibility of open competition.'

The British Foreign Minister Lord Palmerston is reputed to have once said. 'There are only three people who ever understood the Schleswig-Holstein question. One went mad, one died, and I forgot!' A modern-day equivalent of this might well have been the complete ins and outs and the nuances in between of the Australian telecommunications debate in 1990. It was an extremely complex issue with very few people claiming to understand it totally; and even fewer actually doing so. One thing that impressed Beazley's staff from the beginning, however, was how totally he mastered his brief. It was to be a key asset in the coming battle. 'Right from the outset,' John O'Callaghan says, 'when Kim talked about the benefits of his own model, which he did all the time to all sorts of groups, you could see how impressed they were by how much he knew about it.' What was also clear was that it was going to need an enormous amount of such talking to get his model up. While the Beazley model *was* far more cautious than Keating's, it was still daring from the point of view of

---

* *AUSSAT* for Keating was neither here nor there, and he notoriously characterised it as 'space junk'.

being well outside the official Labor Party platform, which had always opposed the privatisation of public entities. That problem could hopefully be dealt with in good time, at a Special Conference of the Labor Party which had been called for 24 September 1990, to discuss just that issue and hopefully ratify whatever model Cabinet endorsed, but in the meantime Beazley had to convince the party that his model was better than Keating's.

It was a rare experience for Beazley to find himself ranged against his good friend Keating on a matter of serious policy debate — a fact that Keating notes. 'During Kim's tenure as Defence Minister,' he says, 'he always had Hawke onside, who was very attuned to American interests, while I was always a believer in the need for Australia's defence self-sufficiency. So, all through his time in Defence he had the Prime Minister and the Treasurer essentially with him for any reasonable proposition.' Clearly that was not the case now, for Keating did not think that on this occasion Beazley was making a reasonable proposition at all. In fact he thought the Beazley model was about as timid as tepid tea, whereas what was needed was a big honest jolt to Telecom that would only come by placing it in the middle of genuine open competition. For Keating, Beazley's cosy duopoly would be just the Two Airlines Policy revisited. 'When we got rid of the Two Airlines Policy in the late '80s and went to open competition,' Keating notes, 'in one year the fares fell by 25 per cent, while the number of passengers rose by 60 per cent. So why would we now go to a Two Telecommunications Carriers Policy instead of open competition? Competition works, and it worked for Labor. I was opposed to lowering our sights.'

Keating's point was strengthened by the fact that not only had the Two Airlines Policy been abandoned, but at the same time as Beazley was garnering support for telecommunications reform, he was also trying to get the party to fall into line behind the notion that the Government should sell 100 per cent of Australian Airlines, and up to 49 per cent of Qantas. In this, he had Keating's full support, but the Treasurer continued to pound away at the notion that it was sheer insanity to be pushing the airlines into the modern age, while consciously putting telecommunications at a point ten years behind them. Why not make the break now? Why not drag all of telecommunications, kicking and screaming if necessary, right slap-bang into the 1990s and expose it to full competition? Why not cut OTC loose to get that competition going? For the very good reason, was

Beazley's line of reply, that when heading off into the global economy, it would be a very bad idea indeed to sell off the Government's international telecommunications institution, and in the process deny Telecom the ability to achieve the crucial 'critical mass' it needed to prosper. 'I thought,' Beazley says, 'we needed to build at least one very big Australian telecommunications company, and the only way we could do that was to give it the seamless operating rights of domestic and international services with the right to do whatever it wants in the field of domestic and international telecommunications, radio communications, wireline communications, the works. You definitely had to keep OTC and Telecom together.' Beazley saw no particular problem with the probability that the telecommunications competitor to emerge to his 'Megacom' would likely be foreign owned in the first instance; he justified this in terms that 'you needed foreign expertise to begin with, because the only telecommunications expertise in this country existed in Telecom and OTC. So you couldn't actually generate an Australian alternative, because they just wouldn't have the expertise'.

Some of Beazley's colleagues, however, saw an inconsistency between this position, and a key decision he had taken at much the same time in another part of his portfolio regarding the level of foreign ownership of Australian television networks. At the time Beazley took over his portfolio, legislation permitted up to 49 per cent foreign ownership and 15 per cent for individual investors. But in June 1990, just four months later, Beazley announced that that level would henceforth be reduced to the blanket limit of 20 per cent foreign ownership. Of all the people that this decision advantaged, the most obvious was Kerry Packer, who was then trying to regain control of the Nine Network after Alan Bond three-and-a-half years previously had paid just over a billion dollars for it. Reducing foreign ownership to 20 per cent meant that a number of Packer's potentially serious competitors like Rupert Murdoch (who was now an American citizen), were knocked out of contention. While the move was applauded by the Labor Left — keeping Australia for Australians etc — it opened Beazley to the charge that he was leaning towards the exceedingly powerful Packer pull. There is no doubt that the monetary value of Beazley's decision to the media mogul was very high — the deal to return the Channel Nine Network to him valued it now at only 750 million dollars. The 'in' political joke of the time ran, 'The ALP Left was so chauvinistic that it overcame its distaste for handing Kerry Packer 200 million dollars; the Centre Left was less chauvinistic, but didn't mind giving him 200 million dollars; and the Right just wanted to *give* Mr Packer 200 million dollars!'[114]

Of course, Beazley rejected any suggestion that he was currying favour with Packer, stating now that 'You've got to take a stand somewhere on foreign ownership. It's already in a sense passed in relation to the newspapers, but television is essential for the culture and if Australians can't own that they can't own anything. And furthermore while technically anyone can start a newspaper, the airwaves spectrum is a limited resource. So it's more appropriate to have heavier regulation in relation to television than it is in relation to newspapers.'

The beat went on. Beazley kept pushing his own model for Australian telecommunications, while the Treasury and the Treasurer continued to push the Keating model. Hawke, in the early part of the struggle, was quite 'hands-off' as the two slugged it out, but as the difference of opinion between the two principals became progressively more pronounced, the Prime Minister used an entirely novel way of informing himself. Hawke organised for his two Cabinet Ministers to have a series of 'moot' debates in his office, whereby each would go at the other over the reasons why their own concept was superior. 'And Paul,' as Beazley recalls, 'would turn up with sometimes seven or eight of his Treasury officials and a whole tray load of documents, while I would go either alone or just with one or two of my people. I did that because I wanted to make the point that I was across it, that I totally understood the subject and that my model didn't need the support of either a lot of officials or a lot of documents — it spoke for itself.' According to Patrick Walters, who accompanied Beazley, the first debate lasted, 'for three hours and 37 minutes. Keating opened up talking about Labor's parlous position in the polls and said that he had a graph showing the continuing downtrend of Labor support. He said "this can't continue if we're going to stay in Government. It's a time when we need to take bold decisions".'

Beazley's reply was that that was all very well, but that it was simply nonsense to hack off the international wing of Australia's telecommunications before trying to take off for the global skies. Let Megacom be formed, and let the competition for it come from another international competitor, with a strong government regulator between the two, to ensure that the competitor wasn't wiped out in the first instance. 'Kim was forceful in his argument,' Walters recalls, 'and Keating was equally forceful, with Hawke interjecting from time to time to ask questions of both of them.' From the beginning it was clear that this was an issue that Keating was never going to back away from, and to many of his colleagues he appeared near-obsessed with prevailing, and if that involved 'crashing through' his old mate Kim as well, then so be it. Perhaps adding to the strength of Keating's vitriol was a fair measure of frustration that he was still not Prime Minister despite — at least in his eyes — having driven the agenda of the Government over the last seven years.

It was an extraordinarily difficult situation for them to get through personally for two such close friends. 'I could sense the air crackling with bloody tension between the two of them,' Gareth Evans remembers, 'and I could sense that things were weighing pretty heavily on Kim'. They were. 'I didn't like the fight, no,' Beazley acknowledges. But as colleagues noted, the Member for Swan never backed off, and persisted in pushing the claims of his own model regardless of the personal cost. For all the strain between them, though, it never broke out into open warfare. 'No,' Keating stresses. 'Kim's relationship with me has always been either very friendly, friendly, cordial or polite. Never anything below that, and on this occasion our relationship was on the lower end of polite, or ... firmly polite.' Beazley agrees. 'To my face and in discussion and before Caucus committees in the moot debates,' he says, 'our discourse was always very correct. Now I don't know what he might have said about me behind my back ... '

As a matter of fact Keating *could* be less than pleasant when telling colleagues about the shortcomings of the Beazley model. When it came right down to it, Keating told some of his Caucus colleagues, not only had Kim developed the wrong model, not only was he all 'piss and wind', but he 'couldn't sell ice-cream in a heatwave' and so had no chance of getting his proposal up. The former Sports Minister, John Brown, though he had by then just left Parliament, remembers being told by Keating at one point that: 'There are four great dinosaurs left in Australia. Telecom, Australia Post, the ABC ... and Kim Beazley — and he runs the first three!' As Graham Richardson portrays it: 'Every jibe was to paint Kim as being weak, as being not strong enough to take the obviously intelligent line which of course equalled whatever Keating was saying. Keating was outraged and 'outrage' is not too strong a word either — he just couldn't believe that Kim would not go with him.' As it happened, Richardson thought that Beazley was being every bit as brave as it was realistically possible to be and still get his proposal through the Special Conference that had been scheduled in September to consider the alternatives, and hopefully to ratify an abandonment of the ALP's anti-privatisation planks of the party.

'My reading of Kim on that occasion,' Richardson says, 'was not so much that he was intellectually committed to his course of action, but he knew from talking to me and others that that course of action was the maximum the Labor Party Conference was going to let him dictate. He was a realist — it wasn't the classic "crash through or crash" approach Keating took, to stand up and dare them to knock you over. I said to Kim many times, "if you try for more than this mate you will get dudded — you haven't got the numbers to go firm on this". Kim was basically trading to find a faction policy with which everybody could live.'

This assessment was backed up by the public comments of two key union people at the time. The head of the Telecom union, Mick Musumeci, was quoted as saying that while the Beazley proposal would mean 'death' for Telecom by 'slow strangulation,' the Keating scheme would rather be death by 'garrotting'.[115] And the then President of the ACTU, Martin Ferguson, said that while they would cop the Beazley plan if they absolutely had to, there was no way they were going to go along with Paul Keating's scheme. 'If Cabinet makes a decision to go any further, it will lose the lot,' he told the *Australian Financial Review*.[116]

Beazley flatly rejects any notion that he had tailored his model as just the best that could be pushed through all the political hoops, rather than the best overall. 'I think Paul particularly always had the view that I was trying to push it as far as the political envelope would permit in the Labor Party tradition,' he says, 'and I am sure that a lot of people in the Cabinet supported me for that reason. But that was *not* my reason, I really think that my model was the best model, full-stop. Neither of our models had a hell of a lot of support in the party, but mine had at least some support. But that wasn't why I was advocating it — I actually happened to think it was right. It got pretty bloody.'

In the middle of the angst, the hassles and the neverending stress, when he was at his home in Perth — rather than with the Wassons in Canberra — Beazley would sometimes find solace in a way surprising to those who did not know him well. He would take down from the wall one or other of the Greek, Russian and Eastern European religious icons — inspirational pictures, often of Jesus or Mary — that he had begun collecting a few years before, and gaze at it for some time. 'I find it enormously refreshing,' he says. 'When I go home I find it helpful to have a look at a number of them and reflect. It is a style of art which is not only beautiful in its simplicity, but also an aid to reflection. While I don't use it as an aid to worship or anything like that, just having them around the place is a calming and settling influence. It also gives you a sense of the longevity of your civilisation, the timelessness of history and the fact that we just fade away . . .'

Something else that gave him such a feeling of serenity, was patting Susie's growing stomach at every opportunity. Their much-hoped-for baby was actually on its way — due early the following year — and few things gave him, or her, as much pleasure as feeling the movement of the baby kicking inside.* (All of the family was delighted with the news of the pregnancy, though Hannah felt a smidgin embarrassed because only a few weeks previously, when they had all been in the car together, Jessica had idly told her father and stepmother that she wanted nothing more from this life than to have another baby sister, whereupon Hannah had interjected to say that she disagreed and would much rather have a puppy.)

Back in Canberra and in the middle of the bitter fight, another consolation to Beazley — albeit a small one — was that he wasn't the only one copping it. 'Keating abused me as well,' Richardson recalls, 'because I spoke very strongly in support of Kim and he said, "You didn't even fucking know what the [relevant phraseology] was, I had to fucking tell you on the phone the other day!" That was partly true but I had to just sit there and let him rave. I was in Perth or somewhere and he spoke to me for about *forty-five fucking minutes*, in fact I was reading the paper while he was going on.'

Mostly though, Keating had Beazley directly in his sights, and was firing volley after volley — mostly from afar, but everyone still knew about it. While Keating was going at his colleague in this fashion, there were many interested observers noting just how Beazley handled Keating's famed 'blow-torch to the belly'. The short answer, was 'not that well,' and the slightly longer one finished with, 'but at least he kept his course, and did not deviate a jot from backing his own proposal'. It wasn't easy for all that. 'He did in fact know his subject on Telecommunications so much more — and better — than Paul,'

---

* This freedom to express his delight and anticipation made a nice change from the way it had once been when Mary had been pregnant with Jessica. On one occasion when he was rather intimately patting Mary's stomach in Lady Molly Paltridge's kitchen, Lady Molly had protested. 'Hang on,' Kim had replied, 'it's *my* baby too, after all.' 'Yes,' Lady Molly had replied rather imperiously, 'but it's MY kitchen.'

Hawke insists. 'And he showed a lot of toughness. He used to come around saying, "this is driving me mad having to go through this", but he never wavered.' Keating commented on his behaviour during this battle on the ABC's *Labor in Power* documentary. 'I was a bit manic about it, probably a bit too manic,' he conceded.

'No, I wouldn't have described his behaviour as manic,' Beazley responded. 'I thought that he was ... I found it quite impressive. He's a very difficult bloke to handle and he was terribly concerned about the appearance of the Government and the directions in which we ought to go, and I respected that. Although I didn't much like being the object of it at the time ... '

The whole battle between the two was complicated further by the role of the media. Usually in such a clash, the media would watch with the same kind of appalled fascination with which others pass car smashes. But in this instance they were more intimately involved than merely observing, with newspapers publishing an almost unprecedented number of leaks from the battle. On successive days, the *Financial Review* published both the Beazley Cabinet submission and the Treasury's counter-submission. All of the media agreed it was not a good look. 'A sure sign of a government in trouble,' the influential political commentator Michelle Grattan noted in *The Age* in the middle of August, 'is when the leaks flow. This week they flooded out.' In one of the Treasury leaks, Beazley was characterised as being guilty of 'McEwenism at its very worst'. As Grattan commented: 'in the Keating lexicon, being a "McEwenite" is nearly as bad as being a child molester.'[117] (Keating's belief was that 'Black Jack' McEwen had been particularly guilty of 'featherbedding' the Australian economy; of being an arch-protectionist who was on the opposite end of the financial management spectrum to an 'economic rationalist'.)

Generally, left entirely to its own commentary, without use of leaked documents, the media savaged Beazley for what they viewed as the timidity of his model, and they portrayed him as a prisoner of the very powerful Telecom Unions. The influential commentator Alan Mitchell, was one who led the charge in the *Sydney Morning Herald*. 'Obviously, [Beazley's] proposed merger of Telecom and OTC is designed to protect Telecom and its unions from serious competition in the short term,' he wrote in mid-July 1990. 'But unfortunately that's not the worst part of the deal stitched together by Mr Beazley and the Caucus's telecommunications committee. Only one firm is to be licensed to compete fully with Telecom. If the Government is not careful, Australian telecommunications will progress from lazy monopoly to cosy duopoly ... '

'That was just not true,' Beazley says with some feeling. 'The Telecom unions found my proposition unacceptable, and I was being constantly opposed by them. In the grab-bag of politics, everybody likes to relate everything to everything else and have things simplified for them — like 'there's Beazley and he's got this model that's acceptable to unions and there's Paul and his offer is acceptable to the ... and so on,' but it was never like that, and it certainly wasn't in this particular case. The unions gave me a lot of trouble over what I wanted to do.' Oddly enough, the airline side of the equation still generated comparatively little heat. All of the howling at the moon that was done seemed to concern only telecommunications, while people generally seemed to accept that the partial privatisation of the airlines was already a *fait accompli*. 'I did find it ironic,' Beazley recalls, 'though I also think that the international economy had changed so dramatically over the previous decade that it was obvious to everyone that the capacity for an airline to survive as an entity without constant capital injections from the Government was minimal and that instead of just letting it limp along, the best thing would be to cut it adrift and allow it to develop its own resources. No Government could ever justify continual financial [subsidies] for an institution which carried so few Australians.'

As the time for the Cabinet meeting on 10 September 1990, drew nearer, Beazley intensified his efforts. In her biography of Bob Hawke, Blanche d'Alpuget wrote of how Hawke's deep belief in his own ability to change things could be so powerful that it was almost self-fulfilling. The belief could transfix others, make them believe too that it was inevitable, so that in a kind of personality domino effect, it actually happened much as Hawke believed it would. To some extent Beazley's approach resembled that, with the difference being that he used logic rather more than charisma, and there was no domino effect — he tended to go and see each domino one by one and personally work on knocking them all over himself if he could. His way was to strap himself into a plane and move. Move and persuade. It was what he had done throughout the whole debate to that point, targeting key unions, factional figures, fellow Cabinet members, and delegates to the forthcoming conference. And now he did some more of it, in a spate of travel that would see him spend a total of only two nights at home in the month leading up to the Special Conference. John O'Callaghan, who travelled with him through most of it, remembers it well. 'It was a kind of classic Kim operation where he just goes from group to group, and convinces them the virtues of what he is about, and builds up the broad consensus behind him. He actually makes them believe, even though it was a very hard process because the majority of union people and Labor supporters didn't want to have a bar of it, because all they could see from their perspective was this icon of Australia, Telecom, going down the gurgler.'

If Beazley was notable for the raw number of people he spoke to in this time, and the number he was able to turn to his point of view, he maintains that it was not purely an exercise in persuasion for him, but also one of listening. 'I think even if you know your course, it is not necessarily based on all the information there is, and if you listen you actually get even better arguments for the direction you want to go in than you've currently thought out. I found that particularly so in Communications ...'

One who Beazley talked to during this time was Wayne Goss, the then Queensland Premier. Goss already had a high enough estimation of the Minister for Transport and Communications that, after the 1990 election — when the State Government north of the Tweed had found to its great annoyance that there wasn't a single Queenslander in Federal Cabinet — his Government had nominated Beazley to be their representative in Cabinet.

'Apart from getting on very well with him,' Goss remembers, 'we thought he understood the problems of a growth or frontier state, coming from the west. It was obviously less satisfactory than having a decent Queenslander, but Kim was the next best thing to keep a watching brief for us.' The telecommunications saga would deepen Goss's respect for Beazley further, and he remembers well his reaction when first becoming acquainted with the Beazley model. 'I didn't know the full details of the telecommunications reform but he came up to Brisbane and saw me and explained what he wanted to do and why he wanted to do it and he *knew it*, he just knew it backwards and you just felt a lot of confidence in the fact that he knew his job. When he left you thought, "okay well whatever this bloke wants, I'll vote for that".'

Significantly, in all this time, Goss had no contact from Paul Keating wanting to sell his own proposal. The very notion that Keating might have made the effort for such a thing would be enough, almost eight years later, to bring an immediate explosion of laughter from Goss.

'Paul's idea of going out and talking to the people was to fly up to Sydney and talk to John Laws for half an hour then get back on the plane and fly back to Canberra. That's the difference between them.'

(That said, Keating was exceptionally busy in that last fortnight of August, organising for the Commonwealth Bank to buy the beleaguered State Bank of Victoria for two billion dollars, with the purchase being funded by the later 30 per cent part privatisation of the Commonwealth Bank.)

If there was a clear difference between Keating's and Beazley's strategies, it is equally clear that this difference lay not just in their personalities, but also in the vast gulf separating their political backgrounds. In the Sydney electorate of Blaxland, Keating had long held one of the safest seats in Labor Party politics, and didn't have to worry if the things he said or did got up the nose of his individual constituents — his seat remained safe. Equally, as a leading light of the most dominant faction in the country, the NSW Right, the Treasurer was used to having the numbers almost automatically behind him for just about everything bar the Prime Ministership itself.

Beazley's background of course could not have been more removed from that. He had come to political maturity without any faction whatsoever protecting his views — and in fact had a big faction against him — and was only ever able to make headway by talking, listening, and gradually convincing people of the inherent rightness of his cause. As to the paper-thin majority he suffered in his own election, he says, 'Being a permanently nervous frontbencher, made me somewhat more sympathetic to those who take the view that you ought to actually test what the electorate thinks before you do something. So I always liked to do a lot of listening . . .' His old Labor colleague Peter Walsh highlights the possible downside of coming from such a volatile background: 'Kim's always been jittery about holding his own seat and because of that he's also been inclined to panic at issues, which are not desirable attributes for someone who has to maintain an overview and remain steady.'

'Kim doesn't like the big fights,' Keating had been telling his parliamentary colleagues in the lead-up to the key Cabinet meeting that was to endorse one or other of their models. But there was at least some evidence to support the contrary view; that at least was the feeling of Robert Ray, on the Saturday just before the meeting. Beazley was in Melbourne to speak at a dinner on the Saturday night, and had asked Ray to see if he could get him a ticket to the big AFL finals football match that afternoon, between his own beloved West Coast Eagles and Collingwood. Ray, laughing to himself, quietly secured him 'a ticket in an absolutely ideal position' — halfway around the ground, equidistant from both sets of goalposts, and right in the very heartland of the Collingwood supporters. 'So I knew his seat number,' Senator Ray recounts, 'and I wandered around the terraces to find him, straight after half-time had gone.' Ray couldn't believe it, for far from trying to merge with the crowd and make himself as inoffensive to Collingwood supporters as possible, there was the Minister for Transport and Communications sitting right in the middle of the fray, wrapped in his halftime purchase. 'He'd bought the biggest Eagles' scarf I'd ever seen!' Ray declared. Oddly enough, the Collingwood supporters, not known for their sensitivity in such matters, seemed to respect the honesty of Beazley's commitment,* if not necessarily its colours. And in the end both brands of supporters had something to boast about at the end of the game, with the result a very rare draw, 90–90. Still the Minister of the moment did not escape scot-free for all that. 'As Kim went to get into his Comcar,' Ray recalls, 'some old Collingwood harridan comes along and says: 'The Labor Party's *fucked* football, it's all your fault!' Beazley drove off into the dusk without a worry in the world. In terms of receiving personal abuse, it was as well to get some practise in . . .

Two days later at the Cabinet meeting on 10 September Beazley and Keating presented their final models to their fellow heavyweight ministers, and then Hawke opened the floor to input from the other ministerial attendees. The vast majority of Cabinet discussions in the Hawke Government to that point had been executed without heat. They were along the lines of: 'Look, I have had a look at Gareth's submission and it's ok, but on page 12, I don't reckon we ought to . . .'

'Yes, but you'll note that I have covered that option on page 14, paragraph 4 . . .'

---

* Another possible reason the Collingwood supporters went easy on him is because the famous Melbourne club was in part established in 1892 by one William David Beazley, who was not only the local Labor MP, but esteemed enough in politics in the latter part of last century to later be the leader of the Victorian Lower House. The portrait of him which hangs in Collingwood Town Hall bears a distinct resemblance to Kim Jnr. W.D. Beazley was born in London — on 7 October 1954, son of a carpenter, and was brought out to the colony as a newborn, arriving in Melbourne in early 1855. The likelihood is that he was at least a distant cousin of Kim Jnr's direct ancestor, John Beazley, who left London as a convict at much the same time.

'But if we do it like that, won't we alienate the ...'

The Cabinet debates on telecommunications reform were not of that order. In Graham Richardson's memory, it was more like ...

'Don't you fucking say that to me!'

'Why the fuck shouldn't I?'

'Because when it comes to this fucking subject you wouldn't know the first fucking thing about it!'

In one of the most dramatic scenes of the Hawke Government, the debate built to the point where it became obvious that the Treasurer was going to lose the argument. As Robert Ray has recalled, 'Paul was doing a very slow burn as the summing up was done.'[118] What really set Keating off, as the then Treasurer remembers it, was the comment by someone that the Keating model, 'was not going to go down well with Bob Pomeroy from the Centre Left in Adelaide'.

'And I looked at Hawke,' Keating recalls, 'like, here we are, done all these big things over the last few years because they were the right thing to do and we had our eyes on the big picture, and here we are now in the Federal Cabinet, being dictated to by somebody from the Centre Left — the *Centre Left!* — in South Australia. So I said "well, if it gets down to this, if you want to sit here and participate in an economic decision of very diminished quality on the basis of a bit of political gobbledy-gook from a boutique faction and a couple of unions that in the past, you and I, Bob, we would have pushed to one side, then I am wasting my time".'

At this point, Keating suddenly threw his pencil on the table, stood up, and gave his considered estimation: 'this a fucking second-rate decision by a bunch of fucking second-raters!' before furiously storming out of the room. 'Spit the dummy!' Senator Robert Ray called out after him. Keating kept walking. It was after all his political hero, Jack Lang, who had always said that if you couldn't win a debate then the thing to do was to wreck it, but by then it was too late to have any tangible effect.[119] In Keating's absence, Cabinet endorsed Beazley's model as the one it would promote. This was a notable victory for the Member for Swan, even if there remained much to do to actually make it all happen.

It was one of the very few occasions when Paul Keating was beaten in a one-on-one policy debate in Cabinet. Some would maintain that you could in fact count such occasions on the fingers of one finger. 'I think that was a very defining moment for Kim because he took Paul on,' Graham Richardson maintains, 'and he had the arguments to prevail in Cabinet at Keating's expense.' While Beazley regretted the falling-out with Keating, he at least was hopeful that their relationship would soon come right again, for despite Keating's image, Beazley maintains that the then Treasurer did not hold grudges. 'Paul was always into the next fight,' he says, 'he was very much a "no permanent allies, no permanent friends" man. So if you had a disagreement with him he'd lick his wounds for a bit of time and then he'd bounce back — there was always something big going on. That was one of the attractive features of him, there was always a fight out there. You just never knew, a fellow who was an opponent on one thing might be an ally on another. So he was remarkably free of that sort of personal vindictiveness.'

Mostly anyway. In the case of the Telecommunications struggle, the way it turned out, Keating himself acknowledges that there 'was some strain' placed on their friendship, but even then the strain was only an undercurrent, and never again broke into open hostility. When, for example, just five days after the Cabinet decision, the great operatic tenor Placido Domingo performed a concert at the Sydney Entertainment Centre, it so happened that Keating and Beazley both attended with their wives. Afterwards, they all ended up having a drink together back at the Park Hyatt Hotel. It hadn't been planned, but when the Keating entourage had spied Kim and Susie seated in the hotel's restaurant with some friends, the Treasurer had brought Annita over to say hello, and they ended up all chatting together for 20 minutes. Keating seemed in a particularly ebullient mood for one who had just suffered a rare defeat in a matter of public policy, but perhaps that was simply because he had enjoyed the Placido Domingo concert so much. He had always been a great admirer of the Spaniard, and opined that Domingo had been particularly outstanding on the night.

For Beazley the concert was a rare break in what was a singularly busy time for him. The next hurdle for his telecommunications reform was the Special Conference to be held in just over a week's time in the national capital, where it would be decided whether or not the party would ratify the telecommunication model that Cabinet had endorsed, and where, also, they would move to privatise the airlines. Nevertheless, in the time between the concert and the conference, Paul Keating had not entirely let the whole thing go. One newspaper report asserted that he was still pushing his own model behind the scenes and saying that it still might pop up during the conference. The report quoted a senior Labor MP as saying, 'You don't have to just *beat*

Keating, you've got to drive a stake through his heart.'[120] As it happened though, come the actual day of the conference, the Treasurer would not say one word on the subject of telecommunications reforms, and instead let Beazley make all of the running.

The latter arrived at the National Convention Centre in Canberra early, left late, and worked assiduously in between times. In his own speech to the other 101 delegates, he began by noting the complexity of the issue they were discussing. 'I do feel very sorry for you,' Beazley began, 'this is like amateurs preparing to deal with brain surgery.' From there he pushed the line that as Australia moved deeper into the global economy, the country simply had to have institutions capable of prospering, and it was absolutely essential that Telecom and OTC merge, and that they be opened to competition. Asia, he noted, was an enormous telecommunications market just waiting to be tapped, if only Australia played the game intelligently.

'If we do not take advantage of the opportunities in our regional markets,' he said, '130 billion dollars spent on hardware, software, and development of systems in Asia over the next five years, if we do not encourage international business to establish itself here — and you cannot do that other than in a competitive environment — we will miss out again.'[121] There was no way that the Hawke Government would ever privatise Telecom he said, because that was the surest way to wreck it, but it simply had to be opened to competition. 'What we are talking about is whether or not we are going to have a vibrant telecommunications industry capable of dealing with the sort of challenges that, with the telecommunications industry growth, we now confront!' For a man who, eight years later, would own neither a mobile phone nor an answering machine, he was certainly passionate about the exciting world of telecommunication, but this was about far bigger things than him. 'This proposal is standard, average, commonsense, democratic socialist policy of how one manages government business enterprises,' he said. John Saunderson, one of the delegates from the Left and a very influential backbencher, was not convinced. 'Why are we here to grease the rails for a Japanese or American telecommunications company to come in on the back of Telecom and take the cream off the business?' he demanded.

Despite such opposition, in the course of the proceedings, Beazley could not have received stronger support from Bob Hawke. In a particularly powerful speech, the Prime Minister thundered that while the anti-privatisation provisions in the party platform had been a sacred cow over the years, that in itself did *not mean* they should survive. The White Australia Policy had also been a 'sacred cow of the ALP,' he began. 'But it was wrong and increasingly as time went on, it was not only morally repugnant, but it was economic insanity. One of the things I am proudest of in my long 43-years membership is that I was part of the fight to throw out the White Australia Policy. It was to the greatest credit of this great Australian Labor Party that that sacred cow was culled from Labor's divine dairy herd, because we were the better party for having got rid of it.' And so too, he went on to say, would the party be the better off once it had agreed to throw off the shackles of its anti-privatisation stance, which in the modern age, was simply no longer workable.

Paul Keating himself came in on the general subject of whether or not the party should overturn the anti-privatisation provisions, an issue which was most pertinent to airline reforms. 'I want to suggest to you,' he said, 'that if you want to get a good belly laugh that you go into Eastern Europe and the Soviet Union and look their good citizens in the eye and tell them that their welfare depends on the maintenance of existing state ownership and the absence of competition.'

The whole thing was over by lunchtime. By a narrow majority, the ALP's ultimate decision-making body had overturned the party's opposition to privatisation; cleared the way for the reform of telecommunications along the lines of the Beazley model; and approved the sale of Australian Airlines and half of Qantas. In respect of the airlines reforms, this was some achievement, given that the previous Labor Party conference had refused to even consider the possibility of privatising the airlines. It was particularly good financial news for the Hawke Government as the telecommunications reforms and the sale of a licence to a new competitor, it was estimated, would bring in about three billion dollars to the Government's coffers, while the part-sale of the Government's airlines holdings would bring in another two billion dollars. The conference turned out to be, or at least as reported in *The Bulletin*, it was 'close to … the biggest moment of Beazley's political career'. 'I was certainly particularly happy with the result,' Beazley notes. 'That was the hardest conference I'd ever been involved in, probably the hardest exercise I'd been involved in, and I was just very relieved that I'd come through ok.'

Yet, for all his relief, hurdles remained. Having conceived the model in Cabinet, and convinced the party's Special Conference that it should be allowed under the ALP's own rules, it remained for Beazley to frame the legislation so that it could successfully pass through both houses of Parliament. This situation was somewhat delicate. Throughout the entire Labor Party wrangle on the subject, the Coalition had strenuously voiced its opinion that Beazley's model simply did not go far enough. Dr John Hewson, the newly elected Liberal leader, had committed his party to selling all three institutions — Telecom, OTC and AUSSAT — and, in the words of Paul Kelly in *The End of Certainty*, Hewson 'rejected Labor's telecommunication duopoly as a policy for wimps'.[122]

The Australian Democrats, meanwhile, took exactly the opposite approach, stridently opposing any privatisation whatsoever. The clear danger was that if those two groups combined they could stop the reform stone motherless dead. To get around this, Beazley put into effect a plan that he had long been formulating whereby he divided the legislation into two parts.[123] The first part of that legislation ensured that AUSSAT could be sold to the new company which would form the second part of the duopoly, and that the new company would have immediate access to the public telephone network, upon which Telecom had previously had a monopoly. The new competitor would pay Telecom fees for the use of their network, at a level that would be set by the government regulator Austel. The Coalition had virtually no choice but to throw their support behind this, because they had long been agitating for the Telecom monopoly to be broken up anyway. The second part of the legislation, to follow shortly afterwards, would contain all the provisions to ensure that the competitor would start on an equal footing with Telecom, and that it would not be swamped from the beginning — something that the Democrats had been saying they wanted, if they failed to stop privatisation in the first place. Under the circumstances they would have virtually no choice but to support it, if they wanted to remain consistent with their previous statements on the subject. This second lot of legislation also set a five year time limit on the duopoly, after which time other competitors could join the fray. This last provision had been introduced largely through the efforts of Paul Keating — as Bob Hawke confirms. 'I believed this concept of giving the new operator a reasonable period to establish itself and then throwing the field open to further competition,' Hawke wrote in his memoirs, 'a position advocated by my own advisers, was one point Keating had right.'[124]

As Keating recollects: 'My preferred policy was an open competitive model with Telstra taking on all comers. When it became clear that the duopoly was actually going to get up, I then broke off engagement on the issue, and focused on where we went in competition terms with the duopoly. In my view, that was making sure that the full telecommunications system would be open and competitive by 1997; making sure that the new competitor Optus got a fair deal, and all the things to make it as competitive a system as possible, even if it was a duopoly at first.'

The Beazley manoeuvre to get both pieces of legislation through would go as he had planned, with both Acts having completed their passage through Parliament by late 1991. In the space of just 18 months, then, the structure of the Australian Telecommunications industry had been entirely transformed. For all the success in getting his model up, seven years later Beazley would not be entirely satisfied. 'Looking back,' he says, 'I don't think that we did enough to actually solidify Optus's position to be frank, I think we left Optus hanging out to dry, and so it's a bit of a worry. We haven't anywhere near diminished Telstra's monopoly in the way in which I thought it would be by now.'

There were some people who remained unhappy with the changes — notably the unions who knew there would always be a smaller workforce with the effect of the increased competition, but as Patrick Walters notes, 'the most remarkable thing was that he got that whole thing through without a single day's industrial stoppage in the Telecom unions'.

One admirer for the way he had handled it all, was Kim Beazley Snr, who would say shortly afterwards: 'He possessed skills that I never remotely possessed'. It was not an untypical comment from Kim Snr, when talking about his son, just as it was always typical of Kim Jnr to return the favour. 'I'm not as good as he was,' Kim Jnr has been quoted in the press as saying about his father. 'I'm not as bright a person as he was and my understanding of history and politics isn't as deep.' Merrilyn Wasson too, had been watching with interest. She regarded her brother's recent triumph with enormous pride and she congratulated him warmly and genuinely.

But there was something even more pressing that she needed to discuss with him at around this time. It was about his nephew, Anton, she said. He was no longer the little boy he had been, and the thing was ... that he needed a bigger room. Kim's room to be precise. Would it be alright if they converted the tiny storeroom down the hall into a bedroom and Kim moved into that? Not a problem replied the conqueror of Paul Keating. He would be happy to move aside for his nephew, and he did do so the following weekend.

Back in Perth, Kim's younger brother, David, was doing quite well. He was still living at home and happy to be there; still fascinated by trains and also now AFL football; and was approaching his 25th straight year of service with essentially the same organisation — although when the General Post Office he had started with had split into Australia Post and Telecom in the mid-70's, he had gone to the latter. Specifically, he worked in the giant warehouse of the Telecom Distribution Services Centre in the Perth suburb of Kewdale — from where all manner of stationery, office supplies and communications equipment could be sent out as required to Telecom offices around the state.

While his older brother had concentrated his energies on trying to make Telecom more efficient, David personally had been finding the going tough, as the distribution process had become progressively more computerised. David's work as a storeman was only 50 per cent physical, and while he had been legendary among his workmates for the prodigious memory he displayed in knowing *all* the serial numbers of the 2000-odd separate items they sent out — and was also highly regarded for, in the words of the warehouse manager, 'never making a mistake' — he just couldn't cop what he saw as the needless complexities of working the computers.[125] While he might say as much to Kim when they saw each other, or when they regularly talked on the phone, their working lives had of course been entirely separate. Until one day ...

David was one of the 85 000 workers Kim Jnr was responsible for within his bailiwick of Communications, and it was around this time that one of his duties as Minister was to open the Material Quality Assurance building which had just been completed within the Kewdale complex. 'David talked about it for weeks beforehand,' the warehouse manager of the time, Clarrie Hair, remembers. 'Normally he wouldn't talk about Kim at all, unless someone might criticise what the Minister was doing on some issue, because David felt very protective towards him and would always defend him, but on this occasion he actually did tell everyone his big brother would be coming to the warehouse.'

True to his word ...

On the day, immediately after he had opened the MQA building, the Minister did indeed make time so that David could introduce him to his workmates and show him exactly what his job entailed. The Regional Manager of Telecom at the time, Len Anderson, who had presided over the opening ceremony and then escorted his Minister back to where

David worked, remembers being singularly impressed. 'There was just a great rapport between them,' he remembers, 'in a very quiet sort of way. It was a brother-to-brother sort of thing, whatever the difference in their levels within the organisation.' Which is much the way Kim remembers the afternoon. 'I think David was pretty chuffed to see me out there,' he remembers. 'I was very proud of him, and I think he was proud of me.' David was, and he would tell his parents later that it was one of the best days he had spent at Kewdale. Nevertheless, only shortly afterwards, David would take a 25-year redundancy package, to live quietly at home with his parents, and, among other things, expand his singularly impressive photo collection of old trains.

Back in his brother's political world, one effect of the whole telecommunications wrangle was an increase in public profile for Kim Beazley Jnr, and recognition of his leadership talents. Only a fortnight after the Special Conference, a Saulwick Poll published in the *Sydney Morning Herald* showed that out of a clear blue sky, Kim Beazley had suddenly sailed into a position of dominance over Keating as preferred Prime Minister, after Hawke. According to the poll, a mere 18 per cent of voters thought that the Treasurer would do a 'good or very good job' as Prime Minister, while a massive 47 per cent thought he would do a 'poor or very poor job'. In contrast, 22 per cent of voters believed Mr Beazley would do a 'good or very good job' as Prime Minister while 27 per cent believed he would do a 'poor or very poor job'. As the article accompanying the poll noted, 'this is the first indication of the relative standing of the two men since Mr Beazley's success over telecommunications reform'.

A follow-up poll in the *Sunday Telegraph* confirmed that the figures weren't rubbery. 'Kim Beazley is the preferred choice to step into Bob Hawke's shoes as the next Labor Prime Minister, according to a new poll released yesterday. The Transport and Communications Minister was a clear winner over Treasurer Paul Keating in a national opinion poll ... 'The Newspoll survey conducted for the *Sunday Telegraph* and published on 16 December 1990, found Mr Beazley, favoured by 25 per cent, was the most popular choice to replace Mr Hawke. Keating was on only 20 per cent, and John Dawkins rated 10 per cent. Hawke fared little better with only 31 per cent satisfied with his performance.' Therein lay the first wisps of wind for a major tornado that would be not long in hitting.

CHAPTER FIFTEEN

ROUND ONE

'I am going to go you, Bob.'
Paul Keating to Bob Hawke, 30 May 1991.

By the end of 1990, it was obvious to all in the Labor Party that Bob Hawke and Paul Keating were rapidly getting to the point where they could no longer work together. While they were not quite giving an impression of two alley cats in a sack, the tension was there for all to see in the inner circle, and apparent to those beyond. The famed 'Placido Domingo' speech to the National Press Club given by Keating on 7 December of that year, where he compared himself to the great operatic tenor and by implication left Hawke as a mere starry-eyed choirboy of national politics, 'tripping over television wires in shopping centres', set the tone. Among many other things the Treasurer asserted that Australia had never had a great national leader, and that one who had previously been nominated in that role, John Curtin, was in fact no more than a mere 'trier'.

It was this comment that went down worst with Beazley, as his regard for his childhood hero in Curtin was still strong enough that now, as a politician himself, he had told colleagues before making a speech at a function to raise money for the John Curtin School of Government in Western Australia, that he 'would find it very difficult to talk about Curtin without breaking down'.[126] He had indeed become quite emotional. Beazley had also, in a speech to the Australian Institute of International Affairs in July of 1985, publicly described Curtin as 'Australia's greatest Prime Minister ...'[127] It was with these feelings that he chipped Keating about his Curtin jibe a few days later when next he saw him, but then left it at that.

Hawke was not nearly so sanguine and attacked Keating both over his needlessly disrespectful comments about the former Prime Minister, and, more pertinently, his blasphemous insinuations about himself. As the tussle started to sink to the mat, one with a unique perspective on the two contestants, was Beazley himself. He says now of their relationship: 'I think they're both very, very complex people. Paul has always taken the view I think that Bob, as President of the ACTU, had been a fairly destructive influence on the Whitlam Government, and for a short period of time Paul had been a Minister in the Whitlam Government — so he carried that resentment with him. He'd said to Bob on a number of occasions, when Bob was trying to be Prime Minister, "Bob you think you are like the one-eyed man in the valley of the blind — the King — but when you come to Canberra you're going to find that most of us here have got 20/20 vision".

'So Paul was always a difficult man to get to support Bob's ambitions — he did in the end, but he was very slow to get there. A very complex person Paul, a very profound sense of loyalty as well as a profound sense of his own destiny. I think he made a substantial contribution as Treasurer, and I think he felt he had Bob's say-so for taking over from him.' He certainly did. Unbeknown to Beazley at that particular time, three years previously on 25 November 1988, Keating and Hawke had reached an agreement at Kirribilli House, before witnesses, that Hawke would stand down in favour of Keating in the next term. It was something that, at the time, had secured an uneasy peace between the two Labor titans. 'Bob I think has basically always seen himself as a man touched by "serendipity," "God", world spirit or whatever to be a natural leader of his nation,' Kim continues. 'He, more than Paul, positioned himself as a prime minister. He had a conception of what a prime minister did, he had a conception of how you organised life as a prime minister to run a government, because he had prepared himself all his life. Paul had not prepared himself for the Prime Ministership, but he felt that he had earned it. So you had their egos clashing. But they were egos that had become complicated by a whole series of other perceptions, loyalties, senses of propriety, senses of process — and these were all very complicated. Really, I think they were just two great politicians — like Muhammad Ali and Joe Frazier — who happened to be around at the same time.'

Others took a less understanding view. Peter Walsh remembers that, 'after the Placido Domingo speech, Keating's incipient megalomania was becoming clearer. As I said at the time, we had a choice between an egomaniac and a megalomaniac. I didn't identify which was which, but it's not all that hard to work out. As time went on Keating turned out to be much more of a megalomaniac than I'd feared.'

A dramatic complication to the Hawke/Keating skirmishes was the outbreak of the Gulf War on 17 January 1991 — resulting from the five-month occupation of Kuwait by Iraqi leader Saddam Hussein's army. Dawn had just broken in South Perth when the phone rang in the Beazley/Annus house. It was the Prime Minister, informing Beazley that the Americans would begin bombing in 15 minutes. After the phone call, Beazley slumped back in his bed. It had come to this then. Here was the first major engagement of the Australian forces since the Vietnam War, forces he had spent six years of his life shaping and preparing for just such an eventuality, and only ten months previously they had been moved entirely out of his province of operations. Senator Robert Ray was now the incumbent Defence Minister, and most of the important decisions would be his call.

Bob Hawke had the impression, just quietly, that it was 'a bit galling' for Beazley to be on the sidelines for this encounter, but this was not correct. 'I could hardly bear it,' Beazley remembers as his main reaction, 'I could ... hardly ... *bear* it.' And nor did he bother trying to hide it from his nearest and dearest. 'It nearly killed him,' agrees Susie Annus. Beazley would in fact spend long hours with Robert Ray discussing the state of play in the Gulf War, a large part of his role was continuing to do what he had done for the previous five months — convincing his Caucus colleagues of the rightness of Australia being involved in the first place. Beazley had always been passionate in his view that it was very much in Australia's interests to commit three ships — two frigates and a support ship — and then mine-clearance divers shortly after the outbreak; as he saw it as an important international cause to save Kuwait and discipline Iraq.

Against this perspective was the view held especially by the Left of Caucus, that it was not an international cause for justice at all; rather, it was the USA pressuring its smaller allies like Australia to get involved simply so that the States wouldn't be seen to be the only one pushing Iraq into the mother of all corners and pounding the living daylights out of it. Just as it had been in the 1950s, '60s, '70s and '80s, the approach one took to America in the 1990s remained one of the main factional friction points of Labor Party politics. True, Beazley had done an enormous amount during his own time as Defence Minister to make it possible for someone to be in the Left wing of the party and still at least tacitly approve of Australia being in a security relationship with America — but this was different. It was one thing to allow America's bases to sit fairly passively on one's sovereign territory, quite another to endorse sending your ships into action in a war that seemed mostly designed to assure that the supply of Middle East oil to America continued unfettered.

Beazley argued strongly against this point of view, both in the Caucus and the cafeterias, to anyone who would listen, and as the longest serving Defence Minister in Australia's history — and arguably the most respected — he was listened to. During those discussions, he framed a three-pronged attack on Labor's Left. First, he argued that while it was admittedly sometimes difficult in international relations to define just what constituted an 'act of overt aggression,' Iraq's invasion of Kuwait was 'about as blatant an act of overt aggression as you could get, and countries that behaved that badly ought to be disciplined'. Secondly, while it was all very well to say blithely that it was all about oil, the simple reality was that the oil supply from the Middle East really *was* critical to the international economy — including Australia's — and if the United States and other allied nations were taking a stand, then it was only right and proper that Australia play its part. 'And the third thing,' Beazley said, 'was to show the nations of this region that if Australia decided that there was a serious national issue at stake, that we were prepared to commit to it.'

Caucus, at least as evidenced by a simple majority, came to share the same view — and Hawke had been able to commit the three ships the previous August. Senator Robert Ray acknowledges the contribution made by Beazley throughout the course of the Gulf War; 'he played a very constructive role in briefings throughout,' he says, but makes one other pointed observation besides. 'I'd have to say it was better that I was in the Ministry at the time of the Gulf War than him, because everyone in Caucus thought he was 'gung-ho', while everyone knew I wasn't. It meant that it was much easier for me to bring the party with me to secure actual overseas commitment for our forces, than it might have been for him.'

With the war under way, Beazley's involvement remained well behind that of Hawke, Ray and the Foreign Minister, Gareth Evans. For the duration of the conflict, however, a Security Committee from within Cabinet met frequently. 'Bob used to use the Security Committee actively during the Gulf War,' Beazley recalls, 'so I at least had a hand in that with Paul Keating and Neal Blewett. That way I was at least kept actively involved and for the period of the time of the war, I spent the time virtually 100 per cent in Canberra following it intimately.'

The upshot of the Gulf War from the political point of view was that as it went on, Hawke consolidated his position as Prime Minister in the polls, and felt such renewed confidence in his stoush with Keating that in a meeting with him on the night of 31 January he felt no compunction in telling Keating that he intended to see out his fourth term as Prime Minister after all, and would not be standing down. As recounted by Paul Kelly, the essence of their conversation, in the Prime Ministerial suite in Parliament House, went as follows:[128]

Keating: 'That's a total breach of your Kirribilli undertaking and the arrangements on which I've relied for the past two and a half years.'

Hawke: 'I recognise this. I'm not trying to hide that. But I believe that I've clearly got the best chance to lead the party to victory at the next election and I'm staying on this basis.'

Keating: 'Bob, you'll never win another election. You're dead meat. You'll just hang around for a punch on the nose.'

Keating left the office, and began to plan his moves. As it was now clear that Hawke was not going to leave of his own accord, there seemed no other way for it than to blast him out. If Kim Beazley, like the rest of the Government, remained unaware of the original Kirribilli pact — still he was aware, as was everyone else, that there was a big storm a'brewing. 'You couldn't miss it,' remembers Beazley drolly. 'It wasn't like the whole Hawke/Keating thing blew up from nowhere.'

Keating did not abandon Hawke in Parliament for all that, and was particularly notable in April of 1991 for mounting a sterling defence of Hawke when the Prime Minister came under attack for revelations emanating from the WA Inc Royal Commission, enquiring essentially into the actions of Brian Burke's Labor Government, which had run from February 1983 to February 1988. As exposed by the Royal Commission, the Burke Government had been involved in dozens of manoeuvrings in the corporate world, which had ultimately done little to ease the burden on the state's taxpayers, but which had certainly enriched many Burke associates, most notably 'Last Resort' Laurie Connell and Alan Bond. When Hawke's name emerged in such a damaging forum — unjustly as it turned out — in Paul Kelly's assessment, '[the Prime Minister] stumbled in Parliament, unable to defend himself, and it was Keating who salvaged Hawke and turned the issue back to Hewson'.[129] Hawke was equally under pressure at this time to dump Brian Burke from his then role as Australia's Ambassador to Ireland and the Holy See, but he refused to do so despite evidence emerging from the Royal Commission that the former Premier had acted at the least highly improperly, and possibly corruptly. The two Hawke ministers who most encouraged the Prime Minister to continue supporting Burke were Graham Richardson and Kim Beazley.

In terms of what ultimately happened (Burke was jailed,) Beazley is clear. 'The fate of Brian Burke is one of the things that mystifies me,' he says. 'Next to Neville Wran, he is the best politician I have ever come across, and that things could have gone so bad still baffles me.' There would be criticism, later, that Beazley was foolish to continue to back Burke when clearly everything the former Premier touched turned to dust. Beazley strongly disagrees. 'If what people mean by that is that I persisted with a friendship with Brian Burke long after,' he says, 'well "bugger it", is my response on that. Burke is not a mate. He is a friend. Mates are people who you pick up with along the line, have a few drinks with, and they might be good nodding acquaintances day-to-day. I have got loads of mates all over the place, but *friends* are different. Friends are people whom you become attached to for other reasons than your simple, normal day-to-day processes. The notion that I would somehow or another disconnect with him because he was in trouble is abominable to me. I didn't run Brian Burke's Government, I didn't run his operations, I wasn't a member of his Government. None of that had anything to do with me, just as it had nothing to do with our friendship.'

Another perspective on Beazley's enduring loyalty to Burke, is provided by Syd Hickman.

'The amazing thing to me was that at the end of it, years later when it became clear what a bucket of shit Burke had left behind, Kim should have realised, must have realised, that if he had agreed about what his old mate Brian suggested — and gone back to WA to become Premier — it would have been him in Peter Dowding's position; him who would have been the one carrying the huge bucket of shit and tipping it all over himself like Dowding had to.' (Dowding, the man Burke had hand-picked to succeed him as Premier, after Beazley had refused — and incidentally another 'son of', this time of Keith Dowding, who had been a one-time fierce political opponent of Kim Beazley Snr — ultimately had to resign as a result of problems arising from the whole WA Inc imbroglio.) 'I felt sorry for Dowding — but that's the slot that Kim would have been put into,' Hickman continues. 'And yet he never once held it against Burke — just incredible — he'd forgive Burke. He kids himself Burke never did anything wrong.'

Perhaps. But back late in 1989, Beazley had been under no illusions about the likely fallout of the collapse of WA Inc on his own political career. As Ross McMullin wrote in *The Light on the Hill*: 'At the end of 1989, opinion surveys confirmed that Labor's standing in the west had deteriorated alarmingly. The concern within the ranks of state Labor was augmented by anxious FPLP [Federal Parliamentary Labor Party] members who were worried that WA electors might express their dissatisfaction with the state government when voting at the imminent national election. One of them, Beazley, who felt vulnerable although a swing of 8.6 per cent was required to unseat him, was particularly animated in urging that something had to be done ...'[130] Something was done. 'The smooth executed removal of [Dowding] ...was a startling manifestation of the ruthless professionalism which had become characteristic of the ALP during the 1980s,' wrote McMullin. Beazley was in no doubt as to the veracity of such an assessment. 'That is accurate,' he says.

In May of 1991, Brian Burke ceased to be the main Labor talking point anyway, as the party started to divide more formally into its pro-Keating and pro-Hawke camps. Some members of the Caucus might have been in a dreadful quandary as to which of the two political titans they should back — and were thus sometimes spotted crossing the river between the two camps — but Beazley was never among them. 'There was no particular problem in making up my mind,' he recalls. 'I was always going to stay with Bob. I always thought that he was a class act, a top politician and he had enormous appeal out there in the community. Paul was very, very good, but I didn't think he had the breadth that Bob had, and there just wasn't enough evidence around that he should go.'

Besides ... 'The party owed him,' Beazley says. 'He was still a great Prime Minister. Also I thought Bob should go of his own choosing.' This last was a theme that he pushed repeatedly with his Labor Party colleagues when they sounded him out on the fight. 'Kim would always say,' recalls Stephen Smith, by then an adviser to Keating, 'that if Paul *just left Bob alone*, then he would go gracefully soon enough. But that if Paul attacked him, unleashed the dogs of war, then Bob would dig in, and there'd be a massive fight.'

Paul would not leave Bob alone. Bob dug in. There was a massive fight. 'By 1991 I had had the better part of a large part of what I thought were the prerogatives of the leader for seven years,' Keating explained on the ABC. 'It was too long a thing — it went on for too long and it was becoming a joke.'[131] It came to a head in the late afternoon of 30 May. A chance conversation in the corridor between Kim Beazley and Graham Richardson alerted the former that Keating was about to launch his attack. Beazley was appalled. 'I raced around to his office to try and talk him out of it,' he recalls. But it was too late. At about 5 o'clock, Keating had already made his way around to Hawke's office where the Prime Minister was engaged in deep conversation with the Queensland Premier Wayne Goss and the head of the Australian Workers' Union, Bill Ludwig. Keating insisted on interrupting the meeting, Hawke asked Goss and Ludwig to excuse them for a moment, and in the course of the conversation Keating once again put to Hawke that it was time for him to honour the Kirribilli agreement, or otherwise he would make their agreement public. Hawke declined. Keating reportedly came back with the immortal line, Australian man to Australian man: 'I am going to go you, Bob.'[132]

Keating left; Goss and Ludwig were ushered back in; Keating made a phone call to Hawke perhaps ten minutes later where Hawke offered to think about it while on a coming trip to Europe. This time it was Keating who declined. It was *on*. Wayne Goss, picking up bits and pieces of the conversation as he went along — in spite of himself — remains stunned at Hawke's ability to turn away from such an exchange, and then resume their previous discussion as if nothing had changed. 'Hawke talked to Paul for a bit,' he recalls, 'said "yes", "right", "good", "okay, well I'll talk to you later", put down the phone and just picked up the conversation! We were talking about a compensation package for World Heritage listing of Fraser Island — and he never missed a beat. After that everybody was running round threatening everybody, but right then, it was calm.'

Beazley, meantime, had at last caught up with Keating in his office and confirmed the news that Keating was going to challenge Hawke for the leadership of the party and the Prime Ministership. Keating, with some theatricality, unveiled to his friend of two decades the news of the Kirribilli agreement. He told him that he and Bob had made a solemn *pact*, witnessed by Bill Kelty and Sir Peter Abeles, to the effect that Bob would stand down for him in this term. And now Bob was going to renege and what did Kim think of *that*? 'Big deal' was the short answer. 'I didn't go on about this at length with Paul,' Beazley recollects, 'because it simply wasn't the moment, but what I thought was that their Kirribilli agreement didn't amount to a hill of beans. It wasn't for them to decide such things — that was quite properly a matter for Caucus — and it was inappropriate of them to have entered into it in the first place.' As the two talked, one thing was clear to Beazley. 'I'd come to the conclusion that these two guys were about to wreck everything they'd created between them, but I also thought that a Government without Keating would be seriously weakened. And it really pissed me off that they were prepared to tear the Government apart. I thought it was pretty unsatisfactory.'

Beazley took his leave of Keating with the mood between them strained, much in the manner of two brothers in a civil war when the time had come to head for opposite sides of the battlelines. Meanwhile, upstairs, Laurie Oakes of Channel Nine was racing to break the story of the Kirribilli agreement on that night's six o'clock news. He had been told the skeleton of the story at around 5.40 pm, and it went to air at 6.06 pm. A long scheduled Cabinet meeting began at 6.30 pm and Hawke had good reason, this time, to be really distracted. Back in his office, his political adviser Col Parks had been watching the Channel Nine television news when Laurie Oakes' story on the Kirribilli agreement ran, blowing the whole thing wide open, and Parks had quickly sent Hawke a note to that effect. Hawke immediately sent back a note with the official company line: Keating's Placido Domingo speech of six months previously had been 'an act of treachery,' which meant that the Kirribilli agreement was rendered null and void. Parks obliged, but was under no illusions about the situation, as he remembers: 'It was now going to be full, open warfare.' Parks was waiting in the Cabinet anteroom, when Keating left shortly afterwards himself, for places unknown.

Back inside the Cabinet Room Beazley remained one of the few who was fully aware of the situation, and remains impressed with the way Hawke handled himself. 'I think he felt confident,' Beazley opines. 'I think in the back of his mind was the view that "I'll win, Keating will go, probably leave politics — and that'll be the end of it". He was also a very tough man, Hawke, much tougher than I'll ever live to be. He was determined that he was not going to be distracted by it, basically.'

When the Cabinet meeting broke up after a couple of hours — with the Prime Minister deciding finally to advise his colleagues that Keating was going to launch a challenge to his leadership — Hawke went back to his office with his core faithful. Everyone now knew it: Keating was going to launch soon, and it was a time for counting heads.

Those heads that Hawke counted in his office included a lot of the party heavyweights. There was Kim Beazley, then Nick Bolkus, Gareth Evans, Gerry Hand, Peter Staples, Simon Crean, Robert Ray and Michael Duffy. They decided that they had to lance the boil immediately, and bring on the challenge as soon as possible. Hawke so advised the Caucus chairwoman, Carolyn Jakobsen, and the meeting was formally set for 8 o'clock the following morning. After the others had gone, Beazley stayed to see how Hawke was holding up under the strain of the challenge, and see if he could offer assistance, but there was no need. 'Bob was fine,' he recalls. 'He was very cheerful, very businesslike, I think he had worked out early on that he was going to survive pretty well. It was all quite calm in his office.'

Perhaps they were in the eye of the political cyclone. For the rest of Parliament House — brand new foundations, building above, and all — started to vibrate. Phone calls, meetings, corridor creepings, whispered conversation, headcounts, lists, the lot — all while the House of Representatives was in session, as it would be until 3.30 am the following morning. For the Federal Parliamentary Labor Party members, the precious hours between the Caucus meeting being called and it actually taking place were focused on the main game, with enormous activity from both camps as they tried to maximise their vote on the morrow. When he stepped back out into the cyclone, Beazley reverted to Beazley of Old, working the phones himself, just as he had done with such enthusiasm back in the State Executive days in Western Australia in the '60s. The tone elsewhere was set by an incident that occurred at around 4 o'clock in the morning in a Parliament House that was still buzzing with an enormous amount of subterranean activity. As recounted by Alan Ramsey in the *Sydney Morning Herald* two days later, Don Russell, Keating's chief lieutenant and numbers man, emerged from Keating's offices at that time and headed off down the ministerial wing on his way to another minister's office.[133] At that very moment, coming the other way, was the near-nucleus of Hawke's senior ministerial loyalists, in Michael Duffy, Nick Bolkus and Gerry Hand. With them was Lisa Barker, the senior private secretary to Bolkus and also, incidentally, Russell's fiancée. Not a word. Not a hand raised in acknowledgement. Nothing. 'We just sort of passed,' Russell told Ramsey, 'we passed in the night.' Such were the times.

When morning broke on 31 May 1991, in Canberra, the cold and clinging fog could have been taken straight from the set of *The Hound of the Baskervilles*. Through it, from all corners of Canberra, came those members of the Federal Parliamentary Labor Party who hadn't spent the night in their offices. And if, together with the fog, there was an obvious tension in the air that early morning, there was something else besides. Bloodlust? The battle call? Something, anyway. These were, after all, a group of people for whom the world of politics had always emitted a siren call, and that political world was never so intense in tone, the siren never so seductive and strong, as when there was a fight to the death over political leadership. It was perhaps unsurprising then that, as admitted by many, some of these people who lived for politics never felt more truly alive than right then. Amid all the hand-wringing there was plenty of pleasurable adrenalin flowing. It *was* on.

Prime Ministers do not arrive first for meetings. They are leaders, the chosen ones, the focal points, and with that in mind they are most definitely not the ones who wait for others to arrive — they are the ones for whom others wait. The Caucus chemistry for the contender, Paul Keating, was different. His only hope of success on the day was to be hoisted on the mob's shoulders, and to do that he had to be right there among them in the meeting from the beginning, which was where he was from 8.00 am, sitting three rows back on the left, blending in. The configuration of the room had Senator Stephen Loosley sitting directly opposite Kim Beazley Jnr, who was seated beside the table at the front of the room set up for the Government leadership. As is correct form in such situations, that morning Beazley was trying to project an air of total confidence. Catching the eye of Loosley — and with that perhaps in mind — he smiled and said to his fellow American Civil War aficionado, in an open and friendly fashion: 'Tell me this, Stephen, do you feel like George Pickett about to go up Cemetery Ridge?' Loosley gave a thin smile, before rejoining, 'Yes, I do as a matter of fact, because I do know what is coming. But equally, Kim, don't *you* feel just a little like Robert E. Lee in his Seven Days on the Peninsula?' Beazley paused in turn, and replied quietly: 'Point taken.'

In Gettysburg, Pennsylvania, on July 3, 1863, Robert E. Lee is leading his forces of the Confederate Army, on the third day of the famous battle at Gettysburg. On the first day, he had assaulted the left flank of the Union Army in the battle of Culp's Hill. On the second day, he had assaulted the right flank at Little Round Top.

Now, for the coup de grace. Lee tells Lieutenant General James A. Longstreet that the Union weakness is to be found in the centre, up on top of Cemetery Ridge. The decision is taken to throw the freshly arrived division from Virginia of Major General George Pickett into the assault, flanked by two other Confederate divisions. The flags of this fresh division are still furled, their guns not yet blazing. The Union has been dealt grievous blows on the first two days, where the Confederates had come within an inch of success. Confidence is high.

So the assault begins, with three Confederate divisions marching straight up the hill, expecting resistance to be minimal at best. In fact not only was the artillery at the top of the hill concentrated straight at the men from the South, but the remnants of the left and right flanks had reformed, angry, and were waiting for them on both sides. It would end up as a near massacre with Pickett's division suffering 7000 casualties, more than three-quarters of his force.

Time passed.

In what became known as the Seven Days on the Peninsula battle of the same war, Robert E. Lee's forces first skirmished and then came to grips with the Union Army under the command of General George B. McClellan. Lee had scored a tactical success by saving the Confederate capital of Richmond, Virginia, and driving McClellan back to the James River. There ensued a defensive battle fought over seven days from White Oaks Swamp to Malvern Hill, where although Lee was able to drive the Union Army of the Potomac away from the Confederate capital of Richmond and back towards the James River, he still suffered more casualties than his opponents. Such was the fragile nature of the South's infrastructure, that they could never replace lost effectives, meaning that the Confederates could never suffer more casualties than their opponents. So while Lee had indeed driven the Union Army back, he knew then that one day they would return in greater numbers.

Time, gentlemen, please. Immediately after the exchange between Beazley and Loosley, there was a restless stirring in the room as Bob Hawke arrived with a flurry of quiet salutations, nods, and meaningful looks at his loyalists — and more importantly at those waverers who might still be counted on to vote for him with the right bit of gentle pressure. The moment of truth was on him.

The previous night, a manoeuvre had been planned by Hawke, Beazley and Robert Ray — after the others had left — to oblige Keating to declare himself a challenger to Hawke's leadership. Under Caucus rules that would mean there would have to be a show of hands for a spill motion that the leadership be declared vacant. All those who wished to vote against Hawke would then be doing it under his beady eye — which would indubitably knock out a lot of the nervous nellies who would not have the courage to do so. So after the preliminaries had been attended to, the Prime Minister got to his feet, and surveyed the room. Superficially at least, the members of Caucus were all pretty much in their normal positions. The Right were generally on the left-hand side of the room as he looked out upon them; the Left tended to stay on the right, while the Centre and Independents were sprinkled around the middle. But where exactly was Caucus now *politically?* With him, or against him?

He began, in a voice of almost unnatural calm, almost as if he were ever so slightly bored with these irritating matters: 'Ok, Paul informed me yesterday afternoon at 5 pm that he intended to challenge for the leadership, so I will invite Paul to move the necessary motion ...' A pause. Then a sole voice rang out from the back of the room. 'That's not what Bill Hayden did in 1982.' It was Peter Walsh, the irascible and fearless Senator from Western Australia, and he had a point. When Hawke and Bill Hayden first tussled for the leadership of the ALP, Hayden had resigned the leadership at the Caucus and declared his intention to re-contest, meaning the leadership could be decided by secret ballot. It had been considered the honourable thing to do under the circumstances, and now that Walsh mentioned it, it escaped no-one that those circumstances now were close to the same. Hawke seemed to waver for a moment, unsure of how to proceed, and it is at that point, in the estimation of Stephen Loosley that 'Bob's leadership expired'.

Keating seized the moment to heighten Hawke's discomfort. He made a slow walk to the front of the room, and in a voice raspy with the fatigue of having made an estimated 80 phone calls to Caucus members the previous night, he put his own view. 'Well Bob I really think you should declare the leadership vacant — that is the tradition. That is what Bill did in 1982 to give you the chance of a secret ballot, and I think that is the appropriate course of action now. There's been talk around of Caucus members having their preselections threatened if they're seen to vote against you. Surely, Bob, you've got to resign and make it a secret ballot.' Again Hawke seemed to hesitate, but then rose and rejected Keating's assertions. That was *not* the way things were going to proceed, he said. Whereupon Carolyn Jakobsen, who was chairing the Caucus, made what is widely regarded as a monumental blunder from the point of view of the Hawke camp, by saying: 'Well if there is no proposition before the Chair I will have to close the meeting.' Richardson, hardly believing their luck, said 'Dead right!' while Michael Lee called out 'Close the meeting!' Yeah! Other Keating supporters took up the cry to 'Close the meeting!' 'Close the meeting!' Jakobsen, to the stunned disbelief of the Keating supporters — glory, glory, hallelujah — did just that. The whole thing had taken less than 15 minutes. The Keating supporters streamed out of the Caucus room, rejoicing that it had gone so well — with their man still standing after the stoush, even though it was expected that he would receive a whipping — while Hawke, Ray and Beazley put their heads together in furious consultation.

Back in Hawke's office the snap decision was taken to hold a second Caucus meeting at 10.00 am where they would indeed go to a secret ballot. Beazley was standing at Hawke's left elbow as he made the call to Keating to make the offer. Foiled again. Keating replied that it was too late, that his camp were already on their way to the airport and they wouldn't be able to get a quorum. Richardson was in his own office ready for just such a manoeuvre and now told that it was happening, immediately worked the phones, furiously punching the buttons with his pudgy fingers and barking: 'Out! Out! Get everybody out! I don't give a fuck what you have to do, get everyone out of the building, they want to have a second Caucus meeting! We will send somebody along to report what happens, but just *get out of the building!* No matter who tries to stop you, just leave. Spread the word.'

Again that is what happened. By the time the Party Whip — himself a strong Keating supporter — moved along the corridors to formally tell Caucus members that the second Caucus meeting would be starting at 10.00 am, he found those offices and corridors oddly empty. Elvis had left the building. And all the Keating supporters in Caucus besides. What went with them was Hawke's definitive chance to slaughter Keating on his chosen field of battle. The fact that Keating and Hawke had met, tussled, and the younger man had walked away neither bloodied, nor bowed, gave Keating an immediate legitimacy for the throne. It also gave him an extra weekend to garner more votes, while lengthening the time that Hawke's leadership would be seriously destabilised. In the words of one Keating supporter, 'We had every confidence that the Hawke Prime Ministership was going to be farcical by the 6 o'clock news ...'

Clearly, this particular episode was a debacle in Hawke's campaign to stave off Keating, and in the words of another of Keating's lieutenants of the time, 'I think Kim has got to bear some of the responsibility for that — he was too clever by half.' Beazley agrees, 'It was a bad move,' he acknowledges, 'and he took us by surprise. We would have been much smarter to declare the position vacant. But Bob's position was basically well held: "*I* am Prime Minister, it is up to *them* to put this on, not me — and if they want to do it they can get up and move it at the meeting." The Keating camp needed more time and what Bob was trying to do was to trap them into moving early. We also canvassed among us the possibility that he would choose not to formally challenge, but the feeling was that he wouldn't do that, because it would make him look weak. But in hindsight the best thing to have done would be for Bob to go in and say "Look, there are all these rumours and whispering around, and here is my resignation. At 6 o'clock tonight there will be a ballot for Leader of the Labor Party".'

Now, even Hawke agrees that they botched it: 'In retrospect we should have seen that a bit differently, but anyway ...' By the time they had realised their bungle, there was no time for recriminations. They had plenty of work to do over the weekend to try to secure a big win in the ballot on Monday, when the next Caucus meeting had been called for 10.00 am. 'Lobbying on my own behalf,' Beazley says, 'I am very average, but lobbying on behalf of other people I am a demon.' So it proved to be that weekend as he worked the phones in his office. Furiously rallying support, it was his task to try to steel the troops to save his leader, mentor and chief sponsor, against the claims of one of his closest friends and the godfather of his second daughter.

In other offices, Hawke's loyalist lieutenants like Gareth Evans, Robert Ray and Nick Bolkus were working their own networks. Karen Bissaker, Beazley's personal assistant, remembers that she and Beazley basically did not stop. 'All day long and into the night, on both days of the weekend,' she recalls, 'I was tracking people down and getting Kim onto them so he could assess their position, and see if they were already voting for Hawke, and if not, if they could be persuaded.' One of Beazley's key political advisers of the time, Gary

O'Neill, was privy to some of his boss's end of the conversations and remembers being impressed with the way he went about it. 'He wasn't like Robert Ray or Paul Keating; he wasn't saying "Listen, if you are not for me then I am going to shoot you and your father and your mother and your dog and then I will burn your house down..." Kim is not like that, and goes about it differently: "these are the arguments, I believe you should do it, you have got a moral duty to do it plus a professional duty to do it" and so on.'

And so on, into the weekend. One of Beazley's jobs was to also work out who could be 'worked on' by the Prime Minister — someone who was wavering in their support for him, but might be prompted to stay with the team if Hawke could come up with the right words of persuasion. Sitting in the Lodge by an open fire, Hawke was himself never off the phone, and was constantly liaising with Beazley.

It was a tough battle for them both — the headline on the front page of the *Sydney Morning Herald* on Saturday 1 June 1991 was '*Stalemate in Canberra. Caucus prepares for a weekend of lobbying after Hawke's ambush fails*'. It highlighted the vulnerability of the Prime Minister, as did the breakout of the paper's editorial on the front page: 'Mr Hawke should stand aside for Mr Keating now ... He is the Party's future; its most respected Minister; and has been a talented and forceful Treasurer.' The only good news was the headline on the other side of the page: *Hawke Streets Ahead in New Poll*, which returned the extraordinary figures that while 65 per cent of the voters thought Hawke would make a better Prime Minister, only 18 per cent of them thought that Keating would. Not surprisingly, it was this line that Beazley pushed most over the weekend, that whatever *they* might think of Keating's claims to the job, there could be absolutely no doubt what the punters thought. Such statistics though, did not tell the whole story as Hawke's public approval rating even then was descending from the stratospheric heights of 75 per cent in 1983–84, to only 26 per cent by the end of 1991. The word increasingly attached to his government at this time was "tired". It would get more tired still that weekend. For it was, by any measure, gruelling for both sides, and by their common estimation, the Keating camp picked up at least another four votes over the course of the weekend, reducing the margin between the two heavyweight contenders for the political champion prize for all Australia by at least eight votes.[134]

On the Monday morning, with Hawke's supporters properly organised this time, the Caucus meeting went off without a hitch.

Actually, just one hitch. When the returning officer announced the result of the secret ballot it showed that Keating had lost to Hawke by 66/44. The hitch for the Hawke camp was the comparative smallness of the margin, where if only a dozen supporters had gone to the other side, the Prime Minister would have been ushered to oblivion at the hands of his own party. For Messrs Hawke, Beazley and Ray, it was exactly the situation that had faced Robert E. Lee in the previous century on the peninsula, knowing that while the goodies might have won the battle this time, it was inevitable that the enemy would return with greater numbers next time.

This crucial point did not escape the media either. When Graham Richardson and Stephen Loosley left the meeting to head back to Richardson's office in the Ministerial Wing, they were quickly and quietly joined by the *Australian*'s highly respected political correspondent, Glenn Milne, who fell in step with them. For perhaps fifty paces the trio walked in a curious but companionable kind of silence. Then Milne lifted up his notebook, and asked the question, while still walking. 'How did you go?'

'We went down this time, 66/44,' Loosley replied.

'That's close enough,' Milne mused.

Richardson paused, looked at him, and replied with some deliberation: 'Yes, that's close enough.'

Milne's assessment highlighted the fact that the Keating camp could probably count on the opinion leaders in the gallery — most notably Alan Ramsey, Laurie Oakes, Paul Kelly, Glenn Milne, and Michelle Grattan — to form the view that Hawke had merely staved off the inevitable until another time. All up, the Keating camp was highly gratified. 'We knew we weren't going to win,' Richardson says directly, 'so what we were about was putting up a reasonable show and also making Hawke look as bad as possible.' Yes, Keating *had* said in his post-ballot press conference that, 'The fact is I only had one shot in the locker, and I fired it.' But in the words of Richardson: 'Everyone knew that was all bullshit and we were going to move on them again. If you don't say it, you're going to be churlish and a bad loser, and you're not a good sport. You don't have to *mean* it, you just have to *say* it.' The rather sombre mood that night in the Hawke camp perhaps acknowledged that the Keating shark was still circling. After all, Hawke had given a similar assurance that he wouldn't challenge Bill Hayden again, after losing to him by five votes in 1982.

Inside the Keating offices by contrast, a soon-to-be-famous party was getting under way. There, the mood was more than merely buoyant. To hell with the fact that it was a nominal loss to the outgoing Treasurer — for Keating had announced at his press conference that he was standing down from the post — no-one there seemed under any illusion that the result was anything less than a major success. George Pickett surely never felt anywhere near *this* good the night after the assault on Cemetery Ridge. In a corner of the offices which were crowded with perhaps 100 people, Keating was holding court among six of his closest confidants. Never a man to drink to excess, it is just possible that on this evening, in the words of one participant, 'he had had a few'. With a glass of wine in one hand, and a broad smile, he was giving his own upbeat interpretation of how he thought the day had gone. His voice was still raspy, bordering on hoarse, and he was giving a singularly good impression of a man who had spent an enormous amount of time over the previous few days talking, talking, talking. 'When I become Prime Minister ...' he was saying, to an audience that included Stephen Loosley and Graham Richardson, 'the first two things I'm going to say to [Hawke supporter] Nick Bolkus, is a) no-one has got any right to be as ugly as you are, and b) you're fucked off to the backbench'. Next, Keating shifted his gleefully malicious mood to other key Hawke supporters in Gareth Evans and Kim Beazley. 'And Kim, I'm going to skewer him,' Keating said, thrusting his right hand forward in a rather vicious and repeated stabbing motion.

As if on cue, there was Kim Beazley himself, making his way into the party of the man who he had been working so assiduously to defeat over recent weeks. He was coolly welcomed by Keating — despite his previous harsh words — and his presence there was in part the mark of the man. 'I think it was reflective of Beazley's personality,' says one of his colleagues 'that while he was so intimately identified with the Hawke camp, he was still on very good terms with all those who were the major Keating backers. It was because of his personality and long-term mateship that he had with a lot of people.' For Beazley it was more a courtesy call than anything, a chance to show that it was nothing personal, that despite the blue, 'we were still good mates after all', even though, as he notes, the atmosphere between them was 'pretty ordinary'. Both knew it was not to be the end of the fracas.

Nearing midnight, long after Beazley had left, one of his advisers, Gary O'Neill, ventured into the party, where now only a few revellers remained. Keating was still in his corner, still going strong, and clearly getting ready to come out for the next round. O'Neill saw him, and hesitated the barest instant — circumstances had, after all, placed him in the opposing camp — but he needn't have. Keating saw him, and waved him over. 'G'day mate, how are you going? Good to see you ...' O'Neill soon ventured the obvious question to Keating about how he might be feeling about the future. 'Oh this was only the first attempt,' Keating replied with a twinkle. 'I will be back.'

Meanwhile, for those who had never left, the business of running the country remained. As Keating has said of that time, 'Now Bob had the ball, and he could kick it himself.'[135] His tactic, to simply absent himself from the game, right back to the backbench, was meant to illustrate to the whole team how they would fare without their opening bowler, opening batsman, gear-steward, chief sledger, coach, chief cook and bottle-washer, all rolled into one; for in Keating's eyes at least, that was what he had become for the Government over the previous decade.

Even Keating though could not have guessed how soon after he hit the backbenches with a thud, the front benches would start to splinter. In the words of one of his chief lieutenants, Graham Richardson, his absence quickly showed that 'while some of us couldn't live with him, almost none of us could live without him ...'

CHAPTER SIXTEEN

ROUND TWO

'In the end we are all sacked and it's always awful. It is as
inevitable as death following life. If you are elevated there comes
a day when you are demoted. Even Prime Ministers.'
Alan Clark, British Minister of State for Defence, 1989–92.

Only two weeks after the leadership spill, Cabinet met to
discuss the issue of whether or not to mine Coronation Hill
for uranium. The issue was whether to grant mining rights to
the huge development in Kakadu National Park — and see the
consequent boost to the economy — or alternatively to respect the
environmental concerns and the rights of the local Aboriginal people,
who were concerned that one of their own most sacred spirits, Bula,
would be disturbed by the mining. Hawke was a great believer that
the rights of the Aboriginal people had to be respected, and put that
argument as passionately as he had pushed any argument in Cabinet
during his whole Prime Ministerial career. Fully three-quarters of his
Cabinet Ministers, Beazley among them, were not of the same view.

The Minister for Shipping and Aviation Support, Senator Bob
Collins, was one who advocated strongly the need to get the mining
going and was relying on Hawke to finally give his endorsement of the
project. Collins was aware, as were all the rest of the concerned
Cabinet Ministers, that Hawke's son Stephen, particularly, was putting
pressure on his father *not* to go ahead with the project. They were
confident though that Hawke's resistance could be overcome if the
right kind of pressure was brought to bear.

The whole issue came to a head in a Cabinet meeting in Canberra.
There seemed a gap in the room right where Keating should have

been — right in the middle of the argument — and after a five-and-a-half hour session had seemed to resolve nothing, the mood in the room was one of acrimonious fatigue. All the ministers had spoken, in the majority on the side of mining, but Hawke was yet to end the debate with his own definitive decision. As told most evocatively by Senator Collins in the *Labor in Power* series, Beazley finally exploded when an exhausted Hawke equivocated that perhaps they should put off the final decision for another day. 'And Kim leant across the table,' Collins recounted with great colour, 'and pointed his finger at Hawke and he said: "Listen Bob, make a decision — it's *make a decision!*" Just devastating stuff for Hawke, this coming from *Beazley*. In other words he was saying to him: "Listen you bloody gormless little shit, *do something!*" and everyone knew that. "We're waiting for leadership Bob," that's what he was saying, "*Lead!*".'

Others remember Beazley's words differently. 'It's an overstatement,' Richardson says flatly. 'Collins always gets dramatic, but what Kim said as I recall, and I don't have perfect recall of all these things but he said words to the effect: "Listen Bob, you know I want to mine it, but if you are going to say 'no' I will go with you on it, but as Prime Minister you are going to have to say what you are going to do and the Cabinet will back you".' Beazley's own memory is much the same: 'What I said at the time really to Bob was, "Ok, well look, we've talked this out as far as we can go. This is a point of time when it doesn't really matter what we all as individual Ministers feel, you've heard our views. Basically this is now a matter for you."'[136]

The upshot was the same. Hawke made a decision to stop the development, and though Cabinet accepted it, by Hawke's own estimation the decision could well have ultimately cost him the Prime Ministership.[137] Elsewhere the Hawke Government would soon be making heavy weather of it.

The symbolism of politics has always been as powerful as its reality, and the fact that Hawke had to find *two* people to replace Keating escaped none of Caucus and was a powerful image. For the Federal Labor Parliamentarians, it wasn't just that Brian Howe had become the Deputy Prime Minister and John Kerin the Treasurer. It was, more to the point that the latter, particularly, was clearly struggling in the role — and he would first be damaged by a very poor response to his August 1991 Budget. But the worst was yet to come. (For the record, Beazley in all likelihood could have gained the Deputy Prime Ministership for himself, but had refused the Right's proposal to nominate him, on the grounds that it was more important that the Left's Howe ascend to the position, so as to keep the Left properly engaged in Hawke's continued leadership. 'I wouldn't run because I thought that it would undermine Bob's position if I did that,' Beazley recalls.)

In the meantime, a kind of Cold War between Hawke and Keating had begun. While Hawke attempted to prove that the Government could in fact function perfectly well without Paul Keating, the former Treasurer was out and about beating the drum at irregular intervals, making speeches and public pronouncements about his own ideas on desired policy, to remind all that he was still there, still circling ...

Keating's close confidant, Leo McLeay, remembers of this time, that 'it hurt Keating more than anything that Kim wouldn't come across to him, because I think he had always seen Beazley as his successor'. Keating himself though, remembers it differently. 'Not really no, it didn't hurt me. Kim was always Hawke's closest friend in Cabinet, and I didn't expect him to deny him, so I didn't ask him because I didn't want to put him on the spot.' It was probably as well, because Beazley's answer would have been a firm 'No'. He says of that time now: 'I thought, with Paul being out of the show, it was actually getting better! You see Paul was not, in public, performing all that well. There was no real sort of momentum building up behind him. He did a couple of public speeches and they were pretty average; there was not a rallying to Paul happening. I think the GST thing probably turned it around for him though ...'

On 21 November 1991, the Opposition Leader, Dr John Hewson, released the Liberal's 'Fightback!' package, which had as its central theme a Goods and Services Tax. Oddly enough for a tax that would soon become marginally less popular than rat poison, no-one in the immediate Hawke Government took the fight right to it. It was the sort of thing that Paul Keating would have delighted in tearing to pieces at once, notwithstanding the fact that he had advocated his own form of a GST six years before. But without him the Hawke Government seemed paralysed, unable to poke holes in it, let alone blow it out of the water, as a lot of the Caucus instinctively felt Keating would have done.

In *The End of Certainty*, Paul Kelly used one of Beazley's actions in Parliament as a symbol of how desperate the situation had become: 'Labor acted like a divided, demoralised and beaten unit. Further humiliation came on 26 November when Beazley repeatedly moved the gag motion in Parliament to prevent the Opposition debating its Fightback! package — this from a Government which had made its reputation demolishing coalition policies!'[138] Beazley disagrees with any assessment that the gag motion was a bad idea. 'I don't think I made a tactical error on it at all,' he says, 'though one thing that did happen on the gag motion is that some of Paul's supporters didn't turn up to vote and so we didn't actually have the numbers to get it up. It was the right motion to move, there was no problem with that — we just wanted to keep the Liberals out of our hair while we got on with our own business — but the absence of Paul's people was a bit of an indication that they were deliberately destabilising us in ways that we hadn't thought before.'

The problem remained. Neither Beazley, Hawke, Howe, Kerin nor Willis was able to make a dent in the Liberals' proposals, and the whole thing descended into farce when Brian Howe, as designated point-man, called a press conference to try to tear down the GST. Not only did the Deputy Prime Minister make no impact, not only did there prove to be a mathematical error in his press release, but when the press conference was over and he went to leave the room, he walked through what he thought was a door ... and into what was in fact a cupboard. Only shortly afterwards, one of Keating's key lieutenants, Senator Stephen Loosley, had a long phone conversation with Laurie Oakes, easily the most influential television political correspondent of his day. 'You had better watch tonight's news,' Loosley remembers Oakes saying, 'because I have got something that is interesting.'

'What are you running?'

'You will keep it to yourself?'

'Of course, excepting Richardson, ok?'

'I have got this footage of Howe walking into this closet after his press conference yesterday ...'

'No!'

'And I said,' Loosley recalls, '"You can't run that, not even *you* can get away with that, that is just too indulgent," and he said "Just watch me". And so I rang Richardson and there was stunned silence and he said "You are fucking joking" and I said, "no, and mate, instinct is telling me that if he does that, Hawkey's had the Richard!" The Deputy Prime Minister made to look like a joke. And he said "I agree and if he does that we are back in it".' And Oakes did. The footage ran, as described, and the Hawke Government began to sway in the breeze.

On 5 December the whole edifice started to positively shake. In a famous public mistake that reflected terribly on the Government, if unfairly on the generally competent and extremely likeable John Kerin, the new Treasurer fluffed his lines when defending the September national account figures, which showed that Australia was in its longest-term economic slump for nigh on 60 years. Unfortunately for Kerin, in a complex world where the seas ran economic tides and the forests grew acronyms, he simply forgot what the acronym of one tree in one forest actually stood for — and it was enough to finish him. He forgot that GOS stood for Gross Operating Surplus. As it showed up on national television that night, it went:

Kerin: 'The gross operating, sorry, the gross, aah ... share rose, gross, aah ... what's GOS?'

Reporters: 'Profit share.'

Kerin: 'The gross profit share rose by 4.1 per cent in the quarter ...'

And that was the end of him. At other times it might have been barely commented upon, but when held in silhouette in front of the large blank space that had been left by Keating's departure, it was judged to be a very big deal indeed, and was a big news story. 'I thought it would do a bit of damage to Bob,' Beazley recalls of his thoughts when he saw the gaffe replayed on television that night.

Hawke clearly felt the same for the following day he moved quickly to sack Kerin from the job of Treasurer, and to install Ralph Willis, while he moved Kim Beazley over to take Willis's previous post of Finance Minister. The reason for Hawke putting Beazley in this role was clear: the biggest problem for the Government was making an effective rebuttal to 'Fightback!' Kim was someone who had never let him down before, and Hawke felt sure he could perform in this portfolio as well. 'I have great confidence in Mr Beazley's capacities,' the Prime Minister told the press, 'and he will ... bring a force and a capacity to that which will overall add to the strength of the Government.' Beazley was under no illusions about what was required in the new post. 'I just thought it was "man the battle stations". I didn't have a sense of ownership of the portfolio, I just had a feeling that the pegs had been put in place for a defensive operation; I was part of it and this was a defensive operation both electorally and also within the party.'

A tiny irony at a time when no-one was much in the mood for ironies of any description was that Beazley became the Minister for Finance on the same day that contracts were signed for the sale of

AUSSAT to Optus — which had emerged as the second telephone carrier to compete with the merged Telecom–OTC (which was called Telstra, instead of Beazley's proposed 'Megacom'.) It meant an enormous thudding cheque of 800 million dollars for the Government, but under the circumstances Beazley barely had any time to bank it, let alone focus on the wider issues of being Finance Minister. With the daily headlines continually heaping new agonies on the Hawke Government, and the Keating forces gaining strength by the day, by Wednesday, 11 December, the six key Hawke loyalists decided — at the behest of Michael Duffy — to meet to find a way out of the impasse.

Initially, Beazley, Duffy, Nick Bolkus, Gerry Hand, Robert Ray and Gareth Evans were to meet in Evans's office, but when the press got wind of it, they suddenly switched the meeting to Senator Ray's house at Yarralumla. They sat in Ray's living room, drinking tea and talking. 'It was just one of those occasions,' Gareth Evans says, 'which was heavy with a sense of the significance of the whole thing and heavy with a sense of the tragedy of someone who had been so electorally successful, potentially being about to lose it. Kim was one of those who was absolutely determined to stay loyal to the last, to totally accept what Hawke wanted to do, while also being prepared to tell him the time was up if necessary. All of us had a sense that the numbers were really loaded against him, and we were there as a major rearguard action to see if it was possible to save it for him, but it wasn't seriously believed.' Not even Beazley believed they could save Hawke. 'Most of us had sort of come to the conclusion that Bob should step aside,' he says of the group's general feelings on the night. 'Some had the feeling that perhaps it was time for a change, others had the feeling that he would lose anyway. My view, was that we should try and talk him out. I didn't think he could win and I didn't like to see him going out like a dirty dishrag.'

So the discussion continued, covering all manner of options. The first option as they saw it was for Hawke to resign immediately in favour of Keating. The second and most preferred option was for the Prime Minister to announce his resignation in a month's time — after US President George Bush's visit to Australia had concluded — and a decent span of time had passed to allow him to go gracefully. The third option, that they at least considered, was for Hawke to resign and publicly anoint Beazley as his successor — 'the third man option' as it became known — though none of them, least of all Beazley, recall this as a particularly serious option. The great problem with it was that the Keating torpedo was still hurtling on its way towards them, and would just as likely hit a person trying to take over from Hawke as Hawke himself — meaning greater casualties, and even more destabilisation than the party was currently suffering. 'It was raised, yes,' Beazley acknowledges. 'They talked about "well can we sort of get Bob to stand down and you can run against Paul and that sort of thing," but it was only a view raised in the way in which you toss out options, and that was tossed out.' The final option, the one they were most reluctant to pursue, was for Hawke to stay put and fight Keating tooth and nail.

Through it all, Michael Duffy noted one key difference in the approach taken by Beazley to that taken by everyone else. Beazley was not focused *only* on the fate of Hawke. Duffy comments: 'He was also concerned about what would happen to Keating, and he was torn by all that because he's that sort of person. Some people would say "oh well, bad luck — this is a fight between Hawke and Keating and I'm supporting Hawke and stuff Keating". But he wasn't like that and I think he probably did it as hard as anybody because he had that tremendously strong loyalty to Hawke, but he also had a lot of concern about what would have happened to Keating too. He would have done it harder than most because, of those six people, nobody would have been as close to Paul as he was.' The meeting concluded around 1.00 am, with a very broad agreement. 'It was somewhat confused, what the strategy should be,' Beazley remembers, 'but our final agreed attitude was that we would support Bob and go down with the ship so to speak. We decided that if Bob said "I am absolutely going to stick with it", then we would back him, but that really we wanted to persuade him otherwise.'

Early the following morning, just before 8 o'clock, Beazley called his political adviser and friend Gary O'Neill into his office to advise him of the meeting the previous night. 'We're all very strong supporters of Bob,' O'Neill remembers his boss explaining, 'but we've nevertheless decided that it's in Bob's best interests to declare publicly that he is leaving some time in the near future, so he can go out gracefully with all of the party behind him. So that's what we're going to do this morning. We're going to go around to Bob and tell him that while he continues to enjoy our total support, we think it's time for him to go.' O'Neill found himself somewhere between bemused and bewildered. At first glance, it didn't seem to him like such a crash-hot idea, and he came straight to the point in reply. 'What are you going to do when he tells you to *piss off*?' O'Neill asked evenly. Beazley paused, O'Neill recalls, for all the world as if this possibility had never occurred to him. 'No, no,' he demurred. 'Bob will understand we're not plotting against him, this is a group of Bob's *supporters*, there has to be a way found out of this situation because Paul is not going to give up, it is causing an enormous amount of damage within the party, so we are going to tell him.'

'And I said,' O'Neill remembers, 'well I reckon he will tell you to "piss off". So he just looked at me sideways, got up and walked out of the room and went around there.'

Beazley returned over two hours later. 'Well, what happened?' O'Neill asked his oddly silent boss. 'He told us to piss off,' Beazley replied, a little morosely. Hawke did pretty much just that, and makes no bones, still, about the reasons why. 'I genuinely believed what I was saying, it wasn't a drastic desire to keep in power for power's sake. I loved the job but I also had this genuine concern about what Keating had become and what sort of leader I thought he would be, and I told them that, I said it would be disastrous.' He told them, and he told them. Again and again. Whichever angle they tried, Hawke would always come back to these two central points. Keating would be a bloody disaster, and he wasn't going anyway.

That very afternoon, it was on again. Again the six ministers met in Hawke's office to discuss the developing situation. Again the staff back in the ministers' offices waited for news. Half an hour after Beazley had left, Gary O'Neill got a call to go to the Prime Minister's office immediately. When he arrived, Hawke was there, behind his big mahogany desk as always — 'smoking a big cigar and looking like he'd just won the Melbourne Cup', as O'Neill remembers it — though he did not speak initially. It was Robert Ray who addressed him, obviously as something of an informal spokesman for the six Cabinet Ministers who were fanned out in a semi-circle around the desk.

'Bob's going to stay on,' the Senator said, glancing towards the beaming Prime Minister, 'and we're going to support him. Somebody has got to go and tell the media that, and we have selected ... [*O'Neill, with a slightly sick feeling in his stomach, knew what was coming next, and instinctively glanced at his boss ...*] Kim. We need you to advise the press that he will shortly be making the statement we have prepared.' O'Neill was privately staggered, but he remembers being publicly meek, saying something trite like 'we're all with you Bob', and exiting. He walked back to the office, shaking his head in wonderment. 'I got very much the impression when I walked into that room,' he recalls, 'that they had said to Bob, "Bob you should go", and he said "forget it, I am staying", and they all said "yes, well, ok fine, we will back you".'*

Thirty minutes later, the journalists, summoned by O'Neill's notice that Beazley would be holding a 'doorstop' at the Ministerial Entrance to Parliament House, had turned up in enormous numbers, not quite sure what to expect. Would Kim Jnr emerge bearing the head of Hawke on a platter, complete with warmed anointing oil for Keating? Would he still have the smoking gun? Would he refuse to comment entirely?

From the southern side of the building at that moment, Beazley was heading towards them, at pace, a little like he did as a far younger man. (Nervous rugby players — of whose number Beazley had once been counted — have an old trick when walking towards a battle that is heavily stacked against them from the outset. That is to go more quickly than normal in the tunnel, moving the body speedily towards the confrontation to trick the mind that they really want this thing, and can't wait for it to start.) 'Kim was moving,' Gary O'Neill recalls, 'really lengthening his stride, geeing himself up that this was the right thing to do. He was saying, "that's it", "that's the decision", "we are going with it", "this is the decision that we all support", "we have made the decision", 'we go forward from here", "we are supporting Bob, that is the message to give them".' When he hove into view at the parliamentary entrance, the seething sea of journalists rustled and then split, and Beazley followed correct form by inserting himself directly in the chasm created. Reading from his prepared statement, only occasionally looking up to see the Lodge over the left shoulder of the assembled media and the Brindabella Ranges beyond, he worked his way to the point. 'At the end of those discussions the Prime Minister expressed the view to the senior ministers in attendance that he intended to remain leader of the party until the next election. Senior ministers endorsed that position and

---

* It had not been quite like that, though a particular seminal moment bears repeating. At one point, Michael Duffy had the floor and was explaining to Hawke the reasons he thought he should go. 'Are you saying you won't vote for me?' Hawke had interjected. 'I'm not saying that at all, I'm simply saying you haven't got the numbers to win.' 'But *you* will vote for me?'
'. . . Yes . . .' Duffy had agreed.
It was, in microcosm, the position of them all, and it was enough for Hawke to refuse to budge.

that is the situation.' There would be criticism afterwards that by using the word 'endorsed' instead of 'supported,' Beazley had ratcheted back by about three cogs the level of commitment to Hawke that should have been given, though as O'Neill notes, 'Kim didn't write it, that's what they all worked out, including Hawke'. On the way back to the office, the minister asked the minder the obvious. How did he think it went?

O'Neill replied that all the journalists seemed to be right 'on the back foot', trying to wrap their heads around the news, but that on a purely theatrical level Beazley's performance was good. And he meant it. 'I thought it *was* good, given the fact that only a few minutes before I guess he was mentally attuned to accepting a situation where Bob had sort of said, "well ok I will announce that I am going to retire from politics".'

The press did not think it was good. For months, if not years to come, starting that very night, and certainly in the following morning's press, Beazley was panned for the ludicrousness of being seen to be the leader of a group 'endorsing', the Prime Minister when it was an open secret that just about every man-jack of them actually wanted him to go. With the benefit of hindsight, Beazley now agrees with this opinion. 'It was a bad idea. I think that it certainly was a bad idea if it couldn't be done in secrecy.' His actions were not well received by his Labor Parliamentary colleagues; but because it was their old mate Kim, there was also an air of forgiveness towards him. Just for him, though, not anyone else. 'Only Kim could have survived that,' Stephen Loosley says, 'simply because no-one wanted to tear him to pieces. Basically people are fond of him and know just how much ability he has got as a thinker, as an advocate, and as a policy maker. But people also understand that he has never had great skills in terms of understanding the intricacies and the byzantine shifts in Labor's internal politics — that's never been his strong point.'

Back in Perth, Susie Annus sat in front of the television, watching the ongoing criticism about Kim's role in the proceedings, and wept. 'I knew that it was taking so much out of Kim,' she recalls. 'I could see it. One of the things about being married to anyone in public life is that the personal criticism levelled at them hits you too, and I remember thinking as they were all saying "this was the worst thing he has ever done in his career" that actually, he really didn't have any alternative, as far as I saw it. I know that Kim, being the sort of person that he is, wasn't concerned with whether his political career was getting a plus or a minus in terms of what his action was — I think he thought that Bob deserved his support — he thought that Bob had won four elections, he thought Bob, given that, had the right to go when he chose to go.'

Others, of course, were not of the same opinion, though they were not necessarily for Keating either. That same Thursday night, in fact, the Labor member for Fraser in the ACT, John Langmore, publicly floated on television the suggestion that Mr Kim Beazley Jnr might be a solution to the current impasse, that he could well be an alternative choice who could offer some solutions. Beazley, absorbed as he was with trying to save Hawke, does not even remember it. By this time, the key problem, as identified by Beazley, was that 'Bob had actually got to a point by then where he just wanted to out-sit Paul come what may'. It was no longer a matter of simply who would make the best Prime Minister, or who would most likely succeed at the polls, it was personal. Keating had forewarned Hawke six months before that he was going to 'go him', and it had now become a matter of honour for Hawke — man to man — that he *wasn't going to go*. The already intense lobbying, and swaying of the Hawke Government, intensified further.

Keating did not directly approach Beazley during this time to switch his allegiance. The thing he did do though, was put it about the party that the Minister for Finance was 'weak,' without the courage to switch his allegiance from Hawke. Even in his own camp, however, this view was never accepted. Graham Richardson's summation of the Keating approach is close to the standard. 'The way Keating saw it, anyone who was not supporting Keating was by definition a moron. And in Kim's case, when it is obviously not possible to say that Kim is weak intellectually — even for Keating that's a tough call — you can't say that, therefore "he must know that he should be voting for Keating but he is too weak to do it" so that is the way these things get rationalised.' There would still be, however, one semi-serious attempt to get him to switch. 'Mick Young spoke to him about it,' Richardson concedes, 'but we more or less knew Beazley wasn't going to move . . . because Kim's not like that. Normally speaking, you have strategies to try and wean someone off someone else, and you will send five people in at different times — and I used to plan all that sort of stuff all the time — but I never thought of it with Kim or Robert Ray or Gareth Evans, because you just weren't going to get them like that.'

As one wretched day malingered into the next, there were many times when Beazley wasn't sure if it was late one night or early the following morning, as he would turn over and over in his head why exactly he was doing this. He was doing it, he told himself, because it was the right thing, because you simply could not dump a Prime Minister who had won the previous four elections, and also because he personally just could never bring himself to vote against Bob. Of that, he was sure. Karen Bissaker, who had been with him for nearly seven years at that point, had never seen him so upset. 'This, I would say, was his worst week in politics,' she says. 'I don't think he had any sleep at all — in fact it was mentioned to me that he hadn't been sleeping and he was going home and changing, and coming back to the office and then we were going home and having 2 or 3 hours sleep but I don't think he had any.' The mood of the office, according to Bissaker, was of course extremely tense, but a lot less concerned with the fate of Hawke or Keating and far more concerned with how their own man was faring. 'You could always tell how Kim's feeling, by the way he slumps his shoulders, the way he walks around, and if he is quiet. Kim is not usually quiet, because he is so friendly and outgoing, so if he's quiet it's then that you know he's really worried about something.'

After five more days of endless phone calls and neverending Machiavellian manoeuvres by both sides — it really had become obvious to all that the writing on the wall read a lot like a Hawke eulogy. Beazley could read it as well as anyone and, on the night of Monday, 16 December, decided to go and see the Prime Minister solo, just the two of them. 'It had become clearer and clearer to me,' Beazley recalls, 'that he was going to find it hard to hold the party together and that he'd probably lose — and that is why I personally decided to try to persuade Bob to stand down.'

It was as quiet as ever when Beazley came to the Lodge at around 11 o'clock on that Monday night. During the day at Parliament House there was nearly always a whirl of activity around and about the very geographical centre of national power that was Hawke's bellybutton. But at night, at home, Hawke could be just like any other man. Beazley found the Prime Minister in the Lodge's study, all carpet, leather and finely crafted Australian wood, with books all around — some of them Hawke's, some dating back to Prime Ministers of up to 60 years before. 'Bob,' he finally mustered, when he got to the point and they were both well into Hawke's cigars, 'this is hard for me to say, but I really do think you should give it away, to preserve your reputation, and your legacy. You deserve to go out on top, not voted out by Caucus, and I've got to tell you that I think that the numbers in Caucus are against you.'

'I was enormously upset for him, personally,' Beazley recalls, 'and concerned that we could find some way where he wouldn't have to go through that.' Hawke, once again, refused to accept this approach, and said, as ever, he simply *wasn't* going, because he genuinely believed that he was the one most likely to take Labor to victory in the following election. 'He was absolutely determined,' Beazley says, 'that if he was going to go, the Caucus was going to have to push him, that the Caucus was going to have to make a deliberate judgement that he should go.' Finally, in desperation, Beazley tried another tack. 'Look Bob, I understand even Hazel is of the same view, and that she wants you to go.'

'No, no, that's not true. Hazel is right behind me, and she too wants me to stay.'

'Well, that's not what I heard.' The two stayed arguing on this point, until eventually, some time after midnight, Hazel Hawke herself was summoned by her husband from bed. She came down to the Prime Ministerial study in her dressing-gown to assure Kim that she did indeed want Bob to stay on, that she backed him all the way.*

There seemed nowhere else to go. Having got to this point, where the Prime Minister's wife had been roused from a deep sleep because Beazley had doubted that she could be really supporting her husband — only to find that she actually was — what was left him? Maybe Hazel Hawke's presence had shifted the emotional balance in the room, or maybe Beazley could now finally see that it was hopeless and that Bob was never going to go quietly (and equally knowing that as his closest colleague and friend in Cabinet and Caucus, he was simply never going to vote against him) but they had clearly reached the end of the line. 'I gave up then,' Beazley recalls simply.

He left shortly thereafter, resolved to support Hawke to the end, though thinking one other thing besides as he drove home along the neatly designed streets of Canberra. 'I did feel that perhaps I would not be in politics a great deal longer,' Beazley recollects. 'I had a

---

* For the record, Hazel Hawke notes that her own backing of her husband on this occasion was not based on any political analysis of the situation. 'Basically,' she says, 'I considered it was his decision. I could see that things were getting really very difficult, but I deferred absolutely to Bob. Partly, this was because I had been in Sydney, I had been ill, I'd had a couple of pretty whammy surgeries and the soonest I could go home was in the middle of all that, so I hadn't been across all of the behind-the-scenes stuff. I had been pressed a bit by others who I don't think I ought to mention to persuade Bob to go, but I just deferred to his judgement in the matter. Kim was not one of the people who'd pressed me.'

feeling that really, I had come to the end of the road; that what was happening was unacceptable, unsustainable. We could have a nasty brawl which Bob would lose, and the party would be terminal from that point on. These were two blokes whom I loved greatly, who were just tearing each other to pieces. I didn't think that Paul could win an election, I wasn't sure Bob could any more either, given the amount of damage done to him. And I just had that depressing view of, "so it has all come to this, has it?" and that everything that we had worked for — what we built to get the show back on the road after Gough's devastating defeat — we had all just knocked over the legacy basically. I couldn't abide the way they tore each other to pieces. I was forced to make a choice between them and I did — I made the choice which I think was the appropriate choice, for me personally anyway.' Gary O'Neill's opinion on Beazley's emotions at the time fits well with this: 'He found it very, very distressing that two blokes that he was very close to in the Parliament — both of them, as he saw it, having enormous talent and legitimate claims to the leadership — were going at it hammer and tongs and destroying the Government. They were destroying the party over what he saw as a leadership issue rather than any great issue of policy or direction or whatever, and it was all *just* leadership, that was all. He couldn't understand it.'

Later that same night, long after Beazley had arrived home to the Wasson's house around 3 am, he was doing what he had mostly been doing at that time of the night lately — not sleeping. Instead he was wandering around the living room, a little aimlessly, going into the kitchen, the dining room, then around again. His sister Merrilyn awoke, she says, not to the sound of the ceaseless tramping, but to the *feel* of 'great sorrow in the house'. Putting on her dressing-gown, she went out to him, embraced him, and they sat down on the couch chatting quietly by the dim light of the side-table lamp.

'Kim,' she remembers saying to him, 'this is obviously really tough for you, what are you going to do? What's happening?' Her brother told her. 'Tonight,' he replied, 'I went to see Bob, and said "look it might be in the best interests of the party if you stand down…" but he rejected it, and he's not going to do that.' They chatted some more, with Kim saying in the course of the conversation, rather doggedly, that 'Bob has got qualities that Paul hasn't'. He allowed, after a while, that Keating might ultimately be better for the party, but averred that his instinct told him that Hawke was the more decent individual and that he should stick with him. Eventually Merrilyn worked up to what had been on her own mind. 'I said to him,' she recalls, '"have you ever considered breaking the deadlock yourself and moving through and becoming Prime Minister?"'

'No!' her brother replied, clearly rejecting the proposition outright. 'It would not cure them of their problem, one or the other has to go through.'

Merrilyn countered: 'But neither one would appear capable of winning the next election, whereas you just might!'

Kim Jnr demurred. And would not be moved. 'I think that in his mind,' Merrilyn says, 'and this may relate back to his childhood, he followed preset patterns and the preset pattern in his mind was that Hawke had been Prime Minister and then at some stage down the line it would be ... Keating. He had only analysed in terms of Hawke and Keating. It was not his style to foresee that he had the capacity, the intelligence to break through himself. He was never ambitious ... I think if it can be traced back to anything, it can be traced back to what we were always told as kids about Curtin and Chifley, to the concept that the people who actually achieve most are those who have the least expectations of achieving a high position themselves and the most expectations of accomplishing something, and I think that that is something that he has really taken to heart ...'

In truth though, she was not surprised at his approach. 'He has always had a sense of something beyond himself,' she says, 'that he isn't the be all and the end all, which neither Hawke nor Keating had. As far as they were concerned they were the answer, they were the panacea. He never saw himself like that. He never doubted that he could do the job if it came to him, but he would never go after it.'

Merrilyn was not the only one who continued to explore the famed 'third man' option. At around that same time, a group of backbenchers who were basically Hawke-aligned were meeting among themselves — among whom was Warren Snowdon, the Member for the Northern Territory. As he recollects, 'there was a general feeling from those very strong supporters that we needed to be contemplating what options we might have available. And one of the options which was clearly available was to try and get another candidate entirely'. Snowdon elected himself to approach Beazley to test the waters, to see if he might be a possible starter. When he got to the newly installed Finance Minister's office there were few people around — it was late in the evening and most of the parliamentarians had either gone home or were bunkered down in their offices — so Snowdon walked straight into Beazley's office and closed the door. After a little chitchat, Snowdon asked him: 'What about *you*, Kim? There's obviously an impasse between Hawke and Keating, it's obviously tearing the party apart, it's beholden on all of us to do what we can to end it, so would you ever consider running yourself?' Beazley replied, at some length, as Snowdon recalls. 'He was not absolutely dismissive, and gave a very considered response.' What that considered response boiled down to though, when it was over, was 'no'.

Snowdon left, and reported back to the backbenchers. Kim was standing shoulder to shoulder with Hawke, and was never going to take a step forward himself. Hawke, for his part, says he was never remotely interested in Beazley as the third man. 'If it had just been a choice between Keating and Beazley, then of course I would have pushed for Beazley,' he says, 'but the fact was if I had stood down for Kim, he would not have had the numbers to beat Keating, so what was the point?'

Wednesday, 18 December 1991. Another night, another meeting, another search for a way to break the dreadful deadlock — to either get Bob up and over and settle the issue for the foreseeable future or, failing that, find a way to get him out of the job with his dignity intact, and keep the Labor Party still functioning. The evening had begun at the Lodge, where the Prime Minister had held his usual Christmas dinner for the Caucus — *sans* Paul Keating, who was doing all possible to ensure that this was Hawke's last supper as Prime Minister. Over the wine and canapés, Beazley and his closest cohorts wrestled with the same old problem, reaching the inevitable conclusion. There was no way out. They had to end this thing.

With this in mind Robert Ray and Beazley made their arrangements with the PM and went to meet him in his office at Parliament House at about 10 pm that night to discuss it. Hawke greeted them warmly and they got down to business. The Prime Minister was in an ebullient mood, a curiosity of this time in his life being that the worse things got for him, the better he seemed to perform, and the more up-beat he became. Ray however, had sobering news to impart.[139] Before arriving Senator Ray had jotted down four points on a piece of paper and now moved methodically through them. First, Hawke had to understand, he told him, that by his best estimates, the best the Prime Minister could hope for if there was a Caucus ballot the following day was a 56–51 loss. Second, it was still possible to avoid that with grace if he wished to announce at the opening of the meeting, as previously discussed, that he would retire on 15 January — though that option too would disappear if he did not grab the opportunity immediately. Third, he had to realise that what was in play here was not just Hawke's future fortunes, but also that of his closest supporters. If he crashed and burned in ignominy, a lot of those supporters too might be found in the wreckage — though he and Beazley specifically exempted themselves from consideration in this equation.

Then to the last point ... Ray chose his words carefully, but proceeded resolutely. 'You've got to prepare yourself for the possibility of defeat,' he remembers saying. 'You have to start thinking now, how you are going to react, how you will carry yourself, what will you do, if you come out on the losing side of the vote.' As Stephen Mills, who wrote extensively of this episode in *The Hawke Years*, notes, 'this last piece of advice was directed as much at the man as the politician'.[140] In reply to the latter, Beazley recalls, Hawke came back with a very dignified, very calm affirmation. 'I accept that possibility,' he said.

What he still did not accept was any notion of standing down either immediately or on 15 January. This thing had gone too far for him to haul up any white flag now, and when it came to it, he simply could not leave the field of battle without taking Keating on, head to head. Their whole history had been leading them to this point, it was always going to happen, and it would be a cop-out to shrink from it now. Nothing concrete was resolved on the spot, and the two visitors soon retreated to Ray's office to assess and discuss. In the middle of it, Graham Richardson called. Another curious feature of the Hawke/Keating battle was how often the chief lieutenants of both sides were in touch with each other. Though sworn to do each other's side down, Ray and Richardson often talked to see where the other was up to; if there was a way to pull back from the brink; and to at least ensure that Hawke and Keating didn't entirely destroy the rest of the party in the course of their struggle. They acted, in short, exactly as two 'Seconds' in a duel of olden times might act, ensuring that all the weaponry of their respective champions was in good working order without necessarily bearing ill-will to the other.

The point was that there had to be something still worth commanding when it was all over, whoever the winner might be. In the course of this conversation though, Richardson confirmed that his camp was right then drawing up the necessary petition to permit the special Caucus meeting scheduled for the following day to decide on the leadership. It confirmed for Beazley that he and Ray had been right in what they had been saying earlier in the evening. Hawke had to put a stop to it immediately, and call on the challenge himself, otherwise the Keating camp would simply hunt him down. 'They needed 37 signatures, one-third of the members of Caucus,' Beazley recalls, 'and Robert and I thought "this is a dirty old way to go". This just wrecks relationships across the party; it means people have to sign something like the King Charles execution document which is just an appalling thing to have on the Labor Party's record. We thought our best chance, both to maintain a unified and unsullied party after all this was over, and our best chance to actually win the situation, was to take an aggressive approach. We decided the only way was to have him go in on the front foot, have Bob requisition a Caucus meeting first thing in the morning and declare his position vacant, to be determined later in the day. So we went to see Bob at about 2 am.'

When they got to his office, the Prime Minister had company. Gerry Hand and Nick Bolkus were there giving Hawke more bad news, from the meeting of the Left that they had attended that night. With the NSW Right falling in fairly tightly behind Keating, the last great hope of the Hawke forces was that the Left would enforce a *bloc* vote on its own members by the system of 'show and tell' — with each member of the faction pairing off with another and showing his or her partner that they had in fact voted for Hawke before putting it in the ballot box. If the Left had locked itself into that system behind Hawke it would have been a massive boost to the Prime Minister, but Bolkus and Hand reported that was not to be. The Left had decided that each member was free to vote as he or she saw fit. Ray, in particular, had expected it, but its confirmation was disappointing all the same. One of the last stanchions holding up Hawke had gone.

Beazley and Ray had had enough, and were now most forceful in their assertions. Hawke *had* to stop the whole debilitating process going on in the party. It was Ray who pushed hardest: 'Just do it completely clean,' he advised the Prime Minister in his own understated, but extremely forceful way. 'Announce tomorrow morning that there'll be a special Caucus meeting tomorrow night at 6.30, release everyone from factional obligations, no "show and tell's", no nothing. Just quick and clean.' Beazley agreed: 'Bob, if you pull it on straight away, we might just catch them napping. They're not expecting it right now!' Hawke, after not the slightest prevarication, agreed. 'I think you're right and I have come to that conclusion myself,' Beazley recalls him saying, 'and I think that launching it immediately gives us the best chance.'

Hawke then wrote a letter to the Caucus chairwoman, Carolyn Jakobsen, informing her of his desire for her to call a special Caucus meeting — above and beyond the normal one already scheduled — for the following evening at 6.30 to decide the leadership. He further wrote, with what was surely a wry inner smile:

At that meeting I will tender my resignation as Leader and offer myself for re-election and go to a secret ballot if anyone wishes to challenge me for this position.
(Anyone like Paul Keating for example ...)
Should there be such a challenge I would ask that all members be released from any suggestion of having to show their ballot paper to any other member.

It was done. Hawke read the letter to an agog Caucus the following morning, and it was set. Wherever it led him, Hawke was taking the high road in the struggle.

In the end, it had come to this. Everything had gone as planned, and they were now in the middle of the special Caucus meeting. Hawke, with great dignity, had resigned his position, and then re-nominated himself, and was quickly joined by Paul Keating, who also put his own name forward. The Caucus returning officer, Senator Jim McKiernan, had then distributed 107 ballot papers, personally initialling each one before handing it over. On the way to the voting cubicle Bob Hawke, with an extraordinary kind of glee under the circumstances, had offered to show Paul Keating his ballot paper.[141] Keating, with a smile, offered the same.

Last votes, ladies and gentlemen, please.

Then they waited.

Just after 7 pm, Gary Punch, who had been acting as one of the scrutineers, came back into the Caucus room, from the small adjoining room where the votes had been counted. Less practised political eyes might have missed it, but not Beazley or Ray; for as they noted, Punch only took a bare two steps into the room, then looked directly at Paul Keating and gave an almost imperceptible nod of affirmation. A split second later, Beazley and Ray simultaneously whispered in the Prime Minister's ear that he had lost. Hawke, in Beazley's memory, had almost no reaction whatsoever, 'but was controlled, incredibly controlled'. The Caucus returning officer Senator Jim McKiernan, then made the announcement: The winner was Paul Keating by the margin of 56 votes to 51. And, for better or worse, for richer or poorer, that was it. The long agony of the party was over. And so was Bob.

John Dawkins, who had been such an ardent Keating supporter, and one of the key antagonists in finally bringing Bob Hawke down, was seen to have tears in his eyes. A long queue of the outgoing Prime Minister's fellow parliamentarians spontaneously formed up, wanting to shake Hawke's hand or give him a hug, many of them too, with eyes misty.

Beazley was not of their number, and was not beset by any such overwhelming emotions of pathos. 'I was angry,' he says. 'I just felt that this is the bloke who had run the party through a large number of victories and he had lost and just felt a great sense of sadness and ... anger that he had gone. I understood what Keating was trying to do and what he thought were his just desserts, but I think it was sad that Keating could not contain himself to allow Bob the courtesy of finishing peacefully.' The one thing that lessened the impact for Beazley was that in the final analysis he didn't think that Hawke was going to get up, so was in a sense prepared for it. 'Robert Ray though,' Beazley recounts, 'thought that Hawke might win and Simon Crean thought that he would. I think their concern was that Bob would win by just two or three votes and the party would be a complete shambles, so I think oddly enough Robert Ray was relieved that Bob lost, but it was very close.'

After a sterling televised press conference performance by Hawke which reminded the nation why it had once so much loved him in the first place, the outgoing PM had one more formal thing to do on the day, and that was to deliver his valedictory parliamentary speech. It was a warm occasion, with the Parliament essentially silent to witness the departure of one of its most legendary members. Among many other thank yous and reminiscences, Hawke paid tribute to his protégé. 'I would also like to mention at this time my hard working and popular Leader of the House, Kim Beazley,' he said with obvious feeling towards the end of his speech. 'He has so many favourable characteristics. He is a model of sartorial elegance. Kim and his able Opposition counterpart could do, I am sure, with the rest that Christmas brings. Their task — yours on this side, Kim, and yours on that side, Wal [Fife] — is truly an onerous one. I appreciate, as I think all members do, the nature of the relationship between you. It is an honourable one of integrity and it helps the functioning of this place. I thank you both very much indeed.'

That night, with a scattered handful of Hawke's closest supporters, Beazley remained into the wee hours in the almost ex-Prime Minister's office, talking over old times, reminiscing of what had been and even what might have been ...

It was the night of 19 December 1991, and it was over. 'Bob was in good form,' Beazley recalls, 'After all, he actually had gone out on his own terms in a way — he had not wanted to hand the show over to Paul, and he hadn't. I think he was also very conscious of the pain in one sense that Paul would be feeling. Having got there, Paul didn't actually win an election, what he had done was overthrow a leader and all of a sudden all the faults of the Government, all the problems of the Government, they were all on his shoulders and without a mandate rather than actually having won a poll. I think Bob was very conscious of that ...'

On April 3, 1865, Union General Ulysses S. Grant captured the Confederate capital of Richmond. General Robert E. Lee, his forces decimated and worse by desertions, deaths, casualties and the lack of new recruits, surrendered his Army of Northern Virginia, at Appomattox Court House on April 9, handing his sword to General Grant at the height of the ceremony.

The Civil War was over.

CHAPTER SEVENTEEN

'ALL THE WAY WITH PJK'

'The theory in the Labor Party was that Hawke always wanted to
have an election because he knew it gave him a chance to front
the electorate, while Keating never wanted to have an election
because he knew it gave the electorate a chance to front *him*.'
Kim Beazley, April 1998.

In the days after Keating took over as Prime Minister, and prepared
to form his first ministry, Beazley was not quite sure what would be
his own fate in terms of which portfolio he would be allocated, or
indeed if he was to get one at all. He had, after all, been close to the
last man left standing of the Praetorian Guard when Hawke had finally
fallen, and it would have been but a rough observance of ancient
tradition, if he too had been put to the sword. Beazley maintains that if
Keating *had* decided that there would be no place for him in his
ministry, then he would have 'copped it sweet' as the Australian
vernacular has it. In this he would have been deferring to Kim Snr's
opinion. 'My father's view,' Beazley says, 'was that if a Prime Minister
asks you to go, you go, you don't sit around and go and fight with him
in Caucus or anything like that. I have always thought my father's
logic on that was impeccable and even though the Caucus rules say
something very different, I have always had that view myself.' Not that
he was overly concerned, one way or another. 'I didn't care all that
much' he says flatly. 'I had done, as Defence Minister, most of what I
wanted to do in politics, so I was able to take a view that was fairly

impersonal and I wasn't at all worried about my fate. I had been very happy to that point with my career and if my fate was to go ... so be it. I was rebuilding a family life with Susie which gave me intense happiness, and if I had to leave politics to go home to them and teach at university — well, what the heck?'

There was an even more basic reason for this blasé appproach — Beazley had simply had a gutful of politics. 'On top of divorce and the absence of Mick,' he says, 'the fight between Keating and Hawke just withered my commitment to politics at that time. I was sickened by elements of it. I was sickened by the fact that my friends had fallen out, sickened by the fact that my marriage had fallen apart. I had got an enormous joy out of politics until about the late 1980s, but after all that, it changed. All of that just about destroyed any joy I had in it, and I have never got it back. What I had left is a hard-armoured sense of responsibility about it, which is a different thing.' As it happened, these feelings were quite academic in more ways than one, because Keating had no intention of dumping Beazley. 'It was important to me,' Keating says now, 'that anyone who had been on the Hawke side of the fight never had any hint or feel of demotion or of distance from me, let alone any notion of retribution.'

With that in mind, one of the new Prime Minister's principal lieutenants, Laurie Brereton, told Beazley in an off-hand conversation that he (Beazley) was to become the Minister for Employment, Education and Training — though Peter Baldwin, as Junior Minister, would have control of Higher Education. Some media commentators interpreted this, when it was announced, as a demotion for Beazley, but Keating says he certainly did not see it that way at all. 'It was one of the senior, major portfolios,' he claims, 'and one of the most interesting. One of the things I believe government should invest in, about the *only* thing government should invest in, is human capital. I always thought education was a key issue for us, the empowerment of the kids from working-class families — especially girls who had for so long missed out.'

Having responsibility for Education, as Beazley noted at the time, once again completed a nice bit of symmetry between his own career and that of his father's. He took some satisfaction in holding the reins of the same horse that Kim Snr had so skillfully and famously ridden for the duration of the Whitlam Government. When asked about his son's assumption of his old position, Beazley the Elder predicted great things for him. 'I believe he will very quickly establish a fine rapport with the universities and the structure of education as a whole,' he told Paul Lynch of *The Australian*, 'and I believe his training at Oxford University gave him the ability to apply rigorous intellectual analysis to the job, which will stand him in good stead. I have always been impressed by the ability of his mind over mine.'[142] Before Beazley could immerse himself in the new portfolio, a far more important thing intervened. He was at home in Perth when the blessed event occurred ...

On the night of 17 January, Susie suddenly went into labour at around 10 pm, and after rushing to the hospital, and working their torturous way through the night, their daughter, Rachel Susanna Beazley, was born at 8 o'clock the following morning. 'It was wonderful,' Kim recounts of the moment and of the time afterwards. 'It is such a very earthy event. Generally speaking we are above the animal kingdom, but in birth I think we all get back to the feral and just as I was absolutely overjoyed when Susie became pregnant, I was knocked out when Rachel was born.' While Susie inevitably bore most of the responsibility for feeding, changing and nurturing young Rachel, Kim made one significant contribution to her safety and well-being in that first part of her life, and that was to get something built — against the day his daughter would start toddling. He organised for a genuine, 100 per cent traditional, white picket fence to be erected between the house and the quiet street on which they lived. 'We needed a fence, and I was very happy with that one,' he says with a laugh.

For all the specific joy of Rachel's birth though, a general melancholy would persist at this time of his life. One of his close friends recollects 1992, 'as the year of his great depression. I have never seen him like that before or since, I practically didn't recognise him. He was not himself; when he would come around to visit, he was lost and wondering if he should still be in politics, wondering if it wouldn't be better to pack up and head home to Susie and the family.' Susie remembers her husband being much the same way: 'That was the most difficult year we've ever had. He was not in the land of the living, his mind was not focused, he'd be home but he wasn't focused on anything. It was also largely due to the fact that he was no longer central to government, as he had been up to that point, and he was at sea for at least 12 months before he and Paul re-established their relationship. He was really still recovering from the Hawke/Keating crash, as it took him 12 months to physically recuperate from it.'

If that was a typical personal perspective, a not atypical political perspective comes from Graham Richardson, who noted the change in Beazley's position from being in the Cabinet under Hawke, to the Cabinet under Keating. 'He'd lost not only the leader, but his *hero* in Hawke,' explains Richardson. 'He had an enormous emotional investment in Hawke and that had gone and you then had Keating in charge and because of what had happened, primarily in 1990 — over Telecom — he and Keating weren't close. So he'd gone from being teacher's pet, to being the arsehole up the back. He found that hard.'

Adding to his general unease at this time was that as happy and contented as he was in his relationship with Susie, there remained some 'clearing of the decks' to do from the first marriage. Although they had ended their legal union in the civil courts, in the eyes of the Catholic Church, his marriage to Mary Paltridge still existed before God. Under Catholic doctrine: *'the remarriage of persons divorced from a living, lawful spouse contravenes the plan and law of God as taught by Christ'*. Susie Annus was a staunch Catholic, but had got around that, to some extent, by marrying Kim in an Anglican Church. Mary, however, now wanted to get married again — to Carl Ciccarelli, a fellow teacher she'd been with at Seton College for the previous five years — and wanted to do so both in, and with the full blessing of, the Catholic Church. There was only one way to do this, for also according to Catholic doctrine:

> *Valid marriage requires EFFECTIVE consent ceremonially exchanged. At times consent may have been INEFFECTIVE. The following twenty reasons render consent INEFFECTIVE and are recognized as grounds of marital nullity which if capable of being proven by credible and available testimony make it possible to declare a marriage null.*

The second of these reasons, reads:

> *2. Grave Lack of Discretionary Judgment Concerning Essential Marital Rights and Duties. You or your spouse, seriously impaired by some factor, were unable to appreciate adequately and evaluate critically the rights and duties of marriage and, therefore, chose to marry imprudently.*[143]

It was by virtue of this clause that Beazley and his first wife chose to try to have their marriage annulled. This involved both of them giving separate testimony to an ecclesiastical court set up in Perth, to the effect that their marriage had been flawed from its beginning — entailing a painful six-hour grilling for both of them, with other friends called as witnesses — but in the end it was done. As extraordinary as it might seem that a marriage of 15 years standing that had resulted in two children could be so altered in status, the Catholic Church figuratively wiped the slate clean and ruled that the marriage had never actually existed in the first place. Although the whole thing had been undertaken at Mary's behest, Beazley himself was very happy. 'From my own point of view,' he says, 'I thought it was important that my own marriage gets respected and registered at the Church.'

Beazley was now a man who had married two Catholic women; had raised two Catholic daughters and was now raising another in that faith. He had received official Catholic blessing to dissolve one marriage. It was all enough for Bob Ellis to pen in his book, *Goodbye Jerusalem*, that the Catholic Church had long been Beazley's 'moral destination'.[144] Beazley does not disavow the notion. 'I think I've always been interested in that possibility,' he says frankly. 'There's no question about that. I'm not sure, because I also get a lot of refreshment and renewal out of the Anglican Church so I suspect I will stay there for a bit. But it's not easy if you actually feel like I do, that you've got to give your kids a chance to arrive at a religious conviction. To not be turning up to the Catholic Church with them, and having them assume that this is something that their mother does, but not their father, is not ideal. So it is a definite possibility, yes.'

Notwithstanding the travails of going through a divorce and then annulment, Mary remained close to both her former husband and his new wife, who had of course also been a long-time friend of hers as well. A measure of how tightly the two families remained linked, was that when the time came for Mary to marry Carl Ciccarelli, the person who provided most of the help with her wedding dress was none other than Susie Annus. The situation was equally free and easy for Jessica and Hannah Beazley. Both young women were based at the home of their mother, but went to their father's house whenever he was in town, and sometimes when he was not, for both also became very close to Susie. If such family times gave Kim great joy — he particularly loved having a young baby in the house again — the pall on his political life remained thick.

For the first time in his ministerial career, his performance received plaudits neither from the press nor his colleagues. One fellow parliamentarian of the time comments, 'He just didn't seem totally absorbed in his portfolio and that is the only time in Kim's whole parliamentary career that I could ever say that.' While he considers such assessments as harsh, Beazley acknowledges that 1992 was not his finest year professionally. 'I had sort of finally got to accept that I would never be Defence Minister again, so I lost a lot of ambition and I stopped straining. And I think the Education portfolio was unsatisfactory from one point of view and that was that John Dawkins really had already steered the big changes, and it was for me to carry them out. I enjoyed Education, but I thought that there was less capacity to achieve in that portfolio than just about any I have had.'

The irony of it all was that back in their days on the Student Guild together, Dawkins — who had himself now gone on to the plum post of Treasurer — had always been a fiend for restructuring *everything*, and though Beazley hadn't particularly agreed with John back then, now it was neither here nor there. His clear duty as minister was to implement the reforms that Dawkins had begun and which were already far advanced. A large part of the Dawkins' vision was to bring all of the state-based technical and further education institutions around the country under Federal control, in return for which the states would be guaranteed an additional one billion dollars a year of Federal funding. The Government hoped that with unified control — whereby there was only one system of tertiary institutions, subject frameworks and accreditation across the continent — that they would be better equipped to assist the rising generation of workers to acquire skills that the nation needed.

A large part of that restructuring had been accomplished by the time Beazley took over, and one of his key roles in the first six months of his tenure was to try and finalise it, with the states formally agreeing to cede their control in return for the money. The restructuring process did not proceed smoothly though, with the states squabbling over the terms of their surrender and the funding arrangements, and in the end Keating personally intervened to bring a conclusion. The states finally agreed to share responsibility for the various TAFEs with the Commonwealth. At Keating's behest, and with Beazley's acquiescence, the Australian National Training Authority was set up to administer the new arrangement. The ANTA established a peak body of people, mainly in business, who became the dispensers of pooled Commonwealth and State funds back to the TAFEs. It was charged with 'establishing a national vocational education and training system, forming a close relationship between industry and training institutions and creating increased job training opportunities and job success rates for those undergoing training, including school leavers'.

'What it did,' Beazley says, 'was to set the seal on the idea that there were national training objectives and that they should be coordinated through a national body, much more oriented to the needs of business. It acted as an umbrella to ensure, above all, that the states maintained their effort; that they didn't just drop away when the Federal Government put in more funds.' Through the process of putting this all in place, though, Beazley would not emerge unscathed — and had taken a particular hit when at one point it had outright stalled.

'*Keating Hands Beazley a Lesson in Leadership*' ran one headline in *The Australian* in June 1992. This looked bad enough, but the story that followed was more personally demoralising from Beazley's point of view because it was written by Helen Trinca, Susie's personal friend of 10 years standing. He and Susie had had a glancing acquaintance with Trinca since they had all been at UWA together, but when in the mid-'80s Susie was briefly living in Sydney she had moved into Trinca's Surry Hills' house and the relationship had grown stronger. 'What is crystal clear,' Trinca wrote, 'is that Mr Beazley, seen as an able minister in the past and a potential Prime Minister, is having trouble pulling it off this time around. He has been unable to control the training agenda, failing to impose his own mark and thus stave off interference ... As time passed and the TAFE issue became increasingly bogged down, the comparisons with his predecessor Mr Dawkins became invidious. Surely something would have been worked out by now if [John Dawkins] had been in charge? The Prime Minister leapt into that window of opportunity with a vengeance, and in recent weeks appears to have increasingly sidelined Mr Beazley ...'

Trinca had been loathe to mount such an attack against someone she knew personally, but in the end felt that she had no choice. 'I was disappointed, as a journalist, that he didn't seem to be putting his whole heart and soul into the portfolio,' she remembers. Though Beazley would never utter a word of reproach to Trinca, he did feel hardly done by. 'There is no doubt,' Beazley says, 'that it was more Keating's initiative than mine. Keating really got it to sing and dance. It was to get that essential national coordination of skills training and a bit of a national judgement on what was valuable. Now Keating really ran with that ball, it is not something that an Education Minister on his own could have delivered. It required being elevated out of the realm of education ministers into the sphere of heads of Government.'

Keating essentially agrees, commenting that: 'Kim was Minister, but again these were negotiations essentially with the Premiers which I had as Prime Minister but on a couple of critical occasions including one that Kim had with [the then NSW Premier] John Fahey, where he drove down to John Fahey's house in southern NSW to get over the final hurdle ... we got up a very ambitious growth strategy for vocational education. Now what I did, what Kim did is really not worth debating because we did it as Prime Minister and Minister. We did it together. We got the system up, but we only got it up because Kim wanted to get it up, and if he had taken the view that he didn't want it up, it wouldn't have got up.' If Beazley was not entirely happy with the final form of the ANTA, at least he believed in the imperatives which had driven the reforms.

Ever and always the nationalist, he had been keen to guide his decisions in this new portfolio by what he thought would most strengthen Australia in the international environment with which it was increasingly connected. 'Our education system is one of the things that will ensure our survival in our region and enable us to compete internationally,' he told *The Australian*. 'It is absolutely important to the continuation of Australian society.'[145] Beazley manifested this belief in a determination to organise education so that as many of his fellow Australians who wanted to avail themselves of it, could maximise their skills. 'Our principal competitive advantage in the world,' he says, 'is not possession of minerals, but that we have the highest skilled workforce in this region, and to go well we also had to have a flexible workforce, capable of quickly learning those new skills. We had to have an education system that basically was designed to open up opportunities for everybody to get themselves in on it.'

If that was the philosophical overview of the portfolio, Beazley was also conscious from the beginning of the portfolio's political imperatives, particularly in regard to school-level education. 'There is no portfolio, with the possible exception of Health,' he says, 'that has the political heft of Education to do you damage or to do you good. It has an enormous voting audience and lots of very adept people politically, with lots of authority within the system: Catholic Bishops, parents' and friends' groups, parents' and citizens' groups, university teaching staff, National Union of Students, Vice-Chancellor's Committee, State governments, the lot ...' And, as he remembers it, it wasn't just the noisy groups he tried to quieten. 'In politics, the dog that doesn't bark is almost as important as the dog that does. One dog out there that wasn't barking but which I knew would absolutely chew our backside off if it did — was the old sectarian fight — or the sense that the Government was in some way or another discriminating against either its Catholic schools or its support for the State school system.'

The 'old sectarian fight' was the issue of Government funding for private schools and while there had long been a debate in the Labor Party about whether or not the Federal Government should fund what many saw as education for the elite and the privileged, Beazley had always taken the same stance as had been taken by his father and that was to strongly support continuing funding for Catholic and other private schools. Gerry Gleeson headed up the Catholic Education Office at the time, and Beazley recalls that he always gave him very specific advice. 'I'd always sit Gleeson down before the Bishops were due to come up and see the Prime Minister, and I used to say, "Gerry, *capital funding*, tell the Bishops it's capital funding, not abortion, not any of the great social issues of the day, it's capital funding for their school that they need and that's what they've got to talk to the Prime Minister about".'

In terms of the State school system, in which of course Beazley himself had been educated, the new Education Minister focused on a couple of key issues. 'One of the things I wanted to do,' he recollects, 'was to attempt to change the opportunities available for schoolteachers in particular. Everybody talks about the need for computers in school, the need for literacy and all these sorts of things — but really the heart of the problem in the education system I thought was the morale of the teaching profession and the sense that they are being under-valued.' With that in mind, Beazley set up pilot studies in universities to examine how best to get teachers with 20 years service back into university to do a certificate course associated with their discipline, and thereby give them an opportunity to update their knowledge. He laboured on. In the words of David Phillips, who acted as one of his key consultants throughout, 'Kim was not a great reformer of education, but he understood the importance of the portfolio and was determined to implement pragmatic reforms where he could'.

While Beazley worked in his portfolio, others in the Labor Party were working on him. At that time, there was a growing feeling that Beazley should move from the increasingly marginal seat of Swan, to one that was safer. From the moments of the first gentle prodding on this subject though, Beazley made it clear that he was not interested;

that of course did not mean that the matter rested there. In July 1992, Ric Charlesworth, the Member for Perth, quietly told the former State Secretary of the WALP, Stephen Smith, that he would not stand at the next election, and that Smith should stand because he'd be a shoo-in after all the work he'd done for Labor in the electorate for the previous 17 years. Smith's most cherished dream in fact was to be the Honourable Member for the seat of Perth, but he knew that others in the Labor Party might well have a different agenda. With that in mind, he tracked Beazley down and said to him over the phone: 'Mate, Ric Charlesworth has told me he is going to tap the mat on Perth, and I have got an obvious interest in putting my name forward; but as your situation in Swan is getting tough, and the next election is going to be *very* tough, I'm wondering if you've got any interest in standing for Perth. If you have, I won't stand.'

Beazley, as Smith recalls, took no time at all to reflect on the offer. 'Thanks very much for telling me,' he replied. 'I appreciate your decency, because I know that's the seat that you have always had in mind. That is your local seat, you have paid your dues and done the work there for years, so there is no way I am going to take it from you. I've made my bed in Swan and I have got to stick it out. I can't swim away midstream. Next year's election is going to be very tough, but if I jump now from Swan to Perth, it will be interpreted as me thinking that we have our backs to the wall and are expecting a big defeat ... so I really will stay here.' Smith received many plaudits from others in the Labor Party once it became known that he had offered to stand aside for Beazley, but as he acknowledges, the action wasn't entirely as 100 per cent saintly as it might at first have appeared. 'Decent of me?' he says. 'Well ... I knew I would get a decent response, because that's what Kim's like.'

Meanwhile, Paul Keating was always concentrating on his famous 'big picture', which in 1992 included issues such as formally gearing the nation towards becoming a Republic and at last achieving reconciliation between black and white Australia by setting up a Government body to work out native title claims resulting from the High Court's *Mabo* decision of that year. With regard to short-term political issues though, the best news for the Labor Party was that there were some signs that the switch from Hawke to Keating as Prime Minister was actually working — on the parliamentary floor, if not necessarily in the wider electorate. Whatever else, Keating had clearly established a psychological ascendancy over John Hewson, and had been entirely merciless in attacking him over the Liberals' 'Fightback!' proposals for a Goods and Services Tax. In the middle of September, 1992 at the National Press Club, Keating devoted an entire speech to demolishing both Hewson personally, and the tax that came with him: 'In a very real sense, 'Fightback!' is just another word for Dr Hewson. I think that may be why he takes every criticism of his policies as personal abuse. It is a case of "I am the Word and the Word is *Fightback!* ... " These are not broad objectives but detailed articles of faith, and collectively they will mean the most radical uprooting of the Australian economy and society in our history ... At its heart, "Fightback!" is essentially a switch in the tax base from income to expenditure, and a clumsy, regressive one at that ... The entire economy is put at risk to deliver one political objective — a 30 per cent marginal tax rate for most taxpayers.'

In Parliament, later that same day, Hewson tried to put the psychological heat back on Keating by noting that if the Prime Minister was so confident that 'Fightback!' was a monumental dud, then there was one obvious course open to him. 'Why don't you call an election?' the Liberal leader shouted at him across the chamber. Keating, clearly amused, replied at his brilliant best. 'The answer is, mate, because I want to do you slowly. There has to be a bit of sport in this for all of us. In the psychological battle stakes, we are stripped down and ready to go. I want to see those ashen-faced performances. I want more of them. I want to be encouraged. I want to see you squirm out of this load of rubbish over a number of months. There will be no easy execution for you.'

And there wouldn't be. The fight over GST would be long and arduous, with Beazley not becoming particularly involved — though he was certainly of the view that the GST was the issue the election had to be fought on. As a matter of fact ... 'He was the first Minister of the Keating Government,' the then ALP National Secretary Bob Hogg recalls, 'who said to me, "we can win the next election on the GST issue". He was very very definite about that, and I remember it very clearly. As a matter of fact he was one of the very few people who said we could win that election at all ...' In the months leading up to that election, Beazley was often notable in television broadcasts of such parliamentary battles, sitting on the front benches just to Keating's left, and appearing to be hugely enjoying listening to Keating speak. Which he mostly was ... 'I always enjoyed listening and watching Paul when he was in action like that,' he notes, 'because he was simply a great parliamentary performer. On his day, there was none better.'

If in his own portfolio Beazley continued to find it all hard going, he was at least reminded from time to time that the party still regarded him highly. The headline and subsequent story in *The Australian* on 11 December 1992, should have been enough to lift any politician.

BEAZLEY NEXT LEADER: RICHARDSON
Graham Richardson yesterday nominated the Minister for Education, Mr Beazley, as 'the logical next leader of the Labor Party. He's been there so long even though he's a young man. He's enormously talented and he's very popular. I think it would be hard for us to go past him ... '

The tone of the story suggested that Richardson would not be at all surprised if the Labor Party were obliged to look for a new leader in the very near future, and there was a good reason for that presentiment. Despite the substantial ground that Keating had made in closing the gap, most informed predictions for the election, which was due to be held in the next few months, came down heavily on the side of the Opposition Leader, John Hewson, becoming the Prime Minister. Whatever Keating's strengths as a Prime Minister in redrawing the 'big picture', there was a growing feeling in an increasingly restive electorate that he was all but ignoring the little pictures that people saw when they looked out the windows of their own day-to-day lives, and as Keating himself notes, 'very few gave me any chance of winning at that stage'. Still, only a year since Keating had become Prime Minister, the polls admittedly showed Dr John Hewson's Liberals only one per cent ahead of Labor; but regardless of that slim margin the common reckoning was that Labor support was soft, and in fact Labor's own privately commissioned polling at that time showed it to be very soft indeed.

Finally, in early February 1993, Keating called the election — hoping this time for 'the easy execution' of Hewson — and it was on again. In Swan, Beazley knew he was up against it from the beginning, as perhaps did many of his Labor colleagues. One indication of their concern came in early March, just a week before the election, when the Minister for Education and Training was working quietly in his Perth office. Gary O'Neill was working there too, and late in the afternoon he took a phone call from Gareth Evans's senior adviser —

who informed him that the Foreign Minister was in town, and as his plane had been delayed and he had a little time on his hands, he wanted to come out and do some doorknocking with Kim. O'Neill tried to put them off. 'Look, we are very, very busy,' he recalls replying, only to be told that Gareth was already on his way. Some ministers demand of their staff a formal bowing and scraping to precede each new conversation. Beazley was not of their number, and shortly thereafter O'Neill was happy to speak his mind: '*Jesus!* Gareth is on his way here to doorknock with you.'

'No, no, I can't, I am too busy,' Beazley replied calmly, barely looking up from his reading. When advised that O'Neill had already tried that, and that Gareth was unstoppable, the two gave in. They decided that Beazley would take him just down the road to the evenly poised suburb of Kensington, where the vision of the Foreign Minister on their doorstep just might winkle out a few extra crucial votes from the constituents. Evans duly arrived, and the two Cabinet Ministers went off together, as O'Neill waited back at the office for the next hour. Presently though, he heard the sounds of the Member for Swan returning. 'So Kim waves Gareth goodbye,' O'Neill recounts, 'and he comes back into the office and he is absolutely white, white as a sheet. And I said, "Jesus, what's the matter with you"!?!'

'You wouldn't believe it,' Beazley replied. 'We walked to the first house, knocked on the door, this woman opened it, but before I could get anything out Gareth said to her, "Now give me three good reasons why you wouldn't vote for Kim Beazley"!'

It was not the Perth man's idea of doorknocking ...

It was Saturday, 13 March 1993, the night of the Federal election. In St Joachim's Primary School in Victoria Park, sitting not too comfortably on the edge between political oblivion and continued existence as a senior Federal Minister, Beazley turned a worried eye once again to the big whiteboard that had been set up, tracking his progress. The television was on in the corner, with workers crowded around monitoring how the rest of the country was going — amazingly well for Labor, was the answer, despite all the dire predictions beforehand. By only ten to eight, Perth time, it was already obvious that the Liberals were going down again, so obvious in fact, that John Howard was asked whether he might consider returning to the post of Opposition Leader, to replace the defeated John Hewson. 'Oh come on,' Howard had replied glibly, while the noise in the

Beazley camp lessened only marginally. 'That sort of thing has run its race.' So it went. The television kept blaring, people made coffee, worked the phones, exchanged news about other candidates' progress. Suddenly though, there really was an abrupt cessation to the hubbub, as on the other side of the country at the Bankstown Civic Centre, at 11.23 pm EST, a clearly delighted Paul Keating stepped to the podium to claim victory. 'This is the sweetest victory of all' the newly re-anointed Prime Minister said, before continuing in his famous fashion, 'This is a victory for the true believers, the people who in difficult times have kept the faith.'

It certainly was a sweet victory for Paul Keating, but the question remained for Beazley — were there enough of these 'true believers' in the electorate of Swan to get him over the line? For a long time it seemed that there were not as he began to fall back in the count — and the ABC presenter Andrew Olle always seemed grim when talking about the 'difficult situation' faced by the Education Minister, Kim Beazley. Hannah Beazley, then 14 years old, barely recognised her father, as he sat, slumped back in his chair watching further results come in. 'Usually,' she says, 'in every kind of situation, Dad wants to break the ice, and is always shaking everyone's hand, having conversations, laughing, joking and all that sort of stuff. But that night he was very quiet and he wasn't really able to speak. It was the first time I'd seen him that stressed out.' By 11 pm, Perth time, as the numbers continued to go badly for their father, both Hannah and 16 year old Jessica began to weep, prompting the candidate to embrace them, as their mother Mary came to them — as always, she had been intimately involved in helping with the campaign, a new husband notwithstanding* — to lead them outside and have a gentle talk. Hannah did as asked, but knew what her real duty was, and was soon back inside attending to it. 'I went to sit in front of the whiteboard and started to will the numbers to come back to Dad. That was what I had always done when I was growing up, and that was what I did then, by really *really* concentrating.' It worked, more or less. As she watched, slowly, slowly, softly, softly, the numbers started to inch closer together, to the point where it at least became possible that her father was going to hold on, although it would take a few more days of twisting in the wind before he found out definitively whether his

---

* Kim's former mother-in-law, Lady Molly Paltridge, would also stay involved, despite the changed marital circumstances, and to this day calls Susie Annus before elections, enquiring what she can do to help, 'even if it's only licking stamps'.

political future lived or died. Something sustaining him in the face of his possible demise was a brief conversation he'd had with Gareth Evans just before the election where, as Beazley recalls, 'Gareth sort of said, "Don't worry, if you miss out we'll make you Ambassador to the US because it's coming up". It was great — I didn't tell Susie or anyone else . . .' No he did *not* tell Susie, and she was not well pleased when he finally did tell her a few days after it was confirmed that he had secured his sixth straight win in the electorate, albeit this time by a mere 290 votes. 'And I know why he didn't tell me,' she says laughingly, 'because he was relying on my vote to get him there, but had he told me, I wouldn't have voted for him and I would have personally knocked on at least 40 houses and said "do not vote for this man" and he knew it!' In the end, with the narrowness of the victory, the Education Minister had every reason to give serious thanks to his great friend, Bob Hawke. In the closing weeks of the campaign the former Prime Minister had journeyed to Swan independently to do some last-minute campaigning for him — which included shooting a television advertisement — and Beazley believed it was that old Hawke magic and his enduring charismatic support that had at last got him up and over the top to victory.

Immediately after that election, things started to get better for Beazley professionally. 'Having had a political NDE, sort of got me going again,' he says. An NDE, he defines as a 'Near Death Experience', and if that heightened the sense of pleasure he got after every election win, this time there was an added fillip. Prime Minister Keating had decided to grant to him the Higher Education role previously held by Peter Baldwin, a move which pleased Beazley no end. 'Getting hold of the universities was pure joy. Higher Education is the central point of the national education portfolio, and I just felt better when I was actually in control of that essential part of it.' Beazley's primary role after regaining Higher Education, as he saw it, was to do 'a certain amount of settling down, and smoothing over the areas where John Dawkins had sort of ruffled people's feathers'. (The Dawkins reforms had seen a massive increase in the number of universities across Australia, as he joined together what had previously been Colleges of Advanced Education and made them into universities. It had been a massive restructuring, that had involved a lot of dislocation.)

In the time following the election and the ALP's extraordinary win, Beazley's energy went towards a programme called 'Job Compact' —

which would later be incorporated into the Keating Government's White Paper on employment entitled 'Working Nation'. The focus of Job Compact was to provide employment and training programmes for the long-term unemployed, on the proviso that they committed themselves to accepting whatever jobs were found for them, or risk losing their benefits. Under the scheme as it panned out, some 233 000 Australians who had been unemployed for 18 months, would be guaranteed either a job or training for a job. Beazley explains: 'Immediately after the '93 election, we realised that we didn't just have an employment problem, because unemployment was actually starting to come down, but we had a problem that long-term unemployment was rising and we risked actually getting stuck with a large number of people permanently out of work, as they lost contact with the workforce. We judged that the best way out of that situation was to make sure that those who found themselves in that situation would be strongly encouraged to get the skills they needed. Job Compact was about reciprocal obligation, it was the idea that if you didn't actually take up the varied training and job opportunities that were presented, then you lost your unemployment benefits. Basically, it was an incentive, because we didn't sort of talk about it as 'work for the dole' or anything like that, we just talked about it as reciprocal obligation.'

A funny thing happened on Friday, 17 December 1993. Beazley was in his office preparing as Leader of the House for Parliament's business of the day, when John Dawkins popped by. 'By the way, Kim,' he said in a very matter-of-fact manner, 'I'll be needing a few minutes today.'

'Eh? What for?' asked Beazley, surprised at the late notice of a requirement to speak.

'Because I'm going to resign,' replied Dawkins.

And that was it. Beazley knew an hour before the rest of the world, and Paul Keating himself had known only an hour before that. The accusation would be made — and it was made strongly — that by resigning when he did, mid-term, Dawkins was having one last shot at Beazley, denying him the safe seat he had always coveted, the family fiefdom that Kim had lost to him almost two decades previously. At the very least, one Caucus school of thought contended, Dawkins should have told Beazley a lot earlier of his intention to resign Fremantle, just as he had told him nearly two decades earlier that he was running for it. Dawkins himself does not see it like that. 'It wasn't going to be possible for Kim to have Fremantle anyway unless I went the full term, because he already had a seat and there was no way in which he was going to resign from Swan to contest a by-election in Fremantle. My objective became "Who can I get in?" and though I have since had reservations about it, I wanted to get Carmen [Lawrence] in, and so the purpose of my resignation was certainly to create a by-election in which Carmen could come in ...' And to keep Beazley out of it? 'No,' insists Dawkins flatly. People like Peter Walsh, one of Dawkins closest political friends over the years, would have none of such explanations. 'Beazley's and Dawkins' political rivalry goes back a long way,' he says, 'but I was surprised that it was so strong in Dawkins that one of the reasons that he pulled the pin when he did, I believe, was to ensure that young Kim did not succeed in the seat of Fremantle.' Beazley, himself, claims not to agree with Walsh's analysis. 'I know they say that and I know Dawkins from time to time has said bitter things about me, but I've always liked John and we've always got on reasonably well and I think John had just decided he wanted out of politics. Now there's no way he could have gone out of politics in the middle of a Parliament and actually given the seat to me, he couldn't do that, as it would have meant *two* by-elections.

'I think John genuinely did not feel the Government and Keating had sufficiently backed him up with his tough budget, six months earlier — a tough budget that was necessary — and so he decided to go. I think he felt that his contribution had concluded, he'd been a big player for a long time, his seat was not going to be lost in a by-election, as far as he was concerned he was off.' He was that, and in the middle of March in 1994, Carmen Lawrence won the seat of Fremantle with an entirely unexpected 1.8 per cent swing *to* Labor.

In terms of those lining up to take over the leadership of the Labor Party whensoever Paul Keating chose to let it go, Carmen Lawrence was clearly a contender from the moment that she arrived in the Federal political arena, and was shortly thereafter made Health Minister. This was also a time when Bronwyn Bishop of the Liberal Party was enjoying her own five minutes of political sunshine, and Labor was looking for someone to counter both her and the exceptionally popular leader of the Australian Democrats, Cheryl Kernot. Added to that though, was Dr Lawrence's obvious intelligence, political experience, her toughness and the fact that she was considered to have done a good job in her time as Premier of Western Australia under difficult circumstances, (from February 1990 to February 1993) despite having lost the previous State election.

One of the very few to emerge unscathed from the smoking ruins of Brian Burke's 'WA Inc' Government — where she had been a Cabinet Minister in its last days — the only possible black mark against her name was the Penny Easton Affair, which dated back to November 1992, when as Premier she was just about to go to the polls. Easton was a Perth lawyer who had driven into the hills outside Perth and, in much the same manner as Kim's childhood friend Col Wilson had almost ten years before, had gassed herself in her car, only four days after a petition had been tabled in Parliament by a Labor backbencher. The petition had maintained (quite falsely as it turned out) that Easton had perjured herself in a previous Family Court matter, and that she had also received confidential documents from Liberal parliamentarian, and then Opposition Leader, Richard Court.

While suicide is of course death by one's own hand, in the case of Penny Easton there was no shortage of people pointing the finger in another direction entirely as to the real cause of her death. The blame, it was said, belonged to Dr Lawrence. The accusation was that the Labor leader had told a bare-faced lie in Parliament the day after Easton's death, when she flatly denied having any detailed knowledge of the contents of the petition. In fact, the allegations continued, Premier Lawrence had actually *orchestrated* its tabling to divert attention from a hugely embarrassing story breaking that very day concerning 5000 dollars worth of travel expenses which she had claimed falsely. It was a highly complicated affair ...

At the time she won Fremantle, however, Dr Lawrence's consistent denials had been widely accepted — despite Federal Liberal Wilson 'Ironbar' Tuckey saying in Federal Parliament during the by-election campaign that she had 'blood on her hands'.[146] Few were listening, and many thought 'The Fremantle Doctor' was in fact just what the Federal Labor Party needed.

For Beazley, though, Lawrence was neither here nor there. The departure of John Dawkins had prompted Prime Minister Keating to reshuffle his Ministry, and the man who ended up filling Dawkins role as Treasurer was Ralph Willis, while Beazley moved across to take Willis's post as Finance Minister. Happy? He was delighted. He had after all, specifically asked for it. 'Kim came to me,' Paul Keating recollects, 'and said "look, I will never be Prime Minister of this country until I climb the economic mountain". He said Treasury was spoken for and that's going well with Ralph Willis, so he said that the other next best job in the broad area of the economy and fiscal policy was Finance ... I said I'd give it to him with pleasure.' Beazley's memory of their conversation is much the same, but thinks that talk of him climbing the economic mountain specifically to get experience for the possible future job of being Prime Minister were Keating's terms rather than his own. 'There is absolutely no doubt I wanted it though,' he states, 'and Paul was a little bit sceptical about whether or not I should take it. I took the view that I needed Finance for two things. Firstly, it advanced your understanding of how a government manages an economy, but more important than that, it was an across the board understanding of all areas of government. If ever I was going to get into a position where I ultimately led the Labor Party, to have that background was invaluable.' When he physically set foot back in the Finance Department, the first words of the first official he saw were a deadpan: 'Welcome back Minister,' prompting Beazley to laugh outright.

The Finance official was referring to the flicker of a fortnight Beazley had spent in the post back in 1991, during the dying days of Bob Hawke's Prime Ministership — and of course now there was no comparison. Then it had all been tumult and hurly-burly. Now it was all quiet on the Western Front. In Finance, the phones did not ring, making for Beazley a very nice change. 'Education had been an intense portfolio,' he explains, 'an enormous people portfolio with a huge array of activity going on all the time, as was Communications, as was Defence. But Finance was just lovely.'

Lovely and quiet.

'It was firstly because Finance is not an operational portfolio so there's nobody that needs day-to-day decisions, and secondly your colleagues do not want to ring you because they're frightened of you.' And for good reason. 'A Minister of Finance is a legally authorised pickpocket,' Paul Ramadier, himself a Minister of Finance in the Fourth Republic of France, once said. So too with Beazley. The role of the Finance Ministry was essentially one of gathering the monies for the Government and then controlling its spending, while the Treasury overlooked the economy generally and determined which levers to pull and buttons to press to make it tick over properly. Yet, as opposed to the way things had been in the good old days at Defence, matters of high finance were not something to which Beazley's mind naturally wandered when he was stopped at traffic lights. His former economics teacher back at Hollywood High, Brian Jenkin, remembers that 'he was a bright enough kid but he wasn't as I recall completely dedicated to it, he sort of coasted ...' and economics had never subsequently been on his list of academic interests. Politically, the only Parliamentary Committee that had ever bored him rigid was the Joint Committee of Public Accounts,* which he had been on briefly during his first term in Parliament. 'I pleaded with him to stay with it,' Michael Duffy remembers, 'because I always had a feeling he was going to be someone of real substance in the Government and it was important to understand that stuff, but he wouldn't cop it'. Beazley had quickly dropped out of it.

Perhaps more significantly, money and its acquisition had never been high on his list of personal priorities. Even at that advanced stage of his successful ministerial career, the net worth of the house he and Susie had moved into in South Perth would have returned plenty of change from half a million dollars, and even then the two had a hefty mortgage on it. Apart from that — and an all but moribund television production company that Susie still had a nominal share of — the financial affairs statement that all Members of Parliament have to fill out at the beginning of every term, was a singularly easy one for Beazley to execute. In it's entirety, it read:

Savings Account — C'wealth Bank.
Savings Account — National Bank
Cheque Account — NAB.

And that was it. No shareholdings, no directorships, no trust funds, no bonds, no equities, no part-shares of businesses, no nuttin'. An unnamed associate, once quoted in an article by Michelle Grattan, had it about right: 'He's not one of your chardonnay and nouvelle cuisine Labor Party people. He's more your hamburger-and-milk-shake-for-lunch man.'[147] And nor, in contrast with some of his colleagues, did Beazley even hang around with very rich people. 'By the time Hawke and Keating had finished their time in politics,' one of their long-time colleagues notes, 'all their mates were very rich people. But in Kim's case that's not true. I know Kim pretty well ... and you just never see him running around with really rich guys, it is not his go.' True enough. Outside of politics his close friends — such people as the Frenchs, Gallops, Tannocks, Pierces and Pascoes — were financially comfortable, certainly, but not one of them would bother looking sideways with intent when passing a Porsche showroom.

---

* This committee is the parliamentary body which examines issues arising from the Auditor-General's report, and is described by Michael Duffy as 'dealing with the nitty-gritty of the economic workings of government'.

It was not that Beazley was — as Labor stalwart King O'Malley once said of Alfred Deakin — 'as destitute of financial knowledge as a frog was of feathers,'[148] but just that matters of finance had never been his passion. In general on matters of economic policy, Beazley considered himself to be neither particularly 'wet' nor 'dry'. As he later described it to ABC interviewer Terry Lane, what he did was 'stand on the seashore and paddle'. In essence, his stance was that while through his ministerial career he had all but totally supported the moves of the 'dry' economic rationalists to reduce tariffs, float the dollar, let in the foreign banks and privatise much of that which had previously been government-owned, he reserved the right to dip his oar in with the 'wets' here and there. He had publicly opposed, for example, the mooted sale of Telstra, saying that it sustained, 'while in public ownership, an improving Australian electronics industry. Take it out of public ownership and it won't. So therefore I want it kept in public ownership.' He also noted that his championing of Australia having 'a decent domestic Australian industry to support a war fighting capability'.[149] was not the decision of a strict economic rationalist, as it had frequently been more expensive to do it domestically than buy it internationally. Basically for him, the star he steered by in making his finance decisions was whether or not he perceived them in making the country as a whole stronger, rather than any ideological commitment to economic rationalism for its own sake. All of that aside, the basics of the Finance portfolio were very basic indeed. First and foremost was the general principle enunciated by Mr Wilkins Micawber in the novel *David Copperfield*:

> *Annual income twenty pounds, annual expenditure nineteen nineteen six, result happiness, said Mr Micawber. Annual income twenty pounds, annual expenditure twenty pounds ought and six, result misery.*

While it is a timeless aphorism for individual households across many cultures, the same cannot *necessarily* be said of the Government's finances. In government life, shortfalls in finances could always be covered by expanding the deficit, which not only delayed having to pay the piper, but gave the Government money to buy the conditions in which elections could be won, resulting in: great happiness, *now*. In the political cycle, Beazley was taking over the post of Finance Minister at a time when the Government would be under a lot of pressure to buy their way out of trouble. In coming times, Beazley would be accused of expanding the deficit up to eight billion dollars in order to do precisely that, but that remained well in the future ...

Going into the job, Beazley as always had a clear idea of how the job should be executed: 'I thought the role of the Finance Minister really is to be Devil's Advocate. It's like the Treasurer sort of chairs and adjudicates and the Finance Minister prosecutes. So it's the job of the Finance Minister basically to present the arguments against things put forward by the other ministers.' The opportunity to show the kind of Finance Minister he intended to be arose in the first Cabinet meeting he attended. Halfway through it, Simon Crean, who had replaced Beazley in the post of Education Minister, put forward his own list of requirements for money to get some of the Education Department's specific initiatives going. New to the post, Crean had, in fact, had very little input into the detail of the requests. As Beazley points out, 'the only thing that had changed on the submission was the name of the submitting minister', and so Crean had every reason to be confident that they would be given the nod anyway. They weren't. Many in the Cabinet, not least Crean, were dumbfounded to see Beazley take his metaphorical razor out, and start vigorously slashing away, saying that Crean was being too extravagant, if not outright wasteful, and that he should rethink some of these things before bringing them before him again. Graham Richardson, staggered, broke in: 'Jesus, Kim, this is a bit rich. These are *your* proposals.'

'Yes, and that's why I know where the bodies are buried,' Beazley replied.

'I'm a realist,' Crean recollects of the episode. 'I know that when people change their functions they've got to fulfil those functions but it *was* a robust debate.'

As well as saving money by slashing and burning ministers' requests, the other side of the Finance portfolio was raising money by privatising that which had previously been publicly held. Beazley took over the portfolio at a time when the ministry was engaged in executing the biggest privatisation programme in Australia's history. The Labor Government, now in office for just on 10 years, continued to work through the contentious issue of privatisation, and with Paul Keating continuing to look at the 'big picture', it was the new Finance Minister's role to get remaining Labor hold-outs to fall in behind the line enunciated by Beazley's predecessor in the post — Peter Walsh.* 'I should state my position at the outset,' Walsh had told an Australian Financial Review Seminar in 1986. 'I have no ideological preference for public or private ownership. In my view, what is important is not whether a business is public or private, but whether it delivers the goods and services required by the public efficiently, i.e., at lower cost.'

Now the time for selling a lot of those former entities had come, and a lot of Beazley's focus during his time in the portfolio was devoted to selling such entities as Qantas, the Commonwealth Serum Laboratories, the Sydney Gas Pipeline, and the last half of the Commonwealth Bank. It was something of an irony that Beazley was now in charge of selling Qantas, because as Minister for Aviation he had sworn that Labor would *never* do any such thing, and then as Minister for Transport and Communications he had begun the process of doing just that. He was not troubled by this, however, as clearly the times had changed, as signified by the decision of the Special Conference of the Labor Party back in September of 1990. As to the privatisation of the Sydney Gas Pipeline — which joined the gasfields of South Australia to Sydney — that was to prove to be a particularly demanding exercise, as it had been established in the time of the Whitlam Government by Minister for Minerals and Energy, Rex Connor, and as Beazley comments, 'we soon found he set it up with all sorts of tricks and traps, so that it could never be privatised by a Tory Government. Basically, he'd put so many different lines of approval in it — of users, of State, of the Commonwealth — that it could never be signed off without them, and we had to line up about a dozen different interests to get the damn thing through. It had all the intricacy of defusing a bomb, because one wrong move, one wrong flick and the whole damn thing would have blown up.'

---

* Beazley always found he had a lot of living up to do in the Department of Finance when it came to the reputation of Walsh. Shortly after arriving, and often thereafter, he was told by varied Finance officials that Walsh was the sort of bloke who would come over and have a couple of beers with the heads of the department, and the next day, the secretary of the department would find a cheque in the mail, to the very precise amount that Walsh had worked out the beer had cost. He was their sort of bloke, and that was the attitude they loved. 'I said to one of the senior officials once,' Beazley recalls, 'just how much did Finance like Peter Walsh? And he said, "Well put it this way, half the department would have died for him, while the other half of the department were not quite so devoted, they would merely have killed for him".'

If such ventures kept Beazley as busy as usual, so too were others starting to get busy on him. In the west, Mark Nolan, the new WALP State Secretary, Stephen Smith and Beazley's long-time campaign manager, John Cowdell, all acted in concert to persuade Beazley that the time had come for him to shift from Swan to the safer seat of Brand. 'Mate, we have got by on the skin of our teeth in the last two elections,' Cowdell remembers going at him with some exasperation. 'It isn't going to happen again, and that is simply because of the demographics. It's nothing to do with you, it's just the way it is.'

And it was true. The evidence was there on the horizon, visible from the top of any high rise in the Perth CBD. As you looked to the south of the city where the electorate of Swan lay, you could see how the waves of development had kept rolling along the South Perth foreshore line, knocking over the older and poorer houses, and leaving in their wake newer, richer establishments. And there was no way around it; the people in them, simply, were all too often Liberal voters. There was *nothing* Kim could do about it, they told him. Mark Nolan showed him, he recalls, 'every bit of research I had on the subject, and it all showed that it was going to be near-impossible to hold'. If Kim was dinkum about continuing in Parliament, they insisted he would simply have to move to the seat of Brand, where Wendy Fatin was about to retire. The seat continues for about 100 kilometres of Western Australia's coastline south of Perth, 50 kilometres inland, and to the north lapped against the seat of Fremantle. Its urban bases included the towns of Mandurah and Rockingham, as well as the heavy industrial centre of Kwinana and the mining town of Collie. 'And Kim, it includes the HMAS Stirling Naval Base! You'll have a fair chunk of the Defence Forces in your own electorate, if you just choose to take it!' Beazley's initial response to them all was the same: 'No. I live here, I have a personal following here, I am the best person to try and hold it and I will stay there. I'm not moving.' They kept at him: 'Yes, you are the best person to hold the seat, the problem is the demographics of the seat and the changing nature of the seat, in the end no Labor person is going to be able to hold it.'

At last, in late October 1994, Beazley was turned around by the irrefutable logic of what they were saying. 'It was more by a process of attrition than anything,' Cowdell remembers. Beazley, too, has a clear recollection of his feelings at the time. 'I looked,' he says, 'at what was happening in the development of Swan. I realised they were right: this seat couldn't be held in the long term. And I asked myself "Am I going to be a leadership alternative?" If I'm going to be a leadership alternative then I have to shift seats. So I shifted seats. It's the only cold-eyed political decision I've ever taken.' The announcement of Beazley's intention to move to Brand, on Sunday, 20 November 1994, seemed to buoy him further. While Brand was certainly not a guarantee that he would survive the next election, at the very least it made it far more likely; he had gone from Labor's third most marginal seat in the 1993 election to the twenty second most marginal, and his energy was renewed for the task at hand. The media, and certain sections of the Labor Party, were less keen, seeing it as perhaps a sensible move for Beazley, but an insensitive abandonment of Swan. 'I am really disappointed that Kim has gone,' the WA State ALP politician, Dr Judyth Watson, was quoted as saying, 'because half of my seat falls in Swan and I just feel that he has turned his back on us here'.[150] Her colleague, Cheryl Davenport, felt similarly, and told the papers so: 'We feel quite angry about the move. We recognise Kim is an outstanding candidate, but I think had he been able to spend time on the ground in Swan, it would not have been as hard to hold it.'[151]

Such rumbling faded quickly though, and as a result of his decision to go to Brand, a change came over him. 'I had a renewed interest in politics,' he says, 'and since then I've got my act together. There was a time, after Bob went, when it was "these fellows put us out of politics, well I'm out of politics, that's life". But I began to come back more heavily to: "ok I am a long-term politician, I've got a long-term career". Really my decision to run for Brand changed me around. It was: "I've got to get myself a new seat and survive and I've got to keep going."'

The decision taken, his own raised spirits occurred at a time when the party around him was starting to feel decidedly poorly. Things were not going well. The most obvious sign of this came on March 25 of 1995, when a by-election was held in Canberra to replace the former Minister for Sport, and close Keating supporter, Ros Kelly, who had decided to retire. The result was disastrous. Labor got thumped by a massive 16.4 per cent — the worst by-election result against a government in half a century. To many independent observers, it really started to seem like something close to a foregone conclusion that the winner of the next election would be John Winston Howard, who 'like Lazarus with a triple-bypass' had replaced the unfortunate Alexander Downer earlier that same year as Leader of the Opposition. Unless, of course, something was done. In the Labor world, the natives, as they say, became restless ...

John Kerin once said of Graham Richardson that one of his principal values to the Labor Party was that he was a warrior who, if he thought it was to the party's advantage, 'would say things and do things that no-one else would contemplate, regardless of friendship and previous loyalties'.[152] Now, in the autumn of 1995, Richardson was of a mind to do just that. Never mind that he had been one of the principal antagonists of Hawke, that he had spilt endless party blood to install Keating in the top post. Never mind even that he had now left Parliament to go and work for Kerry Packer. As Richardson sensed it, there was a growing feeling in the party that Keating's time had not only come, but was now *gone*, that he was out of touch with the electorate, that the Labor Party would get smashed in the next election unless they did something radical. And with all that in mind, Richardson wanted to get rid of Keating, and set about getting his former parliamentary colleagues interested in a coup. 'After the Canberra by-election,' Richardson says, 'Keating was dead in the water. There was no way he would win an election, because no matter when it came, Australia was not going to vote for him. It was obvious, to everyone except the Keating fan club, that Keating was going to lose.'

And it was equally obvious that there was only one man who could replace him — Kim Beazley. 'Certainly,' Richardson states, 'some of them were of the view that if Paul wasn't the leader we had a better chance of winning, and if Paul wasn't going to be the leader there was only one possibility, and that was Kim — there was nobody else who could credibly run as leader. And so I discussed it with [some of them] and eventually we had a talk with Kim.' A key meeting took place one afternoon in April, over tea in Richardson's Canberra flat. 'The difficulty,' Richardson explains, 'is that Kim was never going to let you place him in a position of being an opponent of Keating's. He would never have nominated against Keating, and he was only prepared to take it on if Keating was prepared to agree to go.' In the memory of both Beazley and Richardson it was clear very early that he, Beazley, was never going to launch against Keating so the discussion actually went nowhere.

Yet it was not a manoeuvre carried out in isolation, for others too in the party were circling at this time. 'Gary Punch and Con Sciacca were always at the back of it,' Beazley states. 'They used to drift in to my office, with euphemisms, I think you could say, "veiled references" to the need for me to have a go against Paul. It wasn't direct, just a kind of testing me out, as to whether I would be prepared.' Beazley was less veiled in his reply: 'No.' Part of it was simply an outright refusal to do something so clearly destabilising, and part was a sense that there might be more behind it than a genuine desire to see him in the spot. 'I thought people might use my willingness to run to put pressure on Keating, so that something quite subtle would be going on, in which I would be the "patsy". I wasn't going to do it anyway, but I had an additional vague suspicion that at least some NSW colleagues were of that view. They weren't asking because ultimately they would remove Keating, they were asking because if they could signal to Paul that I was prepared to run against him, then that might energise him to do a few of the things they thought he ought to do, politically.' Beazley's impression of Keating's performance at that time says something about his view of what a Prime Minister should be.

'Paul was massively focused on government, but not on politics and I think that was the difficult bit, that the politics was just hopeless,' he says. 'It wasn't a good political operation being run, even if the last year and a half of his Prime Ministership was magnificent. It was just very difficult ... Basically Paul always wanted things on his terms, he wanted them on his terms in the party and on his terms as Prime Minister and with the Australian people you can't have things on your terms, you have it on theirs and part of the Prime Ministerial job is politics. Bob loved the politics, Bob really enjoyed meeting people and being popular and the rest of it, while Keating despised it. The irony of it though, was that when we needed it, he was good at it actually, particularly with older people. There just wasn't enough of it though.'

If Keating was at all concerned that Beazley was being seen as a possible replacement for him, it certainly didn't show.

On Sunday 18 June 1995, around 7 pm, the phone rang in Beazley's home in South Perth. It was the Prime Minister. He had news — Brian Howe, the scion of the Left, longstanding servant of the Labor Party and incumbent Deputy Prime Minister, was thinking of standing down. It wasn't certain, but that was how it looked at the moment. This would give the new Deputy a chance to use the prestige of the position to further the party's ends in the lead-up to the next election. 'Are you interested in standing?' Keating asked him. 'Yes,' Beazley replied without hesitation. If Keating was asking him, it meant that he had his support, and with the Prime Minister's support it was likely to be his for the taking if Howe did indeed stand down ... so he put his hand up. Keating had already called Carmen Lawrence that day to determine her own ambitions regarding the Deputy's job, and she had declined — as he surely knew she would — entirely submerged as she was in the turmoil of the Penny Easton Affair. (A Royal Commission had been called and was due to start that very week.) On the following day Keating called Simon Crean who, upon consideration, decided not to stand on the basis that he would not have the numbers to topple Beazley even if he had wanted to. 'Howe's decision was a shock to me,' Crean recalls. 'I basically had to make an assessment with pretty short notice. Kim had more notice than me. Paul's point was there's no automatic move from Deputy to Leader, so basically I was given the morning to consider it. By, I think, fairly soon in the afternoon — having taken the soundings and what I considered ultimately to be the smoother transition anyway — I didn't stick my hand up.'

(The historical footnote to this faux contest between Beazley and Crean is that exactly two decades before, Simon's father Frank Crean Snr had contested a Caucus ballot with Kim Beazley Snr to succeed Jim Cairns as Deputy Prime Minister, and on that occasion it was the Crean side of the equation that had triumphed.)

So the scene was set. Lawrence was out, Crean was out, Gareth Evans was still in the Senate and thus not in a position to run for the Deputy's job — although he had announced his intention to stand for a seat in the House of Representatives in the next election. Removing Evans even further from the equation at that time was that he was also in Paris, desperately trying to quell the howls of outrage from the Australian public over what was considered to be the Australian Government's inadequate response to the French nuclear tests being conducted at Mururoa Atoll. It all went as planned — with Brian Howe standing down two days later — but there was one major surprise. During the press conference announcing that Kim Beazley had been elected as the new Deputy, the Prime Minister said that the man standing right by his side, was the 'obvious person' to succeed him. (This, despite what he'd previously told Crean.) Beazley looked clearly surprised at such an official endorsement, as well he might have done. To that point in recent Labor Party machinations there had been an unwritten rule that no-one was to be designated as 'Leader in Waiting'. But Keating's move was part of a carefully calculated policy to draw attention to the high number of heavyweight politicians the Labor side boasted, as opposed to what they perceived to be the embarrassing surfeit of lightweights in the Liberal ranks. Nevertheless, as little as a few hours previously at a press conference with the outgoing Brian Howe, Keating had denied outright any suggestion that Beazley had the right to regard himself as mate-most-likely to ascend to the position of Leader of the Parliamentary Labor Party. Now, however, at this press conference with Beazley, he took an entirely different approach to the same line of questioning: 'I want to make certain first and foremost that if [Kim] is to succeed me, at whatever point that is, that he succeeds me in Government. I think that's what we are both about; winning the next election. I mean, the public insists that the parties deliver quality to them in terms of policies and obviously Kim's standing in the party, his record as a minister in now so many senior portfolios, and now his endorsement unanimously as Deputy Prime Minister makes him, if you like, the obvious person in the longer haul.' Beazley remembers his reaction to Keating's comments. 'I was tremendously flattered. But I was not overwhelmed. I thought actually that Paul would have a good shot at winning the next election, and be leader for quite some time ...'

The journalists for their part were quite certain of the significance of Keating's words. 'And that was that,' wrote Michael Gordon in a long article on Beazley's ascension in The Australian. 'If Howard becomes Prime Minister after the next election, Beazley will be the next Leader of the Opposition, the first Federal Labor Leader [from Western Australia] since John Curtin. There is virtually no doubt on that.'[153]

Other leadership contenders were less enamoured of Keating's public anointment of Beazley. When Gareth Evans returned from Paris shortly afterwards, he made a late-night phone call to Keating to question him closely about why he had made such a public declaration about his heir apparent. Keating replied that after the unanimous vote for Kim, and in the presence of Kim Snr — who by coincidence had happened to be in Canberra at the time and had come along — he had simply been carried away with the euphoria of the moment, and Evans should not read too much into it. Nevertheless, the then Foreign Minister did: 'It was the case that Kim had been effectively anointed at that stage,' Evans says, 'and when he came across to the deputy slot, nobody was in any doubt that that was the succession issue settled. I was surprised at Brian Howe stepping down when he did. I anticipated that occurring maybe before the next election but not as soon as it was — it was a bit of a lightning strike. Any opportunity I may have had to generate a bit more of a hint about myself was out of the question by then because I hadn't managed the shift across to the Lower House early enough and hadn't had an opportunity to establish myself in that kind of context.' Others considered Evans to be well out of the running anyway. In an article in the *Sydney Morning Herald* on the following Saturday, Alan Ramsey put it like this: 'Being a Senator, albeit one switching to the Lower House at the next election, Evans wasn't considered for deputy. Being Gareth, he wouldn't have been considered, anyhow. Evans has more ability and leadership potential than any of them, but he's made such a hash of things lately, one way and another, he couldn't win a Caucus ballot at the moment to shut the door. All this left Kim Beazley as the only candidate still upright.'

Not only upright, but being publicly embraced by his father in front of the whole room, who uttered a throwaway line that, 'it's been a long time since I could get my arms around my son'. To many in the room it had been quite poignant to see the older man there, present at the time of Kim Jnr's elevation to the family's highest position in the Labor Party to that point.

In newspaper reports the following day, there were no quotes from Kim Beazley Snr, about how 'proud' he was of his son. In *The Age*, he went so far as to deny it entirely: 'I have no occasion to be proud of my son. He is his own man, his successes are his own.' Lest that seem harsh, it was more to do with the whole notion of 'pride', than with any regard for his son. 'I dislike the word "pride" in those sorts of situations,' Kim Snr says, 'because this is what happens — I've seen very many good people who never got into those sorts of positions ...'

One of those people perhaps, was the one he saw whilst shaving every morning, and that is certainly the opinion of his eldest son. The two Kims, yet, had a curious relationship at this time of their lives. It was not deferential from younger to older, in the sense of Kim Jnr seeking and getting approval or advice from his father on any particular issue — for that never happened — and as a matter of fact the older man was always careful not to take up too much of his son's time, as he knew how busy he was; but when Kim Jnr was asked by his biographer in late 1997 how old he thought he was when the torch of dominant protectiveness had been passed from his now-elderly father to him, his reply was immediate. 'Never has', he replied softly. 'Never has.'

Through this sudden political elevation, the public persona of Beazley Jnr seemed to change not at all. Yes, the Labor backbencher Mary Easson did give him two bright new ties, both in honour of his 'promotion' and in an attempt to spruce him up a bit, but the man behind the ties remained the same. Aldous Huxley had once said of himself that he was afraid to lose his obscurity, 'because genuineness only thrives in the dark', but Beazley seemed to belie that theory. There was no added swagger to his step, no increased sense of his own self-importance. As his old mate Dr Geoff Gallop describes Kim, 'one of his key features is that he is not obsessed with power, he's relaxed with power but not obsessed with it, which is a real quality'.

Nor had Brian Howe been at all obsessed with power for that matter, but there was a clear difference between the approach taken by Beazley to the job, and the approach taken by his predecessor. Within the party the new Deputy Prime Minister became something of a lightning rod for discontent, a kind of accessible conduit from the Caucus to the sometimes distant and aloof Prime Minister. 'To be fair,' Darryl Melham, then a prominent ALP backbencher, notes, 'both Hawke and Keating also had "open-door" policies where they said members of Caucus were always welcome to drop in when they wanted to, but the difference is that with them, very few members did because they were intimidated by them. With Kim members would drop around all the time, because that was just the way Kim was, the way Kim has always been. He's a naturally open-door kind of bloke, and the Caucus regarded him highly for it.'

If that was the Deputy Prime Minister the Caucus saw, the public saw a different one again; for while Howe had been essentially a 'Prime Ministerial backstop,'[154] to quote one story, there to keep the Left happy — he had been close to invisible to the public eye. The Beazley approach was entirely the opposite. It wasn't that he was out there, campaigning for Labor *per se*, but certainly he took a far more active role in beating the Labor drum than Howe ever had. As Randall Markey put it in the *West Australian* just before Christmas of 1995, 'Mr Keating is showing signs of being tired and bored with the hand-to-hand combat with his political foes. He has done it for 25 years and it is a chore. He believes he has earned the right — indeed it is his duty — to concentrate on the big picture issue of linking Australia with what he regards as its Asian destiny. That leaves the Deputy Prime Minister to take a more central hands-on role on the national political stage. But it has made more demands on his time and curtailed his efforts to campaign in Perth.'

Clearly, there continued to be some within Caucus who thought Beazley did the job so well that Labor would fare better at the coming elections if he were at the helm, and occasionally those views would make their way into the press. The first time the rumblings made their way into the public arena was in Melbourne in early September of

1995, when the *Sunday Age* reported that moves were afoot to depose Keating and put Beazley in his stead. Beazley knocked such speculation on the head, stone-cold dead that same day when he appeared on Channel Ten's *Meet the Press* programme. 'The paramount chief is perfectly secure,' he said. 'Paul Keating is the paramount chief ... and there is no sensible alternative to that course of action. We've got a united team. That's the team that is going to take us into a poll and that's the end of the matter.' And that really was the end of the matter. Footage of the programme shows a man absolutely certain that he would not move against his leader. 'It never entered my mind for a moment,' he says simply, 'and I found all of that kind of speculation most unhelpful to the task at hand of getting us in shape for the coming election.'

For his part, Keating sounded very confident about the Deputy Prime Minister's loyalty. Asked, while on a trip to Bali, what he thought of the newspaper's report, he had chortled merrily: 'If you blokes take that seriously, we could sell you the Town Hall clock, the Sydney Harbour Bridge and a block of flats in Tasmania all rolled into one!'[155] There were no buyers. The story didn't have legs once it was clear that Beazley would not move against Keating, and that was indeed obvious to all. In *The Victory*, Pamela Williams quoted the assessment given to nervous backbenchers, by one of Keating's closest supporters Leo McLeay, about Beazley's chances of taking over from the Prime Minister: 'If asked, won't run, and if drafted, won't serve.'[156] Keating's own view was the same: 'Kim was too honourable to have anything to do with something like that'. Besides, at least in Keating's mind, the succession and its rough timing had already been worked out. If Keating lost the forthcoming election — due in 1996 — then, he said, 'it was obvious to me that Kim should take over'. In fact if he *won* the next election, then Kim would *still* get the job soon enough.

Around the middle of 1995, and affirmed several times over the following six months, Keating had told Beazley something surprising. 'I told Kim,' Keating recounts, 'I said, "if I win, I will stand down for you, in the next term". I didn't dice around with him, I wasn't being tricky or giving him winks. I told him directly "if I win I will give you the job ... "'

This intention, Keating says, was not because he was simply bone-tired after spending literally half of his life in Federal Parliament, and going through many, many bruising and bloody fights over that span. 'I have enough energy to do it all over again,' he would state to the author in late March of 1998. Rather, Keating says he held the view that 'after so many years in office Labor should be turning its leaders over after a reasonable period and not regarding them as fixtures'. He thought the way to fully freshen up a then old party of Government was to periodically come up with a new face in the Prime Ministership. 'The problem for Labor and for me,' he explains, 'was that Hawke had stayed on too long. Just on nine years whereas after five years, by 1988, Hawke had given all he was able to give. Between 1988 and 1991 all that happened was that a void had been created. Gerry Hand and Graham Richardson stuck to Hawke in 1988 and cost Labor its chance to freshen up and by 1991, when the party finally gave the job to me, there was no political capital left in Labor's account with the public. With all that in mind I was determined not to compound the problem by staying on too long myself.

'What happens, is that every time you come up for election, every time you come up for assessment by the public, they strip away more of your political capital. When I was given the leadership, very few people in the Labor Party thought they were giving me anything much at all, just the last 12 months of Hawke's fourth term as Prime Minister. But I turned it into four years by winning election number five. If I'd won election number six we would have been left to the realms of political magic seeking to win election number seven ... and of course I was on the record as saying in mid-1991 that there was almost no life left in it by election number five ...' Besides what he considered would be bleak electoral prospects for him personally, there was another factor though. 'By the time of stepping down,' he says, 'I would have sought to have had the Republic Referendums carried, I would have had most of the things that I regarded as important to do, done — I had most of it done anyway. And I didn't want to make the same mistake with Kim that Bob had made with me, by holding on too long. It was important Kim not be given a political inheritance which had been voided.'

During one long discussion with his Deputy Prime Minister in the Prime Ministerial suite, Keating had also explained why he hadn't stood down for him in *that* term. 'I also told him,' he recollects, 'I said "look if I had thrown it to you in the early part of '95, and let you have the last 12 months of my term as Prime Minister I would have pointed you to defeat. You would have then had to carry the baggage of the last 13 years with only a year to gain the public's confidence, but we are now three years older than when I was able to do that."'

Two years later, Paul Keating was still certain that he'd made the right decision. 'Kim, the next leader of the Labor Party, would have begun as Opposition Leader in all likelihood as the just defeated Prime Minister ... I said to him "if I stay on and lose you will become Opposition Leader with a record of having not lost, as a leader. Don't underestimate the value of not being strapped in to ride in the death seat."' Beazley remembers all of the above. 'He said it to me several times,' Beazley recalls, 'that if he won, he would stand down at some point in the term, and I would take over.' To those who would claim that this was Beazley and Keating's own version of a 'Kirribilli agreement,' Beazley has a clear answer — that was, that an 'agreement,' or 'a pact' would have required two of them to have entered into it, and he, Beazley, had been entirely uninvolved. 'I wasn't pushing for a commitment like that from him,' he says, 'he volunteered it. I didn't particularly want any such commitment. I was enormously flattered that he would say that, but I took the view that if Prime Ministers did from time to time expand on things like that, that's fine, but circumstances may well create conditions where they would want to keep going. He was a very young man, still is a young man ... so I never set any store by it at all.'

Either way, Beazley busied himself in the months remaining to the election doing everything possible to maximise the Government's chances of winning. Generally, he showed a very deft touch when dealing with the public, and was clearly one of their key assets as the time for the election drew nearer. On one occasion, when talking with Year 11 and 12 students of Cranbourne Secondary College, on the southeastern outskirts of Melbourne, he was asked what he would do if he were Prime Minister. 'The first thing you learn as Deputy Prime Minister,' he replied, 'is that you don't speculate about what you would do as Prime Minister ...' To the same group he noted that right from the time he had been their age until very recently, he had always assumed that somewhere there in Canberra, *somewhere*, there would be one wise person who knew just how the Government and the economy actually worked. 'Now, after 15 years,' he told them with a gently self-mocking laugh, 'I am here to tell you that that person doesn't exist.' It was good stuff, and played well when reported in such heavyweight media as the *Financial Review*.[157]

No doubt about it, Labor needed some feel-good publicity at that time; the portents for the coming election were not good. All around were doom and gloom with poll results indicating that the

Government would struggle to hold on in the election already predicted for March of the following year.

In early December of 1995, a sobering insight to Keating's assessment of the future came when Beazley joined the Prime Minister on a flight to Jakarta, where they were to sign a security pact with Indonesia — that country's first bi-lateral security agreement in the region. It was a coup both for Keating and Foreign Minister Gareth Evans, who had organised it, and Beazley was joining them both in his capacity as Deputy Prime Minister, and as the member of the Keating Government who had perhaps been most heavily involved with the Indonesians over the years. Somewhere over the Timor Sea, Beazley turned to Keating and, nodding in the direction of the media in the back of the plane, said: 'Well the journos down the back have been a bit unfair to you, mate. They're saying you've organised all this as some sort of stunt for the election and I know you've been working on it for a couple of years — so I know it is not a stunt ... it has just come to fruition at this time.' In reply, Keating seemed sanguine. 'No,' Beazley remembers the Prime Minister replying. 'They have got a point you know, but not for the reasons they think. One of the reasons why I didn't bring it to a conclusion earlier was because I did want it close to the election, because this bunch don't know how to handle foreign policy and it will give them an automatic proximity to the Indonesians as they find their feet after the next election. We need to leave them with as many institutional things that they can use as possible.' There was a pause, and they left it at that. Each was left with his own thoughts, to the tune of the muted roar of the aeroplane's engines. The way Beazley interpreted the Prime Ministers' words, was that Keating was basically acknowledging that it would likely not be too long before the Liberals — whom he was referring to as 'this bunch' — would be running the show themselves.

A sign of just where Keating was situated within his own party at that time came a fortnight after his return to Australia. The Premier of Queensland, Wayne Goss, declined the Prime Minister's offer to make a campaign appearance in the crucial upcoming Mundingburra by-election, a poll on whose fate Goss's State Government rested. 'I'm not going to put the dingo fence up to try and keep him out,' he was quoted as saying in The Australian, 'but I'm simply going to say that myself and my colleagues in the State Labor Government will put our arguments before the people of Mundingburra and we'll be judged on our performance, not on that of Paul Keating or John Howard.'[158]

If Keating's and Labor's stocks were low, at least going into that summer of 1995/96, Beazley's political and personal stocks were at an all-time high. With Susie, he had as happy a home-life as he had ever known. He delighted in seeing how his two oldest daughters had turned into accomplished young women — with Jessica now at university — and young Rachel had moved from toddler to well-spoken kidlet. Politically, he was not only Deputy Prime Minister and Deputy Leader of the Labor Party, but also highly regarded personally by his colleagues, both in Cabinet and in Caucus. As Malcolm McGregor had written in the *Financial Review*, 'in a party that seethes with factional and personal hatreds, it is almost impossible to find a hard word said about the big, genial Western Australian'.[159] An indication of how highly the party regarded him came early in that summer at a time when Paul Keating and many of his heavyweight Cabinet colleagues were overseas. At one point during their absence, Kim Christian Beazley found himself to be Acting Prime Minister, Deputy Prime Minister, Leader of the House, Acting Treasurer, Acting Minister for Foreign Affairs, and Acting Defence Minister. It wasn't quite '*Kim Beazley, Ruler of the World*', as had once been written on his Primary School exercise books, but it wasn't bad for all that.

Did he like having all that nominal power at his fingertips? 'Loved it,' he acknowledges. With the role of Acting Prime Minister came such accoutrements as a full-time Federal police guard, who followed Kim and Susie everywhere, who set up roadblocks at both ends of their Perth street and asked drivers to state their business before they were allowed to proceed. Two of the Federal police minders were sitting in their car outside on Christmas Day, until Susie went out and insisted they join the extended Beazley family for Christmas lunch. Beazley also called Mick Young on that day, to see how he was getting on, and to wish him and his family the best for the festive season. The two had remained as close as ever, despite Mick having left the Parliament to work as a consultant for a variety of corporations. They saw and talked with each other often, but they had become even more tightly bound lately. Mick was crook. It hadn't yet been properly diagnosed, but all his energy seemed to have gone, and his health was so poor that he had had to take time off work. At least on this day, he was feeling a little better, and they chatted and laughed about anything and everything in much the same manner as they always had ...

On 27 January 1996, the game began again in earnest — and as always all the key participants were playing for keeps. On that day Paul Keating announced an election for 2 March, and Beazley was immediately out on the hustings, touring many marginal Labor seats, while also being careful to spend as much time as possible in his own electorate of Brand. When he was not already committed to official campaigning in other parts of the country Kim, Susie, Jessica and Hannah spent every spare hour in the electorate, doorknocking, being seen, indeed doing what he had done, in one way or another, for the last 40 years of his life. It was difficult finding time to get back to Brand too often though, because he was in such high demand by his colleagues throughout the country. Whatever things Paul Keating had achieved in his time as Prime Minister, widespread personal popularity was not one of them, and Caucus was not queuing up demanding him to appear with them on the hustings. Kim Beazley, on the other hand, was another matter. He was one of the few Labor people guaranteed to engender warm feelings in the electorate, and during this time he visited every marginal Labor seat, many safe seats and some several times over. If one of Paul Keating's problems electorally was a perceived arrogance, no-one ever accused Kim Beazley of such a thing.

Whatever it was, it wasn't arrogance. And it certainly wasn't an inflated ego. When, for example, there had been a flurry of comment when Paul Keating was mobbed by Catholic schoolgirls on the western outskirts of Sydney in the middle of the election campaign, Beazley was asked by radio 4BC in Queensland to take a moment's pause and reflect on his own sex appeal. Beazley replied: 'Paul Keating is a handsome devil and looks good, and I'm just a fat old thing.'[160] At least no-one would ever accuse him of being a mere blow-wave with a suit and tie on. As McGregor put it: 'in a party whose ranks swell with sartorially splendid spivs bereft of souls, Beazley's ramshackle exterior evokes an era of greater decency in political life'.[161]

As the time for the March election drew closer, Beazley was like the experienced farmer looking at the budding wheat-crop for signs of what kind of electoral harvest was going to be reaped this time — and it was not positive. All the signs were bad, but it was equally clear to him that there was a difference between this and other electoral moods he had seen. 'In 1975,' he says, 'the people were out to punish us. They wanted to inflict pain, and they did so without mercy. This time though, it was different. Going into the '96 election I thought their attitude was "look, you've been there a long time, you've been ok, we haven't got a really big gripe with you … but you're gone". People were very friendly, but it was the same message, just … you're *gone*.'

Paul Keating was reading much the same signals, in much the same way — though his own black cloud was still tinged with hope that they could emerge victorious. 'The election in '96 was a struggle,' Keating recounts, 'because the Liberals had turned into a Labor chameleon. Having decided three years earlier to pursue an antipodean version of Thatcher-type policy through things like 'Fightback!' they'd discovered that none of that worked. So for the '96 election, they decided to say, "We're just like the Labor Party! We believe in health the same as they do, industrial relations the same as they do, in fact we're just like them." So in this election instead of having to make a real choice between the two of us, they sought to make it no choice. And people said "Well, if that's the case, and things are going well — inflation's well, growth's well, employment's growing — if that little Johnny Howard isn't going to tear the system up, then maybe we can give the Libs a try."' In Brand, there were plenty of signs that there were plenty of people thinking exactly that, and with only the thin 3.7 per cent margin that his predecessor had left him to defend from the last election, it was always going to be touch and go whether Beazley could hold on.

In the final days he campaigned as hard as he had at any time in his life. Three days out from the election, on the late afternoon of Wednesday 29 February, a rare day for politicking, he was heading home to South Perth with Hazel Hawke beside him. Mrs Hawke, herself Perth born, went back a long way with the Beazley family, at least from a distance. As a young girl she remembers admiring the athlete Betty Judge from afar after seeing photos of her flying form in the paper, and as a young woman newly married to Bob Hawke, she had always paused in her ironing to listen to the 'wonderfully expressive speeches' of Kim Snr in Parliament. A measure of her affection for Kim's and Betty's son — who she had become very close to during her years in the Lodge — was her insistence on coming to Brand to help him campaign. It was an offer the candidate had seized with both hands, and the two had spent this entire day going from shopping centre to bowling club to pensioners' meetings, and on to more shopping centres.

At one point they paused in their conversation to catch the news on the car radio. It wasn't good. The news bulletin informed them that the Treasurer, Ralph Willis, had held a press conference in Canberra, at which he had released copies of two letters that he had received anonymously in the mail that day. One was supposedly from Victorian Premier, Jeff Kennett, the other from Shadow Treasurer Peter Costello's chief of staff, and they were both addressed to John Howard. Both made reference to an apparent John Howard plan to slash federal grants to state governments immediately after the election. If such letters were authentic, they would be extremely damaging to John Howard's electoral chances, but from first hearing about them Beazley was suspicious. 'I had had a bit of a hand in what Ralph was meant to be doing that day,' he recalls. 'It was the last throw of the dice on the Liberal Party costings — that was what Ralph was going to go through and when I heard that there was some sort of leaking letter my concern was, "that's just not on the point, that's an irrelevancy to the campaign". And the whole thing of these letters, just didn't ring true.' When the radio bulletin was finished, and he'd switched it off, the mood in the car was suddenly a lot darker. 'It really put a bit of a hole in it that evening,' Mrs Hawke remembers. 'Kim didn't curse Ralph or anything, because that is not his way of reacting to things, but he was not happy about it.' He would get unhappier still when they arrived home, and a phone call confirmed that his worst fears had been realised — the letters had been all but exposed as a fraud perpetrated by person or persons unknown. It made Willis — together with ALP National Secretary, Gary Gray, and staffer, David Epstein, who had encouraged the Treasurer to proceed without confirming authenticity — look ludicrously reckless, but more importantly it made the Keating Government, by association, seem very ordinary indeed.

Just landed in Adelaide after a flight from Cairns — on the outskirts of which city he'd had an extremely close-call in one of the Australian Army's Blackhawk helicopters that morning — Paul Keating felt the same when told of what had occurred while travelling in a car from the airport to the city. 'When the letters issue happened, I knew we were gone,' Keating recollects. 'Ten days before the 1996 election, Labor had the same standing as we'd had 10 days before the 1993 election. In fact on the major polls there were only 3 per cent points the difference — I had to pick up 1.5 per cent in ten days. A not impossible task. But a number of things happened ...

'One of the big things, that smothered Howard's worst performances in the second-last week was the Super League court decision. Blanket reporting over the final weekend. That blotted out all newspaper political comment and wiped clean a disastrous Howard week.

'So instead of getting marked way down, he got away with it. Then in the final days, the Willis letters. In the last week of the election campaign of course, everything is magnified. In a normal week it would have just been a miscalculation. But in the last week of an election campaign when everything is massively magnified ... it was not recoverable.

'The "Willis letters" have since dropped out of Labor analysis and reckoning. But they are not referred to because Gary Gray and David Epstein who encouraged Ralph Willis to hock his reputation without my consent, don't want to wear the responsibility for their actions. The two officials who ordinarily were the most cautious, the most conservative, who always counselled me against saying anything even mildly controversial, went and hocked the fortunes of a government without so much as a conversation with the leader. In Gray's self-serving analysis in a speech to the Press Club within weeks of the election, [Gray] downplayed the letters, in fact I don't think they were even mentioned. For me though, they were the key.'

That night, Greg Turnbull, who was one of Keating's media advisers, remembers that 'the scene in Keating's room at the Hyatt was like out of a David Williamson play. There was Paul, Annita, Don Russell, Don Watson, myself, all going in and out, trying to work out some way to undo the damage, but there just didn't seem to be any way out. It looked like we were gone.' Others in the Labor Party though, were already of the view that with or without the faked letters, time was simply up. In Melbourne, Senator Robert Ray was more than ever convinced that it was over and that, come election night, Kim Beazley would very quickly emerge as Opposition Leader-elect, provided of course that he held on to his seat. Gary Gray was of the same view, and at the ALP secretary's request, Ray sat down in his office and wrote Beazley a 10-page letter with his own estimations of where Labor had gone wrong in recent times. He further gave his opinion on how his long-time colleague should fill the role of Opposition Leader and in which direction he should steer Labor in order to return it to some form of electoral health as soon as possible. He decided he would give it to Kim the following Monday if he was by then the Opposition Leader-elect, as Ray felt he would be, and would give another copy to ALP National Secretary, Gary Gray.

On the Thursday before the Saturday election, Beazley spoke on Perth radio station 6PR, and made his position clear *vis-a-vis* the leadership of the party should it suddenly become vacant: 'We are the underdogs, there is no question about that,' he said, 'but I have to operate on the assumption of victory and that Paul Keating will continue as Prime Minister.' And if he didn't? 'I am going to be in politics as long as the electorate leaves me there and at any point in time, when the Labor Party leadership becomes vacant I will be a candidate for it if I am still in politics at the time that occurs ...'

It prompted a headline in the following day's *West Australian*, saying 'Beazley Wants Top Job', and while from some people such a statement might be construed as manoeuvring for the top position, that was hardly the case on this occasion, for the reason that there was simply no-one for him to be manoeuvring *against*.[162] Gareth Evans had had a generally successful career to that point — during which he had, among other things, been judged as making significant contributions to securing peace in Cambodia and setting up the Australia Pacific Economic Council, promoting nuclear disarmament and repositioning Australia's diplomatic relations internationally. Nevertheless, recently he had endured arguably the most unfortunate 12 months of his political career. The Foreign Minister had misjudged the Australian public's hostility to renewed nuclear testing at Mururoa Atoll; had created a furore when he had criticised Opposition Leader Alexander Downer's wife Nicki for not becoming a naturalised citizen; had suffered Australian hostage David Wilson being killed by rebel forces in South-East Asia; and had created a diplomatic stir in South Africa when he had publicly criticised the security contingent that had been provided for him. If timing was everything in politics, his misfortune at that particular time was that his watch had simply stopped — in quite stark contrast to Beazley, whose timing was close to impeccable, something that Evans acknowledges: 'I can't remember with any great vividness Kim's trouble and strife [around 1992,]' he says, 'but there is no doubt he did have a bad year, and got it out of the way before the period of transition, whereas I just had my off year I guess in the critical year before the transition. But I never saw myself as a competitor, I knew that way back in the beginning when the die was cast in terms of my senate role. When I moved down to the Lower House it was really just a combination of wanting to round out my own political career ... and ensuring that we had someone there who was experienced and all the rest of it in the event that Kim fell under a bus electorally.'

And Carmen Lawrence's leadership ambitions? By any measure the Easton Affair had debilitated, if not destroyed her political career entirely, and at that time it was out of the question that she run for the leadership. Simon Crean had some support within the Caucus, but clearly not equal to Beazley's, while such mooted 'next-generation' Labor leaders as Lindsay Tanner and Mark Latham were just that — marked down as possible leaders of the next generation but not this.

For Hannah Beazley on election night, it was just like *deja vu* all over again, albeit this time with a couple of slight differences. Again her father was right up against it, again the media and lights and microphones were everywhere. But, 'This time we were in Rockingham, instead of my old Primary School in Swan,' Hannah recalls, 'and it just didn't feel right.' Instead of her father being his usual garrulous self, or being quiet and introspective as he had been during the last election night, on this evening Hannah recalls he was 'very het up, very fraught. He was buzzing around with a lot of nervous energy, wanting to know details, every detail he could get on how he was going and how everyone else in the country was going'.

There was one fact that just about everyone in the country knew at that very moment. Paul Keating, as Prime Minister, was gone. The Labor Government of the previous 13 years was gone. Both had been swept away in a landslide the likes of which Australian politics had not seen since as far back as 1931. That fact, Hannah recalls, focused everyone's mind acutely: 'When you know your Government is gone, you think "well, there's nothing you can do about that anymore, the Government has gone, now it's *personal*, now it's my dad's job, now it is his livelihood — a whole life". It was my Dad, and only my Dad.'

Her father was hanging on, but only just. As the evening wore on, no amount of concentrating from Hannah seemed to make the numbers come together as they had last time. And by around 11 o'clock her father's nervous energy, all energy, had dissipated to the point where he resembled a barely flickering flame, waxing and waning, almost going out before mustering the tiniest burst of light. 'He was slumped down,' she recounts. 'He seemed to give up for a couple of minutes at a time, and say things like "we've lost it", "we can't win it from here", and that is the only time I've ever seen him give up, even for those few split seconds. Then he'd rouse himself, sit up straighter, say "no we haven't, no we haven't, we can do it, because the absentee votes will likely be in my favour and ... "'

And so it went throughout the night, as frequent live television crosses from there to the nation's living rooms reported on how the

Deputy Prime Minister was holding up while teetering on the edge of oblivion. Watching the whole thing in the flesh, inside, Mary Ciccarelli couldn't help but feeling a tiny sense of relief that she was no longer as intimately involved in this kind of life as she had been. 'Perhaps people just don't understand the enormous pressures families of politicians are put under,' she says. 'For not only are you in a situation in a family where your father — or your husband — is constantly out there open to criticism, but every three years his job is literally on the line. I know that a lot of people would say "oh well that's my situation too, *my* job's always on the line", but in politics it is *so public*. That night, we were all sitting there looking at Kim, basically looking to see how he was coping looking at his job going down the drain, and him looking back at us to see how are we coping watching him watching it go down — while everyone else is watching the lot of us. It's extremely hard.'

Making it harder still for Hannah, was being obliged to get a lot of the information from the television; for mixed with the images of the failing Labor force were many images of Liberals celebrating around the country. 'Half of them are there, chucking an absolute party,' she describes, 'while you're still sitting there with no nails left. So you sit there and you start listing off every single thing he's done — and you think "why don't they realise this, why don't they vote for him after he did all these things?" People are chucking a party and you know your dad maybe will lose his seat and you just kind of think, "gee, thanks a lot, that's nice that is".' Jessica Beazley felt much the same as her sister, in a manner reminiscent of the way Kim Jnr, Merrilyn and David had felt when the Liberals led by Sir Robert Menzies had unexpectedly won the 1963 election — upset and angry.

That night, well after midnight, with nothing left to do but go home, get some sleep, and see what morning would bring, the family was heading north to Perth in a chauffeured Commonwealth car. It was surprisingly cold outside beneath an almost full moon and uncomfortably hot inside. Jessica was sitting in the back with Susie and Hannah and was letting off steam, mostly to her father in the passenger seat in front. 'I tell you what, Dad,' she remembers saying, 'the Australian people deserve what they've got coming to them with Howard, they *deserve* this! If they haven't got the sense to elect Labor after everything Labor has done for them, if they're stupid enough to put in the Liberals then they bloody well deserve it.'

The young woman remembers her feelings clearly: 'I just felt humiliated for him,' she says now. 'Angry and bitter and disappointed and humiliated for him that he continually had to be put through this. I know what he's worth and I know he deserves better, he has always deserved better than that.' With such emotions paramount, she continued to rail against the idiocy of the Australian people and how she would enjoy watching what the Liberals were going to do to them.

Her father's mind had drifted off to places unknown, but had now returned and he quietly intervened. Turning his bulk around towards them, as the lights of Perth started to appear on their northern horizon over his left shoulder, he was as firm as he was gentle. 'No, don't talk like that Jessica,' his daughters remember him saying in a voice that had fatigue but no bitterness, 'they don't deserve it. They just don't know what they have done, they don't know what they are getting into.'

CHAPTER EIGHTEEN

OPPOSITION

'In Kim, the Labor Party has a leader for the first time since
Chifley, who doesn't suffer from a major personality disorder ...'
Malcolm McGregor, Financial Review *columnist speaking
on ABC's* Four Corners.[163]

Beazley's situation post-election, has an uncanny resemblance to that faced by John Curtin in the 1940 election. On that occasion, Curtin too had neglected his own seat of Fremantle as he embarked on whirlwind campaigning around the country to try to keep as many of his colleagues as possible safe from electoral harm. In the days after the poll, he had hovered on the edge of oblivion for several days, and to pass the time attended an Australian Rules Football semifinal between Claremont and South Fremantle — when an attendant flashed the news from the radio up on to the scoreboard 'Curtin by 43 votes'. In the case of Beazley, while his electoral circumstances were almost the same, he spent his time waiting at the WACA cricket ground, watching the Western Australian team play in a Sheffield Shield match — and calling John Cowdell at the polling station where the count was taking place, 'about every five to ten minutes,' in Cowdell's estimation.

For over a week the parliamentarian suffered, watching the figures, and thinking 'I'm in, I'm out, I'm gone, I'm back'. At last the returning officer for Brand finally announced the winner — Kim Beazley by only 385 votes ahead of Liberal candidate, Penny Hearne. During that time both he and the Labor Party had examined all number of options to keep him in Parliament even if he lost the seat — from asking one of his WA Labor senatorial colleagues to stand nobly aside and let him have the spot, to replacing the outgoing Paul Keating in his Blaxland electorate when that by-election came — but all had been rejected. 'I couldn't do it to my girls,' he had starkly said to his adviser, John O'Callaghan, when the latter had pushed the Blaxland option. 'There is just no way I'm going to leave them in Perth while I move between Sydney and Canberra.'

At *last* though, he really was over the line under his own steam, in a position to lead the team. From that point, the number of phone calls that Beazley made to lobby his parliamentary colleagues for his own ascension to Opposition leadership could be calculated easily — none. It simply was not necessary. Nearly all within the Labor Party had taken it as given that Kim was the man. On election night both Bob Hawke and Graham Richardson had been endlessly saying as much on the national television coverage, while both Gareth Evans and Simon Crean had also publicly deferred to him as the obvious man to lead them.

'I believed that it was the best decision for the party,' Crean would say to the author over a year later. 'I think he was the right leader for the time.' In the words of his old university colleague and ALP comrade of the previous three decades, Bob McMullan, 'Kim was just the right one for the job. All his political history had led him to that point, and I don't remember any discussion from anyone, considering anyone else *but* Kim.' Senator Robert Ray agrees: 'There just wasn't any contemplation of any other leader but Kim. What we needed after that '96 election was someone who would *not* become a classic Opposition Leader — a moaning, groaning whinger — and secondly someone who could not only be an alternative Prime Minister, but also a real leader of the Labor Party, who could bring all the factions together and have enough personal esteem that people would give him the benefit of the doubt on any particular issue. All of that was Kim.'

On the morning then of 19 March, 1996, after Paul Keating had formally resigned — with a standing ovation both before and after his speech — Kim Christian Beazley was elected unopposed as Leader of the Federal Parliamentary Labor Party, the 16th man to hold that position. In Australian political history, one of the very few parallels to Beazley's ascension was that enjoyed by Harold Holt after Sir Robert Menzies' retirement. 'It was quick, calm — and I climbed over nobody's dead body,' Holt had said at the time.[164] Ditto Beazley. There was no dead body other than that of Keating's political career, no tell-tale drops of blood behind him when he assumed the mantle. On the Labor side of politics such an ascension was close to unprecedented.

Nevertheless, Beazley's decision to stand for the position of Opposition Leader had not been met with universal approval from his family. In sometimes stormy scenes in his parliamentary offices in the days leading up to the Caucus vote on the leadership, his sister Merrilyn, who could always be counted on to give him her honest opinion, had let him have it: '*Don't* do this Kim!' she remembers saying to him. 'For God's sake you almost lost the seat, get out, resign, go and join Henry Kissinger's "think tank", go and be the Ambassador to Washington. If you take on the job as Leader of the Opposition, you'll only have it for three years, and lose the election — you'll never close that big a gap with the Liberals — and then they'll replace you with somebody else! All for *what?!?!*' Beazley listened to his sister, and as she recalls, exchanged a meaningful glance with Susie beside him — as if they had discussed just such a scenario — but held his course. Merrilyn remained unhappy. 'At the time, I thought it was the wrong decision,' she says now. 'He had been in Parliament for 16 years, a minister for 13 years, he was still relatively young, had a brilliant brain, and he should have got the hell out of it to enjoy life. But no. It was like being handed the poison chalice and I was absolutely disgusted with him for taking it. But he had this strong sense that it was his duty to pick up the Labor Party and take it forward. Someone had to do it, and of course it had to be him.'

It was him. Gareth Evans won through to the post of Deputy, by five votes from Simon Crean. One of the first people to ring the new Opposition Leader, to congratulate him on his ascension to the post, was Beazley's old friend and political mentor, Bob Hawke. 'I was delighted, absolutely delighted,' Hawke recollects, 'and so glad, because he really deserved the job.' For the record, Hawke felt entirely vindicated by the landslide against Keating. 'Subsequent events have proven that I was right,' he says, referring to his bitter refusal to stand down for Keating in 1991. 'I certainly would have won the 1993 election. After all I had beaten Howard, I have beaten Peacock twice, I have beaten Fraser, and there was no doubt that I could have beaten Hewson, and the party would not have the subsequent traumas it [did], because in that situation, if I had stayed, Keating would have gone and I would have gone between 1993 and 1996. Beazley would then have come in and I think the party would have been in much better shape. I emphasise in saying that, I am *not* saying that with any bitterness, what happened in 1991 happened, that was the decision and I accepted it and went about my life and didn't interfere with it, but that is my analysis of the situation.'

Kim Beazley set the tone early as to what kind of Opposition Leader he would be, and certainly in terms of personal style, it was as far removed from his immediate predecessor as it was possible to get. Whereas Paul Keating had once said of John Howard that, 'from this day onwards, Mr Howard will wear his leadership like a crown of thorns and in the Parliament I will do everything I can to crucify him'[165] and at other times had called him both 'a dead carcass, swinging in the breeze,' and a 'mangy maggot,' Beazley's approach in contrast, at least at the outset, was extraordinarily conciliatory, even *warm*. 'I have a great deal of respect for John Howard,' he said in his first press conference as Labor leader. 'He is the most substantial conservative politician of his generation.' Such a generous comment about the man who was to be his principal target over the next two to three years, prompted many political pundits to ask the question again: Was Beazley tough enough to be an effective leader? It had been Paul Keating who had once said, 'I suppose most of us would like to be one of those people of whom they say in public life "he never had an enemy in the world, he was one of the sweetest characters you'd ever meet". Yes, but would he knock the big decisions through? Would he knock over the lousy policies? Would he knock over the partisanship and the discrimination? No.' Although Keating had not said this with reference to Beazley — who had after all knocked one very big decision through over the then Treasurer's trampled body — there were still many who would apply the concept to the new Opposition Leader. 'What do you want me to say, that I am a big enough prick?' Beazley countered in an interview with journalist Tony Stephens shortly after taking the post.[166] 'I have had most of the rough portfolios — Defence, Education, Communications, Finance. I've made tough decisions. I've had a better preparation than most for Prime Minister. I understand the conditions for Australia's survival as a nation and have my kids to think of.'

The issue of his toughness was a question mark that had been hanging over him like a poised scythe for too long, and he was jack of it. Still, he never claimed to be as hard as Keating in the first place, and nor did he want to be: 'There is no element of my personality that is anything like Paul's,' he says flatly. 'Paul is pure instinct and very great intelligence, absolutely driven by ideas, with a political killer instinct I don't have. You've got to have the personality for it and I don't. And I can't fake it.' Lest that position be overstated though, Beazley's long-time parliamentary colleague Michael Duffy, puts it in perspective: 'When he was Leader of the House and therefore in charge of business in the Caucus, when he had the numbers he could use the numbers as toughly as anybody, and he used to. He would use the numbers to cut off discussion on an issue if he had to, or he would use the numbers to ram something through. I mean this idea that he is some sort of jellyfish is bullshit. When he has got the numbers he will use them. And people had better understand that ...'

Clearly, Beazley would never try to 'fake' the Keating style of aggression. In the beginning of his tenure as Opposition Leader, he was forthright in his view that the time was not right for that type of aggressive approach anyway. 'This is the '90s,' he told another interviewer. 'This is an insecure time. I think people are looking for a bit of hardness when there are real grounds for disagreement, but not bogus grounds for disagreement. They want a bit of bipartisanship around the place on occasions. And probably that sort of style suits the era. It may not for that much longer, but it suits for now.'[167] He was different from Hawke and Keating, and happy to be so.

'I'm an ideological Social Democrat,' he says, 'and I'm actually about the business, I'm about the policy, I'm about the world view of the Labor Party in a way that they were not. I think in a way both Bob and Paul were ... not necessarily within the Labor Party tradition. They have a radical perspective on the world — a view that wants to change things, and they tend to look at a selection of contemporary ideas that relate to that change. They tend to approach those ideas with a completely open mind — a mind unstructured by other forms of political commitment. Bob's a bit less than Paul that way. I am more conventional in the sense of having a view in the first instance which is an ideological, Social Democratic view and I tend to view an awful lot of things through that prism ...'

Beazley's was a calm, ordered approach that would be viewed as crucial by his colleagues in that difficult period of time after the disastrous election when the temptation, in the words of one member of Caucus, was 'to tear each other's entrails out'. But the real need was to salve and heal the deep wounds within the party and Beazley was regarded by the majority of his colleagues, the man to do this. He had one other key asset to bring to the task at hand. In the words of Leo McLeay: 'Kim's the first Labor leader since Curtin and Chifley that everyone likes, and because they like him it's very hard for people to disagree with him, so there was more of a tendency to follow his lead, and that helped unite everyone.'

In those first few weeks, Beazley spent a fair amount of time reflecting on where the Labor Party had gone so obviously wrong in the last election that they had been trounced so comprehensively. As he did so, a few themes kept pushing their way forward. 'In our last term in office,' he says, 'I think we needed to be more in campaign mode than we were. We'd been a bit exalted: "here is the view, it is coming down from up high and it *is* correct." Most of the views we had were the views which most of Australia holds, but in the run-up to that last election we allowed ourselves to be seen as different from the average Australian, and that was a major campaign failure.'

The way forward, he decided, was to go hard after winning back the hard-core Labor voters, so many of whom had deserted them at the 1996 election. 'Our first point of focus,' Beazley comments, 'had to be the people that we had lost and they were largely men, largely in their forties and fifties and mostly blue-collar workers.' As a general theme to entice them and others back to the fold, Beazley decided on the theme of 'security'. 'I warmed to it in my first press conference,' he recollects, 'and have done since. I wanted to get that word up there in lights, as it related to all sorts of things, the security of your family, the security of your job, the security of your capacity to access education and health. People feel a lack of security now, and I wanted to position the ALP so that we could help provide it.'

Before truly launching on such issues though, what Beazley most needed in that first fortnight after was the very shortest of breaks. He took it over Easter, at a resort up in Broome with his family, and was enjoying it just as much as he always adored this part of the political cycle. 'The most satisfying period is after an election,' he explains, 'when you have been elected to Parliament. It is a period of total relaxation for two or three weeks in which you say "I've survived", and it doesn't matter whether your party has won office or not, the fact is you are still there! After that the reality takes hold and you are back at the wheel again.' On this occasion though, such relaxation was tragically interrupted.

On Good Friday, the phone in their hotel room rang. It was Karen Bissaker, calling from his Canberra office. 'Kim, I've just had a phone call from Sydney about Mick, it sounds very bad. I was wondering if ...'

'I am coming,' Beazley interrupted. 'Get me on the first plane out.'

Within 12 hours he was at Mick Young's bedside at St Vincent's Hospital, listening, talking and telling him stories, as the ex-shearer drifted in and out of consciousness, his body ravaged by the leukaemia that he'd been fighting for the last four months. Beazley stayed there for the next two days. When finally Michael Jerome Young — still a year shy of 60 years old — slipped into a coma that he was clearly not going to come out of, Beazley said his prayers, left his mate to his family, and returned to his own wife and children in Broome. A day after arriving back, the second phone call came. Mick had died in the night. Beazley wept. 'It was so bloody unfair,' he says now. 'Mick never got a break, he *never* got a break.' Prime Minister Howard accorded Mick Young a State funeral, held in St Mary's Cathedral in Sydney five days after his death. As the time drew near for Beazley to deliver the eulogy, he turned to Paul Keating behind him and whispered, with emotion starting to overflow, 'I can't do it, mate ... I won't be able to get through it.'

'You have to, Kim,' Keating had replied gently, 'you owe it to him.'

And indeed Beazley almost did get through delivering the eulogy without being emotionally overcome. Almost. Nearing the end, he nodded to the extended Young family occupying the two front pews of the cathedral, including Mick's wife, Mary, his son and daughter, and his six brothers and their wives. 'In the end,' the new Opposition Leader said, his voice now cracking, 'he belonged to them, not to the party or the nation. But his memory sustains us all ...'

On the way to returning to his pew where Susie awaited, he paused in front of the first pew, where the Young family was sitting and made a long, low bow. ('I thought that was a very lovely thing of him to have done and it just shows you how sensitive and decent he really is,' Mary Young remembers of the moment.) It would be a long, long time before he would fully overcome the loss of Young's death. Even since Mick had left Parliament, the two had seen each other constantly and had talked on the phone almost daily. But no longer. 'I miss him,' says Beazley, 'and I always will.'

Helping him to emerge from the worst depths of his grief was a sense of urgency about continuing to get both the Opposition and himself in shape for the task at hand. Parliament had been back in session barely two weeks, and there was much to do. While he took it as an enormous honour to be Opposition Leader, he was also a keen student of the patterned contours of history, who could see at a glance that those contours would have to be radically changed in the present, if he were to have the Prime Minister's job after only one term of the Howard Government. Clearly, he was up against it. In the previous eight decades, *no* Opposition Leader rising to the post straight after the election of a new Government had ever gone on to become Prime Minister, and he was an Opposition Leader taking the post after the worst result for his party in six decades. One had to go back to the administration formed by Labor's Jim Scullin — thrown out of office in 1931 at the height of the Depression — to find an Australian Government which the electorate had not granted at least two terms.

The portents were grim by any measure, and what it meant for Beazley was that his most likely fate was to find himself sacrificed after a term or two — as most other first-up Opposition Leaders had been — merely serving as a historical doormat for someone else to claim the ultimate prize. Breaking that pattern meant, as a bare minimum, that both he and his team had to learn a few things right off the bat and learn them well.

It is a part of the Westminster system that gets very little press, but just as a new Government must go on a very steep learning curve to understand how things operate, so too must the outgoing Government heading off into the wilderness of Opposition learn how to survive there. As many Labor parliamentarians soon found, the battalions of public servants whose sole job in life had been to facilitate the fulfillment of their desires had now all but disappeared, to be replaced by a veritable skeleton crew. This Labor rump had very few members who had any experience of being in Opposition, one of whom was Kim Jnr just as two decades earlier, when Labor had come into power under Whitlam, they had only two members who had any experience of being in Government 23 years previously — one of whom was Kim Snr. They would have to learn. Thus in the week preceding the formal opening of Parliament, the entire shadow ministry underwent a day-long seminar on the business of being the Opposition. Just what did they need to know?[168] Well, they were told by a series of parliamentary officers, things such as the information technology available to Opposition MPs, how to use the full resources of the Parliamentary Library, how to draft legislation as private members, and understand Opposition procedure in Parliament, etc. And the experts were flown in too. Experts in being in Opposition, like the South Australian State Labor leader, Mike Rann, who came all the way from Adelaide to give them the good oil on just how to make the most of limited opportunities. For men and women who had been running the show for that long, it was all somewhat galling.

'It didn't worry me as much as it worried a lot of our people, who were just demoralised,' recalls Beazley. 'For me it was just swings and roundabouts and while you had a heavy heart about it all, you knew you would be climbing back from the brink, because you also know the Liberals. You know that in the end the Liberals can't help themselves: they are narrow, they are bigoted, they are basically small-minded *Poujardists* when it is all boiled down to it, full of suburban cranks, small-minded Fascists.'* This sense that the Liberals were not in fact up to the role of governing the country was one that would sustain him, particularly in those difficult first few months. 'I don't mean to be terribly insulting but it is not the party it used to be,' he says. 'When Menzies had it, it was a classic, great, governing party, the broad-based Tory Party with a strong appeal to the working class. It had big-minded people, who had been coming through the ranks to be officers in World War II, who saw the good possibilities of government. That's why a bloke like Menzies could create Canberra, why Menzies could focus on universities. He was sort of a classic British Conservative. This current bunch is really narrow and poor-spirited and while there were a number of our people who thought it would be six years before we got back, I thought it would be a year or two.'

That said, he was still back in the seminar with the rest of them, learning how to be an effective Opposition, which of course had as its paramount requirement, an effective Opposition Leader. 'The Leader of the Opposition has possibly the most difficult job in the Parliament,' ran the official line. 'A minister must, of course, be thoroughly conversant with the details of bills or other matters which affect his own department, but the advice and resources of the departmental staff are constantly at his call. The Leader of the Opposition has to make himself master of all the business which comes before the House (not merely that of one or two departments); he has to do this at times at short notice and under constant pressure; and he gets no help from permanent officials. At all times he is the spokesman for those who are critical of or opposed to the Government, and he must be unceasingly vigilant and active.'[169] For all his optimism about winning the next election, settling in to the Opposition Leader's job would take some time. Time, essentially, that

---

* Pierre Poujard was a French bookseller who, according to the Barry Jones' *Dictionary of World Biography*, 'in 1953–54 organised a tax revolt by small businessmen and, in 1956, 52 Poujardist deputies were elected to the National Assembly (with 12 per cent of the vote) on a policy proposing tax cuts, regionalism and vaguely Fascist social policies . . . '

Beazley could never find quite enough of in his new role. 'What I found hard is the sudden massive increase in the demands on you,' he says. 'Basically you are your party's cheerleader and you have got to get around all sections of it, you have to be constantly travelling. I thought I did that as a minister but I didn't know the half of it.'

Bill Hayden had made a remark many years before, at a time before he took the post, to the effect that 'to be Leader of the Opposition you'd have to almost totally destroy your family life. I'm not prepared to do that ...'[170] While that clearly did not happen to the new Opposition Leader, he would come to know what Hayden meant. For inevitably, as always, in the eternal juggling of commitments that was his life, it was time with his own family that suffered most. In his first ten months as Opposition Leader he spent just over one night in ten at home in his own bed in Perth — his worst record in his entire parliamentary career — something that appalled him. While sheer pleasure for him was simply to be at home, dividing his time between his wife and his daughters, pool, books, beach and backyard, there was too little time to do it. On those occasions when he was home, beyond Susie, Jessica, Hannah and Rachel he would also spend time with his parents and with younger brother David, who remained at home with them. Kim and Betty Beazley, by this stage of Kim's life, were not the kind who placed enormous demands on his time. As Susie Annus recounts, 'they have this notion that he is involved in "higher things" and more important things and that they won't call on his time to any great extent'.

With perhaps that in mind, they came at their eldest son in a rather roundabout fashion. If perchance Betty Beazley needed to talk to him, she would call Susie's mother who would call Susie with a message to ask Kim to call his mother when he got a moment. Anything not to impinge. Not on Kim, and as little as possible on Susie.

His two eldest daughters had known what to expect, having been raised already as the children of a particularly busy politician, and they coped in their own fashion. For both — now university students — it was not simply a case of organising their lives to get as much time with their father as they could, but also organising to put as little needless strain on him as possible. 'The thing about being a politician's daughter,' Jessica says, 'is that you actually have to protect the politician from what goes on. When I found a lump in my breast, I was hysterical. My boyfriend was there to support me and Mum and Susie were on the phone — Susie got an appointment for me at the doctor and Mum took me straight away — but it wasn't until Dad got home about three or four days later, and everything was fine, that we actually told him what I had been through. He was completely shocked, he was upset, he needed reassurance that everything was alright, he needed reassurance that everything was checked. He was worried and he kept coming up to me that weekend and patting me "are you alright?", "are you alright?", "how are you going?". You know everything is fine, but this is what you have to do when you are in a family of politicians. You have to protect *them* sometimes from the reality of the situation, you have to go past the reality and *then* tell them what happened so they are not actually *in the reality* — it is easier for them to cope with.' That, Hannah agrees, is just the way it must be.

'You ignore everyday problems, you don't tell him because he has too much to deal with already but we learn to live with it by ourselves and if everything turns out right then we tell him, and if it doesn't turn out right then we take more time to sort it out ... before telling him.'

Rachel also learnt to cope with her father's increased absence the best she could, the same way her father and his siblings had when they were young; the same way her older sisters had. At least for Rachel though, she had the advantage of regularly being able to see her father on television, and not just to hear his voice over the phone. Many an afternoon when Parliament was in session the five year old would find it intriguing to watch the ABC broadcasts of the same, and see her father in action — trying the best she could to wrap her young mind around what he was actually doing. On occasion she would clearly see her father upset with the bespectacled man opposite who she knew was called 'Mr Howard'. 'Doesn't Daddy like Mr Howard?' she asked on one occasion, when the exchange seemed particularly bitter. In reply her mother pushed the same theme she and Kim had agreed on, that while the exchanges *could* be bitter, it was nothing personal.

'No sweetheart, Daddy does like Mr Howard,' her mother replied, 'it's just that Daddy has different ideas, Daddy doesn't like Mr Howard's *ideas*.'

This set off a whole line of questioning in following months whenever a visitor would come to the house of 'Does Daddy like *his* ideas?' On another occasion soon afterwards, when she had started to grasp the concept of 'Prime Minister', and had perhaps heard people say that her father was going to grasp that mantle himself, she proudly proclaimed to her mother that 'Kim Beazley is the Prime Minister!'

'No, sweetheart, Daddy is not the Prime Minister.'

'Well who is?'

'Mr Howard is, darling.'

Rachel looked at her mother and looked at the TV and then once again at her mother before replying, 'Mummy, why didn't you marry Mr Howard?'

In the early months of the Howard Government the man doing most of the shouting at Kim Beazley was not Mr Howard at all, but his Treasurer, Peter Costello. He shouted primarily about the 'Beazley eight billion dollar black hole'. It was a reference to the shortfall between what the Government had spent in the previous financial year and what it had gathered in revenue, and whenever the Opposition made any complaint whatsoever about any stringent Howard Government cost-cutting measure, the Treasurer would — with great theatricality and no little force — wag a finger at Kim Beazley sitting opposite and roar that the Opposition had '*No right*' to criticise when all the Government was doing was trying to make up for the eight billion dollars lost through the Opposition Leader's ineptitude.

As the *Sydney Morning Herald* editorial noted, late in May of 1996: 'Mr Costello has been able to use the bogy of "Beazley's 8 billion dollar black hole" to create an atmosphere of fiscal crisis to condition the public and, more importantly perhaps, his ministerial colleagues, to accept massive spending cuts in his first budget in August.' While this was fine for Mr Costello, Mr Beazley found it more than somewhat irksome. 'There are things in politics which are half-right,' he says, 'things in politics which are right and things in politics which are completely bogus — that is completely bogus. For starters, does anybody in this country, historically or now describe the last two budgets as the [new Finance Minister] John Fahey budgets?'

Beazley's contention was that as the budget came from the Treasury and not the Finance Ministry, it was a bit much to blame the eight billion dollar shortfall on him simply because he was now the Opposition Leader. 'The second point is we in Finance didn't know what the fiscal position was. We did not do repeated analyses of these for the simple reason that it changes by a couple of billion dollars every time you look at it. They are just best estimates and what you are talking about is a budget of 140 billion dollars, and when you are trying to predict three or four years in advance, your estimates are always going to be off, here and there so you don't just keep doing it. You do a couple of points during the course of the year and then you just leave it at that. Now you could if you wanted to go to Treasury and ask what their latest estimate was, but we didn't do that. This is all in contrast to John Howard. John Howard the week before the 1983 election asked for what the figure was going to be from John Stone and John Stone told him that the budget was going to go out — in today's dollar terms — at a 25 billion dollar deficit and John Howard concealed it from the electorate which Kim Beazley did not, he didn't have a figure!'

To paraphrase Peter Costello though, the question was *Why the hell didn't he?* 'Well, we didn't ask for one,' says Beazley, 'and we didn't ask basically because we had been arguing the line that when you do ask for a figure like that you present it and we said there were a couple of stages during the course of the year when we do make those statements. One is the budget and another is around about Christmas, but the point about that is that no Government can put in place forward estimates. Howard argued against putting in place forward estimates when he was Treasurer.' Against the constant attacks of Costello in particular, and to a lesser extent those of the Prime Minister, Kim Beazley essentially gave as good as he got, but the perception in the public mind was that he had made very little impact on the Government. In the words of one Canberra gallery journalist, 'he really spent the first year as Opposition Leader *not* being Paul Keating'. For some this was a plus, for others a negative, but the upshot of his first year in the job was that he looked to be a long way from the man who would be Prime Minister of the country at the next Federal election. It was a perception shared by politicians, public and press alike ...

One morning late in 1996, Fairfax journalist Mike Seccombe spied Senators Robert Ray and John Faulkner in the courtyard opposite Ozzie's Café in Parliament House, and went over to say hello. After greeting them, he looked down to see that there was a third man there, sitting down with his back to him — the Opposition Leader. 'Oh, sorry Kim, I didn't notice you there,' said Seccombe.

'No-one does,' replied Beazley a little morosely.

The opinion polls for Beazley published around that time had indeed been ordinary. John Howard's honeymoon with the Australian electorate had still not finished, and it had to be said that Kim Beazley had made very little progress in romancing the people meantime. In the course of the next 12 months or so though, that began to change as various events not only galvanised his own spirit, but also induced the Australian public to reappraise him as a possible Prime Minister.

The first came with the visit to Australian shores of the American President, Bill Clinton. In late November of 1996, fresh from winning his second term in office, Beazley's fellow Rhodes scholar — although Clinton had not completed his studies at Oxford — journeyed to Australia with his wife for a four-day sojourn of business and pleasure, which included a welcoming luncheon for 600 people in the Great Hall of the Parliament. In welcome, Prime Minister John Howard made what the critics later panned as a particularly pedestrian speech, well across the borderline of banal. 'Our relationship is a very deep and rich one,' the Prime Minister had said. 'It's a relationship that is forged on the basis of many common values, many common elements of our history, our common service on the battlefields of the world in the defence of liberty and defence of freedom ... But as Dr Johnson reminded us, we should always keep our relationships in good repair and never take [them] for granted. We should always work on them, nurture them and water them ...'

Etc ... etc ... etc ... etc ...

Beazley in reply made an essentially off-the-cuff speech from a few notes he'd jotted down the previous day, and rocked the room back in its collective chair. It was personable, had a sense of occasion, and clearly hit the mark. After pointedly also welcoming Hillary Clinton, whom the Prime Minister had ignored, he moved into the main body of his speech, drawing on his own deep knowledge of American politics and history.

'I want to congratulate you on that election victory. I always like to see a fellow win an election. It's a delight for those of us in Opposition to think that these things can occur from time to time. It was a historic one, indeed. Looking back, you are the only southern Democrat since Appomattox to win a second term. And I don't mention Appomattox in a gratuitous fashion here at all. It was a defining moment for the modern American nation, the event which underwrote America's role in the twentieth century ...

'There's another reason I want to mention Appomattox, and note your status as the most successful southern Democratic candidate for President since then. The way in which you reached out to all Americans of all ethnic, racial, cultural and religious backgrounds, and included them in your vision of the United States, is an inspiration to us all ...' He concluded: 'I think you've got quite a story to tell in this country. But don't tell it for too long — get out on the beaches, get out on the golf courses. Get out snorkelling, and have a terrific time here.' Beazley sat down to thunderous applause from the assembled guests, as well as warm nods of appreciation from the American President and his wife.

'It was a great speech,' notes Bob McMullan, who was there for the occasion, 'which caught the attention of the elite, and that is important because it is the elite who communicate their opinion to others. It showed he had absolute dominance as an individual and as a person of international stature, leadership — compared to Howard.'

Lest that be viewed as simply a partisan pump-up, even so often acerbic a critic as Alan Ramsey noted the speech as a turning point for Beazley. Ramsey was a member of the elite of which McMullan spoke, and was positively warm in his acclaim: 'For perhaps five minutes on Wednesday, Beazley looked and sounded more like a leader than in all the eight months since he replaced Paul Keating. It was a single speech, about 600 words. Yet it was a speech that did more for Beazley than maybe all the rest of the Clintons' visit did for the Prime Minister ...

'Beazley's speech was everything Howard's wasn't: warm, humorous, self-deprecating, erudite, even passionate ...

'It wasn't only what he said but the way he said it. Beazley has come to terms with Labor's defeat. He has settled in the Labor leadership. He is now emerging in his own right from the Hawke and Keating legacies of egomania. He knows it will be a long slog. He is starting to behave as a leader at ease with himself and his life, at least until the next election. He could, after all, be a very formidable opponent.' Clinton too, was clearly impressed. When Merrilyn Wasson was introduced to him in a parliamentary corridor shortly after the function had concluded, she remembers the American President leaning close to her and saying, 'Your brother can really, really *speak!*'

Susie Annus noticed the difference in the way people treated her husband almost immediately afterwards. 'I think to that point,' she says, 'most people thought he was a stop-gap leader, that he was there only till Labor could find someone better, but after that speech it changed. People in the party and in the media saw him really shine in that particular forum, and were really impressed. I've probably seen Gough Whitlam, three or four times since then, and each time he says, "that speech ... that day ..." It made a difference.'

If the Clinton speech caught the attention of the 'elite', as McMullan says, it was Beazley's budget reply speech five months later which made a wider impression on the populace at large. The

Opposition Leader took direct aim at what he saw as the inequities of the Government's budget, which most notably had all but dismantled the superannuation contribution scheme which had been set up by the Hawke and Keating governments. Beazley contended that their changes would cost the average Australian worker 110 000 dollars in the lump sum they would receive on retirement. He also took a shot at their announcement of a one billion dollar Federation Fund to go into the infrastructure of the country as well as to go into celebrating the coming centenary of Federation. 'This budget rips off low-income and middle-income earners to fund the Coalition's extravagances and indulgences. How else can you describe the Federation slush fund? People should realise this slush fund is being paid for by their stolen $3.7 billion super contributions, and by increased charges they'll be paying at the chemist and for child care. No money for old people's proper medicine, but a billion dollars for obelisks, fireworks and centennial champagne. This budget is about the welfare of the Liberal Party and not the welfare of ordinary Australians. This is a Sheriff of Nottingham Budget. A budget for the few — and for the very few.'

He also took aim at the Howard Government's record on unemployment, and their sunny predictions that it would fall in the coming financial year. 'Claims of better economic prospects next year do not change the fact that the Government has caused the economy to grow too slowly and, as a result, thousands of Australians are needlessly unemployed,' he said. 'The Government's dismal record in office does not generate confidence that it can deliver on the slightly stronger growth forecasts in the budget. Australians were promised certainty, security, and most importantly, leadership. The Government hasn't delivered on any of these. Rather they have delivered uncertainty, insecurity and indecisiveness and across the country, a mood of quiet anger and frustration.' Again, it wasn't just what he said, it was the way that he said it, and the speech was particularly well received. Michael Lee, the Member for Dobell, remembered the effect in his own electorate — the most marginal Labor seat in the country — as being quite electric. 'It really resonated with the Labor supporters,' he says, 'and got the biggest reaction to that kind of speech that I can remember. All the branch members were enthused by it, and talking about it, they all loved the "Sheriff of Nottingham" line particularly. It was an authoritative, powerful, authentic Labor speech.' Which is how Beazley would like to think of it. 'That speech,' he says, 'was an absolutely rock-rib traditional Labor Party speech, on absolutely straight down the line traditional Labor issues, and I was happy with it.'

So were the voters, or so it seemed. The following day, the Beazley travelling caravan pulled into Melbourne for the day. After an interview in a radio station, they had emerged to find a posse of media waiting for them, and as the Opposition Leader was doing a 'doorstop' on the steps of the building, lots of heads began appearing in the windows above, watching proceedings. 'As soon as the doorstop was finished,' John Flannery, one of his advisers, recalls, 'and [when] we were heading back towards the car there was unprovoked applause and yelling from the windows with people saying "Good on ya Kim", "great speech last night", "you've given us all hope".

'It was around the same time, that people started coming up to Kim and talking to him. In the first six to eight months of being in Opposition he could walk through airports as if he was Joe Blow from the bush and no-one knew who he was, or didn't want to know him, and engaged in conversation amongst themselves rather than acknowledge Kim's presence. But now people began to go out of their way to come over and shake Kim's hand and say "you're doing a good job mate, and things are looking better for you, and we know what you are saying, and we agree with you".'

Another politician who clearly agreed with the thrust of what Beazley had to say was the leader of the Australian Democrats, Senator Cheryl Kernot. In her own budget reply speech in the Senate on the same night as Beazley's, she took aim at the same central targets. 'The Budget completely fails the test on jobs,' she said, while also nominating the Federation Fund as a 'total sham'. Beazley and Kernot had always got on well, notwithstanding the fact that in the previous few months the political pundits had occasionally said she was the *real* Opposition Leader, so invisible had Beazley seemed — and it was only after their dual attack on the Howard Government that he first got wind from Gareth Evans that there was actually the smallest of all small chances that Evans and Senator John Faulkner could convince Senator Kernot to defect from the Democrats and come across to the Labor Party. It was close to the most unheard of thing Beazley had ever heard of, and he was careful not to get his hopes up, being as he remembers, 'sceptical that she would do it'. Still, as Gareth Evans recollects, 'everything in his reaction was positive, there was not a hint of jealously, anxiety or anything other than "this is terrific", and how to make it work'. Beazley also agreed with Evans that it would not be appropriate for him to come in on any of their talks. Kernot was nowhere near to being over the line yet and it would place her in a very awkward position in her future wrangles with the Labor leader if at one time she had talked openly to him about the possibility of her coming to Labor. The thing that was driving Kernot, Evans told him, was the desire to do something to stop what she saw as the colossal damage being done to the country by the Howard Government, and it was her feeling that if she could combine forces with Labor, then there would be a better chance of being able to do something. Beazley at this time was gripped by a similar emotion.

Towards the middle of 1997, he had felt a growing anger towards the approach taken by the Howard Government — most particularly on issues concerning race. One seminal exchange with the Prime Minister in Parliament on 13 May, concerned Pauline Hanson — the Independent Member for Oxley, and leader of the One Nation Party, whose notably simplistic but explosive views had for many, rightly or wrongly, become synonymous with racism.

Kim Beazley: 'My question is to the Prime Minister. The Prime Minister would be aware that today I followed up earlier statements by the National Secretary of the Labor Party that Labor preferences at the next election would not be distributed to the One Nation Party ahead of those for the Liberal and National Party candidates. Will the Prime Minister now join with me and give the same undertaking with respect to the ALP on behalf of the Coalition parties?

John Howard: 'No . . .'

There would be many similar exchanges between the two over the next few days, and indeed over the next months, but the upshot was the same. The Opposition's attempts to resolve the Hanson problem in this manner — or at least to attach a specific sunset clause to it — were rebuffed at the time. In so doing, John Howard had lost Beazley for good.

Beazley had felt an initial surge of anger on the issue the previous year after a speech made by the Prime Minister in Queensland was widely reported. It was at a time when the Prime Minister was under pressure to publicly tear down Hanson as the leader of One Nation, but he had instead rather carefully noted that all Australians had a right to 'free speech'. The Prime Minister had not actually mentioned Hanson specifically at all, but in the eyes of the Leader of the Opposition, he hadn't needed to. 'I was galvanised by John Howard's speech,' Beazley remembers, 'full of self-righteous blah, having had his office first phone Hanson to let her know they were doing it. This country has *always* had freedom of speech, it's got nothing to do with freedom of speech and everything to do with Hanson. That really cheesed me off, because it was just sheer subliminal encouragement to Pauline Hanson, from which, as a country, we've been trying to recover ever since. He went as far as any person could conceivably go, to let all the racist dogs, racial dogs of war loose.'

For all Beazley's vociferous criticism of Howard on this subject though, he too was criticised as Opposition Leader for playing his cards carefully on the electorally explosive issue, and not taking a hard-enough line against Hanson. 'I have been subject to very little unjustified criticism,' he says in reply. 'Most of the criticism I have seen on me from time to time is pretty just, but that charge was complete unutterable bullshit, *complete* unutterable bullshit. The press used to say I was soft on Hanson, and in frustration what I used to get my office staff to do, was to get transcripts of my "doorstop interviews" and all my appearances on talkback radio — none of which had made it into the newspapers — and dump it on their blinking tables. Every time one of those journalists said I was "soft on Hanson", they got a telephone book's worth of transcripts to show I wasn't!'

The other great issue of the time, not unrelated to Hanson's rise in popularity, arose from the Australian High Court's Mabo decision in 1992 and Wik decision in 1996 to recognise the land rights of indigenous Australians. They were decisions that, at least in the first instance, had not gone down well with the broad mass of middle Australia. Substantial political research had shown that one reason Paul Keating had fared so badly in the 1996 election was because as Prime Minister he had totally supported the High Court decision, bringing in the Native Title Act which provided the mechanism whereby those rights could be recognised formally. In reply, John Howard had developed a 'Ten Point Plan', which he aimed to enshrine in legislation and which, if passed, would substantially have repealed those native title rights. Beazley remained a fierce critic and passionate opponent of both the proposed legislation, and the 'Ten Point Plan' which had guided it.

'Of all the things this country has faced in recent times,' he says, 'the native title issue has the greatest potential to be a national tragedy in the making. That is not just simply in terms of the presentation of this country internationally and the coherence of our society domestically, but it also has the capacity, because of the blindness of the Howard Government, to actually do material damage to the economic development of the country. Native title won't go away, no matter how unfair your legislation is — people will merely choose to pursue their objectives in other ways and if they choose to pursue their objectives by moving outside the Native Title Act and go to common law, the potential is there for major disruption to our minerals industry in particular and to a lesser extent to the agricultural industries and pastoral industries.'

In Beazley's eyes at least, Prime Minister Howard was directly culpable. 'Howard has used the issue narrowly, electorally, that has basically been his objective. He has sought to engender a fear and concern in the pastoral community and the community generally, but particularly the pastoral community and the miners and then say only his solution is possible and to try and lock them in by a process of arguing, "either you agree with us or not, you can't go against the Government", "I am really in your corner", and what he is actually getting them to do is to act against their own interests.' Beazley's contention to the Labor Party was that even if the Liberals were successful at the polls in playing that political game, it would still be to their ultimate cost. 'Even if they win, they will then govern without legitimacy. It would be for the Howard Government what the 1975 coup was for Fraser. The Fraser Government struggled for legitimacy between 1975 and 1983, and I think from that if the Howard Government wins a [race] election, in the minds of an awful lot of people in the Australian public they will struggle for legitimacy.'

His eldest daughter, Jessica, noticed a change in her father's whole approach because of the strength of his feelings on the issue. 'I don't think it was actually up until the whole Aboriginal thing and Pauline Hanson,' she says, 'that he actually truly got angry, and with that anger his whole approach changed. He really began to go after the Government on all fronts.'

'There was a time,' Beazley concedes, looking back upon it, 'when I could take or leave the job of Opposition Leader, but I couldn't do that now because I have a consciousness of what I think is the damage done to this country by the Howard Government, and a strong belief that we can win the next one and we have got to get on with it.' In this he was possibly reminiscent of what Gough Whitlam had once said about his own initial nemesis: 'The destruction of the Gorton Government has now become a patriotic duty.'[171]

After the Prime Minister's refusal to guarantee that the Liberals would put Ms Hanson last on their ticket, it meant that by the beginning of winter 1997, Kim Beazley felt much the same as Whitlam had about Gorton. Back in his office, his staff also noticed a distinct change in the Opposition Leader's approach at around this time. 'It lifted him out of the "ho-hum I suppose somebody has to do it", frame of mind,' his senior media adviser, Greg Turnbull says. 'All of the Hanson/Howard stuff began to build up a catalogue of anger and indignation in Kim's otherwise placid, gentle and always decent personality, where he basically said "I want to *do* this bloke".'

Allied with it all was the clear ending of John Howard's political honeymoon. Poll after poll in the middle of 1997 showed the Prime Minister's popularity falling, while the Opposition Leader's was slowly starting to rise. For Beazley's family, there seemed to be the distinct if still distant possibility that he might become Prime Minister as early as the next election. Back in Perth, his older daughters would often teasingly tell him how much they were looking forward to spending the Christmas after next in Kirribilli House, how it would be lovely to sunbake on the expansive lawns while looking down over Sydney Harbour. 'But Dad would always just laugh and change the subject,' Jessica remembers, 'it was like he never wanted to get either our hopes or his hopes up.' Another possible reason is that their father is far from an admirer of the whole idea of Kirribilli House. 'I think it is a useless extravagance,' he says, 'and always has been. It was bought by Menzies to have a place to host foreign dignitaries, but I think in its whole history it's only had two foreign dignitaries stay there, and that's Prince Charles and Tony Blair. It's a very good thing for the National Trust, but it's not a thing a Prime Minister should have, because basically the Prime Minister belongs in Canberra.'

Occasionally in the course of Beazley's first two years as Opposition Leader, there would come reminders of just how good it would be if he actually were the Prime Minister of his country. One such occasion came in late July of 1997 when, on a trip to Britain, he and Susie were invited by his old *compadre* Tony Blair to spend the day with him at the British Prime Minister's country residence, Chequers — a rough equivalent of Kirribilli House. The two talked long and hard about electoral tactics, and just how Blair had managed to achieve the stunning victory of three months previously, when the British Labour Party had reduced the Conservatives to their lowest vote in 165 years.

It was a 'working lunch', but with a twist. 'There was nothing formal about it,' Beazley recalls. 'This is a guy I went to university with, you can't treat them the same way as you do another political leader, even if you are getting on well with them the first time you meet them. I will know this guy after we are both out of politics, and I knew him for ages before.' With such a long friendship behind them, the two on this particular day did what they usually did, in discussing all kinds of non-political things — each other's families, the travails of the British Royal family, the cricket — before getting to more substantive issues. 'I was just picking his brains of all the things he was doing in Government,' Beazley recounts, 'and he wanted to talk to me a bit about the conversations I would be having with some of his folk that week, suggesting things I might talk to them about, like on employment programmes and higher education charters, that sort of thing.' Such 'folk' were in fact Blair's most influential Cabinet ministers, ones that the British PM had arranged for Beazley to see, so there could be an exchange of ideas between the two like-minded parties. They included Peter Mandolson, the mastermind of British Labour's victorious election campaign, Deputy Prime Minister John Prescott, Treasurer Gordon Brown, Foreign Secretary Robin Cook and Defence Minister George Robertson.

'Tony was basically saying,' Beazley comments, '"please tell as much as you can to these folk about your experiences with these various portfolios, as we need to think these things through".' When the time came to return to London, the British Prime Minister walked them out to the waiting car. 'It was late July, on this beautiful day,' says Beazley, 'and we walk out and there's this beautiful vista of these rolling green fields, beautiful thirteenth-century house behind it, and Tony turns to me and says "Kim, I cannot *believe* that I'm Prime Minister of Britain". I thought it was a great line. I was thinking that in the same situation I would probably walk out of the Lodge and say the same thing to any friend of mine who might be walking past.'

In the following week in London, Beazley did confer at length with the aforementioned Cabinet ministers, as well as going to see Blair's public relations expert Phillip Gould — a man credited with helping to shape the whole New Labour image — and was given the good oil about what he most urgently had to do to heighten his own electoral chances. 'He told me to lose weight and to be less long-winded in my sentences,' Beazley explains. 'And I thought he was probably right ...' (Not that he would necessarily do anything particular about the weight part of it, other than continue his reasonably regular exercise doing laps in handy swimming pools whenever he could. 'Kim's view,' Susie Annus explains, 'is that the rest of his life is so hard and disciplined, that eating is the one area where he can let himself go a bit, and it's really no-one else's business but his own.')

One result of such meetings was that Beazley returned to Australia with a different perception of how to tackle the whole role of Opposition. 'I started off with a conception of Opposition, which was Gough Whitlam's conception of Opposition,' Beazley says, 'but after that trip to Britain my view began to change. Gough changed the Labor Party's structure to put in place a Shadow Cabinet, so he could get control of things like the presentation of foreign policy, so that while Jim Cairns and Tom Uren were out there leading the moratorium, people would not think that *that* was representative of the Labor Party policy as opposed to their personal convictions. There's a risk now though that you sideline your people into areas of policy which, though important, are of marginal interest to the electorate. Instead we have to look at the front bench, not quite as an alternative government, but more as a campaign structure, as a bunch of communicators strategising on electoral factors. That's how the British Labour Party uses its front bench, and I think we have to think again about how our front bench operates.'

In terms of how Beazley himself ran that front bench, there was a clear difference remarked by his colleagues, in the way he did it, to the way his two predecessors had done it.

'Hawke was Chairman of the Board, Keating was Leader of the Pack,' says Senator Peter Cook, who served under both men. 'Hawke's thing was for everyone to be in the debate, everyone would contribute, he would summarise, that would become the decision. And in the summary he would pick up little bits from everyone and knit the consensus together, and he would include enough of his own values so that you had an idea of what the Prime Ministerial mind thought about it. Keating came in and said, "I'm not going to do it" [that crappy Hawke way], and he would say, "This is what I think. You can disagree with me, folks" — and again he would accept change — if someone came up with a convincing argument. Whereas Kim is not so easy to categorise. He doesn't fall easily into either of those categories. It involves both styles and it does engage everybody, it's not aloof, it's part of the team. He does speak his mind quite directly, he may not be the first to voice his opinion, he listens to everyone, but when he does speak, that's what settles the question. The important distinction is that he speaks to a general strategy for where he wants to steer the Labor Party, and he judges those decisions against that strategy.' Leo

McLeay agrees with that central analysis: 'Kim's more a consensus person, but in the end, whereas Hawke tended to sort of go with whatever he thought the play was, Kim has opinions and ideas, and wants to get them up, so still provides a direction.'

Even as Beazley began to get into the rhythm of the role, he still found being in Opposition far from easy. 'One of the difficult things about Opposition is that there is nothing that necessarily naturally suggests itself to you,' he says. 'You have got to be thinking all the time, but then your point of activity stops at the exposition of the policy. There is no implementation whatsoever. The truth of the matter is that an awful lot of what really works is unsaleable from Opposition and you actually have to be in Government to get it through and get it operating. For example, I don't think from Opposition you could have suggested that the way to expand university places and give a real chance for working class kids and regional kids to get to university was by introducing the Higher Education Contribution Scheme charges. Because what that would actually mean is that you would be going into a poll telling people they have got to pay a lot of money for their university education which is not a vote-winner on the whole. Get yourself an idea like that in Opposition and you stay in Opposition. When you are in Government you can actually do a few things. It is not the policy so much, because you can do that in Opposition too, it is implementation, it is the routine of actually getting the bricks and mortar in place that provides the thrill.'

On the morning of 3 October, 1997, Beazley was on his way to get a haircut. Several years earlier, Syd Hickman had *insisted* that he discontinue getting his hair done by the local butcher, and had instead found him a Polish hairdresser in Belconnen considered good enough to judge Australian hairdressing competitions. Though it went against the grain to drive as long as 15 minutes from his appointed course straight to Parliament House, he had promised Syd he would and that was that. He had two things on his mind that morning. First the meeting which had been held two nights previously in Senator John Faulkner's office, where Cheryl Kernot had formally committed herself to leaving her position as Leader of the Democrats, to join the Labor Party. The other thing was the 'Travel Rorts' Affair of previous days, where it had been established that several parliamentarians had been claiming expenses for travel and accommodation to which they were not in fact entitled. The Government had already had three ministers resign over the affair, and though Labor had itself come under notable attack — with Peter Costello particularly savaging the Labor Senator from Tasmania, Nick Sherry — Beazley was framing his own *counter-counter-attack* which would have embroiled another three Liberal ministers, two of them heavyweights, in having to explain their own dubious travel claims. Bobbing along through the morning traffic, he rang into the office to check what was happening around the joint, only to find a suddenly choked up Greg Turnbull with appalling news.

'We have got a note here which some people feel may be a suicide note from Nick Sherry which he left with AAP,' Turnbull told him. Beazley could scarcely believe what he was hearing. After all, he had had dinner with Sherry only the night before — at the Tang Dynasty restaurant in Kingston after the Kernot meeting had broken up — and though the Tasmanian had seemed a tad subdued after bearing the brunt of the Government's attacks in previous days, he had not remotely resembled someone considering taking his own life.

Things moved quickly from there. By the time Beazley got back to the office, others of his staff had established that Sherry was not answering his phone, had not caught his scheduled flight home, had not been sighted at any other likely haunts that morning. Beazley's chief-of-staff David Epstein was even then pounding on Sherry's door trying to get a response, with no luck, and all in the office were trying to grapple with the dreadful truth. Senator Nick Sherry was quite possibly ... *dead*. 'It was terrifying, absolutely terrifying,' Beazley recalls. 'I read the note and looked at the time lines and when David couldn't rouse him, I thought he was dead — for a period of time we all assumed he was dead.' Then the call. Summoned by the diminutive Epstein — who was never going to be able to break down the door himself — the police had arrived to break in. They had found the Senator with his wrists slit, but alive. 'I'll never forget the massive, palpable relief,' Beazley says, 'when the police burst in and found him unconscious.'

In the time between the news of the suicide breaking, and Beazley holding a press conference, the Opposition Leader had been touched to take one call from a Liberal minister, in tears, wanting to know news of the state of Sherry, and Beazley had taken his cue accordingly. This was not a time for cheap political point-scoring and in a move that he was highly lauded for afterwards, Beazley declined to score even a single point in that regard. To the contrary, he effectively publicly absolved Peter Costello from all blame, noting that a part of politics was holding the other side accountable for their actions and that the Treasurer had committed no fault in being hard on Sherry. 'I know a little bit about suicide,' Beazley says of the approach he took on that occasion, 'and though it has not touched me directly in my family, other people whom I have known have killed themselves and you know there aren't single causes, that they are always a product of a whole variety of difficulties. So to have gone and ascribed a single cause would have been wrong. It *is* right in politics that we hold each other accountable and we should not be checked or held back by the prospect that somebody might damage themselves. I was also tremendously conscious about the unfairness of the way in which Carmen Lawrence had been treated on the suicide of Penny Easton — so I didn't want to be associated with that level of unfairness.' He wasn't. And again he grew in stature, most particularly with the elite, because of it.

Prime Minister Howard did not take the same approach. Three days later on Channel Nine's *Today* programme, Howard was scathing about Beazley's role in the Travel Rorts Affair generally, and critical that he had not sacked Sherry. 'I was prepared to take action in relation to the people in my team; Kim Beazley wasn't,' the Prime Minister said. 'Because of the unfortunate events affecting Nick Sherry — of course I don't want to dwell unduly on his personal position — but the fact remains that when the crunch came, the heat was on, Kim Beazley didn't have the guts to impose the standards that I had the guts to impose on my team.'

In turn, Beazley was scathing in his reply, stating that the Prime Minister was 'a desperate man lashing out ... He is just not up to the job. There may be a new ministry, but it still lacks a leader'. Such a strong exchange of words notwithstanding, the Travel Rorts Affair was effectively over, with both sides shelving their remaining bombs, and Beazley never did name the three Liberal ministers he had targeted.

A little over a week later, on a Saturday morning in mid-October, 1997, Bob Hawke picked up the phone in his home on Sydney's North Shore to hear Beazley on the other end of the line. The two had remained close despite Hawke's political retirement, so it was no surprise to hear from him, although what did surprise him was Beazley's tone on this occasion. In the wake of the Sherry Affair, Hawke had expected him to be way down in the doldrums, yet as the former Prime Minister recounts, 'In the course of the conversation he said "I am going to win the next election".' Hawke was quite amazed to hear such confidence from his famously worry-wart friend — but didn't press him on it. When Blanche d'Alpuget returned from shopping later on though, he talked it over with her. 'The best thing that has happened today,' he said 'was talking to this professional pessimist who says he is going to win the next election!' It was only on the Monday that he realised the source of the Opposition Leader's sudden surge of optimism, for in a follow-up phone call Beazley told him the extraordinary news. It had only just formally been tied up, which is why Kim had not mentioned it to him before, but Cheryl Kernot was about to publicly jump ship and join the Australian Labor Party! She would leave the Senate immediately, but would stand in the Queensland seat of Dickson in the next election.

This sensational development was — as Beazley thought then, and the pundits agreed — something that could turn the entire election. Its immense significance, even in the context of the near-century of Australia's vibrant Federal politics, was such that it was almost right up there with the celebrated and crucially important defections of Billy Hughes and his followers in 1917 and Joe Lyons and his group in 1931 — both from Labor. The Kernot deal had been set up over the previous three months, most notably by Senator John Faulkner and Gareth Evans, as well as by the ALP National Secretary, Gary Gray — although according to Beazley, Paul Keating had been mooting the possibility from as long ago as 1994. (The irony of the Leader of the Democrats throwing such a lifeline to Beazley's chances to secure victory was that one of the reasons he had nearly lost his own seat in the last election was because the Democrats, with Kernot's blessing, had steered their preferences away from him.)

Beazley had not had a large role in the negotiations with Kernot, and if anything he had been doing everything *but* push her to sign on the dotted line. 'I definitely wanted her to do it,' he notes, 'but for me it was a worry, because I thought she was giving up too much. She had honour as the leader of a political party; she was already making a major contribution to politics, and she was still short of the full 50 per cent pension-for-life you get after eight years in Parliament. If she left politics at that point, then she wouldn't qualify for a pension and that is very important to politicians because, contrary to the general impression, all our salary goes on our job — politicians save nothing. So I was worried by all these things. I was just worried for her that she was jumping off a cliff and imposing an enormous sense of responsibility on me and the others down there to catch her. Really, she was jumping into the unknown; you can't guarantee anything about the Labor Party or the electoral process and here she was leaving all her security behind and her friends to make this gesture against Howard.'

Kernot remembers her conversations with Beazley proceeding along much the same lines.

'Kim pointed out to me what I was giving up by doing this, financially and otherwise, and wanted to be absolutely sure that I appreciated all that. He was very, very concerned that I'd thought everything through before taking such a big step. He was very welcoming to me, and keen to have me in the Labor Party, particularly coming from the Queensland part of it. He's got a generosity of spirit, which always reminds me of my husband. 'I said "yes, Kim, I have thought it through", I feel like I just can't stay for the money. I either have to go from politics or I have to join Labor and be part of the fight, but I can't stay — I feel very, very uncomfortable where I am. I have to come over.'

Kernot's defection from the Democrats to Labor was the biggest political story since Paul Keating had taken the Prime Ministership from Bob Hawke, and really did change the equation to the point where after all known facts were factored into the left-hand side of the equation, it now read on the right-hand side of the equal sign: 'Labor victory now *possible*.' Prime Minister Howard's main retort to the move was aimed squarely at both Kernot and Beazley. Senator Kernot's decision, he said, was 'all about Cheryl Kernot's personal ambition, nothing else'. She had done what she did, the Prime Minister said, because she 'senses a leadership vacuum in the Labor Party and she wants to fill it'.* Beazley could afford to suffer a few such slings and arrows because he was feeling extremely good about the way it had all

---

* Whatever the truth of that assertion, Beazley for his part did not necessarily discourage any of Kernot's hopes that she might harbour about one day leading the Labor Party. At a later point, when Kernot was being savaged by the media after she had in turn savaged them over their coverage of a truck crashing into her Brisbane home, she had shared her angst with Beazley. 'I said to him,' she recalls, "I just can't understand this media hype they're going on with".'
'I can,' Beazley replied. 'There's a deep level of fascination because they think you at least have a chance of being the first woman Prime Minister of Australia.'
'Kim, I'm not going to hang around that long. Labor is led by people with long Labor traditions, like you and Simon Crean, and I haven't done it for that purpose. I'm really happy to be a circuit-breaker, and I don't really want to stay around another ten years in politics.'
'Well I think you should consider staying around at least six … and see what happens,' is her clear recollection of Beazley's reply.

panned out. Whatever misgivings he might have had initially about what the Labor Party was doing to Kernot, there was no doubt about the uplifting effect it had on him. The following Sunday, Beazley did an interview with Laurie Oakes on Channel Nine's *Sunday* programme, regarded as his best interview performance since becoming Opposition Leader. As one member of Caucus noted 'it was the first time the phrase "Beazley Government" came out of his mouth and it actually looked as if he meant it — it didn't seem ridiculous'.[172]

The public clearly felt the same because shortly afterwards the polls started to edge and then leap upwards. A poll taken in the immediate aftermath of the Kernot coup showed more than one-third of Democrat supporters were now more likely to vote for Labor as a result of Kernot's move, and six per cent of Coalition supporters felt the same. In the poll considering Beazley as a potential Prime Minister, he was rated 'highly' or 'very highly' by 35 per cent, while the commensurate news for the Coalition was not good. On two-party-preferred voting intentions, Labor was ahead of the Coalition by 53 per cent to 47 per cent, compared with an even-Stephen 50/50 split the weekend before. Labor generally attracted 42 per cent support, up six per cent, compared with the Coalition's two per cent fall to 38 per cent.[173] These results coincided with a particularly difficult 12 months for John Howard as Prime Minister, over which time seven of his ministers had been obliged to resign.

Beazley, nevertheless, continued to receive his fair share of hits for all that. Despite the improvement in his electoral fortunes, there continued to be trenchant criticism about Beazley's direction of the Labor Party on economic issues, particularly, where he had pushed for a more traditional, interventionist Labor approach. Earlier in the year, he had announced that under Labor, the tariff on imported vehicles and components would be frozen at 15 per cent until at least the year 2005. This went entirely against the tide of the last 25 years which had steadily witnessed reduced tariffs — a tide that had reached its height under the free-market, deregulationist policies of Treasurer Paul Keating a decade before — and Beazley was roundly castigated for it, both from economic commentators and from his own side of politics.

Gough Whitlam, who claimed that the whole process of the internationalisation of the Australian economy had begun properly in 1973 when his own Government had slashed 25 per cent off tariffs across the board, was one who was particularly unimpressed. 'Our appeal to the Australian electorate should not be based on propping up the profits of smokestack industries, but on fostering the growth of high-skill, high value-added, well-paid jobs throughout the economy', the former Prime Minister had said in a speech in Melbourne.[174] Beazley's public reply was pointed: 'Gough put his stamp on the Labor Party for his times — I have to put my stamp on the party for my times.'*

This 'stamp' was modelled by the philosophy that had guided him on most issues throughout his political career — the idea that aimed to situate Australia in ways that consolidated its strength in the sometimes hostile international environment. On this occasion he had applied it to tariffs in the belief that Australia should not further reduce them until many of its Asian trading partners had done the same; but it also applied to wider economic issues. 'I'm not an economic fundamentalist,' he says flatly. 'I do think the Government takes decisions which alter the character of the nation and they should not simply be based on market forces. Market forces might tell this country to go out of steel, for example, for it may be that steel is more effectively produced elsewhere. But if it is more effectively produced elsewhere it will only be because some government has taken some decision to provide a benefit to a steel manufacturer to turn up in that area and exploit what might be actual natural areas of advantage.

'So I don't get embarrassed as the Liberals do, or some of my colleagues have from time to time, about the notion [that] you might pursue a degree of Government activism. But I know this — if we are not steel producers in this country we cut ourselves out of an enormous proportion of manufacturing industry. And if we are not steel producers in the end we are not car producers, we are not ship-builders, and we are probably not manufacturers in just about any other area where steel is an active issue. And in that way you hurt your defences . . .

'Even if you can acquire all that you need from friendly trading partners, at the end of the day you take out of your society essential skills, an essential potential area of innovation, more and better quality steel products, more and more innovation in what you do with steel — these are critical things to a modern manufacturing industry.'

The point for Beazley is that in so crucial an industry as steel, for example, it was simply *out of the question* for the Government — the representative of 'the people' — to allow market forces to dictate

---

* Another who was unimpressed with Mr Whitlam's publically expressed opinion was Deputy Labor leader, Gareth Evans. 'Getting a lecture on economic rectitude from Gough is a bit like getting one on the sanctity of marriage [from Bob Hawke.]'[175]

entirely what happened. 'I believe in a place for Government in the economic arena. People own the Government, they don't own BHP nor do they own any other manufacturing industry. Some may be shareholders in it, but anybody that thinks an individual shareholder is actually a person who controls the company is an idiot. But individual voters do control the Government. And if the Government has decided that it's going to opt out about what ought to be happening in terms of the economic life of the nation, then an important area of popular control and democracy is effectively lost. The Government doesn't want to be stupid about it, it doesn't want to create white elephants and monuments, but with a bit of cleverness the Government's got to take the view that it's in there in the ring, intervening in the economy if necessary.'

One who watched Beazley's political manoeuvres in such fields with intense interest, was Paul Keating. The two had remained, in touch at least every few weeks or so, if not in close contact, as the former Prime Minister had pursued a private life of business consultancy — most particularly business in Asia — as well as occasionally speaking on international politics at the University of New South Wales. Many thought that Keating would be appalled that Beazley was steering Labor away from the economic rationalism that he had made famous, but Keating maintains that this was not the case. 'First of all,' Keating says, 'the Labor Government of the '80s and '90s was about a lot more than just economic rationalism — that was, it was seeking to marry economic demands with social demands and industry policy demands. Observers might have thought it rational rather than rationalist, but we were never into some sort of ideological straitjacket. We did things that we thought were good at the time for the right reasons, and to that extent I think Kim has continued with that approach. Conditions change and your approach has to change with them.'

Keating knew about changes. The most obvious condition that had changed in his life, of course, was that he was no longer Prime Minister, a fact he claims has not troubled him unduly. 'I used to say to my colleagues, "one of these days I'll walk away from it and I won't look back". And I did, and I haven't looked back. I'm young enough, even in my early 50s to be able to make another life for myself away from public life, and I'm trying to do just that.'

In the meantime, Beazley's move towards a more interventionist kind of Labor Party not only did not please everyone, it outraged a few. Some journalists were outright scathing, none moreso than the widely read Terry McCrann, writing for News Limited papers across Australia. 'The once just hypocritical Kim Beazley is developing into a pathetic figure', was the opener of one McCrann column in late October of 1997. While the columnist was taking strong exception to critical comments that Beazley had made in connection with the Reserve Bank's decision to sell off their gold reserves, his column soon widened to an all-out attack on the Beazley approach generally. 'The really depressing feature of Beazley's attack [on the gold sell-off],' he wrote, 'is ... that it is indicative of his stance on every policy issue, from Native Title to nursing homes to Telstra, to tax, to the budget deficit, and many, many more. Forget about trying to find what's good for Australia — grab for the soft popular option ... In short, if he wasn't looking increasingly pathetic, he would be an utter disgrace as leader of the alternative government.'

It might have been a stinging blow ... had Beazley actually read it, but he didn't, for the simple reason that by this time of his life in politics, he basically *never* read newspapers. 'Time is a problem,' he says, 'as it takes a while to read a newspaper. The other side of it is particularly if you think you're under attack you do not want to leave yourself psychologically damaged, [as it's already] hard enough to face the day. You know full well that your minders are going to come in if there's something really important that you should read. But also, politics, particularly when you get into leadership positions, you're just reeling from the punches all the time and reeling from the psychological effects of actually delivering them too, because when you're on the attack that takes it out of you as well. So, you've got to channel your information in a way that doesn't deplete your performance ... and newspapers don't actually fit into that.'

McCrann's — and others' — attacks aside, as 1997 drew to a close Beazley was nevertheless conscious that he had risen in the polls, and that certain events had drawn the public's attention to his position as an alternative Prime Minister. He was equally conscious of what lay behind that rise.

'The press always looks for symbols,' he notes, 'and being Opposition Leader, I suppose I was conscious of seizing opportunities to make those symbols stand out, but the reality of our rise is the graft underneath. We are now an alternative government basically because of that graft, getting our psychology right, getting going on issues again, getting our thinking straight. Every now and then it is nice to get a break, and every now and then you can get a symbolic thing or an issue that gives you a break. But it was the graft that helped us most.'

In late November 1997, as a result of that kind of graft, Beazley had been able to release with much fanfare a revamped version of the Labor Party platform. Though still in draft form, and to that point unratified by the party's forthcoming National Conference — though that would happen in two months time at the National Conference in Hobart — it proclaimed a new direction for the Labor Party. Framed in general terms that were long on principle and short on detail, it nevertheless confirmed without apology that a forthcoming Beazley Government would take a far more interventionist approach than either of its Hawke or Keating predecessors. Among other things it promised to pursue the goal of full employment; enshrined opposition to a Goods and Services tax; promised to maximise Australian control of Australian resources and enterprises; named 11 industries that would benefit from strategic action plans; and three regions (in South Australia, Tasmania and northern Australia) which would also receive specific attention. Together with market forces, the Beazley vision was for the strong hand of Government to be busier than at any time during the last two decades.

'We think we are responding to a changed view in the community,' Beazley had said at the launch at the National Press Club. 'We think this is a community now that cares for each other more than it did in the 1980s, and we think this is a community now that takes the view that there is a valuable role for the Government. I am betting that this is what Mr and Mrs Average in Australia think their governments ought to be like, and if they think that's what they ought to be like then I'm the man for the job.'

In reply, Prime Minister Howard labelled the whole thing as a 'bland collection of motherhood statements ... and ... unfunded platitudes'.

Beazley made reply again, to which the Prime Minister shot back an answer, and when it had all settled down, through 1998, Beazley determinedly grafted on. So it was, so it had been since he was about 16 years old, so it would remain for the foreseeable future. Grafting on.

It is a moot point whether we move through the times or the times move through us. In the rising summer of his fiftieth year, Kim Beazley Jnr could look back on a full life, one that had both changed with the times and been one of the generators of that change. Ever and always the nationalist, he could take some satisfaction when flying back to Australia on an aviation system he helped to organise and to finance, through defence security zones he helped to set up, above regional alliances made with his guidance, at the hands of people he had had a hand in educating and training, using telecommunications systems working on his own basic model, that he had made a genuine impact on the life of the nation he was born to. In so doing he had come an extraordinarily long way from being the little boy who learned the rudiments of politics at his father's knee, and the young man who worried whether he could ever one day match his achievements to his 'overwhelming ambitions'.

Whether it is to be his fate to become the leader of that nation is less in the lap of the Gods than in the hands of the Australian people, and that part of his story remains to be written.

ENDNOTES

Chapter One
[1] As recounted to Mrs Betty Beazley, the morning after Mr Chifley's death.
[2] Research on this subject drawn from Alan Gill, *Sydney Morning Herald*, 28 October 1988.
[3] Rica Erickson, Gillian O'Mara, *Convicts in Western Australia 1850-1887*, 1994.

Chapter Two
[4] Ross McMullin, *The Light on the Hill*, 1991, p. 278.
[5] Alan Reid, *Sunday Times*, 27 May 1956.
[6] Dedman had left Parliament in 1949.
[7] *The Light on the Hill*, p. 278.
[8] *National Times*, 9 September 1983.

Chapter Three
[9] Keith Punch.
[10] Chris Smith.
[11] John K. Ewers 'The Red Road'.
[12] As told to James Valentine, ABC Radio 2CN Canberra, 22 May 1997.
[13] Louise Carbines, *Sydney Morning Herald*, 20 January 1984.
[14] As recounted by Merrilyn Wasson.

Chapter Five
[15] Alan Ramsey, *National Times*, 9 September 1983.
[16] Graham Richardson, *Whatever it Takes*, 1994, p. 55.
[17] As quoted in the *West Australian*, 9 September 1966.

Chapter Six
[18] *Pelican*, 1969, p. 3.
[19] Graham Richardson.
[20] *Sunday Times*, 18 January 1970.
[21] *Pelican*, 1970, p. 33.
[22] Rob French.
[23] As remembered by Peter Walsh.
[24] Stephen Manallack, *Pelican*, 7 October 1970.
[25] As remembered by David Roe.
[26] Bill Hayden, *Hayden: An Autobiography*, 1996, p. 154.
[27] *The Light on the Hill*, p. 403.
[28] Michelle Grattan, *Good Weekend*, 30 June 1990.
[29] Quoted by Gough Whitlam in his eulogy to Lance Barnard, 15 August 1997.
[30] Perth's *Weekend News*, 28 July 1974.

Chapter Seven

[31] *Time,* 12 July 1963.

[32] John Jones, *Balliol College: A History 1263–1939.* Oxford University Press, 1988.

[33] Patrick Walters, *Sydney Morning Herald,* 13 April 1983.

[34] Geraldine Doogue.

[35] *Sydney Morning Herald,* 23 July 1988.

[36] *The Light on the Hill*, p. 346.

Chapter Eight

[37] *The Light on the Hill.* p. 288.

[38] *Sydney Morning Herald,* 13 October 1980.

[39] Perth's *Daily Express,* 17 October 1980.

[40] *West Australian.* (Date unclear) 1945.

Chapter Nine

[41] Jim McClelland, *Who Runs Australia?*, 1972; as quoted in *Macquarie Dictionary of Quotations*, p. 321.

[42] John Brown.

[43] Fred Daly, *From Curtin to Hawke*, 1985, p. 22.

[44] As quoted by Peter Blazey in *The Australian,* 14 May 1983.

[45] Dr Andrew Theophanous.

[46] *Hansard,* 5 April 1981.

[47] *Hansard,* 7 September 1982.

[48] *Hansard,* 21 June 1982.

[49] *Hansard,* 20 October 1981.

[50] Don Whitington, *Nation*, 13 July 1963.

[51] *Sydney Morning Herald*, 25 March 1972.

[52] Bill Hayden, *Hayden: An Autobiography*, Angus & Robertson, 1996, p. 341.

Chapter Ten

[53] As quoted in *Sydney Morning Herald* editorial, 9 March 1989, referring to his comments in 1983.

[54] *National Times*, 9 September 1983.

[55] Peter Walsh, *Confessions of a Failed Finance Minister*, p. 106.

[56] Peter Walsh, *Confessions of a Failed Finance Minister*, p. 107.

[57] Peter Blazey, *The Australian*, 14 May 1983.

[58] Alan Ramsey, *National Times*, 9 September 1983.

[59] Alan Ramsey, *National Times*, 9 September 1983.

[60] John Menadue, *Sunday Age*, 16 February 1997; as quoted by Allan Ramsey, *Sydney Morning Herald*, 19 April 1997.

[61] As quoted by Alan Ramsey, *Sydney Morning Herald*, 1 March 1997.

[62] As quoted by Alan Ramsey, *Sydney Morning Herald*, 19 April 1997.

[63] Bob Bottom, *Without Fear or Favour*, 1984, p. 98.

[64] Bob Bottom, *Without Fear or Favour*, 1984, p. 98.

[65] *National Times*, 24 June 1983.

[66] Anne Flahvin, *Financial Review*, 3 August 1984.

[67] *Sydney Morning Herald*, 11 November 1986.

[68] *The Light on the Hill*, p. 413.

[69] *Sydney Morning Herald*, 18 October 1986.

[70] Alan Ramsey, *National Times*, 9 September 1983.

[71] *Financial Review,* 3 August 1984.

[72] *Financial Review,* 3 August 1984

Chapter Eleven

[73] *Sun Herald*, 6 April 1975, p. 30.
[74] Perth *Daily News*, 13 December 1984.
[75] *The Light on the Hill*, p. 216.
[76] Alan Renouf *The Frightened Country*, 1979. As quoted by Mike Skeketee, *Sydney Morning Herald*, 27 November 1987.
[77] Peter Blazey, *The Australian*, 14 May 1983.
[78] Amanda Buckley, *Sydney Morning Herald*, 5 February 1985.
[79] *The Telegraph*, 7 February 1985.
[80] ABC documentary, *Labor in Power*.
[81] *The Bulletin*, February 26 1985.
[82] *The Bulletin*, February 26 1985.
[83] Mike Edmonson, *D.N. Express*, 24 February 1986.
[84] *Confessions of a Failed Finance Minister*, p. 79.

Chapter Twelve

[85] Edna Carew, *Keating: A Biography*, p. 111.
[86] ABC documentary, *Labor in Power*.
[87] Paul Kelly, *The End of Certainty*, 1992, p. 216.
[88] Based on the account of this incident in *The End of Certainty* by Paul Kelly, p. 216.
[89] *Sydney Morning Herald*, 6 March 1987.
[90] *West Australian*, 20 March 1987.
[91] Stephen Loosley.
[92] Tony Stephens, *Sydney Morning Herald*, 23 May 1987.
[93] *Four Corners*, 22 May 1989.
[94] David Lague, *Australian Financial Review*, 20 March 1990.
[95] *Sydney Morning Herald*, 23 June 1987.
[96] *The Light on the Hill*, p. 344.

Chapter Thirteen

[97] Jenni Hewett, *Australian Financial Review*, 26 February 1988.
[98] See articles by David Jenkins, *Sydney Morning Herald*, June 1989.
[99] *West Australian*, 14 January 1969.
[100] David Jenkins, *Sydney Morning Herald*, June 1989.
[101] *Hayden: An Autobiography*, 1996, p. 404.
[102] As told by the Liberal concerned, to Phillip Scanlan.
[103] Jenni Hewett, *Sydney Morning Herald*, 26 February 1988.
[104] *Sydney Morning Herald*, 25 February 1988.
[105] David Humphries *The Age*, 23 March 1988.
[106] Nikki Savva, *West Australian*, 9 March 1988.
[107] *Sydney Morning Herald*, 19 September 1992.
[108] R. J. Hawke, *The Hawke Memoirs*, 1994, p. 229.

Chapter Fourteen

[109] *The Hawke Memoirs*, footnote 99.
[110] *The Hawke Memoirs*, p. 490.
[111] Paul Kelly, *The End of Certainty*, p. 617.
[112] F.S. Oliver, *The Endless Adventure*, Macmillan, 1931, p. 31, as quoted in Stephen Mills, *The Hawke Years*, p. 208.
[113] Michael Gordon, *Paul Keating, A Question of Leadership*, 1993, p. 191.
[114] Alan Mitchell, *Sydney Morning Herald*, 7 June 1990.

[115] *Australian Financial Review*, 17 August 1990.
[116] *Australian Financial Review*, 10 September 1990.
[117] *The Age*, 18 August 1990.
[118] ABC documentary, *Labor in Power*.
[119] Asserted by Fred Daly, *Sydney Morning Herald*, 29 December 1984.
[120] Pilita Clark, *Sydney Morning Herald*, 21 September 1990.
[121] As quoted by Steve Manchee, *West Australian*, 25 September 1990.
[122] *The End of Certainty*, p. 607.
[123] David O'Reilly, *The Bulletin*, 9 October 1990.
[124] *The Hawke Memoirs*, p. 492.
[125] Clarrie Hair.

Chapter Fifteen
[126] Personal communication from Stephen Loosley.
[127] Speech delivered to the Australian Institute of International Affairs, 27 July 1985.
[128] *The End of Certainty*, p. 626.
[129] *The End of Certainty*, p. 627.
[130] *The Light on the Hill*, p. 438.
[131] ABC documentary, *Labor in Power*.
[132] Stephen Mills, *The Hawke Years*, p. 223.
[133] Alan Ramsey, *Sydney Morning Herald*, 1 June 1990.
[134] Kim Beazley and Graham Richardson both agree on this figure.
[135] ABC documentary, *Labor in Power*.

Chapter Sixteen
[136] ABC documentary, *Labor in Power*.
[137] In Bob Hawke's *Memoirs*, he says 'My stand on Coronation Hill may well have cost me the leadership a few months later.' p. 510.
[138] *End of Certainty*, p. 649.
[139] Stephen Mills, *The Hawke Years*, p. 287.
[140] Stephen Mills, *The Hawke Years*, p. 287.
[141] Stephen Mills, *The Hawke Years*, p. 292.

Chapter Seventeen
[142] *The Australian*, 27 December 1991.
[143] *Catechism of the Catholic Church*, Article 7, 'The Sacrament of Matrimony'.
[144] Bob Ellis, *Goodbye Jerusalem*, 1997, p. 16.
[145] *The Australian*, 4 May 1993.
[146] As quoted by Pamela Williams in *The Victory*, p. 107.
[147] Michelle Grattan, *Good Weekend*, 30 June 1990.
[148] *The Light on the Hill*, p. 71.
[149] Terry Lane, ABC Radio, 4 August 1996.
[150] *West Australian*, 21 November 1994.
[151] *West Australian*, 21 November 1994.
[152] As told to Stephen Loosley.
[153] For an account of Beazley's ascension to the Deputy Prime Ministership, see Michael Gordon's article in *The Australian*, 24 June 1995.
[154] Randall Markey, *West Australian*, 21 December 1995.
[155] Margot Kingston, *Sydney Morning Herald*, 1 August 1995. As quoted by Pamela Williams in *The Victory*, p. 114.
[156] Michael Millet, *Sydney Morning Herald*, 18 September 1995.

157 Malcolm McGregor, *Financial Review*.
158 Mark Riley, *The Australian*, 20 December 1995.
159 Malcolm McGregor, *Financial Review*.
160 Scott Henry, *The Australian*, 23 February 1996.
161 Malcolm McGregor, *Financial Review*.
162 *West Australian*, 1 March 1996.

Chapter Eighteen
163 *Four Corners*, 'Hard Labor' 24 February 1997.
164 *Sydney Morning Herald*, 22 January 1966.
165 *Sydney Morning Herald*, 22 February 1986.
166 Tony Stephens, *Sydney Morning Herald,* 27 June 1996.
167 Clive Robertson, *Radio 2GB*, 28 January 1997.
168 See the article by Alan Ramsey in the *Sydney Morning Herald*, 20 April 1996.
169 From the official web site of the Australian Parliament.
170 Paul Kelly, *The Hawke Ascendancy*, p. 14.
171 *Sydney Morning Herald*, 22 November 1969.
172 Stephen Smith.
173 Craig Skehan, *Sydney Morning Herald*, 20 October 1997.
174 Michael Millet, *Sydney Morning Herald*, 14 March 1997.
175 Alan Ramsey, *Sydney Morning Herald*, 9 April 1997.

ACKNOWLEDGEMENTS

While researching and writing this book I was constantly tapping the knowledge of many of my fellow Fairfax journalists, and they unfailingly allowed me to do so. I thank them for it, particularly Pamela Williams, Paul McGeough, Tom Allard, David Humphries and Alan Ramsey. I ditto did extensive research referring to the many, many articles written by journalists all over the country from as far back as the mid-1940s, though I found particularly valuable the work of Michelle Grattan, David Jenkins, Paul Kelly, Geoff Kitney, Mike Seccombe, Michael Gordon and especially Alan Ramsey.

I used many books as a constant resource. *The End of Certainty* and *The Hawke Ascendancy* by Paul Kelly; *Whatever it Takes* by Graham Richardson; *Confessions of a Failed Finance Minister* by Peter Walsh; *Paul Keating, A Question of Leadership*, by Michael Gordon; *The Light on the Hill* by Ross McMullin; *The Hawke Years* by Stephen Mills (which was particularly helpful for me to understand the logistics of the Hawke/Keating leadership struggle); *From Curtin to Hawke* by Fred Daly; *The Victory* by Pamela Williams and *Hayden: An Autobiography* by Bill Hayden.

I have, I hope, religiously acknowledged whatever I have cited from those books and articles, but inevitably there was also a lot of general background that I was able to draw from them, which is less easy to credit specifically. I was always conscious as I was researching and writing how lucky I was that a good lot of the general terrain I was traversing had already been extensively surveyed by previous travellers.

Both the immediate and the extended family of Kim Beazley Jnr (including his first wife, Mary Ciccarelli) made themselves totally accessible, for which I thank them enormously, most particularly Susie Annus. To Mr Beazley's staff, including John O'Callaghan, Karen Bissaker, Greg Turnbull, John Flannery and Liz Iser, thanks.

I thank Damien Wallace for his advice on the Aviation chapter; Hugh White on Defence; Anne Davies for Telecommunications; David Phillips and Roger Peacock for Education and Brian Toohey for his help overall. To Ross McMullin, for his help on historical accuracy, and much-valued advice and support when I most needed it, my warm appreciation.

All of that said, any errors — if any of the brutes have survived — are mine alone.

I deeply appreciated the Prime Minister of Great Britain, Tony Blair, finding time during historic peace negotiations in Ireland, to pen a much-valued foreword for this book.

Other Labor identities in Australia were also tremendously helpful, especially, Bob Hawke, Paul Keating, Gough Whitlam, Graham Richardson, Stephen Loosley, Stephen Smith, David Combe, Peter Walsh, John Dawkins, Bob Hogg, and Dr Geoff Gallop. In the early stages of the book Barry Cohen was helpful in giving me a crash-course in Labor Party culture, and I thank him for that as well as his forgiving the fact that as a young lad all my own energies at Federal election time were devoted, with my Dad — the local Liberal Party President — to seeing him beaten in the seat of Robertson. He always won regardless.

I found that many of Kim Beazley's personal, non-political friends went out of their way to give me the information and background I needed, particularly Phil Scanlan, Geraldine Doogue, Tim Blue, Professor Peter Tannock, Justice Robert French, Peter Pierce, Ian Pollard, the Reverend Peter Thomson and above all, Rob Pascoe.

To add to that, I also thank specifically everyone quoted directly herein, who — almost by definition — cooperated to the extent of shedding light where I needed it.

I record my gratitude and professional respect to my editor, Belinda Lee. There was a whole team of people at HarperCollins*Publishers* whose efforts helped bring the book into being: Eugenie Regan, Graeme Jones, James Herd, Kate Thomas, Karen-Maree Griffiths, Kylie Corrigan, Darian Causby and Mel Feddersen. Thanks to Geoff Armstrong for initially getting the ball rolling. Thanks also to Vanessa Radnidge and Rodney Stuart for their meticulous proofreading; and Madelaine Davis and Caroline Colton for the index.

I also thank my principal researcher Kevin Brumpton, as well as Samuel Poullay and Rob Schutze who both helped with things Western Australian; Maree Maio for her morale-boosting efforts; Margaret Coleman for her accurate transcribing, and Julian Stuart and Harriet Veitch for their fine subbing work.

Most especially I thank my wife Lisa for her advice, support, painstaking and professional editing of the manuscript — as well as her enormous efforts over 18 months to organise not only our home life but also the birth of our third child, so I could substantially keep working. To Beryl Wilkinson, too, thanks.

Finally, I warmly express my gratitude to Kim Beazley Jnr himself. Within the tremendous constraints imposed on his time he was unfailingly generous in allowing me to pepper him with endless questions; and not once did he try and influence what I wrote, even while sometimes strongly disagreeing with conclusions I was drawing.

There is a famous story told of the former Australian Prime Minister, Billy Hughes, and a portrait photographer. When the photographer mentioned that he wanted to do him justice, the famously gnarled Hughes had replied that 'it's not justice I want, it's *mercy*'.

Allow me to say, that in the case of Kim Christian Beazley, I simply hope that I have done his story justice.

Photographic and Reproduction Acknowledgements

Photo of Gareth Evans, Kim Beazley and Bill Clinton courtesy of David Foote/AUSPIC.

Photo of Kim Beazley and daughter, Rachel, by Robert Garvey.

Photo of Kim Beazley's and Susie Annus' wedding by Frances Andrijich.

Photo of the Hotel Kurrajong supplied courtesy of the Hotel Kurrajong at the Australian International Hotel School.

'The Red Road' John K. Ewers/Edward Black. © 1938 Allans Music Australia Pty Ltd. Used by permission. All rights reserved.

SELECTED BIBLIOGRAPHY

Bottom B. *Without Fear or Favour.* Sun Books, South Melbourne, 1984.

Carew E. *Keating: A Biography.* Allen & Unwin, Sydney, 1988.

Daly F. *From Curtin to Hawke.* Sun Books Macmillan, South Melbourne, 1985.

Department of Defence, *The Defence of Australia 1987.* Presented to Parliament by the Minister for Defence, the Honourable Kim C. Beazley, M.P. Australian Government Publishing Service, Canberra, 1987.

Dibb M.P. *Review of Australia's Defence Capabilities.* Report to the Minister for Defence. Australian Government Publishing Service, Canberra, 1986.

Edwards J. *Keating: The Inside Story.* Penguin, Melbourne, 1996.

Ellis B. *Goodbye Jerusalem: Night Thoughts of a Labor Outsider.* Vintage/Random House, Sydney, 1997.

Erickson R & O'Mara G. *Convicts in Western Australia 1850-1887.* University of Western Australia Press, Nedlands (W.A), 1994.

Gordon M. *Paul Keating: A Question of Leadership.* University of Queensland Press (New Edition), Brisbane, 1993.

Hamilton J. *Burkie: A Biography of Brian Burke.* St George Books, Perth, 1988.

Hawke R.J. *Blanche d'Alpuget.* Mandarin, Melbourne, 1994.

Hawke R.J. *The Hawke Memoirs.* William Heinnemann Australia, Melbourne, 1994.

Hayden B. *Hayden: An Autobiography.* Angus & Robertson, Sydney 1996.

Hurst J. *Hawke PM.* Angus & Robertson, Sydney, 1996.

Kelly P. *The Hawke Ascendency.* Angus & Robertson, Sydney, 1984.

Kelly P. *The End of Certainty.* Allen & Unwin, Sydney, 1992.

McMullin R. *The Light on the Hill: The Australian Labor Party 1891-1991.* Oxford University Press, Melbourne, 1991.

Mills S. *The Hawke Years: The Story from the Inside.* Viking, Melbourne, 1993.

O'Brien P, ed. *The Burke Ambush: Corporatism and Society in Western Australia.* Apollo Press, Nedlands (WA), 1986.

O'Reilly D. *The Woman Most Likely: Cheryl Kernot.* Random House, Sydney, 1998.

Renouf A. *The Frightened Country.*

Richardson G. *Whatever It Takes.* Bantam, Sydney, 1994.

Schneider R. *The Colt from Kooyong. Andrew Peacock: A Political Biography.* Angus & Robertson Sydney, 1981.

Stubbs J. *Hayden.* William Heinemann Australia, Melbourne, 1989.

Walsh P. *Confessions of a Failed Finance Minister.* Random House, Sydney, 1995.

Whitlam G. *Abiding Interests.* University of Queensland Press, Brisbane, 1997.

Williams P. *The Victory.* Allen & Unwin, Sydney, 1997.

INDEX

Australia's Regional Security White
    Paper 293
aviation policy: Sydney airport issues
    198, 222; airline industry
    199–200, 221; Two Airlines
    agreement 201–2, 307

B
Babbage, Dr Ross 181
Bagehot, Walter 216
Baldwin, Peter 367, 380
Baldwin, Stanley 135
Balliol, John 127
Balliol College, Oxford 118, 125–7,
    128, 130, 139
Baptist Sunday School 27
Barker, Lisa 335
Bavadra, Dr Timoci 266
Beaconsfield State School 2
Beazley, Betty (KB's mother): athletic
    triumphs 2, 4; marriage to Kim
    Snr 2; education 2–3; Christian
    beliefs 7; conversion to MRA
    9–10, 26–7; forebears 13;
    marriage difficulties 25–6;
    Secretary of UWA Guild of
    Undergraduates 102; caring for
    David 121
Beazley, David Christopher (KB's
    brother): birth 7; intellectual
    disability 43; work situation
    121, 324–5
Beazley, Hannah (KB's daughter):
    birth 170; relationship with KB
    210–12
Beazley, Jessica Katherine (KB's
    daughter): birth 155;
    relationship with KB 210–12;
    breast cancer scare 419–20
Beazley, John 317
Beazley, Kim Christian (Kim Jnr)
    early life; birth 1; childhood
    11–12, 19–24; family home and
    neighbourhood 16–17; primary
    school 17; stricken with polio
    18–19; childhood friends
    19–20, 45, 50–1, 60, 218–20;

Beazley, Kim Christian (Kim Jnr) *cont.*
    interest in military 22–4;
    backyard air-raid shelter 23–4;
    'arts' education 24; trips to
    Canberra 24–5; religious
    upbringing 27–8; relationship
    with grandmother 28; high
    school 39–40, 41–3; naval
    ambitions 44–5; sport 46–7,
    55–6, 130–1; adolescent
    pastimes 46–51; interest in
    books 51; effect of 1963
    election 53–4; school prefect
    54–5; influence of MRA 56–60,
    101; university years 78–124;
    applications for Rhodes
    scholarship 111, 118; Oxford
    125–52; ambition to become
    Minister for Defence 132–3;
    post at Murdoch University
    154–6, 166–7, 176–7
Moral Rearmament Movement;
    influence of 56–60, 101, 140–1;
    Indian experience 61–5; letters
    from India 63–4, 65, 66, 67, 68,
    69, 70, 73, 75–6; 'Sing Out
    Australia' 64–71; joins
    HIMMAT 71; visit to London
    75–6; Oxford years 140–1;
    waning of influence 186–7
family and personal life; courtship
    110; engagement to Mary
    Paltridge 122–4; second
    thoughts on marriage 136–8;
    marriage and married life
    138–42; birth of Jessica 155;
    birth of Hannah 170; Canberra
    living arrangements 179–80,
    255–6, 323; marriage strains
    183, 212–13, 260; Christian
    beliefs 186–8; relationship with
    children 210–12; weight
    problem 256–7; breakdown of
    marriage 283–5; relationship
    with Susie Annus 287–90,
    291–2; marriage to Susie 296–7;
    birth of Rachel 368;

Defence Department 231–2, 239, 244, 255, 264, 269

Defence Industries 246–8

Defence of Australia, The (White Paper) 262–4, 273–4, 276

defence policy: MX missiles tests 225–6, 232–6, 237; guiding principle 227, 228; defence alliances 229, 230–1, 274–6, 295; self-reliance 229, 231, 232, 254, 274, 294, 295, 299; facilities re-direction to northwest 230, 260; NZ defence relationship 238–9; US/Australian joint facilities 240–2; equipment purchases 244–6, 290, 291, 292, 295; defence industries reform 246–50; Dibb review 252–5, 260, 262, 276; White Paper 255, 260, 262–4, 273–4; Fiji coup (1987) 265–7; regional 274–6, 293–4; Gulf War 328–30

Democratic Labor Party (DLP) 30, 31, 54

Dibb, Paul 239, 294; *A Review of Australia's Defence Capabilities* 252–5, 260, 262, 276

DLP *See* Democratic Labor Party (DLP)

Domingo, Placido 319

Doogue, Geraldine: opinion of KB 95, 110, 123, 162; friendship with Mary Paltridge 124, 135, 136, 137, 138, 139, 148, 165; friendship with KB 145; friendship with Susie Annus 213, 297

Doogue, Peggy 137, 148–9, 287, 288, 297

Dowding, Keith 331

Dowding, Peter 331

Downer, Alexander 390, 406

Downer, Nikki 406

Drewe, Robert 45, 119

Ducker, John 83, 159, 160, 167

Duffy, Michael: opinion of KB 188, 271, 413–14; friendship with KB 220, 385; Hawke/Keating battle 335, 350, 351, 353

E

Easton, Penny 383, 393, 406, 435

economic rationalism 440

Edgerton, Jack 113

education policy: higher education 371–3, 380; state school education 374; teaching profession 374

elections: 1963 federal 53–4; WA State 1967 81; General, Britain 1974 134–5; 1974 federal 137; 1980 federal 171–5; 1983 federal 194–5, 223, 422; 1984 federal 221; 1987 federal 269, 271, 273, 301; 1990 federal 298, 300; 1993 federal 376, 377, 378–80; 1996 federal 402–11, 415; 1940 federal 410

Elizabeth II: Coronation 7; Australian tour (1954) 18

Ellis, Bob 370

employment policy: Job Compact 380–1; Working Nation 381

Epstein, David 404, 405, 434

Evans, Gareth: 197; Colston problem 205, 206, 207; political style 209, 210; Bavadra rescue plan 266–7; Foreign Minister 293, 329, 400, 406; opinion of KB 310; Hawke/Keating battle 335, 340, 343, 350, 355; doorknocking with KB 377–8; US ambassadorship offer to KB 380; Deputy leadership 393, 394–5, 412, 439; deference to KB as leader 411; Kernot defection 426, 427

Evatt, 'Doc' 30

Ewers, John K. 51–2

Outlook (Australian Institute of International Affairs) 94

Overseas Telecommunications Corporation (OTC) 303–4, 306, 307–8, 320, 322, 350

Oxford Movement *See* Moral Rearmament Movement (MRA)

Oxford University 118, 128–9, 150–1 *See also* Balliol College, Oxford

P

Pacific Patrol Boat programme 294

Packer, Kerry 301, 308, 309, 391

Palmerston, Lord 306

Paltridge, Lady Molly, 102, 123–4, 138, 172, 176, 297, 312.

Paltridge, Mary *See* Beazley, Mary

Paltridge, Sir Shane, 95,102,138

Parker, John 219

Parks, Col 334

Pascoe, Robert 155, 254, 289

Pascoe, Susie 172

Paul, John 42

Peacock, Andrew 208, 293, 412

Pelican newspaper 99, 104, 108, 109

Perth Modern School 2, 3, 39, 41, 157, 184

Petrov, Vladimir 30

Phillips, David 374

Pickett, George 336, 337, 343

Pierce, Peter 130, 131, 133, 134, 136, 137, 138, 139

pilots dispute 216–17

pilots' superannuation payments 216–17

Pine Gap 240, 241, 242

Pollard, Ian 130

polls, preferred Prime Minister: 1990 325; 1997 325

Pomeroy, Bob 318

Poujard, Pierre 418

Prescott, John 431

Pritchett, V. S. 98

Punch, Gary 363, 391

Punch, Keith 42

Q

Qantas 199, 201, 221, 222, 303, 307, 321, 388

R

Rabuka, Lt-Col Sitiveni 265

racism 427

Ramadier, Paul 384

Ramsey, Alan 38, 203, 207, 290, 335, 342, 395

Ranford, Janet 50

Rann, Mike 417

Ray, Robert: supports KB on electoral changes 207; AFL finals 316–17; telecommunications debate 318; Defence Minister 328, 329; Hawke/Keating battle 335, 338, 339, 340, 341, 342, 350, 352, 355, 360, 361, 362, 363, 364; support for KB as leader 405, 411

Reagan, Ronald 234, 251

Reid, Alan 29

Republic issue 375

Review of Australia's Defence Capabilities, A (Dibb Report) 252–5, 260, 262, 276

Reynolds, Josh 111, 117

Rhodes scholarship 111, 117, 118, 119

Richardson, Frank 49

Richardson, Graham: Wran/Ducker conflict 83; Right faction 159, 167, 168; opinion of KB 160, 215, 220–1; supports KB on electoral changes 207; MX missile testing 235–6; 1990 election 302; telecommunications debate 310–11, 312, 318–19; support for Brian Burke 331; Hawke/Keating battle 333, 339, 342, 343, 344, 346, 348, 355, 361, 368–9; support for KB as leader 377, 391, 411; education funding 387